LYDIA GINZBURG'S PROSE

Lydia Ginzburg's Prose

REALITY IN SEARCH OF LITERATURE

Emily Van Buskirk

PRINCETON UNIVERSITY PRESS
Princeton & Oxford

PUBLISHED BY PRINCETON UNIVERSITY PRESS
41 William Street, Princeton, New Jersey 08540

IN THE UNITED KINGDOM: PRINCETON UNIVERSITY PRESS
6 Oxford Street, Woodstock, Oxfordshire OX20 1TW

press.princeton.edu

Cover photo courtesy of Alexander Kushner; title page photo by Richard D. Sylvester (from April 1981, Leningrad), also courtesy of Alexander Kushner.

ISBN 978-0-691-16679-7

Library of Congress Control Number: 2015934774

British Library Cataloging-in-Publication Data is available

This book has been composed in Arno Pro

Printed on acid-free paper. ∞

Printed in the United States of America

1 3 5 7 9 10 8 6 4 2

CONTENTS

ACKNOWLEDGMENTS

This book could not have taken shape without the help of many individuals who have generously shared their knowledge and expertise over the years. I would like to begin by thanking Stephanie Sandler, my dissertation adviser, for her wise guidance, excellent insights, strong encouragement, and unwavering support over the years. I have benefited hugely from working on several Ginzburg projects with Andrei Zorin, whose enthusiasm about Ginzburg's prose inspired my research at its initial stages, and with whom I could not imagine a better *sotrudnichestvo.* Kseniia Kumpan shared anecdotes, memories, and insights about Lydia Yakovlevna Ginzburg and her milieu, while generously helping me decipher manuscripts. Irina Paperno offered astute and attentive comments and questions. Caryl Emerson gave me provocative comments on several chapters. William Mills Todd III and Justin Weir provided excellent feedback and support as dissertation readers.

I am deeply grateful to Alexander Kushner for encouraging and enabling my work, and for relating his reminiscences of Lydia Ginzburg. He generously let me work with archival materials while they were in his care, subsequently facilitated my research at the Russian National Library, and has consistently granted me permission to use and publish archival manuscripts. I am also grateful to Marina Lyubimova for her invaluable assistance, and to many other librarians at the Manuscripts Division of the Russian National Library.

Many friends and colleagues have helped me with this project in various ways over the years. I would like to thank the entire faculty of the Harvard Slavic Department, my fellow graduate students at Harvard, colleagues at the Davis Center for Russian and Eurasian Studies, and the faculty of the Princeton Slavic Department, where I got my start in Russian. I am grateful also to my colleagues, my students, and staff members at Rutgers, especially in the Department of German, Russian, and East European Languages and Literatures; the Program in Comparative Literature; and the Center for Cultural Analysis. A special thanks to Carol Avins, Polina Barskova, Alexei Ivanov, Andrew Kahn, Andrei Kurilkin, Stanislav Savitsky, Lidiia Semenova, Maria Svichenskaia, members of the editorial staff at *Novoe literaturnoe obozrenie,* and the contributors to the volume *Lydia Ginzburg's Alternative Literary Identities.* Thanks also to participants in the Zubov seminars at the Institute for the History of Arts as well as in the conference *History and Subjectivity in Russia (Late 19th–20th Centuries)* at European University in St. Petersburg, and to panel and audience members of conferences held by AATSEEL, ASEEES, ICCEES, and NeMLA, for questions and feedback on the papers I delivered there. I am very grateful to Penelope Burt for her truly expert editorial assistance. Thanks also to the anonymous reviewers for Princeton University Press, to copyeditor Jennifer Harris, indexer James Curtis, to my editor, Anne Savarese, and others at the press, including Juliana Fidler and Ellen Foos, who helped guide this book into print.

Many friends of Ginzburg generously shared their memories with me in the course of interviews: Konstantin Azadovsky, Yakov Bagrov, Yakov Gordin, Al'bin Konechnyi, Nikolai Kononov, Nina Korolëva, the late Elena Kumpan, Kseniia Kumpan, Alexander Kushner, John Malmstad, Aleksei Mashevsky, the late Eleazar Meletinsky, Galina Murav'ëva, Elena Nevzgliadova, Irina Paperno, Irena Podol'skaia, Elena Rabinovich, the late Elena Shvarts, the late Nina Snetkova, Zoia Tomashevskaia, Marietta Turian, William Todd, Nadezhda Zolina, and others.

Sections of some of this book's chapters first appeared in article form in *Slavic Review*, *Novoe literaturnoe obozrenie*, and in *Lydia Ginzburg's Alternative Literary Identities*. I am grateful to those who offered feedback on these earlier pieces, which I have subsequently revised.

I extend my gratitude to the many organizations that have supported my research and writing: the National Endowment for the Humanities, the Rutgers University Research Council, the Center for Cultural Analysis at Rutgers, the Davis Center for Russian and Eurasian Studies at Harvard University, the Whiting Fellowship in the Humanities, the Social Science Research Council, and the Frederick Sheldon Traveling Fellowship.

Finally, I would like to express my gratitude to my friends and family, near and far, for their love and support. Thanks to my mother, Faith Knowles, and father, John Van Buskirk, and also to Pete, Eliot, Tom, Lydia, Tessa, Gaby, Haifa, Magali, and other members of the Knowles, Thompson, Van Buskirk, and Bourghol families. I am profoundly grateful for the love and understanding of my husband, Joe Bourghol.

A NOTE ABOUT SPELLING, TRANSLITERATION, AND ARCHIVAL REFERENCES

When transliterating Russian quotations and titles, I have used the modified Library of Congress system. I make exception for names, particularly those already familiar to the English-speaking reader, such as Osip Mandelstam (rather than Mandel'shtam) and Fyodor Dostoevsky (rather than Fëdor Dostoevskii). I have likewise opted for Lydia (rather than Lidiia) Ginzburg.

Ginzburg's archive is located in the Manuscripts Division of the Russian National Library in St. Petersburg, Russia, and has yet to be fully catalogued. To refer to archival materials, I use the Russian acronym of the Manuscripts Division, OR RNB (*Otdel rukopisei Rossiiskoi national'noi biblioteki*) and the basic archival number designating Ginzburg's entire archives, 1377. When referring to the "notebooks," I use the numbering system carried out by Ginzburg ("ZK" for *zapisnaia knizhka*, and a roman numeral). I make reference to loose manuscripts using Ginzburg's titles, when they exist, or descriptive titles of drafts or folders in which manuscripts were located, along with approximate dates. On certain occasions (such as when folders are currently mislabeled, or when I accessed materials after the final archival transfer in 2011), I refer to data from the (still provisional) archival catalogue. I refer to materials from the archives of Ginzburg's brother, Viktor Tipot, and Ginzburg's niece, Natalia Viktorovna Sokolova, at the Russian State Archive of Literature and Arts in Moscow with the acronym RGALI (*Rossiiskii gosudarstvennyi arkhiv literatury i isskustva*) accompanied by complete catalogue information for specific listings.

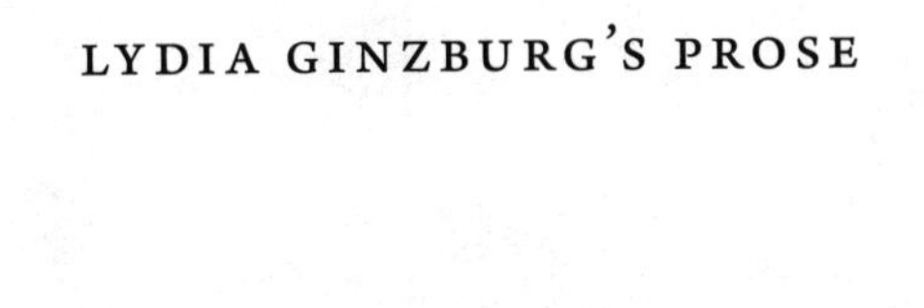

LYDIA GINZBURG'S PROSE

Introduction

For seven decades, Lydia Ginzburg (1902–90) wrote about the reality of daily life and historical change in Soviet Russia. In fragmentary notes and narratives, she exercised what she saw as the unique possibilities of "in-between" genres (human documents, memoirs, essays, autobiographies) to bring representations of new realms of life and thought into literature. She recorded, with an unmatched degree of insight and lucidity, how her contemporaries shaped their personalities and self-images in response to the Soviet experience. Yet in the English-speaking world, she is still known primarily as a literary scholar (author of the book *On Psychological Prose*, whose English translation was published by Princeton University Press in 1991) and as a "memoirist" of the siege of Leningrad during World War II (her *Notes of a Blockade Person* came out under the title of *Blockade Diary* from Harvill Press in 1995).

Ginzburg saw herself as having two callings: as a scholar, but even more vitally as a prose writer. In the late 1970s, taking stock of fifty years of writing "for the desk drawer," she lamented: "For more than half a century I've carried on a dual conversation—about life and about literature. For half a century I've had a double anxiety—when talking about literature, I'm occupied with something other than the main thing; when about life, I'm occupied with something unrealizable."[1]

Ginzburg's reputation has been steadily growing as new dimensions of her literary activities have become more accessible to the public. In the course of this reappreciation, her image has undergone several transformations: she has been seen as a widely respected literary historian specializing in Russian Romanticism, Mikhail Lermontov, and Alexander Herzen; an important scholar of lyric poetry who weaves together historical, textual, and humanistic analysis[2]; the creator of an original theory of in-between literature; a perceptive memoirist who wrote about the leading Russian literary figures of the first half of the twentieth century, including Vladimir Mayakovsky, Nikolai Oleinikov, Yuri Tynianov, Anna Akhmatova; and the author of a groundbreaking philosophical and psychological analysis of life in Leningrad during the blockade, based on her personal experience. Only recently has she been gaining recognition as a writer who created a new kind of prose, bringing together self-examination, philosophical and historical reflection, and her own brand of literary social psychology. Scholarship in both English and Russian is beginning to reposition Ginzburg as a complex and intriguing figure who offers a vantage point on the whole of the Soviet era.

Lydia Ginzburg's significance has been hard to estimate until now because, for all of her formidable publications, the whole body of her work was not known, nor was its shape. This book draws upon a decade of close work with her entire corpus, much of which remains unpublished and is available only in her personal archives. My research has led me to put forth a new interpretation of her personal quest for a different kind of writing, one that would be adequate to the times in which she lived. I place at the center of my analysis not her major works (her better-known narratives, essays, and scholarly monographs), but rather the writings (many of them unfinished) that seem least to fit into the standard literary or critical genres. I believe that these little known writings will have the greatest impact on our understandings of modern life and the Soviet experience.

Ginzburg came of age soon after the Revolutions of 1917 as the most talented student of the Russian Formalists. While she practiced (and made her living through) literary scholarship her entire life, her most profound scholarly contributions reached the public only in the 1970s. Her books *On Psychological Prose* (first edition, 1971) and *On the Literary Hero* (1979) deepen our understanding of how self-concepts travel between literature and life, and how literary characters reflect changing notions of human personality. She demonstrates how the aesthetic structures of *promezhutochnaia literatura*, or "in-between literature," mediate between those of everyday life and of the novel, thus contributing both to literary evolution and self-understanding.

Ginzburg began to experiment with in-between prose in 1925, jotting down witticisms, anecdotes, aphorisms, and reflections on her Formalist milieu in "notebooks" (*zapisnye knizhki*). Her project evolved over seven decades of Soviet history, as she wrote essays and sketches "for the desk drawer" (publication, though desired, was impossible and largely unimaginable until the last few years of her life) in which she critically analyzed the life of the Russian intelligentsia, a group whose values she saw as being under constant assault. Living long enough to benefit from the relaxed censorship of the Glasnost era, Ginzburg stunned Russian readers with ever-expanding editions of her strange stories, witty anecdotes, and probing meditations, which combined the genres of autobiography, fiction, and essay. The literary scholar Sergei Kozlov recalls that in the 1980s, he was not alone in feeling that "Ginzburg gave us the language and conceptual apparatus for understanding ourselves and our milieu." One reader he knew said of Ginzburg, "She explained to me my own self."[3]

Why was Ginzburg so successful in "explaining" the intelligentsia "to itself," even at the end of the Soviet period? For decades, her experiments in self-writing were propelled by two goals that were even more ambitious: (1) to discern a new concept of the self, adequate to the catastrophic twentieth century, and (2) to arrive at a new literary form that would replace the obsolete (as she saw it) psychological novel. She worked on both of these problems inductively, filling her genre-defying fragments with painstaking self-examination and unsparing analysis of her contemporaries. She could explain the intelligentsia to itself because she had developed strong arguments about the connections between personality and history, and had found forms of expression that enabled her to reveal these connections—not the novel, not long forms of any kind, but fragmentary narratives that negotiate between history and fiction.

During World War II, Ginzburg lamented that literature had largely fallen into a state of arrested development and boring repetition. She diagnosed the root of the problem as a failure to discover "a new fundamental concept of the person" (*novaia printsipial'naia kontseptsiia cheloveka*).[4] She discerned a connection between the two interrelated crises—in values and in literature—that permeated her time: both emanated from the absence of a new concept of the self that could express the moral uncertainties amid new historical circumstances, as well as the fragmentation and social conditioning that beset modern identity formation. Wars and revolutions, she wrote, had forever toppled the nineteenth-century ideology of individualism by dispelling the belief in the unconditional value of the unique person, which had ultimately been based on a belief in the existence of divinely ordained absolutes. These events also crushed the dream of positive social change—one had only to look at Stalinist Russia and Nazi Germany to grasp that social evil was ineradicable. From the 1930s through the postwar decades, Ginzburg (in her private writings) urged her contemporaries to put an end to any literary conversation that dwelt on bemoaning the loss of the self-valuable soul in order to reflect on "how ever to survive and endure without losing one's human image."[5] Her concerns run parallel with those of European intellectuals (such as Jean-Paul Sartre) who were also discussing how art must change in response to the total human catastrophe of World War II.

The core of this book centers on an investigation of Ginzburg's concept of the self in the wake of the crisis of invidualism: a self that I call "post-individualist." In Ginzburg's words, this is a "consciousness" that "with all of its subjectivity, hardly dares to wonder at its own finitude."[6] The term "self" has no equivalent in Russian, and Ginzburg herself does not use it. (Russian does have the reflexive pronoun "oneself," *sebia*, a close relative to the word "self" in many languages.) "The self" has been glossed by the scholar of autobiography Paul John Eakin as "a comprehensive term for the totality of our subjective experiences" and by intellectual historian Jerrold Seigel as "the particular being any person is."[7] While invoking these meanings of subjectivity, experience, and particularity, I also draw on Charles Taylor's influential study *Sources of the Self*, where he writes of the "sense of the term where we speak of people as selves, meaning that they are beings of the requisite depth and complexity to have an identity . . . (or to be struggling to find one)."[8] Ethics and narrative are central to both Ginzburg's and Taylor's concepts of selfhood; yet Ginzburg casts more doubt on the stable, permanent identity of the self than Taylor does; she also puts special emphasis on the social dimension (what one might call personality, or compare to William James's "Social Me").[9]

A central element of Ginzburg's theory of the self and of personality structure is that we strive to realize that which we experience as a value, while our sense of values derives from the processes of socialization and interiorization from our milieu. The psychic life of the twentieth-century person consists of isolated moments that fade quickly and are incapable of forming any "lasting association of interpenetrating elements."[10] This detachment from absolute values should not be mistaken for the self-willed freedom associated with Dostoevsky's heroes. The main characters that appear in Ginzburg's documentary prose resemble the fictional heroes of Kafka and Hemingway, who have no time for world-shaking ideas (such as "everything is permitted") since they are condemned to inhabit "a pressing world of the objective horror of life" (from a 1958 essay published in the late 1980s).[11] As she sums it up in her late scholarly work *On the Literary Hero* (1979), the contemporary hero is not defined by ideas, but is instead "governed by the mechanism of socialization, internalization, expectations, prohibitions, the values of his milieu, and his 'reference group.' "[12]

She makes the ethical potential of a post-individualist self central to her writings, following a long philosophical tradition that links ethics, selfhood, and narrative. Ginzburg, an atheist, salvages elements from the humanistic tradition of the nineteenth century and smuggles them into the heart of the twentieth. She jettisons three-dimensional worlds, elaborate plot structures, and representations of individuated literary heroes from within. These departures separate her from her contemporary Vasily Grossman, who wrote traditional Tolstoyan novels about war and the terror using, on the whole, the techniques of psychological prose. In some ways, Ginzburg is closer to the remarkable chronicler of the Gulag, Varlam Shalamov, who argued that readers who had been through revolutions, wars, and concentration camps had no need for novels. Shalamov rejected "literary stuff" (*literaturshchina*) in his documentary prose, minimizing or excluding descriptions of characters' physical appearances and backstories.[13] Ginzburg, too, presents only specific, moment by moment experiences of her fragmentary heroes, and yet, unlike Shalamov, replaces the techniques of fiction with analysis.[14]

External, self-distancing analysis is the key procedure in Ginzburg's approach to the post-individualist self, reflecting a sense that in her era "the conflict of the literary hero has once again become an external conflict, just as in pre-psychological times" (again from her 1958 essay, which overlaps with the scholarly work *On the Literary Hero*).[15] Self-distancing unites Ginzburg's aesthetics with her ethics: external analysis assists in the creation of a personality construct to which one can connect discrete actions, in an effort to retain one's human image. Self-distancing also helps explain her departure from traditional autobiography. As Robert Folkenflik has argued, "the idea of the self as other is a condition of the autobiographical narrative."[16] But Ginzburg takes this "othering" to a new level, approaching the self as a casual specimen—not an autonomous entity, but an inextricable part of the social fabric. The observing self is an abstract analyst, gender unspecified, who usually narrates in the third person. The central character, Ginzburg's alter ego, also relates to himself in the third person, and is slightly fictionalized so as to be more historically representative.

Ginzburg's creative works can best be understood in the context of a crisis in individualism and a crisis in the novel, both of which resonated across Europe in the opening decades of the twentieth century. Osip Mandelstam famously argued in "The End of the Novel" (1922) that the individual in the twentieth century lacked the power and even the very sense of time necessary to sustain a full biography, which formed the novel's compositional backbone.[17] Soviet prose writers seeking to represent their new reality had to contend with the legacy of the nineteenth-century Realist novel, the Formalists' demystification of literary devices, and the cultural impact of the Bolshevik Revolution. Some literary schools came to believe that literature could renew itself by turning toward fact and document (what the more radical ideologues from the Left Front of Arts, or LEF, called "the literature of fact").

While I take account of the full scope of Ginzburg's oeuvre, my focus is mainly on the 1930s and 1940s, when she was actively experimenting in multiple directions. At one point, under the influence of the rising interest in the novel in the Soviet 1930s, she saw writers of notebooks as literary "impotents" lacking in "positive ideas." And yet her open "aversion" to the novel's fictionality led her to favor the incompleteness of the jotting and the note. Her dream, articulated in the 1930s, was to create an unnameable genre closest to "a diary in the form of a novel," where she could "fix the flow of life" "without invention or recollection."[18] I treat in detail, and with reference to archival drafts, the narratives that would have become part of this novelistic diary[19]: "The Return Home" (1929–36), "Delusion of the Will" (ca. 1934), "The Thought That Drew a Circle" (ca. 1934–36 or 1939), "A Story of Pity and

Cruelty" (ca. 1942–44), "Otter's Day" (ca. 1943–45), and *Notes of a Blockade Person* (dated by the author "1942–1962–1983"). These works show Ginzburg's ambition to bridge the novel and personal historiography. She saw both novelists and historians as engaged in "a process of understanding life; that is, a description of facts and an explanation of the connections between them."[20]

Ginzburg's characters belong, like Ginzburg herself, to the humanities intelligentsia raised before the Revolution. The radical historical changes faced by this generation had a way of "estranging" character and making self-images more visible: people outwardly reinvented themselves every decade or so, in order to survive. In the Stalin era, Ginzburg was interested in the central historical plot in each of their lives: as the Soviet State grew increasingly repressive, to what degree could they continue to function as intellectuals? After Stalin's death, she observes how survivors keep adjusting their public statements and images to capitalize on the opportunities of a more liberal time. She is mindful that individuals have very limited freedom in choosing their paths, and yet she holds them accountable for their behavior.

In analyzing her own path, Ginzburg searches for the typical elements in the historical experience of her generation. I discuss her negotiations between the "individual" and "socio-historically typical" most expansively when analyzing her writings about love, a topic that presented a particular set of literary but also personal challenges. To her closest friends, Ginzburg identified as a lesbian, and same-sex desire was taboo in Soviet/Russian literature and society (as it still is today); this constituted an experience of difference that Ginzburg strongly resisted romanticizing, or representing at all. Yet close study reveals that her writings speak specifically, if indirectly, to same-sex love. Ginzburg gives expression to her own private experiences as a lesbian by inscribing her subject position into the masculine third-person singular, thereby creating implicit dramas of apparently heterosexual desire. Her choice to work with mainstream approaches of describing love produces unusual effects—for instance, it intensifies her critique of "normal" women (those who are not "inverts," to use her dated terminology). But the fictionalization of gender and sexuality clash with Ginzburg's ethical pact with the word (words do and should reflect reality and are won through experience and suffering).[21]

The mix of fiction with autobiography also marks my chapter on *Notes of a Blockade Person*, her most popular work (published in English, German, Swedish, French, and Dutch translations). The Leningrad Blockade was a catastrophic experience for its victims, but it ironically gave many people, including Ginzburg, the affirmative feeling of actively participating in a major historical turning point, as the Soviet Union battled to victory over Nazism. For Ginzburg and others, the blockade became a personal test of whether it was possible to "survive and endure without losing one's human image."[22] Ginzburg places at the center of *Notes of a Blockade Person* a male hero named N., who is meant to be a typical member of the Leningrad intelligentsia. This apparent move toward fiction is part of her effort to represent the broadest possible historical experience.

But the unpublished manuscripts show that Ginzburg also orients her work toward fiction in order to conceal her most powerful and tragic experience in the blockade: the death of her mother from starvation. She treats this fateful episode in a quasi-fictional manner in "A Story of Pity and Cruelty."[23] This story reveals the hero's guilt about his aunt's miserable final weeks and death. In *Notes of a Blockade Person,* Ginzburg alludes cryptically and minimally to this experience, while much more fully re-creating the realities of siege existence (realities that may help to account for the hero's flawed behavior in "A Story of Pity and Cruelty"). In other words, across separate narratives, Ginzburg performed her work as historian-novelist, explaining the connections between "facts." In the creation of *Notes of a Blockade Person,* Ginzburg followed a model she knew well from her study of Herzen, who developed out of painful episodes of personal life (a family tragedy, failure, guilt, and remorse) a comprehensive memoir of the history of his time.

I draw parallels between Ginzburg and the authors she studies in *On Psychological Prose* such as Herzen, Tolstoy, and Proust, and yet I also emphasize the many factors that separate her from these models. She made her living as a literary scholar, while writing her prose "for the desk drawer." Her audience often consisted of a small group of listeners, and her poetics were shaped by the habit of oral delivery. These intimate readings appear to have begun in the late 1920s. They most likely ceased during Stalin's Terror (a fact that, ironically, may have liberated Ginzburg to write harsher sketches of her contemporaries), and resumed again in the late 1950s or early 1960s, continuing up through the last years of her life. In the final decades, younger friends typed up her essays with an eye to publication; their tastes influenced the composition of Ginzburg's books. The absence, for so many years, of a broad audience and of the opportunities and pressures of publishing made it difficult for her to create "complete" works. Nevertheless, her genre of the fragmentary essay meant that, before the advent of the word processor, Ginzburg would "cut and paste" sentences, formulations, and essays from her notebooks into works of scholarship, or into longer narratives. Conversely, she was eventually able to publish excerpts of unfinished lengthier narratives as short essays.

Ginzburg once described herself as a person "who has a genuine need to fix his thoughts in words, who has some talent for doing this, and who patently lacks the ability and the desire to *invent.*" She acknowledged that these qualities would seem to predispose a person to write autobiographically—and yet she declared defiantly, "I'm totally incapable of doing that sort of thing; in part from shyness, which it would be possible to overcome, if this were necessary; in part from considerations which probably shouldn't be overcome."[24] In some ways, her mode of documentary prose is a product of these two idiosyncratic pressures: to fix thoughts in words, but without writing autobiographically. Thus, while Ginzburg referred to her writings as a "direct conversation about life,"[25] they bear a quite indirect and complex relationship to the self. As she wrote in 1928:

> It is possible to write about oneself directly: I. It is possible to write semi-indirectly: a substitute character. It is possible to write completely indirectly: about other people and things as I see them. Here begins the essence of *literary reflection*, a "monologuized" view of the world (Proust), which I find probably the closest.[26]

Ginzburg experimented with direct, indirect, and semi-indirect relationships to the autobiographical "I" (she implies that all three are ways of writing "about oneself"). Most often she wrote and reflected "about other people," regarding this as a "direct expression" of her life experience.[27]

It would be extremely difficult to approach Ginzburg's writings with the goal of constructing a coherent or complete biography. Her self-writings are remarkable for their omissions. There are only vague inklings about her childhood, family, and private life. There is little treatment of her political views (her semifictional blockade writings forming the most notable exception) or of the physical circumstances of her life. Though she was by all accounts a talented wit with a wry sense of humor, she preferred to record the witticisms of those around her. (Ginzburg once explained to her good friend Boris Bukhstab that writers should not be their own Eckermanns, following themselves around with a notebook.[28]) The unpublished writings discuss in indirect ways some more details of her biography such as her Jewish identity and failed love affairs with women. In part, Ginzburg was constrained because she wanted to publish, at least eventually, but had her doubts that a fully free press would ever come about. For the most part, however, what look like omissions are the result of her notion of the "range of the depictable,"[29] which was a product of personal and creative considerations.

She once jotted in her 1928 notebook: "Everything that makes a person different is his own private affair; that which makes him similar is his social duty."[30] Early in life Ginzburg had already adopted a distinctly anti-Romantic stance: rather than cultivate eccentricity, she aimed to experience norms and to stand "on the level of the average person."[31] This especially concerned her self-representation in writing. She was eager to write about the typical representative of her generation, and yet felt that she diverged from this model in many ways: "As far as I'm concerned, with all of my sound judgment, even I turn out to be in some respects too eccentric a person for literature."[32] Her position was in some ways similar to that of Alexander Pushkin, who despite his participation in certain aspects of Romanticism, was most un-Byronic in separating creativity from everyday life. As Ginzburg explained in a 1988 interview, "Creativity is the most elevated value for Pushkin, a matter of his higher spiritual life. But in everything else—in everyday life, in the family, in society—he wanted to remain like everyone else."[33] Since her primary output, unlike Pushkin's, was prose documenting everyday life, she ends up writing of an alter ego who "wanted to remain like everyone else."

This book's title is a reversal of one of Ginzburg's own: *Literature in Search of Reality*, her 1987 book uniting theoretical, scholarly essays and prose writings (memoirs, narratives, and essays) under one cover. Ginzburg believed that authors were always striving for greater "realism" (even as she acknowledged the relativity of the term), and saw "in-between" prose as opening up the borders of what is considered to be worthy of representation. Her prose searches for "reality," and yet at the same time it reveals how reality makes its own demands on literature, searching for a new, adequate word. This phrase places the accent on incompleteness and unfinalizability (to use Mikhail Bakhtin's term), on the difficulty of finding a form, whether generic or institutional. It also captures Ginzburg's sense of self as a "shred of social reality."

In order to illuminate Ginzburg's writings on the self after the crisis of individualism, each of the book's chapters takes a different angle on the connections between self-concepts and literary forms. I explicate the in-betweenness of her prose in terms of subject position (between the first and third person, self and other, author and hero) and genre (autobiography, fiction, history, scholarship).

The first chapter contains an explication of the concept of post-individualist prose as a pointed departure from nineteenth-century Realism. This is a fragmentary, documentary literature that restricts itself to the realm of "fact," while being free to range outside the conventions of established genres. The post-individualist person's primary dilemma is a crisis in values, and Ginzburg treats writing as an ethical act. I concentrate on how writing serves as an "exit from the self," a process by which the self becomes another, leaving behind the ego. In the second half of the chapter, the focus turns to two of Ginzburg's narratives ("Delusion of the Will" and "A Story of Pity and Cruelty"), which concern the dilemmas of moral action in response to the death of a loved one. The traumatized subject uses techniques of "self-distancing" to deal with his or her sense of self and of the past by constructing a complete and responsible self-image, embedded within a social milieu, and then trying to connect it with his or her actions. Ginzburg's techniques of "self-distancing" (what I call *samo-otstranenie* in Russian) are examined side-by-side with Shklovsky's concept of *ostranenie* ("estrangement") and Bakhtin's *vnenakhodimost'* ("outsideness").

In chapter 2, I place Ginzburg's diverse notes and essays at the center of the analysis, examining them in three principal ways. First, I examine their genre, in the context of the crisis of the novel, particularly as the Formalists saw it. Second, I elaborate the specific aesthetics of Ginzburg's notes, by articulating the poetics of the "formula," a precise sentence or phrase that encapsulates or compresses a wealth of impressions. Third, I discuss the flexibility and multiplicity of generic orientations in the notes, as evidenced by their publication and reception history.

Chapter 3 undertakes a treatment of the rhetoric of personal pronouns in Ginzburg's writings on love and sexuality, drawing on Michael Lucey's study of the first person in twentieth-century French literature about love.[34] Lucey argues that pronominal usage demands extra attention in matters of literature and sexuality, particularly when same-sex relationships are concerned. Proust creates an abstract "I" in his pseudo-memoir, but Ginzburg chooses a different path, using the third-person masculine singular to articulate her position in between sexual and gender identifications. In my analysis, I bring together questions of genre and narrative, on the one hand, and gender and sexuality, on the other. The chapter divides into two sections, treating writings from two different periods on two kinds of love Ginzburg thought typical of intellectuals: in "First Love," I discuss the unrequited and tragic love depicted in Ginzburg's teenage diaries (1920–23); in "Second Love," I analyze the love that is realized but in the end equally tragic, depicted in drafts related to *Home and the World* (1930s). I examine the models the author sought in literary, psychological, and philosophical texts (Weininger, Kraft-Ebbing, Blok, Shklovsky, Oleinikov, Hemingway, and Proust).

Whereas chapter 3 treats Ginzburg's writing about "the self," chapter 4 focuses on her notes about others—in particular, it examines Ginzburg's character analyses from the 1930s, 1940s, and 1970s, where she tries to explain history through character and character through history. Following the model of two literary landmarks from the nineteenth and twentieth centuries—Herzen's *My Past and Thoughts* (published in installments beginning in 1854), and Mandelstam's *The Noise of Time* (1928)—she tells not life stories, but stories of personality in which history is reflected. At a time when the official doctrine of Socialist Realism and the strict censorship regime had cut off any genuine intercourse between literature and life, Ginzburg's sketches constitute a gallery of portraits of her contemporaries, and a valuable literary history of her social group. They also represent a defense of "true" *intelligentnost'* (an orientation toward higher cultural and social values, ideals, and willingness to suffer for these) against the easy lamentations and lacerations unleashed and made more socially permissible by oppressive circumstances.

Chapter 5 treats *Notes of a Blockade Person*, a heterogeneous narrative in multiple parts that is not only Ginzburg's most important and famous "single" work, but also her most misinterpreted in terms of its genre—it is often taken for a diary or memoir. I conduct a detailed exploration of the layers of this palimpsest in order to identify more precisely the genre of *Notes*, an undertaking that crystallizes the central features of Ginzburg's writings as I investigate them throughout the book. Her techniques of self-distancing create a third-person narrative about a slightly generalized other, in a well-defined historical situation.

LYDIA GINZBURG: A BIOGRAPHICAL SKETCH

This tentative biographical sketch of Ginzburg is based on archival materials and interviews, as well as her own writings.[35] Any kind of straightforward biographical narrative goes against the grain of her poetics. So too does any biography of Ginzburg that separates her from her generational or historical context. With historical participation as her ultimate measuring stick, she summed up her life in a pessimistic way as lacking a biography.[36]

Lydia Yakovlevna Ginzburg was born on 18 March (5 March, old style) 1902 in Odessa into a fairly wealthy Jewish family, which had recovered from two bankruptcies. A brief sketch of both parents' backgrounds from Ginzburg's perspective survives thanks to the efforts of her niece, the writer Natalia Sokolova, who left a short biography of her aunt "resembling a family chronicle" in her own Moscow archive.[37] Born in 1916, Sokolova was the daughter of Ginzburg's older brother Viktor (1893–1960), a playwright known by his literary pseudonym Tipot.[38] Here is the story Ginzburg reportedly told her niece in 1977:

> My father died young, I don't remember him at all.[39] He was, evidently, a talented person. His was a merchant family, grandfather Moisei was a bankrupted merchant. He had lots of children. Grigory, the oldest, somehow recuperated the former wealth, although, probably, not to its full extent. He had a brick factory, and had his own horses. Their home was in Gorodnia, in the Chernigov Region [Ukraine]. [. . .] A huge house, practically an estate. As children, Viktor and I loved to go there with Uncle Mark. More than the successful and rather dry Grigory, I liked the somewhat odd bachelor Manuil, who lived with [his] mother, and she was already completely decrepit, moribund.

> There were a lot of brothers, all became merchants except Yakov and Mark, who chose science, chemistry [. . .] . Yakov was the brighter of the two, Mark stuck with him and was very devoted. They studied in Switzerland, in Bern, where it was easier to get into institutions of higher learning, and cheaper to live.
>
> A rich young lady from Russia traveled to Bern, Raya Gol'denberg, who perhaps wanted to study just a little bit, or to live freely and amuse herself for a while. Her father, a rich merchant, prevented her from studying, and was against her romance with the "pauper" [*golodranets*] Yakov Ginzburg. But in the end he got his way and became her husband. And then Raya's father went bankrupt (like Yakov's father before him). He was in the wholesale business in the export of grain, his steamship sunk. And of all the children of the poverty-stricken merchant Davyd Gol'denberg, Raya turned out to be the most provided for and best established.[40]
>
> Yakov Ginzburg died young, but left his business in running order, and it provided a moderate income: a laboratory for brewer's yeast. And the faithful Mark, who had never married, dedicated his life to mama and to us, his brother's children, and he stayed with mama until his very death. Father had a few inventions, various patents, and I remember advertisements for "viktolydin" (from the names of his two children), I think it was some kind of disinfectant to be used in production."[41]

It is remarkable that Ginzburg does not remember her father, Yakov Ginzburg, who died of a heart attack at the age of forty-five in December 1909, when she was seven years old. His business and family responsibilities were, as she notes, inherited by her uncle Mark, to whom she refers elsewhere as her stepfather.[42] Raya's light-heartedness is a trait Sokolova emphasizes, contrasting it with her Aunt Lydia's firm, decisive character and championing of reason, and repeats one of the witticisms of their friends: "a hen laid an eagle's egg."[43]

In pre-Revolutionary Odessa, the Ginzburgs owned two houses (parts of which they rented out) and employed maids as well as a German tutor.[44] Lydia Ginzburg's youthful diaries show that she read widely in Russian, German, and French (later, she read in English; her multilingualism did not extend to Yiddish or Ukrainian[45]). Together with her brother, she was involved in a semi-domestic theater troupe named Krot.[46] In the summer, the Ginzburgs rented dachas, a practice that continued into the mid- and late 1920s, when many Leningrad-based scholars (some of them originally from Odessa: Boris Eikhenbaum, Viktor Zhirmunsky, Grigory Gukovsky, Boris Tomashevsky, Boris Bukhstab, and others) came for extended visits. Ginzburg enjoyed sports: she was a sailor, tennis player, and an especially fine swimmer.

As a child she was a member of an outdoor scouting club and, as Natalia Sokolova reports, suffered a nearly fatal accident sometime between 1913 and 1915: her group set up a campfire over a hidden unexploded shell that went off just as Ginzburg was bending over it. She recovered after a month-long hospitalization (according to Sokolova, she had been unconscious and near death), but one or both of her eyes were permanently traumatized, easily tearing in her adulthood.[47]

Ginzburg's was a highly secularized Jewish family, some of whose members (but not Lydia Yakovlevna herself) converted to Protestantism, thus making university admissions easier (or even possible) for them.[48] Though she never set foot inside a synagogue as a child, she sometimes attended church on Sundays with her German governess, who instructed her to recite "The Lord's Prayer" at bedtime.[49] By the time she turned 17 (in March 1919), Ginzburg had become an atheist, and remained one for the rest of her life.[50] Never defining herself through her Jewish identity, she also never concealed it, deciding that "the only thing worse than Jewish nationalists are Jewish anti-Semites."[51]

Lydia Ginzburg's views and tastes were shaped by artistic and political radicalism, as was typical for an educated Jewish intellectual of her generation. She admired Blok and Mayakovsky and was sympathetic to both Russian Revolutions of 1917. She wrote of being eager to give up her shameful material advantages, to sacrifice on behalf of "the people" (*narod*). She recalls being most enthralled after the February Revolution, when as a fifteen-year-old she paraded around Odessa with a red ribbon pinned to her dress (only to be rebuked by her schoolmistress).[52] After October, she began to lose her enthusiasm. In Odessa, there were ominous signs of the coming powerlessness of the individual at the hands of the state: sailors strutting about with "gun-cartridge belts dangling from their necks," who "went around the city in packs and entered any home they pleased. This inspired a feeling of helplessness, alienation."[53]

Ginzburg grew up with a fondness and longing for St. Petersburg, the imperial capital since the beginning of the eighteenth century, and the backdrop for the Bolshevik Revolution. She idealized its granite-bound coldness and literary traditions, and fostered hopes that a great new life would begin to take shape for her there.[54] She begins a new diary with this entry:

> Thursday. 19 July 1920. Yesterday for the first time in my life, alone, without relatives, I left Odessa for Petersburg. The strangest thing is that from childhood I pictured it just this way—finishing eighth grade and going to "Piter" to study. And despite the "time" [that is, the Revolution and Civil War] it happened just so. [55]

Full of excitement as an offspring of Revolutionary upheaval, she arrived in a Petrograd that was devastated by famine, economic hardship, and the consequences of the Civil War.[56] At first, she studied chemistry, proving to be a miserable student (by her own account).[57] Three and a half decades later, she wrote about this move, characteristically transforming her autobiographical experience into an abstract case study by shifting her narrative to the third-person masculine and replacing Petrograd with Moscow.

> Here's a case for you, and there are many like it: a person, age eighteen, with keen abilities in the humanities, without any other abilities at all, imagines that in order to educate his mind, to achieve full philosophical development, it was obligatory to establish a foundation in the natural sciences. And so he makes his way, in a heated goods wagon, using the impossible transportation of the 1920s, to Moscow—to establish the natural sciences foundation for a future life in the humanities. Around him are famine and devastation, not yet overcome, and he has no material resources of any kind, and not a single thought about how he, actually, in practice, will transition from this basic foundation (which will likely take a few years to establish) to the acquisition of professional knowledge, and what to eat in the meantime. They thought back then that their minds were gloomy and skeptical. But in fact, without understanding it, they believed enormously in the life that had been flung open by the revolution. In this lies their historical right to be called people of the 20s.[58]

With a sense of a boundless future ahead, she began to sit in on classes with Alexander Vvedensky, the famous neo-Kantian philosopher who taught at Petrograd State University (formerly St. Petersburg University).[59] As was the case with many young people, she started her literary activities by writing poetry and even earned the praise of Nikolai Gumilyov.[60] Yet, even while Ginzburg describes her first year in Petrograd as a multifaceted "lesson"—"the poets' workshop, the poetic soirees, the museums, the city"—she nevertheless sums up all her accomplishments as having a "strangely negative character."[61] She remained obsessed by an unrequited love (see chapter 3), and failed to gain entry into literary circles. After her application to the university was rejected, Ginzburg returned to Odessa in summer 1921. Yet she remained determined to leave behind the "unserious" city of her youth in order to realize her talents.[62] One thinks of the statement by Eikhenbaum several years later, on a visit to Odessa as Ginzburg records it: "I don't understand,—Eikhenbaum said to me pensively,—how you could leave behind the sea, sun, acacias and so on and come to the north with such reserves of good sense. If I had been born in Odessa, it's likely that nothing good would ever have come of me."[63]

In October 1922, Ginzburg was admitted to the Institute for the History of the Arts, and moved back to Petrograd. Friends from Odessa who had already established themselves there helped with her admission.[64] She lived as a poor student (in a city where the population itself was, on the whole, deeply impoverished), staying with family friends or subletting rooms for short amounts of time[65]; her uncle Mark occasionally sent money.

Ginzburg named spring 1923, when Yuri Tynianov praised her very first seminar presentation, as the moment when she fully and seriously committed herself to a literary path.[66] Receiving confirmation of her talents from such a brilliant scholar was both exhilarating and frightening.[67] In her diary, she notes, "I have found an occupation that I like and which suits me, one that I can succeed at, and which might be my future; I have become convinced (at last, *objectively*) that creative forces reside within me, perhaps even significant ones—in any case, the kind that you won't find lying around on the street." On the other hand, now that it had become a reality instead of a dream, her future seemed destined to fall short of what she had imagined in her teenage years: "I believed that I would become a new extraordinary person, in the new extraordinary conditions." (Lest we think that this was a utopian "Soviet New Person," Ginzburg specifies that "what was new would have been external, for other people; while for me, this person was my own familiar ideal person that I carried inside myself.") "But now," she continues, "I am more and more firmly convinced that that person and those conditions will never be." She continues to see herself as "a person who is morally confused, a person who is cut off from the main road of private life." [68]

Yet Ginzburg put aside her doubts and entered a new creative and professional life. At the Institute for the History of the Arts, the birthplace of Russian Formalism, she was by her own account completely remade through contact with the teachers she called *maîtres.*

> The *maîtres* as such, in pure form, changed my life. [...] If there had not been Eikhenbaum and Tynianov, my life would have been different, I would have been different, with different abilities and possibilities to think, feel, work, relate to people, see things.[69]

She recalls much later how the experiences of teaching and publishing gave her group a temporary feeling "that we were becoming actors in a new branch of culture that was just beginning."[70] She describes Formalism as "a current which seemed to be in opposition to the epoch, but in reality was generated by the epoch."[71] However short-lived these experiences turned out to be, Ginzburg believed they determined her future trajectory. Joining an avant-garde movement in literature and scholarship produced a thrill of innovation, discovery, and social participation.

In 1924, a select group of students began to meet in a "house" seminar run by Eikhenbaum and Tynianov, choosing as their main topic nineteenth-century Russian prose. Together this group of pupils, later known as the "Young Formalists" (*mladoformalisty*: they included Boris Bukhstab, Viktor Gofman, and Nikolai Stepanov), produced a volume of articles called *Russian Prose* (*Russkaia proza*).[72] This 1926 volume contained Ginzburg's first article, devoted to the "Notebooks" (*Zapisnye knizhki*) of Prince Pyotr Vyazemsky, a Romantic poet and a friend of Zhukovsky and Pushkin, who at the end of his life attempted a major reconstruction of the epoch of his youth in a series of disjointed sketches, notes, and a collection of famous *bon mots*. In the same year, Ginzburg completed her course of study at the Institute and became a research fellow and teaching assistant there.[73]

While at the Institute, Ginzburg finally gained entry into the Petrograd literary elite, and soon became acquainted with Anna Akhmatova, Osip Mandelstam, Osip Brik, Vladimir Mayakovsky, Nikolai Zabolotsky, and many others. Working on Vyazemsky's legacy, Ginzburg at the same time started to write her own "Notebooks" in Vyazemsky's manner, which were meant to give a vivid and diverse picture of her time and milieu. From the mid-1920s on, Ginzburg's academic pursuits were related to her own literary plans and ambitions. Though she spent her whole life as a scholar and earned her living at it, she always saw her studies in literary history as a projection of the problems that were relevant to her as a writer.

The end of the 1920s saw the crisis and rout of the Formalist School by Marxist ideologues, leading to the closure of the Institute and the decisive silencing of the Formalists in 1930.[74] Even before then, in 1928, Ginzburg was removed from the roster of full-time graduate students at Leningrad State University (where she had begun to study under Eikhenbaum) for her "insufficient use of Marxist methods."[75] In December 1929, Ginzburg was attacked at the Institute by a Marxist ideologue from Moscow, Sergei Malakhov, for an article on the poetry of Venevitinov.[76] In Ginzburg's words, Malakhov, who planned to publish his accusations of her "militant idealism" in *Red Virgin Soil* (*Krasnaia nov'*), had a mission to "wipe her off the face of the earth." [77] Ginzburg was wounded by Malakhov's public pillorying, and by the rumors spread about it by another Marxist (Yakov Nazarenko), but this was nothing compared to her outrage at the fact that her teachers had not been present to help defend her (and she believed they knew in advance about the offensive). She exchanged a series of letters with Eikhenbaum and Tynianov in which she ended her apprenticeship to them, and after which Tynianov withdrew his article from a planned collection, evidently refusing to be published in the same book as Ginzburg.

Even before the final catastrophe, relations between the Young Formalists, especially Ginzburg and the *maîtres* had became strained due to the perennial struggle between "fathers and sons," to enormous political pressures, and to Ginzburg's own turn to sociological methods.[78] This break with her teachers (especially with Tynianov) deeply scarred her, and yet she carefully concealed it and never let it be known publicly, not even in later years. Although personally remote, she remained loyal to them and close to their intellectual tradition throughout her life, even at the risk of damaging her own professional prospects.[79]

Looking back from 1932, Ginzburg realized that by 1928 she had already abandoned her highest hopes of being able to realize her creative ambitions. She articulated three spheres of activity, the subtleties of which she would continue to study and experience for the next half-century: creativity, professional work, and hackwork.[80] In 1930–32, she drafted articles on Proust and on "Writers' Notebooks," which she came to realize were unpublishable.[81] She tried to make a living in children's literature. In 1930, she signed a contract for a children's detective novel, *The Pinkerton Agency* (*Agentstvo Pinkertona*), which she published after some difficulties in early 1933.[82]

In these years (and up until 1970), Ginzburg lived in the center of Leningrad, having officially registered in an apartment on Griboedov Canal (right behind Kazan Cathedral) in 1928. It was a communal apartment in which she had one large room: her neighbors included her intellectual collocutor Grigory Gukovsky, his brother Matvei, and Selli Dolukhanova, the sister of one of her Institute classmates.[83] In 1931, she brought her family nearer—moving her mother and uncle Mark from Odessa (thus helping to rescue them from the coming Ukrainian famine of 1932–33).[84] Ginzburg erected a dividing wall, creating a small room for her mother, who lived there until her death in the Leningrad Blockade in 1942. Meanwhile, she helped set up a sunny one-room apartment for her uncle in a Leningrad suburb, Detskoe selo (formerly Tsarskoe selo and later, the town called Pushkin); he resided there until his death in 1934.

In 1935, Ginzburg became a member of the Writers' Union, as part of a massive membership drive following the organization's 1934 founding. Between 1930 and 1950, she had many lecturing jobs through which she supplemented the publication fees that were her main source of income, which remained meager. Because she had been a Young Formalist (and because she was Jewish), her applications for a professorship at prestigious institutions of learning such as Leningrad State University were invariably rejected. Instead, she lectured at the Workers' Division at the Institute of the Air Fleet (*Rabfak Instituta Grazhdanskogo vozdushnogo flota*) (1930–34), and at the literary circle of the "Red Triangle" Factory (1932–?).[85] At the end of the decade, she was able to take advantage of the approaching centennial of the death of Mikhail Lermontov in 1941 to defend her candidate's dissertation at Leningrad State University based on the monograph *The Creative Path of Lermontov* (*Tvorcheskii put' Lermontova*) published the same year (1940).[86]

Ginzburg survived the years of the Stalinist Terror while living in Leningrad, although many of her friends were arrested and exiled or executed. She herself was arrested only once, in 1933, and jailed for two weeks in connection with a case that was being built against her friend Viktor Zhirmunsky.[87] Ginzburg describes the 1930s as a time that was psychologically more complicated and morally more difficult than the 1920s. On the one hand, there was enthusiasm about building a new society, which produced a tortured desire among the intelligentsia to join in and "Labor in common with all / At one with the legal order" ("Труда со всеми сообща / И заодно с правопорядком").[88] On the other hand, there were the horrors of collectivization, famine, arrests, and the Gulag; these demanded survival strategies of "adjustment, rationalization, indifference."[89] Ginzburg counts herself among those less "enchanted" (*zavorozhennye*) by Soviet ideology in the Stalin era; she attributed this to the fact that her ambitions were intellectual, rather than social or professional.[90]

The end of Ginzburg's Sturm und Drang period and the major shift in her social status and professional aspirations contributed to her literary reorientation. She no longer believed she was a participant in a central cultural trend, and increasingly positioned herself as an observer trying to make sense of history's development. Given her distance from the "common cause," intellectually and socially, she came to know the kind of isolation that is not a pose but rather is "practical, literal, and, what is more, threatens to take away one's piece of bread."[91] Starting in the early 1930s, failure, solitude, and marginality became key factors in Ginzburg's literary identity and self-image. She was marginal as a writer who could not even aspire to publish her work, as a scholar without a regular job in a totalitarian state, as a private lesbian in an increasingly homophobic society, as a Jew in a country where anti-Semitism, only slightly veiled, had gradually become part of official ideology, and discrimination on the grounds of national origins hardened into an established practice. Her approach to all these dimensions of her new social role remained the same throughout her life—she was ready to accept a marginal status, but adamantly refused to romanticize it. She was ready to bear hardships with dignity, but not to search for any consolation in them. Nostalgia for social norms conducive to the kind of ethics she sought defined her position and the structure of her new literary experiments.

In the same period, her interest in notebooks (*zapisnye knizhki*) as a genre faded significantly. While her notebooks for 1925–30 occupy 816 pages, her notebooks for 1931–35 are only half that size—376 pages. In 1935, she stopped writing them altogether (the last one was written after a long interval in 1943–44). What is more, the notebooks themselves change in nature. In the 1930s, we find in them fewer amusing episodes, portraits of great cultural figures, brilliant jokes and witticisms, aphorisms, and dialogues, and more mini-essays, fragments, and reflections on social issues and existential problems. Ginzburg may have begun to view some of these essays and fragments less as finished entities and more as études for larger generic forms.

Ginzburg's first "narrative" (she later coined the term *povestvovanie* to define this type of intermediary literature), "The Return Home" (*Vozvrashchenie domoi*), was written between 1929 and 1936 and dated 1931 for publication.[92] In it, she analyzes the psychology of love and the emotional texture of the meeting and separation of lovers as experienced against a background of different landscapes. It was followed in the late 1930s by at least two more narratives analyzing her personal experiences of the deaths of acquaintances, friends, and close relatives ("The Thought That Drew a Circle" and "Delusion of the Will"). In the late 1980s, Ginzburg would record a dialogue defining her own legacy as a prose writer:

> So there you have it, this person wrote about love, hunger, and death.
> —People write about love and hunger when they arrive [happen].
> —Yes. Unfortunately, the same can't be said about death.[93]

By the time she wrote this note, Ginzburg had already published or was preparing to publish most of her "narratives." However, the reading public did not know that at an early stage they had been designed as parts of one large unified work, which Grigory Gukovsky had greeted as a major novel.[94] A lifelong admirer of Tolstoy, Ginzburg gave to this quasi-novel the title *Home and Peace*, or more accurately *Home and the World* (*Dom i mir*).[95] She envisaged it as something like a diary-novel that would describe her own generation and social milieu, defined elsewhere in her notebooks as "the humanities intelligentsia of the Soviet type and nonofficial mold" (*gumanitarnaia intelligentsia sovetskoi formatsii i nekazennogo obraztsa*).[96]

As is clear from her definition of its genre, Ginzburg intended her magnum opus to be purely nonfictional, where the artistic effect would be created not by invention, but by selection and composition, and by a specific blend of description and reflections on human nature, psychology, ethics, and history. She tried to achieve her goals by elaborating meticulous quasi-scientific methods of analyzing herself and her immediate environment, by sketching and dissecting the characters of people around her and carefully recording their conversations in a stenographic manner. She used techniques of self-distancing in order to treat herself as a specimen, a representative of specific historical trends and tendencies. Ginzburg's "diary-novel" was never completed, but survived in the form of separate "narratives," essays, fragments, notes, and drafts. The drafts and sketches she wrote in the 1940s during the horrors of the war and the blockade could be considered as the continuation of her earlier pieces and the most significant part of her work in this genre.

Ginzburg writes of the onset of World War II as bringing a modicum of psychological respite after the Great Terror of the late 1930s. She survived the Leningrad Blockade by working as an editor at the Leningrad Radio Committee (in the Literary-Dramatic Section)—as a salaried employee from the beginning of 1942 through May 1943, and then as an adjunct editor (*vneshtatnyi redaktor*) until the end of the war. The radio was an important source not only of information, but also of hope and strength for all who lived under the siege. For Ginzburg, her work on the Radio Committee was a valuable experience of "social relevance" (*sotsial'naia primenimost'*)—a chance to feel accepted, even for a short period, within an established order of existence. There was also, momentarily, a slight freeing up of the cultural atmosphere, and it appeared that strong ideological restrictions would gradually ease. After the appalling hardships of the first blockade winter, Ginzburg resumed her work with an intensified creative energy. For a while, she had a feeling that the war had finally resolved the enigma of twentieth-century history, throwing retrospective light on the terror and repressions her generation had endured. Several times in her drafts, she mentions that "only now" could she finally understand the characters she chose for her "narratives" and the meaning of their fate, and thus perceive the full dimensions of her initial design: "Now I know who my typical heroes are: they are people of the two wars and the interval between them"; "Thus, only now has the historical fate of this phantom generation and the symbolism of its fate become comprehensible."[97]

Around 1942–45, Ginzburg wrote what are arguably her two most powerful narratives—"The Story of Pity and Cruelty" and "Otter's Day."[98] The former is a minute description of the blockade death of a close relative and a merciless analysis of the survivor's guilty feelings toward the one who was lost. The second narrative is what Ginzburg much later reworked as *Notes of a Blockade Person*. Both narratives focus on the same character, Ginzburg's alter ego, whose strange-sounding name, Otter, is most likely a transliteration from the French of both *l'autre* and *l'auteur*. She often used it in her autobiographical works of the 1930s and 1940s. Ginzburg analyzes the phenomenology of hunger and the basic structures of human nature and the social order that, from her point of view, were not so much destroyed as discovered and revealed by improbable physical and moral suffering. The sheer volume of essays, fragments, deliberations, drafts, character sketches, and records of conversations that she wrote during these two or three years of endurance and struggle for survival is unparalleled in her literary career.

All these activities nearly came to a halt after the ideological freeze of 1946 and the ensuing anti-Formalist and anti-Semitic campaigns. Seven years, from Andrei Zhdanov's speech against Anna Akhmatova and Mikhail Zoshchenko in 1946 and until Stalin's death in 1953, marked the nadir in the history of Soviet literature and humanities. Because of the new wave of purges following the war, Ginzburg wrote, people began to resign themselves to the fact that the brutality would be never-ending.[99] It seems that during these years, her last hopes, those that had enabled her to keep writing in the horrific time of the Great Terror and the Leningrad Blockade, were extinguished. In the editions of her prose, this entire period is not represented by a single line.[100] Meanwhile, Ginzburg worked on her doctoral dissertation, on Alexander Herzen's *My Past and Thoughts*, with which she faced tremendous difficulties.[101] One of her indirectly autobiographical essays from 1954 profiles an anonymous character who has been struggling for several years to publish his book. Only now that the situation has become less lethal (after Stalin's death) can he allow himself to process the humiliation and pain of those years, when his voice would unwillingly take on a supplicating tone, when friends would avoid talking to him, when he lived in mortifying fear of every phone call and visit with the publishers. She writes of how a person begins to fear "the very process of humiliation" even more than its verdicts or consequences, which included the very real possibility of death.[102]

Ginzburg's only regular academic job came during the anti-cosmopolitan campaign, when her friend Eleazar Meletinsky hired her as an associate professor (*dotsent*) at the university in Petrozavodsk (*Karelo-finskii gosudarstvennyi universitet*) (1947–50). It was deemed safer in these years to remove oneself from view, and she commuted between Leningrad and Petrozavodsk, where she stayed with Meletinsky (according to one source, sleeping in his bathtub).[103] Eleazar Meletinsky was arrested in 1949, and Ginzburg was (in her own words) driven out of the university soon after.[104] At the end of 1952, she was brought in for questioning in a case against Eikhenbaum, but fortunately the death of Stalin a few months afterward (on 5 March 1953) "saved my life, among countless others," as she wrote many years later.[105]

During the Thaw after Stalin's death, Ginzburg's slow rise began. In 1957, she finally managed to defend and publish her doctoral dissertation on Herzen's *My Past and Thoughts* (a book she had described as plagued by a deep-seated lack of freedom).[106] In the 1960s, she wrote and published her book *On the Lyric* (*O lirike*) (1964), which finally established her status as a leading scholar.

She connected with other people of her generation such as Nadezhda Mandelstam, and began spending summers with her and the Meletinskiis in Tarusa (where Mandelstam introduced her to Varlam Shalamov)[107] and Peredelkino. She started reading passages from her notebooks and narratives to a small number of younger admirers, and they soon began to help her type up selections with an eye to future publication. Among these generations of writers, poets, artists, and literary scholars she was revered as a "keeper of the flame," one of the last survivors of the glorious days of the Russian avant-garde.[108] It is from these younger writers and intellectuals that we can still hear reminiscences about Ginzburg today, about her customary hosting rituals (eggs and mayonnaise, a carafe of vodka), a domestic orderliness atypical for the intelligentsia, a conversational style that patiently circled around a thought while acquiring ever more precision, her absolute trustworthiness in keeping secrets, her decency, her mentoring of young poets, and her love of "literary scandal." Many of these friends are able to lovingly imitate her slow, nasal manner of pronunciation.[109]

In the 1960s and 1970s, Ginzburg published several reminiscences, based on material from her notebooks, about her friends and acquaintances of old: Eduard Bagritsky, Anna Akhmatova, Yuri Tynianov, and Nikolai Zabolotsky. She also resumed writing, and during these years wrote some of her best essays, including "About Old Age and Infantilism" ("O starosti i ob infantil'nosti"), "On Satire and Analysis" ("O satire i ob analize"), and many others. The genre of the "note" with its witticisms and *bon mots* reappears (composed now on loose pages, handwritten and then typed, rather than in *tetradi*), as she captures the lives and personalities of both the younger generation and coevals such as Nadezhda Mandelstam, or elders such as Akhmatova. More typical, however, is the longer philosophical or sociological reflection, with a more marked presence than earlier of the first person singular "I," perhaps in response to Ginzburg's rising social status (or decreasing marginality). In these same years, Ginzburg took up amateur photography, as another way of observing and recording her milieu.[110] However, it seems clear that the project of the Proustian "diary-novel" had been abandoned. As Ginzburg wrote in 1954: "Secret little shoots of the future, leaves which are placed inside the desk, are now nothing more than the traces of fallen plans."[111] What was to have been her major work was now split into dozens and hundreds of more or less disjointed fragments. Nevertheless, in the 1960s Ginzburg was once again trying to get one of the most important of these fragments through censorship.

The publication of Solzhenitsyn's *One Day in the Life of Ivan Denisovich* in 1962 significantly shifted the boundaries of the possible in public discourse about the horrors of the past, giving Ginzburg cause to hope that her blockade narrative could also be published. At the same time, she obviously did not want to be perceived merely as one of Solzhenitsyn's epigones and thus had to reject the format of "one day in the life of *x*." In one of the introductions to the new version of her blockade narrative, she wryly remarked: "Compositions that lie ripening and decaying in the desk drawer for decades acquire literary predecessors, just as naturally as published literature acquires successors."[112] She rewrote "Otter's Day" into the text she now planned to title simply "Blokada," replacing her main character with the many voices of witnesses, and thus transforming a personal narrative into a more general description. But while she was working on these changes, the Thaw came to an end. The publication of her blockade narrative was postponed for two more decades.

Literary scholarship—*literaturovedenie* as it was called in the nomenclature of Soviet science (Ginzburg several times mentioned that she hated the word)—was now the only sphere of activity available to Ginzburg as a way both to support herself and to acquire some sort of social standing. In her monograph *On Psychological Prose* (*O psikhologicheskoi proze*, 1971), she tried, as was so typical of her, to find some intermediary ground between the "twofold conversation—about life and about literature" that she had been carrying on for fifty years. Ginzburg called it "the most intimate among her scholarly books," precisely because it spoke about "in-between literature, about the most important questions in life, and the most important writers for me."[113] There is another gap in her "notes" from 1966–73, which appears related to her intensive work on this book; as she once explained: "While my last book was being prepared and written, everything else was put aside for a few years, including these notes."[114] At the same time, some pages of the book came straight out of the laboratory of her earlier notes and essays. The scholarly discussion of intermediary literature was continued in her next book *On the Literary Hero* (*O literaturnom geroe*, 1979), which shows the fruits of her long-standing interest in Western sociology and psychology.[115]

In 1970, Ginzburg's work and living environment changed: the conversion of her apartment building into the Railway Ticket Office forced her to move out, and her friends helped her secure a one-room apartment of her own, the first noncommunal space she lived in during her whole adult life.[116] While Ginzburg had been worried about moving to the outskirts of the city (telling Lidiia Lotman, "It's not Petersburg, not Leningrad. It's a different city!"), she reportedly grew accustomed to her apartment and enjoyed taking long walks in the nearby parks.[117] The walls of her apartment were decorated with avant-garde art from the 1920s, works by David Burliuk, Mikhail Matiushin, Dmitry Mitrokhin, Alexander Tyshler (a portrait of Anna Akhmatova in which the poet had "corrected" her nose[118]), Vasily Chekrigin, Alexandra Ekster, and others (gifts from her friend the art collector Nikolai Khardzhiev).

In spring 1982, on the occasion of her eightieth birthday, her friends and colleagues organized a jubilee at the House of Writers (*Dom pisatelei*) with speeches in her honor, followed by a dinner at the European Hotel (*Evropeiskaia*). Her notes for her speech point out how her interests, which were in fact those of her whole lifetime, were again in fashion. For instance, she talks about how as Tynianov's student, she was influenced by historicism; by her personal disposition, the early Formalists' practice of "immanent analysis did not attract" her. Already in the 1930s she was making "conscious attempts to join historical and structural approaches," which she identifies as one of the "basic problems of contemporary literary criticism." She also talks about her proximity to developments seeking to explore the "intersections of literary scholarship and psychology, social psychology." She specifies her interest in "the problem of historical character, the forms of historical behavior. The semiotics of personality."[119] Despite the proximity of her interests to Yuri Lotman and the Tartu School, she was never embraced by them, a situation, as friends reported, that left her feeling wounded.[120]

Ginzburg had pessimistically concluded in 1980 that she had begun the final, "unhistorical" period of her life. She had no inkling that her reputation was about to undergo a second renaissance, even more significant than her rise as a scholar in the Thaw. The year 1982 marks the first publication of a small selection of her notes in *Novyi mir*. In the same year, she published more notes in a book of articles and reminiscences, *About the Old and the New* (*O starom i novom*).[121] Less than two years later, the Leningrad literary review *Neva* finally managed to publish the abbreviated version of her blockade narrative under the title *Notes of a Blockade Person* (*Zapiski blokadnogo cheloveka*): in the table of contents, Ginzburg was introduced as a "new name."

The sensational success of *Notes of a Blockade Person* stimulated public interest in her work. As a writer, she finally began to reach a wide readership. The policies of *perestroika* and the ensuing collapse of the barriers imposed by censorship made possible further publications. In 1987 and 1988, she stunned the Russian reading public with two successive essays: "Generation at a Turning Point" ("Pokolenie na povorote") and "At One with the Legal Order" ("I zaodno s pravoporiadkom"), providing an acute sociopsychological analysis of the reasons why the Russian intelligentsia sympathized with the Bolshevik Revolution and managed to coexist with the Stalinist Terror. The last years of her life witnessed the publication of three more books with ever-growing quantities of previously unpublished prose; the final volume was prepared by Ginzburg in the last months of her life and published posthumously.[122] In 1988, Ginzburg was awarded the State Prize in Literature and Arts for her books *On the Literary Hero* and *Literature in Search of Reality* (among the dozen or so laureates that year were the director Aleksei German, the poet David Samoilov, and the writer Anatoly Pristavkin).[123] Her scholarly acclaim rose as her interests seemed to coincide with widespread interest in the sociology of literature and with developments in structuralism and in semiotics.

However, even having passed her eighty-fifth birthday Ginzburg could not limit herself to preparing her earlier works for belated publication. As she had said at her birthday celebration three years earlier,

> It's pleasant to tell a person whose jubilee it is that they are young—irrespective of age—and that they have everything ahead of them. I understand that this custom is a mere convention and don't flatter myself. Whatever else is true, it is still good that the desire to express myself in written form has still not deserted me.[124]

Ginzburg continued writing and reflecting about the past and present in the final years of her life. She was also deeply interested in the huge political and cultural changes in the Soviet Union, and acquired her first television, in order better to follow current events. One of her last essays discusses Gorbachev and perestroika.[125]

Ginzburg's feverish activity may have put a strain on her health. Her doctor, Yakov Yurievich Bogrov, reported to me that around 1975 and 1980, she suffered two small strokes, but made an impressive recovery. (These strokes may account for the shakiness of Ginzburg's handwriting in the 1980s manuscripts.) In 1986, she wrote to Natalia Sokolova (who was then occupied with Tipot's archive and trying to collect letters between her aunt and her father):

> I'll certainly search for your father's letters (I can't say whether successfully). I couldn't start doing this yet, because I've been ill. Overexertion and as a result, brain spasms. I'm only now returning to myself. I can't at all get used to the fact that at my age, one has to do everything judiciously—and that includes working. I had to interrupt my reading of my book proofs.[126]

In July 1990, according to Dr. Bogrov, Lydia Ginzburg suffered a minor heart attack followed by a major stroke; she died a few days later on 15 July, at the age of eighty-eight. She was buried in a modest grave in the cemetery at Komarovo, where Anna Akhmatova and many other poets, prose writers, and scholars of Leningrad/Petersburg whom she had known are laid to rest.

CHAPTER 1

Writing the Self after the Crisis of Individualism:

DISTANCING AND MORAL EVALUATION

In a New Year's reflection at the beginning of 1932, Lydia Ginzburg wrote a startling self-description: "My sense of myself is that I'm a piece that's been torn, with its threads still hanging, from the fabric of social reality, which I've succeeded in bringing up close to my eyes, a scrap of reality that's just handy enough for close observation."[1] In sensing that she's a random piece of a whole, she signals her departure from the usual posture of autobiographical subjects, who present themselves in their narratives as uniquely deserving of the reader's attention.[2] And instead of making a neat temporal split between the narrating and the narrated "I"—the "I" now and the "I" in retrospect—Ginzburg offers herself to herself as an object for self-analysis, not as an autonomous entity, but (to explicate the logic of her suggestive metaphors) as an inextricable part of the social fabric.

Ginzburg's approach to herself as a fragment of social reality means that she highlights not what is unique, but rather "everything that is psychophysiologically and historically law-governed." She analyzes her fate and the fate of others as "the point where universal tendencies intersect."[3] At the same time, despite her overwhelming interest in those universal tendencies, she selects the individual person as the unit of analysis. Even in 1934, when pressures mounted to adopt a Marxist methodology, Ginzburg understood that while historians and economists could build theories around mass phenomena, she herself required "a method that's suitable for understanding both the historical process and the fate of a single person as a social being."[4]

Beginning in 1925 and spanning the seven decades of Soviet rule, Ginzburg wrote all kinds of documentary prose—essays, dialogues, and longer narratives bridging the essay and the novelistic diary—containing miniature analyses of individual characters that together constitute a vast canvas of the social realities of her time. Her essays provide rich material for cultural and literary historians alike, who rely on them to understand individual figures such as Osip Mandelstam or Anna Akhmatova, as well as life during the Leningrad Blockade or the working milieu of the cultural intelligentsia.[5] At the same time, Ginzburg's experiments in prose are driven by a larger, more ambitious goal: to describe and portray a new concept of the self, appropriate for her times. This is a project undertaken in response to both a crisis in values and a crisis in literature.

Ginzburg tended to view literary evolution through the prism of concepts of personality and selfhood, and defined the great writers in her pantheon (Rousseau, Herzen, Tolstoy, Proust) as those who discovered and introduced new ways of understanding the self.[6] She lamented the fact that literature after Chekhov and the Symbolists had entered a period of stagnation, due to a failure to arrive at new concepts of the person. During World War II, Ginzburg declared, "The absence of a grand style is the universal characteristic of the whole epoch. It is in general the decline of the culture of the humanities."[7] Here she is not referring to the crisis of the humanities as academic disciplines (so familiar to us now), but rather to a crisis in values and the loss of belief, whether in individualism or social progress. She goes on to describe how the Soviet Union represents the most extreme case, since in it "high literary culture was violently cut off." However, in the West, despite its freedom of expression, literature also suffers from the inertia caused by "the absence of a new fundamental concept of the person" (*otsutstvie novoi printsipial'noi kontseptsii cheloveka*).[8] As I have already noted, Ginzburg does not use the term "self," which has no equivalent in Russian. Her preferred subject is *chelovek*, person or human being, which she uses to refer both to herself and generalized others.[9] On occasion, she uses the first-person pronoun "I" (in its personal and abstract senses), the reflexive pronouns "oneself" (*sebia* and *sam*, within words such as "self-assertion," *samoutverzhdenie*). She frequently speaks of *kharakter* (character, personality, disposition), and on rare occasions, of *lichnost'* (personality, person, individual).[10] The meanings of Ginzburg's *chelovek* could be said to overlap with Charles Taylor's definition of the self as a being "of the requisite depth and complexity to have an identity . . . (or to be struggling to find one)."[11]

For Ginzburg, the interrelationship between a crisis in literature and a crisis in human culture hinges on the concept of the self and its ethical grounding. She suggests that ethics is, in the final analysis, the core content of literary activity: "Literature is concerned with characteristics, personalities, and actions—with every conceivable form of generalized human behavior. And whenever behavior is involved, all basic life values become ethical values."[12] In linking together selfhood, ethical behavior, and narrative, she follows a long philosophical and literary tradition. Charles Taylor remarks in *Sources of the Self* that "Selfhood and the good, or in another way selfhood and morality, turn out to be inextricably intertwined themes."[13] And as thinkers from Aristotle to Paul Ricoeur have shown, we look to existing narratives to teach us lessons about how to be good, and create new ones when examining the ethical challenges of our own lives. Ginzburg makes a link between literature, ethics, and selfhood in the specific social and historical context of the twentieth century, which fomented an acute awareness of social evil, a psychological and philosophical distrust of human wholeness, and—last but not least—a distrust of the narrative form and its habitual categories.

Ginzburg perceived the world around her as morally catastrophic. Even in its periods of relative stability, she viewed everyday Soviet life as a "kingdom of immorality."[14] She describes the people of her generation, who faced two world wars and the horrors of Stalinism, as "twice and thrice smashed to bits" to the point where they realized "the ineradicable nature of social evil and the illusoriness of the individual consciousness."[15] The delusions—that societal reorganization could eradicate social evil, and that the individual consciousness had unconditional value—could both be traced back to nineteenth-century humanism.

Ginzburg inherits and perpetuates the obsessions of the great nineteenth-century Russian authors who sought to portray the person typical of their times, and then to question this self's moral accountability. Yet in her own historical context, the nineteenth-century practice of presenting characters as "self-sufficient souls" appeared to her as "fruitless, epigonic." She sought new ways and forms of perceiving and analyzing the twentieth-century person, with nothing but a shaky "moral routine" to guide his or her thoughts and actions. In plans for her unfinished quasi-diary, quasi-novel *Dom i mir* (*Home and the World*), Ginzburg describes the hero she will portray as a "consciousness that is at once subjectively positive but also nonindividualistic" ("Изображение сознания субъективно-позитивного и притом неиндивидуалистического").[16] He is "positive" in that he refuses to understand his situation as tragic and tends to seek out ways to justify himself, and "subjective" in that his worldview is not rooted in universal values. But it is the last term—"nonindividualistic"—that marks Ginzburg's most significant departure from her predecessors.

Individualism, as Steven Lukes has shown, has a wide variety of meanings, depending on the cultural and historical context. The concept Ginzburg is rejecting emerged from German Romanticism, which celebrated (as Lukes summarizes) "a notion of individual uniqueness, originality, self-realization."[17] Since each person embodied unique qualities or potentialities, he had the obligation to achieve self-perfection and thereby fulfill his role in world history.[18] Herder extended this principle of uniqueness to nations or peoples.[19] The sociologist-cum-philosopher Georg Simmel draws a sharp contrast between the eighteenth-century ideal, promoting the development of the person as a representative of life-in-general or nature ("a mere crosspoint and a resolvable pattern of fundamentally general laws") and the nineteenth-century one, which emphasized difference and "the deepening of individuality to the point of the individual's incomparability."[20] In a sense, with her emphasis on general laws (*zakonomernost'*), Ginzburg brings elements of eighteenth- and nineteenth-century approaches into her twentieth-century prose, while also accounting for intervening developments such as the collapse of religious belief.

In her book *On Psychological Prose,* Ginzburg surveys different philosophies of individualism related to German and Russian Romanticism. She emphasizes the connections between individualism and religious beliefs:

> The commandments of God and the absolute transcended the individual and were therefore beyond dispute. Even the metaphysically understood requirements of the elect personality transcended his individuality, inasmuch as they were requirements of his spirit, to which the empirical individual was obliged to submit.[21]

She goes on to remark that some concept of absolutes that transcend the individual (Ginzburg describes these absolutes as "suprapersonal," or *sverkhlichnye*) persisted even in early positivism, in naturalism, and in Western utopian socialism. Indeed the Decadents, too, at the turn of the nineteenth and twentieth centuries, "could not even avoid reliance on the idea of sin, which is why [the school of Decadence] so easily accommodated itself to dogmatic religion, although the latter would seem to have been fundamentally opposed to it."[22] Yet, starting with the broad ascendance of atheism (under the influence of Schopenhauer, among others) in the second half of the nineteenth century, the most difficult challenge for "nonreligious ethics" was "to establish fresh criteria of value and fresh principles of individual human behavior—to discover, in other words, the reasons for their *necessity*." A "critical impasse" in individualism was caused by the sense that a single life could have no meaning unless the soul had some sort of absolute value or afterlife.[23]

Ginzburg, firm in her atheism, places her twentieth-century hero in a position where this crisis has already lost its tragic quality. In the 1930s drafts of *Home and the World,* she specifies that her hero is a consciousness that is "isolated; nonreligious and nonrevolutionary, disconnected, nontragic (death does not contradict it), extra-moral, infantile, relativistic, etc."[24] In some senses, these attributes correspond to the negative connotations of individualism in French thought. Leaving aside Rousseau (whose main influence in this regard was on the German Romantics), *individualisme* in France referred to the phenomenon of an isolated person inhabiting a disharmonious social order.[25] Ginzburg planned to represent her hero "against a backdrop of the history of personal self-consciousness (Rousseau to the present)—from lofty individualism to decadent subjectivity." I speak of Ginzburg's self as "post-individualistic" (instead of her own term, "nonindividualistic") in order to underscore her awareness of the history of self-consciousness, "from Rousseau to the present," and the enduring power of the Romantic concept.

The most relevant epithet Ginzburg uses for her nonindividualist hero, one that sums up his qualities and predicament, is "immanent." This word often describes the early Formalists' approach to literary texts through the study of factors intrinsic (or "immanent") to the work, while bracketing historical context, the author's biography, and other extra-literary influences. The concept traces back to Kant, who designated as "immanent" those principles limited to the realm of experience, empirically verifiable, as opposed to being transcendentally derived. In one narrative, Ginzburg introduces her autobiographical (yet typical) hero as a representative of the "immanent" consciousness, which is "global in scope." She explains that "people of this mentality lack unconditional values that are posited externally. Their values (and without values no one can act) are either given them by the rules of [social] community [*sotsium*], or are the outcome of their own inclinations, talents and abilities."[26] As she writes in a 1940s draft, the actions of people like this respond to immediate situations—in fact, she speaks at this point of "the person" *as* a "situation," an "intersection of biological and social coordinates" from which behavior and "functioning" arise.[27]

The tragedy of the immanent consciousness is not in its death, for as Ginzburg writes, "it does not dare wonder at its own finitude." It is in the very experience of reality as disjointed, of the moments of one's life as bearing no relation to one another. Ginzburg writes that this consciousness experiences time in the "spatialized" manner that Henri Bergson blamed for preventing our access to time's "duration," and hence to our deeper (*profond*), more fluid and persistent selves.[28] This segmentation and isolation of time seems to devalue one's emotions, pleasure as well as pain. For, as she writes, "there is something even more offensive in the fragility and futility of suffering than there is in the momentariness of pleasure—some kind of disrespect for the person." This immanent consciousness is constantly in a state of perplexity: it cannot rationally get a grip on feelings that pass without leaving a trace. Moreover, "it cannot have a relationship to death, because death doesn't concern it. It is eternally empty—like a sieve, placed below pouring water."[29] Ginzburg investigates the question of this type's "moral victory or defeat in battle with its fatal disjointedness."[30] She makes the predicament of the immanent consciousness—fragmented and uncertain of its own reality—into a central subject of her reflections, whether on the ethical potential of this kind of consciousness, or its import for the justification of art and the literary methods appropriate for her times.

Ginzburg's writings follow in the analytical tradition of documentary prose as practiced by writers such as Alexander Herzen, who made "theoretical, generalizing thought, and the depiction of reality in terms that remain unmediated by the invented world of the artist" into the structural material of his memoir, *My Past and Thoughts*.[31] The techniques she employs in order to represent the immanent consciousness disrupt novelistic conventions of plot and character.[32] The novel in the twentieth century was an impossibility for her just as it was for Osip Mandelstam, who famously argued in "The End of the Novel" (1922) for the "connection between the fate of the novel and the status at a given time of the problem of the individual's fate in history." Since the "compositional measure of the novel is human biography," if a person can have no biography then there can *be* no novel. Mandelstam understood the twentieth-century person as lacking the power and even the very sense of time to sustain a full biography.[33]

Ginzburg's post-individualist self, fluid and fragmentary, is a being whose persistence through time as a connected entity is in question (the permanence that Ricoeur sees as a crucial nexus between notions of "selfhood" and "sameness," *ipse* and *idem*).[34] Anxieties concerning the discontinuous self trace back at least to Locke, who disrupted the unity of person through his arguments about the relationship between mind and body.[35] Ginzburg was certainly aware of being heir to twentieth-century versions of an iterative self (one that varies with every moment of enunciation) which find their current elaborations in theories such as those of Judith Butler (the notion of performative identity).[36] And yet, the freedom to invent/reinvent oneself does not appear to Ginzburg as a positive or comforting value, but rather as a quality that invites moral irresponsibility. Once she identifies this nonindividualistic, fragmented, rootless, "immanent" self, she attempts to explore whether there are structures that could lend it meaning. Ginzburg salvages elements of the humanistic tradition of the nineteenth century and smuggles them into the heart of the twentieth. She herself seems to embody a generalization she makes in a scholarly discussion of twentieth-century prose: "A writer felt the pressure of his time, but he still could not forget the lessons of the 19th century."[37]

The first half of this chapter contains an analysis of Ginzburg's interrelated theories of selfhood, ethics, and literature in response to what she discerned as the predicament of the nonindividualist, immanent subject. Her central argument involves the notion of writing as an "exit from the self," an ethical act that arises from an immanent impulse but then connects immediately to its social underpinning. To explore Ginzburg's ideas about the necessity for new directions and techniques in prose in light of literary and cultural history, I draw largely on several of her essays from the decades following World War II (but published much later, in books such as *Person at a Writing Table*, 1989). I also rely on unpublished drafts from the 1930s, such as plans for the narrative "The Thought That Drew a Circle" ("Mysl', opisavshaia krug") and for *Home and the World* (*Dom i mir*).

Ginzburg's investigations of selfhood and ethics can seem abstract, but they were always grounded in lived praxis, and at times they were remarkably concrete and frighteningly graphic. In the second half of this chapter, I analyze two key narratives, "Delusion of the Will" ("Zabluzhdenie voli" ca. 1934) and "A Story of Pity and Cruelty" ("Rasskaz o zhalosti i o zhestokosti" ca. 1942–44), whose hero (the same in both stories) is driven by repentance to analyze and examine memories that haunt him. Here, the almost cavalier attitude toward one's experiences or personal biography expressed in Ginzburg's statement about the self as "a piece . . . torn from social reality" is replaced by an opposite kind of relationship. When a character feels guilty for the miserable final days and death of another person, he ceases to relate to himself only as social reality. Thus, the author endeavors not to bring her self closer to her eyes but rather, to analyze personal, painful, and chaotic memories in a self-distancing manner, in order to release them. The typicality and "rule-governedness" (*zakonomernost'*) of the hero's experiences have to be actively constructed.

These two narratives—Ginzburg calls them *povestvovaniia*, a form that shifts between essay and short story, between fiction and documentary prose—showcase the unusual effects of her externalized presentation of self. She uses multiple strategies of distancing to analyze and depict episodes in the life of a character who represents the twentieth-century "immanent" consciousness. Ginzburg's methods of "self-distancing" (in Russian, *samo-otstranenie*[38]) have certain commonalities with Shklovsky's theory of estrangement (*ostranenie*), as well as Bakhtin's "outsideness" (*vnenakhodimost'*). And yet, while Ginzburg's *samo-otstranenie* is achieved primarily in the writing process, it is more than an aesthetic device: it is an ethical and psychological strategy. A major aim of perceiving the self from the position of the other is to create a subject with a continuous or unified identity, such that he is capable of feeling answerable for his actions to concrete others and to himself.

AFTER INDIVIDUALISM, A NEW LITERARY "CONVERSATION": POST-WAR REFLECTIONS

Ginzburg's categorical rejection of individualist prose for her era, as articulated in her postwar essays, hinges on four factors that necessitated a break with this literature. The first factor is the very existence of the nineteenth-century past, in which the drama of individualism played out to the point of exhaustion. This past is problematic, furthermore, because its ideologies and personalities helped inspire the Revolution, whose long-term effects have been disastrous. The second factor is the catastrophic present: the world wars and the Stalinist Terror, which shattered any notion of the "absolute value of the individual soul."[39] The third factor is overwhelming state oppression, which reached everywhere and made individuals feel utterly powerless. The final factor is the general crisis in values, signaled by the triumph of moral relativism and social determinism. Let me explore these four factors in detail.

Ginzburg elaborates her demands for a post-individualist prose in an essay called "Celebration of the Sunset" (dated 1958 in the typescript, not published until the late 1980s).[40] She opens with a description of a beautiful sunset, which "gnaws" at her because of its established association—death. Reflecting on the predicament of a writer, now past middle age, who has failed to realize herself, Ginzburg then forbids herself from assenting to the conclusion of nineteenth-century authors that "life is an empty and stupid joke."[41]

> People of the second half of the nineteenth century reviled life and clamored against death. One can excuse them for this contradiction, recognizing that they were people of a lost paradise. Not long ago, in everyone's memory, the paradise of absolutes had vanished into thin air, absolutes ranging from Catholic dogma and the Declaration of the Rights of Man to Hegel. Having lost absolute values and on top of that the immortality of the soul, it makes sense that people could hotheadedly scream for a few decades that life was a lie and a joke. But when they repeat endlessly that life is meaningless, and meanwhile they live on and on, and die very unwillingly, and continue to write about the fact that it is not worthwhile to live, as if to write about this nevertheless were worthwhile,—all of this can nourish neither theoretical thought, nor art.

> Люди второй половины XIX века поносили жизнь и вопияли против смерти. Это противоречие можно им простить, приняв во внимание, что они были людьми потерянного рая. Недавно, у всех на памяти, рассеялся рай абсолютов, разных—от католической догмы и Декларации прав человека до Гегеля. Понятно, что, потеряв абсолютные ценности и, больше того, бессмертие души, можно было сгоряча несколько десятилетий кричать о том, что жизнь обман и шутка. Но когда до бесконечности повторяют, что жить бессмысленно, и притом живут и живут, и очень неохотно умирают, и продолжают писать о том, что не стоит жить, как если бы писать об этом во всяком случае стоило,—то все это уже не может питать ни теоретическую мысль, ни искусство.[42]

This passage gives a colorful, informal history—at once sympathetic, dismissive, and ironic—of the individualist consciousness as expressed in nineteenth-century art. The "classical antimonies of individualism" had lost their power and relevance—art would come to a dead end if all it could do was simply repeat that "life is nonsense, a cruel joke and so on."[43]

Another problem with the nineteenth-century past was its complicity in the ideologically motivated horrors of her own era—a complicity that Ginzburg felt her generation was uniquely positioned to understand and recognize. She expressed this thought most precisely when admiring (in the 1950s) a 1931 poem by Osip Mandelstam, "We'll sit together in the kitchen for a little while": "The genuine word in art—if that word is still possible—probably can be uttered precisely by us. And this is not because we have seen the most dreadful things,—over there [that is, in the West] they have also seen a lot."[44] Ginzburg rejects the idea that witnessing horror alone confers a new understanding of life that can find reflection in literature: writers in the West continued to write individualist prose despite what they had witnessed. Soviet writers could arrive at the "genuine word" because their suffering came from violence that had a basis in lofty ideologies with their illusions of progress: "only we have experienced on our own skin, year by year, the departure of the 19th century. The end of its great illusions, its brilliant prejudices, its arrogance . . . all the banquets of its individualism." The Revolution (which Ginzburg initially supported as a teenager) aimed to overthrow individualistic, capitalist societies and build up socialist ones instead, based on equality and community. Communist ideology drew on various strands of nineteenth-century thought, such as populism, humanism, socialism, Marxism, and even Romanticism, with its dream of a better, more perfect world, its supermen and geniuses.[45] Ginzburg perceived how nineteenth-century humanism, with its high ideals, paradoxically became complicit, in retrospect, in some of the crimes of Communism, since it supported the belief that the ends justify the means, that great sacrifices were needed to build a bright future. "And all of us, the *intelligents* of the older generation," she writes, "are party to this sin."[46]

For Ginzburg, the crisis of individualism, of coming to grips with the nonexistence of God and moral absolutes, belonged to the nineteenth-century past—which meant that artists who still engaged with these questions were making their audiences experience "an unhappy recognition of what has been said about fifty years ago." She writes, "Nothing more can come of this path except for deceptively new repetitions (and 'new' even here only if they are on a high level). Because it is precisely in the 20th century that the conversation about the futility of life, begun long ago, has ended, and another conversation has begun—about *how* ever to [or how one could possibly] survive and endure without losing one's human image [о том, как бы выжить и как бы прожить, не потеряв образа человеческого]."[47] Ginzburg's choice of the word "conversation" does not specify any particular genre but would certainly be fitting for her in-between prose. The final phrase of this passage, "survive and endure without losing one's human image," suggests the second factor that prompts the need for a new twentieth-century prose: the predicament of total moral and physical catastrophe. Ginzburg writes: "A productive art is one that explains why a person should go on living (after all, it cannot be from cowardice alone), and demonstrates or aims to demonstrate the ethical potential of life, at least in the catastrophic circumstances of the twentieth century."[48]

"Celebration of the Sunset" connects with conversations that were occurring across Europe and the United States about human values and about art in the wake of the catastrophic destruction of World War II, and after the Holocaust (an issue epitomized in Theodor Adorno's dictum about the impossibility of writing poetry after Auschwitz).[49] Jean-Paul Sartre wrote in his essay "Situation of the Writer in 1947" of the irony that there existed a painting by Miró called *Destruction of Painting,* while "incendiary bombs could destroy the painting and its destruction together." He states that "We would no longer have dreamed of crying up the exquisite virtues of the bourgeoisie" since there was doubt as to "whether the French bourgeoisie would exist tomorrow." The most burning question among writers was "to know *whether one could remain a man in war-time.*"[50] Vasily Grossman, in his great postwar novel *Life and Fate,* portrays a guard in the Nazi gas chambers who is "dimly aware that if you wish to remain a human being under Fascism, there is an easier option than survival—death."[51] And Varlam Shalamov in his 1965 essay "On Prose," written after he had survived decades in the Gulag, but also with a knowledge of the war, wrote that "the most important thing for a writer is to preserve a living soul."[52]

Ginzburg detected a new "ease of death" (*lëgkost' smerti*) in the twentieth century: the quiet and unceremonious way in which individuals could be wiped off the planet.[53] In her epoch, she argues, despite the persistence of an instinct for self-preservation, *fear of death* ceased to function as an "ideology," as a "measure of things," on account of the growing irrelevance of individualism and the raw visibility of death.[54] The hero of Tolstoy's iconic story *The Death of Ivan Ilych* (1886) famously resisted (almost until the last moment) accepting that he himself, like every individual, was subject to Aristotle's syllogism: "All men are mortal, Socrates is a man, therefore: Socrates is mortal."[55] Ginzburg, in turn, writes of death as the most expected event in the Leningrad Blockade. These kinds of "easy deaths" abound in Soviet (nonofficial) fiction: one thinks, for instance, of Yevgeny Zamyatin's character

Maria in "The Cave," who wants to escape the suffering of the Civil War siege of Petrograd and asks her husband for a vial of death-delivering poison "as simply as if she were asking for tea,"[56] or of the statement in Shalamov's "Dry Rations," "We understood that death was no worse than life, and we feared neither."[57] Ginzburg also speaks of friends, members of the intelligentsia, who were sent to the Gulag and realized how arbitrary their arrests had been. In light of indiscriminate cruelty, camp inmates beheld their fates as typical: "Astonishment in the face of social evil was the offspring of the nineteenth century. [Those who have returned from the camps] tell us about what we should expect from the twentieth. 'The regular patterns are familiar to everyone, and here's another typical case for you, and this case is—I.' "[58] When premature death becomes a common fate, an individual's protest against the cruelty of his own personal misfortune loses its meaning, even for himself. It is not this individual meaningless suffering that Ginzburg wants to make into the theme of her art but rather the logic behind it, together with moral failures and the beauty of life even in periods of extreme hardship.[59]

The truly epochal writers of the twentieth century, according to Ginzburg, were those who reflected the devastations in life as typical, making their heroes into humble everymen. She found this in Osip Mandelstam's later poems,[60] as well as in Chaplin, Kafka, and Hemingway. Ginzburg summarizes the new egalitarian model, starting with an implicit contrast to Dostoevsky:

> Instead of a free world of ideas you have an utterly inescapable and crushing world of life's objective horror. The hero is a sufferer, a little man, simply a human being. His function has radically changed. He has now become the spokesperson for everyone—the great and the small, the stupid and the smart, the well-taught and the barely literate. This is what accounts for the democratism of the contemporary consciousness.[61]

This "democratic" contemporary consciousness was forged through the leveling power of cruelty on a massive scale, whether perpetrated by Soviet or Nazi forces.

The third major factor to which, in Ginzburg's view, contemporary prose should respond was the determining influence of social forces, and the weakness of individual power in the face of oppressive, totalitarian regimes such as that which existed in the Soviet Union. Shalamov in his own essay-manifesto wrote that the new prose should ask, "whether it is possible to actively influence one's fate when it has been pulverized by the cogs of the state machine, the cogs of evil."[62] Reminiscing in 1989, Ginzburg noted how totalitarian pressures had "ground down the personal qualities of human beings. Inherent to the Stalin era was the unification of behavior when people were faced with the threat of torture and punishment. The liars lied and so did the righteous, the cowards cowered in fear and so did the brave, the eloquent and the incoherent both held their tongues."[63] In the 1950s, she reflects: "A person is strong only as the carrier of a social dynamic. . . . There were those who thought this Marxist position was refuted by our practical experience. On the contrary, it is confirmed by practical experience."[64] The fact that a single individual (such as Joseph Stalin, dead by the time Ginzburg wrote this note) could cause an unlimited amount of destruction did not disprove this rule, for "even a four-year-old child, playing with matches, can burn down a village or a wooden city." But the limited constructive power of any individual is dependent on "historical preconditions."[65]

In a 1980s essay, Ginzburg writes: "The twentieth century, with its excessive social pressures, has gradually taken away a person's experience of the absolute value of his own self [переживание абсолютной самоценности]."[66] In this context, instead of individualism, Ginzburg argues, "What turns out to be definitive is a person's social role."[67] When considering the status of moral choices, she adopts a functionalist view of behavior, where "the good" represents no more than the internalized values of one's own reference group and a function of one's social role.[68] In her book *On the Literary Hero*, Ginzburg demonstrates her deep engagement with social and psychological theories that have attempted to explain personality and its formation (by Karl Marx, Wilhelm Dilthey, Sigmund Freud, Eduard Spranger, Max Weber, Karl Jung, Dmitry Uznadze, William James, and others). She also explores the relationships between these theories and novelistic experimentation with character (in the twentieth century, Samuel Beckett, Michel Leiris, André Breton, Jean-Paul Sartre, Nathalie Sarraute, Philippe Sollers, and other members of *Tel Quel*). In particular, she focuses on how novelists have represented the strength of social forces and the decline of the individual's power, whether through absurdism, the abandonment of character as a literary device, or the foregrounding of amorphous and fluid consciousness-as-language.[69]

Ginzburg finds these newer responses less diverse and less interesting, however, than those of the nineteenth century.[70] In both *On the Literary Hero* and *On Psychological Prose*, her vaguely Hegelian story of the evolution of psychological prose begins with Vissarion Belinsky's letters of the 1830s to 1840s (full of self-scrutiny and highly personal encounters with German philosophy), and proceeds along a path influenced by French and German literature and philosophy until it reaches its pinnacle in Lev Tolstoy.[71] Outside Russia, she sees Proust as achieving the highest level in the self-conscious examination of personality. She champions Tolstoy and Proust for investigating "social conditionedness" (*obuslovlennost'*), historical forms of personality, the new types produced in an ever-changing society, and the gaps between a person's fluid identities (or self-concepts) and his or her social roles. Ginzburg argues that the Tolstoyan emphasis on conditionedness, more than any stylistic marker, signifies a writer who continues in the late nineteenth-century traditions that grew out of Realism.[72] She places Chekhov, Gorky, and Proust in this camp. Tolstoy's emphasis on psychology as process, which Chernyshevsky distinguished as a feature even of his earliest prose (in the 1850s), became a dominant approach among twentieth-century writers.[73]

Ginzburg identifies Dostoevsky as an influential writer for twentieth-century Modernists,[74] including the Symbolists (such as Andrei Bely) and the German Expressionists.[75] In this sense Tolstoy's polar opposite, Dostoevsky departs into the freer realm of ideas or metaphysics, where social norms matter less. He rebelled against deterministic theories so prevalent in the 1860s and 1870s, and refused to trace his heroes' actions back to any socially conditioned "chain of causality": "Between the historical preconditions and the behavior of Dostoevsky's hero comes the idea which he, this hero, nurtures and embodies."[76] However, as Ginzburg argues in her book *On the Literary Hero*,

> It turns out that the typical person cannot say "everything is permitted," because he is governed by the mechanism of socialization, internalization, expectations, prohibitions, the values of his milieu, of his "reference group."[77]

Ginzburg had no taste for authors whose heroes possessed an unreal dose of freedom. She followed the Tolstoyan "Realists," rather than the Dostoevskian "Modernists." What she aimed to portray in her twentieth-century poetics were typical personalities in conditions of supreme constriction: the Leningrad Blockade, for instance. Hers is not a psychological literature where individuals get to freely choose their own conflicts, where "the intellectual—not satisfied with the resistance offered by [mere] things and circumstances—preferred to produce the resistance himself and resolve it himself (insofar as he could)." In some senses, her hero's predicament is a throwback to earlier epochs: "In our memory [that is, during our lifetime], the conflict of the literary hero has once again become an external conflict, just as in pre-psychological times."[78] The kind of literary character who is portrayed from the outside, this return to "pre-psychological" prose, she finds in artists like Chaplin and Kafka.

The fourth factor to which Ginzburg responds in fact overarches the previous three: the status of the self in a world where the belief in absolute moral values is absent. In contrast to the crises of values in the past, when Nietzsche unmasked the genealogy of morals, and literary characters protested this loss, she writes that her own generation experienced a need to cling to the hollow shells of moral habits or the "prejudice" (*predrassudok*) from former epochs. "Conventions" might be a better translation than "prejudice," since Ginzburg means it in a positive sense, as a synonym for what she calls "moral routine."[79] From her vantage point, to complain that morality now lacked a metaphysical basis was to misunderstand the use value of moral habits. In the Leningrad Blockade, she realized that reconstructing, reanimating old conventions (a job that was in part being done "administratively," through decrees, initiatives, and special measures) was a tool that society could use in order hastily to construct a defense against selfish and criminal behavior.[80] Ginzburg did not dare to hope for new philosophical principles that might give absolute weight to these conventions.[81]

The acknowledgment of a world constructed around moral conventions accords with a view of the self as shifting and dependent on situational variables. Ginzburg writes: "The person of moral routine is the person of situations, from the biggest historical ones to the most transient everyday ones."[82] She regards herself and her contemporaries as "situational people," fluid arrangements of contradictory qualities, adaptable to changing environments: "a person is not a static arrangement assembled from contradictory parts (still less is he one of a piece). He is an arrangement of changing goals and, depending on these goals, he makes his move from one sphere of value into another, seeking self-fulfillment in each of them."[83] The only consistent attribute of a person was his will to self-realization or self-actualization in any given situation, in the midst of which he might pick his values rather opportunistically.

The great challenge of taking a situational or functional view of character was in maintaining the ethical dimension. As Ginzburg wrote in both her scholarly work and her notebooks, the paradox of nineteenth-century heroes was that on the one hand, they were absolved from responsibility through an analysis that placed the blame for their faults and misdeeds on their corrupting milieu, while on the other hand they possessed the freedom to wrestle with their conflicts and devise solutions and actions. Psychological analysis grew increasingly complex as it explored this relationship between freedom and determinism.[84] And yet Ginzburg sought a clean break from both determinism and psychological analysis. She criticizes the kind of analysis that beholds a person as a whole and from within ("в целом и изнутри")—in order to forgive his or her moral aberrations. Discarding this approach as inappropriate, she presents her key argument about external perspectives:

> We are contemporaries of those who were disposed to make themselves a cigarette case out of human skin. Our deterministic analysis has a limit beyond which it cannot [should not] go. Those who lit the Auschwitz fur-

naces and all those who are like them have no psychology; their home isn't shaken by misfortune, their children haven't died. They are a pure historical function which you have to destroy in the person of its concrete bearers.

But what about the theory of situations? Contemporary ethical sensibility does not accept determinacy as a basis for absolution of guilt. It has more affinity with the deep and cruel words of the Gospel: "Temptation must come into the world, but woe unto the one through whom it must come."[85]

If we examine large historical evil deeds and then everyday moral licentiousness, it turns out that we are in practice looking at qualitatively similar phenomena—now from without, now from within.

Мы—современники тех, кто бывал расположен сделать себе портсигар из человеческой кожи. Наш детерминирующий анализ имеет предел, перед которым он останавливается. У зажегших печи Освенцима и у всех им подобных нет психологии; дом их не потрясают несчастия, у них не умирают дети. Они—чистая историческая функция, которую следует уничтожать в лице ее конкретных носителей.

Ну а как же теория ситуаций? Современное этическое чувство не приемлет детерминированности в качестве отпущения вины. Ему ближе глубокие и жестокие слова Евангелия: «Соблазн должен прийти в мир, но горе тому, через кого он придет».

Если от больших исторических злодеяний обратиться к повседневному моральному блуду, то оказывается—явления качественно близкие мы практически рассматриваем то извне, то изнутри.[86]

Ginzburg makes a stern argument that the writer's role should not be to arouse our sympathies for a person who becomes an Auschwitz executioner, even if his path to evil originates in domestic tragedies. This was the dilemma of the postwar moment—writers recognized the importance of socialization in shaping individual behavior, but they desperately wanted to escape the supreme moral relativism that such social theories encouraged. To explore the character of an executioner from an "inner" or sympathetic point of view, in a psychological novel or documentary prose, was therefore a taboo subject for Ginzburg. She concludes the essay "On Satire and Analysis" by imagining the thoughts of one of those who carried out the 1949 purges and stopping herself: "Enough already! This psychological novel has already been written by the nineteenth century."[87]

Grossman, another ethically minded follower of Tolstoy, arrived at a different solution to this dilemma while writing *Life and Fate*, his novel about

World War II, modeled after *War and Peace*. He draws small portraits (on the scale of the ones he writes about Russian snipers in Stalingrad, for example) of several prisoners who operated the gas chambers, all of whom have some positive qualities and complex biographies that brought them to this position. But Grossman still refrains from portraying the worst sort of guard, who takes pleasure in the executions and whose behavior "could be explained by some terrible, innate depravity." His novel's author-narrator affirms that, despite the overwhelming strength of the State and the inevitability of fate, individuals do bear responsibility and can be judged guilty for their actions.[88]

For Ginzburg, the accursed questions of individualism (freedom, individual value, the loss of absolutes), and the tradition of addressing them through the imaginative analysis of an individual's inner life, could not shape a new "conversation" or a modernist prose adequate to the twentieth century. Overcoming an unacceptable moral relativism depended on achieving an external point of view on one's own actions. In practice, a person regularly comes up with summary images and phrases to judge others, but rarely turns these judgments on herself. Ginzburg, however, saw this as the key to a moral existence.[89] Her endeavor to move beyond individualism produces striking results in her self-writing—which is at once psychological, self-distancing, and philosophical. Writing itself turns out to be a key element of her overcoming individualism, and this is because, as she theorizes, writing is an ethical act as well as act related to selfhood and identity.

ART AS "AN EXIT FROM ONESELF"

Ginzburg's central statement on art, ethics, and creativity focuses on her concept of immanence:

> A person withdraws into the self, in order to exit from self (and the exit from oneself is the core of the ethical act). A person seeks within his very self what is higher than himself. He then finds the undeniable facts of inner experience—love, sympathy, creativity—in his immanence [that is, they are immanent to him], but these facts still do not quench his thirst for finding the ultimate grounds for them in society.

> Человек уходит в себя, чтобы выйти из себя (а выход из себя—сердцевина этического акта). Человек в себе самом ищет то, что выше себя. Он находит тогда несомненные факты внутреннего опыта—любовь, сострадание, творчество—в своей имманентности, однако не утоляющие жажду последних социальных обоснований.[90]

This statement comes from the essay "On Satire and Analysis," designated by Ginzburg as her "writer's *credo*," where she frames the theory of writing within a discussion of ethics.[91] Composed in the 1960s, the essay anticipates the culminating section of her book *On Psychological Prose* (centered on Tolstoy), into which she transplanted formulations, sentences, and even whole paragraphs directly from this *credo*.[92] In the creative act, the artist first retreats into herself, in order to exit from the self (or ego), moving into language, into the sphere of the other. Ginzburg stipulates that creative impulses are immanent, residing within our selves as part of our inner experience or intuition, but that they also demand that we find their social basis in order to justify their significance. Ginzburg writes of this as a paradox of the "individual-psychological realm."[93]

Ginzburg's formulation of art as an exit from the self, and of this exit as an ethical act, has philosophical predecessors in Vladimir Solovyov and Jean-Marie Guyau. In "The Thought That Drew a Circle" (1930s), she refers explicitly to Solovyov's theory of love when remarking that love is the "simplest, most elementary means of exit from oneself."[94] She continues:

> If the principle of love consists in the fact that what is located outside of me becomes me, then the principle of activity (creativity) consists in the fact that I become located outside of myself. And it must be said—this is almost one and the same principle.
>
> Если принцип любви в том, что вне меня находящееся становится мною, то принцип деятельности (творчества) в том, что я становлюсь вне себя находящимся. И надо сказать—это почти один и тот же принцип.[95]

Love and creativity encourage the "overcoming of subjectivity" (*preodolenie sub'ektivnosti*) and "making the world objectively real" (*ob'ektivatsiia mira*).[96] According to Solovyov, when we are in love the very center of our being shifts so that we begin to live not only in ourselves, but also in another.[97] He posits that a person sacrifices his ego in order to offer his "true individuality" (*istinnaia individual'nost'*) to a union with another, which is eternal and immortal.[98]

Ginzburg follows Solovyov in many respects, but rejects his lofty individualism. Instead of the word "individual," she uses the reflexive pronoun *sebia* ("oneself") to designate the entity into which one enters, for preparation or inspiration, and out of which one then escapes into art and love. Love and family are the ultimate test case for Ginzburg (and here she also departs from Solovyov, a mystical advocate of unconsummated love), because they are in themselves extremely egotistical states, even if "this egoism knows that some things are so necessary for the individual life that they already transcend its boundaries." While Ginzburg reflects more often on creativity, that is, creative work, as an ethical act than on love, she notes that the latter is more broadly relevant: "love and family are truly democratic values; for their realization you do not need to be one of the chosen few—or you need to be chosen in a completely different sense."[99]

Before Ginzburg, the French philosopher Jean-Marie Guyau had also argued that artistic impulses come from within, that the artist "is, by an inward force, driven to cast forth his inmost self, to give us of his innermost."[100] Ginzburg almost certainly knew at this point his 1885 treatise, *A Sketch of Morality Independent of Obligation or Sanction*, to which she later makes reference in *On Psychological Prose*.[101] Guyau aimed to establish a postreligious ethics starting from life itself, "to find out what a moral philosophy would be without any absolute obligation, and without any absolute sanction."[102] Ginzburg takes a similar approach when she asks: "Outside of absolutes, outside of the indisputable demands of a common consciousness—how does the ethical act arise in the day-to-day existence of an ordinary person?"[103] Just as Solovyov had found in the case of love, Guyau argued that creative impulses are immanent and universal: they originate in the ego but, as Guyau notes, an individual's life-force and talent seek to extend beyond the self, and require cooperation with others in order to realize themselves:

> Life, like fire, only maintains itself by communicating itself; and this is none the less true with regard to the intelligence than with regard to the body. . . . It is our whole nature which is *sociable*. Life [. . .] cannot be entirely *selfish*, even if it wished to be.[104]

He argues that the irresistible urge to let others know "that we exist, feel, suffer, love" is not egoism, but the "antithesis of egoism."[105]

In her essay "On Satire and Analysis," Ginzburg defines the ethical act as the "sacrifice of the lower for the sake of the higher" (*pozhertvovanie nizshim radi vysokogo*), an overcoming or sublimation of "basic desires" (*pervichnye vozhdeleniia*) in the service of higher values, determined as such by one's social milieu.[106] The creative act, although inspired by immanent impulses, is still an ethical act, because the artist moves beyond basic, selfish needs in order to provide others with something of value. Guyau, too, thought that social values were higher on the moral scale, and even noted a "remarkable characteristic" of "intellectual pleasures": "they are both the most *inward* and the most *communicative*, the most *individual* and the most *social*."[107] Guyau did not place special emphasis on the sacrifice involved in artistic creation (or "intellectual fecundity," as he calls it), but he did propose that there must be a kind of law of the conservation of energy, demanding that intellectual fecundity be balanced against "physical generation" (he writes: "The organism cannot, without suffering, accomplish this double expenditure").[108]

The sacrifice Ginzburg envisions is "not necessarily a sacrifice of the 'Christian type.'" In other words, one is not attempting to martyr oneself to save others, but rather sacrificing one's "free time, peace, and nerves" in order to do creative work.[109] At the end of her essay, Ginzburg alludes to the great sacrifices demanded of Soviet artists by citing the case of Osip Mandelstam. His writings cost him his social position, all means of subsistence, his freedom, and finally his life. After quoting his lines "I have been deprived of the cup at the feast of my fathers, / Of merriment, and of my honor . . . ." Ginzburg continues: "He deprived himself, but carried [his thought/word] to the people."[110] In *On Psychological Prose* (where she is discussing a different theme, the Romantic image of the artist), she says, in a more general vein: "Creative impulses, even though they may be immanent, control a person in ways that the strictest laws of the external world are not always capable of doing."[111]

ART AS PERMANENCE, VALUE, AND MEANING

But the fact that writing is based on "immanent" creative impulses does not settle the question of its meaning or value. Ginzburg comes up with three major solutions to justify creativity, all crafted from the perspective of the immanent self and all relating especially to life-writing. Writing can be justified, according to Ginzburg, as a victory over time, as a socially significant act, and as a way to create meaningful structures. Let me address each of these in turn.

The chief anxiety caused by the crisis of individualism stems from doubt over the self's continued existence through time as a single responsible entity. In drafts for "The Thought That Drew a Circle" from the 1930s,[112] Ginzburg addresses the problem of forgetting, which makes both joys and sorrows impermanent, and results in a constant "dying" (*umiranie*) of the self, which she figures as a series of corpses piling up in one's past.[113] This impermanence, she writes, necessarily leads "to the idea of the meaninglessness of life, which as it were does not exist." Memories, to the extent that one retains them, have no intrinsic meaning, and are doomed to fade away without a trace, like pleasure or pain. However, Ginzburg follows Marcel Proust in combatting this problem through the idea that the self has another faculty, "creative memory" (*tvorcheskaia pamiat'*), which can transform memories into "products" that are "valuable, durable, and that can always be (re)experienced" (*vechno-perezhivaemymi*).

Art then is justified for Ginzburg because it can activate a "creative memory" within the immanent self, so that time can be experienced and reexperienced in an integral and self-conscious way:

> After Hegel, it seems, no one has defined art as powerfully as Proust. In the last volume he explained why art is needed, and by the same token, why it has existed and will continue to exist. Art is time regained, it is a battle with nonbeing, with the horror of not leaving a trace. Objecthood regained, for every object can bring time to a stop. The creative spirit has won its greatest victory—it has stopped the river into which it is impossible to step twice.
>
> После Гегеля никто, кажется, не определял искусство с такой силой, как Пруст. В последнем томе он объяснил, зачем нужно искусство, и тем самым—почему оно было и будет. Искусство—найденное время, борьба с небытием, с ужасом бесследности. Обретенная предметность, ибо всякий предмет—остановка времени. Творческий дух одержал величайшую свою победу—остановил реку, в которую нельзя вступить дважды.[114]

In this definition, art is necessary because it helps the artist to conquer the fear of forgetting, the fear of death (regardless of its social value or ability to transform the reader).[115] But Proust's solution can succeed only if the artist "creates only one work during his or her whole lifetime, so that the past never stops being a single present, which can be experienced an endless number of times."[116] Otherwise, the artist might experience estrangement from his previous works.

Ginzburg refers to her disjointed, fragmentary notes using the singular noun "conversation" (usually, a "conversation about life"). Yet her notion of writing as a stoppage of time seems to depend less on a single work than on the activity of writing itself (whether its relationship to the autobiographical self is direct, indirect, or semi-indirect).[117] Beginning with her teenage diaries, she expresses the urge to live in a maximally conscious way, as well as the fear that whatever fails to achieve verbal expression will fade away and die.[118] At age twenty-seven, Ginzburg asserts: "Everything that is not expressed in words (aloud or to myself) does not have reality for me, or rather, I do not have the right organs for perceiving it."[119] Further, she defines a writer as "a person who cannot *experience life* unless he/she is writing."[120] She describes herself in precisely this way in an unpublished note: "As a result of self-observation, it was long ago established that I am not adapted so much to live as to be conscious of living."[121] And in a 1935 note, she tells her friend Grigory Gukovsky that if she were the sole inhabitant of a desert island, she would write on the sand (he quips that her desk-drawer activities amounted to the same thing).[122]

This does not mean, of course, that Ginzburg experienced no anxieties: she gives voice on several occasions to a fear of her own indifference and of a "cessation of desires" (*ostanovka zhelanii*), including the desire to write.[123] However, the desire always returned—sometimes with a vengeance, as during the Leningrad Blockade, her most prolific period. In many instances, writing seems to have become a means of overcoming a sense of powerlessness by establishing a conscious relationship (*otnoshenie*) to social evil and to death. A person or "ward" (*podopechnyi*) may not be able to control how he or she will be used by the "Leviathan" (Hobbes's term, which Ginzburg uses to refer to the State in her blockade notes), but he or she can decide how to think about it.[124] While struggling to survive the siege, Ginzburg writes: "A relationship is defensive armor" (*Otnoshenie eto bronia*).[125]

In her drafts for "The Thought That Drew a Circle," Ginzburg remarks that it is "rather decadent" to justify experience by virtue of its creative transformation into objects that hold value for the artist alone.[126] For personal memory to be more meaningful, it has to be of "value" to others. Here we move to Ginzburg's second main justification of art, as a socially significant act. She argues that the artistic impulse itself springs from an intuition that the communal holds sway over the individual, from a desire to contribute value to society. This notion reminds us of Guyau, but here Ginzburg refers to the French writer Jules Romains and his doctrine of Unanimism, which posits that even the most individualistic ideas are in fact social, and that art represents a merger with the collective consciousness.[127] The social genesis of all values lends to art a meaning that hedonistic pleasure could never provide. "Only ideology, i.e., a system of values, can organize a person's behavior," Ginzburg claims. Unlike pleasure (which is fleeting), value endures in memory; what's more, it is a social entity, which persists as a timeless and "living ideological reality." Only value, she maintains, "solves the question about happiness and about human behavior" (both related to "the problem of evaluating the facts of life," such as pleasure and suffering). But this theory means that one must renounce individualism: "For in the individual consciousness, it is possible to found the hedonistic criterion of pleasure, but you cannot found the criterion of value." From here, Ginzburg moves on to define creative activity and to justify it ethically: "Creative memory transforms neutral or negative facts of life into value. Creativity presents itself as the most subjective value that grows from within. But, essentially, this is an aberration; certain preconditions are necessary for creativity,—even if they are unconscious,—of the social meaningfulness of this act."[128] Like artworks, values represent "time regained"—but, crucially for Ginzburg, in a nonindividualistic way.

A text takes pieces of one's experiences and gives them an independent social existence (especially when they reach an audience). On the most basic level, the self becomes another in literature through language, which is social in nature.[129] Ginzburg further postulates that artists have the power to effect changes in language, and to bring new ideas into the collective consciousness. In the late 1930s, she writes: "What is an independent [or self-sufficient] human being? [Nothing but] a cave creature. But spiritual life is life in the word, life in the language that has been given to us by society that we might contribute to it some nuances that come from ourselves."[130] While in agreement with structuralist and post-structuralist theorists about the social construction of language and society, Ginzburg does not follow them in sounding the knell for the "Death of the Author."[131]

Ginzburg's third major argument, related to the first two, justifies art as the creator of meaningful structures. She places faith in the concept of structure: "Meaning is itself a structural association, the inclusion of a phenomenon into a structure of a higher and more general order. In a work of art, for example, no element is equal to itself, but is rather placed into a symbolic association of expanding notions." Moreover, art serves as a model for the meaningful organization of life experiences. The fusion of the aesthetic and the ethical is especially important for Ginzburg: "The hierarchical structures of the meaningful interpretation of life, when they come to be embedded in each other, gather height [Структуры иерархического ряда жизнеосмысления, вмещаясь друг в друга, набирают высоту]. Thus meaning and value together form an experience that cannot be dissected into parts."[132] Her logic is circular: meaning accrues when a phenomenon is inserted into a structure of a higher order; therefore structures have meaning. In art, meaning emerges from the interconnections between elements immanent to a work. At the same time, the "expanding notions" into which each element is placed through its "symbolic associations" may also refer to meanings that result from the larger literary, historical, or social context.[133]

The structure and meaning of one's life increase through the creation of a biography—either written down (as an artwork), or enacted in everyday life (as a self-concept). Ginzburg writes: "One can understand death if one understands life as a fact of history and culture. As biography. And biography is a finished structure and thus by its very nature finite." Like her contemporary Vasily Grossman, Ginzburg is attracted by the benefits of emplotment: "This way life is not an assortment of disjointed moments, but a person's fate. And every moment carries in itself the burden of everything that has passed and the germ of everything that is to come."[134] Indeed, each passage in a biography (like each line in a poem) is not equal to itself—it gathers meaning because of its interrelationship to other parts, to the whole, and to "history and culture." To justify one's life in the face of death, it helps to perceive that life as biography, even while it is in progress.

The idea of life as a work of art recalls the Russian Symbolists' concept of *zhiznetvorchestvo* (life-creation), understood, in a Nietzschean vein, as the complete aestheticization of one's daily life. Ginzburg herself defined *zhiznetvorchestvo* as "the deliberate construction in life of artistic images and of aesthetically organized sequences of events."[135] But she (like many in the generations that followed the Symbolists) was skeptical of this specific kind of life-art: "the trouble is that life as a whole refuses to be aesthetically organized."[136] The Symbolists themselves, she notes, knew that in the end their life-art turned into "a mystical joke, buffoonery."[137]

One might rather see Ginzburg's ideas in a different context: they show a close affinity to the little-known work of Grigory Vinokur, the Moscow linguist and literary scholar, who had personal ties to some of the Formalists. In *Biography and Culture* (1927), a book influenced by German *Lebensphilosophie*, Vinokur offers a far-reaching concept of biography as a mental structure, or form of experience, which endows human action with historical and social meaning. True to his linguistic background, he compares the development of personality to a verbal, and in particular a syntactic structure, one that takes shape gradually over time. He distinguishes syntax from chronology: "The logical order itself, in which a biographer groups the facts of development, and all facts in general, is an order that is not at all chronological, but necessarily syntactical."[138] Ginzburg agrees with Vinokur's negative view of chronology, which she calls "the most primitive aspect of structuration," since it leads to the idea that "the only reality for a person would be the last day of his life."[139] In her view, the facets of a life should be ranked by importance (instead of taking the latest developments as most significant), in order to arrive at a "unity of consciousness" (*edinstvo samosoznaniia*).

Ginzburg's ideas (and Vinokur's) share common ground with one of the practitioners of *Lebensphilosophie*, Wilhelm Dilthey and his hermeneutics of art, as it extends into an understanding of life (much of it derived from his studies of psychology and literature). What seems to be most relevant for our purposes in Dilthey's work is the notion that individuals gradually build a "structural nexus" (connected to a sense of their own psyche, values, purposiveness, and creativity) according to which they operate and develop. A researcher who grasps an individual's "psychic unity" could understand not only his past, but could even predict his future development (that is, in Ginzburg's terms, his fate). Dilthey discusses how the individual's "structural nexus" develops in collaboration with "this kind of structural whole which is society." For Dilthey, "The most perfect life would be just that whose every moment would be fulfilled with the feeling for its independent value."[140]

One can understand Ginzburg's reflections on art—its value, meaning, and import for the ethical understanding of life—in this context. She writes, "the only thing that can lead out of the dead-end [of subjectivism] is a governing principle of behavior. The notion of a person's life as the solution to a problem, as the fulfillment of a purpose [осуществление назначения]. Life as a process of becoming, so that everything that has been lived through has meaning as an experience or a stage [in the process]. In this [process of] becoming, the last thing does not cancel out but builds on what preceded."[141]

THE REMORSEFUL SELF: EXPERIENCING THE REALITY OF ANOTHER

Ginzburg's theories about ethics, the immanent self, and writing with an external perspective can be explored in remarkably concrete ways in two of Ginzburg's most powerful narratives, which analyze the moral failings of a character who suffers a death in the family. "Delusion of the Will" and "A Story of Pity and Cruelty" are quasi-fictional treatments of the deaths of Ginzburg's uncle and mother (transformed into the male protagonist's father and aunt, respectively).[142] Guilt and repentance (*raskaianie*) are at the core of the two pieces. Her hero examines how egotism and isolation blinded him to his relative's true existence. He is deeply repentant about his cruel and selfish behavior in the months and weeks leading up to the death that has made his mistakes forever irreparable. Moreover, he feels responsible for the very fact of the relative's death.[143] Ginzburg refuses to release her autobiographical hero from this guilt by placing blame on the environment or uncontrollable circumstances—the Leningrad Blockade, poverty, old age, flawed health care, a cruel state bureaucracy—in a pointed departure from what she perceived as a shortcoming of many nineteenth-century novels.

Tolstoy in *The Death of Ivan Ilych* portrayed a man compelled by his approaching death to reconsider the life he has lived, as well as the very meaning of life. In contrast, Ginzburg obsesses over how the post-individualist, immanent person (represented by her alter ego) experiences the seemingly avertible death of a close relative.[144] "Delusion of the Will" contains an extremely detailed recollection of the physical process of an old man's death, from an observer's point of view. N. (Эн, the narrative's hero, originally called Otter) curses himself for his passivity and inadequate response, but studies the death so carefully that its moments and images haunt him for months and years to come.[145]

Ginzburg calls death a “spotlight” (*prozhektor*) that “sheds a sudden light on the facts of life,” just as a theater’s spotlight illuminates a specific action on the stage. She writes about death’s spotlight as “realistic” and salutary: “consciousness, as it flows in a murky stream, has a need for these projectors.”[146] In “Delusion of the Will,” Ginzburg uses another theatrical metaphor—the tearing down of the curtain—to express the processes of truth-seeking and self-examination that death sets in motion:

> Death tears a piece of being out of the darkness. In order to avoid pain, we don’t allow ourselves to understand the life of the one who is near and dear to us. But the pain that is caused by death is so strong that it does not fear any other pain and tears down the curtain.[147] We seek out a concentration of pain for ourselves, because we experience the death of a loved one as our fault, which demands an internal punishment. Thus death raises up repentance. And repentance loves details and knows how to establish the connection that was overlooked.
>
> Смерть вырывает участок бытия из темноты. Чтобы избежать боли, мы не позволяем себе понять жизнь родного человека. Но боль, причиненная смертью, так сильна, что она не боится никакой другой боли и раздирает завесу. Мы ищем для себя концентрацию боли, потому что смерть близкого человека переживается как наша вина, требующая внутренней казни. Так смерть поднимает раскаяние. А раскаяние любит подробности и умеет устанавливать упущенную связь.[148]

Death can override our usual instinctive avoidance of pain—we masochistically crave this pain as punishment, and as a trigger of the processes demanded by remorse. “Delusion of the Will” and “A Story of Pity and Cruelty” represent attempts of the immanent person to uncover the truth of his relations with the one who is dead.

The goal of creativity in Ginzburg’s theory is similar to the effect of remorse: to recover pieces of reality for the world.[149] She calls repentance “one of the most powerful mechanisms of imagination and memory,” and notes its deep and manifold relationship to artistic creation.[150] Remorse delivers up the “detailed, irreversible, horrible” images that torture one in the present, but belong to the past in being impossible to remedy. Their double temporality means that the “objects of remorse” are “just like those of history or art.”[151] Ginzburg writes of another strange doubling effect brought on by remorse: alongside the person’s life as it actually happened is the life that could have been, had one exerted one’s will to “set it right” or “edit” (*popravit’*) it.[152] Comparisons to art abound: she also likens the guilt experienced by the person who did not exercise this will to the guilt felt by an artist who leaves a work unwritten.[153] This comparison leads the way to an especially forceful imperative to write about one's guilt over the death of a loved one.

Ginzburg's Schopenhauerian title, "Delusion of the Will,"[154] signals the fact that this is not the story of one death (as in Tolstoy's *Ivan Ilych*), but the "story of one guilt," N.'s guilt over the pitiful old age and the death of a parent. It all begins with a well-meaning and sensible act: N. relocates his father, who has been living alone far away and declining in social status and general well-being, to a suburb of the city (presumably Leningrad) in which N. is living. Taking care of him and supplementing his pension with his own meager earnings, N. conceives of the arrangement as mutually beneficial. Since moving to the city as a student, he had dreamed of having a family "home" nearby—a refuge from the loneliness, cold, and hunger that surrounded him.[155] He pictures an enjoyable companionship with his father, described as a democratically minded atheist and materialist, a member of the intelligentsia of the 1880s generation.[156]

Instead, a pitiful reality sets in. Money and food are in short supply, and the living space has to be constantly defended from scheming housing organization (*zhakta*) administrators determined not to allow a pensioner to have a sunny room to himself. The old man—referred to in the narrative most often as *starik* ("old man") rather than *otets* ("father")—suffers from boredom, loneliness, and an inability to work (he had intended to continue researching and writing articles). Meanwhile, paradoxically, just as his father is spiraling downward, N. is in the midst of a new and promising love affair (which soon disintegrates). Things are looking up in his academic career as well after a period of stagnation. Thus, over the short weeks of his father's sharp decline, a number of circumstances, including N.'s general disposition, prevent him from responding adequately and quickly.

Throughout this whole, sad period, N. deludes himself, thinking that he has done his best by providing his father (for whom, as he admits, he did not feel a strong love) with the basic necessities at a time when N. himself often goes hungry. He discovers, however, that he is mistaken and wonders with amazement: "How is it that he had looked right past it at the time, that he hadn't managed to understand the principle of a human life, its main motive power—the conviction of one's own value."[157] N.'s regret is for an error of perception, a failure of understanding. And yet what irritates N. most of all is how his father has internalized his downgraded position. But N., too, perceives his father as weak and pitiful, and hence loses some respect for, and desire to converse with, the old man. In their very last conversation, N. cruelly rebuffs the old man's uncharacteristically open expression of need for his son's company. There seems to be an underlying psychology that explains this insensitivity: in his own life, N. is striving to overcome a sense of his own worthlessness, the image of a "loser" that his deteriorating father represents.[158]

In summertime, N. and his aunt both go on vacation, leaving the old man alone, with insufficient funds. The father's misery impels him to send his son a plaintive letter, which forces N. out of his "loophole of nonunderstanding." Recalling this, N. goes over in detail the tedious, lonely, pitiful reality of the old man's days and nights. And he concludes:

> They *existed*, those slow, old man's nights, when thoughts about worthlessness, his leg, death, flowed in great detail. And it was impossible to pull this link out of the chain of repentance, to erase these days and nights and thoughts. Imagining them clearly as having taken place was enough to make one want to bang one's head against the corner of the table.
>
> Они *были*, эти медленные стариковские ночи со всеми подробностями течения мыслей о ненужности, о ноге, о смерти. И никак нельзя вынуть из раскаяния это звено, чтобы не было тех дней и ночей и мыслей. И достаточно представить себе их ясно как бывшие, чтобы захотелось головой удариться об угол стола.[159]

Death functions as a spotlight: N. now fully perceives another person's miserable existence. It is beyond N.'s power to erase this reality, which is anchored in a time that now seems more permanent and consequential, defying his sense of his own existence as fragmentary and immanent. The all-too-imaginable misery of a concrete human being offers convincing evidence of his own continued existence, in a way that mere theory cannot.

Roughly eight years separate the death of Ginzburg's uncle, which prompted the writing of "Delusion of the Will," and the death of her mother in the Leningrad Blockade,[160] shortly after which she drafted "A Story of Pity and Cruelty," never published during her lifetime.[161] The two works are intimately related. They feature the same hero (Otter, later renamed "N." in the revised version of "Delusion"), who is as consistent over time as any episodic character could be. In both stories, he is guilty of mistakes in judgment, and repentance leads to analysis. His work in the narrative consists of trying to understand and master the memories that haunt him. "A Story of Pity and Cruelty" contains fewer generalizations about pity, remorse, and death—and yet, when they do occur, they repeat and reaffirm Ginzburg's theories from the earlier story. One could even say that the second work is a further illustration of the larger points of the first.

"A Story of Pity and Cruelty" in fact begins with a discussion of how both Otter and the character referred to as Tyotka, or Aunt (*tyotka* is the diminutive of *tëtia* and thus could be translated as "auntie"), experience her approaching death as a repetition of the old man's (the father/uncle). Otter—the third-person narrator—makes the following comparison:

> It was similar and at the same time went immeasurably further in the sense of literalness. The circumstances surrounding the old man's death, like those of many other calamities, had long ago struck Otter with their literalness. Overt social evil took on metaphorical, metaphysical meanings, connected to a complex of poverty, isolation, humiliation. But all of this paled in comparison with the appalling directness and literalness of meanings one had to endure now.
>
> Это было похоже и в то же время это неизмеримо дальше ушло в смысле буквальности. Обстоятельства, сопровождавшие смерть старика, так же как обстоятельства многих других бедствий—давно уже поразили Оттера буквальностью. Откровенное социальное зло реализовало переносные метафизические смыслы, связанные с комплексом нищеты, заброшенности, унижения. Но все это оказалось далеко позади, по сравнению с той ужасающей прямотой и буквальностью значений, которую пришлось пережить сейчас.[162]

It is in the unbearable conditions of the blockade that Ginzburg's hero understands in a most literal way the lack of moral absolutes. Otter asks:

> What criteria can help a skeptic establish a hierarchy of all these intuitions and unmediated moral givens? He can only say that a person's life is necessary for himself, and that people have equal rights to existence.
>
> С помощью каких критериев может скептик установить иерархию всех этих интуиций и непосредственных моральных данностей? Он может только сказать, что жизнь человека нужна ему самому и что в своем праве на существование люди равноправны.[163]

Otter is a middle-aged writer whose theme, like Ginzburg's, is "the rise and fall of the individualist consciousness," and whose death would put an end to his project.[164] His days contain some intellectual pleasures, while Aunt, a seventy-five-year-old "dependent," can only hope for "a certain quantity of gustatory sensations."[165] Otter understands that the lives of two human beings with absolutely the same right to existence are hanging in the balance.

While Otter's mistakes of judgment are similar in both stories, the aunt's personality is diametrically opposed to that of the father. Ginzburg had described the old man as having a weak "life force" (*zhiznennaia sila*, a translation of the term *élan vital* that one finds in both Henri Bergson and Pierre Janet), which is why he accepts his humiliating lot and gives in to self-pity. The aunt, on the other hand, is endowed with a life force so powerful that it encourages one of Otter's major errors. Convinced that her illusions are indestructible, he therefore tells her repeatedly that he does not need her in the least, imagining that his cruel words are "a proper pedagogical tool and a means of self-defense against this life force that whipped him."[166] So, just as with the old man, Otter takes care of his aunt's basic needs, but poisons her existence nonetheless.

The other major problem Aunt poses is that she is an extreme version of the "immanent" type, exemplifying what Ginzburg identifies as a chief problem of the twentieth-century person, without being at all conscious of the problem (unlike Otter/N.). Whereas N. in the earlier story had found the old man's image as a loser threatening, Otter is now keen to resist Aunt's stubborn and indomitable disconnectedness.[167] In her actions, Aunt "always obeys a momentary hedonistic impulse, without taking into account the connection and correlation of things, which persuasion through reason requires. And therefore, no kind of rational persuasion can penetrate this fragmentary consciousness [никакое разумное убеждение не может дойти до этого разорванного сознания]."[168]

This tense personal situation is compounded by the social atomization of the blockade. Otter's cruelty is facilitated by the dearth of witnesses to his behavior: "The psychic mechanism had not assimilated the experience, having taken advantage of an absence of witnesses to the crime, the absence of moral reproach from without, of an external judge, which could have objectified his guilt."[169] Aunt, the major witness and victim of Otter's crimes, lives in forgetfulness. There is no one to assist Otter in turning his guilt into an objective, external fact that he would then be forced to confront; nothing prevents him from disconnecting his individual actions from his more permanent self-image.

The social cues that Otter does receive from the outside drive him further down the moral hierarchy. A friend's offhand remark to the effect that he is saving his aunt at his own expense leads him to regret sharing food with her.[170] The pernicious attitudes voiced by other Leningraders seep into the speeches he addresses to his aunt, alienating him from his own self-image: "This feeling—resembling a theatrical alienation from one's own speech, a stylized imitation of something—found corroboration in the fact that he used words that were not his own, but instead readymade standard formulas, obviously steeped in all the vileness of philistine cynicism."[171] Otter is accustomed to treating words seriously and even with a healthy fear, since he "experienced reality through words."[172] And yet he realizes in retrospect that he had become "theatrically alienated"—the symptom of a moral degradation that comes from a wrong relationship between self and other, and from a lack of self-awareness.

The consciousness of his moral fall is achieved at a later moment precisely through self-distancing analysis. Ginzburg herself had earlier developed the habit of using rationality as a tool for healing in the face of adversity: "I willingly accept accidental joys, but demand logic from misfortunes that defeat me. And logic comforts, like a kind word."[173] She likened the torture of unassimilated and unprocessed experiences to the pain an amputee experiences in a phantom limb.[174]

Both narratives, while containing more of a plot than her other works (since they are structured around an account of a character's death), are driven by psychological analysis and philosophical generalization. They retain the aesthetics of the fragment and the essay.[175] Fragmentariness is the aesthetic correlative of the disjointedness that afflicts the immanent, post-individualist self. As Ginzburg notes in a draft of another narrative, "The Return Home" ("Vozvrashchenie domoi"): "For me, fragmentariness is not a literary effect, but a defect of my worldview. But I do not to want get rid of this shortcoming by way of dead spots and words that are not compressed into clarity. It would only be possible to shake off this shortcoming by perceiving and coming to love the world in a way other than what I am in the position to do now."[176] While fragmentariness may be a "defect," Ginzburg does not feel it can be overcome without falsifying one's texts—in this sense, the fragment is mimetic.[177]

Adding to the sense of fragmentariness in these narratives is a certain disorder and lack of resolution, which reflect the hero's emotional state. Ginzburg presents her hero, Otter/N., as suffering for a long time from a "stream of disconnected thoughts" whenever he begins to think about the death of the loved one.[178] At the end of the earlier story, the author cycles back to list the disordered memories—N.'s mistakes, which are the narrative's painful nodal points—all of which will "keep spinning around in [N.'s] head for an infinitely long time."[179] "A Story of Pity and Cruelty" also has a cyclical structure: Otter's receipt of a postcard from his brother "V." (based on Ginzburg's brother Viktor) launches and concludes the narrative. This circling demonstrates that N./Otter has not achieved full clarity in the course of the narrative, though he has completed a few revolutions in understanding his mistakes and delusions.

The remorse-induced scenes and images in these narratives retain their haunting power, despite having been subjected to logical analysis. The reader of "Delusion of the Will" will recall the oranges, the dead telephone line, the cold bath, the kerosene illegally transported and spilled in the train; and in "A Story of Pity and Cruelty," the cube of lard on the floor, the unwashed food containers, the insufficiently boiled water, the frighteningly light body of Aunt. At the end of the stories, N./Otter has still not mastered this series of painful details: Ginzburg leaves him in a state of grief. She argued that artistic texts could successfully express and inspire pity by freeze-framing sad moments in their concluding pages, as with the mourning Bazarovs in Turgenev's *Fathers and Sons*. This kind of "stabilization," however, seemed to her false, since in real life people carry on normally after the death of another. She praises Tolstoy and Proust as the only ones who show the tragic reality of how "sadness is only slightly more lasting than joy."[180]

Ginzburg leaves her hero in a state of remorse for important reasons, beyond potentially auto-psychological ones: this very failure proves that N./Otter's disjointedness is not total. Or, in Ginzburg's words, the immanent consciousness may lack "common goals," and may think of existence as

> either an empirical muddle of equally senseless moments, or a stupid sequence of moments that cancel one another out. And the last of these moments is death, which cancels out everything.
>
> Such is the logic of individualism at its extreme limit. But existential praxis is stronger than logic. It demands that the human being, here today and gone tomorrow, should live as though his deeds were intended to be part of an infinite historical sequence. It insists on the connections/bonds—which *cannot* be canceled out—of our common existence, of love and creativity, pity and guilt.

> не то эмпирическое месиво мгновений, равноправных в своей бессмысленности, не то тупая последовательность мгновений, поочередно отменяющих друг друга. И последнее из мгновений—смерть, которая отменяет все.
>
> Такова логика достигшего предела индивидуализма. Но сильнее логики экзистенциальная практика. Она требует от мимолетного человека, чтобы он жил так, как если б его поступки предназначались для бесконечного исторического ряда. Она настаивает на неотменяемых связях общего бытия, любви и творчества, жалости и вины.[181]

Both of these stories use "existential praxis," or distressing memories driven by remorse, to prove that an individual does exist through time, and that her actions matter.

"A Story of Pity and Cruelty" and "Delusion of the Will" paradoxically expose both the failures and the power of rational thought. On the one hand, tragically, N./Otter does not manage to benefit from his systematic, analytical mode of being during the period when it matters most; it cannot help him to overcome his egoism and act caringly and humanely toward his father and his aunt. The very fact that the experience of death in "Delusion of the Will" (and the analysis of it) did not prevent N./Otter (or the author) from repeating similar mistakes—as recounted in "A Story of Pity and Cruelty"—shows the inability of rationality, or perhaps memory, to overcome character flaws. In the blockade story, Otter even scolds himself for renewing his own analysis of Aunt in a futile attempt at self-vindication.[182]

On the other hand, rational thought powerfully drives the post-traumatic therapeutic analysis, uncovering past errors or "aberrations" (as Ginzburg calls them in her scientific idiom). Several of the hero's mistakes become visible in retrospect. At a temporal and conceptual remove, and with his relative's death as a "spotlight," N./Otter now draws sensible conclusions from the jumbled impressions torturing his consciousness. He may not achieve the kind of "self-revision" that Max Scheler thought possible[183]—he remains tortured. But these guilt-driven analyses compensate for an otherwise fragmentary, irresponsible post-individualist self. The existence of both narratives—and of the feelings that prompted them—proves a more fundamental, important point about memory and identity, about the continuity and consequentiality of existence.

SELF-DISTANCING, ESTRANGEMENT, OUTSIDENESS

Ginzburg reflects extensively about the mechanics of pity (*zhalost'*), and in particular about the necessity of a certain degree of "distance" from the person and situation to be pitied. She approaches pity as both an aesthetic and an ethical phenomenon: "Like the tragic, the comic, and the sublime, the pitiful transforms the materials of reality, openly making use of aesthetic devices."[184] Painting the imaginary scene of a death on Liteinyi Prospect in the center of Leningrad, she hypothesizes about how the feeling of pity arises (in someone similarly positioned as herself): one notices that the man run over by the tram was carrying apples home in a paper bag; the bag becomes soaked through with blood; the officer rushing to the scene crushes an apple under his boot. . . .

An object needs to be close enough in time and space to achieve the detail, visibility, and relevance that are needed to evoke pity. At the same time, Ginzburg remarks that as a "social fact," pity requires "a feeling of distance and a feeling of responsibility." She generalizes: "As we gain proximity to a person, we often lose pity."[185] Thus, one has to *lack* a certain understanding of another person's condition in order to pity her—there needs to be "an element of surprise, misunderstanding, a sideward glance."[186] An amputee does not pity another amputee, a prisoner in a convoy does not pity his fellow sufferer, even if as a free man he had pitied such people.[187] At the time of the Leningrad Blockade, Otter cannot pity Aunt because he is too close to her and is suffering too much himself. Ginzburg's theory suggests, counterintuitively, that the individuals who are most finely attuned to the needs of those around them, most capable of living in another person's shoes, feel the least pity. Self-distancing is likewise necessary for self-pity: "Pity for oneself is always in part a metaphor or a game, a paradoxical pose of viewing oneself from the side."[188]

Ginzburg's acute sensitivity to the distance from oneself or from another that is needed in order to activate pity turns out to be just one instance of the importance she attributes to perception at a distance. Clear vision requires an external viewpoint on events and characters, which enables the creation of a stable and comprehensive image. She discusses this distanced perception of oneself in the essay "On Satire and Analysis."[189] The important themes of this essay are also the basis for the culminating section of *On Psychological Prose,* which contains a discussion of ethical evaluation in realism. She connects satire, which is "always synthetic with its stereotypes imposed from outside on the everchanging flux of life," with external depiction, and analysis, which "ruthlessly exposes hidden motives from within, at the same time explaining them in a way that to a certain extent 'absolves guilt' " with internal depiction.[190] Ginzburg rejects both satire and nineteenth-century psychological analysis in favor of her own project, aiming for a different kind of analysis that incorporates an external view, a view from the side, while reaching adequate and precise verbal expression.[191] In order to understand how this self-distancing works, it will be useful to turn to *Notes of a Blockade Person* (*Zapiski blokadnogo cheloveka*), which presents this process in unusually physical terms.[192]

Ginzburg's self-distancing in her blockade notes works in some of the same ways as Shklovsky's *ostranenie* (estrangement or defamiliarization), the aesthetic device that allows us to perceive objects anew, reinvigorating our powers of perception. Shklovsky famously declared that the goal of art is to enable us to *see* things, not merely recognize them, by slowing down and making difficult the very process of perception.[193] Both the concept of *ostranenie* (making strange), as put forth by Shklovsky, and Ginzburg's favorite device of self-distancing were devised under the influence of Lev Tolstoy.[194] But self-distancing, which I call *samo-otstranenie* in Russian (from *samo-*, or self, and *ot-stranit'*, or moving to the side), serves a different function.[195] In Ginzburg's blockade prose, it is not just an artistic device or a method of description, like *ostranenie.*[196] It is also an ethical and psychological way of perceiving at a distance and relating to oneself as "other."

Ginzburg makes use of the estrangement or defamiliarization produced by the blockade itself, where Leningraders became highly conscious of the difficulties of existing and moving through spaces that had once seemed so familiar to them. The city could now be seen and sensed, rather than merely recognized. She describes with precision how people's bodies, hollowed out from dystrophy, no longer seemed to belong to them, and how walking, or simply maintaining a vertical position, required conscious, willed effort. Shelled city buildings suddenly resembled Meyerholdian stage sets, in a kind of reverse estrangement. At a certain moment, Ginzburg writes, the city as a whole took on a new, strange countenance: it looked like the countryside, with its elongated distances (once the trams stopped running) and cleaner air (since most factories had shut down). Extreme experiences had an effect on language, too—ossified expressions such as "to break bread with loved ones" ("делиться со своими ближними куском хлеба"), whose metaphorical origins had long been forgotten, regained their literal meaning.[197] *Blokadniki* experienced a disorienting alienation from every aspect of daily life.

Ginzburg considers all of these changes in terms of the extent to which an individual could have any control over his or her experiences and perceptions. Thus, she makes vision into an important theme of *Notes of a Blockade Person*. The hero N., as well as the unnamed narrator of the fragment called "Paralysis" (published in the addenda "Around *Notes of a Blockade Person*"), are nearsighted. On one level, nearsightedness appears to be a convenient device to explain why her male characters are still in the city and not on the front (since they would thus be exempted from military service). But Ginzburg makes more of this quality. In "Paralysis," when the character's glasses are accidentally broken on the tram, he is frustrated by his inability to return to the "monumental Leningrad vistas" the city's "slightly artificial iridescent clarity," an appearance he loved in his former life; and this irritation is so strong that he is ready to dispense altogether with "full-fledged vision" (*zritel'nuiu polnotsennost'*). Alienated, he decides to repel the city himself, pleading: "I was a hurting, irritated surface, and I begged the city not to touch me."[198]

Ginzburg's technique of *samo-otstranenie,* while it relies, like pity, on a controlled calibration, has a different goal from the wounded hero of "Paralysis," however: to sharpen one's lens. Analytical clarity distinguishes Ginzburg's writing in *Notes,* which contain stenographic transcriptions of conversations, minutely detailed descriptions of bodily sensations, and comprehensive treatments of the social and psychological aspects of everyday blockade life. In addition, the conscious adoption of an external perspective may have been a survival technique. The warning signs of dystrophy were more readily visible to others: " 'But he's already swelling up, isn't he,' they say about him—but he doesn't know about it yet."[199] Therefore, in order to assess the state of your health, you had to adopt another's gaze. Some actions became comprehensible only when imagined from an observer's point of view. Ginzburg describes how a person comes to "feel" that he is actually sawing wood only after building a composite picture of the situation: he observes that he has all of the elements of the pose of a sawing person and hears the harmonious sounds. In other words, because he has lost his habitual sense of his body's movement (what Charles Scott Sherrington called "proprioception"), he realizes that he is sawing only through an act of mental imaging and self-distancing.[200] (Shklovskian estrangement is now in fact part of his daily life; *nothing* is automatic any more.[201]) An analogue to this procedure is the gesture that opens *Notes of a Blockade Person*: Ginzburg writes of how one would verify one's sense of the blockade by consulting *War and Peace*—in other words, going outside of one's immediate experience or context in order to comprehend it.[202]

Ginzburg's techniques of self-distancing had their analogues in the moral and physical survival strategies of other *blokadniki*. Not only did many read Tolstoy, but many also wrote diaries, despite the extra expenditure of energy it required in a situation where every ounce of it had to be conserved. One diary published in Ginzburg's lifetime was that of Yura Riabinkin (part of *The Book of the Blockade*, or *Blokadnaia kniga*).[203] This document, whose power Ginzburg noted,[204] abounds with self-criticism and a tortured analysis of the diarist's weaknesses and misdeeds. The sixteen-year-old Riabinkin raises his self-awareness by externalizing his experiences in his diary, by broadening his temporal and spatial perspective beyond the blockade. He imagines his future self, in evacuation, and tries to live up to this image: "In order to become like I was before, I need hope, confidence that my family and I will be evacuated tomorrow or the day after. . . . If there were no hope of evacuation, I would steal, rob."[205] Self-writing for *blokadniki* served as one of "the arts of oneself" as described by Michel Foucault in his study of these practices in first- and second-century Greco-Roman culture: "writing about oneself appears clearly in its relationship of complementarity with reclusion: it palliates the dangers of solitude; it offers what one has done or thought to a possible gaze; the fact of obliging oneself to write plays the role of a companion by giving rise to the fear of disapproval and to shame."[206]

The harsh physical and social realities of blockade life, the struggle for survival that pitted one human being against another, could make it especially difficult to adhere to one's moral routine. In Ginzburg's view, this meant that one had to make a special effort to connect one's discrete acts and feelings into a system or whole, and to adopt a somewhat distanced, observer's point of view. She often observed and experienced the reverse process, where a person would view herself from within, and disown immoral deeds (such as stealing food, or worse) as "temporary and accidental." Ginzburg called this process "psychological doubling," or alienation from one's self-image. She describes an intellectual for whom "the deed bore no relationship to his general understanding of life, and therefore could make no impact on the ethical conceptions and values that had been worked out by his whole biography. He sees himself from the inside, and he sees his act as estranged from his permanent human essence."[207] In moments of adversity, even a person with a capacity to regard himself from the outside and to attain a sense of his biography, weakens and insulates his sense of "life in general" so that it cannot be touched or modified by any "isolated" incident. This same person, however, would easily pronounce judgment on others precisely because of this difference in perception: "he does not see the other from the inside" ("другого же . . . он не видит изнутри").[208]

Ginzburg demonstrates how self-distancing is necessary for moral evaluation, whether the goal is self-critique or self-improvement. Viewing oneself from the position of another helped one to acknowledge oneself as a "scoundrel" when one acted like a scoundrel.[209] Toward the end of the war, Ginzburg observed the opposite phenomenon: collective identities and social pressures were inspiring individuals to live up to higher standards. Leningraders eventually became convinced by people outside the blockade that they were heroes whose daily struggles were contributing to the survival of the nation. They adopted positive self-images based on heroic depictions in the press and the awarding of medals. The negative effect was that they forgot about or repressed any of their actions during the blockade that were not heroic. But they were in fact motivated to act more nobly according to their newly acquired (or reacquired) self-conceptions and values.[210]

As a friend and former pupil of Shklovsky's, Ginzburg must have been aware of the relevance of *ostranenie* to her descriptions of life in the blockade—although she herself contended that it was reality itself that slowed down and made difficult the act of perception. She would have been unaware, however, of Mikhail Bakhtin's idea of *vnenakhodimost'*, explored in his early work "Author and Hero in Aesthetic Activity," written ca. 1924–27 but published only in 1979. That said, she was familiar with works of German philosophers such as Max Scheler who influenced Bakhtin's concept of "being outside."[211] According to Bakhtin's now famous (but still enigmatic) theory, distance—that is, being located outside another—is necessary to transform this other into a visual, aesthetic, or semantic whole. Distance is thus a prerequisite for the creation of a literary hero. Like Ginzburg, Bakhtin pays special attention to the differences between how we tend to perceive ourselves and others, noting: "least of all in our very selves do we have the ability or the know-how to perceive the given whole of our own personalities."[212] Though it is common practice to picture our appearances and actions from another's point of view, to take account of others' reactions to us, and even to imagine the impact of our deaths, the fact is that we then take all of these impressions and "translate" them into our ongoing lives, where we never coincide with ourselves, where we always have a loophole for change.[213] However, for Bakhtin, a literary hero is different from its author, and must be an independent, separate whole. Therefore, to create even an autobiographical hero, "the author must stand outside of himself, must experience himself on a plane other than the one on which he actually lives [or experiences, *perezhivaet*] his life."[214]

Bakhtin and Ginzburg are united in advocating distance as a necessary means for grasping and structuring a person's character. But there are key differences between Bakhtin's *vnenakhodimost'* and Ginzburg's *samo-otstranenie.* Bakhtin's concept functions primarily in the interests of producing a work of art.[215] To the extent that he does bridge the realms of aesthetics, cognition, and ethics, he talks about *vnenakhodimost'* in terms of sympathy or empathy (in a Schelerian vein), not in terms of making moral judgments (about ourselves or others). His most vivid example begins with a person who is suffering. Only from a distance can we see the whole of this person's situation—for example, the blue sky that "enframes" him, which "becomes a pictorial feature which consummates and resolves his suffering."[216] And when Bakhtin discusses our noncoincidence with ourselves, he has in mind a positive notion of our openness to the future, which is certainly important in distinguishing us as subjects. But it does not help in overcoming the uncertainty and fragmentation that Ginzburg finds so troublesome.

Ginzburg's insistence on self-distancing issues from a suspicion that living life as a series of disjointed moments can lead to moral lapses. Especially in an environment where the ethical sense was greatly diminished, she understood the dangers of detaching one's image of oneself from the particular actions that one chose (or was forced) to commit. Ginzburg therefore aimed beyond her immediate context (be it the blockade or Soviet society) in order to submit her actions to a higher ethical standard.[217] Paradoxically, to view the self as other provides a more exact, complete sense of one's "permanent human essence." Through externalization and the systematization of personal experience, Ginzburg communicated to her readers neither a fixed autobiographical image nor a concrete system of values, but something more important: a method for erecting, through writing, a moral structure for the self under any conditions, even in the absence of the absolute.

GINZBURG'S AUTHOR AND HERO: DEGREES OF DISTANCE

Self-distancing, as a concept and technique, is a common thread in Ginzburg's autobiographic aesthetics and ethics. It is crucial for her concept of writing as an exit from the self, an other-directed act in which a product of the self becomes a real thing that circulates in the world. Self-distancing is vital for the creation of a new twentieth-century prose as Ginzburg envisioned it, where the character of an immanent hero and his or her actions could be judged, and not excused by moral relativism, social conditioning, or inner psychology. Distance from oneself and another is also necessary in the experience of pity, and in the post-traumatic process of rationally analyzing past actions.

Another important level on which self-distancing operates is the formal or narratological one, in depicting the complex relationship between author (or author-narrator) and hero. Let us return to "Delusion of the Will," an exemplary narrative that sets out the ramifications of Ginzburg's style for her notions of self in a more straightforward form than usual.

Ginzburg first drafted "Delusion of the Will" in the mid-1930s, and changed its narrative voicing in a number of versions[218] before finally publishing it in 1989. In the early manuscripts, she experimented with the first person. For example, here is what appears to be her initial version of the opening: "When this theme truly comes over me, it flows in a long stream of disconnected thoughts. And it's no longer certain [I can't really tell] whether the stream is flowing now, at the present moment, or whether it's the very same one that droned incessantly in my head in the first days after that death."[219] The draft cuts off too soon for one to determine whether Ginzburg would have proceeded to write a first-person narrative. In a later draft, which provides a more distanced perspective, the narrator still establishes an intimate, autobiographical relationship to his "material": "Here in my hands, in a writer's hands, resided the pitiful life and pitiful death of a person. . . . And in its full scope the death existed for only one person, a person for whom it turned into guilt and the punishment of the will."[220]

In subsequent versions of "Delusion of the Will," Ginzburg introduced her hero Otter, later N. This could be called an act of fictionalization, but because these are not fully fledged proper names, they are more suggestive of autobiography in the third person. "Otter" seems to have been intended as a transcription of the French "author" (*auteur*) and "other" (*autre*). In the drafts, one usually finds the abbreviated form "*Ot.*"—the Russian preposition meaning "away" or "from." Moreover, there is a plethora of recognizably autobiographical details, and a lack of obvious fictionalization, aside from N./Otter's male gender.[221] Even though N./Otter appears as Ginzburg's alter ego across several longer narratives in the 1930s and 1940s (and thus his experiences accumulate over time, just as they do for the writer of a diary), the impetus for creating such a character comes from an obvious desire to separate him from the author. While one can achieve self-distancing even within first-person narration, the third person more obviously removes N./Otter's story from any "inner" consciousness. It signals Ginzburg's stance as a post-individualist writer who wants to achieve a sideward view of the self.

Two principal voices coexist in the published version of "Delusion of the Will": that of the author-narrator who analyzes and generalizes, and that of the semi-autobiographical character (N.), who recounts his past actions and emotions while also analyzing and generalizing. The multiple voices (author-narrator, N. then, N. now) represent so many layers of self-distancing. The author-narrator opens and closes the narrative, and appears to interrupt the storyline with reflections on pity, remorse, guilt, aging, and death. He/she never speaks in the first person (as he/she does in "The Return Home," "The Thought That Drew a Circle," and *Notes of a Blockade Person*). His/her voice is virtually indistinguishable from the voice of Ginzburg's implied author in other narratives and notebook essays, and even, at some moments, in her scholarly work.[222]

The primary voice, that of the hero N., speaks only in the third person as he sorts through his memories.[223] One might label this free indirect discourse, but because of N.'s views on psychology and relationships, and methods of analysis, it is rather as if the author-narrator is a ventriloquist and N. is his dummy, speaking only in the third person. Certain moments when N. attempts to remember events from his past come closer to free indirect discourse, as the voice then becomes more identifiable as his own rather than the impassive author-narrator's. These are moments when it is clearly N. who is reflecting on his own actions and struggling to recall his past. For example, he angrily scolds himself as a "Fool!" (*Glupets*!).[224] In these moments, one finds ellipses and words of hesitation or approximation, such as "somehow" (*kak-to*), "something" (*chto-to*), "probably" (*veroiatno*), "roughly" (as in "roughly two days," *dnia dva*). It is more difficult, however, to distinguish N.'s voice from the author-narrator's when he is engaged in the rational analysis of his past. Consider, for example, the following passage:

> Once N. had guests over, and one of the guests, one of the women, said that the old man was looking terrific, that he was getting younger, and this pleased the old man.
>
> No, these kinds of memories just don't stick, they are faint and forced. The structural work of repentance forcibly sweeps aside everything that doesn't suit it. But what does suit this repentance perfectly is the time when the old man once said, not directly to N., but to his aunt,—probably meant for him; he said: it would be better if he gave me a fixed sum each month, and not just haphazardly as it comes. Better—that means more

like a pension or salary, in any case it wouldn't be so insulting. . . . How could he, how could he let it come to the point of an insult. . . .

> Как-то у Эна были гости, и кто-то из гостей, одна из женщин, сказала, что у старика отличный вид, что он молодеет, и тому это было приятно.
>
> Нет, такие воспоминания явно не клеятся, они тусклы и насильственны. Структурная работа раскаяния с силой отметает все, что ему не подходит. Зато раскаянию вполне подходит то, что однажды сказал старик, не Эну прямо, но тетке,—вероятно, для передачи; сказал: лучше бы он давал мне определенную сумму в месяц, а не так, как случится. Лучше—это значит, больше похоже на пенсию или на зарплату, во всяком случае не так обидно. . . . Как можно, как можно было допустить до обиды. . . .[225]

Here we find different types of discourse: first we see N. as he attempts to recall a pleasant scene from his past. But then he, or perhaps the author-narrator, interrupts to say that such memories cannot function as we would like them to. This is a more distanced view, which gives way to an even more distanced generalization—perhaps once again belonging to the author-narrator—about the structure of repentance, which "forcibly sweeps aside everything that doesn't suit it." And yet, a quick reversal follows: with the next sentence, we are back with N. as he remembers a more typical and painful conversation. After recalling and interpreting his father's complaints, N. involuntarily returns to the emotional present, chiding himself repeatedly in disbelief ("How could he, how could he . . .")—and we are back to the difficult, unceasing work of repentance.

Another instance of vertiginously shifting levels of narrative distance occurs near the end of the story. Here we see the anticipated response of a "fictional" character, Liza (N.'s girlfriend), to what appears to be an authorial generalization:

> *Père Goriot* is a very untruthful book. Are there really, could there ever really be children who because of a dinner party don't want to go visit their dying father? In reality it is much worse and much simpler: children always go to see their dying father, rush to their dying father, only after they have ruined his life while he lived.
>
> Liza will understand this, she is just the same. Liza once said to him:
>
> —You've surely noticed that people who really loved their parents relate to their death quite peacefully. The ones who suffer are the egoists—instead of thinking about the person who has disappeared, they think about their own guilt.

> «Отец Горио»—очень неверная книга. Разве бывают, разве могли быть когда-нибудь дети, которые из-за званого обеда не хотят пойти к умирающему отцу. На самом деле все хуже и проще: дети всегда идут к умирающему отцу, спешат к умирающему отцу, после того как испортили жизнь живому.
>
> Лиза это поймет, она сама такая. Лиза когда-то сказала ему:
>
> —Ты заметил, люди, которые в самом деле любили своих родителей, к их смерти относятся довольно спокойно. Мучаются же эгоисты—вместо того, чтобы думать об исчезнувшем человеке, они думают о своей вине.[226]

The reflection on Balzac seems at first to belong to the author-narrator, and yet it may be that N. himself is quarreling with Balzac. In either case, Liza is imagined as responding to this thought. The perfective phrase "Liza will understand . . ." opens up the narrative to the future, implying that N. hopes to find sympathy and reassurance from Liza. The generalization about how a person provides much-needed affection and care only when it is too late also turns up in "A Story of Pity and Cruelty," and seems to be attributable to Ginzburg's usual author-narrator.

Much of the time the voice of the hero and Ginzburg's author-narrator are virtually indistinguishable. They appear to be simply at different distances from the experience or the events. N. has a present that opens into a future beyond the narrative: he exists in story time. And yet he analyzes himself in a way that is consistent with the author-narrator's methods and views. There is a similar blending or consistency of voices in "A Story of Pity and Cruelty." In this raw blockade narrative, the generalizing voice of the author-narrator is only minimally present. And yet, given the close relationship between the two narratives, one might say that the philosophizing in "Delusion of the Will" provides the frame for "A Story of Pity and Cruelty."

This multiplicity of voices (Otter, N., the author-narrator) demonstrates multiple layers of distancing—or fragmentation of the author's voice—without a clear separation or differentiation in "character." Ginzburg creates a hero, seeming to detach the story from her authorial position using a technique reminiscent of fiction, but then she returns to a documentary aesthetic, because of the proximity between the author and the hero. The detachment means that as the author, Ginzburg takes no responsibility for the actions in the text, at least in front of the reader. In other words, she depicts a fragmented, immanent character, even while arguing that we must all do our best to connect experiences, and to create responsible identities.

Inspired by Bakhtin's discussion of *vnenakhodimost'*, one might posit that, in order to bring her narratives into existence, Ginzburg needed a "creative consciousness" that transcended her episodic narratives (in this case, about guilt) and could observe her literary hero in action without being an actor herself. A splitting of voices, between an author whose experiences are unknown but whose views form generalizations, and a hero who is the subject of the action but who also partakes in reflection and generalization, may have been aesthetically or psychologically necessary to a narrative treatment of guilt over the deaths of Ginzburg's uncle and mother. Ginzburg as author had to isolate a fraction of experience and organize it coherently (embedding relationships to the whole through certain generalizations and consistencies across narratives). This would mean that there is an attempt on the author's part to gain clarity on experiences (to establish a defensive "relationship") while her character was gaining distance from his—a real act of self-distancing, accompanying the represented one.[227]

The fictionalization of personal experience through the creation of a hero combined with a (partial) split between hero and author appear to create a necessary level of transcendence for explaining the structures of the immanent person. The degree to which the authorial voice manages to escape or separate itself from the sphere of the individual would seem to indicate the possibilities for transcending an immanent situation.

CONCLUSION

The twentieth-century person whom Ginzburg analyzes and places at the center of her experiments in prose is the post-individualist self, with whom she identifies, and whom she sees as typical of her time. This anti-Romantic, immanent person must navigate historical catastrophes and life in an oppressive state, while possessing only socially conditioned values and a tentative, intermittent notion of its own existence. Under pressure (historical or personal or both), this kind of self has a propensity to act irresponsibly and then to rationalize or forget about its actions. Ginzburg reflects this fragmentation in her prose with her third-person episodic heroes, but without dissolving character into speech or thought, as in the *nouveau roman*. In both her essays and her semi-autobiographical narratives about Otter, she posits the construction of a coherent self-image as the only safeguard against irresponsible, selfish behavior. Techniques of self-distancing enable the creation of this image and are instrumental in making moral judgments (even if only in retrospect). A measure of distance is also needed before experiences can be presented as typical, and subjected to clear, rational analysis. In a larger sense, writing itself is a form of self-distancing: it is an exit from the self and communion with others; a way to live actively and self-consciously; a product of "creative memory" that has structure, meaning, and value.

Because of their rhetorical structure and approach to the self, the products of Ginzburg's "creative memory" have some resemblance to autobiography in the third person, whose effect, according to Philippe Lejeune, is to expose to plain view the indirectness of all autobiography and the ambiguity of identity. He asserts that "the first person always conceals . . . a secret third person" and that "we are never really someone else, nor really the same person."[228] Or, in the words of Robert Folkenflik, "autobiography will often take shape as a way of dealing with the otherness of the figure in the past."[229] In Ginzburg's case, the way to "deal" with otherness is to distance this other from the "I" through the creation of an episodic character, while creating a near-identity of distanced voices and perspectives on these experiences. Not only does the third person highlight otherness, but it also works particularly well when one wants to tell a story of failure (whereas most first-person autobiographies are in some manner success stories).[230] In Ginzburg's quasi-autobiographical texts, the "he" is a traumatized self, who is trying to understand his moral failures through a division into actor/sufferer and critic/judge. In life, as her theory goes, this self-distancing move makes possible the creation of a structural whole to which the "I" can then connect future actions in the struggle to be morally responsible, to preserve a "human image."

Ginzburg's narratives featuring a third-person character are episodic and were never brought together in a single work, a fact that highlights the very fragmentation that her hero is battling against. On these grounds at least, Ginzburg's attitude toward autobiography was similar to that of Roland Barthes, another practitioner of in-between genres. Barthes delighted precisely in narrative discontinuity, in claiming that his autobiographical text should be thought of as spoken by characters in a novel, and denied the possibility of uttering of a "final word" about himself.[231] Ginzburg's avoidance of traditional autobiography could be interpreted as an act of reserving for herself narrative freedom, which enabled a harsh and exacting representation of the self that would have been impossible under a regime of "sincerity." This avoidance is also in line with her notion of the self as situational, of personality as historical, of identity as unstable, and of meaning (and social values) as inhering in immanent structures on any scale, however fragmentary.

CHAPTER 2

The Poetics of Desk-Drawer Notebooks

At a private gathering sometime in the early 1930s, after Ginzburg had begun experimenting with longer narratives, she read a draft of "The Return Home" ("Vozvrashchenie domoi")[1] to a group consisting of Anna Akhmatova, Nikolai Punin, Nikolai Oleinikov, Grigory Gukovsky, Boris Engelgardt, and at least six others.[2] After the reading, she recorded (in an unpublished note) her listeners' opinions and characterizations of her narrative's theme, style, and genre.[3] Grigory Gukovsky chose to describe the genre of the innovative piece as a "novel" (*roman*) whose material was "human thought" rather than experience. (It was Gukovsky who proceeded to spread the rumor—which has circulated to this day—that Ginzburg was writing a Proustian novel.[4]) However, one female friend (referred to simply as "L.") said she preferred the notebooks, and added, "This isn't a novel at all. It's basically the same as the notebooks, only more uniform." Akhmatova commented on Ginzburg's striking descriptions of love, calling them "so revelatory that it's even unpleasant to hear about" ("Очень разоблачительно, так что даже неприятно слушать"). [5]

While "The Return Home" is oriented toward a number of genres (for example the essay, diary, memoir, and novel or tale), Ginzburg's friend "L." was correct in calling it more "uniform" than the notebooks. In an unpublished article "On Writers' Notebooks" ("O zapisnykh knizhkakh pisatelei") (ca. 1930–32), Ginzburg herself identified what was "distinctive of the notebook": the "multiplicity of genres" (*mnogozhanrovost'*) that "mix and interrupt one another." In this chapter, I discuss the heterogeneity and flexibility of Ginzburg's notebooks, examining what happens when a "note" (*zapis'*) migrates from one composition to another and acquires new neighbors. I explore her "theory of the note" in her early scholarship on Pyotr Vyazemsky (1925–26, 1929) and in her article "On Writers' Notebooks"—her first scholarly reflections on in-between prose, later to become the area of her most significant contributions to literary scholarship.

Ginzburg's early scholarship, and the inception of her notebook project in 1925, coincided with a perceived crisis in the novel and a rising interest in documentary literature. A focus on the late 1920s will allow us to trace how Ginzburg's notebooks were shaped by this crisis and sought to emerge from it. Though several aspects of the traditional novel did not appeal to her as an artist, she sought ways of bridging the distance between the notebook and the novel in both her notes and her longer narratives. A key role in the novelization of the note is played by the distinctive poetics of the "formula," a concise sentence or phrase that encapsulates or compresses a wealth of impressions. The formula shares some of the novel's qualities: it attempts a retrospective gaze and an expression of those aspects of a person's fate that conform to more general laws (*zakonomernost' chelovecheskoi sud'by*).[6] Crafting a formula involves finding a logic and underlying structure in the messiness of life's flow, and thus helps connect Ginzburg's prose writings to her scholarly interests. Later in this chapter, I take the example of her deeply personal formula on the color of the sea to show that the formula is a fixed phrase that changes meaning in relation to the developing self and to the long-term project of desk-drawer writing.

In 1954, with three decades still separating her from her breakthrough to publication, Ginzburg despairingly remarked that a "fifty-year old author already counts several periods of creativity for the desk drawer—early, mature, late. . . . He can follow how the writing lying in the desk loses its contemporaneity [. . .] how substance that never saw the light of day [*nezhivshaia materiia*] decays."[7] And yet, when she finally got the opportunity to reach a broad audience in the 1980s, her multigeneric fragments turned out to answer a demand for documentary prose and possessed a flexibility and openness that allowed for multiple kinds of publication. In the final section of this chapter I take account of the various generic orientations in the publications of Ginzburg's notes from 1982 to the present.

DOCUMENTARY PROSE DURING THE CRISIS OF THE NOVEL

In the opening decades of the twentieth century, in both Europe and Russia, the novel was perceived to be in a state of crisis.[8] As theorists in the 1920s pointed out, the viability of the literary form that had so dominated the second half of the nineteenth century was now challenged by the rapid social changes attendant upon the upheavals of war and revolution as well as by a broad crisis in subjectivity. The self was no longer viewed as a discrete and concrete individual, but rather as a loose arrangement of discontinuous impulses and sensations.[9] Osip Mandelstam, in his famous essay "The End of the Novel" (1922), identified the key issue confronting the novel: the impossibility of individual biography and psychology, resulting from a combination of twentieth-century phenomena—the rise of mass movements, the splintering of social relations, and a new understanding of time and space, as expressed in Einstein's revolutionary theory of relativity. Since biography was the backbone of the novel, its disintegration due to social forces as well as the uncertainty of time and space would lead to the novel's obsolescence.[10]

Mandelstam's definition of the traditional novel hinged on its completeness or unity: "What distinguishes the novel from the tale, the chronicle, memoirs, or other prose forms is the fact that it is a compositionally closed narrative, extensive and complete in itself, about the fate of one person or a whole group of people."[11] But the new idea of a fractured human subject, accompanied by a modernist aesthetic of fragmentariness and multiplicity, led to a belief in the impossibility (or undesirability) of completeness, closure, and unity. Instead of aiming for an organic whole, Russian writers such as Viktor Shklovsky and Boris Pilnyak began to create "novels" by throwing together pieces from different compositions, written for different purposes and even by different people.[12] Their experiments attempted to prove that a "work" could be made by the simple act of framing a group of heterogeneous texts as such, rather than by telling the complete, logically connected story of a person's fate. Shklovsky provided a memorable image of authorship as contingent compilation when he described the genesis of his quasi-novel *Zoo* (first edition, 1923): "When I put the pieces of the finished product on the floor and sat down on the parquet floor to stick the book together, another book resulted—not the one which I had been making."[13]

In Russia, the crisis of the novel coincided with the birth of literary studies as an independent discipline or science (*nauka*). Beginning in 1915, the Formalists established their new science by isolating what was specifically literary about the literary work, to see "how it was made," and to discover the immanent "laws" of its creation.[14] Displacing the author, they entered the text as if it were a workshop, rather than assuming the traditionally secondary role of the scholar who researches the creator and his or her intentions. They dissected a text into its component parts, stylistic methods, and devices, in particular those that helped to heighten the reader's awareness of its artistry. For the Formalists, the novel became a testing ground rather than a hallowed form: many felt that the ultimate proof of their credentials as scholars would be to compose one. In her notebooks, Ginzburg relays Shklovsky's opinion that every "decent" literary scholar should be capable of writing a novel—"if not a good one, then at least one that is technically correct."[15]

In fact, in their early phase (roughly from 1915–21) the Formalists were not necessarily interested in theorizing the novel.[16] As their school was developing, they gave precedence to the study of poetry, whose language and structure are most distinct from everyday discourse. In demonstrating the operation of "devices" in prose, they mostly concentrated on the short story. (Eikhenbaum, for example, wrote articles on Gogol, in 1919, and O. Henry, in

1925.) When the Formalists did analyze novels, they tended to select those that clearly defied convention (Shklovsky wrote on Sterne and Cervantes). Shklovsky in 1929 made the claim that the Russian novel had remained "outside theory" (*vneteoretichen*), even though serious study of the novel in Russia had been inaugurated in the 1890s with the work of Alexander Veselovsky.[17] While a book called *The Theory of the Novel* by Boris Griftsov came out in 1927, the mid-1930s were the more important period for theories of the novel, the leading critics of which were György Lukács and Mikhail Bakhtin.[18]

When Lydia Ginzburg arrived at the Institute for the History of Arts in the fall of 1922, there was not only a crisis in the novel but, as she recalled in 1982, a crisis in Formalism itself.[19] Members of OPOYAZ (the Society for the Study of Poetic Language, in which the theorists known as Formalists grouped together in 1916) realized the "bankruptcy" of their earlier positions on the immanence of the literary text (the idea that it could be studied in isolation, as a self-sufficient object) as soon as they "transitioned from pure theory, from poetic language, to the history of literature."[20] Already Yuri Tynianov's 1922 article on the ode had suggested one way out of "immanence" by noting the importance for the "literary system" of the "closest neighboring" extra-literary series [*vneliteraturnyi riad*], the spoken word and "everyday speech" [*bytovaia rech'*][21] And his 1924 article on "The Literary Fact" marks a definitive turn toward the history and evolution of literary genres (a turn that continued in "On Literary Evolution," 1927). Here he argues that even when it comes to devices, historical context determines their perception and function, so that "the whole essence of a new construction might be in the new use it makes of old devices, in their new constructive significance."[22]

Tynianov's emphasis in "The Literary Fact" is on how definitions of genre—and of literature itself—change drastically in the hands of writers and the minds of readers of different epochs. Reception of fragmentary genres can show extreme variability: sometimes they are perceived as parts of longer works (such as the *poèma*), sometimes precisely as *fragments*.[23] Tynianov argues that when defining a genre, we should look at those secondary or deeper features usually taken for granted. Thus, we should define the novel by its size and energy, "by the fact that it is a *large form*," rather than by its content (say, the story of an individual's fate) or other features that might dominate only in a specific period.[24] Simply taking account of size can open onto complex interpretations, since "depending on the size of the construction, each detail, each stylistic device, has a different function, a different force, and a different load is laid upon it."[25] As Tynianov moves to the broad, indefinite concept of energy, he continues to understand the work as a single, complete entity—in particular, as a "dynamic speech construction."[26] Meanwhile, defining the novel as a "large form" means that it can be created by aggregating smaller parts, in the absence of unifying plot structures. In Tynianov's view, a tendency to perceive a collection of fragments as a "large form" arises (paradoxically) when "small forms" have become dominant and thus automatized.

Following Tynianov's logic, it would be a testament to the ascendancy of the fragment in the 1920s that Ginzburg, in a 1926 article on Vyazemsky, chooses to draw attention to his achievements in prose by way of a hint about the novel. She writes: "In the aggregate, the disconnected fragments of the Notebooks are almost monumental—a sort of large form of a small genre."[27] Ginzburg seeks to define Vyazemsky's genre as monumental without overshadowing his achievements in brevity, which is precisely the quality that made his "Old Notebooks" fit the contemporary moment. In her notebook from early 1927, Ginzburg defines brevity as a twentieth-century trait, remarking that contemporary prose is written in sentences that resemble lines of poetry, each of which can be evaluated separately. Ginzburg's characterization agrees with that of her contemporary Yevgeny Zamyatin, who drew a connection between brevity and the modernist fascination with speed and energy in 1923 when he declared, "the old, slow, creaking descriptions are a thing of the past; today the rule is brevity—but every word must be supercharged, high-voltage.... The image is sharp, synthetic, with a single salient feature—the one feature you will glimpse from a speeding car."[28] The trend toward short sentence-paragraphs was pioneered in Russia by Shklovsky, who, according to Ginzburg, "gave contemporary Russian literature a short sentence that's basically un-Russian."[29] Tynianov even confided to Ginzburg that Shklovsky's experimental autobiographical novel *Third Factory* (1926) should have been published as separate sentences rather than as a novel.[30]

Tynianov himself, later a writer of historical novels, also had aspirations toward "very small" forms, which he found "very difficult."[31] Ginzburg indicates the demands small forms place on the writer in her critique of Dmitry Lavrukhin's novel *In the Hero's Footsteps* (*Po sledam geroia*, 1930), the first half of which consists of fragmentary notes written by the hero: "*You can swallow down the boredom of a three-volume novel, but in a three-line note, boredom is unbearable.*"[32] Ginzburg herself, who dazzled with her aphorisms and witticisms, felt that she would fail precisely with longer forms, confessing, "I am confident that [...] I would fail when it comes to the plot and in general making connections between things."[33]

In the Soviet 1920s, it seemed to many that *all* literary genres and institutions were in crisis, not just the novel. Boris Eikhenbaum noted in 1924, "There is no literature—there are only writers, whom readers do not read."[34] With her specific creative ethos and orientation toward "the word," Ginzburg saw around her in October 1925 no like-minded prose writers who were working to "squeeze from every word the greatest expressivity." Instead, she writes, they were busy collecting or mimicking linguistic oddities, whether "folk" speech or the uneducated syntax and lexicon of workers struggling to adapt to their new Soviet reality (she mentions Mikhail Zoshchenko). She laments an infectious dilettantism, which in her opinion reached its fullest expression in Ilya Ehrenburg ("a son of a bitch," according to her) with his melodrama *The Love of Jeanne Ney* (*Liubov' Zhanny Nei*, 1924).[35] Ginzburg expresses astonishment and frustration at this dilettantism:

> *By what means* do they write, these people without language, without style, without characters, without imagination!
>
> In essence they are simple-minded boys, though they imagine they are *clever as snakes*, because theoreticians trained them up to use a few "Sternean" tricks, which no one needs in the very least.
>
> What do they understand about things like Tolstoy's work in the archives, the notebooks of Goncourts, authors' studies that go on for years, the persistent accumulation of non-literary material, in which any novel is clothed, the scope of the large form—or a book that takes 10 whole years to write!

> *Чем* они пишут, эти люди без языка, без стиля, без характеров, без фантазии!
>
> Они в сущности простодушные мальчики, хотя воображают, что *мудры как змии*, потому что теоретики натаскали их на несколько никому не нужных «стерниански» трюков.
>
> Что они понимают в таких вещах, как работа Толстого в архивах, как записные книжки Гонкуров, как авторские штудии, длившиеся годами, как упорное накопление внелитературного материала, которым одевается всякий роман, как размах большой формы—как книга, которая пишется 10 лет![36]

Ginzburg's ideal is the Tolstoyan novel, built on careful preparation and serious historical research. Tolstoy, in a 1908 letter to Leonid Andreev (quoted in Shklovsky's *Third Factory*), had instructed the popular writer to avoid the "desire to be special and original, to surprise the reader" and also to avoid haste, which is "not only harmful but also indicative of the absence of any genuine need to express the thought in question."[37] Ginzburg's mention of the need to accumulate nonliterary material tempts one to imagine that her notebooks may have been, in part, a novelist's research.

Ginzburg also follows Tolstoy in her rejection of fiction in contemporary prose. Tolstoy, who had given the world so many compelling fictional characters, events, and three-dimensional worlds, predicted fiction's demise in a 1905 statement: "It seems to me that with time, people will stop *inventing* belletristic works. People will be ashamed to make up stories about some thought-up Ivan Ivanovich or Maria Petrovna. Writers, if there are any, will not invent, but will only tell stories about anything interesting or significant that they happened to observe in life."[38] Tolstoy cast doubt on the future of imaginative literature, and suggested that it was more honest and decent to report one's observations directly rather than through the mediation of fiction.

Like the later Tolstoy, Ginzburg finds fiction shameful. In 1933, she reports a conversation with the poet Nikolai Oleinikov on this topic: "We spoke for a long time about how impossible it was to figure out how to write prose. Surely nothing could be more shameful than to write: so-and-so walked up to the desk and sat down. And, really, all of the existing ways of depicting a person are a forever-compromised fiction."[39] She uses "fiction" here in the sense of "falsification," but to use the techniques of fiction seemed an especially "compromised" way of representing reality. In the following year, Ginzburg's personal feelings about fiction grew even more negative: "Invented people and situations [...] fill me with a kind of disgust."[40]

Ginzburg's aversion to fiction echoes the spirit of the 1920s, when readers were impatient to see their contemporary moment reflected in texts, and demanding that this new material be treated in a hyper-naturalistic manner.[41] As she generalizes in her draft article "On Writers' Notebooks,"

> Interest in the document from everyday life is usually connected with a rise in the demand for *material* in literature; the demand for material is characteristic of periods of big historical shifts, when literature cannot keep up with the social demands placed upon it [*sotsial'nyi zakaz*].

> Интерес к бытовому документу связан обычно с повышенным требованием *материала* в литературе; требование материала свойственно периодам больших исторических сдвигов, когда литература не поспевает за предъявляемым ей социальным заказом.[42]

The Formalists were influenced by an energetic movement that burst onto the scene in 1922–23: the Left Front of Arts (LEF), led by Osip Brik, which advocated a "Literature of Fact," or the creation of everyday, traditionally nonliterary and nonfictional genres (newspapers, journals, memoirs, letters, diaries, etc.). In the 1920s, what was previously considered to be "nonliterature," a mere part of "everyday life" (*byt*), came to be viewed as "literature" (a reorientation Tynianov discusses in "The Literary Fact"). Both Tynianov and Shklovsky spoke of how journals and newspapers could become the new "large form" to replace the novel; articles by various authors could be conceived of as a single work, designed by the editor.[43] Eikhenbaum even wrote an experimental "thick journal" of the self, *My Periodical* (*Moi vremennik*) (1929).[44]

An important direction in the "literature of fact" was the move away from plot-oriented prose (which Shklovsky consigns to "the warehouse of old habits") in favor of genres such as the memoir, which are "perceived aesthetically."[45] Brik argued that there was a direct correlation between the "growing interest in individual facts, in individual details" and "the disintegration of the plot scheme." Texts from everyday life could supposedly incorporate "raw" material without distorting it through artificial plots.[46] Brik wrote of the plot as a force that violently suppresses the fact: "Every plot construction necessarily does violence to the material, choosing from it only what can aid in developing the plot, and what's chosen then goes on to distort the material toward the same end. . . . People will not allow the plot to cripple real material, they demand that real material be given to them in its original form."[47] Facts, according to Brik, did not need the artificial unity conferred by plot—instead, they could form a different kind of unity in their simple aggregation.

In her notebooks, Ginzburg reports a conversation (from 1926) with Brik about Shklovsky's experiments combining fiction and fact. In a bemused manner, she writes: "The literature of facts, in which Brik believes (if he *does* believe in it) has a need for ethics instead of (bourgeois) aesthetics. It must be honest."[48] Brik tells Ginzburg of how one of Shklovsky's readers felt duped and angered after meeting the author: Shklovsky's merry demeanor was nothing like the moroseness projected in *Third Factory*. Ginzburg quotes Brik as saying, "the reader is right, it's not ethical to deceive the reader." She then concludes the note by saying that the LEF theory is so opposed to basic literary conventions that it demands further consideration: "The patent absurdity of this theory wins you over. It's so anti-literary that you feel an urge to get to the bottom of it and find some kind of healthy roots."[49]

Ginzburg's ironic stance, as she casts doubt on whether Brik sincerely believes in sincere literature, causes the reader to detect her skepticism about whether a sensible basis for a "literature of fact" could be found. In her 1929–30 desk-drawer article on Proust, she directly expressed doubt that new material could lead to an exit from the literary impasse: "What's at issue is not the material, but the creation of a new structure of meanings and the heightening of the cognitive possibilities of the literary word."[50] Ginzburg's own turn toward documentary prose reflected her Tolstoyan sense that writing fiction in the transformed world of the twentieth-century was shameful, as well as her understanding that literature could renew itself only by turning toward *byt* (which she conceived as the psychology of the everyday) and the traditionally nonliterary. What she was after was not material itself, but a new way of expressing the reality around her—a heightening of literature's "cognitive possibilities"—which seemed to require breaking out of the constraints of the novel.

GINZBURG'S "THEORY OF THE NOTE"

In 1925, Ginzburg began to work on her first full-length article on Prince Pyotr Vyazemsky (published the following year), and in 1929, she edited and wrote the introduction for an abridged, selective publication of his *Old Notebook* (*Staraia Zapisnaia Knizhka*). She presents to the public a previously "undiscovered Vyazemsky." As she writes, the prince's own contemporaries only read his "second-rate" poetry and criticism while missing his main achievement, and over time he came to be regarded solely as a friend of Pushkin.[51] Ginzburg promotes Vyazemsky's aphorisms, anecdotes, and reminiscences about the oral and literary culture of his era as his true achievement, and remarks that even he knew that his contributions were not on the "main road of Russian literature."[52] She continues the theoretical tradition of her teacher Yuri Tynianov by attending to the function of "peripheral" or marginal genres and the incorporation of oral speech as sources of literary renewal.[53]

In 1982, Ginzburg recalled how her work on Vyazemsky "led me to the idea of starting something like a notebook."[54] Certain similarities in their literary circumstances may have encouraged this choice, and yet there were also significant differences. Prince Vyazemsky was an aristocrat surrounded by a salon culture, which cultivated the art of conversation. Ginzburg's 1920s lively milieu of Formalists, Futurists, Acmeists, and OBERIU (the group's name is an abbreviation of *Ob'edinenie real'nogo iskusstva*, or Union for Real Art) poets celebrated verbal eloquence, but this culture soon disintegrated and was brutally destroyed. Vyazemsky's self-appointed mission in recording and commenting on rumors and anecdotes was to advance the state of Russian letters, which he thought lagged behind its oral culture, not to mention the literature of other nations.[55] He intended his notes as material and inspiration for future writers in other prose genres.[56] Ginzburg's documentary prose about the social reality of the intelligentsia is meant to chart the way out of a literary impasse, the crisis of the novel, and yet it is doubtful whether she ever envisaged her notes as material for others' writings. (If she at any point conceived of her notebooks as preparation for other works, she surely pictured herself as their author.) Vyazemsky wrote his notes from 1813 to 1877, a long period encompassing the beginnings of the professionalization of Russian literature as well as its highest achievements in the great Realist novel. Ginzburg's notes, written from 1925 to 1990—as fate would have it, almost the exact same number of years as her predecessor—span nearly all of Soviet literary history, from the years of the "literature of fact" to the grandiose myth-building of Socialist Realism to the turn toward memoir and documentary prose of *perestroika*.

Ginzburg was self-consciously aware of the parallels between her contemporary moment and the previous century, the turn from the 1820s to the 1830s. She characterizes the 1830s as a decade of heightened interest in "material" and in "genuine feeling," not "neutralized" by aesthetic form (reminding one of her conversation with Brik about Shklovsky).[57] Adopting Tynianov's term for the 1920s, she calls the 1830s a *promezhutochnyi period* or "in-between period": "a period of using, reworking, and overcoming the high achievements of the previous decades."[58]

Ginzburg adopts a somewhat ambivalent relationship to LEF in her 1929 introduction.[59] On the one hand, she refers to LEF's "literature of facts" and to montage and writes of how "our contemporary literary moment, with its indefinite belletristic forms and heightened interest in memoirs and materials creates auspicious conditions for the reception of Vyazemsky's unofficial activities."[60] On the other hand, she refuses to follow the LEF tendency to equate the "literature of fact" with the *poèma* or the novel, discussing Vyazemsky's *promezhutochnost'* as a "self-imposed limitation" (*samoogranichenie*). She positions his works precisely as intermediary, between fact and the novel.

The most important part of Ginzburg's article on Vyazemsky is her characterization of his in-betweenness: "The thrust of the *Notebooks*, and their basic technical problem, is the creation of finished verbal constructions that neither kill the fact nor render it literary."[61] Ginzburg wants to argue that Vyazemsky remained admirably closer to "fact" and "reality" by avoiding "literariness" and "stylization." She even uses violent language—"kill the fact"—reminiscent of the LEF ideologues. And yet, she shows herself as a good student of Tynianov in maintaining that Vyazemsky was crafting a literary work by creating "finished verbal constructions" (*zakonchennye slovesnye konstruktsii*) and taking "full responsibility for the verbal structure of his notes."[62]

The Romantic tradition celebrated the fragment for its *incompleteness*, which was said to paradoxically portend the existence of a mystical whole. Ginzburg speaks of Vyazemsky's notes as "finished" in the sense of being "perfected" as aesthetic structures rather than being "finalized" or "complete." Ginzburg's purpose is to classify his notebook as a literary genre that escapes the restrictive conventions of established genres such as the novel or *poèma*.

She also highlights Vyazemsky's talent for brevity and wit, achieved through careful and economical word choice. While as editor Ginzburg maintains the "note" as the compositional unit, she nevertheless asserts that his poetics operate on the level of the individual sentence (a trait she characterized as belonging to the twentieth century).[63] She singles out as an example his "four-word masterpiece": "The fabulist Izmailov is a tipsy Krylov" (just four words in Russian, which form two lines of anapestic dimeter: "Баснописец Измайлов—подгулявший Крылов"). Ginzburg unpacks the sentence in a full-page endnote, the essence of which is that Alexander Izmailov had a reputation in the 1820s for reflecting the coarse language of the people in his naturalistic prose (and, adopting a stance of familiarity toward readers, joked about journals issues being delayed by drunken celebrations), whereas Krylov knew how to "refine" this simple speech in his fables.[64]

The poetics of the "finished verbal structure" also allow the *Notebooks* to escape many of the constraints of literature by way of their "negative constructive principle." In her Vyazemsky edition, Ginzburg follows only a rough chronology. She arranges the notes in her own order, creating her own rhythms and juxtapositions. She numbers each note, reinforcing the boundary of the "verbal construction." She takes her cue from what she considers to be Vyazemsky's most important innovation: his decision not to organize his notes into groupings based on themes or other categories. As Gary Saul Morson has noted, witticisms demand an element of surprise: their impact is enhanced when they are included within, or border on, other kinds of utterances.[65] Ginzburg argues that if Vyazemsky had grouped notes belonging to specific genres under separate headings (such as reminiscences, portraits, aphorisms, collections of sayings, political essays), it would have been easy to conceive of his work according to preexisting models. It was his purposeful disorganization that made his prose seem innovative even in the twentieth-century literary environment. He wrote finite miniatures, combined into a collection of infinite variety.

Ginzburg continued her study of notebooks, a subject holding immediate importance for her, in an article "On Writers' Notebooks" (ca. 1930–32) that treats Vyazemsky alongside writers such as Andrei Bolotov, Alexander Pushkin, Anton Chekhov, Alexander Blok, and Vasily Rozanov, who all practiced notebook writing, whether as a laboratory for their other compositions or as a literary form in itself.[66] Though the article was destined for the desk drawer, she includes common tropes of literary publications of the time (though no references to Marxism-Leninism), arguing that notebook-writing techniques deserve attention since they have both "historical and practical" value.[67] Contemporary writers should study notebooks, she says, in order to learn "the very principle of a sharpened observation of the world. How to freely face material that has been extracted from associations that have passed through literature."[68]

Ginzburg begins with the most self-evident definition of the notebook: "Everyone knows that a *zapisnaia knizhka* is a small notebook, notepad, or little book of a certain (necessarily small) format, which you carry in your pocket and where you write down various things you don't want to forget."[69] She proceeds to argue that there is a continuum that runs from datebooks, address books, notepads filled with "to-do" lists, the "writer's notebook" containing sketches of future literary works, to the notebook as a literary genre.[70] The notebook's origins in practical daily life, as well as the material conditions of its use, help shape the writing and the author's image in the text. The notebook's size and format and the way in which it is written (whether carried on one's body and penciled on the go, or drafted at a writing table with a jar of ink) exert "pressure on the selection of material, on the ways of distribution and combination, and, finally, on the character of the individual note."[71]

Ginzburg writes that in the notebook, "least of all does one find the individual person," discovering instead the person who belongs to a certain historical formation, socioeconomic class, and profession. This is consistent with how she had characterized Pyotr Vyazemsky's self-portrait in his notes—as a social or "outer biography," a presentation of himself as a public figure and citizen, rather than a portrayal of his personal or emotional life.[72] Ginzburg also observes that the notebook writer, like the everyday keeper of datebooks, is frequently attempting to solve "some problem immediately posed by the surrounding environment."[73] She herself often singled out the practical necessity of her own notebook writing as "a process of finding the best solution to a problem."[74]

The draft article on writers' notebooks is jotted in a pad containing grades for Ginzburg's Rabfak (Workers' University) students, showing how her desk-drawer scholarship coexisted with the mundane tasks of her practical and professional life. Over the seven decades of her notes, her material conditions (the very availability of notebooks or ink) and professional activities changed dramatically several times. Ginzburg's *zapisnye knizhki* began as hardbound books of various sizes with high-quality paper, but in the 1930s and 1940s were in less durable notepads with rough paper. She sat at a desk with a pen and inkwell (which became, in the Leningrad Blockade, a pencil, and in the postwar years, a typewriter), recording finished notes that she had usually drafted first on scraps of paper (scraps that allowed for her to make initial jottings in various settings around the city and beyond).[75] When Ginzburg published a book of notes in 1989, she chose the title *Person at a Writing*

Table, emphasizing the image of a meditative and solitary writer.[76] This is far from the image, say, of Mayakovsky in *How to Make Poetry,* carrying a writer's notebook on the tram. In her notebooks, Ginzburg habitually left facing pages blank (despite paper shortages) in order to further edit her fragments, or to insert new entries. She often juxtaposed notes of heterogeneous genres and recorded them out of chronological order. She also used scissors and glue to cut and paste entries, and used thick black ink to blot out some fragments. Only sporadically would she date entries, often removing these dates before publication.

In "On Writers' Notebooks"—a piece that can be read as an indirect attempt to theorize her own notebooks—Ginzburg discusses how readers in her time would bring to notebooks a dual code of interpretation, perceiving them simultaneously as "raw material" and as constructions.[77] Contemporary writers and readers alike have difficulty "*operating with the concept of pure material, so strong is the tendency to understand it as a construction.*"[78] "Every author writing documentary notes of any kind," she continues, "senses their double orientation (even one and the same note) in the direction of the construction, and in the direction of the draft."[79]

"A DIARY IN THE FORM OF A NOVEL"

The notebook's capacity to incorporate a multitude of genres, and the note's simultaneous orientation toward draft and "finished verbal construction" make this format a suitable laboratory for a writer's experimentation. Reminiscing around age seventy, Ginzburg suggests that she conceived of some early writings as drafts and preparations: "And the most wonderful thing is that you don't yet know what these casts molded out of love and pain, victory and humiliation will be good for—because you still don't know what you can and cannot write."[80] The notebooks as originally conceived under the influence of Vyazemsky could not thrive in the absence of a vibrant literary culture. And over the years, Ginzburg experienced a gravitational pull toward different genres and intellectual projects. The flexibility of her in-between prose allowed her to pursue these plans within her established format.

While still at the Institute, Ginzburg imagined that a novel was *inevitably* in her future. In the summer of 1927, she noted with a certain amount of bravura: "I, for instance, know that I will write a novel,—and this is one of those essentially terrifying expectations that doesn't terrify me simply because it is so natural. It's how people think about the fact that they will inevitably age, survive their loved ones, die."[81] Little did she suspect that the only novel she would ever write (given the reality of her historical circumstances) would be a children's detective story, *The Pinkerton Agency* (begun in 1930, published in

1932).[82] It was Ginzburg's belief that people's limitations, what they cannot do, could be just as revealing as what they can do.[83] *The Pinkerton Agency* was not a natural occurrence along the clear path of her development as a Russian author who begins with poetry and ends with prose, nor was it part of her role as a Formalist (who writes a novel to demonstrate her expertise). It was, rather, a way to survive and earn a living in an increasingly hostile and restrictive literary and academic environment. She describes *Pinkerton* as "not her own" work (and its style is indeed far removed from that of her notebook entries), as a "conscious literary falsification."[84] "With every move," she laments, "what keeps showing through and coming to mind is not things that you can call by name, but the abstract rules of the genre."[85] This type of novel was an endeavor she could never undertake again, "because I don't know whether it is possible, with any sense of engagement, to twice write a thing that is not your own."[86]

What Ginzburg longed to write was *another* kind of novel, although this would remain an elusive goal. In 1928, she dreamed of a novel that would have something in common with the form as the German Romantics understood it: a "highly responsible summary of thoughts about life, ideas about life, relationships to life." She goes on to say that in the work she wanted to write, "a person stands before the universe and freely speaks about the universe, reasoning, retelling and describing—that's what the novel is, after all" ("Человек стоит перед вселенной и свободно говорит о вселенной, рассуждая, рассказывая и описывая,—это и есть роман").[87] By early 1933, Ginzburg expresses frustration, as she disparages the Vyazemsky-esque note that sparkles with "eloquence and wit," and dreams of replacing it with "cognition and expression of reality."[88] She observes that since "Notebooks etc. are the literature of impotents," it would be "impossible" for her to "live without writing a novel." She acknowledged a problem, however: "to write a novel, I now understand, is also nearly impossible. I just don't see the kind of reality—or even traces of it—that could be put into form with the words I have at my disposal."[89]

In addition to the larger problem of finding a language to describe the reality around her, Ginzburg ran up against the conundrum of how to achieve the completeness of the novel. In sheer practical terms, it was difficult to achieve a "finished" product because of external conditions: the opportunity (and even the pressure) to publish was simply not there. But a creative problem also arose, given her orientation toward the documentary writing of the self. She notes, "The diarist advances by guesswork, not knowing his own fate or that of his acquaintances. This is a forward dynamic, full of chance and untested events. The novel possesses a retrospective dynamic, which presupposes regularity [law-governed-ness] and evaluations."[90] The author of the novel, furthermore, possesses an "ultimate creative knowledge (*poslednee tvorcheskoe ponimanie*), being in the position to evaluate actions and pronounce the "last word."[91]

Ginzburg had always resisted writing memoirs, rejecting memoir time as "cold."[92] The ideal creation she imagined would combine the retrospective/historical dynamic of the novel with the forward-moving one of the diary. She wanted to represent, in a single consciousness, an event that was both complete and continuing to happen.[93] Her best approximation to a descriptive term for this genre was the diary-novel or "diary in the form of a novel":

> If only—without invention or recollection—one could fix the flow of life . . . the feeling of flow, the feeling of the present, the authenticity of multiple and indissoluble aspects of being. Translating this into a specialized terminology you again come up short: *a novel in the form of a diary, or the version I like better—a diary in the form of a novel.*[94]

Ginzburg's discussion is hypothetical, and it is unclear whether she conceived of certain of her own works as this "diary in the form of a novel."

Outlines in Ginzburg's archive testify to her plan in the 1930s to write a large interconnected opus. A white folder labeled *Home and the World* contains several outlines, drafts of individual scenes, and character sketches related to this unfinished work.[95] Ginzburg's title opposes "home" as a fragile sphere of comfort, emotion, and creativity to "the world" as a social arena that is threatening but indispensible for survival. One of the central themes of *Home and the World* would have been the fate, or the possibilities for self-realization, of a group of intellectuals (*gumanitarnaia intelligentsia*), formed by the Revolution, in the years when it was no longer possible to be a "fellow traveler." The characters would have been modeled on Ginzburg, her mother, her past loves, her friends and colleagues.[96]

In her drafts, Ginzburg refers to the work as a "novella" and also as a "five tales" (*piat' povestei*), but never as a "novel" or "diary in the form of a novel." The drafts and outlines do not point to a single unified work, but rather to a series of interconnected narratives (most likely the *piat' povestei*) that draw on her life experiences:

> <Home and the World>
> 1. Theoretical Introduction—Epigr[aph]
> 2. Return to the Homeland—Epigr[aph] from M.
> 3. Death—Epigr[aph] from La Rochefoucauld
> <4. Home and the World I. Epigr[aph] from M. and *Faust*>
> <5. Home and the World II.>[97]

The first three sections of this work have since become known to readers, in different forms, as separate narratives. Items four and five are further described in an adjacent plan as concerning the "five categories of existence: daily life (*byt*), love, profession, creativity, self-consciousness."[98] Most of the extant drafts (dialogues and character sketches) in the folder relate to love and daily life[99]; there are also outlines of a day in the professional life of the hero.[100] The form and style of these three texts, which one reader described as "rationalistic impressionism,"[101] are highly fragmentary. As such, they attest to the nature of Ginzburg's oeuvre: all the pieces that make it up can easily be shifted from one work to another, while the whole is highly interconnected.

The diary—factual, unpredictable, open, and fragmentary—and the novel—fictional, structured, complete, and extended—are the two poles between which Ginzburg's prose fluctuates. At the same time, elements of the note—as draft and construction, and a reflection of the social person—continue to have a place in her experiments. The uncertainty and flexibility of the moment are keenly sensed in the diaries, but "regularity" (*zakonomernost'*) and evaluation (*otsenka*) are difficult to attain. In order to create finished, generalizable texts in a diary, one must somehow achieve a retrospective glance at life as it is being lived. This dilemma led Ginzburg to the poetics of the formula.

THE FORMULA: MAXIMS AND MICROCOSMIC PLOTS

Ginzburg was a master of brevity and wit. Her anecdotes often capture a truth about society at the same time as they reveal the character of a given personage. For example, her one-liner from 1928 about a professor of hers—"I attend only my own lectures, says Vinogradov, and even then, not always"—seems to speak to this particular scholar's arrogance, as well as to the self-absorbed and overextended lifestyle that is a professional malady.[102] Ginzburg's anecdotes sometimes approach the aphorism or maxim, which go a step further in their generalization.[103] (She was a devoted admirer of La Rochefoucauld, whom she saw as having "the terminology of a moralist but the acumen of a psychologist").[104] One particularly characteristic genre of note in her repertoire is one she defines as the "formula," which shares with the witty one-liner its poetics of brevity. Ginzburg practiced the formula throughout her creative life.

The formula is the end product of the search for regularity or structure that approximates the attempted retrospective glance at one's life as it unfolds. It is an observation, truth or opinion that has been finished or compressed into a single line, which Ginzburg then frequently explains or embeds within different compositions. The formula is a microcosmic representation that seeks to explain a complicated story with a short expression. Here are a few examples:

> Talented people are always professionally more honest than people without talent.
> (Талантливые люди профессионально всегда честнее бездарных.)
>
> When misfortune strikes, the worst family is handier than the best of friends.
> (Когда доходит до беды, самая плохая семья удобнее самых лучших друзей.)
>
> What we can and cannot do determines the limits of our consciousness.
> (То, что мы можем, и то, чего мы не можем, определяет границы нашего понимания.)[105]

These formulae have an emotional quality to them, bringing logic to painful situations.[106] Thus Ginzburg's younger friends recall her in old age speaking the second formula, as she was becoming frail and dependent on their help, in the absence of family members. Her formulae speak to a wealth of life experiences while combining two key ingredients common to verbal art (both of which she identified as characteristic of the novel)—emotionality and generalization.[107] They are the product of both creativity and analysis.

The formula combines observations of oneself and others. It is therefore especially appropriate for a writer who early on defined her project as the analysis of neither the "uniquely personal" nor the "typical," but rather "everything that follows psycho-physiological and historical laws. A person's fate as the point where universal tendencies intersect."[108] As a writer of notebooks, Ginzburg balances the inevitable "accidental" elements (*sluchainosti*) with depictions of life's regularities.[109] She writes that the diarist or writer of notebooks must "tiptoe behind his own life," always cognizant of the fact that his or her life "is not obliged to be edifying."[110] The writer-analyst must also have an eye turned toward the lives and fates of others, in order to discover the typical.

The formula has a delicately complex relationship to time: it combines the forward-moving (*postupatel'naia*) dynamic of the notebooks with something more stable, reflective, and final—but not so final that it becomes a dead-end. Ginzburg enunciates her notion of the formula in its relationship to reality and to verbal expression in a key passage from the summer of 1929:

> Each formula of internal experience is compressed out of a large mass of undifferentiated and seemingly pointless impressions. Sometimes you

need to squander two months, live them in a chaos of abrupt sensations, in order to think up one sentence.

I am speaking about the sentence because for me a formula found is the best of rewards. Everything that is not expressed in words (out loud or to oneself) has no reality for me, or rather I do not have the receptive organs for it. To express a thing in a word does not mean to name it terminologically. It is necessary in each case to think up a formula, a little structure, a microcosm of plot, with its own denouement. When I see a splendid landscape and don't have a formula for it, I experience the feeling that what's happening is not really necessary, as if I were sitting on a bench in a dusty public square chewing sunflower seeds. All the joys and sorrows of life come with their own verbal clusters, which are like obsessive quotations that have been congealing for a long time in my consciousness.

Всякая формула внутреннего опыта является выжимкой из большой массы недифференцированных и как будто бесцельных впечатлений. Иногда нужно загубить два месяца, прожить их в сумбуре обрывающихся ощущений, для того чтобы придумать одну фразу.

Я говорю о фразе, потому что для меня найденная формула—лучшая из наград. Все, не выраженное в слове (вслух или про себя), не имеет для меня реальности, вернее, я не имею для него органов восприятия. Выразить вещь в слове—не значит наименовать ее терминологически. Необходимо в каждом данном случае выдумать формулу, маленькую структуру, микрокосм сюжета, со своим собственным разрешением. Когда я вижу прекрасный пейзаж, не имея для него формулы, я испытываю ощущение ненужности происходящего, как если б я грызла семечки на лавочке в пыльном сквере. Все радости и горести жизни доходят какими-то словесными сгустками, как бы навязчивыми цитатами, надолго застывающими в сознании. [111]

This extraordinary passage describes a nearly utilitarian attitude to the world as material for creative verbal expression. This material does not obey the laws of economy or labor, since the transformation into words requires an apparent, if not real waste of energy. The search for formulae becomes the uninterrupted activity of a writer's mind. After all the time spent discovering the right formula (during which there can be a temporary feeling of futility and meaninglessness, expressed through the metaphor of chewing sunflower seeds), the words that do finally arrive seem to have long existed in the consciousness, in some warehouse of thought-expressions. Ginzburg's idea about the formula as a "microcosmic plot" indicates a possible relationship to fiction, or the expansion of characteristics of fiction of its categories into documentary prose.[112] As a product, the formula interrupts the continuity of time (an epiphanic moment that is crystallized and clung to); it is further disloyal—one could say fictive—in relation to time, since it compresses it (*vyzhimka*).

The first definition of "formula" in the seventeen-volume Academy of Sciences Dictionary reads: "A short, general definition of any position, law, or relationship, etc., applied to individual cases; a short, exact verbal expression, a definition of something."[113] Ginzburg's own usage of the word "formula" shows that her definition also includes the clichés that everyone repeats in everyday life such as "this too will pass" ("все проходит") or "time heals all" ("время—лучший целитель").[114] (She notes that while these formulae may express general truths, they cannot be used in concrete situations to comfort others or oneself; they seem vulgar [*poshlyi*] and false.) She also discusses the compression of a scholar's theories into isolated formulae as a regrettable phenomenon, since this can "devour the diversity of ideas, capable of actively living and working as they enter into unforeseen relationships."[115] In the dictionary entry, the first example of usage comes from none other than Alexander Herzen (one of Ginzburg's models), who defines it as a rule for living, a maxim: "Adopt for yourself a general outlook, a general formula, and you will almost never err in applying it to a particular application."[116] The formula has a practical and ethical goal of helping one to operate in the world and to better oneself, and thus it connects the activity of notebook writing, as a literary genre, with the more practical origins of note keeping.

"Formula" is a word that readily evokes the disciplines of science and mathematics and reminds us that Ginzburg originally went to Petersburg to study science, and that she came from a family of chemists. It also reminds one of the scientifically oriented Formalists. Further, both *formula* and *zakonomernost'* (law-governed-ness or regularity) have Hegelian and Marxist overtones, alluding to the idea that history advances according to certain laws, and can produce formulae for the future when scientifically analyzed. (The word "formula" took on negative connotations when it referred to Marxist-Leninist commonplaces, or *shtampy*, the compulsory but hollow jargon that crept into speeches and the forewords of books.[117]) Ginzburg's use of the term speaks to what Alexander Zholkovsky has called the pseudoscientific element of her prose.[118]

The habit of looking for logic and underlying laws connects with Ginzburg's occupation as a scholar. Yuri Lotman defines the scholar as a person who organizes messy material such as an artistic text into "regularity" around a certain system or structure, the work of scholarship.[119] And yet the scholar's work remains akin to the novelist's task, which is to create a world more ordered than the one outside the text. Barbara Hernnstein Smith, in her theory of fictive discourse, reminds us that: "the artist creates structures that are relatively free of those irrelevancies, irregularities, and monotonies that often frustrate and attenuate our satisfaction in cognitive activity, but structures that are, at the same time, sufficiently complex, rich, or subtle to engage and exercise our cognitive faculties."[120] As a practitioner of in-between literature, Ginzburg wrote of art as always constituting a "struggle with chaos and nonbeing, with life's onward flow, which leaves no trace behind" ("борьба с хаосом и небытием, с бесследным протеканием жизни"), and of fictional prose such as novels or tales as the highest expression of aesthetic structure.[121]

Lotman goes on to argue that artists invent, while scholars discover. One may in a scholarly way recover old formulae, or in a more artistic way invent new ones. When she was young, Ginzburg was especially fond of discovering formulae "readymade": "Others' words are always a find—you take them as they are; in any case there's no way to improve or remake them. The words of others, even if representing our own thought only distantly and inaccurately, act like a discovery or a formula that we searched for and found long ago."[122] One example of such a "found" formula comes from one of Tolstoy's epiphanies: "one must not, must not, must not live the way I am living,—this alone was the truth," about which Ginzburg remarks, "Here it is, the formula of individual moral responsibility for social evil. The formula of true humanism. The precondition for pity. A formula that has been lost."[123] Ginzburg not only rediscovers the formula, she also reflects on its importance, use value, and cultural history. Another example shows how she often takes a formula that exists as a Russian proverb and adds her own personal dimension to it. Thus, "The well-fed do not understand the hungry" is a common adage, but Ginzburg's blockade experience allows her to say: "The well-fed do not understand the hungry, oneself included" ("Сытый не разумеет голодного, в том числе самого себя").[124] In the poetics of the formula, the speech of others is mediated by personal experience, a feature that the formula shares with the essay (discussed later), which is similarly open to experience in a way that traditional scholarship is not.[125]

THE SEA-COLORED SEA: A PERSONAL FORMULA

Not all of Ginzburg's formulae attempt to generalize from experience or to instruct. Some of them are chiefly personal and idiosyncratic. One such formula describes the sea, which is a locus of intense emotion and reflection in her writings. Ginzburg grew up in Odessa on the Black Sea, and was a superb swimmer, rower, and sailor. As a twenty-year-old, she wrote in her diary of the sea as unmasking life's frightening essences. When you are alone by the sea, she remarks, "it's as if everything has been laid bare, and for a few minutes you're aware of what you really always are—a lost person, surrounded by a thousand dangers."[126] Nature is a rare subject in her notes, and she relates to it with ambivalence, as a force that may provoke either calm or anxiety.[127]

One of Ginzburg's most extended treatments of natural space (sea, mountains, and countryside) is in "The Return Home." In her main passage on the sea, she declares that she prefers the sea not when it reflects the pink of the sunset, nor when it is gray from a storm, but precisely when it prevails as the "sea-colored sea." She writes, "I prefer the sea in the broad and dim glitter of the sun when it is rising to its zenith, the morning sea the color of sea."[128] Her preference is a variation on the theme of "regularity" (*zakonomernost'*), since what she is describing could be thought of as the "law-governed sea," one that does not pose as a Dostoevskian eccentric or put on masks.

Ginzburg likes the sea-colored sea because "you cannot compare it with anything else or name it otherwise (making a lot of comparisons is pointless, really)."[129] She generally avoided metaphors, and described their excessive use as a stylistic danger for prose writers. (She criticized Vera Inber, and even Osip Mandelstam, for this fault.) The danger for writers who "didn't know how to leave a thing in peace" until they had "herded it into a metaphor" was that they would generate "irresponsible comparisons, false proportions, cabinets of curiosities, and witticisms."[130] Metaphor in prose could obstruct the path to the Tolstoyan or Pushkinian clarity and adequacy of the word. If in a metaphor, a = b (one thing is made equal to or substituted for another), then in a formula, as Ginzburg interprets it, a = A (a thing is equal to a more generalized version of itself).

Ginzburg's description of the sea associates its natural color with the "formula" for a healthy attitude toward life and death: "the sea-colored sea, in a short and strong wave, helps one find the formula of health and the formula of overcoming fear. Health is the courage of the organism which lives, though it knows about possible and unavoidable calamities, including its own death."[131] Later in this passage, Ginzburg describes how the swimmer becomes self-conscious of the precariousness of his position in the water. Suspended over an abyss but remaining on the surface because of the maneuvers of his own body, he exists by the force of his own will. The neutral "sea-colored sea" characterizes the human relationship to a body of water as absence, and this helps a person grasp death, and therefore life.

There is another passage about the sea where Ginzburg, casting herself in the guise of a hypothetical writer, tests her mettle. She drafts the passage as part of a "Theoretical Introduction" (ca. 1939) to "The Return Home" (the first section of *Home and the World*).[132] She presents a writer dissecting his experiences as he methodically analyzes his impressions:

Let's imagine a person lying on the beach. On his back he's sunk into the sand that prickles his back. His knees are relaxed. The sun has halted on his lips and eyelids. Closing his eyes, he hears how the wave hisses and dies out. Opening his eyes, he follows a wave, at first moving in a row of others. The wave is ever clearer and closer; it comes at last as the first wave of the surf. Growing larger, suddenly it turns in on itself and blazes up in foam; leveling off, it turns over, flows back, leaving behind it bubbly foam, soaking down into the sand. The person on the beach likes lying in the sand, in the sun, and looking at the wave. But some kind of movement going on within him cannot stop at this. What do I really need the sun for? Because it gives me pleasure. And why experience pleasure? . . . Most probably, the hypothetical man on the beach does not pronounce this internal monologue. But this is the most precise way of deciphering his internal anxiety. In his anxiety he begins to think; he thinks about the sand and to himself calls it prickly, tickling, hard, or, on the contrary, soft; it occurs to him that the skin of the lip responds to the sun's rays with greater sensitivity than the rest of the body's surface, and he formulates: the sun halted on the lips and eyelids. It occurs to him to dissect the surf into a few sequential motions. And when this is done—there is nothing more to be anxious about. The sand, sun, and sea have found their use.

With equal success the hypothetical person could have posed the question . . . and why did I call the sand, on which I am lying,—soft, or crumbly, or prickly? Is this interesting? And why should it be interesting. . . . He could have asked, but he doesn't. This means he has found what in various contexts they call sense, happiness, value, meaning,—the undissectible end-in-itself of the life process.

Представим себе человека, лежащего на пляже. Спиной он ушел в колющий спину песок. Его колени расслаблены. Солнце остановилось у него на губах и веках. Закрыв глаза, он слышит, как шипит и как потухает волна. Раскрывая глаза, он следит за волной, сначала движущейся в ряду других. Волна—все отчетливее и ближе; она идет, наконец, первой волной прибоя. Увеличиваясь, вдруг заворачивается вовнутрь и вспыхивает пеной; разворачивается плоско, течет назад, оставляя за собой пузырчатую пену, всасывающуюся в песок. Человеку на пляже нравится лежать в песке и на солнце и смотреть на волну. Но какое-то происходящее в нем движение не может на этом остановиться. Зачем мне, собственно, солнце? Затем, что это доставляет мне удовольствие. А зачем испытывать удовольствие? . . . Скорее всего, гипотетический человек на пляже не произносит этот внутренний монолог. Но так точнее всего расшифровывается его душевное беспокойство. В беспокойстве он начинает думать; он думает о песке и про себя называет его колючим, щекочущим, жестким, или, напротив того, нежным; ему приходит в голову, что чувствительная кожа губ сильнее, чем остальная поверхность тела, отзывается на солнечные лучи, и он формулирует: солнце остановилось на губах и веках. Ему приходит в голову разложить прибой на несколько последовательных движений. И когда это сделано—беспокоиться больше не о чем. Песок, солнце и море нашли себе применение.

С таким же успехом гипотетический человек мог бы задать вопрос . . . зачем я назвал песок, на котором лежу,—нежным, или рассыпчатым, или колючим? Это интересно? А зачем, собственно, чтобы было интересно. . . . Он мог бы спросить, но он не спрашивает. Это значит, что он нашел то, что в разных контекстах называют смыслом, счастьем, ценностью, назначением,—неразложимую самоцель жизненного процесса.[133]

In this deeply layered passage, a vivid image serves to illustrate how such a description takes shape in the writer's head, and how the writer feels during this process. Ginzburg's approach to both the external and internal worlds (the sea and the writer's mood) is dissection (of the wave's motion and the writer's anxiety). The mode is also one of explanation: the "formula" for lying on the beach—"the sun halted on his lips and eyelids"—turns out to have a clear logic, in that the skin on these parts of the face is especially sensitive. The whole scene is a set of questions and solutions.

For all of its analytical flair, the passage has an enchanting consonance and a poetic quality.[134] The first line overflows with the sounds of "s," "l," and "n," which are focused in the overarching *Solntse*. In the fourth short sentence, the "y" (ы) sounds (and one "i" [и] sound) and hushings predominate ("*Zakryv glaza, on slyshit, kak shipit*"). On the whole, there is a preponderance of hushings and the "v" and "s" sounds, perhaps evoking waves splashing on the sand ("p" and "s" sounds). Later, there are internal rhymes, such as the repeated *-vorachivaetsia* (*zavorachivaetsia, razvorachivaetsia*) and the three stressed syllables, all open "a" sounds, in *pliazhe nravitsia lezhat'*. Not only sounds, but also actions are multiplied. The sun stops (*Solntse ostanovilos'*), but something within the writer cannot (*kakoe-to proiskhodiashchee v nem dvizhenie ne mozhet na etom ostanovit'sia*). This motion (*dvizhenie*) within the writer is doubled in the motion of the wave that he breaks down into parts (*razlozhit priboi na neskol'ko posledovatel'nykh dvizhenii*). The dissected (*razlozhit*) flow is opposed to the indivisible end in itself (*nerazlozhimuiu samotsel'*).

The contrast between motion and stasis, a focus of this passage, resonates with the relationship of time to writing. The fixed formula near the beginning, which is an image of stasis ("The sun halted on his lips and eyelids"), is set in motion through the act of dissection. Its meaning is different the second time around, when we find out exactly how it occurs to the mind of the writer. In Ginzburg's mini-plot, the writer's anxieties dissipate after he has found a formula for the scene. Paradoxically, despite her talent for analysis, she equates happiness with the cessation of mental activity afforded by the successful formula; for a moment, her journey ends with the hypothetical writer's. However, she hints at an unraveling of the writer's reluctant satisfaction, since it would only take one more question, one more "what for?" (*zachem*?) to undo the finality of the ending. Ginzburg's tendency to punctuate continuous motion is reflected in two images: the sun halting on the lips and eyelids, and the breaking wave, itself broken down into its constituent motions. And yet the passage as a whole, which appropriately follows upon a comparison of the writer to Proust's hero, unfolds the thought process as it occurs in the present moment. The description of a single breaking wave can serve as a metaphor for the treatment of the flow (*protekanie*) of life in the entire work—fascinating precisely because its motion is so continuous and difficult to capture.

A temporal expansion is achieved here through analysis, through breaking the scene down into its component parts. The unceasing questions and the lyricism of analysis are reminiscent of Tolstoy.[135] Ginzburg's "hypothetical writer" seems to share the sensibilities of Tolstoy's Irtenev in *Childhood*, since it is as if he is learning how his perceptions of the world work, becoming aware of this process for the first time. In her scholarship on Tolstoy, Ginzburg noted that his analysis was "synthetic in its own way" and that by breaking down a "unitary phenomenon" into parts, he achieved a depiction greater than the sum of these components, since they could now enter into new aesthetic relationships.[136] In this passage about the sea, Ginzburg achieves the same kind of analytical synthesis that she admired in Tolstoy.

Decades later, Ginzburg's memory of her earlier "formula" of the "sea-colored sea" triggers a reflection on her perceived failure to realize herself as a writer. In an essay from 1960, she describes being on a boat trip when her "distant efforts to describe the sea" and to "grasp its color" suddenly come back to her:

> And it all ended, it seems, in a formula: the sea-colored sea. Back then it seemed that [my] cognition of the world was beginning, that there was nowhere to rush to; it seemed that an experiment had been set up, and that

it could be drawn out for a long time. Since then a life has passed, mainly consumed by other things. A consciousness existed, which could become aware of things—and it lost heart, under the pretext of causes outside of its control.

И все это, кажется, кончилось формулой: море морского цвета. Тогда казалось, что начинается узнавание мира, что спешить еще некуда; казалось, поставлен эксперимент, который может надолго затянуться. С тех пор прошла жизнь, в основном занятая другими делами. Существовала сознание, которое могло осознать—и смалодушествовало, под предлогом не зависящих от него причин.[137]

The subject of this passage is Ginzburg's sense of failure, which she treats by holding up the example of her earlier self as aspiring writer, becoming conscious of the world by formulating it in words. It is no coincidence that she refers back to "The Return Home," which marked her first attempts to become a kind of novelist. Significantly, she posits the formula as the end result of a thought—which mirrors her feeling that the "experiment" was already finished, even as it seemed to be just beginning. (The formula is a small victory, but it is also a problem, as one cannot go any further or abandon it; it is finalized, unless and until it resurfaces.) And yet counteracting the sense of an ending is the fact that the formula resurfaces at a much later moment in time as a memory with a new meaning and pathos. At this moment, then, Ginzburg has found in the "formula" a memory trigger and a phrase that summarizes an earlier encounter with nature, one that reflected her own potential as a writer.

Once Ginzburg had found or invented a formula, a precise expression of her thoughts or observations, she was likely to repeat it in various prose works and contexts—even in a work that was so highly conditioned by generic templates, and so heavily subjected to editing from the cultural gatekeepers in the early 1930s as *The Pinkerton Agency*.[138] She was aware that her formulations and thoughts did not belong in this alien book, and tried to resist placing them there: "I already had a lot that I'd thought out about life; many preparations, especially descriptions. Consequently, the relentless temptation was to insert them."[139] In *The Pinkerton Agency*, the hero Crane suffers from hunger, and borrows money from his boardinghouse roommate in order to eat a square meal before his recruitment interview at the spy agency. Ginzburg writes:

Crane ate a warm breakfast on the Irishman Tommy's dollar; now as he sat across from his future boss he was alert, with a clear head and obedient

> nerves. Hunger was behind him, that prolonged hunger which resembles a disease and does not at all resemble the desire to eat. Crane gritted his teeth: I have to find work.
>
> Крейн съел горячий завтрак на доллар ирландца Томми; теперь он сидел против будущего хозяина настороженный, с ясной головой и послушными нервами. Позади голод, затянувшийся голод, похожий на болезнь и уже совсем не похожий на желание есть. Крейн сжал зубы: я должен найти работу.[140]

Ginzburg was well acquainted with hunger from the years of War Communism, as well as from her student years in Petrograd; even into the 1930s, she often went hungry as she struggled to provide for her mother and uncle on her small earnings.[141] She inserted her insight about prolonged hunger, and its unsettling psychological effects, into a book whose young audience might have skimmed past it to follow the plot (though they may also have been experiencing hunger themselves, in these difficult years).

Ginzburg suffered from hunger on a different scale in the Leningrad Blockade. In writing about hunger in *Notes of a Blockade Person,* she inserts her formula from *The Pinkerton Agency*.

> Real hunger, as is well known, does not resemble the desire to eat. It has its masks. It could turn into melancholy, indifference, an insane hurry, cruelty. It most resembled a chronic disease. And, as with any disease, one's mental makeup was very important here.
>
> Настоящий голод, как известно, не похож на желание есть. У него свои маски. Он оборачивался тоской, равнодушием, сумасшедшей торопливостью, жестокостью. Он был скорее похож на хроническую болезнь. И, как при всякой болезни, психика была здесь очень важна.[142]

The psychology and physiology of hunger is a central theme in *Notes of a Blockade Person,* where this generalization fits integrally and is explained at length. The temptation to insert cherished thoughts, positions, and observations into multiple compositions, which faces authors in general, must be especially intense for those who have to write some prose for the desk drawer and other prose for publication.

NOTES, ESSAYS, FRAGMENTS: GROUPINGS AND COMBINATIONS

The flexibility of the fragment becomes readily apparent in view of Ginzburg's use of it to sustain so many of her diverse publications. Attending to

Ginzburg's selection, editing, arrangement, and titling of her notes for publication will shed light on their aesthetics and generic orientations. As she wrote in *On Psychological Prose*, "It is not invention that is necessary for aesthetic significance, but organization—the selection and creative combination of elements reflected in and transfigured by the word."[143] One way to bring the "formula" into life was to spin out its genesis in a longer narrative and to place it in a larger context (the act of swimming in the "sea-colored sea"). Ginzburg's "finished" notes could also take on new life and offer up new creative possibilities by their selection and combination.

Between 1982 and her death in 1990, Ginzburg published about twelve editions of her "notes," ranging from two-page selections in journals to the 350-page compilation *Person at a Writing Table*. Due to her growing popularity as well as to diminishing censorship, she released more and more notes, touching on an increasingly broad range of subjects (one of her last publications during her lifetime included an account of her brief arrest in 1933 and her interrogation in 1952).[144] The sheer number of Ginzburg's publications creates the impression that she had an enormous warehouse of "finished" miniatures that could be infinitely edited, varied, collected, and recombined. After her death there remained vast amounts of unpublished notes. She had withheld certain of these because their themes (such as same-sex love) still tested the boundary of the publishable, or because they could have offended or upset her subjects or their friends, or because of a lack of time. She spent the final weeks of her life working with Nikolai Kononov on the book *Transformation of Experience*, and plans from her archive show that she was sketching out still other publications.

Though conditions were wildly different when she began publishing in the 1980s from when she started writing in 1925, they had again grown favorable to in-between forms. For one thing, literature was once again in search of new directions and genres. Introducing the first small selection of her notes, Ginzburg expressed a hope that the concerns of the twenties and thirties would resonate with the contemporary literary process.[145] Second, as she observed in her book *On the Literary Hero*, the boundaries of literature had opened up such that autobiographical and documentary prose were now established genres.[146] Third, during *glasnost'* readers thirsted for documentary prose about the past.[147] Ginzburg gave preference in her earliest publications to her "old" notes from the 1920s and 1930s, especially those containing sketches of famous literary figures (many of whom had been taboo topics for years): Akhmatova, Mayakovsky, Mandelstam, Shklovsky, and Oleinikov. She thus created an unfortunate parallel between herself and Vyazemsky, often conceived of merely as a wellspring of anecdotes about Pushkin, Vasily Zhukovsky, Nikolai Karamzin, and Ivan Dmitriev.

When editing her notes in the 1980s, Ginzburg was certainly influenced by the changes in her public identity as a writer—from a member of the Formalist circle, to a representative of the post-revolutionary intelligentsia and witness of the Leningrad Blockade, to a cult figure in her own right. The fragmentary nature of the notes allowed her to do "constructive" work on them through combination and selection. Nevertheless, out of respect for the human document, she never rewrote her notes from the 1920s with the concerns of her more mature period (for example, oral speech or the post-individualist person) in mind, editing them only slightly (mostly by cutting). (Her reminiscences, which she explicitly framed and dated as such, are a different story, but even they privilege and quote from the notes.)

How did Ginzburg choose and arrange her "notes" for publication? Her early notebooks themselves observe the "negative constructive principle" that she had identified as the innovative ingredient in Vyazemsky's notebooks. Notes of diverse kinds (anecdotes, witticisms, reflections, essays) on a range of subjects border one another. In preparing them for publication, she had to choose whether to group the notes thematically or chronologically, or by some other principle, or simply to make a random arrangement. In practice, she combined the same notes in different ways for different publications (and sometimes slightly modified individual notes stylistically). In addition, she published her longer pieces—the "reminiscences," longer "essays," and "narratives" such as *Notes of a Blockade Person*—in several different versions, usually including more material as opportunities arose.

The debut publication of Ginzburg's notes in *Novyi mir*, "Person at a Writing Table: From the Old Notebooks," showcases episodes from her early literary life. The designation "old notebooks" is undoubtedly meant to evoke Vyazemsky's use of the term. Ginzburg's publication almost fits into the category of memoir, typical of the Russian intelligentsia, that Barbara Walker has called the "Contemporaries" genre.[148] In a preface, Ginzburg writes a brief reminiscence about the atmosphere at the Institute for the History of Arts, which paves the way for her selection of about thirty-five notes, most of them portraying famous Leningrad poets and scholars from the late 1920s to the early 1930s. Not only does the theme of literary life serve to unify these miniatures, but Ginzburg creates several small groupings around important figures: there are two consecutive notes about Blok, three in a row about Mayakovsky, six about Akhmatova, and four about Oleinikov. Within each grouping, the order of notes (printed without dates) does not follow chronology.[149] Ginzburg opens and closes the publication with a different kind of note, showing that the author is no mere chronicler: she begins with a note reflecting on how reading habits in youth differ from those in adulthood, and moves into a list of books she lived by, including any and all of Tolstoy's writings.[150] The concluding note is about nighttime writing habits and the "person at the writing table," who feels alive and free from the tyranny of daytime routines.[151] This note contains the phrase that lends its title to the publication, and subsequently to Ginzburg's book.

The book *Person at a Writing Table* (as well as other, longer publications) follows a "negative constructive principle" to a much greater degree than this initial publication. This principle does not imply that Ginzburg just scattered her notes on the floor and picked them up at random like Shklovsky (or rather Shklovsky's conceit of himself as an author, since the pieces of *Zoo* in fact demonstrate a progression or plot)—rather, she appears to have sequenced them with deliberate care. Often, she alternated different kinds of notes to create variety: a serious note borders a comic one, the historically significant is next to the more intimate, short next to long, quoted speech next to reflection. Interestingly, the note about "the person at the writing table" that so poignantly ends the journal publication appears in the book haphazardly in the midst of notes from 1929, with no special demarcation.

Unlike the journal publication, introduced by a preface and a meditative note, the book opens informally, with an account of a conversation with Yuri Tynianov that could have taken place in the halls of the Zubov Institute. The note, thirteen lines long, begins:

> Tynianov is a student of Vengerov (like everyone else). He assured me that Semyon Afanasievich [Vengerov] would say: "Really! You plan to prove Katenin's influence on Pushkin . . . but after all Katenin is an unsympathetic personality!"[152]

From these very first words, Ginzburg seems to be speaking to two audiences: her Formalist peers, and readers in the 1980s who found the 1920s milieu fascinating.[153] Readers need to bring along their cultural-historical knowledge in order to catch the irony that the Formalists were trained by the very academics whose methods they proceeded to reject. In an economical, amusing, and informal way, the note goes on to treat the methods and ethics of literary scholarship. Tynianov speaks of how Vengerov had higher expectations for his students' research, reading, and mastery of material than the Formalists ever did.

The first several pages of *Person at a Writing Table* indirectly introduce the author, who was intellectually shaped by her years at the Institute, with a series of notes about the Formalists (as scholars, writers, and colorful personalities). Ginzburg selects notes that make a special hero of Shklovsky, who played a larger role than her other teachers in inspiring her prose. Tynianov, who influenced her scholarship to a greater degree, features more prominently in the original notebooks. Not until the sixth page of the book does one find a different kind of note: an unattributed witticism with no apparent relationship to specific contemporaries.[154] Two similar notes follow: one-liners with psychological insights, taken from Ginzburg's life: "X is one of those people who, having beheaded a person, is interested to know whether the part in his hair got messed up in the process"; and "How strange that we see one another so rarely and part so often (from a letter)."[155] Clusters of notes about a single personage occur less frequently than in the *Novyi mir* selection. Meanwhile, chronology serves as more of an ordering principle, perhaps because the book covers so many more decades. In *Person at a Writing Table,* something akin to chapters are created by temporal divisions. These sections are asymmetrical (consisting of just one or two years between 1926 and 1936, but then pairs of decades beginning from the 1950s), which has the effect of framing the early decades as more important historically and personally.[156] (The decade of the 1940s is not represented by the usual kinds of notes—only by *Notes of a Blockade Person.*) It should be noted that Ginzburg never follows a strict temporal chronology in her arrangement of notes within a given section. She also places certain fragments under the "wrong year," usually with clear motivations.[157]

Let's take a sequence of four notes from *Person at Writing Table,* featuring Viktor Shklovsky as their "hero," and analyze the results of Ginzburg's juxtapositions. None of the notes carries a specific date, though they are placed in the section "1925–26."

> Shklovsky became a director at the Third State Film Factory (in Moscow). Sources confirm that he telegraphed Tynianov: "Keep writing scripts. If money is needed—I'll send it. Come immediately." And that Yu. N. Tynianov answered: "Money is always needed. Why come immediately, I don't understand."
>
> "I specialize in not understanding," says Shklovsky.
>
> Shklovsky says that his entire ability to be unhappily in love was used up on the heroine of *Zoo;* since then he can only love happily.
>
> He said about the first (Berlin) edition of *Zoo* that he was so in love with this book that he couldn't hold it in his hands without burning them.
>
> It's completely false that Shklovsky is a cheery person (as many people think). Shklovsky is a sad person. When I asked him about it, in order to dispel conclusively any doubt, he gave me his word of honor that he is sad.
>
> Шкловский вошел в дирекцию 3-й Госкинофабрики. Уверяют, что он телеграфировал Тынянову: «Все пишите сценарии. Если нужны

деньги—вышлю. Приезжай немедленно»—и что Ю. Н. телеграфно ответил: «Деньги нужны всегда. Почему приезжать немедленно—не понял».

«Моя специальность—не понимать»,—говорит Шкловский.

Шкловский говорит, что все его способности к несчастной любви ушли на героиню «Zoo» и что с тех пор он может любить только счастливо.

Про «Zoo» он говорил, что в первом (берлинском) издании эта книга была такая влюбленная, что ее, не обжигаясь, нельзя было держать в руках.

Совершенно неверно, что Шкловский—веселый человек (как думают многие); Шкловский—грустный человек. Когда я для окончательного разрешения сомнений спросила его об этом, он дал мне честное слово, что грустный.[158]

There is a certain consistency in the way these four separate anecdotes work: each contains reported speech (first- or secondhand) that is compressed and "perfected." Brief statements produce humorous effects, similar to the unexpected result of Shklovsky's telegram (where brevity is strictly required)—so as to become almost aphoristic. And just as Tynianov takes the second line of Shklovsky's telegram out of context, answering a specific question about money for a journey to Moscow with a generalization about always needing money, the rest of the fragments are ripped from their original place, time, and context. As Barbara Hernnstein Smith would say, this removal from context is a procedure that makes the notes into literature: they are "depictions or representations, rather than instances, of natural discourse."[159] We recognize Ginzburg's fragments as snapshots of Shklovsky, written with a mind to the historian's task of illuminating Shklovsky's enigmatic character and its relationship to his authorial persona.

The four juxtaposed notes about Shklovsky in fact originate from two different notebooks, and cover a two-year period, 1925–27.[160] The second note here, "I specialize in not understanding," was inscribed on a page that also contained a fragment on the subject of Shklovsky's rift with "the old OPOYAZ," and in particular from Tynianov and Eikhenbaum (which Ginzburg left unpublished).[161] In its original setting, this note seems to comment on Shklovsky's scholarly method, his stubbornness, and his difference from the other Formalists. But in the published version, the anecdote now seems to comment—through Ginzburg's juxtaposition—on Tynianov's sarcastic response to the telegram (which ends with the word "understand"). Further, Ginzburg conjoined two paragraphs on *Zoo*, diminishing their importance as "finished" miniatures and making them more telling of Shklovsky's relationship to *Zoo,* as well as of his mercurial character. The fourth note, in its original location in the manuscript notebook, follows the fragment discussed earlier in this chapter, where Brik reports to Ginzburg about a dissatisfied reader of *Third Factory.*[162] By moving her note about Shklovsky's word of honor that he is sad, just like his authorial persona (which does nothing to settle the question), Ginzburg removes this comment from the context of the polemic with Brik over the "literature of fact." At the same time, publishing the note next to the discussion of Shklovsky's *Zoo,* she maintains an echo of this context: the comparison of Shklovsky in life to Shklovsky in his autobiographical novels. Other groupings, those that favor variety and incongruity, could be analyzed in a similar way to highlight their different, but purposeful structures.

Just as one finds shifting generic orientations in Ginzburg's 1982 journal publication and her 1989 book based on the selection of notes, one finds shifts in generic labels. Thus in her early publications, as well as in books such as *Literature in Search of Reality* (1987), she uses the designation "notes" (*zapisi*), which alludes most obviously to Vyazemsky, but also to fictional works (such as Turgenev's *Hunter's Notes* or Dostoevsky's "Notes from Underground") and to the documentary prose of Alexander Herzen.[163] In *Person at a Writing Table,* Ginzburg reclassifies her fragments as "essays" (*esse*). She thus carries out a subtle shift and draws an explicit connection to the French tradition, to the genre made famous by Montaigne.[164]

Reda Bensmaïa, surveying the use of the lexeme "essay" since the seventeenth century, recounts that it has "been used to describe any prose of medium length wherein an informal tone prevails and the author does not attempt an exhaustive treatment."[165] As an in-between genre, the essay has prompted arguments over whether it belongs more to art or science. György Lukács describes it as a subtle art; Theodor Adorno argues that it "distinguishes itself from art through its conceptual character and its claim to truth free from aesthetic semblance," but that its unsystematic quality separates it from the purely scientific.[166] Most theorists agree that while the essay may address and interpret other texts, it demonstrates a more direct relationship to life than either criticism or other art forms. Following Montaigne, the essayist traditionally relies on her own faculties of reflection and the knowledge base of her own experience, putting ideas "to the test."[167] This idea of the essay (and the essayist) evokes Ginzburg's "direct conversation about life" (*priamoi razgovor o zhizni*), the fluidity of genres that she practiced (since she saw no firm boundary between her scholarship, notes, essays, or other prose forms), and her tendency toward philosophical reflection.[168]

Montaigne's *Essays* have been described as a loose arrangement of "stories, examples, maxims, and other elements,"[169] and may be said to demonstrate what Ginzburg called a "negative constructive principle" in relation to Vyazemsky's notebooks.[170] Montaigne affirmed chaos as his basic principle (or lack of one), writing, "I seek out change indiscriminately and tumultuously. My style and my mind alike go wandering."[171] The essay is also fragmentary: in Bensmaïa's terms, the essay's word is only ever "sufficient," never total or complete.[172] Even when the essayist gives titles to the essays (such as Montaigne's "Of Drunkenness," or "On Some Lines by Virgil"), the musings that follow touch on a multitude of themes that do not exhaust or define the title.

The essay, in part through its title, simultaneously flaunts its excess and its incompleteness. One sees this dynamic at work in Ginzburg's publications. In *Person at a Writing Table*, the first heading to appear is "Poets" (*Poety*), which one imagines will introduce a series of notes or a longer essay. But in fact Ginzburg uses it to introduce a single anecdote about Mandelstam's excitement over his discovery of Konstantin Vaginov, which compels him to call Eikhenbaum in the middle of the night.[173] Several of the notes that surround this one (and lack headings themselves) also feature poets as their main subjects (Pasternak, Tikhonov, Mayakovsky); all of them deepen our understanding of how poets live and interact, as well as of particular works and personalities. It is possible that this heading indicates that this single note—which ends "There you have it, a living history of literature, the history of literature with illustrations"—should be read as an epitome of the life of poets. But it is also possible that the heading is meant to extend to several of the surrounding essays or notes, drawing our attention to one of their recurring themes.

SHIFTING GENERIC ORIENTATIONS IN THE POSTHUMOUS EDITIONS

While *Person at a Writing Table* was the fullest collection of her prose published during her lifetime (in 1989) and appears to be the culmination of the editions she released beginning in 1982, the fact that Ginzburg was still at work on further editions at the time of her death means that there is no "definitive" version of her notes. And their inherent quality as essays or notes is to resist final or authoritative form. The reception of Ginzburg's notes and essays has been evolving over the three decades and more that have passed since their first, limited publication. The shape given to the posthumous publications of her writings testifies to the range of orientations toward her fragmentary oeuvre: there are readings of the notes as a "novel," as "diaries," as essays, and as historical-literary document or "archives." Ginzburg's "journals" have been called a "consummate prose form for the new age," in tune with feminist and post-modernist theories of the journal as an engendered form of autobiography, and as a particularly contemporary narrative art.[174] She has been seen by some as a link connecting Vyazemsky, Herzen, Eikhenbaum, and Shklovsky to Russian scholars writing in a more post-modern or eclectic key such as Mikhail Gasparov, Alexander Zholkovsky, and Mikhail Bezrodny.[175] However, she is most often valued as a thinker offering unique historical, psychological, and social analyses of Soviet life.[176]

Nikolai Kononov, a poet and novelist who entered the public scene in the era of *glasnost'* (and in post-Soviet times founded a press in Petersburg), worked together with Ginzburg on *Transformation of Experience*. As co-editor he influenced the selection of notes, their titles, and their arrangement in the book. The volume came out in 1991, a year after her death.[177] Kononov regards Ginzburg as primarily a writer, even a novelist, and champions her as such. In a postscript to the book, he argues that Ginzburg's scholarly works serve only as a commentary to her innovative prose. He regards *Person at a Writing Table* in its entirety as "quite genuinely a novel with a nearly detective-type plot" whose hero is "Thought calling itself into existence."[178] In *Transformation of Experience*, Kononov and Ginzburg observe the "negative constructive principle," presenting the notes out of chronological order. The ordering amplifies Ginzburg's image as a creative force. For instance, the division "Notes from Various Years" begins with the following note: "On the subject of these notes I said to Andrei Bitov, 'A person records people's conversations, and is praised for it. It's unjust!' to which Andrei replied, 'But, after all, first you need to invent them.' "[179] If one assumes Ginzburg agreed with or was flattered by Bitov's remark, this prominent note tilts the genre toward fiction, suggesting a more positive attitude toward invention than the "aversion" discussed earlier.

In 1992, Alexander Kushner, a prominent poet and Ginzburg's long-time friend (who is also the executor of her estate), selected previously unpublished notes from the 1920s and 1930s for publication in *Novyi mir*. Describing her prose as a kind of "novel" organized by her powerful intellect,[180] he establishes a continuity across her notes and narratives, and further argues that there is no clear division between Ginzburg's occupations as literary scholar, memoirist, essayist, or prosaist. He initiates a semi-archival approach to her work, publishing the "leftovers" from the notebooks in chronological order, an arrangement that deemphasizes the aesthetic structures created by Ginzburg's ordering of her notes in her own publications. He encourages the reader familiar with *Person at a Writing Table* to imagine "the place of the notes published here in their general context," and to understand that many of the lacunae in the section of posthumously published fragments could be "filled by another part of the text, published earlier." Protective of Ginzburg's legacy, he presents the author as a person of such stature that even her "immature" opinions (for example, that Pushkin's lyrics were inferior to Batiushkov's and Baratynsky's, or that Fet was a "bad" poet), which she herself excluded from publication, could be aired. Her tastes in her early twenties, he argues, were in tune with the epoch. And yet he by no means publishes all notes excluded by Ginzburg, and in making his selection he continues to shape her image and to respond to the interests of the imagined reader.

In his introduction to the commentaries in *Novyi mir*, Alexander Chudakov—known as a Chekhov scholar, co-editor of academic editions of Formalist scholarship, and later in life as a novelist—showcases the interrelationship between Ginzburg's theory and her prose. He positions her not as the writer of a diary, but of a special kind of in-between prose of which she was also the preeminent scholar. Chudakov's commentaries, by restoring the context of the 1920s, show how a knowledge of the history of Formalism and of the Leningrad literary elite enhances one's appreciation of the notes.

In 1999, the first selection of Ginzburg's notes to be published in English (translated by Jane Gary Harris) came out in the anthology *Russian Women Writers*.[181] Titled "From the Journals" (and prefaced by an article on Ginzburg's life and work), this introductory selection attempts to initiate new audiences into the world of Ginzburg's notebooks by featuring notes accessible to the general reader, complete with editorial headings and appearing in chronological order. In the same year, Igor Valentinovich Zakharov, a publisher whose press issues the popular detective novels of Boris Akunin and who is outside Ginzburg's circle of friends (and regarded by them with some suspicion) created a very different edition with *Zapisnye knizhki: Novoe sobranie*.[182] He claims to be presenting the most accessible notes, "texts that don't require a specialist's knowledge." Zakharov opts not to respect the ordering principles and divisions Ginzburg had created; he removes the titles of her essays, and offers only excerpts from them. *Notes of a Blockade Person* appears within notes from the 1940s. On the dust jacket, he introduces Ginzburg as a witness to Soviet history, and in some sense reinforces her work's status as historical document by grouping the notes in sequential order. Meanwhile, the jacket sensationalizes Ginzburg's prose as "scary" (*strashnaia kniga*) and "sharper than any novel" (*pokruche liubogo romana*). Zakharov's edition, which Kirill Kobrin justifiably calls "monstrous in its principles and execution" for the liberties it takes with Ginzburg's oeuvre,[183] does show how her fragments can be fitted into bizarre and arbitrary formats.

Kobrin, a writer, critic, and journalist who came of age during the Soviet Union's dissolution, describes his own experience of the 1990s as framed by Ginzburg's books.[184] The decade of the 1990s, however, saw a lull in the publication of Ginzburg's works. This picked up with formidable intensity in 2002, the centenary of her birth, during which the single largest volume to date came out, *Zapisnye knizhki. Vospominaniia. Esse*, bringing together under one cover all of her previously published notes, essays, narratives, and reminiscences.[185] It respects Ginzburg's constructive principle by leaving intact sections from *Person at a Writing Table* and *Transformation of Experience*, while also including unchanged Ginzburg's posthumous journal publications, which were organized on other principles.[186] In the same year, more notes were extracted from the 1925–34 notebooks for publication in *Zvezda*, selected and introduced by Kushner. Once again, he tried to replicate more or less the order of notes in the original notebooks. Going back into the notebooks—and violating not only Ginzburg's, but his own, previous principles of selection, he justifies this decision by remarking that while these may be "leftovers of the pie," such leftovers are "sweet" (*ostatki sladki*, a Russian idiom). He voices the fear that these posthumous publications might "disrupt the general fabric" of Ginzburg's "strong text" with "less substantial, more incidental" ones, but finds a precedent in his earlier role as editor, during Ginzburg's lifetime.[187]

Those who speak of Ginzburg's prose as a novel or single work are in many senses following Ginzburg's lead.[188] She had long held the ideal of creating a "single" work, a "conversation about life."[189] In the preface to her book *Literature in Search of Reality* (*Literatura v poiskakh real'nosti*), she states that there is a connection between the first division, containing theoretical articles, and the second, containing essays and memoirs: "I do not sense an impassable rupture between the genres of the two parts. To me, it is all prose, in its many varieties."[190] Comparisons to the novel, however, run counter to an opposite and more widespread trend—that of conceiving of Ginzburg's notebooks as diaries. The "diary" approach has been used at times by Ginzburg scholar Stanislav Savitsky,[191] but it is a reading more commonly performed by scholars who extract single notes from Ginzburg while studying the history, literature, or culture of any of the decades about which she writes.[192] American Slavist Sarah Pratt has argued, meanwhile, that one might read Ginzburg's writings in diverse genres as forming a single "autobiography": she proposes that the book *O starom i novom* (*About the Old and the New*, 1982), containing theoretical studies, articles on specific literary figures, reminiscences, and notes, might well be renamed *O Lidii Ginzburg* (*About Lydia Ginzburg*).[193]

The decade or so since 2002 book has seen several small publications of Ginzburg's essays.[194] Published in 2011, *Passing Characters. Prose of the War Years. Notes of a Blockade Person* directs its attention not to the *zapisnye knizhki* of 1925–36 but rather to the war years (the 1940s, which turned out to be Ginzburg's most prolific, though perhaps least Vyazemsky-esque, decade). The book presents archival notes and unfinished drafts, compiled from notebooks and scattered pages that survived the blockade and subsequent decades.[195] According to the critic and scholar Inna Bulkina, *Passing Characters* seemed to mark a new "archival-sociological wave of interest in Ginzburg."[196]

The poetics of the fragment mean that readers of any of Ginzburg's publications are free to read notes out of their published order, either randomly or according to some principle, for example, of length or subject (indexes of names are included in the 2002 and 2011 books). Downloadable versions of Ginzburg's text make it possible to read according to word searches (though Ginzburg's abbreviations often make it difficult to search and find the names of people).[197] One's choice of how to read, and one's impression of the arrangement of Ginzburg's notes depends in part on one's orientation toward genre, whether one inclines toward the multigeneric or the novel, diary, note, or essay.

One more sign of the flexibility, versatility, and openness of Ginzburg's genre and the unfinalizable quality of her oeuvre is the online site Lidia_Ginsburg, a live web journal in Russian, initiated in 2004 and still active today (though decreasingly so, perhaps because Ginzburg's rising popularity makes her less of a niche name). Irina Paperno describes Lidia_Ginsburg as "a community of online diarists (men and women) who borrow Ginzburg's identity, her words, and her photo image to help them in self-expression."[198] Users post individual notes and then exchange comments that demonstrate how Ginzburg and her writings prompt personal memories, confessions, reflections, and historical commentaries. Occasionally, they create a "dialogue" by juxtaposing Ginzburg's notes. Thus, one user ("arpad") posted on 16 August 2007 a fragment from Ginzburg's "Around *Notes of a Blockade Person*," making a "note" out of a longer narrative, about the difference between a normal, beautiful winter and an "unconquered" (that is, blockade) winter of hauling buckets through the cold and dark. Another user ("anonymous") posts on 27 September 2007: "But all the same, spring will come," thus introducing a fragment from a postwar note by Ginzburg about the wonder of that time just before spring, *predvesna*.[199] The second user apparently wanted to comfort the first through this reminder that spring always follows winter, and created a new, personal meaning by juxtaposing fragments outside of their original contexts and conjoining them into a new narrative “plot.”[200]

CONCLUSION

Ginzburg’s writing procedure often began with observations and note-taking, which she would then pass through the expanding prism of commentary or the compressing device of the aphorism, in order to arrive at the thought with its illustration, or the scene with its formula. Roland Barthes, in one of his third-person essays, speaks of a “procedure” characteristic of his thought: “he rarely starts from the idea in order to invent an image for it subsequently; he starts from a sensuous object, and then hopes to meet in his work with the possibility of finding an *abstraction* for it, levied on the intellectual culture of the moment.”[201] In her book *On the Literary Hero*, Ginzburg remarks upon a similar trajectory in documentary prose, as opposed to fiction, or invention:

> In the sphere of belletristic invention the image arises in the movement from the idea to the particular unity that expresses it, in documentary literature—from a particular and concrete unity to the generalizing thought.[202]

Ginzburg’s thesis, so close to Barthes’s, helps to explain why her observations of her surroundings and of social and individual behavior (the particular and concrete unities) often end in formulae (generalizing thought). The scientifically disposed scholar who works inductively also begins with what is “given” and moves from there to “thought.”

In her description of the opposing procedures followed by documentary and fictional prose, Ginzburg uses two different words: “idea” (*ideia*) and “thought” (*mysl’*), placing the former within the province of the novel, and the latter within the domain of documentary prose. While she highly valued thought that was grounded in social reality (one recalls in this connection her preference for Tolstoy over Dostoevsky), one finds hints in this distinction of a certain inferiority complex from the 1930s, when she upheld the ideal of the novel. In those years, despairing over her form, she complained that writers of notebooks were “impotent.” They merely accompanied reality, whereas novelists were demiurges who could create “whole worlds.”[203] At that time, Ginzburg implicitly placed herself in the camp of Vyazemsky, who “was incredibly smart, learned, talented—and even so, never wrote anything worthwhile in his life” (“который был через голову умен, учен, талантлив—и так за свою жизнь ничего путного не написал”).[204] In another unpublished note from this period, she laments: “In any case, this future novel won't be written by me. It will be written by people with positive ideas, whose shoelaces I'm not fit to untie."[205] She lacked confidence in herself as a writer—even declared at one point that she was not a writer at all, but hoped to become one.[206]

Meanwhile, despite her envy of "people with ideas," Ginzburg in her prose did not enter the "sphere of belletristic invention," which would have meant beginning with the "idea" and moving "to the particular unity which expresses it." She renounced both invention and recollection when planning her "diary in the form of a novel" in these years.[207] She certainly knew she could not escape from a reliance on memory even in her notebooks, and admitted that all reported dialogues were invented to some extent.[208] She also embraced a certain quotient of fiction by creating a semi-autobiographical hero of a different gender (male) and in her selective presentation of characters from her own life. However, there was, for her, an element of principle here in basing her prose as closely as possible on the "reality" that interested her. Ginzburg's prose is thus built on a deliberate renunciation of certain means and procedures. This is similar not only to Vyazemsky's "negative constructive principle," but also to Proust's ability to write nine thick volumes without resorting to certain "constructive elements."[209]

Lydia Ginzburg never completed her "own" novel, nor did she frame her fragments as such. She was, however, at home with what Roland Barthes has celebrated as the "novelistic," which, like the essay, emphasizes method over result, the unfinished and unmastered over the systematic or complete work.[210] Ginzburg and Barthes both grew up in the shadow of World War I, became readers during the crisis of the novel, and rose to public prominence in the 1960s. Ginzburg practiced novelistic techniques in highly idiosyncratic ways within her documentary and fragmentary aesthetic, so that their effects are far from what one expects in a novel. Sometimes, she followed the impulse to compress her thoughts, experiences, and generalizations into a "formula," which acts as a finished piece, capable of approaching the force of a maxim. But she often incorporated and reincorporated her formulae into fragments, essays, and narratives that are inherently incomplete. As a writer with no publication outlet for decades, the variety of ways in which her work has finally reached an audience attests to the fact that her essays and notes answer "to the no doubt properly modern idea that the incomplete can, and even must, be published (or to the idea that what is published is never complete)."[211]

While Ginzburg, unlike Barthes, remained frustrated with her notebook mode for decades, she also recognized the fragment as most suitable form for her way of thinking. In 1928, she wrote, "It would hardly be possible to find a form more fitting for my tendencies than these notebooks,—but meanwhile

I can't make peace with them. Everyone knows that comic actors want to play Hamlet, draughtsmen want to produce large battle paintings. Derzhavin wanted to compose a heroic *poèma*. What's more, I'm bothered by their not being published."[212] Six decades later, when Ginzburg finally entered the public realm, it was in large part these notebooks that so delighted readers. She must have realized from her readers' praise in the late 1980s that she had succeeded by failing.

Ginzburg began her notebook project in the atmosphere of the novel's crisis, in a time of the literary "in-between" or "interval" (*promezhutok*) when experimentation was seen as a way out of a literary impasse. While she soon quested after the novel out of certain frustrations with the notebook form (and in line with her creative ambitions at the time), the question of form per se was not the important one for her. Rather, she sought for a mode of writing that would enable her to craft adequate depictions of her world and, if possible, arrive at new ways of understanding personality, character, and society. Her interest in the law-governed aspects of personality, rather than individual eccentricities, and her constant search for the features in her life that had generalizable social and historical significance for the predicament of the nonindividualist self pushed Ginzburg's prose closer to historiography and sociology. The same tendencies toward generalization and typicality encouraged another important creative decision when she came to draft her not-quite "diary in the form of a novel": to inscribe her experiences into a subject position that is grammatically and formally male. The next chapter is devoted to Ginzburg's dilemma of how and whether to represent same-sex love in her quasi-novel–quasi-diary. Focusing on Ginzburg's teenage diaries, as well as her 1930s drafts for *Home and the World*, the chapter aims to trace the development of her views on gender and sexuality through several literary encounters and life experiences. It will study how her embrace of certain aspects of literary tradition functioned in concert with the generic innovations of her analytical, documentary prose.

CHAPTER 3

Marginality in the Mainstream, Lesbian Love in the Third Person

In 1925, Ginzburg wrote, for the desk drawer, a critique of André Gide's famous defense of homosexuality, *Corydon: quatre dialogues socratiques.* The focus of her attack is not so much his overall purpose, but rather one of his main arguments: the claim that homosexuality is an irreproachable way of being since it is "natural," and present throughout the animal kingdom. With obvious sarcasm, Ginzburg counters that "in essence, all good things are not natural: art is not natural, [. . .] using a fork or a napkin is not natural, [. . .] the steam engine and electric generators are unnatural to the highest degree." Reducing Gide's argument to the absurd, she taunts: "But what if the male dogs who salvage your argument had confined themselves to the favor of their bitches—what then?" ("А если бы спасительные собаки ограничились бы благосклонностью своих сук, что тогда?").[1]

Ginzburg also targets Gide's lack of attention to the question of lesbian sexuality. While Corydon, Gide's hero, acknowledges infinite "shades and degrees" within and between sexual orientations, his ultimate goal is to elaborate the social, aesthetic, and personal superiority of what he calls "normal pederasty."[2]

> Gide, following custom, barely touches upon the question of female perversion. Probably, it does not satisfy his requirement of a higher erotic (Plato!).
>
> But meanwhile if one wants to find "the sublime" in any of the forms of homosexuality, in comparison to normal feeling, then it is here most of all.
>
> (Already Weininger took account of this with great precision in his unique, inspired book that cannot withstand any criticism.)
>
> For better or worse, but without a doubt, to this day women look to men in order to measure their intellectual stature.
>
> And sometimes in this measuring they arrive at the necessity of male love—the only valuable, complete, and literary love—which is insurmountable not so much physically as psychologically.
>
> And at this point there sometimes forms a "psycho-physical" disgust for one's own natural role. But not always.
>
> Pushkin loved to repeat Chateaubriand's adage: "Il n'y a de bonheur que dans les voies communes."[3]

Ginzburg seeks to belong to the tradition epitomized, for her, by Alexander Pushkin, whose Romantic poetry both aestheticizes and spiritualizes women. Keen on inhabiting a heterosexually male subject position, Ginzburg appeals to a cultural heritage different from Gide's. Her statement that the psychologically insurmountable nature of "male love" can foster disgust for one's "natural role" implies that this feeling might cause a woman to aspire to the model of the heterosexual male, regardless of her sexual orientation or physical desires.

Roughly a decade later, Ginzburg sets out to write her own brief Socratic dialogue, a reply to Gide, in which she treats the taboo subject of same-sex love more directly than anywhere else in her oeuvre, at least among surviving texts. She invents a voice of male authority (grammatically masculine, if in no other obvious way) in order to tell the story of the typical process through which gay and lesbian teenagers of her generation gradually reach an understanding of their sexual orientation after the sudden discovery of "something foreign [*postoronnee*], something impossible."[4] Imagining the opportunity to counsel a gay youth, Ginzburg's speaker discusses what kind of attitude leads to the happiest possible relationships (his answer is: resignation), while warning of a basic underlying problem. Great, lasting love (says the teacher) is the rarest of exceptions, and therefore a relationship can become stable and secure only when transformed by various institutions and life events. However, "two inverts [a term then common in psychological and sexological discourse] are united primarily by love that is alienated from everything, love that is not secured by anything: children, family, formalized daily routine, social recognition, duties and obligations. But love, if it cannot be transformed into anything else, does not stay in place; it crumbles from its own self-centeredness." Lesbians face this problem most acutely, the teacher continues, since "a normal woman" has a psychological need in her everyday or domestic life for "forms that are organized, defined by the social status of her partner."[5]

Along with their dialogue form, Gide's and Ginzburg's divergent treatments of same-sex desire also share the device of metafiction. Corydon, visited by a former friend (who is initially rather bigoted) in search of guidance in thinking about a certain "scandalous" trial (most likely a reference to Oscar Wilde's), answers by testing out the arguments of his book-in-progress, *Defense of Pederasty*.[6] Ginzburg's unnamed male speaker, on the other hand, is first asked about whether he is in the process of writing a novel. The entire discussion of same-sex desire and identities transpires under the pretext of answering the question: is this a set of problems one can treat in a novel? Would the male speaker, who has taken a special interest in this topic, use it as material for his prose fiction? The reply is negative. Not only is it not a "problem" for the novel, it is

> not even a theme. Well, maybe it is a theme for a humanistic novel about the mercilessness of society. But I am indifferent toward such novels. In part because, in this case, more merciless than society are the regular patterns of these relations themselves. As far as the psychological novel is concerned. . . . If I wrote a psychological novel, I would put aside this theme [я отвел бы эту тему]. This substitute, dubious theme of a special love, which is as if unlike any others.[7]

The verb that the speaker uses to describe his hypothetical rejection of this theme, *otvel*, is somewhat ambiguous. It can mean: lead, lead aside, lead back, divert, or avert (as in averting one's eyes). It suggests that there is some effort or trickery involved in *not* writing about this "special love," or that it can be "put aside" without being entirely rejected. In fact, as it turns out, Ginzburg planned to include this dialogue—about not writing a gay novel of any kind—in the "diary in the form of a novel" that she was composing at the time, which treated (in barely fictionalized form) one of her love affairs as a heterosexual relationship.[8]

If Ginzburg had chosen to create a "humanistic novel about the mercilessness of society," she could have found ample material. As the contemporary sociologist Igor Kon has written, Soviet society was highly intolerant of any kind of difference, and among those who behaved or thought differently, homosexuals were the most stigmatized group.[9] At the beginning of the twentieth century, as an adolescent, Ginzburg briefly took part in a cultural environment that was relatively liberal in matters of sex, when gay themes visibly entered Russian literature and philosophy through figures such as Mikhail Kuzmin, Nikolai Kluiev, Lydia Zinovieva-Annibal, Sophia Parnok, and Vasily Rozanov—even if, outside of a certain literary milieu, homosexuality was still regarded as an illness.[10] After the Bolshevik Revolution, there came what Simon Karlinsky calls "a total retreat to the bourgeois sexual mores of the Victorian age."[11] As Karlinsky reports, not a single openly gay or lesbian literary figure began a publishing career after the Revolution.[12] In December 1933, a law was passed making male homosexuality a punishable offense, with sentences ranging from three to eight years of hard labor (on a par with sabotage or espionage), and this law remained in effect throughout the entire Soviet period. Less than two decades of socialism were supposedly sufficient to eradicate homosexuality, according to the commissar of justice Nikolai Krylenko, who declared in 1936 that all remaining homosexuals were "remnants of the exploiting classes."[13] Laws making divorce prohibitively difficult and banning abortion further implemented the return to "family values" in Soviet society.

While female homosexuality was not explicitly outlawed, a lesbian could expect "ridicule, persecution, expulsion from college or work, threats to take her children away," according to Kon.[14] The general silence that descended around same-sex love by the 1930s was even more total where it involved women. Diana Burgin writes: "Not only did no one write or talk about lesbian love, but no one even implied it during the course of the entire Stalinist epoch and later, up to the 1980s."[15]

Thanks to the evidence from her archive, we now know that Lydia Ginzburg did write about lesbian love—for the desk-drawer—in this atmosphere of silence and repression, both in her prose experiments of the mid-1930s and in her sketches from the Leningrad Blockade (1941–44). Yet she did so only in order to repudiate the importance of same-sex themes for literature, or at least for the kind of literature she had an interest in reading or writing.

The 1930s "Dialogue about Love" poses several paradoxes. For one, Ginzburg again seems to have written this piece mainly to renounce its theme. What is more, she invented a male speaker to argue authoritatively about lesbian love. How can we make sense of the directness of this enunciation within the framework of indirection provided by fictionalization, the dialogue form, and the use of the other's voice? Is this an instance of Ginzburg's claiming to belong to what she sees as an elevated masculine literary tradition, and is it somehow a subversion of this tradition?

THE NEXUS OF GENDER, SEXUALITY, AND PERSON

"Dialogue about Love" includes observations and opinions that are based on personal experiences, painful moments from Ginzburg's teenage years. This autobiographical aspect is counterbalanced by her method of abstraction, consisting most obviously of a grammatically male speaker. She thus irrevocably removes any female identity from the "I," and places the speaker in the hypothetical realm of a Socratic dialogue. She also distances her piece from confession by using a speaker who claims to have learned about homosexuality through careful data gathering rather than anything experienced on his own skin ("I took a special interest in all of this. I collected observations," he says).

This rhetorical creation—a framed first-person male speaker—exists on a continuum with Ginzburg's most common autobiographical surrogates. She summarily avoids bestowing proper names upon her alter egos, which would be an unmistakable sign of fiction.[16] Instead, she populates her notes and narratives with characters who have quasi-names such as "N.", "Y." (usually spelled out, that is, *En, Igrek*), or "Otter" (Ginzburg's "other" or "author," both from the French) and often abbreviated as "Ot." or "O."[17] These heroes are grammatically male, but they are not marked by any other distinctive features of "maleness." Their love interests, if any, are exclusively female, when they are mentioned at all. Their traits, personalities, and concerns, meanwhile, are recognizably autobiographical.

In much of her writing, Ginzburg often reaches for an even greater level of generalization, replacing "I" with the generic word for "person"—in Russian, *chelovek*, a grammatically masculine noun with a gender-neutral meaning. Since *chelovek* requires the use of the masculine singular in the third person, this pronominal usage can become the most fluid mode for analyzing a generalized instance of oneself. By using initials and the pronoun "he," Ginzburg can thus extract her (female) individuality from the text without abandoning the poetics of documentary prose for the conventions of fiction.[18] In certain narratives, she affirms this orientation toward documentary literature by inserting a first-person narrator alongside her O.'s or N.'s (for example, in *Notes of a Blockade Person*). At the same time, this "I" has a minimal role in the narrative, and its gender goes unspecified. To accomplish such a feat of indefiniteness in a language where gender is grammatically marked in most forms (including past tense verbs), Ginzburg resorts to noun phrases, oblique cases, passive clauses, the present tense, and dialogues in the ungendered second-person plural. The verbal acrobatics necessary to conceal gender sometimes produce awkward constructions that underscore the obstacles faced by a female writer attempting to join the mainstream Russian literary tradition. Meanwhile, Ginzburg's decision to treat her experiences through the generalized perspective of what appears to be a heterosexual male prevents her from speaking directly to the disadvantaged position of women and lesbians in Soviet society.

In his book *Never Say I: Sexuality and the First Person in Colette, Gide, and Proust*, Michael Lucey suggests that both literature and sexuality are "arenas in which pronominal usage requires special attention."[19] He argues that the desire of authors to speak about same-sex relations and the question of whether they should use the first person to do so are both central to the evolution of twentieth-century French prose.[20] While the histories of French and Russian literature differ markedly in their treatment of eroticism and sexuality, Marcel Proust—the central figure in Lucey's book—is supremely relevant to our discussion of gender, sexuality, and genre, especially since *In Search of Lost Time* (published between 1913 and 1927) powerfully affected Ginzburg's own approach to writing, particularly in the 1930s.

When Proust learned that his friend André Gide was planning to write a treatise about homosexuality (*Corydon*), he is reported to have uttered the following injunction: "You can tell anything . . . but on the condition that you never say: *I*."[21] Proust's initial design for his own novel, which treats same-sex love in overt and covert ways, involved a frame narrative. Called *Jean Santeuil*, it was to contain the story (of Santeuil) as told by a fictional author (C.). Gérard Genette has suggested that Proust had to overcome certain obstacles posed by the autobiographical tradition of first-person narratives in order to "win the right to say 'I,' or more precisely the right to have this hero who is neither completely himself nor completely someone else say 'I.' "[22] Lucey builds on this argument by adding that the impossibility of saying "I" was compounded for those twentieth-century French authors who were trying to find ways of speaking about, for, and from the perspective of same-sex sexualities. In the novel *In Search of Lost Time*, Proust constructed an unnamed narrator (who, in one passage, is tantalizingly but only conditionally called Marcel) in order to blur the lines between memoir and novel, and to make his "I" into an abstract and fictional instance.[23] The shift is acknowledged as a triumph despite, or even because of, the novel's tensions and inconsistencies, between the first and third person as well as between the limited and omniscient points of view.[24]

Proust obscures the distinction between the unnamed narrator and the author, between fiction and autobiography, while using an "I" of the masculine gender, reflected everywhere in his French. Moreover, the narrator's great loves, for Gilberte and Albertine, in many ways emulate and expand the mainstream, heterosexual models of world literature. For this reason, Ginzburg's speaker in her "Dialogue about Love" represents himself as a follower of Proust, who "demonstrated that there is only one love, that deviant love only magnifies the features of natural feeling." While the French author investigates the social aspects of Baron de Charlus's milieu, Ginzburg writes, he nevertheless presents same-sex desire as no different from heterosexual varieties: "the social plane here does not correspond to the emotional one, in which Charlus's love for Morel does not at all differ from Swann's love for Odette, from the narrator's love for Albertine; who moreover has been transposed from Albert."[25]

Ginzburg's pronouns, the grammatically masculine "he" and barely gendered "I," are pointedly more abstract than Proust's "I," which has nevertheless been hailed as a "figure, a procedure, a technique, more than a subjectivity."[26] But even after encountering Proust's model, Ginzburg did not adopt this figure of the "I" that mimics autobiography or memoir. There are several possible reasons for her rejection. First, as Lucey acknowledges, women in particular were subject to the general charge against first-person authors, of a "failure of artistic autonomy," and a privileging of "the object of representation [. . .] over the mode of representation."[27] It is hard to imagine that a female Proust would have tried or succeeded in creating an abstract instance of a feminine *je*. Second, if Ginzburg had chosen to write openly about lesbian love in this way, aiming subtly for abstraction, it would have prevented publication into the foreseeable future, and possibly endangered her life (or in any case undercut her already precarious social standing). Third, the mimicry of autobiography was not a suitable model for Ginzburg's post-individualist prose, with its ethics and aesthetics of self-distancing.

As she searched for new forms in which to analyze the personality of the post-individualistic self, one of Ginzburg's main tasks was to design an intermediate (and to some extent indeterminate) level of including the author, a compromise between concealment and openness, as well as between particularity and universality, subjectivity and objectivity.[28] This intermediacy was essential for representing the typical, generalizable elements of her experiences. Her attempts were conditioned and complicated by the self-imposed constraints of her documentary prose: mainly, her decision not to create a "second reality" of invented heroes or narrators operating in a fictional world. These aspirations, particularly when combined with her desire to write about experiences of love, led her to create an alter ego who was both "I" and "not-I."

The goal of this chapter is to illuminate Ginzburg's manipulations of the rhetoric around "person," especially as they relate to questions of gender, sexuality, and the representation of love. The relationship of rhetorical structure to genre is extremely complex, and cannot be examined solely on the basis of the first versus the third person. Nevertheless, voicing is a central problem in autobiographical or documentary prose, and indeed in everyday self-presentation. Studying point of view opens up new questions related to tone and narrative effects, particularly where gender and sexuality are concerned.[29] I argue here that Ginzburg's choices were driven by her relationship to cultural tradition, from which she drew in unusual ways—thus both adopting and subverting it to some degree. As we shall see, her prose makes adjustments to the patterns she finds, and thereby manages to express certain specificities of same-sex love while striving to remain indeterminate and universal. The importance of gender and sexuality to Ginzburg's rhetorical choices is a topic that deserves more attention, especially since most writing about her work, if it makes any mention of her private sexual orientation, does so in passing, in parenthetical phrases, and in relation to other aspects of her marginal identity.

To understand how Ginzburg solved the narrative dilemma of how to write about same-sex love in her own way (differently from Proust, and from pre-Revolutionary Russian gay and lesbian authors), we need to analyze some of her early writings, from the 1920s and 1930s. In her teenage years, a set of key textual encounters (with Alexander Blok, Otto Weininger, and others) shaped Ginzburg's notions of the psychology and representation of sexual and gender identities. Elements of her early ideas endured even as she turned to the work of other writers (Shklovsky, Oleinikov, Hemingway, and Proust) who could help her overcome the Symbolist heritage, with its strains of decadent individualism, art-life confusion, and apocalyptic mysticism. In the 1930s, Ginzburg does not attempt to exalt the pain of her unrequited love, but rather to connect it to the emptiness experienced by an intellectual of her generation as well as to the larger dilemmas of self-realization. We take account of Ginzburg's models and metaphors in different periods and focus on the intended and unintended effects of her rhetorical choices, drawing upon three groups of materials never published by the author: her teenage diaries, her earliest fictions (1922–23), and fragments of *Home and the World* (1930s), including "The Stages of Love" and "Dialogue about Love."

These writings treat two loves, which Ginzburg defines typologically as the "first" and "second." According to her theory, which does not differentiate for sexual orientation, "the classic first love of an intellectual is grand, unrequited, unrealized (secretly it does not want to be realized)," whereas the second love, which need not be the second in number (it could be the third, fourth, and so on), is "when a person retrieves his losses. It must, without fail, be happy, mutual, realized."[30] Ginzburg marshals support for her theory from Proust's novel, where Gilberte is the hero's first love, and Albertine the second.

PART I: FIRST LOVE

Love in the Time of War Communism (and NEP)

The course of Ginzburg's first love unfolded in the chaotic environment of the immediate post-Revolutionary period, as a new empire and society were taking shape in a wartorn country. The years of War Communism, from 1918 to 1921 (when the New Economic Policy [NEP] was instituted, bringing moderate relief), were marked by mass deprivation and hardship, resulting from war, a severe grain crisis, and the nationalization of private property and enterprise. It was a time when, in the words Ginzburg borrows from Mayakovsky's poem "Very Good!" ("Хорошо!" 1927), a man would arrive at his lover's door holding the green stems of a gift of two carrots (an inverted bouquet). In a pseudo-fictional account of her first love written in the late 1930s, Ginzburg sketches the impact of the harsh conditions: "It was love in the epoch of War Communism. When love could be weighed and measured by a piece of bread, a little log of firewood. A person was surrounded by very few things, the most essential. And when vital necessity met with love, it appeared grand."[31] Here she seems to be saying that impoverishment lent greater meaning both to the material things, exchanged in the economy of love, and to the object of one's infatuation (a person who was nearby and essential).

It was a time of hunger and of making do. The atmosphere, paradoxically, fostered a spirit of improvisation and levity in her generation:

> In the years of War Communism, when the practical [*polozhitel'nye*] and long-established [or inherited, *nasledstvennye*] professions turned out to be utterly precarious and in part irrelevant, the young intelligentsia went in droves into jobs as accompanists, actors, writers, and journalists, turning their homegrown talents and amusements into a profession. In all of this, there was a kind of lightness and instantaneous adaptation, something akin to the crazy pressure and fickleness of the time, something corresponding to the spectacle of the old world that had crumbled forever.
>
> В годы военного коммунизма, когда положительные наследственные профессии оказались сугубо непрочными и частью неприменимыми, интеллигентская молодежь толпами шла в аккомпаниаторы, в актеры, в писатели, в журналисты, обращая в профессию домашние дарования и развлечения. Здесь была какая-то легкость и мгновенная применимость, что-то похожее на сумасшедший напор и переменчивость времени, что-то соответствующее зрелищу навсегда обвалившегося старого мира.[32]

Between two attempts to move from Odessa to Petrograd, in order to study science and then literature, Ginzburg became involved in an amateur theater run by her older brother. The troupe, named "Krot" (an acronym for Konfreriia Rytsarei Ostrogo Teatra, or "Brotherhood of the Knights of Witty Theater"), put on satiric miniatures and operatic parodies in a basement theater.[33] As a young intellectual who was also an athlete, Ginzburg worked primarily as a stagehand. She wrote one play in the German Romantic style: "And while my verse play—in which the main role was played by a skeleton—was running, I also operated the curtain—which is probably the only such case in the history of world theater."[34]

There may be an aspect of what Ginzburg would call "conformity to the laws of the times" (*istoricheskaia zakonomernost'*) in her dalliance with the theater. As Katerina Clark has written, the theater in these years moved from the margins and basements into the very forefront of Revolutionary culture. Moreover, since most individuals had to assume new roles after the disappearance of the old world, life itself acquired a theatrical aspect. Enthusiasts such as Nikolai Evreinov, a leader of the experimental theater in Petersburg/

Petrograd, were calling for the institution of a "theatocracy."[35] And as we know from her diaries, Ginzburg spent New Year's Eve, 1920–21, reading Evreinov's *Theater for Oneself* (*Teatr dlia sebia*, 3 volumes, 1915–17), in which he advocates the theatricalization of everyday life.[36]

Ginzburg wrote several diaries between 1918 and 1923, from the ages of sixteen to twenty-one. The two largest volumes—the first (225 pages) extending from August 1920 through September 1922, the second (138 pages) from September 1922 through May 1923—cover the period of her infatuation with Rina Zelyonaya (1901[?]–91), a young woman who was launching what would become a successful acting career.[37] Near the end of her life, Ginzburg signaled the distinctive status of these diaries by leaving a note when sealing them for a decade after her death (a step she took with no other writings). She warned those who would come to know the contents of this folder—"the later, the better"—that in preserving them she was motivated solely by her "disgust for the destruction of human documents."[38] What had tempted her to destroy the diaries, it seems, was their prevailing subject matter, along with the psychological state of their author at that time: "an unrequited, rejected feeling flowed unceasingly from my psychic apparatus." This experience of desperate, unreciprocated love, Ginzburg declares, was a unique one in her life—"both in strength and in structure." To love in this way again would be "to appear on the border of the ridiculous."[39]

Lydia Ginzburg and Rina Zelyonaya met in Odessa in late 1919 or early 1920 through their involvement in Krot.[40] Ginzburg's older brother, Viktor Tipot (soon to become a fairly prominent director), wrote and directed one-act plays; Vera Inber (soon to become an officially recognized poet) was the other main playwright; Tipot's wife, Nadezhda Bliumenfel'd, worked as a costume and makeup artist as well as a translator. In an Odessa hardly touched by the NEP, the theater scraped together costumes by raiding family wardrobes; with paper in short supply, the young Ginzburg drafted her play on order-and-delivery slips from a yeast factory connected to her family's business.[41] Zelyonaya had recently arrived from Moscow, suffering from typhoid fever, and lived in utter destitution with her mother and younger sister (the father, a military officer, had abandoned them).[42] As she describes it in her light-hearted memoir *Scattered Pages* (*Razroznennye stranitsy*, 1981), her life began to turn around only after she met up with the intelligent and relatively well-off theater crowd that included the Ginzburg siblings. Lydia Ginzburg is a minor character in *Scattered Pages*. Zelyonaya portrays her as "modest and shy," in contrast to her ebulliently witty older brother, and remarks on the comic incongruity that a maladroit stage worker—"an awkward girl, clumsy"—blossomed into a renowned scholar, with a doctoral degree.[43]

The "relationship"—in her diary from these years, Ginzburg calls it "that which was not" as opposed to "that which was" (Diary I, 204–5, 17 August 1922)—seems to consist of Ginzburg's serving "R." in every way, from buying cosmetics for her performances to providing food for her and her family (and virtually living in their apartment as a caretaker).[44] The diarist never writes the full name of her beloved (in fact, she seldom gives the full names of anyone), employing a series of initials, E., K., R., xxx, or simply the pronoun "She."[45] (Henceforth, I use the initial "R." when I refer to Zelyonaya as reflected in Ginzburg's diaries, as a reminder of the fact of representation and the techniques of concealment.) R. sometimes treats her with tenderness (*nezhnost'*), and accepts her friend's total care while ignoring its obvious emotional basis. Ginzburg writes:

> It took a lot of intelligence, intuition and a sort of freedom or breadth, and a lot of egoism to do what she did: to take everything from me, without ever asking for anything; to be exacting, without demanding anything. [. . .] And at the same time, to reduce to a minimum my feeling of what was strange and bewildering in my position. After all, just one refusal, one question, one glance showing surprise or lack of understanding, would have sufficed to make the relationship impossible, to make my life unbearable. (Diary I, 219–20, 23 August 1920)

In fact, as we find out, R. welcomes favors and gifts from an array of men. Ginzburg the diarist, however, perceives that a special mixture of ego and understanding was needed for R. to accept such largesse from a young woman. R.'s flirtations make Ginzburg painfully jealous, especially when they involve "V." (brother Viktor), who for some time lives with R. in Moscow (in one apartment with his wife), and even voices his desire to marry her.[46]

Aside from focusing on this "first love" of hers, the crucial factor that sets these early diaries apart from the mature writings is their use of the (feminine) first-person singular and their overriding concern with self-analysis. The young diarist uses the first-person pronoun and possessive pronouns in an entirely unproblematic fashion, without restraint. These self-centered forms accord with the author's belief that she is cultivating a "great and complex" soul (Diary I, 146–47, 15 February 1922). She writes: "my existence cannot be a dead lump of life, it must be an atelier of the soul" (Diary II, 40, 16 October 1922). One of Ginzburg's chief exercises is to record and analyze her emotional states, the most frequent of which is *toska*—the untranslatable Russian word whose meanings include "longing," "melancholy," and "depression." She values this *toska* as a sign of the reality and grandiosity of her suffering, and therefore laments its inconstancy: "It vexes me that I have no trouble dulling my *toska* with human company; it somehow cheapens it in my eyes; it cheapens the drama in which I am now playing a role" (Diary II, 32, 16 October 1922).

Looking back from 1930, Ginzburg attributed her youthful self-absorption—or in her words, "deep psychology, nervous lacerations [*nadryvy*], extreme interest in psycho-analyzing oneself"—to the influence of Decadence.[47] Yet, at the same time, there were limits to her self-analysis and self-exposure. For example, the diarist neither discusses her sexual orientation directly nor the degree or manner in which her family and friends understood this. She does, however, use certain phrases that indicate a self-deprecating attitude toward her personal traits, writing of her "humiliating 'particularities'" (*unizitel'nye 'podrobnosti'*) (Diary I, 56, 10 December 1920), and describing her life as "peculiar to the point of monstrosity" (*do urodlivosti svoebraznaia*) (Diary II, 35, 16 October 1922).[48] She appears to allude subtly to sexuality in a passage on the tragedy of her love:

> The love of such people as I is too senseless and bitter to dare be called an exit [from the self]. It is a second circle, which is harder than the first, because you travel along it outside yourself, at the same time confirming your insanity; you travel it with another person, although this second person might merely be present, thereby accepting shame and learning how to be shameless. (Diary I, 217–18)

The inability to carry over one's feelings into a genuine self-other relationship grieves all hopeless lovers. The talk of insanity, senselessness, and shame, as well as the phrase "such people as I" suggest the exacerbating factor here: this particular love dare not speak its name.

Ginzburg later characterized the mood of her generation ca. 1917 as prone to chaos: "a giant confusion reigned in our minds. [. . .] What is there that did not find a place in fifteen-year-old heads—socialism and solipsism, the Futurists and Lev Tolstoy's sermons, [the terrorist] Sofiya Perovskaya and 'Joy, O Joy-Suffering / the Pain of unexplored wounds.'"[49] Her diaries indeed give evidence of her extensive reading in these years, in several languages and genres, from the Gospels and Pushkin to Knut Hamsun and Anatole France. And yet there is curiously little mention of Socialism, Revolution, or Futurism. After joining an audience of 100,000 people to witness the third anniversary celebrations of the Revolution—the largest mass spectacle of all time, "The Storming of the Winter Palace," directed by Nikolai Evreinov (whose works she read in this same year), Ginzburg notes that her presence at this "Mystery Play" was valuable in terms of understanding gained, but that the experience was completely unpleasurable.[50] The words "brotherhood" and "unity" are alien and irritating to her, since she suspects that others must be as she is: alone and particular (Diary I, 59, 10 December 1920).

At the age of eighteen to twenty, caught at the crossroads of Russian Modernism, Ginzburg is pulled in a multitude of directions as she searches for cultural resources to help bring clarity to her self-image and her situation. She appears to arrive at a primary antagonism, between Symbolism or, more broadly, Romanticism, on the one hand, and Realism or Acmeism (a contemporary aesthetic movement opposed to Symbolism), and, more broadly, Rationalism, on the other. Ginzburg mentions a host of Russian and French Symbolists (Fyodor Sologub, Charles Baudelaire, and others), and speaks of such telltale themes as the apocalypse and the Nietzschean will.[51] She often turns to Blok—particularly his dramas and his semi-epic poem "Retribution" ("Vozmezdie"), which she heard him recite in person.[52] And yet she also reads and quotes Acmeists such as Akhmatova and Gumilyov. In the winter of 1920–21, she attends the latter's workshop in Petrograd, and hands him some of her youthful verse, which she characterizes as "rather Gumilyovesque" (*dovol'no gumil'evskie*).[53]

In a statement that epitomizes this clash of viewpoints, Ginzburg uses a key term in the language of Symbolism (*zhiznetvorchestvo*, "life-creation") to describe her anti-romantic longing for moral perfection and her attempts to acquire healthy and productive habits. She writes: "Perhaps the deepest task of my life-creation [*zhiznetvorchestvo*] is to stand at the level of the average person." (Diary II, 9). The confrontation between a self-invention based on theatricality and one based on moral guidelines (and normalcy) traces back to the classic opposition, Dostoevsky versus Tolstoy:

> Tolstoy's dazzling simplicity and harsh irony are both comprehensible to me, but this is all at certain heights of my spirit [*na nekikh vershinakh moego dukha*], where I devoutly love and understand Tolstoy, but on the hysterical and fantastic middle level of my soul, I'm a person out of Dostoevsky: I love schemes, I love pathos, the game of ideas, the conventional romanticism of words, the artificial romanticism of relationships. (Diary II, 13)[54]

Ginzburg understands the debased relationships and nervous strain among the principal characters in her life (herself, R., V., and V.'s wife, N. Bliumenfel'd) through the prism of Dostoevsky's novels. Meanwhile, following the young Tolstoy, in his diary, she composes behavioral guidelines and mottoes designed to improve her moral and intellectual life. She detects falsity in Romantic effusions—"it is one step from the beautiful to the vulgar"—and thus wants to avoid this lexicon despite its palliative effects on her nerves.[55]

Lydia Ginzburg's early diaries present a self in turmoil, one that alternates between what her contemporaries saw (after Nietzsche) as Apollonian and Dionysian currents and that feels the temptations of Symbolist culture most acutely in relation to love and its expression. With a divided mindset, and in a state of romantic suffering that endures throughout the years of War Communism and into the early days of the NEP, the young Ginzburg encounters a set of readings that shapes her approaches to sexuality and love, and gives her a new justification for an interest in the self.

Choosing One's Tragedy

In a retrospective note from the 1960s, Ginzburg summarizes her generation's relationship to Freud, whom she had read as a teenager:

> Freud's compositions were a guide in which adolescents of the 1910s who were wise with thought chose their future tragedy. The clinical complexes of the Viennese bourgeoisie were magically transformed, in the consciousness of the Russian *intelligent* (who, according to Blok, still bled cranberry juice back then), into complexes of ideas, into ideology, for example, the idea of unquenchable yearning.[56]

Ginzburg speaks here to the notorious tendency of Russian intellectuals to live by ideas, a trait shared by Proust's hero. Freud's powerful writings, growing out of his therapeutic work with his bourgeois Viennese patients, took on an aura of spirituality and abstraction when transplanted into the milieu of the Russian intelligentsia. His theories were food for identity formation: people's tragedies did not exist as such until he informed them of the menu of possibilities. This "magical" transformation was effected through the writings of Symbolists such as Alexander Blok, who ascribed desire not to physical or sexual urges, but to spiritual thirst, the ideal of the Eternal Feminine, and anxieties about Russia's future. Ginzburg's reference to "cranberry juice," (from Blok's play "The Puppet Booth," to which we will return), alludes at the same time to the dynamic of theatricality undercutting the *intelligent*'s plight, and to the confusion between art and life cultivated by the Symbolists. The expression "back then" (*togda*) hints at the real tragedies that would strike this generation in the coming decades.

In addition to Freud, the adolescents of Ginzburg's generation, it would seem, also found a template for their tragedies in the pages of Richard von Krafft-Ebing's famous manual of sexual pathology. In her 1930s "Dialogue about Love," where Ginzburg discusses the discovery in general terms, the speaker says that awareness of same-sex preference comes in the form of an epiphany, often at the age of seventeen or eighteen. Thereafter, it becomes impossible to suppress "strange" feelings or sensations of which one has been aware for a long time: "something impossible is discovered. The curtain was torn [*razorvalas' zavesa*]." Ginzburg's theatrical metaphor recalls the final scene of Blok's "The Puppet Booth" (when the backdrop tears, and then all the decorations also "fly away"). This teenager's next step into this territory of the "frightening" and the "strange" would be a trip to the library to check out Krafft-Ebing's *Psychopathia Sexualis*, a book first published in German in 1886 and quickly translated into Russian as *Polovaia psikhopatiia* (that is, *Sexual Psychopathology*, printed in numerous editions between 1887 and 1919). In this exercise in taxonomy, the Viennese sexologist classifies forms of homosexuality along with other "perversions of the sexual instinct." *Polovaia psikhopatiia* was extremely popular in Russia, inspiring discussions and fictional stories in the thick journals.[57] Of great interest to readers of the time, as Evgenii Bershtein has demonstrated, was the extensive body of confessional letters, sent to Krafft-Ebing by "sexual psychopaths" and included in his book.[58]

Remarkably, Ginzburg does not describe the discovery of her own deviant sexual desire in her youthful diaries. However, two months before her twentieth birthday, she notes in her diary a two-day span of "intensified reading of Krafft-Ebing," which—combined with cigarettes and a splitting headache—"is creating a rather muddled state—nevertheless, my moral feeling is not too nasty" (Diary I, 140, 4 January 1922). In the 1930s "Dialogue about Love," pointedly distant from autobiography and confession, the male speaker paints a detailed and tragic picture of this reading. He states that certain teens would stay up at night reading this book with unparalleled interest, until their eyes burned red: "They read this thick, rather boring book—with pain, with passion, and a kind of terrible ecstasy at the spectacle of the gaping abyss. This book—they'll never read anything else in the same way—not *Faust*, not Proust, not 'The Bronze Horseman.'"[59]

As in her discussion of Freud, Ginzburg implies that one reaches an understanding and articulation of one's identity, one's psychology, with the help of preexisting models. With a sense of urgency, teenagers consulted Krafft-Ebing's judgmental, clinical, and "boring" account of sexuality in the absence of a visible community, of any coming-out ritual. And readers found confirmation of their own reality or—to paraphrase Ginzburg—a guide to their own sexual tragedy, in the autobiographical "confessions," the letters cited in the book.

Ginzburg's diaries provide no evidence about the precise lessons that she took away from her readings of Freud and Krafft-Ebing or how she adjusted their theories on the basis of her own experiences. But the 1930s dialogue does provide a larger window onto her views on homosexuality. Appropriately, her speaker emulates the sexologists who base their theories on case studies, on careful observations of others. He articulates a general idea of sexual preferences as biologically inherited, and of love as socially constructed. The process of internalizing group norms, he says, makes heterosexual and homosexual love essentially the same. Ginzburg's speaker firmly opposes the dominant theory (held by Krafft-Ebing, Havelock Ellis, and others) that homosexuality was a disease:

> However, homosexuality [*gomoseksual'nost'*] is not a disease. [. . .] Its organic forms yield neither to a cure, nor to coercion. External or internal pressures lead only to debilitating neuroses. The disease begins with the attempt to heal. By itself, it is not a disease—it's a matter of one's constitution [*ustroistvo*]; it is almost always purely psychic, and therefore allows for ambivalence.[60]

Ginzburg agrees here with Freud, who found that psychoanalytic therapy was largely ineffective in "converting" homosexuals to heterosexuals (or vice versa), unless the person was "in a still oscillating or in a definitely bisexual organization."[61] The fluidity and complexity offered by Freud's notion of "organization" is echoed by Ginzburg's word *ustroistvo* (arrangement, structure, constitution), which she uses elsewhere to define the human personality.[62] Moreover, while Freud categorized a variety of behaviors as "perversions," he nevertheless maintained, as Ginzburg does, that neuroses were "the negative of the perversions," caused by the repression of love-choices and love-acts.[63] Elsewhere, Ginzburg writes that same-sex love is not a question that needs answering, but rather a fact that requires no justification.[64]

"Dialogue about Love" describes self-discovery as a process of finding a name for the "unnameable," for the "impossible." A plethora of words for denoting male and female homosexualities circulated in the Europe of Ginzburg's youth.[65] Ginzburg in her 1930s dialogue characteristically employs a term with a scientific and taxonomic resonance as a label for homosexual people of both genders: "inverts" [or "inverted," *invertirovannye*].[66] The terms "sexual inversion" and "inverts" were used by Krafft-Ebing, Freud, Weininger, and others to describe "people whose sexual objects belong to the normally inappropriate sex."[67] Ginzburg employs the categories of active and passive inversion, which one assumes to mean (in the case of women) desire for a woman versus the desire to be desired by a woman. However, her authoritative male speaker opines, "in female homosexual relationships, one side is, as a rule, normal [. . .] female passive inversion practically does not exist." Ginzburg does not specify what motivates "normal" women to love "inverts," or whether her concept of "normality" takes account of Freud's notion of universal bisexuality. Presumably then, Ginzburg saw herself as an "active invert" and R., for example, as "normal."

If the young Ginzburg found the language and affirmation of her reality in Freud and Krafft-Ebing, she discovered ideas with a broader aesthetic application in Otto Weininger's *Sex and Character* (1903), which, like Krafft-

Ebing's *Psychopathia Sexualis,* was widely read and discussed in Russia. Weininger's book had a defining influence on her conceptualization of love and of the sexes. She first mentions that she is reading *Sex and Character*—"a book that is not without interest for me"—on 31 December 1920 (Diary I, 79a).[68] Two years later (3 October 1922), she launches an eight-page excursus, which begins with a critique of *Sex and Character*[69] as unconscionable, full of sloppy reasoning and fanaticism. It is "dead, a one-day wonder [*ona mertva, ona odnodnevka*]," in relation to science and logic, but alive "in its tragic truthfulness, in its intimacy that is full of suffering; there is an undying emotion [*pafos*] that is passionate, cruel, and touching" (Diary II, 19). Counterintuitively, she finds that it is primarily a book for women, for whom it can serve as a "whip that beats in the truth of self-understanding"—a remarkably masochistic and ascetic readerly relationship—and a source for the concept of "the tragedy of femininity": "Every person is to a greater or lesser degree the conscious bearer of personal tragedy, which in part has its roots in the tragedy of science, class, religion, estate [*korporatsiia*], sex." No woman engaged in constructing her life (*ne odna zhenshchina, kotoraia stroit sebia*) should ignore this misogynistic tract.

Weininger portrays "Woman" (the pure type) as an entirely sexual creature, whereas "Man" can posses something else—talent, intellect, genius, or a soul.[70] He hypothesizes that every person is fundamentally bisexual, in the sense of having different proportions of masculine and feminine elements. The ideal romantic pairing would consist of two people whose combined elements add up to 1M + 1W. A proponent of gender fluidity, Weininger argues that women could emancipate themselves by cultivating their "masculinity" (M). In his view, the most gifted women were the most masculine, and were either attracted to women or to highly effeminate men.[71] He writes of how men "create" women as a projection of their own sexuality and guilt (misogyny is thus a result of self-hatred). As Tolstoy had done in "The Kreutzer Sonata" (1889), but for different reasons, he carves out a moral and spiritual path of complete abstinence: women were to reject sexuality because it enslaves them, and men ought to renounce it so as not to use another human being as a means to an end.[72]

Weininger opened up emancipatory possibilities unseen by Tolstoy. Ginzburg was not alone in singling these out: as Judy Greenway demonstrates, at the beginning of the twentieth century, many advocates for women's and homosexual liberation found support in his work, despite its unabashed misogyny and anti-Semitism. Ginzburg clearly approved of Weininger's elevation of intellectual women who departed from traditional feminine roles and stereotypes. She applauded him for rehabilitating the "despised and ridiculed mannish [*muzhepodobnaia*] woman" and for unmasking "the male egoism in the ridicule of this woman and in the cultivation of a specific kind of femininity as a source of pleasure."

In her approach to Weininger, Ginzburg may have been unique in her focus on the universal tragedy that women face:

> The grounds for tragedy are obvious: if a woman has enough elements of M. [Man] to be horrified at her own unreality, does that mean she has enough to accept humbly all of the work, self-renunciation, and asceticism not of political emancipation, but of intellectual-moral-physical emancipation? Because if "C'est un dur métier d'être belle femme" (I understand *belle* here not in the literal sense of beauty, but in the sense of a "genuine" [*nastoiashchaia*] woman), then to be a man is even more difficult, though less degrading.

Transgendered identity is "even more difficult" than what Baudelaire called the "difficult profession of being a beautiful woman" or, as Ginzburg would say, a "genuine" one. Embracing one's inner "M" demands moral, physical, and intellectual work, and can require a life of renunciation and suffering. Moreover, not being understood socially as a "Man" constricts one's life paths and emotional outlets—Ginzburg laments in her diaries that she cannot escape her suffering by entering the navy or going on a drinking spree.[73] Becoming an "M" requires a kind of double renunciation, of aspects or privileges of both genders.

Departing from Weininger, Ginzburg launches her own reflections about gender, and specifically the question of who is allowed to occupy the dominant aesthetic position.[74] In a move that prefigures the theories of Laura Mulvey and the turn in Feminist film criticism of the 1970s,[75] she observes that men, at least in contemporary society and in literary culture, have monopolized the aesthetic gaze, while women have the patent on beauty:

> For a man, everything in a woman: her body, movements, voice, smile, and gait constitute an object for aesthetic admiration; while a man, at least a contemporary man, is outside of aesthetics. This phenomenon, in my opinion, is clearly reflected in the literature common to humankind and in the morality common to humankind. Male fetishism is aesthetically justified, female fetishism is automatically classified as perversion. (Diary II, 23)

The twenty-year-old Ginzburg goes on to say that when women make a fetish of male beauty, they are perceived as "arrogators": "a woman's fetishism appears as something unfeminine, as a kind of usurpation of a pleasure not designed for her." To possess an aesthetic eye or "I" is already to abandon the traditional female position, to suffer from "perversion," even if one is describing a male body. The aesthetic viewpoint and literary tradition, she observes, present and represent female bodies as objects of desire. It is only a small step from here to Laura Mulvey's hypothesis that women readers become thoroughly habituated to trans-sex identification.[76]

In her diaries and early prose, Ginzburg aims to describe her own emotions, and yet she finds no models in literature for doing so from a female perspective: "Literature . . . reveals the depth, the intensity, the idealism, the drama of male erotic experiences and the utter poverty and flatness of female ones." While the male aesthetic position originates in the erotic, it then becomes the primary viewpoint from which one describes the world. Yet here, already in 1922, Ginzburg recognizes literary tradition and language as easily adaptable to her own aesthetic inclination: to write as if from a male perspective. While Michel Foucault and others have taught us to appreciate the constricting power of the cultural patterns embedded in language and literature, Lydia Ginzburg senses a liberating potential in the ability to craft fictions and adopt transgendered authorial personae. She fashions from *Sex and Character* a new way of looking at gender and sexual identity, and finds a justification for cultivating her aesthetic impulses. While she criticizes Weininger's reasoning, her creative interests encourage her to borrow and adjust his theories in order to write about female same-sex desire.

In an entry from 16 October (two weeks after the discussion of Weininger), she writes of her past relationship with "xxx" (R.), at the time when she was trying to isolate herself in order to bring things to an end:

> If I knew then how everything that has been experienced would become invaluable intellectual baggage, the experiential material for generalizations, the source of aesthetic Reminiscences; how from there threads would stretch forth, connecting me with the world's art and the impulses of my own personal creativity, then I would not have tried to rob myself, but would have thought about how to augment the precious moments.[77]

Ginzburg's exhilarated realization that experiences of unrequited love could furnish her with literary material, could form the basis for Reminiscences (with a capital "R"!), was a temporary upsurge that would eventually run up against her impulse for self-distancing and her rejection of the memoir genre. And yet the drive endured—to create value out of her "intellectual baggage," to generalize from her own experience, and to connect to world art. Ginzburg's decision to cultivate a male subject position put her in the mainstream of Russian and world literature. Not only did a male aesthetic perspective dominate in Russian art, but there was widespread misogyny concerning women writers and poets in Ginzburg's milieu. As Catriona Kelly has observed, Weininger's theories had fueled the "post-Symbolist backlash against women's writing, which was to have far-reaching effects, attaining its apogee after 1917 in the writings of the left avant-garde."[78]

"The Puppet Booth": A Literary Model of Tragic Love

Like Weininger's *Sex and Character*, Blok's "The Puppet Booth" (*Balaganchik*) plays a major role in Ginzburg's early conceptions of love and aesthetics. The play, hovering between tragedy and farce, and baring all of its devices, features a central triangle of Comedia dell'arte characters—Pierrot, Harlequin, and Columbine—entangled in a net of relations with each other, and also with the character of the "author" and a chorus of mystics. Pierrot is in love with Columbine, his bride, and wants to abscond with her, but is repeatedly prevented—by his friend Harlequin, by the "author," by the curtain, and by the mystics, who interpret Columbine as the incarnation of death, a long-awaited herald of apocalypse. The triangular relationship appears to echo the one involving Blok, Andrei Bely, and Blok's wife, Liubov' Dmitrievna, with its complex admixtures of spiritual and earthly desire.[79]

On 20 January 1921, Ginzburg mentions that she is writing an essay about Blok's dramas. She works on this essay, which appears primarily to concern "The Puppet Booth," for nearly a year before having an epiphany about the play's personal significance. On 20 December 1921, she hints enigmatically at her new understanding of this "intimate" meaning:

> At last I understand in essence what Pierrot is, or rather *who* Pierrot is. It is that word which I somehow did not dare to find.
>
> And above all this word is a key to a great many things. It clarified for me this disbelief in happiness, the incapacity for happiness and the inability to go on the offensive, and the desire to always defend oneself, to be wounded in order to incite pride, to be unloved in order to be tortured by neglect.

> Поняла же я собственно что такое Пьеро, вернее кто, Пьеро. Это то слово которое я как-то не смела найти.
>
> И главное это слово ключ ко многому. Оно объяснило мне это неверие в счастье, эту неспособность к счастью и неумение наступать, и желание всегда защищаться, быть обиженным для того чтобы бунтовалась гордость, быть нелюбимым для того чтобы мучила заброшенность. (Diary I, 138)

While Ginzburg's discovery about Pierrot's *real* identity remains vague, her very omission of the word behind the "who" ("that word which I somehow did not dare to find") suggests something "unmentionable." According to Douglas Clayton, the pale and androgynous Pierrot—who entered Russian culture as a type through French Symbolist and Decadent poetry—showed "strong hints of homosexuality."[80] These resonances certainly reached Ginzburg. Perhaps she reads Pierrot as in some way "inverted," or simply as weak and impotent in his love for Columbine, possessing a secret wish that his desire for her go unrealized.[81] Possibly, the mystery behind the "who" would simply have been the pronoun "I."

Ginzburg then hints that she herself has a competitor, a version of Harlequin. And in relation to her own rival and Pierrot's, she wonders:

> What if Harlequin could feel ashamed, could sense that he should give way to Pierrot with bared head, not dare to do anything while he's around. But after all it's not about Harlequin, it's about the fact the Pierrot, "for obvious reasons," can't be Pierrot all the way.... And maybe he is internally even bigger on account of this, even more hopeless.

> Что если бы Арлекин мог устыдиться, почувствовать что он должен с обнаженной головой уступать Пьеро дорогу, ничего не сметь при нем. Но ведь тут не об Арлекине речь, а о том, что Пьеро «по известным причинам» не может быть Пьеро до конца.... А может быть он внутренне от этого еще больше, еще безнадежнее. (Diary I, 139)

When Ginzburg uses the mysterious phrase "can't be Pierrot all the way," does she mean that Pierrot cannot fully embrace his spiritual nature by renouncing his earthly desire? Or the opposite: that Pierrot cannot be a "man," is incapable of consummating his desire, a failure that increases his tragic aspect? The phrase "for obvious reasons" euphemistically alludes to a sexual "complex," arguing for the second interpretation. Mapping Blok's triangle onto Ginzburg's personal life yields a different geometry: a woman ("Ginzburg"-Pierrot) yearns hopelessly (and with a secret wish for the desire to go unanswered) for romantic love from another woman ("R."-Columbine) and is tortured by male rivals ("V."-Harlequin) who have easier access to her and more outlets for expression. Ginzburg concludes that her discovery of the play's personal significance has elevated her respect for Blok. She now wishes for these characters to accompany her through life: "Only now do I love Blok's dramas. I want to take the images of Pierrot, Harlequin, and Columbine as Eternal Companions" (Diary I, 137–40).

Through her readings of Weininger and Blok, Ginzburg finds reasons to aestheticize the tragedies spawned from the gap between the ideal and the real: the imbalance of desire, the impossibility of sexual realization, the unquenchable thirst. She imports her Blokian companions into her imaginative world, fusing their identities and complexes onto those of the real characters in her life. Thus, she proceeds in her diaries to refer to R. as her Columbine.[82] Meanwhile, she fetishizes aspects of R.'s appearance—her narrow feet and delicate hands as well as her gloves, yellow stockings, furs, and perfumes—that connect to other images from Blok's poetry such as "The Stranger" ("Neznakomka").[83] Ginzburg adores R.'s "feminine" excess and impracticality: her spoiled and luxurious tastes during a period of deprivations that should have called for stern discipline (Diary II, 57). At the same time, she describes R. in ways that show the influence of Weininger's misogyny—she imagines saying to her beloved: "as a real woman [*nastoiashchaia zhenshchina*], you are cruel, duplicitous, forgetful, and demanding" (ibid., 86, 5 January 1923).

Blok's Columbine in "The Puppet Booth" serves as a canvas for the simultaneous projection of divergent desires. In the realization of a metaphor that parodies Symbolist ideas, she turns out to be made of cardboard. Ginzburg appropriates Blok's metaphor to refer to her own "cardboard sins" (*kartonnye grekhi*) (Diary II, 46, 23 October 1922). Because her love for R. was unrequited and unrealized, even her sins were chimerical. In a 1936 sketch of Zelyonaya (now "K."), Ginzburg defines her as a "woman who is loved" (*Zhenshchina, 'kotoruiu liubiat'*); in other words, she too is a canvas for the projection of others' desires.[84]

Beyond its central triangle, "The Puppet Booth" was a compelling model for the adolescent Ginzburg because of its foregrounding of theatrical conventions, its self-conscious blending of life and art. In her diaries, she talks about the "drama in which she plays a role" (Diary II, 32), and describes R. as heavily costumed and the center of attention even when offstage (ibid., 56). The young Ginzburg often portrays herself as both player and playwright, constructing "scenes" in which she acts in a premeditated manner—and usually fails to achieve her desired goal. As she designs elaborate ruses to attract R.'s attention and affection, her entries follow the drama of emotions within the autobiographical subject. One of the most colorful episodes even plays out in a theater foyer, when R. heartlessly passes off to V. the cigarette lighter Ginzburg had bought for her that day, at a sacrifice of time and money, on Nevsky Prospect. The author rejoices in spite of it all—a Dostoevskian moment: "I experienced the familiar aesthetic ecstasy at the magnificence of her carelessness" (Diary II, 77, 31 December 1922). (She then buys R. a compact mirror, certain that she could not regift this item at least to V.)

Ginzburg's Tolstoyan strain surfaces when she discusses her anxieties about the unreality of the dramas she has created. She speaks about how she lacks a real life, possessing only the "illusion of living through play" (*illiuziia zhizni cherez igru*, ibid., 80). The experience of life as artifice relates to Symbolist "life-creation," the "projection of poetic symbolism into life." In her chapter on Blok in *On the Lyric,* Ginzburg notes that Blok feared this "mixture of life and art," which he considered the most characteristic feature of Decadence.[85] Blok's life and Pierrot's serve as warnings that imaginary tragedies and cardboard brides can end in real pain.[86]

Ginzburg may have sensed that "The Puppet Booth"—in part a critique of Symbolist philosophy and its muddles—offered an outlet for her anxieties that Romantic effusions were always "on the border of the ridiculous" (to quote again the note to future readers she left with her youthful diaries). As she matured, she became increasingly critical of Symbolism, and by the 1940s even accused the movement of wholesale *poshlost'*. She defined this specifically Russian concept (roughly meaning "vulgarity," "triviality," or "banality") as an "incorrect relationship with value," a quality that "tears values from their organic context."[87]

Ginzburg's diary entries about her first love represent one possible mapping of desire onto a traditional cultural model, a drama fusing the sublime, the tragic, and the ridiculous. Finding a model—even if an imperfect one—was a joy, a comfort. Equipped with her reading of Weininger, she adapted her "Eternal Companions" by interpreting Blok's short Symbolist play, rich with ambiguity, through the lens of personal experience. In retrospect, she may have found herself guilty of submitting to *poshlost',* since she was not "organically" connected to Decadent values or to a Symbolist style, which were themselves alien to the values of post-Revolutionary Russia.

Ginzburg's Early Fictions about Love: Enter the Male Protagonist Narrator

After constructing a framework for understanding the relationships among gender, point of view, and her own love tragedies, Ginzburg began to pen her first fictions (and lyric poems as well) about love. Adopting the scale from Ginzburg's *On Psychological Prose,*[88] one could say that the aesthetic structure of these early fictional fragments is more complex than the diary entries about "The Puppet Booth," involving more decisions about representation and form. In these fictions, Ginzburg begins to remove her authorial image from the text through the creation of narrative frames and a male alter ego.

The first fictions are a set of four small sketches that carry the title "From the Disorderly Notes of N.N." ("Iz besporiadochnykh zapisok N.N."), which appear to date to the second half of 1922.[89] Written on loose pages that were tucked into the second diary, the sketches are indeed disorderly and their temporal sequence is unclear. Instead of a continuous plot, the sketches are built around alternating moments of hope and despair in the male narrator's relationship with his beloved. At the beginning of the first sketch, Ginzburg betrays, by a slip of the pen, the novelty for her of adopting a male narrator: she writes a feminine ending that she then crosses out (*Ia znala* becomes *Ia znal*). Unlike most of his successors, the main protagonist bears a proper name—Vasya, which is revealed simply (in un-Proustian fashion) when others address him.

As a narrator, Vasya is doubly framed—he is distinct from both N.N. (whose notes these purport to be) and the author. In relation to Proust, who considered using this timeworn technique for his novel, Genette writes that it testifies to a "certain timidity at novelistic writing and an obvious need for 'distancing' "—a comment that seems to apply to Ginzburg.[90] She encloses each episode in quotation marks (though not with complete consistency), and begins three of them with long ellipses, which suggests that Vasya is telling his story to some fictional N.N., who then records his notes, with lacunae, in random order. Since N.N. is given no separate voice or character and the act of telling is not depicted, this disarray has no psychological motivation on N.N.'s part, instead reflecting Vasya's hopeless love and the influence of Decadent aesthetics. Vasya's goal of achieving "moments of happiness" (while consciously sensing the egoism of his position) fits in with the fragmentary form as well as the Decadent ethos of enjoying life's "moments."

Vasya appears to be Ginzburg's first male autobiographical hero; he speaks in the masculine first-person singular but is in other respects similar to the "I" of the diaries. He is an outgrowth of the theatricality of the diary entries and of Ginzburg's self-modeling on Pierrot. Vasya's drama unfolds in similar ways to the love story in the diaries: he plans ways of extracting affections, but often fails and appears weak in the face of the spontaneous words and gestures of his beloved.

In these sketches, as in her later writing about love, Ginzburg makes communication into a central theme, exploring the limits of self-expression. As Proust reveals brilliantly, the drama of love unfolds subtly in communicative and interpretive acts, as individuals ascribe deeper meanings to straightforward utterances. Ginzburg's Vasya endeavors to study the heroine's every word and gesture. He constructs a semiotics of kisses and embraces, reading certain varieties as apologies and admissions of guilt, and others as meaningless acts. He endows his own utterances, however formulaic, with hidden meanings: "Then her voice, it must have been her voice, called me upstairs. 'What for?' [I asked.] These words could have expressed quite a lot, if only she wanted to understand them."[91] The first-person voice helps to capture Vasya's painful state of desire and his difficulty in expressing himself. Years later, as a literary scholar, Ginzburg would analyze Tolstoy's dialogues, explaining each phrase or gesture.[92]

In her "Disorderly Notes," Ginzburg pays special attention to the significance of the absence of gestures, a kind of negative semiotics that is instructive in reminding us of how one can give expression to same-sex love even when it is, on the surface, nowhere to be seen. During the crowded farewell scene at a train station, Vasya interprets the special treatment by his beloved—"the absence of a kiss" ("Iz bezporiadochnykh zapisok N.N.," 21)—as a sign that she is not indifferent to him. This Romantic posture of the hero—rejected and therefore elect—is germane to Ginzburg's period of experimentation with the first person. This fictional scene seems to compensate for the less Romantic analogue in the diaries, where Ginzburg expresses dismay when R. casually sends her greetings in correspondence with others: "She not only could not find the time to write me a few words, but could not even find the time to think about not writing me at all" (Diary I, 207).

The most dramatic section of "From the Disorderly Notes of N.N." describes the heroine's departure at the train station. As his beloved takes her leave of the others, Vasya carefully watches from a distance. His own farewell is mechanical and dictated by the heroine's action: a firm handshake, at arm's length. However, after the third bell signals the train's imminent departure, Vasya suddenly enacts a more intimate final gesture:

> Without looking at anyone, I pressed up close to the window, in order to be able to push my head inside the coupé.
>
> I don't remember her face at that moment, nor do I remember how her hand looked, and precisely how it lay on the ordinary wooden plank that serves as a table in the railway carriages, it must be that I didn't even see it, but I distinctly remember the familiar feeling of the tender and almost slightly cold touch of this hand to my lips, and that my kiss was longer and more expressive than ever before.
>
> I somehow lost consciousness in the kiss, when unexpectedly something else arose that cut short this slow and deep sensation—the light sensation of her kiss on my disheveled hair. So light that it seemed to come wafting from afar and then instantly faded away.
>
> That was a highpoint.
>
> Pulling my head out of the window I painfully hit it against the edge and this completely unexpected physical pain gladdened me.
>
> People were asking her for flowers. She started to hand them out to everyone, and in her excitement she managed badly with all of those stems and thorns.
>
> —Have this one, Vasya!
>
> And I took from her hand a bunch of *vasil'ki* [blue-bonnets]. Five dark *vasil'ki,* not counting the buds.

> Ни на кого не глядя, я притиснулся вплотную к окошку, так чтобы просунуть через него голову во внутрь купэ.
>
> Не помню ее лица в ту минуту, ни того как выглядела ее рука, и как именно она лежала на обычной деревянной дощечке, заменяющей стол в вагонах, должно быть я ничего этого и не видел, но помню отчетливо знакомое ощущение нежного и как будто несколько холодного прикосновения этой руки к моим губам, и то что мой поцелуй был как никогда долог и выразителен.
>
> Я как-то забылся в нем, когда неожиданно обрывая это медлительное и глубокое ощущение, возникло другое—легкое ощущение ее поцелуя на моих спутанных волосах. Такое легкое, что казалось оно донеслось издалека и тотчас же погасло.
>
> Это была точка.
>
> Вытаскивая голову из окошка я больно ударился о край и это совсем неожиданная физическая боль обрадовала меня.
>
> У нее просили цветов. Она стала раздавать всем, от волнения плохо справляясь со всеми этими стеблями и колючками.
>
> —Держите, Вася!
>
> И я принял из ее рук кучек васильков. Пять темных васильков, не считая бутонов. ("Iz bezporiadochnykh zapisok N.N.," 22–24)

In this moment, Vasya awakens from his numbness, passing from a state of watching without experiencing to a state of experiencing without seeing. He abandons his self-consciousness in order to push his head boldly into the coupé. He then performs a nearly wordless farewell, the only words spoken being the heroine's as she hands over the flowers. The symbolism of the hero's name now becomes clear: it refers to *vasil'ki* (blue-bonnets). This act has a biographical basis: in her diary Ginzburg writes of preserving the *proshchal'nye vasil'ki* that R. gave her on her departure for Moscow (Diary I, 164). By naming her hero Vasya, she amplifies the power of Zelyonaya's gesture: R. has unknowingly determined the identity of Ginzburg's alter ego.

This passage evokes the visually palpable, three-dimensional world typical of Realist fiction, which Ginzburg abandons in her later writings about love. In other passages that intricately detail every kiss, we see that creating a fictional world through Vasya seems to have liberated the author to describe subtle physical dimensions of love that are absent from most of her other writings. But at the same time, the first-person narrator differs from later heroes such as Otter and N. in valorizing a moment of self-forgetting and lack of analysis. The heroine's kiss is ephemeral, and in this way both spiritualized and lightened, exemplifying the Eternal Feminine. Vasya's sensations are heavier, but Her kiss inoculates him against the pain of bumping his head, against the awkwardness of the moment.

In the "Disorderly Notes" narrated by Vasya, Ginzburg seems to cede to the temptations of Romantic effusions, with their palliative effects. The choice to fictionalize frees the author to "augment the precious moments," along the lines of her interpretation of Weininger. Ginzburg was wary of Romantic heights (as she said: "it is one step from the beautiful to the vulgar"), an uneasiness that additionally motivates the comedy of Vasya's bumping his head at the peak of his ecstasy. On the whole, though, Vasya embraces his individuality and even his state of rejection.

In her second semi-fiction, Ginzburg experiments with the dialogue form, which becomes a mainstay of her mature prose about love. This piece records a nighttime conversation on 1 February 1923, and was drafted directly into Ginzburg's diary the next morning. Introducing the dialogue, she writes: "I will relate the quintessence of this conversation, which is so dear to me, from the moment when it becomes important. If there is to be an element of selection and stylization in the transmission, then I enter into it consciously." (Diary II, 103).[93] The moment of fiction thus occurs not through the creation of a male hero, but through selection and omission, aspects more distinctive of documentary prose.

Here, contrary to her usual manner, Ginzburg does not mask the same-sex desire. While the women address each other as *Vy* (the formal "You" pronoun whose nongendered plural endings afford the grammatical possibility of concealment), the author reveals and highlights their female genders by setting out the dialogue as a play with two characters, identified as "I" and "She" (she also reveals gender in other ways, such as the first-person past tense, and a discussion of how things would change if Ginzburg were a man). The use of the first-person singular in a text of such immediacy and intimacy produces a direct kind of authorial inclusion. Meanwhile, it is significant that the author does not use Rina's name, and yet "She" utters Ginzburg's name in adjectival form ("There goes your Ginzburgian vileness [*merzost'*]").

Much later—judging from handwriting, in two different decades, the 1960s and 1980s—Ginzburg returned to recopy this dialogue, perhaps intending to publish it. She made several minor revisions, and added the title "Conversation (at Night). For a Tale about Nervous People" (*Razgovor [nochnoi]. Dlia povesti o nervnykh liudiakh*).[94] She probably never wrote this larger "tale," but the revisions shifted the work's orientation away from the autobiographical, and historicized it by designating its belonging to the NEP era, for which "nervous people" is a catchword.[95] Her most significant revision was to remove the personal pronouns I/She (*Ia/Ona*) introducing each utterance (she also removed the adjective "Ginzburgian"), thus making the characters more abstract and anonymous—and less pointedly female.

In the diaries, this nighttime dialogue is the climax of the love plot. Communication suddenly transcends the muted signals, the one-liners, the failures to become a true, open exchange. As she sets out to record the conversation, the author notes her surge of happiness, perhaps resulting from the Bakhtinian potential of dialogue, which emerges from the unpredictability of another living human being, who can be more loving and forgiving than the version we generate in our thoughts. Columbine comes to life and shows that she is not simply "cardboard."

The person who now comes alive gives several grounds for relief and happiness. First, "She" appears as witty, smart, and full of understanding, which reassures Ginzburg that she has not been cheapening herself by adoring an unworthy woman. Second, "She" flatters the author's dream of family belonging, and semi-normalizes her eccentricity by equating her with Viktor, even while she calls the siblings loathsome and rotten. Third, "She" acknowledges Ginzburg's potential as a writer, instructing her to preserve herself because she is "infinitely capable" ("Вы беспредельно много можете"). Fourth, "She" adopts a motherly posture, inviting Ginzburg to rest her head on the fur jacket covering Her lap, physically caressing and comforting her. Finally, the "I" succeeds in extracting these gifts from "Her" not through self-abasement and persistence, but by daring to talk about a range of feelings, from fear to gratitude. In the next entry on 3 February, she reflects: "it is especially striking that I suddenly told her about myself with simplicity and trustfulness, almost with disinterestedness [*s prostotoi i doverchivost'iu, pochti s beskorystiem*], because I am so accustomed to the bad and cruel that I did not expect mercy" (Diary II, 116).

The climactic moment of the dialogue involves an avowal of same-sex desire that the "I" had not dared to enunciate. The relationship remains no less tragic.

SHE—Yes, loneliness is the most horrible thing.

I—As a matter of fact I don't care about that. I don't need anybody. That is, not nobody . . . I don't know whether I can call things by their names.

SHE—No, please don't.

I—In essence, I didn't want to say anything frightening.

SHE—I know what you wanted to say. You wanted to say that you don't need anyone except me. Please don't say that.

I—You just said it yourself. How incautious you are. . . .

Here the exact sequence of the conversation is lost. What follows are its fragments, in order when possible.

ОНА—Да, одиночество самое ужасное.

Я—Как раз это мне все равно. Мне никто не нужен. То-есть не никто . . . Не знаю можно ли называть вещи их именами.

ОНА—Нет, пожалуйста, не надо.

Я—В сущности, я не хотела сказать ничего страшного.

ОНА—Я знаю что вы хотели сказать. Вы хотели сказать, что вам не нужен никто, кроме меня. Так, пожалуйста, не говорите.

Я—Вы же сами это сказали. Как Вы неосторожны. . . .

Здесь точная последовательность разговора теряется. Нижеследующее суть его фрагменты, по возможности в порядке.[96]

The prohibited discourse of homosexual desire and the unacknowledged basis of the one-and-a-half year relationship generate a remarkable pathos of enunciation. This "incautious" act grows in significance because it is uttered, and acknowledged, by "Her": it is She who enacts the prohibition ("Please don't say that") and immediately breaks it ("you don't need anyone except me"). The urge, on the part of "I," to speak the truth of her desire is fulfilled in an unexpected and more satisfying way—through the words of her beloved, which carry a greater reality. The emotional intensity of this moment seems to render the author/subject incapable of faithfully recording what follows ("the exact sequence of the conversation is lost . . .").

While Vasya provided a model for interpreting gestures and their absence, this dialogue demonstrates the intense power of enunciation. Ginzburg attributed supreme importance to verbal realization—she wrote a few years later that things not verbalized did not exist for her.[97] This view helps explain her concern with taboos (*zaprety*), barriers, and with what it was possible to say when face to face with another person. In the Leningrad Blockade, Ginzburg summarized the power of conversation in an impersonal, yet uplifting way: "Conversation is wish fulfillment. In a conversation over a cup of tea or a glass of wine, impregnable barriers are lifted, goals are reached that in the world of actions would take many years, failures, and exertions."[98]

In her early fictions, Ginzburg tests out two aesthetic modes as she explores failures and occasional breakthroughs in communication. In the "Disorderly Notes of N.N.," a fictional male hero (Vasya) acts as narrator and focalizer, while describing scenes of verbal and nonverbal interaction in their physical and psychological dimensions (for the hero). In "Nighttime Conversation," written into her diary, she constructs a dialogue between two women, one of whom is identified as "I." She abandons the conscious fictionalization through the male gender for the documentary aesthetic of selection and omission. In the first piece, the influence of Blok and of late Symbolism are evident in her use of the first person and in the emotional excess of her autobiographical hero. But when Columbine comes to life in the second piece, a verbally enriched reality proves (at least momentarily) more attractive than illusion. Elements of these experiments would find their way into the later fictions, which nevertheless differ significantly from these youthful attempts.

PART II: SELF-REALIZATION AND THE SECOND LOVE

After 1921–23, the most intensive concentration of Ginzburg's writings about love occurs in the 1930s. Her return to the subject came on the other side of the seven or so years she spent at the Institute for the History of Arts, which determined her life's course as a writer and literary scholar.

Ginzburg characterized her move to Petrograd in 1922 to study at the Institute for the History of the Arts under Yuri Tynianov, Boris Eikhenbaum, Viktor Shklovsky, and others as a move into history from a "prehistoric" provincial existence.[99] As a "Young Formalist," she experienced "the thrill [*pafos*] of an unexpectedly acquired social relevance,"[100] undergoing a "second socialization" after childhood. Her entry into the vibrant cultural life of the northern capital paved the way for her escape from the Decadent aesthetics and the tragic pose of Romantic sufferer that had held her in provincial thrall. As she later recalled, the spring day in 1923 when Tynianov praised her first oral presentation propelled her out of her humiliating obsession with her unrequited love (for R./Zelyonaya).[101] Her new career as a *littérateur* offered a sphere of realization quite apart from the frustrating realm of romance. Ginzburg felt that she had received the gift of a separate "world to own and govern."[102] The notebooks of 1925–28 chart a "group romance with the *maîtres*"[103]; erotic love becomes a minor theme, the source of an occasional aphorism or anecdote.

In the 1930s, Ginzburg depicts and analyzes a love affair (for a woman whose biographical correlate remains unknown) built on an idea directly opposite to that of the first: the "second love" must be "happy, mutual, realized."[104] These writings about love include no diary entries or poems. In fragmentary notes, semifictional essays and narratives, Ginzburg foregrounds not isolation and uniqueness but rather the plight of her whole generation and the universal laws of love. Her alter ego remains an erotic failure, but lacks Pierrot's tragic aura. The quest for emotional fulfillment falls by the wayside as Ginzburg's new hero, in a compensatory move, now conceives of love as a realm of self-realization. And she consistently describes her experiences from an increasingly deindividualized masculine third-person perspective.

The Impotence of a Formalist

Ginzburg's male autobiographical heroes in the 1930s (and 1940s) are sexually inexperienced and prone to erotic failure. We see this most clearly in the 1933–34 essay "The Stages of Love," which recounts four case studies—all of them failed love affairs—in the life of "A." The first case, a rewriting of Ginzburg's unrequited love for Zelyonaya, is followed by analyses of two "affairs" lacking in any element of the physical or sensual. The fourth case is the "second love." The alter ego A., like Ginzburg at the time, is thirty-one years old, with a wounded self-image: "In A.'s past—a series of erotic calamities. Utter lack of realization. An awareness of sexual impairment [*ushcherbnost'*], psychic impotence. Because of this, he has the sense: not a real person [*nenastoiashchii*], not a grown-up. Attempt to overcome this feeling and to burnish his self-esteem [*raspravit' samoliubie*]." From A.'s side, the relationship with his lover B. hinges on its being a requited, exclusive, physical love, because only this will allow him to overcome his traumas of impotence and immaturity. But the relationship eventually fails for this very reason: "love was a secondary phenomenon in relation to the instinct for realization. It was not the object that begot desire, but desire begot the object." What A. really wants is not pleasure or happiness but a mature self-fulfillment.[105]

In this period, the frustrated Ginzburg often regards herself as a creative failure, as "impotent" (using the masculine/general term rather than the markedly feminine "barren"). In 1933, she observes that novelists like Tolstoy, Flaubert, and Dickens felt an "urgent need to create worlds," whereas writers of notebooks and in-between prose were "impotent."[106] She describes her desire to produce a novel as a rejection of this stigmatized status: "Notebooks, etc., are the literature of impotents [*literatura impotentov*]. Therefore it's impossible for me to live without writing a novel."[107] Only the writing of a novel would constitute for her an act on a par with sexual reproduction: the novel, like the "second love," is here motivated by the desire to achieve maturity and to demonstrate one's powers.

As Ginzburg faced the increasing intolerance of Soviet society, she conceived of her professional fate as a scholar and her personal fate as a lesbian under the overarching tropes of impotence and Formalism. Both tropes connect to her main concern with self-realization. In 1931, Ginzburg likened her professional tragedy to misfortune in love: "They've devised for us the torment of the unlucky profession, to replace the unlucky love of our predecessors. The burden of a fruitless creative will."[108] To understand this historical generalization, we need to understand the trajectory of her career in an increasingly repressive state, and why Formalism became associated with the feelings of impotence and the dilemmas of sexuality.

The Revolution ushered in radical cultural changes and further encouraged Ginzburg's break with decadent moods. Gone were the liberalism and relative permissiveness accorded to nontraditional lifestyles and minority sexualities. Gone too, as Ginzburg saw it, was the whole culture of love, since it depended on the existence of leisure time.[109] The model citizen—the New Soviet Person—was strong, healthy, and machine-like, with the power to conquer irrational forces, weakness, and illness. This aesthetic inspired writers such as Mikhail Zoshchenko to attempt to purify and purge themselves of phobias and sicknesses, as Keith Livers has discussed.[110] In August 1930, Ginzburg remarks on her new respect for normality: "it is curious that for the current 'system of myself' the concept of the normal is just as important as were kinks and quirks [*vyvikh i vyvert*] that served as preconditions for my earlier life."[111]

Ginzburg perceived a silver lining in this cultural turn toward conservatism. She wrote of how fortunate it was that history was now turning against "the structure of a person with a deep soul and a tendency to self-psychologize," which she had cultivated from the ages of fourteen to twenty.[112] At the same time, in early 1929, she noted that social norms had turned into coarse, mechanized rules. And by 1929–30, she and her cohort experienced a decisive loss of profession and a concurrent sense of isolation and irrelevance. To publish as a scholar, one had to adopt Marxist sociological methods. To write fiction or even documentary prose, one had to employ, exclusively, the method of Socialist Realism and to celebrate the State's achievements. But she and her friends were too "eccentric" [*sdvinutye*] to regard the "fulfillment of norms" as something joyful or productive; they felt that only their "aberrations" could "preserve their humanity."[113]

In 1933, after Socialist Realism became the official doctrine, Ginzburg describes the fate of her generation of intellectuals as a tragedy contained in a single question: was it possible to operate in accordance with the "path of the October Revolution"—since it was impossible to act outside of it? Many writers felt the temptation to join the "new order," an urge encapsulated by Boris Pasternak in his 1931 poem, "More than a Century Ago—Not Yesterday" ("Stolet'e s lishnim—ne vchera").[114] The lines Ginzburg often quotes—"Labor in common with all / And at one with the legal order" ("Труда со всеми сообща/ И заодно с правопорядком")—express the intelligentsia's agonizing desire to become part of the toiling masses. At this point, Formalism was already an "historically abandoned" path and, if she still identified with it (and she did), Ginzburg was definitely not "at one with the legal order." The classic dream of the *intelligent*, which Herzen so keenly felt and propagated, of becoming a "person of action," haunts her.

Sexuality figures in complex ways into Ginzburg's contemplation of the paths of intellectuals in relation to the dominant order. For example, when she tries to pinpoint the quality that empowered a small minority to resist compromise in the creative realm, she arrives at "giftedness" (*talant*) or "abilities" (*sposobnosti*). These are almost biological attributes, in her reckoning.[115] As one note shows, she lightheartedly discussed with Boris Bukhstab, her close friend, Freud's theory that "giftedness comes from the combination of sexual deviance [*seksual'nykh uklonenii*] and a capacity for work."[116] In a 1934 essay elaborating a typology of six major personality types, Ginzburg identifies sexual deviance as a common attribute of the intellectual type: "Intellectualism, probably, is most often the result of social irrelevance [*neprimenimosti*] and irresponsibility, combined with certain sexual defects [*s nekotorymi seksual'nymi defektami*]—with the kind of qualities that divert a person from achieving straightforward sexual goals [*priamykh seksual'nykh tselei*]."[117] She names Marcel Proust and his hero as intellectuals *par excellence*—they spin out a thought for its own sake, without trying to propagate an "idea" (that belongs to another type: "people of ideas" or "ideological people"). Ginzburg classifies herself as a mixture of the "intellectual" and the "active" types. The latter are doers, builders, writers who are governed by a "will to action" (*volia k deistviu*).[118] Intellectuals take pleasure in "thought as such" (*samovitaia mysl'*), an allusion to the Futurists' "word as such" (*samovitoe slovo*), and to the Formalists' stance of autonomy and anti-utilitarianism.

Ginzburg directly links Formalism and sexuality in her "Dialogue about Love," where the speaker asserts: "Inverts can have a peaceful existence [. . .] if they are Formalists in love, believing in the reality of the moment, and separating the means from the ends (in art, after all, Formalism is also the emancipation of the means)."[119] A moralistic reading of this statement (where the means are sexual pleasure and the ends are biological reproduction and "social usefulness") might be justified.[120] The advice that "Formalism [unlike Symbolism] in love" can deliver a peaceful existence, points to a significant dilemma. Ginzburg resisted *samovitost'*—living in the moment, a-politically and a-socially—and subjected hedonists and characters who failed to live connected lives to the harshest criticism. She sought to overcome the fragmentariness of life through self-distancing and the creation of a cohesive self-image, which she could then submit to moral judgment. Ginzburg's writings, as an offering to society and a method of viewing the self as other, are themselves an attempt to overcome *samovitost'*, solipsism, and the immanence of the post-individualist person. Paradoxically, disconnectedness serves as the basis for Ginzburg's critique of both Symbolism and Formalism, in the context of love: the Symbolists adopted values torn from their organic contexts and magnified them through mysticism, and the (early) Formalists attempted to separate a thing from its social and historical context.

For Ginzburg, then, Formalism and homosexuality are both associated with inaction and impotence. They intensify the distance she senses between herself and the ideal "hero of her time." Closing this distance becomes one of her creative goals:

> But I am very far from being an altogether social or generally successful contemporary. For obvious reasons, my psychological preconditions are such that on the whole they make me a person of *inaction*. But these primary psychological traits, instead of becoming organizing factors, as they might have done in other circumstances, have become disorganizing residues. (For example, what in a different, more personal and more decadent epoch, could have been a dominant of my existence, is now more or less pushed into the depths of the psyche.)
>
> One such remainder in me, as a person of inaction, is my sense of humor. [. . .]
>
> I distinguish my "primary" psychological traits from "secondary" ones (which are more socially conditioned) mainly by the fact that they do more to prevent me from becoming a genuine contemporary of my time.
>
> The problem of the socially and historically conditioned, and how it gets layered on top of the personally given (inherited)—should even become the next subject of investigation for a novel—whether for a social or psychological novel, I'm not sure yet—but for the kind of novel that is most needed.

Впрочем, я очень далека от того, чтобы быть вполне социальным и вообще благополучным современником. Мои психические предпосылки таковы, что, по понятным причинам, они в общем делают меня человеком бездействия. Но только первичные психические свойства, из организующих принципов, какими они могли бы быть при др<угих> обстоятельствах, становятся дезорганизующими остатками. (Напр<имер> то, что в другую более личную и более декадентскую эпоху могло бы оказаться доминантом моего существования и моего сознания, сейчас более или менее задвинуто в глубины психики.)

Таким остатком у меня, как у человека бездействия, служит, например, юмор. < . . . >

Я различаю в себе «первичные» психические свойства от «вторичных» (то есть в большей степени обусловленных социально) главным образом потому, что они в большей степени мешают мне стать действительным современником своего времени.

> Проблема социального и исторически обусловленного, как оно накладывается на лично (наследственно) заданное,—и должна стать ближайшим предметом исследования для романа, уж не знаю—социального или психологического, словом для того романа, который очень нужен.[121]

In this intimate and autobiographical fragment—which Ginzburg never published—there is no mention that sexuality is a discordant "primary" psychological trait. The idea that a different self might have formed in decadent times alludes to homosexuality (a stronger marker of decadence than humor). The phrase "for obvious reasons," as in her remarks on Blok's Pierrot, may serve as code for "inversion." Ginzburg seems to possess an almost physical awareness of the processes of social conditioning (*obuslovlennost'*), which here suppress, if incompletely, elements that might have become dominant in other times. The use of an impersonal, passive construction (*zadvinuto*, "pushed") to describe this suppression makes the subject into both specimen and observer.

Models for Catastrophic, Twentieth-Century Love

In the 1930s, love becomes a theme within the framework of other vital questions that taxed Ginzburg at the time: the structure of personality around "value" and the fate of subjective consciousness in a "post-individualist" world. She turns to a new set of male authors—Viktor Shklovsky, Nikolai Oleinikov, Ernest Hemingway, and Marcel Proust—who, different from each other as they are, share Ginzburg's suspicion of the mystico-religious Romantic and Symbolist ideologies of love.

Lydia Ginzburg once noted that her friend Viktor Shklovsky's[122] epistolary novel, *Zoo, or Letters Not about Love* (first published in 1923), was one of the few books that had, for a time, fully inhabited her consciousness.[123] As in her reading of Blok's "The Puppet Booth," she must have found personal meaning here in the themes of unrequited love and prohibition. In *Zoo*, love is doubly forbidden. First, the female correspondent Alya, in real life Elsa Triolet, agrees to tolerate receiving letters from a man she does not love only so long as he avoids the subject of his feelings, and preferably if he imparts his insights on literature instead.[124] The second prohibition emerges from Shklovsky's sense of literary history. He himself finds love to be an impossible topic, because all the "good words" about it—the tropes, symbols, and psychological convolutions—are "faint with exhaustion."[125]

Shklovsky, along with his autobiographical character, forges a relationship between love and writing, whether one calls this sublimation, seduction, or revenge.[126] He sets out to confront his romantic defeat with words, to create a psychological distraction from love—a subject he nonetheless smuggles in, against both prohibitions, by using irony and metaphor. Love turns up everywhere as the motivation and subtext for every word about Berlin, the zoo, literature, or technology. And as much as Shklovsky laments the constraints of literary tradition, his novel dazzles us with its original blend of literary theory, fact, and fiction.[127] His success in writing about love while confronting the crisis in literature is similar to Blok's double treatment, in "The Puppet Booth," of the crisis in both the theater and late Symbolism.

Ginzburg never offered an extended analysis of *Zoo*, but she noted the appropriateness of Shklovsky's indirection in his treatment of love: "The erotic theme in its pure form cannot be sufficient in the present time. It is characteristic that in *Zoo*, Shklovsky constantly props up love with profession. Alya parades under the cloak of the formalist method and the automobile."[128] But she did not interpret these metaphorical substitutions as pure play, and discerned the book's underlying emotions (as she did with Weininger's theories).[129]

The other contemporary Russian writer whose treatment of love Ginzburg studied closely in this period was her friend Nikolai Oleinikov. In 1933, she composed a lengthy analysis of his ballad, "Gluttony" ("Chrevougodie").[130] As she saw it, Oleinikov, like Shklovsky, was performing an operation on language and style with a goal attuned to the Formalists': "to clear the path for a new word" by "killing the old ones" ("Для того чтобы расчистить дорогу новому слову, ему нужно было умертвить старые").[131] The "old words" had sunk under the strain of their heavy Symbolist baggage. They needed to be removed: "[Oleinikov's masks] were needed in the battle that the literary generation of the 1920s waged against the yet-to-be overcome heritage of symbolism with its otherworldliness, and against the aestheticism of the 1910s." On the face of it, his poems are comic, and exhibit a stylistic "naiveté" similar to Primitivist paintings (lacking perspective, and made up of crudely drawn figures), and to the syntax of Velimir Khlebnikov.[132] And yet, beneath all of the buffoonery, Oleinikov is for Ginzburg a highly serious poet. She notes humorously to her friend, "You tied yourself in knots so that at least some kind of word could ring out" ("Вы расшиблись в лепешку ради того, чтобы зазвучало какое-то слово").[133]

In "Gluttony," a philistine forges a direct relationship between his caloric consumption and his ability to be a lover, all the while trying to employ a lofty register as he asks for food. Ginzburg characterizes the speaker's language as *galantereinyi*, a word applied to an uneducated person who is trying to sound or act "sophisticated." She writes of this faux-"gallant" culture in ways that recall her concept of *poshlost'*: both involve an incorrect relationship to value, and an ignorance of the sacrifices through which the responsible use of language is earned. Oleinikov uses this kind of "gallant" language, she writes, "in order to compromise and splinter inherited symbolist meanings. Because nothing in the world can smut up an ideology like 'gallant' language."[134] Showing his fine sense of this linguistic register, Oleinikov uses it to create a serious, sublime piece about love, hunger, sadness (*toska*), and death.[135] In Oleinikov, Ginzburg finds an ally in her battle against the Symbolist ideologies to which she was prone in her youth, and evidence for the relationship between renewing language and renewing language's relationship to value.

Another congenial writer on love is Ernest Hemingway, whose *Farewell to Arms* (1929) Ginzburg recalled receiving from Anna Akhmatova as soon as it was translated (1936),[136] and he features prominently, along with Proust, in the original "Theoretical Introduction" to *Home and the World*, dated 1939.[137] It was Hemingway who, according to Ginzburg, revealed the disconnected and superficial nature of conversation in the twentieth century, and also the nature of love for people who had no idea of whether they would still be alive the next day (in his case, soldiers, but one could easily think of Soviet subjects under the Terror).

> Hemingway, a truly contemporary writer, as a counterweight to medieval and modern times, affirms physical love as something that needs no justification. But this affirmation is inseparable from the tragic essence of love, which Hemingway revealed in twentieth-century society. Love, especially a great love, is a state that cannot last. It is intended to unite two people; in order for this pair to remain united, love must fasten onto other social material (daily life [*byt*], home, children). That original feeling, totally unalloyed—just try, in your head [*myslenno*], to keep it going to infinity. What you get is a strain [*napriazhenie*] that is immediately tragic, beyond anyone's strength, and which leads nowhere, bordering on the necessity of catastrophe.[138]

Here Ginzburg is ascribing to Hemingway the insights that she herself had made in her 1934 essay "Stages of Love"; and thus it is possible that the American writer did not so much influence her writing as confirm for her the accuracy of her intuitions. In this sense, and apart from all chronology, he becomes for her one of her predecessors. Both writers place love in the context of catastrophic historical experience, where love becomes a catastrophic experience in itself. Ginzburg's 1939 description of the hero of *Farewell to Arms* echoes the sketch of Otter in *Home and the World*. Living in a hostile world, both characters try to overcome their isolation through the love of one other person. What results is "no longer homebuilding, but the clinging of each to the other, the coupling of two people in the void" ("уже не домостроительство, но цепляние друг за друга и сцепление двух человек в пустоте").[139]

But the writer with perhaps the greatest significance for Ginzburg in the 1930s was Marcel Proust. Her first encounter with his writings probably dates from 1927,[140] and a 1929–30 article "for the desk drawer" shows the evolution of her thought on Proust at a pivotal stage of her creative development, when she was trying to become a kind of novelist-researcher.[141] She aims to view the author from the perspective of a contemporary seeking to "assimilate" aspects of his method for Russian literature: "in this article I am interested in Proust as method, and as the possibility of a method" ("в данной статье меня занимает Пруст, как метод и как возможность метода").[142]

This draft article shows how Ginzburg learned from a writer through scholarly analysis. She sees Proust as a radical innovator in literature, an author who liberates his novel from the constraints of plot and literary character. He achieves this, above all, through the techniques of the pseudo-memoir. While soothing the potentially disoriented reader with a surface-level familiarity, these techniques allow him to shift the realm of the novel from representation to reflection, from "showing" to "telling," from a drama that transpires in the world to a drama of consciousness and memory. The pseudo-memoir enables Proust to create a hero who is "free . . . of personality" (*osvobozhden . . . ot kharaktera*),[143] but who is at the same time no longer an "empty space"—the fate, she notes, that has befallen all first-person narrators (*skaz* narrators excepted). The narrator is now one who "judges and evaluates"—a factor that was secondary in other first-person narratives, and that Proust made into a constructive principle. Unlike Tolstoy's *Childhood,* Ginzburg notes, Proust's emphasis is on the "narrating I" rather than the "narrated I," and this shift frees the author from the temporal and spatial demands of the chronicle, a traditional construct in memoir and autobiography. By turning the narrator's consciousness into a focalizer, the "researcher's method" (*issledovatel'skii metod*) enables the author to explain the motives of behavior and to examine personality in a way less bound to particular characters than the psychological novel. Hence, Proust destroys the unities of plot and character, and replaces them with a unity of intonation and style, of poetic sentences filled with analogies and metaphors.[144]

Ginzburg's interpretation of Proust showed another way out of the quagmires of Symbolism—this time not, as in Oleinikov, through the lyricism that underlies the comic mimicry of a philistine's "sophistication," but instead through a more earnest investigation into the intellectual constructs, and personal memories or associations, that make objects in the world meaningful. As Ginzburg writes in *On Psychological Prose*, "Proust's materiality is . . . a sensuousness that invariably gives way to [or is sublated by] intellectual symbolism" ("материальность Пруста < . . . > это чувственность, всегда снятая интеллектуальной символикой"). Objects such as "spire, apple tree, and raindrop" "are not allegorical, but representational. Their symbolic meaning emerges from context, inasmuch as they belong to the hallowed landscapes of the 'lost paradise' of Combray."[145] In her 1929–30 article, she is not just taking aim at Symbolism but at contemporary Soviet literature as well, which sought to respond to the demands of the new society ("'социальный заказ' революции") by attending to the material alone, a trend exemplified by the LEF ideologues of the Literature of Fact movement. For Ginzburg, "What's at issue is not the material, but the creation of a new structure of meanings and the heightening of the cognitive possibilities of the literary word."[146]

None of Ginzburg's discussions of Proust dwell on his treatment of same-sex love. She briefly alludes to the character of Charlus in explaining how Proust shows the intersection of the social with the "psycho-physiological": Charlus's Germanophilism is a result of both his homosexual orientation and his status as an aristocrat. She thus seems to agree with Proust's somewhat inconsistent position that the forms of love are universal, but that sexual identity as it manifests itself in society can be analyzed on a sociological and linguistic level.[147] In her notebooks, she defends him against the charge that he has written a "pornographic" memoir-novel, claiming that the work can be considered indecent only if one allows that an anatomy textbook is obscene.[148] She applauds Proust's ability to approach love while largely steering clear of the ethical complexes characteristic of Russian psychological novels.

Jean-Paul Sartre and Simone de Beauvoir, two writers and thinkers whose interests are in some ways similar to Ginzburg's, and who write about love in the third person, criticized Proust for his approach to love as universally the same, because it prevented him from treating sexuality as socially constructed. Sartre writes: "We are of the opinion that a feeling always expresses a specific way of life and a specific conception of the world that are shared by an entire class or an entire era, and that its evolution is not the effect of some unspecified internal mechanism but of those historical and social factors."[149] This statement accords so closely with Ginzburg's theory of social and historical conditioning that it highlights the inconsistency of her position on love. At the same time, Ginzburg's use of the third person, departing from Proust's example, may allow her to represent the social and historical conditioning of love even as she attempts to analyze its anatomy in a universalizing way.

The Rhetorical Structures of Dom i Mir *(*Home and the World*)*

In the 1930s, Ginzburg worked on a series of narratives, planning to combine and unify them into her quasi-diary–quasi-novel called *Home and the World,* at whose center would be representations of the "nonindividualistic" (*neindividualisticheskii*) person.[150] Under the heading "On the Contemporary Novel," she jotted down a reflection that the "greatest achievement of the psychological literature of the nineteenth century" was literary character, or the sense that each person's fate was singular. But this approach was now outdated, she argued, because it was "bound up with the the whole humanistic concept of the person in terms of individuals" ("Это связано со всей индивидуалистически гумманистической концепцией человека, и сейчас неприменимо"). A contemporary approach should emphasize those common structures and elements that combine and intersect to make up a personality. It is these structures, acted upon by social pressures, that produce behavior. Proust's characters do not have those Tolstoyan "qualities that individually and independently belong to them as psychically unique and unrepeatable beings" ("у основных героев нет характеров в толстовском смысле, т.е., индивидуально и независимо им принадлежащих свойств, им как психически единственному и неповторимому явлению").[151] Despite the fact that Tolstoy, like Proust, had revealed the social and historical conditioning of his characters, it was the latter whose example Ginzburg followed more closely, by emptying her characters of any qualities that might mark them as unique, in order to emphasize the socially typical and the psychologically universal.

In moving away from the individualist philosophies of the nineteenth-century novel, Ginzburg—like Proust—chooses a quasi-autobiographical genre. But she sets different priorities for herself: "I want to analyze a person, his behavior, and the things that surround him into rationally cognizable elements. Factors of scientific thought. [. . .] It's different in Proust. For him, the most important thing is the world in consciousness. For me, the most important is the world in cognitive categories."[152] While consciousness in fact remains one object of depiction in Ginzburg, her desire to capture "the world in cognitive categories" signals a change in focus, away from the inner, subjective world of the hero and toward the analysis of the personality structures of others, as shaped by social factors.

It is possible that Ginzburg's drafts are more systematic than the final prose work she planned (but never completed) would have been. Evidence to this effect can be found in the finished narratives, such as "The Return Home," which portray the thoughts, memories, and perceptions of the hero

(Otter, Y., N., or "I") in a semi-personal way that is neither alienating nor schematic. "The Return Home" shows the strong influence of Proust's novel in its freedom from plot and character, in its emphasis on the representation of the thought process, in its use of dialogue as illustration, and in its style, mixing scientific generalizations with ornate and well-nigh poetic descriptions of landscapes. Ginzburg's narrator is more emotionally restrained than Proust's, and more scientific when dissecting perceptions belonging to him/herself and to the illustrative character (Y.).

Ginzburg's outlines for *Home and the World* clearly testify to this intended "scientific" approach. In one of them, she explains her method as follows: "A person is analyzed in those manifestations of his that are accessible to external observation and generalizing reason. The basic elements are the analytic discussion and recording of human speech, accompanied by an analytical commentary."[153] The characters in the sketches and dialogues (who have real-life counterparts in Ginzburg's circle) are indeed analyzed in their external manifestations, most of all in their speech. The one exception is the autobiographical hero, Otter, whose thoughts and emotions, narrated in the third person, accompany the dialogues.

The most extensive surviving fragments of *Home and the World* treat love and daily life (*byt*): two of the five "categories" of existence posited by Ginzburg (the others are profession, creativity, and self-consciousness).[154] The central relationship is modeled on her "second love." Here the characters are not A. and B. (as in "The Stages of Love"), but Otter and Lialia—the first heroine who actually has a name in Ginzburg's writings on love. Otter's primary personality trait—and a recognizably autobiographical one—is that he is "a person who perceives the world in words" ("От.—человек, воспринимающий мир в слове"). Otter is also a *littérateur* (литератор), a writer and scholar with a talent for psychological analysis.

Ginzburg's plot bridges Herzen's concerns with "creative action" (or *odeistvotvorenie*, or coming into being through "an act that had historical and social significance")[155] and Hemingway's exploration of the emptiness experienced by the twentieth-century subject. *Home and the World* tells of "the battle of people with emptiness and in emptiness for self-realization," where love is just one instance of the universal "battle" (and not simply a Romantic "quest") for self-realization. Ginzburg elsewhere defines self-realization as the maximum that a person can achieve, the highest possible fulfillment of one's talents and abilities within a real environment with its inevitable obstacles, often accompanied by a feeling of social validation (but which may prompt a defensive posture—conscious or unconscious—against things one cannot achieve).[156] Like Proust's hero, Ginzburg's Otter is able to find fulfillment and an escape from emptiness through a clear-eyed self-awareness, which can illuminate every realm of life, public or private, and can find its best outlet, perhaps, in writing. In the romantic sphere, he needs to sense his partner's inexhaustible love in order to confirm that the relationship is real. He can overcome his complex of "impotence" with nothing more than this validation—he does not need an audience.

Since Otter is a person of the "intellectual type," his erotic psychology is not determined (as Ginzburg would have it) by the external circumstances surrounding his love. Lialia has a sexual inferiority complex of a different kind. She fears being regarded as "a woman whom no one wanted to marry," and therefore requires a publicly acknowledged relationship. Having had no visible relationships with men, and lacking confidence in her own attractiveness, she has a psychological need to avoid having a reputation as a virgin—a position that combines infantilism with old age (the stereotypical and much-maligned "old maid"). However, Lialia cannot admit to all of this without sexually humiliating herself. Thus, it is only Ginzburg's analysis that finds the lie in her explanation that she wishes to marry for "social position" and material security. As her authorial commentary shows, Ginzburg judges Lialia's behavior to be outdated: "in our living conditions, these types of things [independence, a social position] for women only partially depend on marriage and can be created or destroyed independently."

Communication is a central theme in *Home and the World*, as it was in the early fictions about the "first love." And speaking in the register of romantic love is (and should be, according to Otter) impossible. Those lofty words have lost their meaning—they are "dead," particularly since the period of their happy love has ended. Hence, when Lialia asks, "Do you love me?" she confronts Otter with a dilemma:

> Silence. For Ot., with his agonizing sensitivity to the word, it's impossible to pronounce this word as an empty one. This word in its pure form can only be torn from him by a momentary surge, a changed consciousness; otherwise he utters it with the reservations characteristic of an ironic and skeptical consciousness. But it's impossible to be silent indefinitely. It's rude, insulting. And so he says quietly, in a completely unnatural voice: *Liubliu* [I love (you)]. Before he pronounced this word, his thoughts tossed about, seeking a context, a way around it. And found nothing. So he pronounced this word completely, in pure form. But a strange, dead intonation served as his way around it. The intonation expressed the fact that he was pronouncing this word as unreal. Intonation saved him from a lie. He pronounced this word, feeling as if he were letting it drop into the void.
>
> And Lialia said, "Oh no, no, you don't have to . . . ."

Молчание. Для От. с его мучительной чувствительностью слова невозможно произнести это слово как пустое. Это слово в чистом виде у него может вырвать только мгновение подъема, измененного сознания; иначе он выговаривает его с оговорками, свойственными ироническому и скептическому сознанию. Но молчать до бесконечности нельзя. Это уже грубость, обида. И он говорит тихо, совершенно неестественным голосом: Люблю. Прежде чем он произнес это слово, его мысли метались, обыскивая контекст, оговорку. И не нашли. И он произнес это слово полностью, в чистом виде. Но странная, мертвая интонация послужила оговоркой. Интонация выразила, что он произносит это слово, как ненастоящее. Она предохранила его от лжи. Он произнес это слово с таким ощущением, как будто роняет его в пустоту.

И Ляля сказала:—Ах нет, нет,—не надо . . .[157]

In this scene, Otter attempts to satisfy two moral imperatives: to be polite and not to lie. The utterance "I love you" (or the single Russian word for "I love," whose ending reveals the first-person governance) should have real signifying power, but is now meaningless and "empty." Through intonation designed to express his disagreement with his own word, Otter creates a double-voicedness. He fills the word with his emptiness. His voice communicates to Lialia that she has forced him into an unpleasant predicament. This scene is in stark contrast with Vasya's communications in the "Disorderly Notes" and with Ginzburg's early diary entries, which aim to convey hidden desires and to enhance the symbolism of a great, tragic love. Otter is bent on breaking this spell, on bringing the external world into alignment with the purer resolutions that he has inwardly made.

The passage detailing Otter's intense physical and ethical response to the word *liubliu* exemplifies the kind of viewpoint Ginzburg provides on her hero. His third-person voice heightens the tone of analysis, detachment, and even despair, while it gives access to the hero's emotions. But the passage also provides other perspectives on Otter: there is a generalizing voice that summarizes his type as ironic and skeptical, a subjective voice that traces his thoughts and expresses his discomfort, and an indeterminate voice that may either express his own judgments or the author-narrator's. (This ambiguity arises for example with the adjective "agonizing," and with the statement "Intonation saved him from a lie," which could be interpreted as either Otter's hope or the narrative truth.)

But despite her bold experimentation with prose form, Ginzburg falls into line with the literary "legal order" by depicting a homosexual love as heterosexual, and maintaining a traditionally gendered approach to her characters.

Home and the World also includes discussions of stereotypically gendered forms of self-realization: Ginzburg generalizes that as a rule, women seek fulfillment in love and everyday life, while men express themselves in their work and professional lives. Ginzburg does criticize this "atavism" (which, she says, is reinforced by biology), but her critique is not reflected in her depictions of Otter and Lialia. The author compares Lialia to women in bourgeois societies because her psychology is prone to "parasitism and complete infantilism." Her irresponsibility and selfishness stem from her dominant quality—light-mindedness (*legkomyslennost'*), which Otter tells her is "when a person gives in to the impulses of the moment." (Many of Ginzburg's principal female characters, most of all the one modeled on her mother, share this flaw.) Lialia totally lacks an "understanding of the iron necessity of choice"—a lack which the author claims is "generally characteristic of women."[158]

In a surprising move, but in line with mainstream approaches to gender roles, Otter and the author prescribe marriage for Lialia as a corrective to her character flaws. By creating inevitable and irrevocable responsibilities, marriage and children could bring her "salvation." Otter lectures Lialia, not sparing her feelings in voicing his convictions:

> —Listen, it's the same as with work. Just as you can't do a damn thing on your own, but when you're in the office you work well—in the same way, you need a family, a child, responsibilities that are totally obligatory; so that you can't avoid them with words. When a child whines, you can't talk your way out. Maybe you'll be a good wife and mother. How could I know? It's like punching a clock. The only thing that can save you.

> —Ты пойми это то же самое, что с работой. Так же как ты сама по себе не черта не можешь делать а на службе работаешь хорошо; так же тебе нужна семья, ребенок, обязательства совершенно принудительные; чтобы нельзя было от них отделаться словами. Когда ребенок пищит, тут не поговоришь. Может ты будешь хорошая жена и мать. Почем я знаю? Это как номерок вешать. Единственное, что тебя может спасти.[159]

We have traveled a long way from the Dostoevskian temptations of the early diaries. Otter's advice sets forth Ginzburg's current theory about the use value of "norms" for average people. Otter himself, however, is one of the elect: he takes words seriously, seeks realization in his creativity, and his sense of responsibility does not depend on the dictates of institutional arrangements (although this does not protect him from erotic failure).

The reader might wonder: since Ginzburg conceived of personality structures as determined in complex ways by the environment, why was she not willing to abandon the tradition of a male aesthetic position, inherited from Weininger and from the literary past? Given her ethical pact with the word (words do and should reflect reality and are won through experience and suffering), why does Ginzburg seemingly violate it by fictionalizing her gender and sexuality? The answer seems to be that despite the fact that in daily life she must have spoken with grammatically feminine inflections, she nevertheless saw her position in love and literature through the lens of cultural models, which still prevailed in defining the male viewpoint as the subject position. One recalls Ginzburg's favorite adage from Chateaubriand, as quoted by Pushkin (in an unsentimental letter to a friend about his impending marriage): "Il n'y a de bonheur que dans les voies communes." For her, the only "valuable" and "complete" love had been constructed in literature and society from a male perspective. She quotes an anonymous N.N. as saying: "Love is not a female affair: or if you wish, not an affair of the female mind" ("Любовь—не женское дело: если хотите, не женского ума дело").[160] Her choice also speaks to her overwhelming desire to represent experiences that she saw as socially and historically typical, rather than to appear as a radical.

But Ginzburg's creative decisions can produce noticeable incongruities. In *Home and the World*, there is no explanation as to why Lialia's relationship with Otter must remain "secret" and thus cannot provide her with the appearance of being sexually desirable and experienced. In the description of the relationship based on the same biographical experience (Ginzburg's relationship with the woman Lialia represents) in "The Stages of Love," problems caused by "rumors" and "the internal abnormality of the situation" motivate B., the female, to take up with a third person (presumably male) in order to effect "the unconditional negation of the very essence of the relationship." The hypothetical reader who does not sense the camouflage of homosexual content within heterosexual role-play in *Home and the World* might wonder why Otter does not consider marrying Lialia. Does it not sound strange for him, as her lover, to recommend that she save herself by marrying someone else and bearing someone else's child? The reader familiar with Ginzburg's methods of transforming her experiences would understand that she is attempting to represent one of her relationships without fictionalizing the whole of it.

Ginzburg's decision to portray lesbian relationships using a heterosexual model limited what she would call "the range of the depictable" (*okhvat izobrazhaemogo*).[161] For instance, there are gaps in the explanations of the pressures on the relationship between Otter and Lialia—pressures that are partly responsible for driving them apart. Another consequence of Ginzburg's decision to portray her experiences through a male autobiographical hero is the intensification of her critique of women. If she had presented Otter as a woman, she could have created a positive female character—more positive than the male version, since this figure could have served as a model for overcoming traditional gender stereotypes and paths to self-realization. Ginzburg could then have treated the obstacles blocking Otter's self-realization as other than self-inflicted. But, let us recall, Ginzburg's alter ego was "indifferent" to "humanistic novels about the mercilessness of society."[162] Otter, who fulfills all the male stereotypes as he dominates and instructs Lialia, thus becomes yet another messenger of society's "mercilessness."

Ginzburg's attempts to make her personal experiences the basis of far-reaching generalizations reach their height in "The Stages of Love." Intended in some form to become part of *Home in the World,* this piece essays a universal theory of love's course—how romantic attachments take shape, and how they inevitably crumble and sometimes manage to re-form.[163] Her four basic stages are: (1) "the beginning" (or initial knot); (2) the moment of forming (*oformlenie,* a term she proposes as an improvement on Stendhal's "crystallization"); (3) "the catastrophe" (a crisis caused by hindrances to the fulfillment of desire, by incompatible desires, or by the fading of desire); and (4) the "dénouement (disintegration or re-attachment)."[164] Ginzburg devotes particular attention to the second phase, where the intellectual's tendency to formulate an "idea" (an erotic concept that shapes desire) is most in evidence. As it turns out, her autobiographical hero's predicament is in fact due to his extreme propensity to construct symbolic structures and to desire according to a specific erotic concept. Thus, in the fourth case, when A.'s lover realizes that A.'s physical needs are secondary to his concept of "happy love," this concept is destroyed. A.'s desire then fades, and the third stage, the "catastrophe," is reached (it would be the first of several).

Paradoxically and yet characteristically, "Stages of Love" is not only Ginzburg's most expansive and abstractly conceived theory on love but also her most intimate in its details, however sparing they are. The draft's positioning in the notebooks reveals what motivated the piece: her need to understand four of her relationships, and in particular the most recent one. She writes the piece in two entries. In the second of these, dated 23 December 1934, she begins by asking, "why did this love so resemble heartsickness, heaviness, fear? . . . Returning to our ideas about the 'stages of love' " ("почему эта любовь так похожа на болезнь сердца, на тяжесть, на страх? . . . Возвращаясь к соображениям о 'стадиях любви' ").[165] An agonizing personal question abruptly gives way to a case study with a dry, scientific structure and style. The account is harsh and analytical, since only honesty could bring about the desired therapeutic effect (reminding one of "A Story of Pity and Cruelty" from the blockade, a subject of chapter 5). Ginzburg unflinchingly represents her alter ego as a character with low self-esteem, who is damaged by his tragic first love and his overall failure to find sexual fulfillment or mutual love before age thirty-one, and who aches to rid himself of "the yoke of infantilism." We also see that A. has an "old habit of mixing love with other feelings—tenderness, solicitude, etc., developing precisely though the suppression of more direct erotic manifestations; he even has a need to apply and exercise these blocked [*glokhnushchie*] capacities." In her portrayal of A., Ginzburg seems to reach an unprecedented level of openness and intimacy, perhaps made possible by the high level of abstraction. A similar level of intimacy (paired with wishful thinking) appeared in the earlier sketches about Vasya, a more fictionalized text detailing physical caresses. Now, Ginzburg makes a barely fictional confession of the most difficult kind, regarding sexual inadequacy: a physical love had seemed necessary to A., but as it turns out, he desired not sex but only the experience of "happy love" as a concept, to overcome his "infantilism."

Ginzburg's generalizations about romantic dynamics and emotions succeed in achieving universality, and yet the informed reader might discover in them patterns typical of lesbian love. For example, one of A.'s attachments, a "camaraderie amoreuse" without physical intimacy, may be common in a repressive society. And the emotion of "tenderness," which looms so large in the "The Stages of Love," had been called an unfortunate tendency of lesbians who fear "formalism in love" by the speaker of "Dialogue about Love."[166] Moreover, the reader with a knowledge of the archival manuscripts discussed in this chapter would be able to fill out the details of the compressed episodes that both illustrate and serve as material for the generalizations. Thus one can find here a thumbnail sketch of Ginzburg's first love (Zelyonaya), which began with the concept of a younger admirer's servitude (*sluzhenie*) to a "magnificent woman," and which A. transformed into a "grandiose symbolic structure" that "swallowed up his consciousness" for several years. Ginzburg attributes A.'s "erotic groveling" primarily to the lack of other spheres for his self-realization, such as a successful intellectual career. After repeated rejections, a new concept takes hold of A.: a great unrequited love (*velikaia neschastnaia liubov'*), which eventually fades after a long period of suffering. Ginzburg then comes up with a formula: "Joy turned into a habit—that's a way of building up the conditions for a normal life. But suffering turned into a habit—that's an absurdity" ("радость, обращенная в привычку,—это жизнеустройство. Но обращенное в привычку страдание—это абсурд").[167] She has pared down a personal experience, framed it in general terms without any gender-specific markings (other than grammatical ones), and subordinated it to the project of demarcating the stages of love.

I would argue that the way in which this piece—without any markings of the first person—relates to autobiographical experience gives rise to its particular power or, as Ginzburg would say, "pathos." It is, Ginzburg notes elsewhere, a person's fate that the reader finds to be the most emotional and compelling aspect of literature, and the most difficult to examine in fragmentary in-between prose.[168] The psychological urgency that is so apparent in "The Stages of Love" lends the piece a particular poignancy. One of the more powerful lines comes near the end:

> A. renounced, in succession, happy love, love, and physical intimacy. Probably, it's his final renunciation. It is that uttermost point that exists in every feeling (a point might be located at various degrees of distance from the direct erotic objects), a point that people approach but never overstep, because it is the final form of erotic accommodation, and beyond it there's nothing but meaningless sufferings.

> А. отказался последовательно от счастливой любви, от любви, от физической близости. Вероятно, это последний отказ. Это та крайняя точка, которая есть в каждом чувстве (она бывает расположена в разной степени удаления от прямых эротических объектов) и до которой доходят, но ее не переступают, потому что она последняя форма эротического приспосабливания, и за ней нет ничего, кроме бессмысленных страданий.[169]

The poignancy of this passage comes in the second sentence. The word "probably" (*veroiatno*), expresses a hope, or possibly a fear, that this will not be the final renunciation, that the relationship will find a way of surviving this latest catastrophe. The ambiguity of this passage suggests that A. does not foresee physical intimacy in his future. Ginzburg uses the third-person plural to fold A.'s behavior into a generalization whose sad implications are thereby softened. At the same time, her techniques of understatement and concealment may even heighten the reader's sympathy: A. is not, after all, simply an abstract variable.

"The Stages of Love" and *Home and the World* depict the kind of semifictional male alter ego that is typical of Ginzburg's narratives. It is this character who enables her to represent her experiences, and it is exclusively this character's thoughts to which the reader has access, his psychology and emotions being the focus of her analysis. She generalizes her experiences through exclusion, paring down, rather than through fictionalization or building up a social or physical world. Exploring how her experiences imperfectly translate into a certain point of view and framework helps one to better fathom what may be lost in these analyses and what may be gained, how the personal may intersect (and clash) with the more "universal" structures of love.

Turning briefly now to "The Return Home," a narrative she published during her lifetime, unlike the other works discussed here, we find Ginzburg drawing from and portraying the experiences of her "second love." There are scenes and dialogues in "The Return Home" that read like revisions—now compressed and distanced—of the draft materials for *Home and the World*. From different angles, Ginzburg investigates the psychological (almost physical) state of anxiety, indifference, and the fear of a "cessation of desires" (*ostanovka zhelanii*), creating a Hemingway-esque sense of emptiness. Halfway through the narrative, she introduces the character "Igrek" (Russian for the letter "Y") to illustrate and develop the theme of love, and more specifically a person's anxious return to his lover. Igrek's relationship with a woman referred to only as "She" closely resembles Otter's with Lialia, and A.'s with B.

"The Return Home" shifts between perspectives and characters, setting up the rough configuration that Ginzburg will use in subsequent narratives, including *Notes of a Blockade Person*.[170] Ginzburg's narrator is grammatically neutral; Igrek is grammatically male, but otherwise has no specifically gendered characteristics.[171] At certain moments, Igrek and the narrator seem to draw closer in their physical, emotional, and intellectual points of view. For example, when Igrek returns to Leningrad, we notice that the narrator also appears there, walking the streets alone in some indefinite temporality. And sections of Igrek's diary, interpolated into the story, are then discussed by the narrator.[172]

Ginzburg achieves what Gérard Genette regards as typical of the contemporary novel: a prose style that "does not hesitate to establish between narrator and character(s) a variable or floating relationship, a pronominal vertigo in tune with a freer logic and a more complex conception of 'personality.'"[173] For Ginzburg, this pronominal indeterminacy reflects the need for a new model of personality, one that moves beyond nineteenth-century notions of literary character. The tension between the first and third person in her prose is at once a statement about the implicit gendering of perspective in traditional representation, and a "making do" in order to express a nontraditional sexuality—a way of improvising in a cramped and impoverished situation, which may have an analogue to Ginzburg's early attraction to the theater during the years of War Communism.

CONCLUSION

Though Ginzburg wrote several notes and essays on love in the 1920s and 1930s, she excluded them from her published oeuvre. Perhaps she was aware that, despite her assertions to the contrary, and even after her processes of fictionalization and abstraction, her accounts speak in a tragic way to same-sex desire, or to tabooed love that is prevented from expression. Another reason Ginzburg may have left these writings unpublished is that she had already abandoned them by the 1940s, when she realized her dream for the quasi-novel in a different form, in "Otter's Day," which later became *Notes of a Blockade Person.* As she began to publish in her eighth decade, with a sense of the limited time remaining to her, she chose to give priority to the notebooks and other, more finished narratives that she could publish as separate fragments, as she did with "The Return Home."

Ginzburg's relation to her readership is another factor in her exclusion of these works from publication. A small number of loyal and enthusiastic younger friends had begun typing up sections of her notebooks in the 1960s. Ginzburg marked the manuscripts, indicating essays that her helpers should skip. These included most of her essays on love, perhaps from reticence about sexual matters. In interviews I conducted with Ginzburg's friends in younger generations (in 2003 and later), some said the topic of same-sex love was almost never broached in conversation; others recall frank discussions on homosexuality. Some generally open-minded friends of hers nevertheless spoke to me of Ginzburg's sexual orientation using the code word "eccentricity" [*chudachestvo*]; a few denied it adamantly.[174] Or perhaps Ginzburg ordered these manuscripts to be disregarded by her typists because they had come to seem less vital to her. In the 1980s, she excluded even many of these already "censored" typescripts from publication. It is important to realize that the treatment of same-sex love was subject to official censorship even at this relatively late date. Another of Ginzburg's considerations could have been her reluctance to "out" other women. In general, she honored and respected her friends' and partners' right to privacy and published only what would have been acceptable to them.

Many questions remain concerning Ginzburg's thinking on gender and sexuality and its place in her work. Since she appears to have left almost no new reflections about same-sex love in the postwar years, one wonders whether and how Ginzburg modified any of the views she expressed in the 1930s. Does the absence of further writings indicate that her views underwent no significant changes? Did she ever rethink the importance of the "norm"? One does see a reemergence of the first-person singular in the notebook essays of the postwar period, which may be related to her changing social status and attitudes toward self-presentation. It would be surprising if her perspectives on writing about love did not change as the twentieth century wore on, producing a broader distribution of aesthetic positions than before and more women writers who broke the taboos against writing directly about lesbian love.

Ginzburg herself never explained (at least in writing) her views on being a woman author, but implied through her choice of male perspectives and autobiographical heroes that gender and sex were fluid—that she could write successfully for or from the male perspective, becoming a transgender or genderless writer. She once recorded the opinion of her friend Anna Akhmatova, perhaps the quintessential example of a woman poet in Russia: "A.A. got upset, understandably, when people called her a *poetess,* and on the topic of *women's poetry* (Karolina Pavlova, Akhmatova, Tsvetaeva), she said: 'I understand that there must be male and female toilets. But in my opinion, this has nothing to do with literature.' "[175]

Natalia Sokolova, Ginzburg's niece, recorded the following conversation: "Liusia the prose writer in her *Notes of a Blockade Person,* in her 'narratives' was fond of writing from the first-person masculine, from the 'I' of a man. 'Like Gippius in poetry, so I do in prose,' Liusia said, laughing. 'It's just handier for me that way' " ("Люся-прозаик в 'Записках блокадного человека,' в своих 'повествованиях' любила писать от первого лица мужского рода, от 'Я' мужчины. 'Как Гиппиус в стихах, так я в прозе,' сказала как-то Люся, посмеиваясь.—'Так мне сподручнее' ").[176] It is telling that Sokolova makes an incorrect generalization: *Notes of a Blockade Person* is mostly written in the third person, with a few sentences introducing a first-person, genderless narrator. Only one small section "Paralysis" ("Otsepenenie") is written in the masculine first person.[177] In the manuscript version, this fragment was in fact written in the third person, about "Otter." In the 1960s, Ginzburg had carried out a revision, crossing out every instance of "he" and replacing it with "I."[178] This simple replacement demonstrates the fluidity of these two "persons," or voices, for her poetics—she may have sometimes thought of her "I" as a "he," and vice versa.

Indeterminacy and indirection, concealment and revelation, as well as disavowal and avowal, are significant elements of both Proust's and Ginzburg's prose in the treatment of autobiographical material.[179] Ginzburg inhabits and disinhabits a subject position with indeterminate gender, which complicates the generic orientation of her prose. Ginzburg herself argued that documentary literature possesses a unique dynamic of double understanding. Through the use of various signals orienting the text toward fact, authors grant their readers permission to supply extra-textual knowledge—from archival manuscripts, biographical research, historical sources, and so on—to their interpretations (even if some, like Rousseau, might dissuade their readers from creating independent accounts of events, they nevertheless invite such investigations through their choice of genre). Ginzburg offers many such signals: the existence of a first-person alongside the third, minimal fictionalization and lack of full-fledged proper names, the interconnection of pieces and their relationship to the notebooks, and the scholarly or scientific approach in analyzing the generalized "person of her time." Some of her techniques, however, can be regarded in the opposite way, as orienting her prose slightly away from fact: the masculine third person, the use of semi-fictional names, and the fragmentation of the works.

The creation of characters who are "not-I" seems to have been a crucial step in Ginzburg's writing process. Yet, the reader with a knowledge of her biography or her thoughts on Weininger will constantly be finding the "I" (or "she") hidden in the "he." Still, in some respects, Ginzburg's "I" fits uncomfortably and incompletely in the male shell. Ginzburg had written in her early diary that the world of men was not hers to own in real life: "if I were a man (no, better not get carried away, because with this kind of 'if,' I would already not be myself)" (Diary I, 46). The rhetorical impact of "he" is different from "I"—the abstraction and fictionalization are firmer and more irrevocable than Proust's abstract first person. The third person affords greater opportunity to explore the social conditioning of the nonindividualist person. Even if Ginzburg prefers to elaborate a universal psychology of love, she uses the third person to treat other "categories of existence" such as professions and everyday life, in their social dimensions. She creates a fragmented, distanced self, in order to analyze, harshly and painstakingly, experiences from her own life.

Our examination has brought into focus the logic of Ginzburg's rhetoric of person and the importance for her aesthetics of the question of how to write about love. She sought to inhabit a traditional male perspective and to employ literary conventions while writing about a nontraditional love. In certain ways this is surprising, since—according to her own theories—documentary prose tends to be ahead of the curve; it "strives to reveal those relations in life that have not yet been mediated by the plot inventions of artists."[180] Yet, in writing about love, one factor that binds Ginzburg to tradition is a desire to connect to the broadest possible readership. She was aware that, just as in the Terror, people were indifferent as long as they remained personally untouched by events,[181] the same is true when it comes to love: "No one cries over what doesn't concern him" ("Никто не плачет над тем, что его не касается").[182] Over the half-century during which she composed her desk-drawer writings, she constantly appealed to an imagined audience of the broadest possible kind, and also to the lawful order that she was certain would outlive her. The grammar at her disposal was inadequate to her experiences of gender and sexuality, and her usage of the conventions of the masculine first and third person reflected the in-betweenness of her position.

CHAPTER 4

Passing Characters

In her book *On Psychological Prose,* first published in 1971, Ginzburg articulates the realm in which life and literature dynamically interact as we model our personalities: in daily life, people understand themselves and others through "creative constructs," carrying out the aesthetic work of "selection, correlation, and symbolic interpretation of psychic elements." The processes through which we compose and project our self-images resemble the creative acts authors perform when designing literary characters or lyric personae. Not only are these processes similar, they are symbiotic, since a personality "shapes itself, both internally and externally, by means of images, many of which have already passed through literature."[1] These images have a more intricate aesthetic structure in novels than in everyday life; the personality constructs in *promezhutochnaia literatura,* or in-between literature (for example, memoirs, diaries, letters, essays, confessions), tend to fall somewhere "in between" the two. Many of Ginzburg's own writings approach case studies, directly addressing selfhood and identity with a high degree of structure, blending the aesthetic and the scientific. And in her book, she asserts that great writers of in-between prose (Rousseau, Herzen) pioneered new conceptions of the self, which later entered into canonical literary genres such as the novel.

Ginzburg envisions an individual's self-construction (both the internal process and the external projection) as historically and socially conditioned through and through, but also as a set of willed acts. A person chooses, with varying degrees of conscious awareness, which qualities to invest into his image, and which to conceal, based on the requirements of "his milieu, his time, his actual situation, and his own abilities and potentialities."[2] External circumstances impose the "rules of the game" and limit choice. In her late essay "Generation at a Turning Point," Ginzburg describes how personalities took shape and diverged after the Revolution: "In one and the same social milieu, different historical characters are formed—depending on the situation, on personal qualities, on chance. *But this set of possible formations is not unlimited.* Personal psychological qualities fell into several varieties, which formed a stable typology."[3] The creative process of self-invention generally results in imperfectly fitting models and leaves a residue of discordant elements that are pushed aside but not entirely excluded from consciousness.[4] It is feasible that an individual living through dramatic historical times, or transitioning from one milieu to another, might change her image by reactivating formerly suppressed qualities, or suppressing those that were manifested earlier (changes occur in less dramatic time horizons as well—for example, between home and the workplace).

In this 1971 book, her most personal work of literary scholarship, Ginzburg elaborates a theory of personality formation while discussing French and Russian traditions of "psychological prose."[5] How are her notions of character and personality reflected in the sketches and analyses she wrote for the desk drawer? While in chapter 2 we looked explicitly at the genre of Ginzburg's notes, and in chapter 3 we looked at the rhetorical choices involved in the expression and analysis of an autobiographical other, this chapter will examine Ginzburg's concern with character and personality structure in relation to historical experiences.

The genesis of the ideas Ginzburg expressed in her scholarship of the 1970s had come decades earlier, in fragments she wrote beginning in the 1930s, where she attempted to understand how her contemporaries crafted themselves in response to external demands and changing situations. In these years, she sought to bridge history and the novel, asserting that both "are a process of understanding life; that is, a description of facts and an explanation of the connections between them." What's more, she continued, the same "facts" or subject matter (human lives) are central to each, though "taken on different scales."[6] She used the scale of the single person, and sought "a method that would be of use for understanding the historical process and for understanding the fate of a single individual as a social entity."[7]

In an environment where sociology did not exist as an academic discipline, and psychology was largely restricted to Pavlovian reflexology, Ginzburg improvised a far-reaching methodology.[8] She learned from the writers she admired most (chief among them Marcel Proust, Herzen, and Lev Tolstoy), while using the skills she had acquired as a Young Formalist, such as how to identify dominants and functions to describe literature as a complex system and dynamic historical phenomenon. Her analytical approach was influenced by social psychologists and philosophers popular in pre-Revolutionary and early Soviet Russia, many of whom fell out of favor in the thirties. Her conceptual vocabulary for discussing the components of personality and psychology includes Freudian notions such as repression and sublimation; concepts of "will" influenced by Friedrich Nietzsche (the "will to power," the "will to pleasure"); the idea of a weak or strong "life force," similar to Henri Bergson's creative "vital impulse" (*élan vital*), as an essential part of character (and not only among artists); and the universal drive to self-assertion, found in the theory of Alfred Adler as well as the novels of Tolstoy. Her constellation of typologies based on the chief ways in which a person experiences value appears to be inspired by Eduard Spranger's *Lebensformen* (1928).[9] Also important for her is William James's concept of a person's multiple social selves, and of the dynamics of self-seeking and self-estimation. Ginzburg's discussion of how a person's sense of self depends on a particular "group consciousness" is similar to George Herbert Mead's notion of the "generalized other" (though it is unknown whether she was aware of his 1934 volume, *Mind, Self, and Society*, at the time).[10]

In the 1930s, Ginzburg studied friends, acquaintances, and colleagues by observing their speech, attitudes, and behavior in everyday interactions or in settings such as a Writers' Union meeting. At this time, when she was moving away from the notebooks to more sociologically or analytically oriented work, Soviet society was becoming increasingly closed, hierarchical, rigid, and authoritarian.[11] Always looking to understand how social values are layered upon the individual, Ginzburg asks how various qualities "fall in" with a set of available identities, whether professional (for example, teacher, actor, administrator, *littérateur*) or personal (for example, wife, husband, mother, romantic partner, rival). She analyzes why intellectuals project images of, say, the "decadent," the "fatalist," or the "Don Juan." She titles one of her blockade-era notebooks "Passing Characters" (*Prokhodiashchie kharaktery*), emphasizing the transient nature of self-images, as well as the fragility of people whose everyday survival was always at risk.[12] Her title alludes to Jean de La Bruyère's *Les caractères* (1688), which Ginzburg later called "the greatest achievement of seventeenth-century social and moral typology."[13]

Neither of her books *On Psychological Prose* and *On the Literary Hero* treats Socialist Realism (with the exception of Gorky's *Klim Samgin*),[14] or the question of what happens to self-construction when restrictive policies prevent the flow of certain personality concepts between literature and life. In "The State of Literature near the End of the War" (written in 1944), Ginzburg discusses the unique and unprecedented situation that arose in the Soviet Union: it was not just actual censors, but their own "inner censors" that prevented many writers from incorporating their experiences into their literary works. This silencing severed the meaningful connections between literature and life.[15]

Lydia Ginzburg's notes from the archives (some still unpublished, others appearing recently) not only contribute to the understanding of personality in relation to historical circumstances, they also allow for a rare glimpse into the social history of Soviet Russia—in the microcosm of one Leningrad *intelligentsia* milieu—during Stalinism and in wartime. The most notable and unusual feature of the personality constructs Ginzburg identifies is their origin in some kind of failure, a fact that may be due to her obsessions, as well as to the harsh difficulties posed by Soviet society. Her subjects have suffered tragic fates: they forfeited material wealth and social status after the Revolution; during the blockade, they suddenly and dramatically lost their beauty and sexual attractiveness; they shed self-images undesirable in Stalinist Russia, such as that of "decadent." Again and again, Ginzburg analyzes people for whom "a different fate had been prepared" before history made its turn. To express the plight of a generation, she quotes Anna Akhmatova: "Just like a river, / I was deflected by my stalwart era" (the fifth of the "Northern Elegies" [1945]).[16] Historical changes afford Ginzburg the insight that "there are not only people who are born-again and resurrected, but there are also people who die again, and die repeatedly."[17] Nevertheless, paradoxically, her notes testify to people's resiliency in reinventing and reasserting themselves after every symbolic death.

The notes from the 1930s (at least those extant) contain little or no mention of such dangerous subjects as collectivization, the orchestrated famine in Ukraine, mass arrests, or purges.[18] They do, however, treat the policies and institutions that shaped the daily life of the Leningrad intelligentsia, such as the functioning of the Writers' Union, the university, communal apartments, and the organization of cemeteries and death rituals. During the relative cultural freedoms of wartime in the 1940s, Ginzburg reflects openly on the war's progress, both on a grand historical scale and as it relates to matters of life and death in besieged Leningrad (the distribution of food and housing, transportation, censorship, and directives concerning literature). And yet she addresses totalitarianism and absolute state power only obliquely, for example in the passages on the Leviathan (a term Ginzburg borrows from Hobbes as an allegory for the totalitarian state)[19]; she refers to Stalin only once, in a coded way (as "st" in "The State of Literature near the End of the War").[20]

The catastrophes of Stalinism and of the war manifest themselves profoundly in the studies of her contemporaries' confrontation with personal and professional failures. Ginzburg's notes give evidence of what Alexander Zholkovsky has termed the "power-ridden cultural atmosphere" of Stalinism.[21] Her characters must find ways to master their fates and prevail over the formidable obstacles in their way. For all of its fragmentariness, the post-individualistic self was still prone to self-assertion, to the promotion of its own ego and personality. Nadezhda Mandelstam, in her memoir, noted that the loss of the "I" inflicted on Soviet subjects by an "era of wholesale slaughter and death camps" paradoxically gave rise to widespread egocentrism. For a majority of people, she writes, "the most important thing in life is self-preservation: everybody looks after himself, by whatever means he pleases." In most, the loss of "self" and "atrophy of true personality" led to "blatant individualism with its extremes of egocentrism and self-assertiveness."[22]

Ginzburg demonstrates in her notes that the strategies people employ to assert themselves and strengthen their social standing as they adapt to the conditions of Stalinism are subtle and varied. Writing in 1980, she described the typical historical behavior of her generation as a combination of adaptability (motivated by "a dual mechanism: the evasion of suffering and the pursuit of pleasure"), justification, and indifference.[23] Her own strategy in the 1930s and 1940s seems to have involved acceptance, withdrawal, cynicism, and patience.[24] Her strongest survival tool was her analytical mind, which she used, as an observer, to dissect the strategies of others.[25] The notes discussed here must have served a dual purpose for Ginzburg: part coping mechanism, part études for a future novel. (The *Home and the World* manuscripts group certain characters under the rubric "Ruined" or "Damaged" [*Povrezhdennye, iskazhennye*].) While they offer insights into the psychology of her milieu, they are equally if not more revealing of the author's personal fixations. That she tended in the 1930s and 1940s to analyze failures (despite having many acquaintances who experienced success at least temporarily, such as Grigory Gukovsky, Olga Berggolts, and Konstantin Simonov) speaks to her struggle with the public expression of her own failed social realization in her professional and personal life.

An examination of Ginzburg's "passing characters" allows me to educe four crucial paradoxes in her representation of Soviet society. The first two paradoxes have already been suggested earlier: (1) Ginzburg's subjects are strong and determined to prevail, even if they have self-images of failure; (2) they are overwhelmingly self-willed individuals, even though they must choose their identities from a limited set of historically determined identities. The next two paradoxes are related to Ginzburg's own identity and her modes of writing: (3) she places exclusive emphasis on visible, social forms of existence, while the most essential part of her own identity (and existence), that of being a writer, had to remain hidden—a situation that finds a parallel in relation to her private lesbian sexuality[26]; and (4) Ginzburg's representation of everyday life allows for no interaction that is not infused with self-assertion. People are engaged in a Hobbesian battle with one another.[27] Meanwhile, her prose is built on self-distancing and the avoidance of self-assertion in every way. Her work allows one to perceive a difference (not posited by or verbalized in her theories) between social life and writing about it, in the sense that writing is not *necessarily* interested or implicated in power struggles. Ginzburg's impersonality and attempts at generalizing her self-image, especially in the works she designated as *povestvovaniia* (narratives), remove the autobiographical self as much as possible from the social battlefield of power.

GINZBURG'S THEME: THE FATES OF THE *INTELLIGENT*

Before examining particular self-images, it will be useful to make some observations about how Ginzburg identified her subject or hero more generally. Her notes and sketches document the lives of intellectuals who saw themselves as descendants of the nineteenth-century Russian intelligentsia, whose members Ginzburg defined as "conscious bearers of goal-oriented social ideas" who demonstrate a "readiness to suffer" for these ideas.[28] As historian Martin Malia has explained, the intelligentsia had fought for many of the goals that the Revolution realized in perverted form. It gradually ceased to exist as such, since opposition (the intelligentsia's previous function in relation to the tsarist regime) was punished, and the tradition of introspection had no place in a system where all questions had (purportedly) been answered.[29] Ginzburg's notes and sketches also tend to focus on people of her own generation who had undergone the same process of formation, whom she called, adopting Alexander Herzen's neologism, her *soplastniki* (a metaphor from nature evoking layers of rock that mark geological time, and here referring to a "historical layer").[30]

Ginzburg's collective literary hero is, thus, the Russian cultural *intelligent* of her generation who, like her, had welcomed the October Revolution as a teenager, and had flourished amid the new opportunities of the early 1920s. This was the type famously described in Boris Pasternak's poem "A Lofty Malady" ("Vysokaia bolezn' ") as being at once "fool, hero, *intelligent* . . . ," an idealist who had "Printed and penned placards / About the joy of his own sunset [demise]."[31] Beginning in the late 1920s and early 1930s, the humanities intelligentsia composed of the so-called fellow travelers (*poputchiki*) of the Revolution was faced with its main dilemma: whether (or not) to join the dominant "legal order" (*pravoporiadok*) under Stalin. For Ginzburg, the temptation to participate under Stalinism was encapsulated in Pasternak's lines: "Labor in common with all / At one with the legal order."[32] But then, since it was impossible according to Ginzburg to operate "outside the Revolution," how could the intelligentsia continue to function within or alongside it, while retaining its principles and its historic function?[33] She tracks her heroes' methods of navigating through a narrow set of choices in order to live, work, and create in the harsh conditions of the 1930s, 1940s, 1950s, and beyond—regarding this as her generation's tragedy. She also studies other problems of self-realization: how women make choices between career and family, and how unmarried women, sometimes closeted lesbians, escape feelings of sexual humiliation as a result of others' misperceptions. In the catastrophically devastating Leningrad Blockade, she analyzes how traumatized subjects reinvent new self-images after narrowly escaping starvation and death. Throughout the decades, she traces how intellectuals interact with the institutions of power in their field: universities, publishing houses, the Writers' Union.

The fact that Ginzburg studied members of the intelligentsia helps explain her bias toward perceiving self-conceptions as conscious and intentional constructions: she postulates that intellectuals exhibit a higher degree of self-conscious artistry than others when crafting their self-images. Here is her rough articulation of the idea of *avtokontseptsiia* (self-conception) from a 1936 notebook:

> A person (especially an *intelligent*) is an ideological creature. He can exist as fragmentarily and haphazardly as he wishes, but he must think of himself in a web of connected elements; these connections form a self-conception. The self-conception is a conscious awareness and aesthetic configuration of the empirical chaos of psychic life. The aesthetic configuration gives a person that which he needs so much—a sense of his own value. A person adorns himself psychologically with strength, if he is strong; if not, he adorns himself with his weaknesses; in any case he gets his way [claims what is his own].
>
> Человек (особенно интеллигент) есть тварь идеологическая. Существовать он может как угодно разрозненно и случайно, но, но [*sic*] мыслит себя он в обязательной связи элементов; связь элементов образует автоконцепцию. Автоконцепция это осознание и эстетическое упорядочение эмпирического хаоса душевной жизни. Эстетическое упорядочение дает человеку то, что ему так нужно—ощущение самоценности. Человек психологически украшается своей силой, если он силен; если нет,—он украшается своими слабостями; во всяком случае он свое возьмет.[34]

Here, the self-concept appears as an aesthetic embellishment but at the same time something vital and inescapable. In her notebook "The Word" ("Slovo"), from besieged Leningrad, Ginzburg writes similarly about the construction of a self-conception that goes beyond one's physical and psychological qualities as a way to "experience [*perezhivat'*] one's value," as well as for the sake of "beauty and interest."[35] Strong self-images act as armor in an embattled social sphere, allowing people to "claim what's theirs" (hence characters who are good at doing this should be destined to succeed). The stakes are high: the self-concepts analyzed here are formed in a time Ginzburg frequently refers to as one "lacking in stable daily life" (*bezbytnoe vremia*), and without a culture of leisure.[36] In framing self-construction as an aesthetic process, Ginzburg may be overplaying the fictional or symbolic aspect of self-images at the expense of the real pain and suffering experienced by individuals. This was a tendency of which she was self-critically aware.[37]

THE STRUCTURES OF HISTORICAL PERSONALITIES: GINZBURG'S METHODS

In a 1928 note, Ginzburg had declared the need to analyze that which was "governed by historical and psycho-physiological laws," rejecting two alternatives: exploring the unrepeatably personal, which could not be expressed in language, and constructing typologies, which would overwhelm or stifle her human material.[38] Nevertheless, in her research on psychology and behavior in the 1930s, she gravitated toward typification, seemingly driven by a desire to achieve order and clarity even as she knew that reality was more complex and fluid. She identified the dominant elements in her subjects' personalities in order to use them as a starting point for understanding their choices among the historical roles available to them at the time.

The articulation of types forms an explicit part of Ginzburg's unpublished "Method of Examining a Person" ("Metod rassmotreniia cheloveka"), dated January 1935. The first and most fundamental step of her analysis involves studying the ways in which a person experiences and realizes that which constitutes "value" to him or her.[39] The importance of value originates in Ginzburg's theory that what moves people to act is the "primary human need to realize the maximum of one's potential as a social being."[40] As she explains, people differ most of all in their ways of experiencing socially constructed value and pleasure, which then determine their reactions to their environments. In another programmatic essay from 1933, she divides people into six types on these grounds: empirical, sensual, emotional, intellectual, active, and ideological.[41] She placed these types on a hierarchical scale of value, from low to high in the aforementioned order, asserting that this was not simply her own personal judgment—such were the preferences of her historical era. (This interest in looking at types within a specific historical framework distinguishes Ginzburg from Eduard Spranger, to whose typology she makes reference.[42]) According to Ginzburg, the empirical, sensual, emotional, and intellectual types are better suited to bourgeois societies, since they thrive on luxury, decadence, and individualism: they are all in her opinion antisocial. Her elevation to the highest level of the ideological type, those whom she also calls "people of ideas" and "people guided by ideas," who derive fulfillment from experiencing and introducing valuable ideas into society, clearly stems from the tradition of the intelligentsia.[43] Curiously, she offers no example of this type as she does with the others. As a "type," Ginzburg describes herself as a combination of the intellectual (prototype: Proust) and the activist (prototype: Tolstoy). The intellectuals resemble ideological people, except that they enjoy the word as such (*samovitoe slovo*) instead of the idea.[44] Ginzburg's activists are professionals, builders, those who aim to be socially responsible and relevant, and who want to have an impact on other people. Both the activists and ideologues are capable of sublimating their immediate desires into social or creative values.

Following this first step of Ginzburg's 1935 method (studying a person's primary way of experiencing value), six more steps then follow: (2) studying how a person fights for the realization of his or her values, dealing with obstacles along the way; (3) studying the interaction between a person's biological and social qualities and changing social conditions; (4) building up a scheme and a structure that can organize the "nebulous mass of elements" composing a person's spiritual life, consciously selecting items that are repeated and interconnected, and omitting others; (5) distinguishing both primary and secondary characteristics in a person's structure (for instance, ambition is derived as a secondary characteristic from the primary trait of being action-oriented); (6) studying a person as existing on different layers or levels, on which she can react differently at the same time, giving rise to complexity and contradictions; and (7) studying a person as a historically changing entity, and as a historical actor. This last step involves understanding that different parts of a personality can enter into one's historical identity at various points during one's lifetime.[45]

This seven-step method forms the backdrop for Ginzburg's identification of the people in her midst, both in terms of their own self-images and in terms of their personality types and dominants of which they may be less aware. She often encapsulates these images in a single word, though she does not discount the greater complexities or the fact that the self is a fluid and complex arrangement of elements. Ginzburg's attempts to identify dominants form part of her concurrent work as self-styled literary sociologist, psychological essayist, and novelist-historian. The first two images I shall analyze are concentrated in sketches from the mid- to late 1930s.

INTELLIGENT WITH *NADRYV*

In a notebook entry from 1930, Ginzburg comments that the "intellectual with *nadryv*" was a common type in the milieu of her youth, characterized by "soulful depths, extreme interest in self-analysis, misfires of the psychic apparatus, which are immediately aestheticized."[46] The new epoch, fortunately in her opinion, was teaching her contemporaries a contrary lesson: "respect for the health of body and soul, health that delivers results; an interest in the common good [*interes k obshchemu*]; a perception of life in its social dimensions [...] professionalism, an unsqueamishness in relation to work that pays by the hour or to rough drafts; a slight squeamishness in relation to soulful depths, and to self-absorption and aestheticism."[47] Soviet ideology emphasized human civilization's mastery of a chaotic nature, whether through large-scale industrial, infrastructural, and agricultural projects, or programs of personal transformation directed at the human body and psyche. The consciousness of the New Soviet Person would be forged through overcoming weakness, illness, and irrationality (with the help of the word). This ethos affected writers such as Mikhail Zoshchenko, who tragically welcomed the turn toward an ideology of health as a way of overcoming his own psychological complexes.[48]

Nadryv, a Russian word defying simple translation, is rendered most effectively as "lacerations"[49]: it is most immediately associated with Fyodor Dostoevsky's *The Brothers Karamazov*. As indicated by translator David McDuff, alternative renderings include "ruptures," "harrowings," or "hysterias."[50] Robert Belknap remarks that in the novel *nadryv* is similar to buffoonery in its "perversity, willfulness, self-consciousness, self-dramatization, and absurdity," different only in that pain rather than laughter is now the moving force.[51] Through its association with Dostoevsky, *nadryv* contains its own parody: it can be either a sincere emotional outburst or the inauthentic travesty of one.[52]

The cognitive linguist Irina Levontina correlates the rise of *nadryv* with the rise of the class of *raznochintsy* in the 1860s. If Pushkin and the other noble members of the Arzamas society (1810s) idealized restraint in verbal expression and resolved questions of honor through duels, Vissarion Belinsky and Nikolai Chernyshevsky, as archetypal *raznochintsy*, strove to lay bare the ugliest stains on their souls in letters that call to mind Rousseau's *Confessions*. After its apotheosis in Dostoevsky's novels, this mode of being died out in self-parody, according to Levontina, who supports this assertion by adducing the late Soviet and post-Soviet writings of Viktor Erofeev, Sergei Dovlatov, and Joseph Brodsky, members of the 1960s generation. If we are to believe Ginzburg, however, *nadryv*—to whose manifestations she seems finely and critically attuned—retained its relevance to concepts of personality in both post-Symbolist and post-Revolutionary times. And while we possess scant evidence of Ginzburg's own image as understood by her contemporaries in the 1930s and 1940s, it was most likely the opposite of *nadryv*: she strove for health, control, and restraint, what one might call *sderzhannost'*. Her own self-concept was probably closer to the one she describes it in relation to both Pushkin and her contemporary, the poet Nikolai Oleinikov: "Oleinikov was formed in the twenties, when there existed (alongside others) a type called the 'diffident person' [*tip zastenchivogo cheloveka*] who was afraid of lofty phraseology, whether official-bureaucratic, or leftover-intelligentsia [phraseology] [(*frazeologii*) *perezhitochno-intelligentskoi*]. [. . .] A taboo was placed on any direct expression of the sublime, when it wasn't balanced by laughter."[53] The "diffident type" used irony and humor instead of overwrought confessional outpourings. In Ginzburg's aesthetic attitude toward verbal expression, evidenced in her writings, one also finds elements of Acmeist poetics, which Ginzburg terms *profil'trovannost'*—that is, the filtering or purification of feeling into plain words.[54]

In 1936, Ginzburg sketched a character "K.," a cipher for Rina (Ekaterina) Zelyonaya. (Here and elsewhere in this chapter, I will preserve Ginzburg's use of initials, since at times she intended this stylistic choice not only to preserve anonymity, but also to reserve a right to quasi-fictionality.)[55] Ginzburg had a special investment in (or obsession with) scrutinizing K.'s character, since K. is the figure whom Ginzburg describes in private diaries and encoded passages as the object of the most intense and devastating passion of her youth (1921–25, from the age of nineteen to twenty-three): a first, unrequited love that nearly destroyed her.[56] The 1936 sketch is cold, sardonic, and condescending. Ginzburg begins by quoting at length an encyclopedic dictionary entry on "hysteria," which in her view fits K. perfectly (*toch' v toch'*). Among the hysteric's traits and "ethical defects," the entry lists an inability to contain passing impulses, an unaccommodating nature, a desire to be the focus of others' attentions, mendacity, and eccentric behavior. Ginzburg elaborates on the character of the hysteric (which she detaches from gender) in her analysis of K. as childlike, egotistical, and narcissistic, a person who lacks in her "natural state" even the minimum ability to restrain her selfish urges. She believes K.'s proclivity for unrestrained Bohemian living stems from her "uncultured and disorganized" upbringing in a "time lacking in stable daily life" (*v bezbytnoe vremia*).[57] These tendencies were exacerbated by her choice of the acting profession, "the profession of women and hysterics—with the sole exception of those truly great people of the theater." K.'s "sexual narcissism" grows into "social narcissism," as she develops an addiction to the immediate satisfactions of occupying center stage. Ginzburg writes, "Professions have a deep correspondence to character (which does not hinder a profession from breaking a character, or a character from adapting to a profession)." In K.'s case, this was an appropriate career, based on her "sensual" personality type and her physical attractiveness.

After her role in the popular film *Podkidysh* (*Foundling*, 1939), Rina Zelyonaya would find success and fame, most of all for her mimicry of children's voices.[58] But in 1936, Ginzburg pities her situation: K. lacks a real home (she lives in one room with her mother and sister, who are dependent on her), a husband, and true friends. Her voice is half-wrecked (*na polovinu sorvannyi golos*)—a fitting physical manifestation of *nadryv*—as a result of the vocal acrobatics in her performances. She has not raised her profession to the level of true creative work (this also satisfies Levontina's description of *nadryv*)[59]: "In her professional life, K. rushed around, held several jobs [*sluzhila*], got tired, earned money—and never worked [*nikogda ne rabotala*]."[60] K. is a personal and professional failure who has taken the easiest road to value through the self-image of *nadryv*:

> Lacerations [*nadryvs*]—this is a surrogate of moral value and a kind of self-justification. [. . .] Neurotics gladly adorn themselves with lacerations. This term is in need of more precise definition, but in any case an element of conscious poking around at and harping on one's suffering enters into this concept. Nervous laceration [*nadryv*] is an aesthetic superstructure erected by neurotics over their failure. Hysteria is especially dangerous because it is a counterfeit of a higher psychic life. It is most dangerous in Russia, where in the cultural traditions of Dostoevsky, a pernicious equation has taken hold between suffering and value. In Russia this is available to all. K. is not very literary, but in her psychic existence the rampant "Dostoevsky-itis" is firmly implanted. She seeks a sense of self-worth in a self-conception of psychic imbalance, fateful doom and so on.

> Надрывы—это суррогат нравственной ценности и род самооправдания. < . . . > Невротики охотно украшаются надрывами. Термин этот нуждается в уточнении, но во всяком случае в это понятие входит элемент сознательного разглядывания и педализации страдания. Надрыв—эстетическая надстройка, воздвигаемая невротиком над своей неудачей. Истерия особенно опасна тем, что это фальсификат высшей душевной жизни. Больше чем где бы то ни было она опасна в России, где в культуре традиций Достоевского закреплено пагубное равенство между страданием и ценностью. В России это общедоступно. К.—мало литературна, но в ее душевном обиходе ходовая достоевщина привита очень прочно. Ощущение самоценности она ищет в автоконцепции психического излома, роковой обреченности и проч.[61]

Ginzburg's preliminary concept of *nadryv,* a gaping at one's own suffering, lines up with the definitions of Dostoevsky scholars and cognitive linguists. What is unique to Ginzburg's concept is the idea that a person forms an enduring aesthetic structure, something akin to a self-concept, which is meant to substitute for some other value.

In Ginzburg's reckoning, K. suffers most because of her unbridled will (*raznuzdannaia volia*)—composed of the will to influence (*volia k vozdeistviiu*) and the will to power (*volia k mogushchestvu*)—while lacking a will to self-constraint or self-compulsion (*volia k samoprinuzhdeniiu*). Though loved and admired, K. does not love in return; therefore, she heartlessly and selfishly mistreats others, and is not committed to her career in any higher sense. Ginzburg writes that K.'s absolute egoism has not been sublimated: the result is emptiness. Relying on Dostoevsky's legacy, she is able to advertise and magnify her distress through the self-concept of the hysteric, which flaunts the value of suffering.

In the blockade, Ginzburg refines the concept of *nadryv* while examining another "failure," G.B. Ginzburg redefines *nadryv* as "a condition and behavior that arise from experiencing a lack of correspondence between one's own value and the possibility of realizing this value."[62] Returning to the root of the word (*ryv* or *r/v*, tear), one might imagine that an outburst emerges from the gap between potential and actual achievements. And, as Ginzburg argues, *nadryv* is a mechanism for broadcasting, through a show of suffering, one's potential, unrealized value.

In G.B.'s case, the primary value whose realization has been obstructed is that of her "femininity" or womanhood—which had earlier been ensured by her beauty and "sex appeal" (*zhenshchina krasivaia i seksapil'naia*). Ginzburg places G.B., as a typical historical phenomenon, into two categories: (1) the déclassé bourgeois intelligentsia; (2) women who fail in family life but are then incapable of attaining self-fulfillment in professional life either, due to weak impulses and an absence of specific talents. Ginzburg writes that, as a weak, submissive, and dependent character, G.B. pleases men only temporarily, before being inevitably jilted. Married at the young age of sixteen, she had an unhappy and childless union with her husband. Like many women in this position, according to Ginzburg—who clearly identifies with what she defines as the more typically masculine manner of self-realization—G.B. has two choices for "ersatz-realization": to get a job (*sluzhit'*) or to study. She entered graduate school, only to be expelled for acting and speaking like a "*lady*" (*dama*), behavior that provoked the powers-that-be into failing her on a political exam.

A "hysterical narcissist" (Ginzburg consistently links *nadryv* with the hysteric), G.B. builds a self-concept around failure precisely because she has full confidence in her "feminine value."[63] Ginzburg argues here that *nadryv* is "affirmation through denial." As the hero of Dostoevsky's *Notes from Underground* teaches us, overt self-humiliation amplifies one's significance, by making obvious the lack of correspondence between what one deserves and one's actual fate.[64] G.B.'s *nadryv* manifests itself in lamentations, sometimes adorned by the speech habits of the intelligentsia (acquired in her youth), but often laying bare primitive concerns: fulfilling her appetites—whether for food or sex. In the Blockade, interests in food and physical comforts take on a general, socially acceptable or even heroic significance (tied to the city's survival), and thus her self-image develops in the direction of greater self-exposure. Ginzburg imagines G.B. justifying her self-concept thusly: "life has brought me, an educated woman (a graduate student), to the point of talking like a whore." Her *nadryv* is therefore partly naïve, partly conscious. G.B. is able to delight doubly: "in the satisfaction of primitive impulses" (speaking openly about sex and food), and "in the experience of her own self-conception."

KHAMSTVO

Like *nadryv*, *khamstvo* is a Russian behavioral concept that does not lend itself to a one-word translation into English. Though our focus here will be on the 1930s, the later reflections on *khamstvo* by Sergei Dovlatov, a Russian émigré writer who lived in New York City, can help us understand this phenomenon (which he considered to be virtually absent from American society):

> *Khamstvo* differs from rudeness, insolence, and impudence in that it is unconquerable, in that it is impossible to do battle with, that faced with it all you can do is retreat [...] it is none other than rudeness, insolence, and impudence all in one, but meanwhile—multiplied by impunity. [...] Precisely with its impunity, *khamstvo* kills you on spot, you cannot oppose it with anything except your own humiliation, because *khamstvo* is always "from the top down," it is always "from the strong to the weak," because *khamstvo* is the helplessness of the one and the impunity of the other, because *khamstvo* is inequality.[65]

Khamstvo, which one might translate as "offensive boldness," or "selfish impunity," is built from the noun *kham* (boor, heel, swine)—originally referring to Ham, one of Noah's sons. Contemporary usage, which extends far beyond the biblical reference, has also produced a verb, *khamit'* (to act rudely, with impunity). While the *kham* is a powerful figure, many thinkers have seen this boorish behavior as emerging from weakness. In a 1906 essay "The Approaching *Kham*" ("Griadushchii kham"), the Symbolist and Christian thinker Dmitry Merezhkovsky defined *khamstvo* as the worst of all possible slavish behaviors—that is, the philistinism that he saw (following Herzen) as common to positivists and the petty bourgeoisie in Europe and Asia.[66] Yuri Lotman, in a television lecture from 1989, aligned *khamstvo* with "the psychology of a slave [...] , the psychology of a person who has been humiliated, who therefore does not respect himself and tries to compensate for his lack of self-respect by humiliating others."[67] Lotman finds the opposite of *khamstvo,* a widespread twentieth-century phenomenon (common to both slaves and colonizers), to be *intelligentnost'*, whose characteristics are "civility, psychological sensitivity, the ability to suffer not only from physical pain."[68]

The *kham* assumes a position of such superiority and invincibility that the natural response, if it is to be a vocal one, is none other than *nadryv*, since "you cannot oppose it with anything but your own humiliation." *Khamstvo*, in its contemporary meaning, is more or less a post-Revolutionary phenomenon, having become a way of life during the era of great social transformations, of shortages and poverty administered by an indifferent or cruel bureaucracy, of ideological lies, and high stakes.[69] It seems to combine in a particularly toxic mix with communist ideology, if the latter becomes a tool for abusing one's personal enemies, neighbors, family members, or colleagues. Yet it may also be used simply for the pleasure of experiencing the power of one's position. One finds the *kham* in the satirical prose of Mikhail Zoshchenko and Mikhail Bulgakov.[70] Shifts in social norms seemed to give free reign to *khamstvo*.[71]

What relationship might *khamstvo* have to a person's own failure? Is it a self-image, or a personality "dominant" diagnosed by another? As Ginzburg writes in *On Psychological Prose*, "the individual does not say to himself, 'I am a scoundrel, a toady, a troublemaker, an envious person' "[72]—it is most commonly a judgment we make about others, an epithet bestowed by the injured party, in speech or in writing (where the injured may take revenge).[73] Identifying oneself as a *kham* would most likely be an act of self-judgment, as a prelude to self-improvement. Alternatively, negative self-images can be a form of bravado, an attempt to embellish oneself or make oneself more "interesting."[74]

The Soviet-styled Romantic poet Vladimir Mayakovsky constituted a prominent model of the *kham*, possibly popularizing and elevating this image just as Dostoevsky was seen to do with *nadryv*. Whether or not he used the word in reference to himself, many recognized his image as a *kham*. Writing in 1927, the poet and critic Vladislav Khodasevich criticized Mayakovsky's *khamstvo*, which he painted as a harmful version of the "cretinism" and "romanticism" of the *zaum* ["transsense"] poets (among whom, incidentally, Mayakovsky did not belong): "[Mayakovsky] was the first to make vulgarity and rudeness not the material, but the very meaning of poetry. [. . .] He filled the zero, empty meaning of *zaum* poetry with a new content: horsey, swinish, 'simple, like mooing.' A *kham* stood in place of a cretin. And the *kham* became 'the voice of the masses.' "[75] Alexander Zholkovsky, in part launching his analysis from Khodasevich's, has explored the image or myth that Mayakovsky created for himself as that of a *kham*, who advertises his hatred for children, the elderly, nature, the city, "normal life," and literary tradition.[76]

In August 1989, Ginzburg summarized Mayakovsky's image as congruent with the Romantic's pose of loneliness and separation from the crowd, with a Soviet-era spin, where the abject poet on stage hurls insults at the audience. She writes: "Mayakovsky is a romantic, with all of the basic signs—a hypertrophy of the lyric I, the conflict between the poet and the crowd, the opposition of higher love to base desires. Mayakovsky is the romantic model in its *kham* variety [*eto romanticheskaia model' v khamskoi ee raznovidnosti*]."[77] Perhaps Mayakovsky's *khamstvo* was, in part, a response to the pain of feeling unloved.[78]

To be an effective *kham* requires a position of some power or authority. It is a suitable self-concept for those who have lost stature in the past, and then risen again (sufficiently to oppress others with impunity) in professional or social hierarchies. In Ginzburg's record and analysis of the Writers' Union Meeting that took place in Leningrad from 6–7 August 1943, she characterizes the poet Alexander Efimovich Reshetov as a *kham*. He has "a years-long condition of being wounded (he did not succeed at becoming an administrative leader) in combination with organic *khamstvo*. Thanks to his marriage to a prominent literary bureaucrat, he's found himself in a peculiar (unofficial) position, on the strength of which he can play dirty tricks on anyone."[79] Reshetov, as Ginzburg describes him, is a poet who conforms exactly to the official line. Vera Inber, a poet who is more senior and slightly more independent (yet still publishable), suggests to him at this 1943 meeting that the time for ultra-militant war poetry (with its refrain "Beat the enemy!") has passed. Reshetov, who poses as the "fine young fellow" of folktales (*dobryi molodets*), boosts his macho image with the ideology of patriotism, which is on the rise. Ginzburg detects strains of racism in Reshetov's comment that Inber does not understand truly Russian feelings, together with his passing remark about her "languishing voice" (*govorit s 'tomnym golosom'*). (The official, massive anti-Semitic campaigns were still a few years off.) He implies that she is "a rotten female intellectual and a Jew" (*kak gniloi intelligentka* . . . *kak evreika*).[80] His impudent style, in Ginzburg's opinion, recalls that of RAPP, the Russian Association of Proletarian Writers (1923–32), whose poets may have taken their style from Mayakovsky.

In roughly the same period as she wrote the sketch of K.—that is, in the years of high Stalinism and the Terror—Ginzburg analyzed "S.," a long-time neighbor inside her communal apartment and the older sister of a close friend from her student years.[81] S. hailed from a wealthy Armenian family in Tbilisi. In the sketch, Ginzburg imagines a counterfactual biography for S.—the life for which she was destined had the epoch not diverted it: "High society life [*svetskaia zhizn'*] with all of the fictitious yet complex activity it presupposed; all sorts of other activities, such as studying in the conservatory, pleasant because optional; marriage, without the unpleasant aspects caused by poverty, i.e., without taking place in one single room (half for the wife, half for the husband), in general without the necessity of being cramped."[82] It was an "empty" life, but it would have been compensated for and lightened by the sheer multitude of pleasant and distracting "fictions" usually found in "everyday life."

Instead of this enjoyable existence, S., who is nearing forty, has "achieved loneliness and cold," and predicts for herself a gloomy, solitary old age. In Ginzburg's schema of personality types, S. is sensual (but not in the realm of erotic love) and in possession of an active, strong life force. Marriage is an unrealistic prospect for her due to her "absolute egoism," whereas life as a casual flirt is also out of the question, "since in our time people have neither the time, nor the money, nor the taste, habit, or ability" for such a thing. In Ginzburg's view, sexual independence has come easily to S. because of her "frigidity."[83] Economic independence has required more effort. S., who has become a teacher, has formed an image of herself as a "female toiler who sprouted from a society woman" (*obraz truzhenitsy, prorastaiushchei iz svetskoi zhenshchiny*). She fell into the teaching profession almost by accident and proved to be good at it, with her verbal gifts and "clear practical mind." Teaching in fact allows her to realize her "feminine" impulses to be the center of attention, and to satisfy her "thirst for power," her tendency toward *khamstvo.* As a pedagogue and an "interesting woman," Ginzburg writes, S. can permit herself to "yell, interrupt others, and bang her fist on the table," while still being liked by her students and viewed as "something exotic." S.'s *khamstvo* is linked to her practicality and directness. Ginzburg finds in S. a redeeming quality: she does not tolerate falsehood, whether for the sake of ideology, literariness, or pettiness.

The *kham* and the "*intelligent* with *nadryv*" would seem to flourish in unequal, hierarchical societies—like those of pre-Revolutionary and Stalinist Russia. Interestingly, for the women she analyzes, Ginzburg finds the roots of these personalities in the relationship between pre-Revolutionary upbringings (or class identities) and new Soviet realities. For instance, S.'s self-image as a *kham,* in Ginzburg's account, results from the fact that she was raised with a sense of entitlement (conscious or unconscious), seemingly predestined to be a "master" of life (*khoziain zhizni*), only to be subsequently crushed by reality, where both a comfortable marriage and a joyful, easy life prove impossible. S., unconventionally, channels her aristocratic style and verbal flair into this *khamstvo*, adapting her image to her workplace environment. From the example of S. and others, it becomes obvious to an observer how self-conceptions change across biographical time in response to external, historical pressures.

Though Ginzburg does not hint at the Terror, her sketch contains vague references to a bleak social environment: S. has a gloomy outlook on social reality, because she has been prevented from living her life hedonistically: "her way of thinking is to transfer blame to the circumstances and grow angry at the circumstances. There can be no hedonistic life, and therefore life is horrible, everything is a lie, it would be better to die."[84] The fact that her psyche was "adapted for a light and merry passage through life" makes her "spite and gloominess" emerge ever more sharply:

> The sight of others' happiness, the sight of carefree and merry-making people calls up in her a particular spite. She considers this a mistake, an act of thoughtlessness or vulgarity, bad tone. She senses with her whole organism that she should have had a good life, that she is predestined and suited for having a good life. And she can only understand that things are bad for her if they are bad for everybody, if nothing can be good in principle, and if people who imagine that they have it good are stupidly deluded or are stuck on some lower level of development.

> Особенную злобу вызывает у нее вид чужого счастья, вид беспечных и веселящихся людей. Она считает, что это ошибка, недомыслие или вульгарность, дурной тон. Она всем организмом ощущает, что ей должно было бы быть хорошо, что она предназначена и приспособлена к тому, чтобы ей было хорошо. И понять, что ей плохо она может только исходя из того, что всем плохо, что хорошо не может быть принципиально, и люди, воображающие, что им хорошо глупо заблуждаются или стоят на неком низшем уровне развития.[85]

Ginzburg's critique takes on an especially macabre, almost perverse quality when one considers that she was writing her sketch during the Terror. S.'s sister fell victim to the repressions during this period (arrested on 4 February 1938, executed on 28 June 1938 in Leningrad), a fact that of course could not be mentioned even in desk-drawer notes. Despite S.'s dismal outlook, Ginzburg writes of how her positive sense of life and strong will find "loopholes" (or ways of being expressed) in three primary areas: smaller pleasures (concerts, and so on), verbal brilliance (which runs in the family), and a strong work ethic.

We see in the case of S. how *khamstvo* can be combined with the positive self-image of a person who is practical, captivating, and who speaks the difficult truth. As Ginzburg observes it, *khamstvo* in its Soviet variety can grow out of the confrontation between a pre-Revolutionary past and the difficult present of the 1930s. Her notion that Mayakovsky was following "the Romantic model in its *kham* variety" likewise shows an orientation toward the past, as she finds the poet adapting an older model to the embattled post-Revolutionary cultural sphere.

PASSING CHARACTERS IN THE SIEGE: THE "DYSTROPHIC WHO SURVIVED"

In the blockade, Ginzburg observes how Leningraders rapidly transition among different self-conceptions, while acclimating to new bodies, social positions, and environments. In her notes from 1942–43, she depicts people who have narrowly escaped death from hunger, cold, and bombs, and who have lost their previous identities along with their spouses, their jobs, and their habitual outer appearances.[86] She writes, "Now people have to define themselves anew in the most difficult circumstances, when all surrogates and fictions [*zameniteli i fiktsii*] have been lost."[87] The construction of a self-image is, in a sense, a search for new fictions, the most banal of which still promise to adorn or beautify one's life. Some of the blockade self-images Ginzburg identifies are the "dystrophic," the "fatalist" and the "troglodyte." What distinguishes these siege identities from those of the 1930s is their universality and their minimalism, as faint hints at reemerging personality structures.

The term "dystrophy" (*distrofiia*) was coined by Leningrad's medical community to refer to starvation as a deadly disease, and was widely adopted by Leningraders.[88] Meant to refer to the condition of the body, the term was extended to indicate the psychological sufferings and moral shortcomings associated with starving people: "moral dystrophy." As Ginzburg writes of the character A.O., "He came to know intimately everything that dystrophics knew—waiting for death, lethal indifference, lethal egoism."[89] "Moral dystrophy" was considered by many *blokadniki* to be a voluntary and avoidable disease. The architect and siege diarist Esfir' Levina writes, "There's a new term: moral dystrophy. Many use it as a cover, to justify dirt and laziness. It's difficult to find the border between suffering and speculation based on the circumstances [that is, crafty attempts to elicit pity and avoid responsibility]."[90] Ginzburg writes of N.K., who herself had avoided dystrophy: "She does not even understand moral dystrophy. She never, even in the worst times, understood that brutality [*ozverenie*] when people would hide a piece of food even from loved ones. Toward dystrophics she feels pity and involuntary hatred, the mild hatred of a good person."[91]

Ginzburg uses the phrase the "dystrophic who survived" (*utselevshii distrofik*) to refer to an identity common in the latter part of the blockade (and shared by her alter ego).[92] The phrase refers to a transitional or liminal status—one has survived "whole" (the root of *utselevshii*), while remaining attached to the symptoms and suffering of the "dystrophic" past. One example is the character Nina V—ts, an actor who was booted out of the theater in the 1930s because of her undesirable "class background" (descent from the nobility). She is now merely "one of many office workers, emaciated, and no longer young." According to Ginzburg's theories, Nina is an emotional and aesthetic type, whose earlier basis for self-realization was her feminine attractiveness. When this asset suddenly disappears, leaving little time for adjustment, she struggles to latch onto a new psychology. Ginzburg writes:

> In short, she has no psychic state. Only dystrophy remains, and only in the form of remnants. And now she tries to hold on to these remnants as if they were the only content of life and the possibility of realization. It is a concept that serves to justify emptiness and a premature feminine ruin. This ruin is mitigated by the fact that it is an illness—which means, perhaps, something temporary?—and, moreover, a *universal* illness. This ruin is sublimated by the fact that it is a social tragedy.
>
> Словом, у нее нет психического состояния. Осталась одна дистрофия, и то в виде остатков. И вот за эти остатки она хватается как за единственное содержание жизни и возможность реализации. Это оправдательное понятие для пустоты и для преждевременного женского крушения. Это крушение смягчается тем, что оно болезнь—значит, может быть, и нечто временное?—и притом всеобщая болезнь. Это крушение сублимируется тем, что оно социальная трагедия.[93]

In the situation of the blockade, one has to work to overcome one's existence as a mere animal struggling for survival before achieving any psychological state whatsoever. The self-image of the "dystrophic who survived" often accompanies the first step of reentry into society. Nina's utterances, as Ginzburg records (or reconstructs) them, center around her losses, and thus accentuate her belonging to the common tragedy. For instance, she used to "live for" the Hermitage, but now brags about her indifference to art, in order to broadcast just how much she has lost. She speaks of how she cannot take care of her appearance, expressing amazement that some women will now pay extraordinary prices—two kilos of bread—for stockings. Nina's knowledge that her fate is a common one satisfies the selfish goal of elevating her own imagined value.

Nina's sister "Tata," an intellectual type, exercises her self-image by telling colorful, aesthetically crafted stories replete with metaphors, generalizations, paradoxes, and humor. When she recounts how she survived bombings, her underlying theme is that she is an incompletely recovered human being, a "dystrophic." Her reactions are no longer "normal"; what's more, she is not yet ready to appreciate art again, though she has already started to read books. A third woman, T., had a prewar image as a "Don Juan."[94] Ginzburg discusses with B. (her friend Boris Bukhstab) how T.'s image as a "gentleman," her super-erotic charge, lends her an exoticism that produces a uniquely powerful affect on women. Before the war, "Don Juanism" was a compensatory model explaining her failure to achieve loftier goals—"family splendor" or success in literary affairs: "Don Juanism served for her whole life as a justificatory concept for intellectual vacuity and fruitlessness. That was in the past, and in the present—dystrophy." While she occupies a respectable administrative position in the National Library during the blockade, T. uses dystrophy as an excuse for her romantic failures, as well as for her inability to write books.[95]

A final "dystrophic who survived" is A.O., one of the smaller number of male characters Ginzburg analyzes. Blockade men in general, she writes, sooner or later fall prey to an inferiority complex because of their absence from the front. In response, they either adopt the pose of *nadryv* or redouble their search for a justificatory concept. What helps in the latter move is "exceptional self-satisfaction" or a position with responsibility, power, and command (which, as we have seen in the case of Reshetov, can end in *khamstvo*). Ginzburg interprets the fact that men are abandoning *nadryv* as a self-concept toward the end of the blockade as a sign of a rising "common will."

A.O., a literary scholar who had studied at the Institute with Ginzburg, worked at the Radio Station during the blockade. A "passive" type according to Ginzburg (with a diffuse will, despite his strong desires and capacity for pleasure),[96] he demonstrates the classic predicament of Soviet intellectuals: they had to mold new self-images every five or ten years in order to survive. In A.O.'s case, his 1920s self-image had been that of a "small everyday decadent" ([*byl*] *malen'kim bytovym dekadentom*), a poet who projected "spiritual bankruptcy and a touch of demonism." He was a "decadent with *nadryv*"—wrote poetry and fragmentary diaries and had "confused relations with women" (*zaputannye otnosheniia s zhenshchinami*). In the 1930s, A.O. worked at a publishing house, the type of place where the *apparat* prevented almost all culturally meaningful activity. He forged a new self-conception as a cynic and failure who had "buried his talent," finding comfort in the widespread belief that there was no other way to survive. While "conceding to the terrible world and acting by its evil laws" at his job, he tried meanwhile to erect his own private niche, where he could see himself as a card-player, book collector, epicure, and poet.

The third metamorphosis was ushered in by the war: he spent these years starving in the blockade, intensely fearing death. At the time of Ginzburg's note, A.O. was a dystrophic whose personal image consisted of *appearing* to possess a deep "psychology":

> He is an utter *intelligent* and an utter hysteric and therefore even now, no doubt, he has his lacerating self-concept [*nadryvnuiu avtokontseptsiiu*] (as a failure, a broken person, etc.), which allows him even now to count himself among the chosen, among those who are endowed with an inner life, who have a "psychology."
>
> Он сугубый интеллигент и сугубый истерик и потому он и сейчас, несомненно, имеет свою надрывную автоконцепцию (неудачник, сломленный и т.д.), которая позволяет ему и сейчас числить себя среди избранных, наделенных внутренней жизнью, имеющих «психологию».[97]

Ginzburg next argues that this self-image of a failure, which would allow for membership in the elite intelligentsia, has drawbacks for A.O., since it is socially unacceptable for a forty-five-year-old head of household. In order to hide his degradation, he cultivates his reputation as an eccentric, as someone who collects books at the expense of food—even if, as a still recovering dystrophic, he sinks to the level of accepting soy-oil cakes [*shroty*] from others in the Writers' Cafeteria (who thereby feel superior).

ATTITUDES TOWARD DEATH: THE "FATALIST" AND THE "TROGLODYTE"

The self-image of the "fatalist" exemplifies people's tendency to transform inevitabilities into self-conceptions that afford them a sense of the beauty and value of their position.[98] Ginzburg interviews several of her companions about their attitudes toward death and discovers that they have different ways of making sense of, or making self-images of, their lack of fear. For instance, N.P., a person with a "large life force," takes pleasure in revealing that she is a "fatalist" (an image popularized in Russian culture by Lermontov's *Hero of Our Time*)—she does not fear air raids, since she has no control over her end, which will inevitably come when it will come. The fact that a savage war with a massive death toll produces fatalists is no surprise, and one can find evidence of this self-image in several siege diaries.[99]

The rarer self-image constructed under death's shadow is the "troglodyte." This position—the opposite of fatalism, yet also a weapon for confronting the fear of death—is exemplified by N.K., who boasts that her instincts are so highly developed that she can sense that her time is not now. N.K. is an intellectual, one of Ginzburg's former classmates from the Institute, who during the blockade worked at Leningrad State University and then at the library (Volodarskii Raikom VKP[b]) and the Writers' Union. In her concluding remarks, Ginzburg says of her position: "All of this is the raising-up of one's qualities into a self-conception, into superstructures of value over a biologically indubitable fact—people with a large, greedy life force and a capacity to resist often do not fear death at all, and vice versa."[100]

Ginzburg probes into the constructions intellectuals build over "biologically indubitable facts." In the stark circumstances of the blockade, even a "psychic state" seems to be a hard-won attribute. She refers to "psychology" (in quotation marks) as a quality that some *intelligents* project in order to elevate themselves in the eyes of others. It does not matter how basic or simple the self-image is: what's important is that it can do the work of self-elevation in situations of everyday life.

A MEETING AT THE WRITERS' UNION: MULTILEVELED CHARACTER ANALYSES OF THE 1970S

Ginzburg's analyses of the self-conceptions of her "passing characters," locked in a battle for survival and social superiority, show traces of their author's own position and struggle. If she is a historian-novelist, she is one very much embedded in her moment; if she resembles a social scientist, then she is a "participant observer."[101] Her position is not unlike that of her models, in-between writers like the memoirists Alexander Herzen and the eighteenth-century Rationalist the Duc de Saint-Simon, who sketched and evaluated members of their own generation (*soplastniki*, to repeat Herzen's neologism) who participated in the same social sphere. This resemblance is heightened in certain of Ginzburg's essays written from the vantage point of late socialism, when she can evaluate in retrospect the entire careers of people she had known for decades. In this final section of the chapter, let us turn to the essay "A Meeting" (1974–75),[102] where Ginzburg shifts her focus—from how people battle in particular conditions to realize their own "values"—to longer-term relationships between individual fates and historical possibilities. Starting from the contemporary moment (a meeting at the Writers' Union), when her subjects make speeches that are similar on the surface, she exposes and demystifies the different types of relationships to power that underlie these speeches. Moving from there to survey the careers of various participants in the cultural-literary sphere, she goes on to suggest that a person's "positive" historical function can somehow trump their negative behaviors and personal attributes.

In "A Meeting," Ginzburg places herself in dialogue with the Duc de Saint-Simon, which suggests that she saw parallels between the hierarchical cultural-literary establishment in Leningrad and the aristocratic court of Louis XIV. In her book *On Psychological Prose,* Ginzburg distills Saint-Simon's method of character depiction into a tripartite structure: "somewhere at the foundation lies the most general social-moral typology of the age, then comes the 'social machinery' that Saint-Simon investigated at the French court and that he regarded as the main subject of history, and last is individual character, in which particular, sometimes whimsical features are woven into a fabric of recurrent formulas. The stable typological schema and its undercutting by continual differentiation—that is Saint-Simon's method."[103] Though the three levels of character are often coordinated, Ginzburg finds it most interesting when Saint-Simon portrays individuals whose personal qualities are at odds with their "social machinery."

As Ginzburg notes, Saint-Simon was directly engaged in the "social machinery" he portrayed, and made judgments based on his position in the aristocracy and on the values that circulated in his ever-evolving milieu. Saint-Simon casts himself, Ginzburg argues, as "an ideal representative of his group and party [. . . who] reserves the right of judgment over everything that happens in his book, since he is the most 'faithful' to his caste and is endowed with all the qualities necessary for that role."[104] She argues that the memoirist subjects his characters to moral judgment based on three criteria: "historical function, personal relationships, and individual attributes."[105] To judge characters according to their attributes and relationships may be straightforward, but judging one's contemporaries in terms of their historical function would seem to present problems of perspective. Ginzburg clarifies: this function amounts to a person's "place in the array of forces that define the Saint-Simonian world, in the basic conflicts of that vast yet self-enclosed arena where positive principles (the great aristocracy) are disposed against negative ones (the bourgeois upstarts, the king's ministers [. . .])."[106] Saint-Simon evaluates a person's position in a highly differentiated but small (and important) milieu, the court of Louis XIV, which is itself connected to larger forces, classes, and values.

Like Saint-Simon, Ginzburg makes herself into an "ideal representative" in her own essays through the implicit standards by which she judges others. Her own criteria seem to have had their main sources in two sets of traditions: those of the Russian intelligentsia, and those of the modernist (more specifically, the Formalist-Futurist) culture of the 1920s. Emphasizing her connection to the first tradition, Sarah Pratt argues that Ginzburg was a traditional nineteenth-century *intelligent*—"a geological find, an element of an earlier age left visible in spite of the apocalyptic upheavals of the early twentieth century."[107] Above all, Ginzburg shares the intelligentsia's central concern for "*sotsial'nost'* . . . connectedness, moral values, and structures."[108] Kirill Kobrin has presented an alternative view of Ginzburg as a typical member of the 1920s generation, whose most important characteristics were "unlimited enthusiasm, wild energy, surprising passion [*pafos*]."[109] Kobrin further identifies in this generation's intellectuals and writers a love of scientific methods and instruments, as they attempted to merge the social revolution with a scientific and aesthetic one.[110] A better picture of Ginzburg might emerge from combining as well as modifying Pratt's and Kobrin's representations of her: she was a 1920s *intelligent*, straddling two divergent traditions, both of which are in turn complex and diverse. Her understanding of her 1920s generation differs from Kobrin's, however—for example, for Ginzburg the category of energy and "life-force" appear to be psycho-physiological attributes unrelated to generational belonging; also, she names the distinctive characteristics of her particular milieu as love for the "word as such" (*samovitoe slovo*), irony, and skepticism.[111]

In "A Meeting," Ginzburg analyzes public figures of the literary world (academics, editors at publishing houses) while taking into account several decades of their activity and behavior. She treats the themes of the intelligentsia and the "social machinery" (the bureaucratic institutions in which they had to operate), making ethical evaluations using a subtle and multilayered scale. She uses (and presents as her own) an evaluative method with a tripartite structure that is almost identical to the one she had discerned in Saint-Simon:

> First there is a person's historical function, his place in the array of forces, which people of a certain evaluative orientation consider positive or negative (the concept is completely relative, of course). Next, there is a person's concrete social behavior, correlated with his function, but not identical to it, deviating under the pressure of circumstances. Finally there are a person's individual qualities.
>
> The evaluative signs of these three layers may or may not be congruent and may enter into different combinations. There are plusses and minuses, established from a relative, but not at all subjective, point of view. In its own way it is an obligatory point of view (group consciousness).
>
> Есть историческая функция человека, его положение в расстановке сил, которую люди определенной ценностной ориентации считают положительной или отрицательной (концепция вполне релятивистическая, конечно). Есть, далее, конкретное общественное поведение

> человека, соотнесенное с его функцией, но ей не тождественное, отклоняющееся под давлением обстоятельств. Есть, наконец, личные свойства.
>
> Оценочные знаки трех этих пластов могут совпадать, могут не совпадать и вступать в разные сочетания. Плюсы и минусы, проставляемые с относительной, но вовсе не субъективной, а в своем роде обязательной (групповое сознание) точки зрения.[112]

Ginzburg notes that her judgments are relative but not subjective: they represent a community, a milieu (in other words, the views of what Mead would call the "generalized other"). She credits "contemporary sociology" with the insight that a person is a "social organization" who acts according to values instilled by the groups to which he belongs.[113] Where Saint-Simon's judgments about behavior rely on personal interactions and relationships,[114] Ginzburg creates the more scientific category of a person's "concrete social behavior," which purports to be independent of the person's relationship to her (though in practice this must have been impossible). Her notion of her contemporaries' "historical function" appears to depend on a person's predominant social role, his or her career position (for example, academic, administrator, writer, or editor) in cultural institutions, or even his or her role in unofficial literary affairs, which she also believed capable of revealing "social regularities."[115]

Unlike Saint-Simon, Ginzburg makes allowances for behavioral changes under pressure from external circumstances—an acknowledgment of the limited choices available in her milieu. Of one person's change from fellow-traveler to bureaucrat, she wrote: "Again a choice, and what a choice!—essentially, between the possibility—or impossibility—of living" ("Опять выбор. И какой!—в сущности, между возможностью жить и невозможностью").[116] According to Ginzburg, the Soviet system had produced the following types: "decent people (who basically have not survived), semi-decent people, scoundrels who willingly did what they did, and semi-scoundrels who unwillingly did what they did and therefore did it a bit less."[117] She thus tries to correct for her generation's tendency toward "naïve realism," and also for the view of younger intellectuals who, from a distance that obscured nuances, were slotting Stalin-era subjects into the categories of good and evil.[118] She reminds us that a "person cannot invent for himself a nonexistent form of behavior, but he can choose his historical character from the models that history has prepared." It is only within these parameters that one can select one's behavior based on motives that are "social and biological, conscious and unconscious, law-governed and fortuitous." Ginzburg pays great attention to generational belonging, since every five- or ten-year period in Soviet history presented different possibilities and molded different kinds of actors (those who came of age in the 1930s being the most frightening). Historical shifts can have a disproportionately large effect, to the point of completely reversing a person's function and behavior.[119] But Ginzburg also sees the individual actor as having some degree of influence. Thus, while she agrees with theories of functional sociology about how people receive their social roles in line with the expectations of their milieu, she maintains that "social roles are also forms of acting on one's milieu" ("социальные роли—это также формы воздействия на среду").[120]

In "A Meeting," Ginzburg addresses several questions that are central to her approach to history and selfhood. For example, how does history act on people through their specific milieu? What attributes, what events in people's lives, can determine their responses to the limited historical options presented to them? How do different relationships to power motivate a person's professional actions and public speeches? And above all (in this essay), what differences in behavior and personality lay beneath a person's fulfillment of a "positive" historical role? She examines how personality traits (positive ones such as kindness and sympathy, or negative ones such as egoism and coldness) combine with various situations to produce different behaviors over time. Accepting an important job often meant being complicit or active in interrogations (*prorabotki*), character assassinations, and the propagation of intellectual falsehoods. Positive behavior then amounts to (reluctantly) fulfilling the unsavory requirements of functionaries and bureaucrats, but to the most minimal possible extent. (One should not forget that Ginzburg's own livelihood often depended—directly or indirectly—on some of the relatively powerful figures undergoing analysis.)

The first part of Ginzburg's essay dissects the "array of forces" at a meeting of the Critics' Section of the Writers' Union. The meeting has been called to address the "illusionary" problem of the dearth of young critics and the aging of the old cadres. As Ginzburg points out, however, the real problem is not what the speakers say it is: that universities, journals, and the *apparat* are not doing the right things to encourage critics to develop and join the organization—but rather that the overall situation of literature is stagnant. The topics on the meeting's agenda are, in her opinion, "counterfeit themes,"[121] which will "create the appearance of activity, which is a practical necessity for those gathered here, and the appearance of saying things that are smart, even liberal and noble—which is always pleasant for the one who is spouting them."[122] Ginzburg analyzes the speeches of members of different ages and relationships to power: "those who had power, those who have it now, and those who wish for power" ("власть имевшие, власть имущие и только еще хотящие иметь") and how this affected the judgment of their historical function.[123]

The first speaker is someone who once believed in communist ideals: in the typescript he is deciphered as Lev Abramovich Plotkin (1905–78).[124] His fate was "deflected" by the Revolution, but toward success rather than failure. As Ginzburg describes it, he came from a poor provincial family and started work at age fourteen, but subsequently managed to graduate from the university and to begin a career in Leningrad. His participation in the trials of the 1930s was mitigated by the fact that he was not among those who wished death on his opponents—he just wished they would clear out of his way. He became an administrator (the de facto director) at Pushkin House, was dismissed and then reappointed, and was also promoted to professor at Leningrad State University before being forced out again. Ginzburg writes of how the trials he had undergone brought on two heart attacks, but that he had still played the role of harsh interrogator in cases such as Mikhail Zoshchenko's. He had served as a gatekeeper at the university: immediately after the war, he asked an applicant to graduate school "how things stood with the nationalities question" (that is, whether the person was Jewish), but with some degree of embarrassment. At the 1970s meeting, this pensioner (in the category of "those who had power") could have chosen the genre of self-criticism, but instead his speech is optimistic and full of praise for other critics. Ginzburg interprets this move as his attempt, consciously or unconsciously, to demonstrate that he has the approval of the current hierarchy.[125]

Ginzburg enlists four other figures to show how the various shades of criticism or optimism in their speeches reflect in unexpected ways the positions people have held, hold, or are seeking to hold. The two subjects who "currently hold power" both came of age in the 1930s: the typescript identifies them as Vasily Grigorievich Bazanov (1911–81) and Grigory Panteleimonovich Makogonenko (1912–86). Both figures came from similar backgrounds: born in small villages, they worked in factories before coming to Leningrad and joining the Komsomol. And yet Bazanov turned into a tyrant of a bureaucrat (another *kham*), whereas Makogonenko became an excellent teacher (with a positive historical function according to Ginzburg). Their paths apparently diverged due to one chance circumstance: Makogonenko fell under the influence of his teacher Grigory Gukovsky, who opened up for him the road to becoming a mesmerizing speaker and an academic. Both Bazanov and Makogonenko speak according to the script—the former about the need for greater contact between scholars and writers, and the latter (speaking passionately as usual, even under these stultifying conditions) about the mission of journals to support young critics.[126] The final two figures are from the next generation, born around 1930 and entering the scene in the 1960s (hence falling into the category of those still in search of power): they are more cautious and self-critical. Ginzburg shows that underneath the general agreement about how to conduct a meeting dealing with an "illusionary" problem (that is, the dearth of young critics rather than the real problem: literary stagnation), her subjects still have different relationships to power and have followed career paths that turned out very differently, despite their similar ambitions.

In the second half of the essay, she turns to an analysis of the behaviors and personalities of three people roughly of her own generation (one of them slightly older)—fellow-travelers who had all been forced to adjust to the precipitous changes in the country in order to stay active. These figures were not only interlinked as members of the Leningrad intelligentsia: in the 1920s, they were all connected to the Institute for the History of Arts, a place that Ginzburg describes as reshaping its students, giving them a "second socialization" after childhood. First, there is the "dignitary" (Ginzburg uses a term here—*sanovnik*—with tsarist overtones) called "N.," whom the typescript reveals to be Vladimir Orlov (1908–85), one of Ginzburg's fellow students at the Institute, later a researcher (*nauchnyi sotrudnik*) at the Institute of Russian Literature (Pushkin House), and finally the editor of the "Biblioteka poeta" series. Second, there is "N.N.," the "orator," who can be decoded as Grigory Gukovsky (1902–50), who also studied and lectured at the Institute, and worked as a professor at Leningrad State University until he was repressed in the anti-cosmopolitan campaigns of 1948–49. Finally, there is the "charmer" Boris Eikhenbaum (1886–1959), who was one of Ginzburg's most influential teachers at the Institute, also made a professor at Leningrad State.[127]

As usual, Ginzburg constructs a typology, identifying three personality types: organizers (*organizatory*), flatterers (*obol'stiteli*), and creators (*sozidateli*).[128] However, Ginzburg's complex view of the ethical dimensions of the self takes account not only personality types (in which she attempts to discern values, inner motivations, and self-concepts), but also of how characters act on their environment as participants in historical dramas large and small.

"Organizers" seem to be related to her earlier category of active types, except that their will to action is of a specific kind: the desire to direct and rule over others. Orlov, who represents this type, is a person who Ginzburg believes in other times would have become a "resourceful organizer of daring literary enterprises." "Flatterers" want to produce an unmediated and instantaneous effect on other people through their bodies and minds (they are actors, prophets, charmers). This appears to be a reincarnation that combines Ginzburg's earlier emotional and sensual types. "Creators" are defined as needing neither to rule nor to flatter: they represent an ideal category (similar to the earlier "ideologue"). They may have negative personal qualities (such as "working egoism"), but they are higher types because they do not require immediate gratification or social success, and the manifestations of their will are "mediated in the products of their creativity and work."[129] Ginzburg's valuation of creativity, work, and the ability to see beyond the present moment relates to her concerns with the ethics of the post-individualist self. Ginzburg identifies Gukovsky and Eikhenbaum, both deceased by the time of this essay's composition, as flatterer types, who at times doubled as "creators."[130]

Ginzburg demonstrates the unexpected effects of being an organizer or a charmer within one's role or job in the Soviet official humanities intelligentsia. Orlov and Gukovsky both have more or less "positive" personal qualities: they are essentially kind and capable of sympathy. Yet their desires for self-realization—whether through organizing other people in Orlov's case, or charming them with his voice, intelligence, and body, in Gukovsky's[131]—produce negative behaviors. For example, Orlov performs the necessary dirty work (writing slanderous or ridiculous things in introductory articles, or participating in show-interrogations) so that he can use his position to get unrecognized writers published. Both players tried to bracket off their moral attitudes in the unofficial sphere from their behaviors in their jobs, but in both cases these strategies failed to protect their careers and well-being (and in Gukovsky's case, fatally so: he died in an isolation ward in Lefortovo Prison while awaiting his final sentence). The fact that both remained to some extent *intelligents* in their private lives seeped uncannily into their official identities and produced jealousies and resentment among the "herd-like bureaucrats," who had a vague intuition that they did not belong, were not *svoi*.[132] In Ginzburg's evaluation, both Orlov and Gukovsky had positive historical functions on the whole for their work in the literary and academic spheres.[133]

In the end, Ginzburg endows Eikhenbaum, too, with a "positive" historical function as "great scholar" and "avant-gardist," but he receives negative marks in the category of personality—his self-centeredness makes him completely indifferent and even cold toward others. Nevertheless, his behavior, unlike Orlov's and Gukovsky's, is "positive" on the whole. His desire to accentuate his uniqueness produces an effect bordering on resistance. He denies the status quo in order to defend his reputation as refined and brilliant, rather than to protect any strong values or ideas. Ginzburg describes one scene:

> But then his social behavior was one of a kind. His behavior was elevated into a conscious historical role. He paid the price of deprivations and risk in order to preserve his *persona*. This was a truly fearless person. Which does not contradict his nature—spoiled women were at times especially

> fearless. A meeting. The chairman opens with the ritual formula. Who is for, who is against? No one is against. It is unanimous. And just in the non-existent space between "no one against" and "unanimous," he raises his hand—alone in the hall that's holding its breath.[134]

The refusal to be completely intimidated into conformity, even if the motivation is egotistical, must be called nothing other than brave. Ginzburg does not indicate when this incident occurred, but one imagines the late 1920s to early 1930s; she suggests that the traditions of OPOYAZ kept Eikhenbaum honest for a while. Later, he began to "concede," after "his scholarly reference points were lost. The school slid out from under him." And more broadly, this capitulation came at a time "when everything had already exceeded the boundary of the human."[135]

Earlier, toward the end of the war, Ginzburg had sketched a scathing portrait of Boris Eikhenbaum in which she studies the effects of state recognition and social hierarchy on an individual's relationship to power and bureaucratic officialdom.[136] It reflects a moment when Eikhenbaum has successfully established himself in a high position and yet, as an *intelligent*, he is embarrassed to betray his interest in such careerist matters. Whenever possible he tries to show his independence through an ironic attitude to bureaucratic language.[137] Eikhenbaum faces a psychologically trying moment in June 1945: he has been awarded a medal, thus entering into an elite group, but has not been invited to the celebratory banquet, which shows that he is not one of the very select few. Ginzburg explains the extreme psychological difficulty of this in-between position.

> If one doesn't receive anything, one can withdraw in a proud and mocking indifference, but once one falls into the hierarchical mechanism, one can no longer do this. The hierarchical feeling, especially in an uneasy and unstable environment, is a continual feeling of a double-sided pressure. From below, it lifts you up, and from above it again presses and hurls you back down.[138]

Hence Eikhenbaum is stuck in a singularly dissatisfying place in the hierarchy. He is not among the ignored, nor fully among the "decorated."

When Ginzburg observes the others around her who are in one camp or the other, she notices that they shift their projected self-images, depending on whether they are succeeding or failing at the moment. In this way, *intelligentnost'*, which brings the ability to brush things off with humor, becomes a mask to be donned when necessary:

> In this way, they have two contradictory impulses—one is irrepressible delight, corresponding to their real function and situation as bureaucrats;

> the other is mockery (it is at yourself that you laugh . . .),[139] corresponding to their fictitious (imagined) function as *intelligents* with its fictitious traditions. This impulse is supported by the professional obligation and habit of finding these traditions touching, but these traditions would specifically prohibit this kind of delight. One also should not forget that the second impulse carries the supremely valuable experience of moral superiority.[140]

Here Ginzburg's vision penetrates to the cynical core of the *intelligent*'s persona: the thirst for superiority, which motivates any seemingly moral stance. She also explains the psychological contradiction for the *intelligent*-bureaucrats who have experienced professional success. Their cultural and intellectual tradition, especially in the case of the Formalists, would call for them to reject authority and despise the parceling out of "success" by an official bureaucracy. To be truly faithful to the Formalists' tradition, and not just seemingly moved or touched by it, would require suppressing all outward expressions of joy over professional advancement (or not having these feelings in the first place). In this analysis, one can sense Ginzburg's pain at her isolation and lack of recognition, the result of her attempts to stay loyal to the old ways.[141]

Ginzburg's sketches testify to the disintegration of the traditions of Formalism under the pressures of the Stalinist order. By the 1970s, when she wrote "A Meeting," Ginzburg declares that the intelligentsia has also lost its trademark behavioral principle. The willingness to suffer for one's ideals that traditionally characterized the intelligentsia had largely disappeared among those in intellectual circles. While she finds some intellectuals willing to undertake acts of protest (such as signing petitions), they fail to accept suffering as a possible or inevitable consequence of their action.[142] History leads one to predict, Ginzburg writes, that smaller measures of intimidation—such as obstacles to publication, or the prevention by the authorities of a planned trip abroad—would discourage resistance almost as well as more drastic measures. And yet she still finds talented people in this group, people who are interested in real, substantive matters (*interes k delu*)—even if they are driven by fashion (and fashion, she notes, is a serious thing).[143]

CONCLUSION

In her character sketches from the 1930s and 1940s, unpublished during her lifetime, Ginzburg analyzes personalities in difficult and catastrophic historical situations, where strong-willed subjects attempt to "claim what's theirs."

At the same time, these analyses of embattled subjects demonstrate Ginzburg's obsession with failure, including her own.[144] Many of the failures inherent in the life of the intelligentsia of her generation (and the self-conceptions meant to compensate for failure) appeared to Ginzburg as products of clashes between the personality models inherited from pre-Revolutionary times and those formed under the pressures of the new epoch, which deflected (to recall Akhmatova's metaphor of the river) or blocked any drive for self-realization in the professional, social, sexual, and physiological sphere. It was these dramatic changes that made self-conceptions especially visible and perhaps added to Ginzburg's sense of their fictitiousness.

The *intelligent* with *nadryv* and the *kham,* who appear most prominently in Ginzburg's notes from the 1930s, have personalities that seem at home in the hierarchical and violently antagonistic atmosphere of Stalinism. The atmosphere of doom surrounding the purges can be sensed indirectly through her characters' struggles to transform and overcome positions of helplessness and failure. Whereas the *intelligent* with *nadryv* advertises this failure in order to make others suffer (from sympathy or pity), the *kham* uses the power of a higher position (often temporary) in order to humiliate or take advantage of others.

One finds images of these characters in the blockade as well, though at that time (and especially from 1942–44) there were also characters that had a more direct relationship to starvation and death: the dystrophic who survived (*utselevshii distrofik*), the fatalist (*fatalist*), and troglodyte (*troglodit*). Not only are these character images less complex as aesthetic structures, they are also less dependent on a rigid hierarchy: the *distrofik,* for example, garners value precisely by being one among many, part of a general tragedy. All of these three images originate in a person's relationship to mortality, though they also become the justificatory mechanism for maintaining a vulnerable social position (especially for men who had not gone to the front, or women who had failed to realize themselves in career or family). The images, and Ginzburg's writing about them, speak to the lifting of taboos during the blockade, in the realm of literature and public speech (the "mini-thaw" and the decreasing importance of the NKVD, or Peoples' Commissariat of Internal Affairs, a predecessor to the KGB, though it still operated).[145] Ginzburg's writings also demonstrate the loosening of traditional taboos imposed by the sensibility of the *intelligent* (food preparation, for example, would have been a topic undeserving of particular attention).

These sketches, as Ginzburg's later analysis of the Duc de Saint-Simon helps to underscore, represent a defense of "true" *intelligentnost'* against the easy lamentations and lacerations unleashed and made socially permissible by oppressive circumstances. One might look at these writings of hers as a substitute self-realization, full of bitterness toward herself and toward her less self-conscious contemporaries. The essay "A Meeting" seems to contain one or two jabs at those "semi-scoundrels" who in the 1970s were forgetting and forgiving themselves for their wrongdoings in the Stalinist years, and who were now assuming the right to judge others. For instance, Ginzburg remarks on Orlov's renewed cultivation of his self-image from his Formalist youth. He seeks out the company of people from his past, and speaks admiringly of those who chose to remain outside the circles of power and recognition:

> About such people he speaks fondly, with an intonation of self-judgment: "I respect this person. He built his life as he wanted." Yes, as he wanted. Only, the greater part of his life was wasted on obscure work. Only, there were times when he didn't have a ruble to spend on dinner. But he didn't go telling you about this.[146]

There are moments where Ginzburg may seem to risk striking a note of self-pity or self-righteousness, and yet she guards against this by her lack of direct reference to her own situation. Where she refers, indirectly and in a generalizing manner, to her own profile and experiences, she presents these as inevitable. Speaking about an anonymous alter ego, she writes of merely possessing a researcher's mind together with a large life force. Therefore she worked for herself, on her own, no matter what the circumstances—she could not do otherwise.[147]

In a slightly more direct autobiographical passage, Ginzburg indicates that a person in this situation perceives himself as acting through weakness, rather than strength:

> The main thing is that a person involuntarily fulfills the conditions laid down by his talent. From the inside it even seems to him—he only behaves well from weakness, from languor, or from the fact that he is shy, and lacks the courage to suddenly do an about-face and begin to speak otherwise. We are experts in this. All of our life went by in fulfilling these conditions, and never was this accompanied by a haughty sense that we were carrying out some ethical act.

> Главное, человек непроизвольно выполняет условия, поставленные его талантом. Изнутри ему даже кажется—это он от слабости, от вялости ведет себя хорошо, оттого что стесняется, храбрости не хватает вдруг перевернуться и заговорить другими словами. В этом мы знаем толк. Жизнь вся прошла в выполнении условий; и никогда это не сопровождалось горделивым переживанием осуществляемого этического акта.[148]

Ginzburg presents herself (in the first-person plural, alongside others) as simply following the imperatives of her talent, without any sense of moral superiority. The spirit of judgment, which is present in these notes, appears to be overpowered by the desire to explain and understand how these choices and differences were shaped, and how they affected the milieu (and the actors themselves). Though she does not enter here into her own biography, one imagines it next to the others as "a typical case, one variety of the epochal person," as she presents herself in "At One with the Legal Order." And in this famous essay's ending, she writes that a life such as hers, with its alternation between the "passive experience of inordinate historical pressures and a semi-illusory active participation" can barely produce a biography. If there is one, it is "a biography very much against the subject's own will."[149] Ginzburg's sketches of her contemporaries demonstrate their deliberate attempts to mold successful or effective self-images in the face of failure, while her self-reflective essays evince another mood that frequently assailed the subject in this era: the feeling that historical pressures are preventing her from having any kind of 'biography' at all.

CHAPTER 5

Transformations of Experience

AROUND AND BEHIND *NOTES OF A BLOCKADE PERSON*

Toward the end of the blockade, Ginzburg observed that Leningraders were beginning to form a collective identity of themselves as heroes, and that this process encouraged forgetting. She wrote of how *blokadniki* were "already eliminating a whole series of inner states" from their memories of the worst period, the winter of 1941–42.[1] They were forgetting that "they vacillated, that many of them remained in the city for reasons that were external, coincidental, or personal, that they lived in fear and despair, that for months they were interested only in food, that they were mean, pitiless or indifferent, that they passed through the most humiliating and darkest psychological states."[2] Ginzburg found that in fact these collective erasures of memory had value in that they created a morally uplifting effect: self-identified "heroes" who had "freely" chosen to stay and bravely defend their city at any cost had now begun indeed to act more bravely and nobly, eager to maintain their hard-won identities. And yet she worried that this group identity was likely to be exploited: "Of course, people will abuse, boast about, profiteer on this. It's a general human quality to abuse and boast. But better that people boast about this than all sorts of nonsense."[3]

In a subsequent essay, drafted in 1944, Ginzburg criticizes *blokadniki*-writers who were beginning to capitalize on their experiences as Leningraders. Sensing the historic nature of their trials, they began indulgently exposing them to the public: "shameless profiteering [*spekuliatsia*] on other people's and even their own sufferings somehow gets combined with a sincere need to realize in writing what they feel to be their most elevated and difficult life experience."[4] Siege writers such as Olga Berggolts, Vera Inber, and Vera Ketlinskaya led relatively privileged existences (which is not to say that they did not undergo extreme suffering): this is in fact what gave them the physical strength and fortitude to write their novels, diaries, and poetry.[5] During the blockade, Ginzburg notes, they sometimes flaunted their privileges to assert their self-worth, and yet avoided hints of this in their writings, where they publicized their belonging to the suffering collective.

In 1943–44, Ginzburg was a keen and critical observer of how memories, identities, and literary representations began to distort the lived experience of the blockade. She understood the impulse to transform "the instinct for self-preservation and a vaguely manifested common will for victory" into something "much more purified and conscious"—but at the same time she found in this process something not wholly naïve or earnest.[6] Ginzburg's sensitivity to the complex decisions around memory and representation of the blockade compelled her to work painstakingly on navigating relationships among personal, collective, and historical representations when she sat down to compose her own blockade narratives. In some of her earliest writings, driven by guilt and remorse, she aims to retrieve personal experiences and to reconstruct the fuller context of the blockade situation. At the same time, as she continued to work on her siege narratives with an eye toward their eventual reception, she went to great lengths to avoid laying bare her own sufferings, since this would seem like an attempt to inscribe herself into the collective identity of the heroic Leningraders. Ginzburg was determined to describe the general experience of the blockade without "purifying" her own experiences, but also without indulging in self-exposure. Confessions and autobiography went against the grain of her general aesthetics, and not even the blockade could lift her taboo on these modes. Hence her style could be seen as a response to the blockade writings of women writers like Berggolts. In 1944, Ginzburg criticized Berggolts's *February Diary* for assuming the right to "a personal heroic intonation . . . , which is hard to do without in women's art, since women need to embody themselves personally, concretely, physically; to embody themselves as objects of erotic admiration and self-admiration."[7]

In her own published siege narratives, Ginzburg delves into an extraordinary level of detail, drawing not only on memory, but also on the notes, transcriptions of conversations, and sketches of various Leningraders she had made during the latter part of the blockade, when she was recovering from the worst period of suffering. Studying herself and others, Ginzburg documents the physiological and psychological dimensions of hunger and cold, the never-ending battles for self-assertion among *blokadniki*, and their changing perceptions of time and space. Her nuanced and comprehensive observations contributed to the success of *Notes of a Blockade Person* in the 1980s (when much had long been suppressed or forgotten).[8] Ginzburg crafted this heterogeneous three-part composition from drafts she had begun during the blockade and revised several times between her first serious return to them in 1962 and her death in 1990.[9]

In *Notes* as published in 1984–89, Ginzburg investigates some difficult topics (such as attitudes toward death), but she avoids those with a tinge of the dramatic or the sensational (the ubiquitous corpses are mentioned only twice, for example).[10] She goes to great lengths not to romanticize suffering or martyrdom, especially her own. Not only does she abstain from self-aggrandizement: she builds up an image of herself that is neither positive nor negative. Ginzburg's narration contains scant first-person references, and focuses around a "composite and conventional" (*summarnyi i uslovnyi*) male hero named N., designed as a representative blockade intellectual. Introducing him, Ginzburg mentions the need to show "not only life in general, but also the blockade existence of a single person."[11] Whenever this individual risks appearing too autobiographically oriented, she abandons him for the more universal (but still grammatically male) *chelovek*, or "person."

And yet the desire to present an impersonal and universal historical narrative is sometimes at odds with Ginzburg's simultaneous attachment to concrete particulars and illustrative examples. She aspires toward universality while regarding crucial realms of experience, such as intimate relationships, as largely outside her "range of the depictable."[12] The tension between the general and the particular, composite images and personal details, illuminates some of the fundamental aesthetic dilemmas in documentary and psychological prose of the kind that *Notes of a Blockade Person* strives to be. In her scholarship, Ginzburg had noted the importance of "selection, judgment, and point of view" in the creation of a documentary account.[13] As scholars of Gulag and Holocaust literature have shown, writing a witness-based documentary account of a historical event, particularly one of collective trauma, involves difficult negotiations between personal reflection and historical representation, memory and forgetting, autobiography and fiction.[14] Moving from personal experience to historical narrative requires a process akin to fictionalization, and, in Ginzburg's case, a move toward typification, rather than individuation.

The processes of selection and generalization in *Notes* come sharply into focus when one reads "A Story of Pity and Cruelty," the powerful narrative about death and remorse she wrote during the blockade, but never published (nor, it seems, made known to others).[15] This narrative, which dissects the relationship between the hero (Otter) and his aunt (named in the story simply as Aunt—Tyotka in Russian) during the final weeks of her life, is a quasi-fictional account of the death of Ginzburg's mother in November 1942. It appears that Ginzburg drafted this narrative before composing "Otter's Day" ("Den' Ottera"), the 1940s predecessor to *Notes of a Blockade Person*, which focuses on a completely different set of the same character's experiences.[16] Comparing "A Story of Pity and Cruelty" to "Otter's Day," and finally to *Notes*, one can trace the processes of transformation involved in the generalization of experience. In *Notes*, where she speaks of guilt and remorse, Ginzburg includes only summary descriptions and small, scattered examples involving anonymous characters. Every single one of these turns out to originate in "A Story of Pity and Cruelty." The title derives from one such instance: in *Notes*, there are a few lines presenting a thumbnail sketch of the relationship between a certain O. and his much older sister, which Ginzburg labels "a story of pity and cruelty."[17] This sketch portrays in miniature the dynamics between Otter and his aunt in the unpublished "Story of Pity and Cruelty."

Few published accounts broach the territory of resentment and hatred that blockade conditions could inspire between family members.[18] Ginzburg furnishes her story with dialogues that transgress the boundaries of human decency. Otter yells at his aunt that he wishes she would die, and complains that she is more likely to drive him to the grave first ("and when I croak you will be in difficult straits, you'll feel what it's like with your dependent's rations").[19] Aunt's use of pet names and tender words only shame and rile him; he perceives in them a manipulative ploy, so distant are they from reality. The small sections on family ties in *Notes* speak to this relationship in a generalized manner:

> So painful, so horrible was the physical contact between people that in the closeness, the proximity, it became difficult to distinguish love from hatred toward the one whom one could not leave behind. It was forbidden to leave—but you could insult, wound. And the bond did not disintegrate. All possible relationships—camaraderie and apprenticeship, friendship and love—fell away like a leaf; but this one remained in force. Either writhing from pity, or cursing, people shared their bread. Cursing, they shared, sharing, they died. Those who left the city bequeathed these domestic sacrifices to those who remained behind. The insufficiency of sacrifices (if you survived it meant you sacrificed yourself insufficiently), and together with that insufficiency—remorse.[20]

While Ginzburg does not erase the brutal emotions of pain, hatred, and resentment from the blockade experience, she compresses whole pages of analysis from "A Story of Pity and Cruelty" into this summary. As usual, she treats a powerfully emotional experience with a distanced, impersonal voice, combining analysis with lyricism.[21] But a rare use of simile ("fell away like a leaf"), hypnotic repetitions, and near-syllogisms lend this pattern of relations a ring of inevitability.[22]

Indeed Ginzburg postulates that remorse was universal among siege survivors: "For those who lived through the blockade, remorse was just as inevitable as the changes in a dystrophic body. Moreover it was the most oppressive kind of remorse—the uncomprehending kind. A person remembers a fact and cannot resurrect the experience; the experience of a piece of bread, candy, which inspired him to cruel, dishonest, humiliating acts."[23] She suggests a motivation for both *Notes of a Blockade Person* and "A Story of Pity and Cruelty" in the relationship between "facts," experience, and remorse: an individual was more likely to be haunted by shards of memories when integral experiences were forgotten, leaving only facts behind. Repentance then drives one to recall the difficult past more completely (thickening facts with context) in order to reconcile it with one's present identity. Hence guilt and remorse compel a person to write, to connect fragmentary moments of experience.[24] In *Notes,* where Ginzburg removes any direct autobiographical treatment of her family tragedy, she "resurrects" the conditions enabling cruelty, the context in which a piece of candy acquires an entirely new meaning. The psychology of food is the dominant theme in part 1 of *Notes,* and could be said to issue from "A Story," where food is bound to remorse, serving as the material source of arguments and reconciliation between Otter and Aunt.

What might have prompted Ginzburg to abandon "A Story of Pity and Cruelty" and to rein in its remarkable power when creating her more general, historiographical *Notes of a Blockade Person*? Can we reconcile the incongruity between Ginzburg's insistence on the centrality of remorse in the Blockade, and the almost total exclusion of details on this subject in her otherwise detailed *Notes*? My discussion of these questions will touch upon issues of genre, which have plagued the reception of *Notes* since their very first publication. In all of Lydia Ginzburg's scholarly work on "in-between literature" (*promezhutochnaia literatura*), such as her book *On Psychological Prose,* a concern with genre is subordinate to her main interest: concepts of human character and personality, and their reflection or discovery in literature. The fragmentation of different parts of experience between *Notes of a Blockade Person* and "A Story of Pity and Cruelty" reflects Ginzburg's complex notions of character in twentieth-century literature and history. A comparison of these texts casts light on her innovative approach to character, which strives to encourage ethical responsibility while reflecting a radically partitioned and fragmented subject. In Ginzburg's documentary narratives, self-examination battles against self-exposure, while a commitment to the literature of fact withstands an aversion to autobiography.

GUILT AND HISTORY: HERZEN'S MODEL

The most obvious literary texts informing *Notes of a Blockade Person* are Lev Tolstoy's *War and Peace* and Marcel Proust's *In Search of Lost Time.* Ginzburg famously opens with Tolstoy's notion that personal and even selfish actions can acquire national-historical significance, aiding a war effort. The parallel between 1812 and 1941–44 provides justification and cover for her exploration of subjective experiences and battles for social superiority. Ginzburg closes part 1 of *Notes* by gesturing to Proust. She compares the act of writing with "time regained": "In the abyss of lost time—something found."[25] Her narrative charts an intellectual's return to health and suggests an impending breakthrough of the empty (blockade) circle of egoistic gestures aimed solely at survival. She stops short of having her hero sit down to write the narrative, making ambiguous the "person" of the title *Notes of a Blockade Person*. The most relevant model of documentary prose and historical self-representation for *Notes*, though, is Herzen's *My Past and Thoughts* (*Byloe i dumy*). Irina Paperno has argued (in part through a discussion of Ginzburg) that Herzen's work served as a kind of "textbook" for generations of Soviet readers, inspiring them to turn their experiences into historical testimonies. One finds his influence in the development and popularization of a group consciousness, a particular brand of catastrophic historicism, and the "notes" genre itself.[26]

Though Ginzburg's aesthetic was deeply historicist in the 1920s and 1930s (as she looked for reflections of history in her own life), during the war she experienced the satisfaction of participating in large-scale events and an increased desire to understand history's course and its intersection with her life. Not coincidentally, it was during this time that, as a literary scholar, she began to study *My Past and Thoughts* and its unique combination of autobiography, historiography, and fiction.[27] She commenced work on her doctoral dissertation on Herzen in 1944, which she finally defended and published in 1957, subsequently revising part of it into a chapter of *On Psychological Prose*.[28]

"Whoever managed to survive must have the strength to remember": Ginzburg quotes this line from Herzen in the middle of part 1 of *Notes of a Blockade Person*, and considered using it as an epigraph.[29] Remembering, for Herzen, elicits a narrative act, and thus the "strength to remember" means the "strength to write."[30] He inscribes this line into his memoirs before addressing the years from 1848 to 1852, when his world came crashing down around him. He lost his beliefs and ideals in the wake of the failed revolutions in Europe and the destruction of his family circle (which he had sought to establish as an alternative ideal). His mother and son perished in a shipwreck in November 1851, shortly before the revolution ended in France. His wife Natalie was swept up in a stormy love affair with their friend, the Romantic poet Georg Herwegh, and then she contracted pneumonia and pleurisy and died in May 1852, after giving birth to a boy, who died on the same day. The dictum should be understood in the strictest sense, given the events to which Herzen was referring (and how he interpreted them): a survivor is morally responsible for providing a voice or a historical record for the deceased, who no longer had a voice.

In "A Story of a Family Drama"—part 5 of *My Past and Thoughts*, which was published in its entirety only posthumously—Herzen nearly implicates himself in his wife's death, showing how he did nothing to alleviate her suffering, perhaps worsening it through his iron will and unsympathetic ear.[31] Nevertheless, he portrays himself as a rational, positive hero, and defends his and his wife's honor, showing how they were preyed upon by morally bankrupt, petit-bourgeois Westerners (Georg and Emma Herwegh).[32] Ginzburg, in her 1957 book and in *On Psychological Prose*, argues that guilt motivated the composition of "A Story of a Family Drama" and by extension the voluminous *My Past and Thoughts* (since, as Herzen explained, the first text begot the second). Remorse, however, as she reminds us, remains external to the text. It can be sensed only in the depiction of Natalie's death (a "self-torment by slow remembering"): "Herzen forces himself to take a close look at a continually shifting sequence of painful details, so that their reconstruction [*vosstavlenie*] and re-experiencing [*povtornoe perezhivanie*] becomes a kind of moral duty, a creative expiation of guilt [*tvorcheskim iskupleniem viny*]."[33]

Ginzburg's analysis of Herzen places his tasks as an artist front and center.[34] She explains his exclusion of the psychological realm by his mission to depict a model figure of the new Russian revolutionary.[35] Herzen "saw himself as a champion of enlightenment, and a pathology humiliating to the rational person therefore had no place in his approach to the examination of spiritual life."[36] Ginzburg describes his sublimation and even erasure of guilt as an artistic victory.[37] And she writes: "Herzen's strength, like that of every great artist, is in making the personal take on a general, objective significance."[38] Herzen's historicism, which can be traced back to Hegel, includes the idea that the minutiae of one's domestic life reflect history and have a place in the historical record, taking on an objective meaning.[39]

The concluding passage of *On Psychological Prose* offers a sweeping statement on historicist impulses and aesthetics. Ginzburg's words seem to speak doubly for her inspiration to write "A Story of Pity and Cruelty" and *Notes of a Blockade Person*:

> It is through knowledge and action that suffering, guilt, and failure are expiated [*Deianiem i poznaniem snimaiutsia stradaniia, vina, neudacha*]. It was from this conviction that the initial plan for *My Past and Thoughts* emerged (subsequently evolving into the book's enormous canvas of social life). The book as planned was not, however, intended merely as vengeance and atonement, but also as an act of artistic cognition that would recover the past for the future [*spasaiushchii proshloe dlia budushchego*], that would transform that past into history and art. That sense of the past as something the creative person *does not have the right* to allow to disappear without a trace, that historicism in its most particular and personal manifestation, is correlated in *My Past and Thoughts* with a Herzenian

> sense of history as the shared awareness of a common past [*s Gertsenovskim chuvstvom istorii kak obshchego proshlogo, zhivushchego v obshchem soznanii*].[40]

Ginzburg implies that Herzen succeeded in his plan to preserve (or recover) the past for both history and art by writing and publishing a grand narrative.[41] Ginzburg does not specify *which* past—that is, which parts of one's past—the creative person cannot allow to disappear, but surrounding passages point to the most difficult moments, those haunting ghosts of remorse. And yet her lofty conclusion paradoxically implies that even if guilt and failure were motivations (or the "psychological impulse" behind the text), Herzen's concealment of his most devastating experiences, and abstention from psychological self-analysis, do not diminish (from the perspective of world or national culture) his accomplishments as a historian and activist.

If one keeps in mind Ginzburg's blockade writings, one is tempted to interpret the passage cited earlier in the following way: *My Past and Thoughts* and "A Story of a Family Drama," not published in Herzen's lifetime, constitute a "trace" of the past sufficient to satisfy the historicist imperative. A writer, even a writer-activist *intelligent,* is under no moral obligation to stand trial in public, as long as he processes his guilt creatively on the way toward crafting a more elevated and far-reaching reflection of experience. As she wrote these lines on Herzen, in both the 1950s and the 1970s, Ginzburg underplayed the distinction between "A Story of a Family Drama" and the rest of *My Past and Thoughts,* that is, between "traces" published in one's lifetime and posthumously. In her decades-long experience of writing for the desk drawer, she had to hope that unpublished writings mattered vitally, as did words uttered and heard by no one. She believed that our writings survive us, independently of our wishes: "Those who write, like it or not, enter into a conversation with what is outside the self. For those who have written die, and that which was written remains, without asking their permission."[42]

FROM FACTS TO EXPERIENCES: "A STORY OF PITY AND CRUELTY"

In a 1986 interview, Lydia Ginzburg responded to a reader's question about the triple date—1942–1962–1983—she appended to *Notes of a Blockade Person* when it was finally published in 1984.[43] She explained: "In 1942, when things became a bit easier, I began to write down facts, conversations, details of blockade life—preparations for a future work I had not yet defined."[44] She went on to describe how she restructured the composition in 1962, creating a unified narrative through the creation of a single, composite hero. This account is not quite accurate, however, since her 1940s draft "Otter's Day" already contained a single hero, though a less generalized one than the later version in *Notes*. As the archives show, she not only recorded "facts" between 1942 and 1944 but was already trying to reconstruct experiences in continuous narratives using an autobiographically based hero. This was especially the case in her narrative about guilt.

"A Story of Pity and Cruelty" depicts two individuals locked in psychological warfare as they struggle desperately for survival in the impossible blockade conditions. The middle-aged hero is tormented by guilt over his behavior in the period leading up to his aunt's death from emaciation and starvation. Otter recalls that it was easy for him to share his small food ration and preserve his aunt's life through the deadly winter, but when conditions improved in the spring, he began to resent her as a force of chaos and a parasite. In the absence of witnesses, he behaves cruelly, hurling verbal insults and threats at her. The narrative is written from Otter's point of view, as he tries to break through repetitive and disordered thoughts to dissect his emotional state in the belief that it is better to "systematize" than to "blindly drive needles under one's fingernails."[45] He engages in something akin to post-traumatic psychotherapy, but with this difference: since it is Otter's character to be analytical, rational, and self-aware, anything like a clinical state of denial is unthinkable.[46] Rather, he attempts to master his disturbing memories, separating self-pity from pity for his aunt, guilt from remorse, and explaining (and to some extent even excusing) the facts by recreating the fullness of experience.

"A Story of Pity and Cruelty" is written as a third-person monologue, which incorporates remembered conversations. Otter conducts his own analysis, and converses with himself (*razgovor s samim soboi*) in what is not a confession, since it lacks an addressee. Walled off from the reader or any other interlocutor, he is capable of brutal honesty. This narrative isolation mirrors his predicament in the blockade, where he dreams of breaking out into the world of social relations outside the home. Unlike in Ginzburg's published *povestvovaniia* (narratives), there is no philosophical preamble or separate author-narrator introducing the main character as an example. In a sense, Otter needs no introduction, being the usual hero of Ginzburg's longer draft narratives from the 1930s and 1940s, including the early versions of what became *Notes of a Blockade Person*.[47] And yet Ginzburg keeps all these Otters separate from one another—in the case of the blockade, his life experiences in "A Story . . ." conflict with those in "Otter's Day."

In assigning blame for the tragedy, Otter hones in on his aunt's "bad" (*durnoi*) character, which conditioned his behavior to some extent, and blurred his judgment. He claims that Aunt's stubbornness and strong "life force" blinded him to the fact that she was deteriorating, and provoked him to habitually oppose her. Because she treated everything as a playful fiction (*igrovaia fiktsiia*), his use of language grew careless. With great power, "A Story of Pity and Cruelty" poses a philosophical question that concerned Ginzburg deeply: can one remain true to "oneself" in the absence of external witnesses and while lacking any belief in the "absolute value of the individual soul"?[48] Can the twentieth-century intellectual, the Russian *intelligent* whom Otter represents, act humanely toward his family members without a strong feeling of love and a firm sense of duty?[49] Can he "survive and endure without losing his human image" (as Ginzburg was to formulate the question after the war)?[50]

The Leningrad Blockade, and in particular Otter's life with Aunt, provides the ultimate testing ground for Ginzburg's moral philosophy, based on the notion that an "immanent" person—one who adheres to no religion or other absolute principle—can escape from egoism only through love and creativity. These states or activities allow a person to "become another," to "exit from the self," and to sacrifice selfish needs.[51] Otter strives to lead a moral life, which means that he must live consciously, applying a standard of decency to his thoughts and actions, and connecting them into a stable identity. Being a writer with unrealized talent (Otter is described as writing "on the rise and collapse of the individualistic consciousness"), he must try to offer something of himself and his ideas to others through art. In order to recommence writing in the midst of the blockade, Otter needs to conserve precious energy and time by organizing his affairs. Aunt, the epitome of chaos, hedonism, and "asociability" (Ginzburg uses *asotsial'nost'*, referring to her selfishness, despite being a social butterfly),[52] is his nemesis, and yet she provides meaningful proof of his social value, offering him a very concrete "exit from self." Otter feeds his aunt but cannot find the strength for kindness. His irritation is directly related to his "working egoism," resulting (ironically) from the desire to contribute to the broader social good.[53] Her life stands on one side of the balance, his life and "cruel creativity" on the other.[54]

The circumstances of Ginzburg's life suggest direct parallels with this story. The basic situation in "A Story of Pity and Cruelty" is this: Aunt, who is seventy-five, has two nephews: V., who is the elder, and Otter; she is also a great-grandmother. This latter fact may be an authorial slip, as no children of hers are mentioned (making her only a great-aunt).[55] Aunt is a spoiled, bourgeois lady of the old world whose family had suffered bankruptcy. V., described as a "person of oral speech" (*chelovek ustnoi rechi*), lives outside the blockade and occasionally sends money. Otter, proudly, feels wholly responsible for Aunt's existence. But her frivolity (*legkomyslennost'*), impetuousness, and lack of consideration for others exasperate him.

Ginzburg was famously reticent about her personal life, but her niece Natalia Viktorovna Sokolova's spirited, unceremonious "family chronicle," deposited in a Moscow archive, helps fill in the gaps.[56] Lydia Ginzburg's mother, Raisa Davydovna Ginzburg (born Rakhil' Gol'denberg), died of starvation in Leningrad in November 1942.[57] She was born in 1867 (making her seventy-five in 1942) and grew up in a relatively wealthy Jewish merchant family that came to financial ruin around the time of her marriage to Yakov Moiseevich Ginzburg. She never worked, and was supported by her husband (who died in December 1909), then by his brother, Mark Moiseevich (who died in 1934), and finally by her two children, Viktor and Lydia.[58] Natalia Sokolova singles out "light-spiritedness" as her grandmother's signature quality: "The main thing about grandma Raia—she was light in spirit [*legkaia*]. Grandma-butterfly. Grandma-moth." She also notes that Raya (the common nickname from Raisa, which came from Rakhil') and her daughter Liusia (as Lydia Yakovlevna was known to her family and close friends) had sharply divergent personalities.[59] Ginzburg's brother, Viktor Tipot, a fairly successful dramaturge, moved to Moscow from Odessa ca. 1922, and by the time of the war had a daughter (Natalia Viktorovna) and two grandsons.[60] As letters testify, he occasionally sent money to support his mother at his sister's request. Lydia Yakovlevna was her primary caregiver: from the early 1930s until her death, Raisa Ginzburg lived with her in a communal apartment at 24 Griboedov Canal.

These are only the most essential biographical correspondences.[61] The autobiographical dimension is in keeping with Ginzburg's documentary aesthetic. One cannot know what aspects of the story, other than the change of a mother-daughter relationship to that of an aunt and nephew, were intentionally fictionalized by the author. But it is instructive to consider a statement Ginzburg made about another story that dealt with remorse, "Delusion of the Will," based on the death of Mark Ginzburg.[62] When this story was published, Natalia Sokolova recognized the prototype, and wrote to her aunt for confirmation. The latter replied: "Mark is indeed present in 'Delusion.' Aside from you there is no one, I think, who could guess this. But, of course, a lot has been transformed and extended [*mnogoe transformirovano i domysleno*]."[63] Ginzburg's readers and friends in the 1980s knew so little of her private life in the 1930s that not much fictionalization was required to disguise any biographical referents. Ginzburg's vague expression—"Mark is indeed present"—leaves ample room for poetic license. And her choice of the word *domysleno* ("thought through," "extended") seems significant given her voiced aversion to "invention" (*vydumka*, something thought up): she was more likely to fictionalize by omission and selection than by the addition of wholly fictional characters or situations.[64]

Ginzburg's "A Story of Pity and Cruelty" is what Herzen promised his "A Story of a Family Drama" would be: "a narrative from psychological pathology" (*rasskaz iz psikhicheskoi patologii*).[65] Along with the marked differences from Herzen—for example, the fact that his story involves a cast of colorful characters and takes place over several years and in multiple countries, while Ginzburg's features just two isolated beings in a section of a communal apartment over several weeks—there are also parallels. Herzen's autobiographical character stands for a politically active young Russia while his enemy represents the petit bourgeois West.[66] Aunt (whom Otter describes as "imperialistic") represents the selfish pre-Revolutionary bourgeoisie, whereas Otter shares the values of the *intelligentsia* of the 1920s generation. Otter is not a positive hero—even given his capacity for self-conscious reflection and selfless sacrifice, his moral foundations are tenuous and he acts cruelly and egotistically. Still, he fits into Herzen's mold: he tries to find a basis for moral behavior in coherence or interconnectivity, judging Aunt for living too much in the moment (a phrase Ginzburg uses to describe Herwegh in her scholarly work).[67] Beyond this, there are several passages in Ginzburg's narrative that have close relatives in Herzen's text: for example, where Otter laments caring for his aunt's dying body after having abused her living one. Ginzburg writes, "care came too late, and for a body that was already unfeeling, things were done that the body needed while still alive." This thought resembles Herzen's regret, "If I had tended her sick soul with half the care I gave afterwards to her sick body, I should never have let this rankling sorrow send out roots in all directions."[68]

In Ginzburg's book on Herzen, she notes that the compositional unevenness in his "Story of a Family Drama" produces an unmatched impression of authenticity.[69] The draft of her own "story," with its raw emotional power, possesses this quality to a heightened degree, and seems to have been written shortly after the death of Ginzburg's mother. Even while sticking to the outline stated in the story itself (to analyze self-pity, pity for Aunt, the process of her death, guilt and remorse), the last section balloons out of all proportion. She repeats certain passages, adding to the unfinished quality of this unpublished text. One interpretation might be that Otter's repetitions of certain scenes and phrases are thematically motivated by his difficulty in working through the haunting details of his relationship to Aunt. And yet it is difficult to separate Otter's repetitions and excesses from the author's:

> In the world where everything was horribly literal, each of these complexes struck Otter as catastrophic, as threatening his ruin. And against these complexes he conducted a struggle that was cruel, rude, desperate, breaking his strength—and completely in vain. For against him

> there stood a *stubbornness* that was monumental, irrational, elemental, moved by the dark intuition of desires that sought momentary satisfaction—a stubbornness against which persuasion, pleas, and rage were all powerless.

> В мире страшных буквальностей каждый из этих комплексов казался Оттеру катастрофическим, грозящим ему гибелью. И он вел с ними жестокую, грубую, отчаянную, надрывавшую его силу—и совершенно тщетную—борьбу. Ибо против него стояло монументальное, иррациональное, стихийное, движимое темной интуицией мгновенного удовлетворения желаний—упрямство, против которого были бессильны и убеждение, и мольба, и злоба.[70]

These long, perhaps excessive, lists of adjectives and nouns seem to express Otter's (and perhaps Ginzburg's) lingering frustration and desperation. In fact, the nephew's fundamental grievance against his aunt is that she fails to account for him as a person. This conflict has a long history: even in unfinished 1930s sketches for *Home and the World*, Otter feels that Aunt neither fears nor respects him (unlike his older brother V.), nor does she reckon with his needs or desires, such as those connected to his vocation.

Otter's frustration can be read in terms of the ethical ideal of connectedness, since in Aunt he confronts a person, living in a state of forgetfulness, for whom words do not seem to matter. Otter frets that to give advice to her is "like throwing a pea against a wall."[71] And yet his guilt stems from the perception that his verbal abuses are crimes. Even if *no one* were to hear his screaming insults, it would still count, because he is a writer and a person for whom the word is an ethical act.[72] It is these ghosts, these "ineradicable events of memory,"[73] as Herzen put it, that force one to find the strength to reckon with the past. For Herzen also, secret crimes matter (though in his life, in contrast to Ginzburg's, almost nothing was secret). For example, his friends Engelson and Orsini hatch a secret plot to do away with Herwegh, but Engelson makes the mistake of seeking Herzen's blessing. In the story, Engelson regrets opening his mouth: "Engelson: 'My damned weakness, but anyhow nobody will ever find out that I've told you.' '*But I know*,' said I in answer, and we parted."[74]

If personal life reflects large-scale history, then private, personal crimes become highly meaningful. In Herzen's worldview, behavior in domestic life is completely relevant to, and has consequences for, a person's public undertakings as a political activist.[75] In the blockade, Ginzburg describes a chain of evil extending from "plates thrown on the floor" in disgust to the worst crimes of war.[76] And yet there are oceans separating Ginzburg's narrative methods from Herzen's. Even if he cleansed most of his memoirs of guilt,

Herzen sought to make sense of his failures and successes in public, in his voluminous first-person memoirs. Ginzburg's task was different, in part because she was not a public figure (especially before the 1960s). Departing from Herzen's style of self-presentation, Ginzburg writes in the third person about a semi-fictional character, and limits the scope of her narratives to a single situation. Hers is a different, fragmentary sense of biography, born of a post-individualist era. She never gives a character's life story, only the traits that are "functional"—that is, relevant to the current conflict. And so she divides up her hero's experiences, keeping "A Story of Pity and Cruelty" separate from "Otter's Day" and from *Notes.*

THE MAKING OF *NOTES OF A BLOCKADE PERSON*

The plot of "A Story of Pity and Cruelty" is structured around the central event of Aunt's death and Otter's efforts to overcome his trauma. In contrast, "Otter's Day" is written as a "day in the life," a model with a rich history including Victor Hugo's *The Last Day of a Condemned Man,* Tolstoy's "A History of Yesterday," and, more recently, Solzhenitsyn's *One Day in the Life of Ivan Denisovich* (1962).[77] "Otter's Day" reads like a first draft of *Notes of a Blockade Person* and provides most of the material for N.'s day in the later work (specifically, part 1 and "Intervals of a Siege Day" [*Otrezki blokadnogo dnia*]). *Notes* is thus more expansive and generically more heterogeneous, and the single narrative strand concerning N. and his typical day becomes less important. What is remarkable is that the main timeframe in "A Story of Pity and Cruelty," "Otter's Day," and *Notes of a Blockade Person* is unfailingly spring–summer 1942, designated everywhere as the "breathing space" (*peredyshka*), a period of relief after the harsh and deadly winter of 1941–42.[78] And yet while the narratives coincide temporally, they describe alternative realities. The Otters of the two latter texts experience no family tragedy or remorse, even though their days take place in what was the worst period for the first Otter.

In "Otter's Day," the conflict so exhaustively explored in the earlier story is condensed into a single paragraph differentiating the two aspects of Otter's relationship to Aunt: antagonism (because she symbolizes chaos) and dependency (because supporting her gives value and meaning to his life). Despite Aunt's minor role, the simple fact of her existence allows Ginzburg to delineate clearly the difficult routine of her hero's day (which she cannot do in *Notes* without adding elements of fiction), a routine that provides the basic structure of the narrative. After the morning chores and breakfast, Otter's regimen leads him from home to the office, to a cafeteria for lunch, to a second cafeteria, home for Aunt's lunch, back to the office, and finally home for the night.[79] It is a double circle, and doubly exhausting. There are no scenes showing the hero's rudeness; each time meals at home are described, Aunt is either not mentioned or is lying in bed, feeling weak.

In creating *Notes of a Blockade Person* from "Otter's Day," Ginzburg entirely removes Aunt as a character. Instead she speaks in general terms of the distinction between those who returned home with "booty" to impress their loved ones, and those who lived alone.[80] N. experiences an "after-lunch depression" (*posleobedennaia toska*) because of the painful brevity of the meal that in peaceful, more leisurely times would have broken up the day.[81] But the cause of his despair has no evident interpersonal element.

Excising Aunt's death and, eventually, her entire existence, from the narratives gives rise to strange features in "Otter's Day" and *Notes of a Blockade Person*. There is a curious moment in "Otter's Day" during the winter of 1942–43, when the hero suddenly acquires full bread rations and extra cafeteria coupons. His genuine food trauma begins in the wake of this abundance. Ginzburg gives a reason for the increased rations (Aunt's relocation to a hospital), but her decision not to develop the Aunt theme prevents her from giving sufficient reasons for the trauma. She writes: "The worst time for Otter set in when, objectively speaking, better times set in (it was this way for many). At that time, he already received 400 grams of bread. His aunt was in the hospital, and he moved to the office, because at home temperatures were already far below zero." In "A Story of Pity and Cruelty," the ailing Aunt wants to move to the hospital, but Otter does not allow it. He dreads the difficulties involved in procuring a spot for her and delivering food across the city, and privately he fears being without her. Nor does he want to interrupt their relations in this most horrible phase, leaving nasty feelings on both sides. After her death, his decision not to arrange a hospital stay for her plagues him. Ginzburg herself lived at the radio station after her mother's death. In an interview, she describes the move in a way that resonates with "Otter's Day," where the radio station is an oasis of life: "After my mother's death (she died of starvation), I took up residence at the radio station, like some other writers who worked there. It is precisely this, I think, that helped [me] survive. At home there was frost, darkness, a deafening silence, but here there were people all around, and this was very important psychologically."[82] In *Notes of a Blockade Person*, she writes that the sound of voices and the presence of other people at the radio station provided a spiritual lift during the difficult hours after lunch, but there is no mention of a death at home as having produced this stark contrast.[83]

Ginzburg reintroduces into *Notes* the theme of guilt, which was absent in "Otter's Day." In addition to the generalized passages discussed at the beginning of this chapter, she offers several fragmentary illustrations, most of them concerning the food-related traumas of anonymous individuals. In some cases, she directly discourages autobiographical readings. For example, she prefaces the small sketch summed up as "a story of pity and cruelty" with a statement distancing it from her own experience: "Among the blockade stories that I have collected is the story of O."[84] Near the end of part 1, however, the reader may detect that Ginzburg is alluding to experiences that were drawn directly from her own life (and now we can read fuller portrayals of these moments in her earlier, more autobiographical narratives): elliptical statements erupt as if out of the void about burnt cutlets and a piece of candy that was greedily withheld.[85]

An examination of two similar passages from different texts will further showcase the dynamics involved in Ginzburg's transposition of her story about guilt. In "A Story of Pity and Cruelty," there is a passage near the end of the narrative, when food supplies increase—too late to reverse Aunt's fate. Otter recalls bringing home chocolate and butter, her favorites, while she lies dying and unable to eat. He makes a mixture of the two ingredients, and eats it alone:

> He ate, and he was rent by anguish. This was the most acute sensation of anguish and grief he ever felt in connection with this death. Food, the experience of food was intimately associated with her, and now it had come to an end, the interest had ended, the human interest in food; what remained was something dark and animal-like. And at the same time it seemed to him that food was drowning his anguish, physically blocking it, that this food was sealing it up, passing deep down somewhere there to meet the gnawing anguish. He chewed and swallowed, but the anguish rose up in response. It was the saddest of all the sad moments that he experienced in those days.

> Он ел, и его терзала тоска. Это было самое острое ощущение тоски и горя, которое он испытал в связи с этой смертью. Еда, переживания еды были тесно ассоциированы с ней, и вот это кончилось, и кончился интерес, человеческий интерес еды; осталось что-то мрачное и животное. И в то же время ему казалось, что еда заглушает тоску, физически забивает ее, залепляет ее эта пища, проходящая вглубь куда-то туда навстречу сосущей тоске. Он жевал и глотал, а тоска подымалась навстречу. Это была печальнейшая минута из всех в эти дни пережитых.[86]

Ginzburg and her character seem to be searching for words to capture the intertwining of physical and emotional processes in eating. The "saddest moment" connects the aunt's final sickness to her death, since in both periods

Otter experiences the dehumanizing effects of eating alone. Simply ingesting food will not help to alleviate his suffering; the whole process exacerbates his grief and reminds him of his shared meals with Aunt. Food has become nothing but an animal substance and cannot perform the emotional work he requires. In "Otter's Day," the hero also experiences an "animal relationship" to food after the worst period of hunger has ended. Already living at the radio station (while Aunt is in the hospital), he is "maniacally focused on food." Ginzburg writes: "On better days he shoveled three portions of porridge onto one plate, so that it looked like there was a lot. And he fell into despair because there was still not enough."[87]

This detail about multiple bowls of porridge also appears in a scene from *Notes of a Blockade Person* in a variation on the passage from "A Story of Pity and Cruelty." The character here, however, is not O. or N., but an anonymous person in the Writers' Cafeteria.

> In one of the nooks of some office or other there stood a woman, wrapped in scarves. With a dark, impassive face she ate porridge from a tin, spoonful after spoonful. For those times, it was considered a lot of porridge.
>
> —My mother died,—she said as she stopped an unfamiliar passerby,—this porridge is from her coupon. . . . Such anguish, unimaginable. And it won't pass, not for anything. I thought—what happiness to eat three bowls of porridge, four bowls. . . . But I can't, I don't want to. . . . I swallow and swallow, because the anguish, it's down there, deep inside: I keep thinking—it will get better. This porridge, this mush will sink down there, below, will press down the anguish, smother it maybe. I eat, eat, but the anguish won't pass.

> В каком-то из закоулков какого-то из учреждений стояла женщина, обмотанная платками. С темным, неподвижным лицом она ела ложку за ложкой из банки кашу. По тогдашним понятиям, каши было довольно много.
>
> —А у меня мать умерла,—остановила она проходившего мимо малознакомого человека,—каша вот по ее талонам . . . Такая тоска, невероятная. И ни за что не проходит. Думала—какое счастье съесть сразу три каши, четыре каши . . . Не получается, не хочу . . . Глотаю и глотаю, потому что тоска, она там глубоко, внутри: мне все кажется—станет легче. Эта каша, жижа опустится туда, вниз, придавит тоску, обволокнет ее, что ли. Ем, ем, а тоска не проходит.[88]

For the first time, the pain of eating is connected to grief over the loss of a mother (rather than an aunt or a sister). Ginzburg cloaks this character in headscarves and places her in some vague corner of an unspecified office, as if literally to mask her identity. These gestures of concealment and overdetermined anonymity prepare (or allow) for an unusually direct confession of grief made by a female character, albeit in halting phrases addressed to a perfect stranger. What probably began as a painful personal experience, and was translated into an expressive scene in the introspective "A Story of Pity and Cruelty," has now been transformed into faltering spoken utterances. Ginzburg intends for the voice of this anonymous coworker, confessing her trauma to a stranger, to be indistinguishable from those of historical others in this documentary piece.

We see from this example how, in revising bits of "Otter's Day" to produce *Notes of a Blockade Person,* Ginzburg added details from her "story of pity and cruelty," while carefully limiting its explosive power, and dissociating any grief from the leading character, N. (after first dissociating him from herself). There are other cases where she completely reverses her hero's experiences. A scene from "A Story of Pity and Cruelty" describes Otter's daily preparations for work, in which he runs up against his aunt's inability to perform the task he has begged her to carry out:

> For example, every time when he had to get ready for work and at once gather the lunch tins to take with him, the inattentiveness complex came into effect. It turned out the lids weren't ready, and he had to search for the string-bag. This was repeated day after day, regardless of entreaties and promises. It reduced him to despair. The person [Aunt] who was supposed to help was standing in his way. The rational system was destroyed.
>
> Например, каждый раз, как надо было собираться на работу и заодно брать с собой обеденные банки,—вступал в силу комплекс невнимания. Крышки оказывались неприготовленными, авоську надо было искать. Это повторялось изо дня в день, несмотря на просьбы, на обещания. Это приводило его в отчаяние. Человек, который должен был помогать,—мешал. Рационализация рушилась.[89]

When Ginzburg later describes this scene, she transforms and idealizes it. In "Otter's Day," where there are no obstacles to the hero's success, the packing of the containers is resoundingly triumphant:

> In this area, Otter has everything well-organized. The tins—a one-liter tin for soup, half-liter for porridge (for his aunt's lunch). Each tin is matched with a tightly fitting lid from a jar. The string-bag is placed among the containers, wrapped into a ball—in case there are any additional hand-outs—and a tin box, with a spoon across it. It is an uncomplicated arrangement, of which Otter is proud. It is a small victory over chaos, over a piece of chaos. It is the beginning of orderliness, of sociability. It is the beautiful

> beginning of organization, which defeats the cursed isolation of an egotistical person, uniting him with the system of the social whole.
>
> Здесь у От. все хорошо подобрано. Банки—литровая для супа, полулитровая для каши (это обед тетки). К банкам подобраны плотно налезающие на них консервные крышки. Между банками кладется свернутая в клубок авоська—на случай каких-нибудь дополнений и жестяная коробочка, поперек ложка. Это нехитрое устройство, которым От. гордится. Это маленькая победа над хаосом, над частицей хаоса. Это начало стройности, социальности. Это прекрасное начало организации, которое побеждает проклятую изоляцию эгоистического человека, приобщая его к системе социального целого.[90]

The despair from the previous narrative has been replaced by a fantasy of technical order. Aunt's disastrous role has been removed (though the past-passive participles leave unclear who arranges the tins). We sense Otter's joy over the well-organized, beautiful arrangement (*ustroistvo*) that has emerged out of chaos. There is discernable delight in the very process of describing every physical detail, down to the spoon lying crosswise.

The corresponding scene in *Notes of a Blockade Person* is abbreviated and subdued, and yet there is still something jubilant about how N. gets ready for work. Ginzburg portrays as "pleasant" and "automatic" the gestures with which he does up his tie and combs his hair. She writes: "The bag, packed with tins of various sizes and a string-bag wrapped into a ball, gets swung across his shoulder. This area of his life, detached from the chaos, is pretty well organized."[91] These are uplifting moments because they are mechanisms for extracting the territories of the body from the "chaos of things" (and the chaos of other real people). Instead of being part of the difficulty of domestic life, as in "A Story of Pity and Cruelty," these preparations for leaving home lead to entering the happier realm of social organization on the outside, where some things (trams, the Radio Station, the cafeteria) function autonomously, greased by others' efforts. N. is proud of his arrangement and the evidence of his "sociability."[92] These later revisions appear to carry out wish fulfillments, cancelling out the frustrations Ginzburg experienced.[93]

HISTORICAL LESSONS LOST, REVISED

When making *Notes of a Blockade Person*, Ginzburg revised and minimized the evidence not only of her personal traumas but also of her hopes that the country had reached a historical turning point. Andrei Zorin has gone so far as to argue that in 1942–43, she was trying to find a "theoretical justification for Soviet history," a meaning in the mass destruction of life in which the state had involved its citizens (and not only in the war against Nazism and Fascism).[94] While Ginzburg, unlike Herzen, did not hope for a social revolution, she did hope that the war and the blockade would bring about an internal change in people, who would develop a new kind of self-consciousness. She includes an autobiographically infused passage in "Around *Notes of a Blockade Person*" about how members of the *intelligentsia* had inherited from the nineteenth century a wish to rid themselves of egoism and isolation, dreaming of an "exit from the self, of responsibility, of the supra-personal." And the war seemed to offer an opportunity to realize this dream: "The *intelligent* now had to want the same thing that the common cause wanted from him. The old utopian problem (how it had enticed Herzen!)—would it not be solved by the synthesis of the state's logic with the logical absurd of the self-valued personality?"[95] Alienation and separation from society had to be overcome because the state now required its citizens to participate in the war effort and prepare for the ultimate sacrifice. Even as the worst days of the siege passed, Ginzburg observed around her new behavioral norms, taking shape around a Leningrad group identity, which discouraged cowardice and selfishness.[96]

In her notes from the second half of the blockade, Ginzburg observes several times that people are "maturing" or "ripening" inwardly to a stage where they can understand "that egoism as a standard of conduct is equal to death, that hedonistic individualism and humanistic socialism are untenable; and this is owing to two factors that have emphatically been revealed for people—the illusory nature of individual existence and the ineradicability of social evil."[97] Though Ginzburg sees no documentable evidence that any changes in people's attitudes have occurred, she believes that "deep historical shifts"[98] have produced a desire for change and an understanding among a select group that what is needed is nothing short of a "rebirth": "People thought that they would change, they passionately wanted to change, but it didn't happen. . . . But they have ripened for change, and the best among them understand the necessity of the rebirth of humanity."[99]

The new consciousness that Ginzburg glimpsed "ripening" around her was "civic" in nature. In a draft for the theoretical section of "Otter's Day," the words she uses are "ascetic civil awareness" (*asketicheskaia grazhdanstvennost'*), "civic consciousness" (*grazhdanskoe soznanie*), and a "new Spartanism" (*novoe spartanstvo*). It is hard to imagine that she would have idealized Sparta's total militarization of society and regulation of citizens' behavior. And yet, as Herzen had said of Sparta, "The individual personality [*lichnost'*] was lost in the citizen, and the citizen was an organ, an atom of another, sacred, deified person, the person [*lichnost'*] of the city" ("Личность индивидуума терялась в гражданине, а гражданин был орган, атом другой, священной, обоготворяемой личности—личности города").[100] Ginzburg had no utopian dreams that any social organization could be completely benign, writing that the new Spartanism "does not refute the inevitability of social evil and unfreedom." Instead, it "demands that the individual person put himself at the disposal of the community" as the new Spartanism "searches for the correct dialectic of social evil, the substitutes that are most favorable for the given historical formation."[101] It is unclear what kinds of "substitutes" she has in mind.

Ginzburg worries that her whole concept of civic consciousness is too abstract to function on a mass scale: "*Grazhdanstvennost'* in terms of its positive content is too abstract and rationalistic. It has genuinely controlled the human masses only in its religious variant (the ancient world). The *downfall* of pure belief in the state and in social utopia lies in its abstractness." She had noticed how it was love for the motherland rather than ideals of citizenship that had successfully mobilized the Soviet people: "The consciousness of the modern person finds the idea of the motherland, of the nation, to be the most adequate form of communal life. The motherland is an emotional bond that does not fear irrational, irresolvable residues."[102]

There were no contemporary models for the kind of civic consciousness Ginzburg was hoping for. And she herself documents the failure of this consciousness to actually develop. First, there is the devastating individual case of Otter in "A Story of Pity and Cruelty," which demonstrates that even an individual who intends to act morally cannot do so. Then there is the behavior of her fellow writers and radio station workers, who were desperate to assert themselves by climbing higher up the social hierarchy than their peers: "They hastily, greedily grasp at any sign of differentiation, at anything that ought now to separate them [from the crowd], protect them."[103] And in an essay from January 1944, she writes that even though people have inwardly changed, they haven't realized it yet—and so instead they "rush to recover their previous position."[104] One of her acquaintances, "A.O.," imagining how things will change when the war ends, speaks about the competition for jobs (fearing that blockade survivors will lose out to those returning from the front), as well as the need for material comforts and family life. She notes, "This person thinks not about the future forms of self-consciousness, but thinks—and justifiably so—about how he will live, how he can exit from that socially diminished position in which he has found himself."[105]

And even as writers seek to give shape to their experiences of the war, Ginzburg observes that the Writers' Union continues to function according to its prewar norms. Writers continue to repeat the usual slogans: they complain of a lack of productivity in literature, of the failure of Soviet writers to produce new epics, and propose that an increase in production can be attained through fulfilling plans and combining the correct ideological position with a sincere will to work. She remarks of a Writers' Union meeting in August 1943: "Despite the rise of a common will, everything continues to take place according to official and bureaucratic order. For all its shortcomings, this is a form that has been worked out, and now is not the time to reconsider it, and who knows whether it will be reconsidered in any sort of near future."[106]

When revising her drafts between 1962 and 1983, Ginzburg left intact the section about the illusory nature of the individual consciousness and the ineradicability of social evil—the lessons that she had drawn from the war and which she thought her generation of the *intelligentsia* had absorbed. But she modified the sections about the ripening of a new civic consciousness. Instead of an actual shift, what she now describes is an intense thirst for change, a tentative desire for "purification in the common will," the search for a new solution that proved elusive. In the published version of "Around *Notes of a Blockade Person*," we read: "The person who has been destroyed, tested by catastrophes, does not have the strength to believe in the beauty and absolute value of the individual soul. It is much more natural for him to feel disgust for this naked soul and a bitter and vain thirst for purification in the universal, in some kind of desired system of connections—in religion? In existential self-projection? In a new *grazhdanstvennost'*?"[107] She justifies the impulse to search, instead of being able to recount the successful adoption of a new model or the realization of a new consciousness. The reality that awaited the country was much darker. In the published version of *Notes*, Ginzburg uses the benefit of hindsight to note the sad historical turn: "This tormented country won. And without even knowing it, the country was preparing to enter a new frenzy of social evil."[108]

CONCLUSION

Readers have long interpreted *Notes of a Blockade Person* as a memoir, a diary, or some other form of documentary prose.[109] The title of the published English translation, *Blockade Diary*, may be responsible for some misunderstandings and for shorthand references to the work as a "diary."[110] The fictional aspects of the text are generally brushed aside by historians who rely heavily on Ginzburg as they seek to understand and characterize life during the blockade. And *Notes* does appear to be a veritable gold mine, containing, in neatly compressed and generalized form, testimony (corroborated elsewhere) on shifting gender roles, changing identities, reading habits, methods of food preparation, and the physical transformation of the city.[111]

And yet, as we have seen, Ginzburg performed complex transformations of personal experience within her generalized narratives (which were also based on her observations of others), sometimes even reversing or idealizing it. Though she characteristically avoided generic labels, she designated *Notes of a Blockade Person* as a *povestvovanie,* a form she described as "something that lies between a novel, a tale, and an essay [*esseistikoi*]."[112] She labored over the generic ambiguity of her composition and was bothered by critics who were too quick to categorize it.

> E. S. Ventsel' is among those who noticed my prose and rated it highly, but even she published a review of *Notes of a Blockade Person* under the title "Prose by a Scholar." Kaverin wrote to me about the striking physiological exactitude "which, *strangely enough* (italics mine), does not hinder the artistic quality of perception."
>
> Especially insistent have been the attempts to classify this work as a memoir, despite the obvious fact that the leading character is not memoiristic. Just a few days ago at a meeting of the Critics' Section, Ninov called *Notes* memoir-documentary prose. To call it simply prose would apparently contradict the social status of the author.[113]

Ginzburg wanted *Notes* to be read as "simply prose," and blamed her reputation as a literary scholar for inspiring readers to view it otherwise. She insisted on the text's fictional aspects, perhaps exaggerating the significance of her composite character N., whose male gender was meant in part to broadcast his nonidentification with the author. Ginzburg's avoidance of traditional autobiography could be understood as a move to preserve her own freedom in narrative, so that she could present a representation of her experience without falling into the trap of self-exposure or catering to the heroic myth of the blockade survivor.[114]

Over the years, Ginzburg tested out various direct statements to discourage autobiographical readings. In the 1960s, she drafted the following note to introduce two major sections of what later became *Notes*:

> The two psychological episodes that follow were recounted to me by two people who knew nothing about one another. Both episodes were written down by me according to convention [*uslovno*] as continuously constructed confessions [*sviazno postroennykh priznanii*] (the first in brief, the second at some length). They were set down by me and, probably for that reason, these narratives have come to resemble one another and everything else that I have written about the blockade.[115]

This discarded note announces intentions that diverge from Ginzburg's usual creative practice. In the 1940s drafts, the hero of both "confessions" was Otter, and the character remained consistent (though not identical) across all later versions, even after the name changed. The "brief" narrative, which readers know as "Paralysis" ("Otsepenenie"), concerns a single psychological state: the disease of the will that plagues a person recovering from starvation.[116] When she later published "Paralysis" as a narrative in the first person, Ginzburg framed it as a "psychological episode" constructed on the basis of stories told by several "blockade people."[117] The second narrative, written "at some length," resembles part 1 of *Notes*, and is neither a "continuously constructed confession" nor a "psychological episode." It is fragmentary and disjointed, covering the psychology of winter and spring, of food and work, as experienced by many Leningrad intellectuals.

This note is telling for other reasons. Ginzburg invokes the "continuously constructed confession" as the narrative convention to which she adheres, even as she is creating something entirely different (here she uses the word *priznanie*, referring to a confession in a social or legal setting, such as a confession of love or of a crime, and not *ispoved'*, which refers primarily to Christian confession, and is used for example to translate Rousseau's *Confessions*). Her discontinuous, heterogeneous, generalized narratives may have begun with a series of confessions, but they have been utterly transformed and hidden among observations and descriptions of other people. Ginzburg states that what ties these "confessions" together is their singular voice or manner ("They were set down by me, and for that reason . . ."). This indicates a traditional notion of authorship, which persists despite her radical approach to character and self-presentation.[118]

Ginzburg's usual mode in her notebooks, to a much greater extent than in her *povestvovaniia*, is to "write completely indirectly: about other people and things as I see them."[119] The "I" is often a hidden observer, an analyst—still a kind of unifying presence. Meanwhile, when Ginzburg writes of an autobiographical self, it is usually an observed self (or multiple selves) that is split off from the observing one and held at a distance. Otter and N. become objects, "substitute characters."[120] Ginzburg is then free to partition their experiences and spread them across separate narratives.

In certain cases, perhaps, the reader can postulate Otter-N.'s identity across the texts (for example, relating parts of "A Story of Pity and Cruelty" to *Notes*). And yet by dividing these narratives and making them contradictory in places, Ginzburg was attempting to show two things at once. First, that one's individual experiences and words matter and have historical relevance: this is an article of faith she inherited from Herzen. At the same time, it need not matter (to readers) precisely whose experiences these are, which individual is being depicted, or whether the specific detail or word can be traced back to a single biological or biographical organism. One should note that Ginzburg specifically allowed Herzen the right to separate out and elevate his experiences, to conceal and transform embarrassing elements of his biography, since he was investigating the relationship of the personal to the historical.

In the 1940s, working on the drafts for *Notes of a Blockade Person*, Ginzburg was trying to design a new way of analyzing personality:

> The new method of examination corresponds to the new (at this point still predominantly negative) concept of a person. The psychological novel of the 19th century arose on the great illusions of individualism. Now the examination of a person as a closed, self-sufficient soul has a sterile, imitative quality. The contemporary understanding is this: not a person, but a situation. The intersection of biological and social coordinates, from which the behavior of a given person is born, the way this person functions. A person as a function of this intersection. This dismal analytical method does not occur to me as valid for all times, but as the most adequate for the negative concept of a person that exists at the present moment.

> Новому (пока еще преимущественно негативному) восприятию человека соответствует новый метод его рассмотрения. Психологический роман 19 века возник на великих иллюзиях индивидуализма. Сейчас рассмотрение человека как замкнутой самодовлеющей души имеет бесплодный, эпигонский характер. Современное понимание—не человек, а ситуация. Пересечение биологических и социальных координат, из которого рождается поведение данного человека, его функционирование. Человек как функция этого пересечения. Этот унылый аналитический метод не мыслится мне действительным на все времена, но лишь наиболее адекватным существующей в данный момент негативной концепции человека.[121]

This concept and method of investigation—of a person as a function, an intersection of biological and social "coordinates"—was roughly the one to which Ginzburg adhered. Even if heroes of the psychological novel were influenced by their environments, they were nevertheless organically connected to traditions of individualism. The nineteenth-century concept of a "self-sufficient soul" was not adequate to a new age: in a later formulation of Ginzburg's, the person was now an *ustroistvo,* that is, an organization or arrangement.

In her documentary writing, Ginzburg investigates personality as shaped by the social and historical context. While constructing *Notes of a Blockade Person,* she strove to create a historical narrative out of a personal experience. She left behind "traces" of a recovered past (her own personal drama)—

many of which would be deciphered only in the twenty-first century. Even if Ginzburg maintained the notion that a writer's actions, behaviors, and words matter, and should have a bearing on his or her writings or public activities, she felt no obligation to engage in confession (in fact, she felt an aversion to this activity, as we have seen in her reaction to other women's accounts of the blockade). Her own autobiographical self becomes representative of the twentieth-century "immanent person," who exists only in a particular situation. Her total isolation, her hidden identity as a writer, and the hidden nature of her drama—in contrast to Herzen's—were part of what made possible the successful partitioning and fictionalization of personal experience, as well as the creation of a character who was condemned to isolation and failure. For this character, it was a battle, and not an inalienable right, to exist as a single connected individual.

Conclusion

SUSTAINING A HUMAN IMAGE

Lydia Ginzburg is a writer whose techniques of analysis and ethical evaluation aim to overcome the catastrophic predicament of the "post-individualist self." This person is fragmented but anti-Romantic, and lacking moral absolutes; he is "immanent," meaning that he can experience life's value only empirically, in and through himself. He is crushed and tested by the external circumstances of war and terror, and has no grounds on which to base a hope for a revolutionary transformation that could bring about a more just society. As Ginzburg wrote during the Leningrad Blockade—and just a few years after Stalin's purges: "when you grumble about social evil, beware: this evil may be serving as a placeholder for something even more deadly."[1] Despite her skeptical outlook, Ginzburg's narratives rest on the optimistic notion that one can learn to act in a more decent way, and acquire a better understanding of one's mistakes, through systematic, probing thought aimed at discovering guidelines by which one could truly live. In an environment where strong core values and beliefs are lacking, these efforts find their inspiration in remorse and guilt, which inspire a repentant subject to connect actions across time; applying analytical thought to memories provides the most promising guide to responsible, ethical behavior.

With her sense of reality as hopelessly fragmented, Ginzburg found it possible to make sense of—or even defend against—the threatening world around her through writing. She also felt she had little choice in the matter. In 1934, for example, she remarks, "A person's possibilities are defined by what he cannot do, at least as much as by what he can do. A writer is a person who cannot experience [*perezhivat'*] life without writing."[2] The double negative is significant here: she cannot *not* write, since writing allows her to experience life. Writing is thus an inevitability but also a deed (*postupok*), which accompanies active living. To write is to make real, or to make available to consciousness, the surrounding world (recall Ginzburg's claim that whatever was not expressed in words did not have reality for her).[3]

She also conceived of her personal need to write as having a wholly social underpinning. Discussing Tolstoy in *On Psychological Prose*, Ginzburg wrote, "the undeniable necessity of giving one's thought and one's creativity and labor to the outside world bears witness to the social human being's primary awareness of communal bonds and of himself in terms of those bonds. Whether he wants to or not, a person acquires that awareness along with the social and cultural contents of his mind and with his language as the carrier of shared meanings." But she goes on to point out a paradox of writing's social aspect: "To be sure, that sense of connection excludes neither the conditions of loneliness and isolation that are psychologically opposed to it, nor the most cruel and powerful of egoistic impulses."[4] Note that the writer may experience not just loneliness, but "loneliness and isolation"; not just egoistic impulses, but of the "most cruel and powerful" sort. This kind of pathos in a book of late Soviet scholarship makes sense to readers only in retrospect: Ginzburg was writing about her own experiences as a prose writer. Soviet literary culture, with its censorship, its official directives, and its collusion at times with the evils of the State, made the social basis of her writing at times seem an impossible dream.

Ginzburg's deep awareness and constant theorization of her own position is part of what prompted Alexander Zholkovsky to remark that Ginzburg "has left us no room for meta-transcending her text. . . . All one can pretend to is the role of grateful connoisseur of the findings, which, so un-Picasso-like, have disguised themselves as mere searchings."[5] It is true that Ginzburg was at once author and critic of the very genre she practiced, and left behind insights that help to illuminate her own experiments. And yet scholars need not feel at a loss to add to what she is able to say about herself. This study, while drawing on Ginzburg's own theories of in-between prose, has aimed to shed light on unexpected relationships among her choice of genres, her rhetorical strategies, and her search for what I call the post-individualist self.

This book has also brought to light several paradoxes attending Ginzburg's creations, and I would like now to expand on a few that have been only implicit until now. Ginzburg was rather skeptical about the individual writer's ability to transcend the discourses and conditions of her time—and in fact, she saw this rootedness in the present as a positive sign of the individual's connection to his or her culture. At the same time, in many ways she appears to have cultivated an alternative ethics and way of writing, strongly connected to the tradition of the intelligentsia and the literary giants of the previous century such as Tolstoy and Herzen. To repeat her words: "A writer felt the pressure of his time, but he still could not forget the lessons of the nineteenth century."[6]

Ginzburg's approach to character, even as she endeavors to overcome the legacy of individualism, is traditional in certain ways. The main problem with naturalistic psychological novels for her was their presumption of "the crude fiction of the objectivity of what is being represented. The objectivity of sensations, of the thought process, of people who sit down at and get up from a table. People who are understood not as a constructed system, but as a thing."[7] Her distrust of techniques that presuppose anything but a subjective reality and her view of people as "constructed systems" make of her a modernist writer. Ginzburg analyzes her heroes with attention to functions, mechanisms, and structures—deindividualizing operations typical of both social science and Tolstoy's methods. Diminished in stature from the typical nineteenth-century variety, this "hero" is a democratic "everyman" in the spirit of Kafka or Hemingway.

And yet Ginzburg's concept of the "new prose" was that it should preserve the formal unity of personality or character, something akin to the literary hero. The contours of this hero's personality are not erased. A minimal level of structuring of personality was necessary, given Ginzburg's interest in values, and also made aesthetic sense to her. As she writes in her critique of the *nouveau roman* and other twentieth-century experiments in *On the Literary Hero*, certain elements of form inhere in writing despite all attempts to abolish them. A narrator or narrative subject must have features or signs (*priznaki*), and these signs become characteristics that he or she possesses (*svoistva*). Moreover, the "materials of a composition inevitably aspire to be concentrated in separate nodes, points."[8]

And even as her fragmentary style reflects a modernist spirit, Ginzburg's attempts to achieve maximum clarity in her own verbal formulations show the influence of Pushkin's prose aesthetics, which champion "precision," "brevity," and "thoughts."[9] In 1934, she criticized the logical endpoint of Modernist or Formalist prose—fanciful combinations of words that are hollow signifiers, which have lost their relationship to reality and to ideas. Her ideal was to squeeze each word out of experience: "a new cognition of reality is possible only when each verbal formulation is obtained through new experience, not like the unwinding of a runaway ball of verbal yarn, but like immediate relationship to the thing (Tolstoy is frighteningly good at this continually renewed measuring up of words and realia in experience)."[10]

One of the results of this constant measuring of words and reality is the "formula," which captures penetrating observations about human behavior in historically contextualized situations. Ginzburg once observed that readers only *seem* to "recognize" the phenomena authors describe when they read something and think to themselves "yes, that's just how it is in life." In fact, she wrote, readers would not be able to perceive these things at all if authors did not first reveal them.[11] Ginzburg's mission to describe the reality around her may have gathered a certain intensity due to the fact that official, publishable literature had only a tenuous link to this reality, or one that was distorted by ideology. Now that her writings have finally come to light, they have become a valuable document of Soviet reality—of the experiences, impressions, and fiercely analytical observations of a person who lived through it. Many of her "formulas" are so apt and so clearly codified that her readers might even come to take for granted her efforts to help them recognize the truth in the behaviors and phenomena she pinpointed. For instance, one thinks of her one-liner to describe the silence around the purges during the terror: "No one talks about those things that you don't talk about."[12] Or her observation that in the Stalin era, scholars were guilty of subtle lies that consisted not in embracing an ideological worldview, but rather in "intonation," "in a hurried display of agreement, in the use people made of the occasion or the moment to declare 'I think so too.' "[13] One thinks also of her keen diagnosis of the effects of literary censorship and the situation of literature at the end of World War II: "In conditions of absolute unfreedom, it is very hard and very easy to be daring. For everything is daring, every unregulated breath is daring."[14]

A further paradox inheres in Ginzburg's understanding and practice of in-between genres. She had observed that the author of in-between literature was freer from stylistic conventions than the novelist or the poet, and hence could nourish the discovery of new themes and ideas of personality. Ginzburg's études and sketches of the personalities around her seem to gain from the stylistic freedom of her form. And yet she often runs up against constraints imposed by other kinds of conventions. Hence Ginzburg found her abilities to express same-sex desire constrained by literary and cultural tradition (not to mention the kind of self-censorship internalized by Soviet writers). Already in her teenage diaries, she adopts heterosexual models in her attempt to understand and represent lesbian love. Her writings on love for *Home and the World* retain these models, which prevent her from representing the external circumstances (for example, the reasons her characters need to keep their relationship secret, and their inability to build a life together) that would have made her prose more direct and possibly more powerful. Moreover, even at the end of her life she left these writings on love unpublished. Documentary prose has fewer constrictions, but literary tradition still affects it, and social convention still determines which experiences can be depicted there and how. Ginzburg tries not to give her readers access to the particular pathos of her fate—in any autobiographical way—but then she communicates it inadvertently because of the gaps that result from measuring up her personal experience against general cultural models.

Other paradoxes of Ginzburg's approach arise from her notion of the self-image. She describes the process of constructing an image as a necessary step in the twentieth-century self's overcoming of fragmentation, which enables a person to judge her actions according to some chosen standard. And yet the self-images she documents in others are intended to be mechanisms for survival, for navigating the treacheries of social hierarchies. These self-images are used to assert one person's ego over another, to "claim one's own"; they are convenient assemblages that exclude and excuse unpalatable acts as not belonging to oneself. The armor-like quality of these self-constructions intensifies as the personal failures in life multiply. Ginzburg's notes take an analytical approach to this problem, and demonstrate a brutal honesty toward herself and others. She wrote of herself as a person typical of her generation, whose members experienced a catastrophic history and were cognizant of "the ineradicable nature of social evil and the illusoriness of the individual consciousness." While many of her more autobiographical writings reflectively treat problems of identity (in the sense of questioning continuous selfhood), memory, and responsibility, her studies of her contemporaries focus to a larger extent on the "relational" aspects of the self.[15]

Her particular sensitivity toward her contemporaries' experiences of hierarchies may be related to the fact that in the central decades of her life (the 1930s, 1940s, and 1950s), Ginzburg experienced hindrances to realization in most of her spheres of activity—professional and creative. She occupied a relatively marginal position, in part because aspects of her identity were not tolerated by the regime (her Jewishness, her sexuality, her attachment to the Formalists), and in part due to her unwillingness to make ideological or moral compromises. Meanwhile, she watched carefully as others rose and fell in the professional hierarchies, driven by their different wills, ambitions, and personalities. In her sketches of the experiences of the intelligentsia under communism, she was finely attuned to the issue of "self-actualization": the degree to which a person could fulfill his or her talents and abilities within the system—and whether one could still work within the system while maintaining a moral self-image. With a curiosity that sometimes bordered on resentment, she sketched her friends' rise and fall, all the while remaining critical of her own marginality, egoism, and thirst for recognition.

Ginzburg contemplated the problem of self-actualization in ways that blended philosophy with psychology. In "Notes on Prose," one of the central meta-statements about her project from the late 1930s, she writes: "The correspondence between the impossible, the possible, and the insistently necessary forms the line of fate. This line is drawn by the regularities of a person's realization [*zakonomernost'iami realizatsii cheloveka*], the hindrances to his realization, the overcoming, the circumvention of these hindrances or their triumph." It seemed impossible not to write, but equally impossible to publish; it seemed perhaps possible to survive as an independent scholar and lecturer, but these activities sapped energy from the "insistently necessary" vocation of writing. This dynamic—of the possible, the impossible, and the insistently necessary—could also surround questions of love, or of survival in the Leningrad Blockade.

A final paradox of success and failure deserves further reflection, since it enters into debates on Ginzburg's legacy[16] and overlaps with the paradox of traditionalism and innovation. My work on Ginzburg, concentrating as it does on the decades of the 1930s and 1940s, brings to the fore the problematic of failure in her career as a writer. The notebook project, begun in the lively atmosphere of the 1920s, was in some ways destined to come to an end in the 1930s. As Ginzburg knew, the role of *littérateur* was possible only in a vibrant literary culture, and her efforts to document this culture were bound to fade when that culture physically disappeared.[17] On the face of it, the 1930s, when Ginzburg was "in search of a novel," was a decade occupied by two failures: *The Pinkerton Agency,* because it was not "her" novel (though she made a living from it), and *Home and the World,* because it was never completed. During the blockade, Ginzburg continued to work on her ambitious set of narratives, embedding some of her insights on the post-individualist self into "Otter's Day" and "A Story of Pity and Cruelty," and continuing to develop her theories through the close study of oral speech and self-assertion. She was unable to publish most of her drafts from these years, even as she incorporated some of them into *Notes of a Blockade Person* and other works.

The 2011 publication of these blockade-era sketches and drafts in *Passing Characters* inspired the scholar Sergei Kozlov to perceive the extent of Ginzburg's failure:

> It turns out that from this point of view life in the blockade was for her not a terrible misfortune, but an exceptional opportunity, which gave her unprecedented experience. And it turns out that in the end she was unable to fulfill her goal. This historical fiasco of Ginzburg's is staggering in scale, specifically on the strength of the scope of the results that were achieved. Why did she suffer defeat where more traditional writers—from Bulgakov and Pasternak to Grossman and Solzhenitsyn—each in his own way, achieved their goals? But this kind of analysis is a task for the future.[18]

The current study allows us already to propose answers to Kozlov's question. It may be fair to say that Ginzburg failed in some sense to bring her ambitious project of the 1930s and 1940s to fruition. And yet, one must state that this project would never have become a novel like *Doctor Zhivago* or *Life and Fate,* or even like *In Search of Lost Time* (despite Grigory Gukovsky's notions, based on his acquaintance with "The Return Home"). Given Ginzburg's aesthetics and her understanding of her historical context, any novel of that kind would have been impossible for her. And if she succeeded, she succeeded precisely in *not writing* a novel. Her characters have no biography: they are constructions and systems; her world can be accessed only through a consciousness where the sense of time is refracted by guilt and remorse. She inclines toward the documentary, toward direct, quasi-scientific analysis, and indeed toward the fragment. The "essays" show an unwillingness to overcome this fragmented experience or to be dishonest about it.

Summing up his reaction to the 2011 collection of Ginzburg's blockade writings, Kozlov also speaks of how it presents a "new" Ginzburg. This "new" Ginzburg, most evident in the archives, is capable not only of explaining the psychology and outlook of *Homo Sovieticus,* but also the history of its formation. The new Ginzburg has an early, a middle, and a late period instead of being seen as the author of a single, undifferentiated mass of essays. The present volume makes this Ginzburg available—and other Ginzburgs too: the writer whose reflections on the historical dimensions of individual personality have implications beyond the Soviet context; the one who reflected the catastrophic twentieth-century experience of the post-individualist self; and one of the few writers to analyze lesbian experience in Stalinist Russia. Ginzburg's systematic and careful approach to the psychology and language of hunger, loss, humiliation, and remorse make her writings worthy of future scholarship by those working in trauma studies.

The Ginzburg archive is still being catalogued. The quantity and quality of the materials warrant much further study and informed publication. Not only will future literary scholars find valuable materials in Ginzburg's legacy of letters, manuscripts, and fragments, but cultural historians would find material to enhance our understanding of the Soviet literary environment as a whole and the Leningrad cultural sphere in particular.[19]

Ginzburg's case as a scholar-writer differs from those of figures such as Viktor Shklovsky, Roland Barthes, or Susan Sontag. I believe that her prose takes precedence over the scholarship for which she was once exclusively known, and which sustained her material existence for more than a half-century. And yet, further directions for productive scholarship on Ginzburg include the study of the intersections between belles-lettres, in-between prose, and scholarly theory and analysis—from which we could draw lessons about the interpretation of literature. We can also examine a larger question: to what other purposes—creative, ethical, psychological—can the analytical techniques of literary scholarship (of Russian Formalism for instance, or of those acquired through a liberal arts education) be fruitfully used? We can broaden our consideration of Ginzburg's "formula" or maxim and further the study of how it might bring inductive scholarship closer to fiction (for example, through generalization).

In Ginzburg's notebooks, begun at a moment when literary studies were becoming a separate discipline, we have seen a return to a moment before the professionalization of literature and history, a connection to authors like

Vyazemsky and the Duc de Saint-Simon. As she continued on her creative path, Ginzburg tried to combine the occupations of historian and novelist. She leaves us with the sense that creative thought, autobiographical prose, and semi-fictions are vital for understanding the "facts" of human experience as well as the connections between these facts.

One of the largest aesthetic and ethical questions Ginzburg faced at the outset (and to which she continually returned) arose from the problem of a fragmentary identity, the loss of the unified subject and of transcendental values. She addressed, head on and through various narrative techniques, the dilemma of how to found an ethics that could work for a disconnected subject, in a morally bereft environment. Ginzburg's strategy of self-distancing can be productively studied in the context of ongoing dilemmas of identity, selfhood, narrative, and ethics. Her attempts to show how we can achieve some degree of connectedness and coherence, at least in our ethical relations with others, have some relevance in a world where we as persons sometimes seem to be just collections of data, both to ourselves and to the powers that be. Ginzburg's notion of art as an exit from the self, an escape from egoism into social value, shows that her solutions are life affirming, even if they are neither as utopian nor as radical as the ideas of Mikhail Bakhtin. She acknowledges that we are above all social and ideological beings, but her conclusions do not agree with those suggested by Michel Foucault's theories, which can make the individual appear practically powerless. For her, the social realm is not a trap: common values and a common language are in fact what save us.

Ginzburg's now oft-quoted call for literature to start a conversation about "how to survive and how to endure without losing one's human image" ("как бы выжить и как бы прожить, не потеряв образа человеческого") is remarkable. There may be no human essence, no stable identity, and yet the preservation of a human image is essential. As she wrote in the blockade, using a biological metaphor that speaks doubly for the body's recovery, one can work backward from images to values and motivations: "under a once-empty membrane, something like a living nucleus that corresponds to it gradually forms."[20] Egoistic acts may be given a heroic meaning in retrospect, and then one's self-image (as a Leningrader, in this case) may inspire moral behavior in the future; an ideal concept can generate real motivations.[21] In a post-individualist, catastrophic environment, one can begin with the leftover shards of earlier value systems and build the depths.

NOTES

INTRODUCTION

For an explanation of my system for referring to archival materials, please see "A Note about Spelling, Transliteration, and Archival References." Some of the material for this introduction originally appeared in the introduction to Emily Van Buskirk and Andrei Zorin (eds), Lydia Ginzburg's Alternative Literary Identities (Oxford: Peter Lang AG, 2012) and is reproduced here with permission.

1. Ginzburg, "Variation on an Old Theme," in Lidiia Ginzburg, *Zapisnye knizhki. Vospominaniia. Esse* (St. Petersburg: Iskusstvo-SPb, 2002), 269. Henceforth, I refer to this volume as "Ginzburg 2002." All translations are my own unless otherwise noted.

2. See Richard F. Gustafson, "Ginzburg's Theory of the Lyric," in *Canadian-American Slavic Studies* 19, 2 (Summer 1985): 135–39.

3. Sergei Kozlov, "Lydia Ginzburg's Victory and Defeat," trans. Emily Van Buskirk, in *Lydia Ginzburg's Alternative Literary Identities*, eds. Emily Van Buskirk and Andrei Zorin (Oxford: Peter Lang AG, 2012), 23.

4. Lidiia Ginzburg, 1943–46 notebook, in *Prokhodiashchie kharaktery. Proza voennykh let. Zapiski blokadnogo cheloveka.*, eds. Emily Van Buskirk and Andrei Zorin (Moscow: Novoe izdatel'stvo, 2011), 204. Henceforth, I refer to this volume as "Ginzburg 2011."

5. Ginzburg 2002, 198; from "Celebration of the Sunset."

6. In Russian: "При всей субъективности это сознание, в сущности, неиндивидуалистично,—оно не смеет уже удивляться собственной конечности." Ginzburg, "The Thought That Drew a Circle" in Ginzburg 2002, 574.

7. Paul John Eakin, *Living Autobiographically: How We Create Identity in Narrative* (Ithaca, NY: Cornell University Press, 2008), xiv. Jerrold Seigel, *The Idea of the Self: Thought and Experience in Western Europe since the Seventeenth Century* (Cambridge, UK: Cambridge University Press, 2005), 3.

8. Charles Taylor, *Sources of the Self: The Making of Modern Identity* (Cambridge, MA: Harvard University Press, 1989), 32. Ellipsis added. Taylor defines identity as follows: "My identity is defined by the commitments and identifications which provide the frame or horizon within which I can try to determine from case to case what is good, or valuable, or what ought to be done, or what I endorse or oppose. In other words, it is the horizon within which I am capable of taking a stand." Ibid., 27.

9. William James, *Psychology: Briefer Course* (Cambridge, MA: Harvard University Press, 1984), 161–63.

10. Ginzburg 2002, 583; from the narrative "Delusion of the Will."

11. Ibid., 199; from "Celebration of the Sunset."

12. Lidiia Ginzburg, *O literaturnom geroe* (Leningrad: Sovetskii pisatel', 1979), 135.

13. Varlam Shalamov, "O proze" (1965), in Shalamov, *Sobranie sochinenii v shesti tomakh*, vol. 5 (Moscow: Terra—Knizhnyi klub, 2005), 144–57.

14. Though Shalamov rejects "literary stuff," his minimalist tales resemble short stories in many ways, with characters—who sometimes lay bare their thoughts for the narrator, a sign of fiction—moving in a three-dimensional world. His distance from Ginz-

burg is evident in his declaration, "The analysis of Kolyma Tales is in the very absence of analysis." Ibid., 154.

15. Ginzburg 2002, 198–99; from "Celebration of the Sunset."

16. Robert Folkenflik, "The Self as Other," in *The Culture of Autobiography: Constructions of Self-Representation*, ed. Robert Folkenflik (Stanford, CA: Stanford University Press, 1993), 222.

17. Osip Mandel'shtam, "The End of the Novel," in Osip Mandel'stam, *The Complete Critical Prose and Letters*, ed. Jane Gary Harris, trans. J. G. Harris and Constance Link (Ann Arbor, MI: Ardis, 1979), 198–201. Russian in Osip Mandel'shtam, "Konets romana," *Sochineniia v dvukh tomakh* (Moscow: Khudozhestvennaia literatura, 1990), 201–5.

18. Ginzburg 2002, 142. See my discussion of this important passage in chapter 2.

19. I avoid the term "diary novel" since it has connotations of a *fictional* narrative in the form of a diary. See for example Lorna Martens's definition of a diary novel as "a fictional prose narrative written from day to day by a single first-person narrator who does not address himself to a fictive addressee or recipient." Lorna Martens, *The Diary Novel* (Cambridge, UK: Cambridge University Press, 1985), 4.

20. Ginzburg, unpublished entry from ZK VIII–IX (July 1933–January 1935), 37–38. OR RNB 1377.

21. Ginzburg writes, for example: "a new understanding of reality is possible only when each verbal formula is obtained on the basis of new experience." In Russian: "новое понимание действительности возможно только когда каждая словесная формулировка добывается из нового опыта." ZK VIII–IX (1933–35), 35–36. OR RNB 1377. She writes in a 1935 note critical of Symbolism: "Empty words like annuled currency, words that are no longer justified by creative efforts, or suffering, or social upheavals, which at one time gave a basis to their values." In Russian: "Слова, пустые, как упраздненные ассигнации, слова, не оправданные больше ни творческими усилиями, ни страданием, ни социальными потрясениями, в свое время положившими основания их ценности. " Ginzburg 2002, 125.

22. Ginzburg 2002, 198; from the 1958 essay "Celebration of the Sunset" (quoted earlier).

23. Unknown until my discovery of this narrative in the archives, "A Story of Pity and Cruelty" was published in the 2011 volume edited by Andrei Zorin and myself, *Prokhodiashchie kharaktery*.

24. Ginzburg 2002, 400. In Russian: "Я совершенно лишена этой возможности; отчасти из застенчивости, которую можно было бы преодолеть, если бы это было нужно; отчасти из соображений, которые, вероятно, не нужно преодолевать."

25. Ibid., 201, 269, 344.

26. Ibid., 400. In Russian: "Можно писать о себе прямо: я. Можно писать полукосвенно: подставное лицо. Можно писать совсем косвенно: о других людях и вещах, таких, какими я их вижу. Здесь начинается стихия *литературного размышления*, монологизированного взгляда на мир (Пруст), по-видимому наиболее мне близкая." The original note is in ZK III (1928), 61. OR RNB 1377. The full note (beginning on ZK III 57) includes an important reflection on the novel that Ginzburg published: see Ginzburg 2002, 60.

27. Interview with Liudmila Titova in *Smena* 13 November 1988 (262, 19112): 2. Ginzburg says: "In contemporary prose the sense of the author is very much on the rise. That being said, the author does not necessarily have to speak about himself. He takes the

floor for a conversation about life. Not autobiography, but a direct expression of his life experience, his view of reality." In Russian: "В современной прозе очень возрастает ощущение автора. При этом автор не обязательно должен рассказывать о себе. Он берет слово для разговора о жизни. Не автобиография, но прямое выражение своего жизненного опыта, своего взгляда на действительность."

28. Johann Peter Eckermann was Goethe's friend and personal secretary, who recorded and published his conversations with the poet. Ginzburg wrote:

"Boria: It's a mistake that you so rarely write down your own witticisms and aphorisms. . . .

Me: I'm afraid of damaging my own sense of humor. You see, it's no good when a person follows himself around with pencil and paper. And in general, when each person becomes his own Eckermann."

In Russian: "Боря: Напрасно ты так редко записываешь свои остроты и афоризмы. . . .

Я: Боюсь повредить собственный юмор. Понимаешь, нехорошо, когда человек сам за собой ходит с карандашом и тетрадкой. И вообще, когда каждый сам себе Эккерман."

Unpublished note from ZK III (1928), 73. OR RNB 1377.

29. In Russian: "охват изображаемого." Lidiia Ginzburg, *O psikhologicheskoi proze* (Leningrad: Khudozhestvennaia literatura, 1977), 204. English translation in Lydia Ginzburg, *On Psychological Prose*, trans. Judson Rosengrant (Princeton, NJ: Princeton University Press, 1991), 163.

30. Ginzburg 2002, 24. The full note in Russian:

"Для того чтобы быть выше чего-нибудь—надо быть не ниже этого самого. Н. Л., человек с самой благородной оригинальностью, какую я встречала в жизни, говорила:

—Прежде всего нужно быть как все.

Добавлю: все, чем человек отличается, есть его частное дело; то, чем человек похож,—его общественный долг."

N.L. from this note can be decoded as Nina Lazarevna Gurfinkel', Ginzburg's closest childhood friend and confidant.

31. Diary of September 1922–February1923, 9–10. OR RNB 1377.

32. In Russian: "Что касается меня, то, при всем моем здравомыслии, и я оказываюсь в некоторых отношениях чересчур раритетным человеком для литературы." ZK III (1928), 59. OR RNB 1377.

33. "Pisatel'skaia mysl' i sovremennost': Chto est' chto?" ("A Writer's Thought and Contemporaneity: What's What?"), Interview, *Literaturnaia Rossiia* 51, 1351 (23 Dec. 1988): 8. In Russian: "[Неромантическая пушкинская модель] в том, что пока поэт не занят своим творчеством (а это—высочайшая для Пушкина), то он должен быть в жизни как все люди < . . . > Потому что творчество—эта высочайшая ценность для Пушкина, дело его высшей духовной жизни. А в остальном—в быту, в семье, в свете—оставаться, как все люди < . . . >." Ginzburg explains that Pushkin died while proving he was like other people. For he agreed to a duel with Georges D'Anthès ("a fop and a scoundrel"), who he knew could kill him, because he wanted to act according to the behavioral model of his milieu, and not to place himself as a poet above such actions.

34. Michael Lucey, *Never Say I: Sexuality and the First Person in Colette, Gide, and Proust* (Durham, NC: Duke University Press, 2006).

35. The first published biographical sketch of Ginzburg, starting with childhood, was Jane Gary Harris's "A Biographical Introduction," in *Canadian-American Slavic Studies* 28, 2–3 (Summer–Fall 1994): 126–45. Though it has some inaccuracies, it represents an important first biography that draws on interviews with Ginzburg and family photographs from Ginzburg's collection, as well as published essays.

36. Ginzburg 2002, 296.

37. Natalia Viktorovna (whose mother was Nadezhda Germanovna Bliumenfel'd) was married for a time to the famous poet Konstantin Simonov. Later, she married Pavel Sokolov. In her Moscow archive, she prefaces the biography in the following way: "Taking up this work, I don't at all pretend to analyze Lydia Ginzburg's style or range of ideas; others will be able to do this without me. I simply know some things about Liusia as a person, and do not want this to be lost or to die with me. According to my beliefs, grains of the past, even insignificant ones, should be preserved with care. Maybe it will come in handy for someone. In places my work resembles a family chronicle. Well, so be it." RGALI. F. 3270 Op. 1, delo 27. Sokolova Nataliia Viktorovna. N. V. Sokolova, "Lidiia Ginzburg, rodnia, znakomye. Materialy k biografii." (1990s, 93 pages), 2.

38. The story behind Viktor Ginzburg's stage name is that it evolved from the Russian word for "boss," *nachal'nik*, shortened to *chainik*, or in English, "teapot."

39. Lydia Ginzburg's father died on 14 December (old style) 1909 at the age of 45. He and his brother not only owned a brewer's yeast factory and laboratory but also were editors of a trade paper called *Vestnik vinokureniia.* An obituary of Yakov Ginzburg appeared in *Vestnik vinokureniia* 6 (30 May 1910), 62–67. A short notice of his death had appeared in *Vestnik vinokureniia* 20 (31 December 1909).

40. Elsewhere in the memoir, Natalia Sokolova describes three of Raisa's siblings she remembered: Avenir, Liuba, and Sonia Gol'denberg, who lived together in Ostankino (where they moved in the mid-twenties), near Moscow. None of them ever married. Avenir taught mathematics. One sister died before the war; the other one, after. Lydia Ginzburg visited them when in Moscow and sent Avenir money from time to time. Natalia Sokolova knew of one other sister, a favorite of Lydia Yakovlevna's, named Iul'tsa. She had emigrated with her husband and lived in Czechoslovakia, and did not have children.

41. N. V. Sokolova, "Lidiia Ginzburg, rodnia, znakomye," 3–4.

42. See Ginzburg's "autobiography," written for official purposes, reproduced in Ginzburg 2011, 503.

43. N. V. Sokolova, "Lidiia Ginzburg, rodnia, znakomye," 5.

44. As a sign of their prosperity Sokolova cites the fact that they served ice cream at home, in a silver bowl. Nevertheless, they were not wealthy enough to have box seats at the opera (unlike the Bliumenfel'ds, her other grandparents). Photographs of the house where Ginzburg grew up, as seen from the courtyard and the stairwell, survive in the archives. According to Alexander Kushner, one of her younger friends traveled there in the 1980s and brought the photographs back for Lydia Ginzburg to comment on and identify. About the German tutor, see Ginzburg 2002, 393.

45. See Ginzburg's attempts to read a Ukrainian review in her letter to Boris Bukhstab: "Pis'ma L. Ia. Ginzburg B. Ia. Bukhshtabu," commentary and introduction by Denis Ustinov, *Novoe literaturnoe obozrenie* 49, 3 (2001): 355.

46. See Nataliia Sokolova, "Ogliadyvaias' nazad . . . ," in *Voprosy literatury* 5 (1994): 285–92. See also chapter 3.

47. A strange but telling sign of how Ginzburg's sexuality could be regarded even by

a close relative: in recounting this accident Sokolova cites it as a possible cause of her aunt's homosexuality. N. V. Sokolova, "Lidiia Ginzburg, rodnia, znakomye," 29.

48. Ibid., 4. Viktor Tipot, who studied in Darmstadt (Germany) to become a chemist, chose Lutheranism ("the Augsburg faith of Melanchthon," as Sokolova calls it); he was already an atheist and regarded this as a practical matter, according to Sokolova. Avenir Gol'denberg converted to Russian Orthodoxy in order to study mathematics; his sisters followed suit. Ibid, 7.

49. Ginzburg 2002, 393.

50. Ginzburg, 1918–19 Diary. OR RNB 1377.

51. Ginzburg 2002, 392. This posthumously published note comes from ZK II (1927), 74–77. OR RNB 1377. Ginzburg wrote little on Jewish identities. An exception is the essay "The Jewish Question" from the Blockade period, published in Ginzburg 2011, 191–94. My English translation appeared in *Lydia Ginzburg's Alternative Literary Identities*, 353–57. Another exception is a 1989 essay published posthumously, which includes reflections on the different relationships of Pasternak, Babel, Mandelstam, and others to Judaism and their Jewish identity. Of herself, she writes here, "Just as I have external racial features, so do I, probably, have Jewish traits of mind and character. But this is a biological fact; for me they have not been socialized, not elevated to a structural meaning. And I know that I carry in myself a part of the fate and thought of the Russian intelligentsia. But the contradiction still won't release [me] . . . ." In Russian: "Так же, как у меня есть внешние расовые признаки, так, вероятно, есть еврейские черты ума и характера. Но это факт биологический; у меня они не социализированы, не подняты до структурного смысла. И я знаю, что ношу в себе частицу судьбы и мысли русской интеллигенции. А противоречие все же не отпускает . . . ." Ginzburg 2002, 427–28.

52. Ginzburg 2002, 277. English in *Lydia Ginzburg's Alternative Literary Identities*, 371.

53. Ginzburg 2002, 281. English in *Lydia Ginzburg's Alternative Literary Identities*, 375–76.

54. It appears that she actually lived not in the city, but in the suburb of Pargolovo, with her aunt, Liubov' Gol'denberg. 1920–22 Diary, 21. OR RNB 1377.

55. She continues: "Petersburg was for me a kind of turning point, the fount of *real* life, the fantastical city of Pushkin and Dostoevsky, in which there loomed for me some big spiritual ordeals, a creative longing that lay in wait for me. [*added:* I found this longing too, but it was morbidly boring instead of creative—20 September 1920] There everything was supposed to be reborn and begin. The word Petersburg (I do not like 'Petrograd') has a rather plain association for me. I always pictured some dimly lit not quite masses, not quite columns, as if made from cold, gray granite, and longing, longing, but in this longing is the solution to everything."

In Russian: "Четверг. 19. VII. 20. Вчера я в первый раз в жизни одна, т.е. без родных выехала из Одессы в Петербург. Страннее всего, что с детских лет я именно так и представляла себе окончить 8-ой класс и в Питер учиться. И вот несмотря на «время» именно так и произошло.

Петербург был для меня каким-то поворотным пунктом, кладезем настоящей жизни, фантастическим городом Пушкина и Достоевского, в нем мне мерещились какие-то большие духовные испытания подстерегающие меня творческая тоска. [insert: Я и нашла тоску, но не творческую а скучную мертвую 20. сент. 20г.] Там все должно было перsignal, начаться. На слово Петербург (Петроград я не люблю) у меня довольно плоская ассоциация. Мне все представлялись какие-то мутно светлые не-то громады не то колонны, как из холодного, серого гранита и тоска, тоска, но в этой тоске и разрешение всего."

I have corrected orthographical errors and archaisms. Ginzburg 1920–22 Diary, 1. OR RNB 1377.

56. For instance, there was a dramatic population decline, as men left for the front (World War I and then the Civil War), and families retreated to the countryside in search of food. During the Civil War, the city was briefly under siege by the White Army under General Yudenich. For a remarkable portrayal of the cold, hunger, and suffering in Petrograd during the siege of 1919, see Viktor Shklovsky's 1920 essay, "Petersburg during the Blockade," in *A Knight's Move*, trans. Richard Sheldon (Normal, IL: Dalkey Archive Press, 2005), 9–20, or Yevgeny Zamyatin's short story, "The Cave" (written in 1920, published in 1922). English translation in *The Portable Twentieth-Century Russian Reader*, ed. Clarence Brown (New York: Penguin Books, 2003) 90–102. Russian in Evgenii Zamiatin, "Peshchera," in *Sobranie sochinenii v 5 tomakh*, ed. St. Nikonenko and A. Tiurin, vol. 1 (Moscow: Russkaia kniga, 2003), 548.

57. Ginzburg 2002, 72. One of Ginzburg and Tipot's friends in their student years in Odessa was Alexander Naumovich Frumkin (whose first wife, Vera Inber, was also a friend of the family). As Ginzburg told her niece, "Shura" Frumkin spoke about chemistry with a level of inspiration that few have when speaking about poetry. Sokolova, 5.

58. In Russian: "Вот случай, один из многих: человек восемнадцати лет, с резкими гуманитарными способностями, с отсутствием всяких других способностей, вообразил, что для воспитания ума, для полного философского развития необходимо заложить естественнонаучную основу. И вот он в теплушке, по фантастическому графику 20-го года, пробирается в Москву—закладывать естественнонаучный фундамент будущей гуманитарной деятельности. Среди еще неизжитой разрухи и голода у него никаких материальных ресурсов и ни единой мысли о том, как же, собственно, практически от заложенного фундамента (на это уйдет, очевидно, несколько лет) переходить потом к освоению профессиональных знаний и что есть при этом . . . Им казалось тогда, что они мрачные и скептические умы. На самом деле, сами того не понимая, они гигантски верили в жизнь, распахнутую революцией. В этом как раз их историческое право называться людьми 20-х годов." Ginzburg 2002, 192.

59. Ibid. Also, Ginzburg 1920–22 Diary, 42–43. OR RNB 1377.

60. Ginzburg 2002, 21. Ginzburg stopped writing poetry at age 22, when she had decided on a career and a vocation.

61. Ginzburg, 1920–22 Diary, 67. OR RNB 1377.

62. Ibid., 128–30.

63. In Russian: "Не понимаю,—сказал мне Эйхенбаум задумчиво,—как это вы могли от моря, солнца, акаций и проч. приехать на север с таким запасом здравого смысла. Если бы я родился в Одессе, то из меня бы, наверное, ничего не вышло. *(Июль 1927, Одесса)*" Ginzburg 2002, 41.

64. These were the Trotskiis, later Tronskiis (the change was because of Leon Trotsky). One of Ginzburg's closest friends growing up was Nina Lazarevna Gurfinkel' (1898–1984). (The two continued to be friends after Nina Gurfinkel'/Gourfinkel emigrated to Paris. For biographical information about Nina Gourfinkel and a bibliography of her works as a Slavist, see Ruth Schatzman, "Nina Gourfinkel," *Revue des études slaves* 63, 3 (1991): 705–23.) Ginzburg was also friends with Nina's older sister, Maria Lazarevna, who married Joseph Trotsky/Tronsky, a classicist. This was the couple who

helped Ginzburg get into the Institute. As I learned from Kseniia Kumpan, who has studied the history of the Institute, there were rolling admissions in 1922, and many students joined in November and December. It is possible that Ginzburg was not even examined. It helped that she already knew French and German. Ginzburg made a note in her 1929–31 notebook that supports the version that the Tronskiis helped with her admission: "Dear Kolia [Kovarskii], he too, though not suspecting it, participated in my professional resurrection: during my presentation he got up to turn on the light in the darkening auditorium—this seemed flattering to me. And on the next day he went up to Maria Lazarevna [Tronskaia], bowed and said: "Allow me to thank you for the gift you made to the Institute for the History of the Arts." And just as on the previous visit, he had told her as he wrinkled up his handsome nose and smiled genially: "Fie! You know, I haven't taken a liking to her at all, this girl of yours." In Russian: "Милый Коля [Nikolai Kovarskii], и он, сам того не подозревая, участвовал в действе моего профессионального воскресения: во-время доклада он встал, чтобы зажечь свет в темнеющее аудитории—это показалось мне лестным; на другой день он пришел к Мар. Лаз. расшаркался и сказал: Позвольте вас поблагодарить за подарок, который вы сделали Инст. Ист. Искусств. В предыдущий же раз он говорил ей, морща свой красивый нос и добродушно улыбаясь: Фу! Знаете, она ужасно не нравится мне, эта ваша девочка." ZK V (1929–31), 48. OR RNB 1377.

65. Interview with Kseniia Kumpan.

66. In the final entry of her journal from 1922–23 (from May 1923, p. 136), at age 21, Ginzburg writes of having received objective confirmation of her talents. She left a fuller account of this moment in ZK V (1929–31), 40–41. The presentation was on Gottfried August Bürger's "Lenore," in the Russian translations by Vasily Zhukovsky and Pavel Katenin. Ginzburg writes: "Never again have I experienced and never will I experience anything equal or even similar to that which I experienced in spring 1923, when Tynianov lavished praise on 'Lenore,' my *first* presentation as a student. [Author's insert from verso page: "On the whole, I got much loud praise in my student years, and then it stopped abruptly. That's how we commemorate the onset if not of academic maturity, then of academic adulthood. The last time I was praised was in 1926, for my first article on Vyazemsky."] [Back to recto page] [. . .] To some degree, this evening decided my life. I don't consider my life a brilliantly solved problem, but in any case I didn't go to the devil, whereas I could have; I wasn't far from it." In Russian: "Ни разу больше я не испытала и никогда не испытаю не только ничего равного, но и ничего похожего на то, что я испытала весной 1923 г., когда Тынянов расхвалил «Ленору,» мой первый студенческий доклад. [Insert from verso page:] Вообще меня много и шумно хвалили в студенческие годы, потом сразу перестали. Так у нас ознаменовывается наступления, если не академической зрелости, то академической взрослости. В последний раз меня хвалили в 26-ом г., за первого «Вяземского.» [Back to recto side:] < . . . > В какой-то степени этот вечер решил мою жизнь. Я не считаю свою жизнь блестяще разрешенной задачей, но во всяком случае я не пошла к чертям, а могла пойти; ходить оставалось не далеко." Dated: "Yalta, 14 September, 1929." OR RNB 1377.

67. Denis Ustinov notes that Tynianov was the theoretician most revered by the students of the Formalists, even though Eikhenbaum took more care in teaching and mentoring his students. See Denis Ustinov, "1920-e gody kak intellektual'nyi resurs: v pole Formalizma. Formalizm i mladoformalisty," *Novoe literaturnoe obozrenie* 50, 4 (2001): 303.

68. In Russian: ". . . мне удалось то, что удается далеко не всем—найти дело,

которое мне нравится и которое мне подходит, дело которое мне удается, и которое может быть мне будущее; я убедилась (наконец-то *объективно*) в том, что у меня есть силы творческие, м.б. и большие, но уже во всяком случае такие, которые на улице не валяются. < . . . >

Что у меня может быть в будущем? Что может быть в будущем у человека морально запутанного; у человека, для которого закрыта большая дорога личной жизни. < . . . > Вся идеология моей ранней юности лежала в этом—я верила, что я стану новым необычайным человеком, в новых необычайных условиях. Т.е. новое-то должно было быть внешне и для других, для меня же, этот человек был родной и знакомый тот идеальный человек, которого я вынашивала в себе. < . . . > А теперь мне все тверже кажется, что того человека и тех условий уже никогда не будет. Это я знаю только сейчас, впервые в жизни, как вывод из этих последних месяцев, и это потому, что моя жизнь а не «приготовление к жизни» очевидно началась и началась так по другому." 1922–23 Diary, 137–38 (recto and verso pages). OR RNB 1377.

69. In Russian: "Они же, метры, как таковые, в чистом виде, изменили жизнь. < . . . > Если бы не было Эйхенбаума и Тынянова, жизнь была бы другой, то есть я была бы другой, с другими способами и возможностями мыслить, чувствовать, работать, относиться к людям, видеть вещи." Ginzburg 2002, 56.

70. Ibid., 295. In Russian: "Нам показалось—и недолго казалось,—что мы начинающие деятели начинающегося отрезка культуры."

71. Ibid.

72. The group continued under Eikhenbaum's sole leadership until late 1927, when they broke with him over his turn toward the study of "Literary Environment" (*literaturnyi byt*) and continued on their own, with Viktor Gofman leading the other students. See Ginzburg 2002, 444–45 (from "Problema povedeniia"). See also Denis Ustinov, "1920-e gody kak intellektual'nyi resurs: v pole Formalizma. Formalizm i mladoformalisty": 302–5, 313–14.

73. In 1926, Ginzburg completed the "Higher State Courses in Art History of the State Institute for the History of the Arts." She became a research fellow (*nauchnyi sotrudnik II razriada Otdela slovesnykh iskusstv GIII*) and a teaching assistant at the Institute (*prepodavatel'-assistent VKGI*), leading courses and seminars on the history of Russian literature. See Ginzburg 2011, 504.

74. For the classic account, see Victor Erlich's *Russian Formalism: History and Doctrine*, 3rd ed. (New Haven, CT: Yale University Press, 1981 [1955]), esp. 118–39. See also Carol Any's discussion of Eikhenbaum's experience of this crisis in *Boris Eikhenbaum: Voices of a Russian Formalist* (Stanford, CA: Stanford University Press, 1994), 80–103.

75. Eikhenbaum was temporarily removed as well, as a consequence of the March 1927 "Dispute" between the main leaders of the Formalists and some Marxist representatives from the University. On Ginzburg's history with the University in these years, see the commentary of Denis Ustinov, "Pis'ma L. Ia. Ginzburg B. Ia. Bukhshtabu," 345, 385–86. See also *Rossiiskii Institut Istorii Iskusstv v memuarakh*, ed. I.V. Sepman (St. Petersburg: RIII, 2003), 266. On the Marxist dispute, see Denis Ustinov, "1920-e gody kak intellektual'nyi resurs: v pole Formalizma. Materialy disputa 'Marksizm i Formal'nyi metod,'" in *Novoe literaturnoe obozrenie* 50, 4 (2001): 247–78.

76. Ginzburg's article was "Opyt filosofskoi liriki (Venevitinov)," in *Poetika*, ed. V. Zhirmunskii (Leningrad: Academia, 1929), 72–104. For a history of the Institute for the History of Arts in this period of its destruction, see Kseniia Kumpan, "Institut istorii

iskusstv na rubezhe 1920-x–1930-x godov," in *Instituty kul'tury Leningrada na perelome ot 1920-x k 1930-m godam* (2011), at www.pushkinskijdom.ru/LinkClick.aspx?fileticket=lSfRoURS2-k%3d&tabid=10460, accessed 21 September 2014.

77. See Ginzburg's letter to Shklovsky in Denis Ustinov, "1920-e gody kak intellektual'nyi resurs: v pole Formalizma. Formalizm i mladoformalisty," 314. See also Stanislav Savitskii, "Spor s uchitelem: Nachalo literaturnogo/issledovatel'skogo proekta L. Ginzburg," *Novoe literaturnoe obozrenie* 82, 6 (2006): 129–54.

78. Denis Ustinov explores the complexities of the relationship between the "young Formalists" (*mladoformalisty*) and their teachers—given the Formalist teachers' own orientation toward radical innovation—in his article "1920-e gody kak intellektual'nyi resurs: v pole Formalizma. Formalizm i mladoformalisty": 296–321.

An additional reason for the rupture, Ginzburg thought, was that her teachers wrongly perceived her to be under the intellectual influence of Viktor Zhirmunsky, the editor of the volume where her article on Venevitinov appeared (she pleaded with Tynianov that she was *his* student, and merely Zhirmunsky's friend). Ginzburg explains the conflict to her niece in a letter quoted in Sokolova's memoir. It is in its way a commentary to a letter Sokolova had discovered to Tipot from a friend of the Ginzburg siblings, Lena Gernet.

"The conflict in 1930 was between us (the younger ones) and the maîtres. Its causes were both historical (the inevitable conflict that sets in between teachers and students) and psychological (they were angered by our rapprochement with the Zhirmunskiis and Gukovsky, we were angry at their indifference). In a word, what was going on was everything you'd expect in breakups, whether romantic or academic.

At the time I still possessed the capacity for strong reactions, and I reacted with letters (enormous ones)—a letter with explanations to Boris Mikhailovich [Eikhenbaum] and a letter with explanations of these explanations to Shklovsky. Shklovsky, as you can see, managed to frighten our relatives [that is, by calling Tipot to ask whether Ginzburg was okay]. From the whole history I saved Tynianov's letter, which is an extremely angry one."

In Russian: "В 1930 разбирался конфликт между нами (младшими) и метрами. Причины у него были как исторические (неизбежно наступающий конфликт между учителями и учениками), так и психологические (они сердились на наше сближение с Жирмунскими и Гуковским, мы—на их равнодушие). Словом, налицо было все, чему полагается быть при разрывах любовных и академических.

Я тогда обладала еще способностью к сильным реакциям, и реагировала письмами (огромными)—Борису Михайловичу с объяснениями и Шковскому с объяснениями объяснений. Шкловский, как видишь, даже напугал родственников. От всей истории у меня осталось и хранится письмо Тынянова, весьма сердитое."

N. V. Sokolova, "Lidiia Ginzburg, rodnia, znakomye," 42.

79. Confessing the whole ordeal to Shklovsky in January 1930, she wrote: "For me, the war is already over. The liquidation was for me a deeply personal, internal act (therefore I did not want to make it public); it was a liquidation of apprenticeship, of the excitement, of the years of study, of the Institute. It does not have any external consequences for me, it did not remove any of my external obligations. In public appearances, in the press, in conversations with people who weren't involved I consider myself to have just as little a right to show my disrespect as two months ago. And this is not at all from 'generosity'; even less is it from meekness . . . it is because for me, commitments to traditions outlive commitments to people." In Russian: "Для меня война уже конч-

илась. Ликвидация была для меня глубоко личным внутренним поступком (поэтому и не следовало его опубликовать); она была ликвидацией ученичества, пафоса, годов учения, Института. Никаких внешних результатов она для меня, разумеется, не имеет, никаких внешних обязательств она с меня не сняла. В публичных выступлениях, в печати, в разговорах с посторонними людьми я сейчас также мало считаю себя вправе проявить неуважение, как два месяца тому назад. И это отнюдь не из «благородства»; тем менее из кротости . . . это потому, что для меня обязательства к традициям переживают обязательства к людям." Ginzburg's letter to Shklovsky was published by Denis Ustinov in *Novoe literaturnoe obozrenie* 50, 4 (2001): 315–19, quotation on p. 319. The year "1929" in the manuscript and the publication is wrong; Ginzburg wrote the letter in January 1930.

80. See Ginzburg 2002, 114–15.

81. See ibid., 414.

82. The official publication date is 1932, but Ginzburg's notes recount that the first copies went on sale in February 1933. ZK VIII (1933) 1, note dated 18 February 1933. OR RNB 1377. I discuss Ginzburg's difficulties with this book in chapter 2.

83. Her address was Griboedov Canal 24, Apartment 5. She lived on the top floor. There is a letter from Ginzburg to Tipot dated 21 October 1928 that confirms this move. RGALI F. 2897. Op. 1 dela 88. Tipot Viktor Iakovlevich. Sokolova states in her account that the Gukovsky brothers, knowing they would be forced to take on apartment mates, preemptively chose their own. In Russian: "[решили] самоуплотниться (не ждать же, когда жилотдел их уплотнит, вселят кого попало)." N. V. Sokolova, "Lidiia Ginzburg, rodnia, znakomye," 22. The Gukovsky brothers then moved to Vasilevsky Island.

84. Ibid. See also the letter from Ginzburg to Tipot dated 23 March 1931. RGALI F. 2897. Op. 1 dela 88.

85. The end date of her work at the factory is not specified in her official "autobiography." See Ginzburg 2011, 503–5.

86. Her original plans were to write on "Tolstoy in the Sixties," after which she chose another unrealized dissertation topic: lyric poetry of the 1830s. She wrote in January 1932: "Not long ago, so recently that it is absurd, I first uttered the words that my dissertation—a book on poetry of the 1830s—would never be written." In Russian: "Совсем не так давно, до смешного даже недавно, я впервые выговорила словами, что моя диссертация—книга о поэзии 1830-х годов—никогда не будет написана." Ginzburg 2002, 99 (she published this note under the year "1931"). Her plan of study, including the description of her dissertation, was published, with commentaries, by Denis Ustinov in *Novoe literaturnoe obozrenie* 49, 3 (2001): 380–83.

87. See Ginzburg 2002, 338–41.

88. This line from Pasternak's poem "More than a Century Ago—not Yesterday" ("Stolet'e s lishnim—ne vchera"), a take on Pushkin's 1828 "Stanzas" ("Stansy"), is quoted in Ginzburg 2002, 116–117, 285, 289–90, 514.

89. Ibid., 292–93. Of the moral difficulties, Ginzburg wrote: "But the paradox is that when we sympathized [with the revolutionaries], we were much more moral—in everyday life and in political aspirations—than later, when we began to understand and our understanding turned into a mixture of indifference and fear. We were more moral in our living experience of the hierarchy of high and low, sacrifice of lower for higher, which makes up the essence of the ethical act." In Russian: "Но парадокс в том, что, когда мы сочувствовали, мы были гораздо нравственнее—и в повседневности, и в политических мечтах,—чем потом, когда мы стали понимать и понимание оказа-

лось смесью равнодушия и страха. Мы были нравственнее живым опытом иерархии высшего и низшего, пожертвования высшему низшим, что и составляет сущность этического акта." Ibid., 279.

90. Ginzburg 2002, 282. English translation in *Lydia Ginzburg's Alternative Literary Identities*, 377.

91. Ginzburg 2002, 289. English translation in *Lydia Ginzburg's Alternative Literary Identities*, 390.

92. Ginzburg affixed the date 1931 to this narrative's 1989 publication in *Chelovek za pis'mennym stolom* (Leningrad: Sovetskii pisatel', 1989). She had earlier appended the date 1929 to its publication in *Literatura v poiskakh real'nosti* (Moscow: Sovetskii pisatel', 1987). The second date appears to be a correction to the first.

93. In Russian: "Вот человек написал о любви, о голоде и о смерти.

—О любви и голоде пишут, когда они приходят.

—Да. К сожалению, того же нельзя сказать о смерти."

Ginzburg 2002, 336.

94. See Ilya Serman, "Writer-Researcher," *Canadian-American Slavic Studies Journal* 19, 2 (1985): 187–92.

95. See "Chetvertyi 'Razgovor o liubvi,' " 154–68. See also chapters 2 and 3 of this book.

96. Loose manuscript of 1933 essay tucked into the folder with Ginzburg, ZK VIII-2 (Sept. 1932–Nov. 1932). OR RNB 1377.

97. In Russian: "Итак, только теперь понятен исторический смысл этого выморочного поколения и символика его судьбы"; "Теперь я знаю кто это такие мои типовые герои—это люди двух войн и промежутка между ними." Ginzburg 2011, 294, 303.

98. Both titles were selected by Andrei Zorin and myself on the basis of textological research.

99. Ginzburg 2002, 285.

100. The fact that the years from 1944 to 1957 appear to have been by far the most arduous of Ginzburg's career and intellectual life has been corroborated by interviews—for example, by my conversations with Nina Pavlovna Snetkova, who met Ginzburg in 1957 just after the Herzen book came out. Snetkova was working in the division of the publishing house (Gosudarstvennoe izdatel'stvo khudozhestvennoi literatury) that brought out Ginzburg's Herzen book (it was located on Nevsky Prospect, 28 in the Singer building, which was also Dom knigi).

101. From 1944–47, Ginzburg was a doctoral student at the Institute of Literature at the Academy of Sciences. She described the topic of her dissertation as "Herzen's Creative Work, 1830–1850s."

102. Ginzburg 2002, 203.

103. Interview with Kseniia Kumpan, summer 2003. In Leningrad, Ginzburg led one seminar at the University (1948–50). She had also lectured in Leningrad at the All-Russian Academy of Arts (1944–46).

104. Ginzburg was attacked together with Eikhenbaum in *Zvezda* in 1949. See Any, *Boris Eikhenbaum: Voices of a Russian Formalist*, 195. Mikhail Gasparov recorded Ginzburg's explanation of the reason for her expulsion from Petrazavodsk University as follows: "it was because she gave *credit to the the bourgeois West for our reactionary Romanticism.*" In Russian: "за то, что она *отдавала на откуп буржуазному западу наш реакционный романтизм.*" Mikhail Gasparov, *Zapisi i vypiski* (Moscow: Novoe liter-

aturnoe obozrenie, 2001), 43, quoted in Lidiia Lotman, *Vospominaniia* (St. Petersburg: Nestor-Istoriia, 2007), 182.

105. Ginzburg 2002, 338–41.

106. Ibid., 294.

107. See Harris, "Biographical Introduction," 126. Ginzburg and Shalamov exchanged letters in the 1960s. A letter from Shalamov is in the archive as Op. 3, ed. khr. 491. Shalamov Varlaam Tikh., 21 August 1966, 1 l. The draft of an unfinished letter from Ginzburg to Shalamov is there as Op. 3, ed. Khr. 121, Ginzburg L. Ia, Pis'mo Varlamu Tikhonovichu Shalamovu, 27 June 1967, 1 l. OR RNB 1377.

108. Ginzburg uses this phrase in "At One with the Legal Order" in Ginzburg 2002, 296. English in *Lydia Ginzburg's Alternative Literary Identities*, 399.

109. These qualities (and others, including occasional flashes of a "Southern" temperament, certain fears and superstitions connected to the Terror, an appreciation for food despite an inability to cook, a typical Leningrad/Petersburg habit of rising late, and more) were described in several interviews (some of which are still ongoing) I conducted with the following younger friends of Ginzburg, in 2003 and 2004: Alexander Kushner, Elena Nevzgliadova, Eleazar Meletinsky, Elena Kumpan, Kseniia Kumpan, Al'bin Konechnyi, Galina Murav'ëva, Aleksei Mashevsky, Nikolai Kononov, Konstantin Azadovsky, Elena Shvarts, Nina Korolëva, Irena Podol'skaia, Nina Snetkova, Yakov Bogrov, Irina Paperno, John Malmstad, William Mills Todd III, Yakov Gordin, Elena Rabinovich, Marietta Tur'ian, Zoia Tomashevskaia, Nadezhda Zolina (phone interview), and others.

Some of the more noteworthy reminiscences include those by Ilya Serman, Victor Erlich, and Irina Paperno in *Canadian-American Slavic Studies* 19, 2 (Summer 1985); by Mikhail Gasparov, Andrei Bitov, Alexander Chudakov, Boris Gasparov, Alexander Zholkovsky, Alexander Kushner, and Aleksei Mashevsky in *Canadian-American Slavic Studies* 28, 2–3 (Summer–Fall 1994) (some of these were published earlier in *Literaturnoe obozrenie*); by Alexander Chudakov, Sergei Bocharov, and Andrei Levkin in *Novoe literaturnoe obozrenie* 49, 3 (2001); and by Elena Kumpan and Elena Nevzgliadova in *Zvezda*, 3 (2002). See also Elena Kumpan, *Blizhnii podstup k legende* (St. Petersburg: Izdatel'stvo zhurnala "Zvezda," 2005): 62–104; and Lidiia M. Lotman, *Vospominaniia*, 178–87.

110. Tipot wrote to Ginzburg in 1955, "Send some samples of your photo-activities" In Russian: "Пришли какой-нибудь образчик твоей фото-деятельности." RGALI F. 2897 op. 1 del. 88, Tipot Viktor Iakovlevich, Pis'ma i telegramma Tipota V. Ia. Ginzburg Lidii Ginzburg (sestre) 26 Nov. 1928–August 1960, 30 ll. A few dozen photographs from Ginzburg's oeuvre are preserved in her archive. OR RNB 1377.

111. In Russian: "Таинственные ростки будущего, листы, которые складываются в стол, теперь не более, чем следы павших замыслов." Ginzburg 2002, 193. One hears echoes in Ginzburg's sentence of Vasily Rozanov's *Fallen Leaves* (*Opavshie list'ia*), as he titled his fragmentary, autobiographical writings, whose genre bears some resemblance to Ginzburg's. Rozanov's metaphor describes the sometimes accidental or random relationship between autobiographical texts and the self. And yet Rozanov compares his fragmentary "fallen leaves" (or sheets of paper) to involuntary exhalations from an individual soul, a formulation quite at odds with Ginzburg's. See Vasily Rozanov's explanation of his metaphor in *Uedinennoe* (Moscow: Politizdat, 1990), 22.

112. In Russian: "у произведений, десятками лет созревающих и распадающихся

в письменных столах, за это время появляются предшественники, столь же естественно, как у печатной литературы преемники." Ginzburg 2011, 453.

113. Ginzburg 2002, 303.

114. She continues: "I considered that my readers would wait for me. But now, renewing my work, I see that psychologically, my readers ceased to wait for me. They stopped being a value-oriented milieu, and each person separately is no longer interested." In Russian: "Покуда готовилась и писалась последняя книга, все другое на несколько лет было отложено, в том числе эти записи. Считалось, что мои читатели меня подождут. Но сейчас, возобновляя работу, вижу, что читатели психологически меня не дождались. Они перестали быть ценностно ориентированной средой, а каждому в отдельности уже неинтересно." Ginzburg 2002, 267.

115. See William Mills Todd III, "Between Marxism and Semiotics: Lidiia Ginzburg and Soviet Literary Sociology," *Canadian-American Slavic Studies* 19, 2 (1985): 159–65. See also idem, "Discoveries and Advances in Literary Theory, 1960s–1980s," in *A History of Russian Literary Criticism and Theory*, eds. Evgeny Dobrenko and Galin Tihanov (Pittsburgh, PA: University of Pittsburgh Press, 2011), 230–49. An expanded version of this article appears in the Russian edition of this volume: "Otkrytiia i proryvy sovetskoi teorii literatury v poslestalinskuiu epokhu," in *Istoriia russkoi literaturnoi kritiki: sovetskaia i postsovetskaia epokhi*, ed. Evgeny Dobrenko and Galin Tihanov (Moscow: Novoe literaturnoe obozrenie, 2011), 571–607.

116. The story of her move is recounted in detail by Elena Kumpan in "Vspominaia Lidiiu Iakovlevnu," *Zvezda* 3 (2002), 143–49, and in her book *Blizhnii podstup k legende*, 76–88. Ginzburg's new apartment was on Prospekt Shvernika (now called Vtoroi Murinskii Prospekt). Her full address was 27 Prospekt Shvernika, Apt. 20.

117. See Lidiia Lotman, *Vospominaniia*, 179–80. The Kumpans took me to one of the parks in which they recall walking with Ginzburg, the Park Lesotekhnicheskoi Akademii. The larger Udel'nyi park is among others nearby.

118. I have seen this portrait and the other artworks Ginzburg owned, now in the care of Alexander Kushner. On how Akhmatova corrected her nose, see Alexander Zholkovsky, "The Obverse of Stalinism: Akhmatova's Self-Serving Charisma of Selflessness," *Self and Story in Russian History*, ed. Laura Engelstein and Stephanie Sandler (Ithaca, NY: Cornell University Press, 2000), 49.

119. The emphasis on history and "creation of forms" receives articulation in her important late essays, "On Historicism and Structuredness" ("Ob istorizme i strukturnosti. Teoreticheskie zametki"), in *Literature in Search of Reality (Literatura v poiskakh real'nosti)* (Leningrad: Sovetskii pisatel', 1987), 75–86.

Ginzburg's notes for her speech are in all capitals, but I have restored normal capitalization. There are also a few pages where she made sparse notes about what others (Kushner, Gordin, Chistov, Ivanov, Chudakov, Vatsuro, and Ninov) said about her. In the archive, there is a bill for a dinner for sixteen people at the European Hotel. It may be considered a piece of Soviet history to pass on what was consumed, which was probably quite typical for such events: "Hotel «Европейская»—Торжественный обед, 19:00, для 16 человек. 7 апрель 1982. Водка, икра, осетрина, язык, ветчина, колбаса, жульен, салат из свеж<их> огур<цов>, салат витаминный, соус—хрен, цыпленок, пломбир «Европа», Напиток из сиропа, Водка «Пшеничная», Шампанское, Сухое вино, Минер<альная> вода, Кофе с сахаром, Фрукты, Хлеб. " All of these documents are in OR RNB 1377.

120. See Elena Kumpan, *Blizhnii podstup k legende*, 99–102. Also, interviews with

Kseniia Kumpan. There is a different version of events (relating to Lotman's failure to cite Ginzburg's work *On Psychological Prose* and his insufficient attention to her scholarship) in Lidiia Lotman, *Vospominaniia*, 186–87, where there is also an anecdote about the reconciliation between the two figures.

121. *O starom i novom* (Leningrad: Sovetskii pisatel', 1982). The journal publication was "Chelovek za pis'mennym stolom. Po starym zapisnym knizhkam," in *Novyi mir* 6 (June 1982): 235–45.

122. These books are *Literatura v poiskakh real'nosti. Stat'i, esse, zametki* (Leningrad: Sovetskii pisatel', 1987); *Chelovek za pis'mennym stolom: Esse, iz vospominanii, chetyre povestvovaniia* (Leningrad: Leningrad: Sovetskii pisatel', 1989); and *Pretvorenie opyta* (Riga: Avots, 1991).

123. In an interview, Ginzburg is asked how she feels about being awarded an official State prize, and she mentions that she feels good about being in the company of these other laureates. "Nravstvennost' svobodnogo cheloveka," interview with Il'ia Foniakov, in *Literaturnaia panorama* 2, 5224 (14 January 1989): 7.

124. In Russian: "Приятно говорить юбилярам, что они молоды—независимо от возраста—и что у них все впереди. Понимаю условность этого обычая и не обольщаюсь. Как бы то ни было, хорошо и то, что меня пока еще не покинула привычка выражать свои мысли письменным образом." OR RNB 1377.

125. Lidiia Ginzburg, "Prezumptsia sotsializma" ("The Presumption of Socialism"), publication, commentary, and introductory article "Ginzburg i perestroika" ("Ginzburg and Perestroika") by Emily Van Buskirk and Andrei Zorin, *Novoe literaturnoe obozrenie* 116, 4 (2012): 416–26.

126. In Russian: "Письма папы я непременно поищу (не знаю, с успехом ли). Не могла этим пока заняться, п.ч. болела. Переутомление и мозговые спазмы в результате. Только что прихожу в себя. Никак не могу привыкнуть к тому, что в моем возрасте все следует делать благоразумно—в том числе работать. Пришлось прервать чтение корректуры книги." RGALI F. 3270. Op. 1. Ed. Khr. 40. Sokolova Nataliia Viktorovna, Pis'ma Ginzburg Lidii Iakovlevny Sokolovoi N.V., 9 Feb. 1933–1 Sept. 1989, 43 ll.

CHAPTER 1. WRITING THE SELF AFTER THE CRISIS OF INDIVIDUALISM

1. In Russian: "Я ощущаю себя как кусок вырванной с мясом социальной действительности, которую удалось приблизить к глазам, как участок действительности, особенно удобный для наблюдения." Lidiia Ginzburg, *Zapisnye knizhki. Vospominaniia. Esse* (St. Petersburg: Iskusstvo-SPb, 2002), 99–100. Henceforth, I refer to this edition as "Ginzburg 2002." Original note dated 3 January 1932, ZK VI, approx. 41–45. OR RNB 1377.

2. Philippe Lejeune defines autobiography as "Retrospective prose narrative written by a real person concerning his own existence, where the focus is his individual life, in particular the story of his personality." Philippe Lejeune, "The Autobiographical Pact," in Lejeune, *On Autobiography*, ed. Paul John Eakin, trans. Katherine Leary (Minneapolis: University of Minnesota Press, 1989), 4.

3. In Russian: "... все психофизиологически и исторически закономерное. Фатум человека, как точка пересечения всеобщих тенденций." Ginzburg 2002, 60–61. This note is from 1928.

4. Lidiia Ginzburg, "Stadii liubvi," publication and introduction by Denis Ustinov, *Kriticheskaia massa* 1 (2002), 34. Original note ZK VII–IX, 1933–35, ca. January 1934. OR RNB 1377.

5. On life in the blockade, examples include numerous articles by Polina Barskova, such as "Nastoiashchee nastoiashchee: o vospriiatii vremeni v blokadnom Leningrade," in *Neprikosnovennyi zapas* 2, 76 (2011); "Avgust, kotorogo ne bylo, i mekhanizm kalendarnoi travmy: razmyshleniia o blokadnykh khronologiiakh," in *Novoe literaturnoe obozrenie* 116, 4 (2012): 130–45; and "Chernyi svet: problema temnoty v blokadnom Leningrade," in *Neprikosnovennyi zapas* 2, 70 (2010): 122–38. Also using Ginzburg as a source on blockade life are Cynthia Simmons and Nina Perlina in *Writing the Siege of Leningrad* (Pittsburgh, PA: University of Pittsburgh Press, 2002); and Lisa Kirschenbaum in *The Legacy of the Siege of Leningrad, 1941–1995: Myths, Memories, and Monuments* (Cambridge, UK: Cambridge University Press, 2006). Svetlana Boym cites Ginzburg as a source on mechanisms of survival of the Stalinist Terror in *Common Places* (Cambridge, MA: Harvard University Press, 1994); on the history of Formalism and life in the 1920s in *Future of Nostalgia* (New York: Basic Books, 2001); and on intonation in "'Banality of Evil,' Mimicry, and the Soviet Subject: Varlam Shalamov and Hannah Arendt," *Slavic Review* 67, 2 (Summer 2008): 342–63. Zholkovsky makes use of Ginzburg's notes on Akhmatova in "The Obverse of Stalinism: Akhmatova's Self-Serving Charisma of Selflessness," in *Self and Story*, ed. Laura Engelstein and Stephanie Sandler (Ithaca, NY: Cornell University Press, 2000), 46–48. These are just a few representative cases.

6. In the book *On Psychological Prose,* as well as her notebooks, Ginzburg speaks of great artists as discoverers. On Rousseau in this regard, see for example *O psikhologicheskoi proze* (Leningrad: Khudozhestvennaia literatura, 1977), 201, 204. Henceforth, "Ginzburg 1977." English translation in *On Psychological Prose,* trans. and ed. Judson Rosengrant (Princeton, NJ: Princeton University Press, 1991) 157, 161, 190, 163. Henceforth, "Ginzburg 1991." On Tolstoy as discoverer, ibid., 271; in English, 221. A sample notebook list of such "discoverers" includes Cervantes, Shakespeare, Tolstoy, Dostoevsky, Proust, Chekhov, and Kafka, while excluding Nabokov. Ginzburg 2002, 317.

7. Lidiia Ginzburg, *Prokhodiashchie kharaktery. Proza voennykh let. Zapiski blokadnogo cheloveka.* ed., commentaries, articles by Emily Van Buskirk and Andrei Zorin (Moscow: Novoe izdatel'stvo, 2011), 204. Henceforth, "Ginzburg 2011." From notes connected to ZK 1943–46.

8. Ibid.

9. As Jerrold Seigel notes, "person," as the singular form of "people," can mean "any individual among others, whether she or he bears any particular qualities or not." The English word "person" also has a connection to the Latin *persona,* meaning mask, or literally, "animating the mask 'by sound,' and referring by extension to the occupant of a particular social position or status. Modern usage makes personhood or personality sometimes a dignity conveyed by social recognition, and sometimes a quality deriving from individual talents or gifts." Seigel, *The Idea of the Self: Thought and Experience in Western Europe since the Seventeenth Century* (Cambridge, UK: Cambridge University Press, 2005), 16. The word *chelovek* in Russian has no connection to the Latin *persona.*

10. The word *lichnost'*" has specific associations with individualism that are not present in the English word "personality." On the history of personality, personhood, and *lichnost'* in Russian culture, see Nikolai Plotnikov, "Ot 'individual'nosti' k 'identichnosti' (istoriia poniatii personal'nosti v russkoi kul'ture)," *Novoe literaturnoe obrzenie* 91, 3 (2008): 64–83. See also Derek Offord, "Lichnost': Notions of Individual Identity," in

Constructing Russian Culture in the Age of Revolution: 1881–1940, ed. Catriona Kelly and David Shepherd (Oxford: Oxford University Press, 1998), 13–25. When I write of "personality," I invoke the sense of "character" (*kharakter*) and "person" (*chelovek*) more than the Russian *lichnost'*. Peter Brooks has written of the complex semantics of the word "character," calling it a concept in which, as it enters into literature, "all our aesthetics and ethics converge," in *Enigmas of Identity* (Princeton, NJ: Princeton University Press, 2011), 3.

11. Charles Taylor, *Sources of the Self: The Making of Modern Identity* (Cambridge, MA: Harvard University Press, 1989), 32. See my brief discussion in the introduction. Ginzburg's notion of the "self-concept," or *avtokontseptsiia*, is related to identity. See Ginzburg, 1936 notebook with sketch of "K." OR RNB 1377. I discuss *avtokontseptsiia* in chapter 4.

12. Ginzburg 1977, 385. Translation in Ginzburg 1991, 318. See also Lidiia Ginzburg, *O literaturnom geroe* (Leningrad: Sovetskii pisatel', 1979) 131. Henceforth, "Ginzburg 1979."

13. Taylor, 3.

14. "On Satire and Analysis" in Ginzburg 2002, 253–57. Ginzburg gives the examples in this essay of how scholars had to make intellectual compromises in order to secure their works' publication. They would include obligatory phrases about Lenin's contributions to a given topic, sometimes augmenting their sense of independence by omitting the qualifier "ingenious." They depended on administrative organs for positions and livelihoods. No one avoided complicity in the repressions (whether through votes, speeches, or silence).

15. In Russian: "Дважды и трижды превращенному в крошево поколению открывалась неизбывность социального зла и призрачность единичного сознания." Ginzburg 2011, 429.

16. Ginzburg, "Dom i mir" folder. OR RNB 1377. She repeats the term "non-individualistic" in the published narrative "The Thought That Drew a Circle" (*Mysl', opisavshaia krug*), in Ginzburg 2002, 574.

17. Steven Lukes, "The Meanings of 'Individualism,'" in *Journal of the History of Ideas* 32, 1 (January–March 1971): 54.

18. Karl Weintraub, "Autobiography and Historical Consciousness," in *Critical Inquiry* 1, 4 (June 1975): 821–48, 839. See also idem, *Value of the Individual: Self and Circumstance in Autobiography* (Chicago: University of Chicago Press, 1978), 334.

19. Karl Weintraub, "Autobiography and Historical Consciousness," 847.

20. Georg Simmel, "Individual and Society in Eighteenth- and Nineteenth-Century Views of Life: An Example of Philosophical Sociology," *The Sociology of Georg Simmel*, trans. and ed. Kurt H. Wolff (Glencoe, IL: Free Press, 1950), 78–83. See also the discussion of Simmel in Lukes, 55.

21. In Russian: "Сверхличны, тем самым непререкаемы веления бога, абсолюта, сверхличны даже метафизически понимаемые требования избранной личности, поскольку это требования ее духа, которым эмпирический человек обязан подчиниться." Ginzburg 1977, 389. Translation in idem 1991, 321.

22. Ginzburg 1977, 385. Translation in idem 1991, 318.

23. Ginzburg 1977, 389; idem 1991, 321.

24. In Russian: "Сознание изолированное; нерелигиозное, и нереволюционное, бессвязное, нетрагическое (смерть ему не противоречит), внеморальное, инфантильное, релятивистическое и.т.д." "Dom i mir" manuscripts. OR RNB 1377.

25. As Lukes notes, *individualisme* in French nineteenth-century thought referred to "what Durkheim identified by the twin concepts of 'anomie' and 'egoism'—the social,

moral, and political isolation of individuals, their dissociation from social purposes and social regulation, the breakdown of social solidarity." Lukes, 53.

26. "Delusion of the Will" (*Zabluzhdenie voli*) in Ginzburg 2002, 583. In "The Thought That Drew a Circle," Ginzburg and one of her learned interlocutors (a classicist) contrast "immanent" (*immanentnye*) people to "transcendent" (*trantsendentnye*) ones—the former must experience value "in themselves," and the latter need the ultimate value to reside outside of themselves, to be externally posited. Ibid., 572–74. Their discussion is philosophical (they make reference to Schopenhauer, for instance), but it is unclear whether they are referring to Kant's definition of the "transcendental subject" as that which is prior to or beyond the bounds of experience. The Russian word *trantsendentnyi* is used to translate Kant and also for the related general philosophical and religious meaning of that which goes beyond our empirical experience of the world. Ibid, 572–74.

27. Draft "Theoretical Section" of "Otter's Day," in Ginzburg 2011, 294.

28. "Delusion of the Will," Ginzburg 2002, 583. See Henri Bergson, *Essai sur les données immédiates de la conscience* (Paris, 1888), and its explication in Seigel, *The Idea of the Self*, 517–22.

29. "Delusion of the Will," Ginzburg 2002, 583. There is a similar description of this type in "The Thought That Drew a Circle," where Ginzburg again points to the relationship between problems of identity and responsibility, and a sense of time. She writes: "In an unmediated way [this impressionistic soul] has been given only a chaotic sense of life, a sense whose ownership cannot be determined; some kind of insanely incomprehensible substance, which a person carries in himself, in relation to which his whole conscious mental life is only a doubtful phenomenon." Ibid., 574.

30. "The Thought That Drew a Circle," ibid., 572. Ginzburg identifies the "transcendent" types in her midst as those who thirst for belief, whether in God or in some other externally posited value. Notebook drafts for "The Thought That Drew a Circle." OR RNB 1377.

31. Ginzburg 1977, 249. Translation in idem 1991, 201.

32. In his analyses of identity and narrative, Paul Ricoeur devotes much attention to the close relationship between plot and character—and demonstrates how efforts to remove the fixity of character simultaneously undo plots, particularly endings. The most experimental treatments of characters occur in novels that approach essays—such as Musil's *Man without Qualities* and the autobiographical experiments of Michel Leiris. See Paul Ricoeur, *Oneself as Another* (Chicago, University of Chicago Press, 1992), 148–49. See also Paul Ricoeur, "Narrative Identity," in *On Paul Ricoeur: Narrative and Interpretation*, ed. David Wood (London: Routledge, 1991), 196.

33. Osip Mandelstam, "The End of the Novel," in *Mandelstam: The Complete Critical Prose and Letters*, ed. Jane Gary Harris, trans. J. G. Harris and Constance Link (Ann Arbor, MI: Ardis, 1979), 198–201. Russian in Osip Mandel'shtam, "Konets romana," *Sochineniia v dvukh tomakh* (Moscow: Khudozhestvennaia literatura, 1990), 201–5.

34. For Ricoeur's initial definition of these terms, see *Oneself as Another*, 2–3. For a concise statement of his thesis, see Paul Ricoeur, "Narrative Identity," in *On Paul Ricoeur: Narrative and Interpretation*, 188–99.

35. See Charles Taylor on Locke in *Sources of the Self*, 49, and 159–76.

36. On performativity of identity, see for example Judith Butler, *Gender Trouble: Feminism and the Subversion of Identity* (New York: Routledge, 1999).

37. Ginzburg 1979, 81.

38. Some elements of the present chapter have previously appeared in " 'Samo-

otstranenie' kak eticheskii i esteticheskii printsip v proze L. Ia. Ginzburg," *Novoe literaturnoe obozrenie* 81, 5 (2006): 261–81.

39. Ginzburg 2011, 429. English in Lidiya Ginzburg, *Blockade Diary*, trans. Alan Myers (London: Harvill Press, 1995), 88.

40. I adopt this title following a draft list of essays (perhaps a plan for publication), where Ginzburg refers to this essay by its opening words, "Celebration of the Sunset" ("Torzhestvo zakata"). There is a faint echo of Oswald Spengler's popular work *Der Untergang des Abendlandes* (1918, 1922), translated into Russian as *Zakat evropy,* or *Europe's Sunset.* The tradition of adopting titles from opening lines belongs to Russian poetry. This title appears in several lists in the archives. In one place, there is a fuller variant: "Торжество заката. Как если бы все прекрасное . . ." ("Celebration of the sunset. As if everything beautiful . . .").

41. As Caryl Emerson has noted, this phrase is a quotation from the famous 1840 lyric by Mikhail Lermontov, "I skuchno i grustno." Emerson, "Lydia Ginzburg on Tolstoy and Lermontov (with Dostoevsky as the Distant Ground)," in *Lydia Ginzburg's Alternative Literary Identities*, ed. Emily Van Buskirk and Andrei Zorin (Oxford: Peter Lang AG, 2012), 45.

42. Ginzburg 2002, 198.

43. Ibid., 199–200. Ginzburg's chapter in *On Psychological Prose* contains a condensed version of this same discussion. Ginzburg 1977, 389–90. Translation in idem 1991, 321–22.

44. Ginzburg 2002, 214. Mandelstam's short poem paints a scene of a simple meal of bread in a kitchen lit by a primus stove, before a trip to the train station to escape a search ("Мы с тобой на кухне посидим, / Сладко пахнет белый керосин. // Острый нож да хлеба каравай . . . / Хочешь, примус туго накачай, // А не то веревок собери / Завязать корзину до зари, // Чтобы нам уехать на вокзал, / Где бы нас никто не отыскал.") In O. Mandel'shtam, *Stikhotvoreniia* (Leningrad: Sovetskii pisatel', 1974), 151. The poem was first published in 1964. Presumably Ginzburg knew it earlier through her acquaintance with Osip and Nadezhda Mandelstam and friendships with people in their circle such as Nikolai Khardzhiev.

45. Soviet scholars eventually identified a strain of "revolutionary Romanticism" or "democratic sentimentalism" (represented by Radishchev and Ryleev, among others), opposing it to a more conservative Romanticism (Karamzin and others). See Lauren Leighton's discussion in "The Great Soviet Debate over Romanticism: 1957–1964," in *Studies in Romanticism* 22, 1 (Spring 1983): 41–64.

46. Ginzburg 2002, 343.

47. Ibid., 198.

48. Ibid., 200.

49. For a useful treatment of Adorno's dictum, which attempts to return it to its original context, see Michael Rothberg, "After Adorno: Culture in the Wake of Catastrophe," *New German Critique* 72 (Fall 1997): 45–81.

50. Sartre, "Situation of the Writer in 1947," in *What Is Literature?* trans. Bernard Frechtman, intro. David Caute (London/New York: Routledge, 2001), 164. While Ginzburg's essay sketches the trajectory of values through German philosophy and Russian literature, Sartre's essay builds on an analysis of French writing beginning from World War I. Sartre stood in a very different place from Ginzburg, and his degree of freedom in choosing the terms of *engagement* would have been impossible for her, but he held similar views: on the need for writers to bear witness, to think metaphysically,

and to exercise their power carefully and responsibly through the prudent choice of words. Sartre's negative evaluations of both surrealist prose and official Soviet literature also would have resonated with Ginzburg's views. I do not know whether (and if so, when) Ginzburg read this essay by Sartre. In the 1970s, she does write about *La nausée* and *Les mots,* as well as his 1946 essay "Existentialism Is a Humanism." See for example Ginzburg 1979, 136–37.

51. Vasily Grossman, *Life and Fate,* trans. Robert Chandler (New York: New York Review of Books, 2006 [1995]), 535. Russian original: "Он смутно знал, что в пору фашизма человеку, желающему остаться человеком, случается выбор более легкий, чем спасенная жизнь,—смерть." Vasilii Grossman, *Zhizn' i sud'ba* (Moscow: Knizhnaia palata, 1989), 404.

52. Varlam Shalamov, "O proze," in Shalamov, *Sobranie sochinenii v shesti tomakh,* vol. 5 (Moscow: Terra—Knizhnyi klub, 2005), 153.

53. Ginzburg 2002, 197–98.

54. In "The Thought That Drew a Circle," Ginzburg's first-person narrator speaks of how fear of death *as an ideology* (not just as an instinct for self-preservation) was "thought up in the second half of the nineteenth century, out of egocentrism." Ibid., 546. It then faded in her time. See also ibid., 82, where she attributes this insight to Tynianov.

55. Solovyov also discusses this syllogism in "The Meaning of Love." Information connecting Aristotle, Tolstoy, Kiesewetter, and Solovyov can be found in a short footnote in Vladimir Solovyov, *The Meaning of Love,* ed. with revised translation by Thomas R. Beyer, Jr., intr. Owen Barfield (West Stockbridge, MA: Lindisfarne Press, 1985), 69.

56. Evgeni Zamyatin, "The Cave," in *The Portable Twentieth-Century Russian Reader,* ed. Clarence Brown (New York: Penguin Books, 2003), 100.

57. Varlam Shalamov, "Dry Rations," in *Kolyma Tales,* trans. John Glad (New York: Penguin Classics, 1995), 33.

58. In Russian: "Удивление перед лицом общественного зла было детищем XIX века. [Вернувшиеся из лагерей] же рассказывают о том, чего и следовало ожидать от двадцатого. 'Закономерности всем известны, а вот вам еще характерный случай; случай этот—я.'" Ginzburg 2002, 208.

59. Ginzburg wrote that beauty and happiness should be part of art because they are real experiences, and because they create a dialectic outside of which suffering loses its power. Ibid., 198.

60. Ibid., 274.

61. In Russian: "Вместо свободного мира идей—предельно необходимый и давящий мир объективного ужаса жизни. Герой—страдательный, маленький человек, просто человек. Функция его в корне изменилась. Он стал теперь выразителем всех—больших и малых, глупых и умных, умудренных и малограмотных. В этом демократизм современного сознания." Ibid., 199.

62. In Russian: "Возможно ли активное влияние на свою судьбу, перемалываемую зубьями государственной машины, зубьями зла." Shalamov, "O proze," 153.

63. In Russian: "В XX веке размывание характера, быть может, сопряжено с непомерным тоталитарным давлением, перетиравшим личные свойства человека. Сталинской поре присуща унификация поведения перед всем грозящей пыткой и казнью. Лгали лживые и правдивые, боялись трусливые и храбрые, красноречивые и косноязычные равно безмолвствовали." Ginzburg 2002, 345.

64. Ibid., 196. Ellipsis in the original. At the heart of the passage about an individu-

al's constructive potential is one of Marx's foundational statements, often repeated by Marxist-Leninists, that "It is not the consciousness of men that determines their being, but, on the contrary, their social being that determines their consciousness." Preface to *A Contribution to the Critique of Political Economy*, in *The Marx-Engels Reader*, 2nd ed., ed. Robert C. Tucker (New York: Norton, 1978), 4.

65. Ginzburg 2002, 196.

66. Ibid., 319. Ginzburg here is in the midst of self-quotation from her essay "Avant-garde," in ibid., 337.

67. Ibid., 319.

68. Ginzburg 1979, 135.

69. Ibid., 129–49.

70. In one of her essays from the late 1980s, she puts it this way, "Twentieth-century prose (the noveau roman, Beckett . . .) attempted to do away not only with character [in the sense of personality], but with characters [in the sense of literary characters]. This was a futile attempt, because the subject of the process of the plot could not be abolished,—even if he only appeared as an amorphous magma of consciousness" In Russian: "Проза XX века [новый роман, Беккет . . .]) попыталась отделаться не только от характера, но и от персонажа. Попытка тщетная, потому что неотменяемым оказался субъект сюжетного процесса,—даже если он представал аморфной магмой сознания." Ginzburg 2002, 345.

71. Ginzburg 1991, 82, 340. Russian in idem 1977, 106, 412–13. Vissarion Belinsky (1811–48), one of the first Russian literary critics and literary historians famous for his writings on Gogol, Dostoevsky, and others, is often credited as the founder of Russian Realism (including by Ginzburg). Ginzburg's chapter on Belinsky in *On Psychological Prose* is devoted to his letters, in which the lack of censorship and of the demands of his readers allowed him to give expression to "a series of psychological conflicts that were remarkable for their intensity and their degree of conscious realization . . . to this vast work of the soul." Ginzburg 1991, 58; Russian in idem 1977, 76. The case of Belinsky bolsters Ginzburg's argument that "psychological insights not yet possible at a certain stage in the established, canonical genres, or only beginning to come to light in them, are often possible in the more peripheral forms of literature—in letters, diaries, memoirs, and autobiographies." Ibid.

72. Idem 1979, 81–82.

73. Ibid., 129–30.

74. When introducing the term "Modernism," Ginzburg notes its shortcomings (ambiguity, and the diversity of movements included as Modernist), but finds no better alternative. Ibid., 79.

75. Ibid., 83 and 127–28.

76. Ibid., 83. Ginzburg gives credit to Bakhtin and Engelgardt for their work on Dostoevsky's novels of ideas. She also discusses Dostoevsky in the context of social psychology on 135.

77. Ibid., 135.

78. In "Celebration of the Sunset." Ginzburg 2002, 198–99.

79. Ginzburg 2011, 177.

80. Ibid., 178.

81. Ginzburg 2002, 375. Here, Ginzburg distinguishes moral principles from moral prejudice by the fact that the former can be *explained*, even if in subjective terms, by those who hold them.

82. Ginzburg, "On Satire and Analysis," ibid., 254.

83. In Russian: "человек не есть неподвижное устройство, собранное из противоречивых частей (тем более не однородное устройство). Он—устройство с меняющимися установками, и в зависимости от них он переходит из одной ценностной сферы в другую, в каждой из них пробуя осуществиться." Ginzburg, "Generation at a Turning Point" (dated 1979), ibid., 282.

84. Ginzburg 1977, 412. Translation in idem 1991, 339–40.

85. Luke 17:1. Ginzburg had felt the importance of this passage even as a sixteen-year-old. A diary entry from 18 February 1919 reads: "In the gospels it says something like (I don't remember the exact wording), 'evil must come into the world, but woe unto the one through whom it comes.' In my life, I would like never to forget these words for a single moment. Maybe they are unjust, but in them is located the whole meaning of personal self-perfection." In Russian: "В Евангелии сказану [*sic*] не помню точно, но смысл таков: зло должно войти в мир, но горе тому через кого оно войдет—Мне бы хотелось никогда ни на одно мгновенье своей жизни не забывать этих слов. Быть может они несправедливы, но в них вложен весь смысл личного самосовершенствования." Diary 1918–19. OR RNB 1377.

86. "On Satire and Analysis," Ginzburg 2002, 256.

87. Ibid., 259.

88. Grossman, *Life and Fate*, 535–37. Russian in *Zhizn' i sud'ba*, 404–6.

89. Ginzburg 2002, 255.

90. Ibid., 253. Italics added.

91. This designation of the essay "On Satire and Analysis" as Ginzburg's "writer's credo" ("Писательское *credo*") appears for example on a scrap of paper located in the folder together with drafts for "Mysl', opisavshaia krug" in what looks to be an outline for publication, most probably from the 1960s. OR RNB 1377.

92. In the English translation, this section of *On Psychological Prose* carries the title "Ethical Valuation" (in Russian, it is the untitled third section of the book's final chapter, "Problems of the Psychological Novel"). One reason for Ginzburg's transposition may have been that in the 1970s, she was still uncertain that her desk-drawer writings would reach an audience in her lifetime.

93. Ginzburg 2002, 253.

94. Solovyov propounded his theory of love in *The Meaning of Love* (*Smysl liubvi*, 1894) and not, as Ginzburg writes, in *Justification of Love* (*Opravdanie liubvi*), a conflation of the titles of two of Solovyov's books: *The Meaning of Love* and *Justification of the Good* (*Opravdanie dobra*). This error is present in every published edition of this work—beginning with its first partial publication in Lidiia Ginzburg, "Dolgii den'. Otryvok," *Avrora* 4 (1989): 105. Repeated in Lidiia Ginzburg, *Chelovek za pis'mennym stolom*, 464, and in Ginzburg 2002, 569.

95. Ginzburg 2002, 569.

96. Ibid. In Solovyov's words: "In the feeling of love . . . we affirm the absolute significance of another personality and, through it, of our own." While we habitually idealize the beloved, he or she is at the same time "as real, concrete, and objectivized as we are." English translations in *Russian Philosophy*, vol. III, ed. James Edie, James Scanlan, and Mary-Barbara Zeldin (Chicago: Quadrangle Books, 1965), 92, 89. Russian in Vladimir Solovyov, "Smysl liubvi," in *Russkii eros ili filosofiia liubvi v Rossii*, ed. V. P. Shestakov and A. N. Bogoslovskii (Moscow: Progress, 1991), 47, 35.

97. Vladimir Solovyov, "Smysl liubvi," 34.

98. See ibid., 41.

99. Ginzburg 2002, 569. For Solovyov, love that joined male and female complementary halves had the potential to engender a perfect and spiritual union with the universe (*vseedinstvo*), instead of sexual reproduction or family.

100. Jean-Marie Guyau, *A Sketch of Morality Independent of Obligation or Sanction*, 2nd ed., trans. from French Gertrude Kapteyn (London: Watts & Co., 1898), 83.

101. Dozens of editions of Guyau's works appeared in Russian around the turn of the century, including his collected works. *A Sketch of Morality Independent Obligation or Sanction* (*Nravsvennost' bez obiazatel'stva i bez sanktsii*) appeared as a separate edition in 1923 (Moscow). In *On Psychological Prose*, Ginzburg specifically mentions Guyau's argument that morality springs naturally from a person's need for expression and self-realization, and not from social pressures. Her discussion of Guyau contains language very similar to that in her writer's credo: "The life force is realized only when the individual 'emerges from himself' by means of love, creativity, or heroism. In love, something that is external to the individual absorbs him; in the act of creation, he himself becomes something external." Ginzburg 1977, 399. Translation in idem 1991, 329.

102. Guyau, 208.

103. In Russian: "Вне абсолютов, вне непререкаемых требований общего сознания—как возникает этический акт в обиходе обыкновенного человека?" Ginzburg 2002, 254.

104. Guyau, 210.

105. Ibid., 84–85.

106. Ginzburg 2002, 251–52. Cf. the definition in *On Psychological Prose* of the ethical act as "the rejection of the lower for the sake of the higher." Ginzburg 1977, 419, and idem 1991, 345.

107. Guyau, 94–95.

108. Guyau believes an artist's lack of biological progeny is made up for by the existence of books and ideas that travel in the cultural consciousness. Ibid., 83.

109. Lydia Ginzburg, ZK VII (1932), back side of 30. OR RNB 1377. The entry, while undated, falls within notes from February 1932.

110. In Russian: "'Я лишился и чаши на пире отцов, / И веселья, и чести своей . . .' Сам лишился, а до людей донес." Ginzburg 2002, 259.

111. In Russian: "Творческие побуждения—пусть имманентные—распоряжаются человеком так, как не всегда им могут распорядиться суровейшие законы внешнего мира." Ginzburg 1977, 425. Translation in Ginzburg 1991, 350. Andrew Kahn explores Ginzburg's image of Mandelstam in "Lydia Ginzburg's 'Lives of Poets': Mandelstam in Profile," *Lydia Ginzburg's Alternative Literary Identities*, 163–91.

112. Ginzburg wrote several drafts of this important narrative. I date the manuscripts using a number of clues: handwriting and materials, the subject matter treated (for example, the death of Mark Moiseevich Ginzburg in 1934, Kuzmin's 1936 death in "The Thought . . ."), Ginzburg's own dating (for publication) of "The Thought That Drew a Circle" to the end of the 1930s, and the interconnections between these narratives and pieces that are dated in the notebooks, such as "The Stages of Love" from 1934. See also my discussion of "the novel" in chapter 2.

113. Ginzburg writes: "All of the people that a person once was, all of these corpses, enter into the vacated consciousness and oppress [it]." In Russian: "Все те люди, которыми был человек, все эти мертвецы, входят в опустошенное сознание и гнетут." Folder with drafts for "Mysl', opisavshaia krug." From the first of two notebooks.

Pages are not numbered. Under points 5–7 corresponding to Ginzburg's outline. OR RNB 1377.

114. Ginzburg 2002, 224. Note from the beginning of the 1960s. This same thought occurs in similar phrasing in drafts for "Mysl', opisavshaia krug" and "Zabluzhdenie voli."

115. Ginzburg's mentors, the Formalists, have been characterized as generally ignoring the question of reader reception. See the discussion in Carol Any, *Boris Eikhenbaum: Voices of a Russian Formalist* (Stanford, CA: Stanford University Press, 1994), 69–70.

116. Drafts for "Mysl', opisavshaia krug." OR RNB 1377. There is a similar passage in Ginzburg 2002, 141 ("Zametki o proze") and in the final version of "The Thought That Drew a Circle," 569–70.

117. See Ginzburg 2002, 400, a passage quoted and discussed in the introduction.

118. On the ideal of conscious living, see for example Ginzburg 2001, 581 ("The Thought That Drew a Circle"). In her teenage diary, she writes, "The meaning of life is in happiness, and happiness consists in becoming conscious of everything as intelligible . . ." In Russian: "Смысл жизни в счастье, счастье в том чтобы все осознавалось как осмысленное . . . ." Diary 1920, 14–15. OR RNB 1377.

119. In Russian: "Все, не выраженное в слове [вслух или про себя], не имеет для меня реальности, вернее, я не имею для него органов восприятия." Ginzburg 2002, 74. Original note in ZK V (1929–31), 26. Late August or early September 1929. OR RNB 1377. This statement—while it would seem to oddly cancel out the reality of music and unverbalized emotions—points to semiotics and post-structuralism.

120. In Russian: "Писатель—это человек, который, если не пишет, не может *переживать жизнь*" (italics added). Ginzburg 2002, 147, ca. 1934.

121. Ginzburg ZK 1933–35, 67. OR RNB 1377. She concludes this passage by writing of how things and emotions are replaced for her by empty shells, unless she writes about them. This passage comes within a section whose published version compares to Ginzburg 2002, 147.

122. Ginzburg 2002, 126. For another take on writing as an essential part of life for Ginzburg, see Irina Sandomirskaia, "The Leviathan, or Language in Besiegement: Lydia Ginzburg's Prolegomena to Critical Discourse Analysis," in *Lydia Ginzburg's Alternative Literary Identities*, 193–234, esp. 203–8.

123. Ginzburg, "Vozvrashchenie domoi," in Ginzburg 2002, 528. English translation by Alyson Tapp, "The Return Home," in *Lydia Ginzburg's Alternative Literary Identities*, 324.

124. See for example Ginzburg 2011, 431–32, especially the variants in the notes.

125. Draft of "Teoreticheskii razdel," in Ginzburg 2011, 295.

126. Draft of "Mysl', opisavshaia krug." OR RNB 1377.

127. Ginzburg mentions Jules Romain by name in drafts for "Mysl', opisavshaia krug." OR RNB 1377.

128. Draft notebook of "Mysl', opisavshaia krug" OR RNB 1377.

129. Ginzburg 2002, 730.

130. In Russian: "Что такое самостийный человек? Пещерное существо. А духовная жизнь—это жизнь в слове, в языке, который нам дан социумом, с тем чтобы мы от себя вносили в него оттенки." Ibid., 132. Cf. ibid., 730 (Translation in Ginzburg 1995, 88). There is also a strong expression of this idea in the 1943 notebook (with notes from 1943–46): "Creativity is a free, goal-oriented, individual act of a person on the world [or individual way of impacting/affecting the world: *individual'noe*

vozdeistvie cheloveka na mir], "I" on "not-I"; whereby as a result of this individual action expedient [*tselesoobraznye*] changes take place in the world, which have communal [*obshchie*] meanings and belong to communal connections." See Ginzburg 2011, 176.

131. For definitive statements in this line of thought, see Roland Barthes, "The Death of the Author," and Michel Foucault, "What Is an Author?," collected in *Authorship: From Plato to the Postmodern*, ed. Seán Burke (Edinburgh: Edinburgh University Press, 1995), 125–30, 233–46. The first to treat Ginzburg's polemic with this viewpoint was William Todd in "Between Marxism and Semiotics: Lidiia Ginzburg and Soviet Literary Sociology," *Canadian-American Slavic Studies* 19, 2 (1985): 178–86.

132. Ginzburg 2002, 568–69.

133. For a discussion of this concept of meaning production in immanent verse as "poetry of meanings," in the poetry of Venevitinov, see Lidiia Ginzburg, "Opyt filosofskoi liriki," in Lidiia Ginzburg, *Raboty dovoennogo vremeni: Stat'i. Retsenzii. Monografiia*, ed. Stanislav Savitskii (St. Petersburg: ID "Petropolis" 2007), 157. Originally published in *Poetika* 5 (Leningrad, 1929), 72–104.

134. Ginzburg 2002, 578.

135. Ginzburg 1991, 20. Russian in idem 1977, 27.

136. Ginzburg 2002, 133.

137. Ibid., 261. In his essay "The End of Renata," Vladislav Khodasevich famously subjected the practice of *zhiznetvorchestvo* to an ethically charged analysis, performed from the vantage point of post–World War I, post-Revolutionary experience. The essay, dated "Versailles, 1928" by the author, was published in Paris in 1939 in a collection of memoiristic essays, Necropolis [Nekropol']). On the Symbolist concept and practice of *zhiznetvorchestvo*, and its critique, including the one by Khodasevich, see Irina Paperno and Joan Grossman, eds., *Creating Life: The Aesthetic Utopia of Russian Modernism* (Stanford, CA: Stanford University Press, 1994).

138. G. O. Vinokur, *Biografiia i kul'tura. Russkoe stsenicheskoe proiznoshenie* (Moscow: Russkie slovari, 1997), 40. Scholars are still to explore this part of Vinokur's scholarship and its philosophical sources. Irina Paperno (oral communication) maintains that Ginzburg often spoke of *Biografiia i kul'tura*, lamented its obscurity, and loaned her copy of what was then a rare 1927 edition to others. Ginzburg cites this book in *On Psychological Prose*. See Ginzburg 1977, 22 n. 2; translation in idem 1991, 368 n. 20.

139. Ginzburg, draft notebook for "The Thought That Drew a Circle." OR RNB 1377.

140. I quote Dilthey's very compact rearticulation of his main points in chapter VIII of *A Descriptive and Analytic Psychology* (1894): See for example Wilhelm Dilthey, *Descriptive Psychology and Historical Understanding*, trans. Richard Zaner and Kenneth Heiges (The Hague: Martinus Nijhoff, 1977), 99.

141. Draft notebook for "The Thought That Drew a Circle." OR RNB 1377.

142. "Delusion of the Will" (*Zabluzhdenie voli*) was first published in an abbreviated version in *Novyi mir* 11 (November 1988): 137–54. It appeared in full in *Chelovek za pis'mennym stolom* (Leningrad: Sovetskii pisatel', 1989), 481–516, and again in Ginzburg 2002. All translations from this story are my own. The narrative has been published in English translation by Ludmilla Groves and Mary Plume as "Conscience Deluded," in *Present Imperfect: Stories by Russian Women*, ed. Ayesha Kagal and Natasha Perova (Boulder, CO: Westview Press, 1996), 41–67.

143. This aspect, one should note, to some degree defies Ginzburg's generalization about the powerlessness of the twentieth-century self (or perhaps, affirms its potential solely for destruction).

144. Ginzburg had criticized Tolstoy for his "optical illusion" (*obman zreniia*) in *The Death of Ivan Ilych*: the fact that death concerns only Ivan Ilych, and not his relatives—the daughter, wife, doctors, servants are all presented as if immortal, as if they will never go through the torments of approaching death. This is why, she asserts, the reader finds them so distasteful. Ginzburg 2002, 275.

145. Ibid., 608. The careful description of another's death reminds one of Herzen's study of his wife's death, which Ginzburg saw as motivated by guilt. Ginzburg 1977, 267–68. Translation in idem 1991, 216–17.

146. Ginzburg lists a plan in her outlines to write about "С<мерть> как прожектор." One of her drafts contains the following sentences: "Death acts as such a strong impression that it sheds a sudden light on the facts of life. Like a spotlight that is suddenly directed at this or that zone." In Russian: "См<ерть> столь сильно действующее впечатление, что она проливает внезапный свет на факты жизни. Как прожектор, внезапно направляемый на тот или иной участок." Drafts for "Delusion of the Will." OR RNB 1377.

147. This torn-down curtain appears also as a metaphor for epiphanic knowledge in relation to sexuality, and may have its origin in the final scene of Blok's "The Puppet Booth." See chapter 3.

148. "Delusion of the Will." Ginzburg 2002, 599.

149. "The Thought That Drew a Circle." Ibid., 581.

150. The German philosopher Max Scheler, especially popular in the 1920s, had called repentance "the most *revolutionary* force in the moral world," since it offered a chance for a person to be reborn "whole," after expiating his guilt. Max Scheler, "Repentance and Rebirth," in *On the Eternal in Man*, trans. Bernard Noble (London: SCM Press Ltd, 1960), 35–65. The cited phrases are on 56 and 53. Ginzburg, an atheist, does not attribute liberating or transformative powers to repentance; rather, she uses it to help prove the continuity of existence.

151. Ginzburg 2002, 584.

152. Ibid.

153. Guyau makes a similar point in his treatise: "Let us, for example, think of an artist who feels genius stirring in him, and who is condemned to manual labor for the whole of his life. This feeling of a lost life, an unfulfilled task, of an unrealized ideal, will beset and haunt his sensibility more or less in the same way as would the consciousness of a moral failure." Guyau, 189.

154. Ginzburg writes: "Schopenhauer had the idea that repentance is a punishment of the will that has done what it did not want to do. The deep-laid will, grasping its unity with others, did not recognize itself. It became muddled by the superficial desires of spite, greed, vanity, faint-heartedness, laziness." Ginzburg 2002, 584. Ginzburg discusses the importance for Tolstoy of Schopenhauer's "Wille" (as Tolstoy confronted determinism to see humans as morally responsible, though conditioned) in Ginzburg 1991, 341; Russian in idem 1977, 413–14.

155. Ginzburg 2002, 593.

156. Ibid., 590.

157. Ibid., 592.

158. In the blockade (around New Year's Day, 1944), Ginzburg writes an essay about Otter as a loser, which she called "Résumé of Failures" ("Itogi neudach"). Ginzburg 2011, 164–74. Also published as "Loser" ("Neudachnik") in *Pretvorenie opyta* (republished in Ginzburg 2002, 151–60).

159. Ginzburg 2002, 596.

160. Mark Moiseevich Ginzburg died in 1934 (spring), and Raisa Davydovna Gol'denberg/Ginzburg died in November 1942. I treat this biographical data in chapter 5.

161. I found this story in the archive in 2006. For a description of the manuscript, see Ginzburg 2011, 557–58. I treat "A Story of Pity and Cruelty" extensively in chapter 5, and thus confine myself to a few observations here. Otter was in this period a unifying hero, appearing in manuscript versions of *Notes of a Blockade Person* (or in its 1940s version, "Otter's Day"), sketches for *Home and the World*, and some notebook essays. On the autobiographical features of Otter, see chapter 5; on the male gender of this character, see chapter 3.

162. Ginzburg 2011, 17.

163. Ibid., 23.

164. From another blockade text about the same hero, "Den' Ottera," in ibid., 223.

165. Ibid., 23.

166. Ibid., 36.

167. Aunt has a very weakly developed "extended self," to borrow Ulric Neisser's term (and the extended self, he reminds us, built on "autobiographical recall," is socially adaptive, because it makes strong interpersonal relations possible). Ulric Neisser, "Five Kinds of Self-knowledge" in *Philosophical Psychology* 1, 1 (1988): 46–48.

168. Ibid., 46.

169. Ibid., 40.

170. Ibid., 30.

171. In Russian: "Это чувство как бы театральной отчужденности от собственной речи, как бы стилизации под что-то—подтверждалось тем, что он пользовался не своими словами, а готовыми стандартными формулами, заведомо пропитанными всей мерзостью обывательского цинизма." Ibid.

172. Ibid.

173. In Russian: "Я охотно принимаю случайные радости, но требую логики от поразивших меня бедствий. И логика утешает, как доброе слово." Ginzburg 2002, 81. The original is in Lidiia Ginzburg, ZK V (1929–31) 89–90. OR RNB 1377. The note is not dated, but a neighboring note on p. 95 of the notebook is dated July 15, 1930.

174. Ginzburg 2002, 570.

175. In the draft manuscript for "Delusion of the Will," Ginzburg indicated clear divisions between sections, with the following headings: "Introductory Tale" ("Vvodnaia povest'"), "The Introductory Tale Breaks Off" ("Vvodnaia povest' preryvaetsia"), and "Introductory Tale (Continuation)" ("Vvodnaia povest' [Prodolzhenie]"). These headings themselves mark self-conscious fragmentation. In the published version, she does away with these markers, but the style remains no less fragmented—in fact, the shifting only becomes more fluid and less obvious.

176. In Russian: "Для меня отрывочность—не литературный эффект, но дефект мировосприятия. Но я не хочу избавляться от этого недостатка путем мертвых мест и слов не дожатых до ясности. От него можно отделаться только поняв и полюбив мир иначе, чем я в состоянии это сделать сейчас." Draft in a folder labeled "Vozvrashchenie domoi." OR RNB 1377.

177. In a blockade note, Ginzburg writes: "All the same, we will have to bear this chaos as the essence of our soul and as its sickness to the end of our days. It is our

cursed inheritance, going back to Tiutchev." 1943 notebook, published in Ginzburg 2011, 150.

178. Ginzburg 2002, 584–85.

179. Ibid., 609.

180. Ibid., 587.

181. Ibid., 610.

182. Ginzburg 2011, 43, reads: "And in the search for self-justification, in an attempt to alleviate his guilt, piling even part of it on the deceased,—he again analyzes her character." Tyotka, or Aunt, is analyzed in several of Ginzburg's texts, most extensively in drafts for *Home and the World*.

183. Scheler, 40.

184. Ginzburg 2002, 586.

185. Ibid., 587.

186. Ibid., 587.

187. Ibid., 588.

188. Ibid., 587.

189. Ginzburg 2002, 251–59. Richard Gustafson includes an interesting discussion of this essay in terms of Ginzburg's relationship to Tolstoy, and of Ginzburg's need for an analysis that is both sociological and moral in "Lidiia Ginzburg and Tolstoi," *Canadian-American Slavic Studies* 28, 2–3 (Summer–Fall 1994), 204–15; see especially 207.

190. Ginzburg 1991, 333–34; Russian in idem 1977, 405.

191. Ginzburg 2002, 251.

192. I analyze *Notes of a Blockade Person* in chapter 5, specifically in relation to "A Story of Pity and Cruelty," and questions of genre. Here I limit myself to an analysis of several distancing techniques within this narrative.

193. See Viktor Shklovskii, "Iskusstvo kak priem," in Viktor Shklovskii, *Gamburgskii schet. Stat'i. Vospominaniia. Esse* (Moscow: Sovetskii pisatel', 1990), 58–72. Originally published in 1917. The key passage about estrangement/*ostranenie* is on p. 63. English translation in Viktor Shklovsky, *Theory of Prose*, trans. Benjamin Sher (Normal, IL: Dalkey Archive Press, 1990), 6.

194. Kobrin compares the treatment of war by Ginzburg in *Notes of a Blockade Person* and Tolstoy in *War and Peace* in his article, contrasting the "total war" of the twentieth century with Kutuzov's "people's war" of the nineteenth. Kobrin 2012, 240–45. Richard Gustafson discusses Tolstoy's influence on Ginzburg in general, and *Notes of a Blockade Person* in particular, in "Lidiia Ginzburg and Tolstoi," 204–15. Gustafson notes that "Ginzburg's experience of the blockade is intimately associated with her professional turn to Tolstoi," 215.

195. Shklovsky's neologism *ostranenie*, though it is spelled with one "n," has as its root the word *strannyi*, or "strange." However, Svetlana Boym discusses alternative etymologies, including those that derive from *strana*, or "country," making *ostrananie* a kind of *dépaysement*. Shklovsky himself discusses the confusion between his *ostranenie* and the word *otstranenie*: "There is an old term, ostranenie, that was often written with one 'n,' even though the word comes from strannyi. Ostranenie entered life in such a spelling in 1917.When discussed orally, it is often confused with otstranenie, which means 'distancing of the world.'" Quoted in Boym, "Poetics and Politics of Estrangement: Viktor Shklovsky and Hannah Arendt": 581–611, 599. Russian in Viktor Shklovskii, "Iazyk i poeziia" in *Izbrannoe v dvukh tomakh*, vol. 2 (Moscow: Khudozhestvennaia literatura, 1983), 188.

196. Scholars have attempted to broaden the meaning of Shklovsky's *ostranenie*: for instance, there have been discussions of the possibility of understanding this device as an ethical principle in connection with Bakhtin's *vnenakhodimost'* (discussed later in this chapter). See for example, Svetlana Boym, "Poetics and Politics of Estrangement: Viktor Shklovsky and Hannah Arendt," *Poetics Today* 26, 4 (Winter 2005): 581–611; Caryl Emerson, "Shklovsky's *ostranenie*, Bakhtin's *vnenakhodimost'* (How Distance Serves an Aesthetics of Arousal Differently from an Aesthetics Based on Pain)," ibid.: 637–64; Galin Tihanov, "The Politics of Estrangement: The Case of the Early Shklovsky," ibid.: 665–96.

197. From "A Story of Pity and Cruelty," in Ginzburg 2011, 17.

198. Lidiya Ginzburg, *Blockade Diary*, trans. Alan Myers (London: Harvill Press, 1995), 98, 100. Henceforth, I refer to this translation as "Ginzburg 1995." Russian in idem 2011, 435–36. One could note that the hero's attempts to reject the city that has wounded him allow us to draw parallels between "Paralysis" and canonic examples of what is known as the "Petersburg Text" such as "The Bronze Horseman," "The Overcoat," and *Notes from Underground*.

199. English in Ginzburg 1995, 10. Russian in idem 2011, 315.

200. See the discussion by Oliver Sacks in "The Disembodied Lady," in *The Man Who Mistook His Wife for a Hat* (New York, NY: Simon & Schuster, 1998), 43–54, and in his autobiographical account, *A Leg to Stand On* (New York: Harper Perennial, 1994). See also Paul John Eakin, *How Our Lives Become Stories: Making Selves* (Ithaca, NY: Cornell University Press, 1999), 26–42. Also relevant is Ulric Neisser's concept of the "Ecological Self" in "Five Kinds of Self-knowledge," *Philosophical Psychology* 1, 1 (1988): 37–41.

201. Kirill Kobrin argues that the defamiliarization produced by the city under siege is so exhausting and mortally dangerous—because of the destruction of routines and habits—that " 'Blockade person' could only survive by defeating defamiliarization." Kobrin 2012, 240.

202. Ginzburg 2011, 311.

203. *Blokadnaia kniga,* edited by Ales' Adamovich and Daniil Granin, was published first in 1979, and then in several subsequent editions, subject to decreasing amounts of censorship. The first two publications were in Moscow, since the work was turned down by all the Leningrad journals. On this history, see Arlen Blium, *Kak eto delalos' v Leningrade: Tsenzura v gody ottepeli, zastoia i perestroika 1953–1991* (St. Petersburg: Akademicheskii proekt, 2005), 167.

204. Lidiia Ginzburg, Interview with G. Silina, *Literaturnaia gazeta* 3, 5069 (15 January 1986).

205. *Blokadnai kniga*, ed. Ales' Adamovich and Daniil Granin (Leningrad: Lenizdat, 1989), 382. Fragments from Riabinkin's diary had been published in the newspaper *Smena* in 1970. Ibid., 266.

206. Michel Foucault, "Self Writing," in *Ethics: Subjectivity and Truth*, ed. Paul Rabinow, trans. Robert Hurley and others, *Essential Works of Michel Foucault 1954–1984*, vol. 1 (New York: The New Press, 1997), 207.

207. In Russian: "Поступок не имел отношения к его пониманию жизни вообще и потому не мог отразиться на этических представлениях и оценках, выработанных всей его биографией. Он видит себя изнутри, и он видит свой поступок как отчужденный от его постоянной человеческой сущности." Ginzburg 2011, 186.

208. Ibid. Ellipsis added. Cf. Ginzburg's discussion in *On Psychological Prose*: Ginzburg 1991, 335–36; idem 1977, 407.

209. "On Satire and Analysis." Ginzburg 2002, 255.

210. Ginzburg 2011, 188.

211. Ginzburg mentions Scheler in "The Thought That Drew a Circle" in reference to consciousness of death. Ginzburg 2002, 553–54. Scheler uses a visual-spatial metaphor when discussing self-improvement through repentance. He writes, "Just as, when climbing a mountain, we see both the summit's approach, and the valley sinking beneath our feet, each picture entering our experience under the control of the one act, so in Repentance the Person mounts, and in mounting sees below it the former constituent Selves." Max Scheler, "Repentance and Rebirth," in *On the Eternal in Man*, trans. Bernard Noble (London: SCM Press Ltd, 1960), 48. On Bakhtin, Scheler, Nicolai Hartmann, and others, see Brian Poole, "From Phenomenology to Dialogue: Max Scheler's Phenomenological Tradition and Mikhail Bakhtin's Development from 'Toward a Philosophy of the Act' to His Study of Dostoevsky," in *Bakhtin and Cultural Theory* (Manchester, UK: Manchester University Press, 2001), 109–35. See also Craig Brandist, *The Bakhtin Circle: Philosophy, Culture and Politics* (London: Pluto Press, 2002). Valentin Voloshinov in his book on Freudianism called Scheler "the most influential philosopher of our time" (in Poole, 112).

212. M. M. Bakhtin, "Avtor i geroi v esteticheskoi deiatel'nosti," *Sobraniie sochinenii*, vol. 1 (Moscow: Russkie slovari, 2003), 89. The English translation is my own.

213. Ibid., 97–98, 117–18.

214. Ibid., 97. My translation.

215. The principle of *vnenakhodimost'*, as Bakhtin discusses it, is about making art, rather than ethical deeds, possible. It is in this aesthetic sense that Caryl Emerson has drawn a parallel between Bakhtin's *vnenakhodimost'* and Shklovsky's *ostranenie*. Caryl Emerson, "Shklovsky's *ostranenie*, Bakhtin's *vnenakhodimost'*."

216. Bakhtin, "Avtor i geroi," 107. English translation in *Art and Answerability: Early Philosophical Essays by M.M. Bakhtin*, ed. Michael Holquist and Vadim Liapunov, trans. Vadim Liapunov (Austin: University of Texas Press, 1990), 27. A very different, fairly radical analysis of Bakhtin's "Author and Hero" has recently been performed by Irina Sandomirskaia, who decribes this work as an apology of repression, finding the author's control over the hero to represent a "manifestation of terror" common to works in the Stalinist era. According to Sandomirskaia, Bakhtin's "author" turns the "hero" into a "thing" in order to create the totality of the novel. Irina Sandomirskaia, *Blokada v slove: Ocherki kriticheskoi teorii i biopolitiki iazyka* (Moscow: Novoe literaturnoe obozrenie, 2013), 111–72, esp. 145, 156, 161.

217. On Ginzburg's ability to remove herself to another realm, see Andrei Levkin, "Shkola dlia umnykh," *Novoe literaturnoe obozrene* 49, 3 (2001): 421–26. On Ginzburg's belonging to the nineteenth-century traditions of the Russian intelligentsia, see Sarah Pratt, "Lidiia Ginzburg, a Russian Democrat at the Rendezvous," *Canadian-American Slavic Studies* 28, 2–3 (Summer–Fall 1994): 183–203.

218. It is evident that there are different narrative strategies between these two versions, both appearing to be from the 1930s: one of them a more or less full draft, and the other consisting of a few pages of an earlier draft within one of the manuscripts for "The Thought That Drew a Circle." The pages clearly show that "Delusion . . ." would have at that point been part of, or an outgrowth from "The Thought . . . ." These drafts, which I studied in Kushner's archive, were part of the second archival transfer and are listed in

the provisional catalogue under Op. 2. ed. khr. 41 and ed. khr. 42. (They are mislabeled as "Zapisnye knizhki" of the year 1936, 66 pages and 53 pages, respectively.) Another, later set of drafts was part of the first archival transfer to the RNB (Op. 1) and is listed, without a number, under "Mysl', opisavshaia krug" (278 pages). OR RNB 1377.

219. In Russian: "Когда эта тема по настоящему находит на меня, она идет долгим потоком разорванных мыслей. И уже неизвестно—теперешний ли это поток или тот самый поток, который непрестанно гудел в моей голове в те первые дни после этой смерти." This opening occurs within a draft of "The Thought That Drew a Circle." Ginzburg archive, folder for "Mysl', opisavshaia krug" (Op. 2 Ed. khr. 42). OR RNB 1377. The remaining paragraphs of this draft opening consist of generalizations as well as a disembodied dialogue between "repentance" and "self-justification" (such a dialogue also appears in the finished version).

220. In Russian: "Вот в моих руках, в руках писателя побывала жалкая жизнь и жалкая смерть человека. < . . . > И во всем своем объеме она [смерть] существовала для одного только человека, для которого она стала виной и казнью воли.". First page of manuscript in folder labeled "Zabluzhdenie voli." OR RNB 1377 op. 2 ed. khr. 58.. In the final version, Ginzburg uses the first person plural throughout this passage. For example, "[This other's life] is like a valuable thing that we held in our hands, but threw away in ignorance." Ginzburg 2002, 584.

221. On N.'s gender, see chapter 3. On the autobiographical basis of this story, see chapter 5.

222. Sarah Pratt has noted this effect in her argument about the autobiographical nature of *Notes of a Blockade Person*, where, as she puts it, there is a "quintessentially Ginzburgian analysis" similar to what one finds in *On Psychological Prose* and *On the Literary Hero*. Sarah Pratt, "Angels in the Stalinist House: Nadezhda Mandelstam, Lidiia Chukovskaia, Lidiia Ginzburg, and Russian Women's Autobiography," *Auto/biography Studies* 11, 2 (1996): 73.

223. There are some additional incidental voices: for example, the utterance of one anonymous woman (a reflection about aging parents) suddenly intrudes into the story. Her speech is seemingly quoted by the author-narrator. Narratologically, it would be more consistent if she were speaking to N. Ginzburg 2002, 597. On the whole, in both "Delusion of the Will" and "A Story of Pity and Cruelty," which are singularly focused on one person's guilt, there are many fewer such voices than in works such as *Notes of a Blockade Person* or "The Thought That Drew a Circle."

224. In the manuscript, "*Durak*!"

225. Ginzburg 2002, 595.

226. Ibid., 610.

227. A related question, which I investigate in chapter 5, is: what is the interrelationship between fiction and ethics in the process of self-examination—can one provide a record of one's guilt through the creation of a clearly fictional, rather than an autobiographical or historiographical narrative?

228. Lejeune, "Autobiography in the Third Person," in *On Autobiography*, 35–36.

229. Robert Folkenflik, "The Self as Other," in *The Culture of Autobiography: Constructions of Self-Representation*, ed. R. Folkenflik (Stanford, CA: Stanford University Press, 1993), 234.

230. Folkenflik, 222–24. Folkenflik uses *The Education of Henry Adams*, a rare third-person autobiography, to argue that a major reason behind this rhetorical choice is Henry Adams's incredibly low self-esteem. Jean Starobinski, on the other hand, uses the examples of Caesar's *Commentaries* and the second part of La Rochefoucauld's *Mé-*

moires to make the point that third-person autobiographies can, under a mask of modesty, glorify "the hero who refuses to speak his own name." Jean Starobinski, "The Style of Autobiography," translated by Seymour Chatman, in *Autobiography: Essays Theoretical and Critical*, ed. James Olney (Princeton, NJ: Princeton University Press, 1980), 76–77. Somewhat in line with Starobinski's argument, Sarah Pratt, in her article "Angels in the Stalinist House," asserts that Ginzburg (together with Lidiia Chukovskaia and Nadezhda Mandelstam) was "enhancing" the self through seeming to "deny" it: "as these Russian women 'denied the self' in preserving the Word and experience of others, they become creators of the Word themselves, and they themselves came to embody the highest values of Russian culture." Pratt, "Angels in the Stalinist House," 81.

231. See *Roland Barthes by Roland Barthes*, trans. Richard Howard (Berkeley: University of California Press, 1994). For example, he writes: "Once I produce, once I write, it is the Text itself which (fortunately) dispossesses me of my narrative continuity," 4. "All of this must be considered as if spoken by a character in a novel—or rather by several characters," 119. "What I write about myself is never *the last word*: the more 'sincere' I am, the more interpretable I am, under the eye of other examples than those of the old authors, who believed they were required to submit themselves to but one law: *authenticity*," 120. All three examples are used by Folkenflik in his discussion of Barthes on 232–33 of "The Self as Other." Candace Lang puts it well when she writes that "the Barthesian subject is not an entity, it is a relationship," in "Autobiography in the Aftermath of Romanticism," *Diacritics* 12, 4 (Winter 1982): 15.

CHAPTER 2. THE POETICS OF DESK-DRAWER NOTEBOOKS

1. When publishing this narrative in *Literatura v poiskakh real'nosti* (1987), Ginzburg appended the date 1929. In *Chelovek za pis'mennym stolom*, she changed the date to 1931. I believe she wrote parts of it between 1929 and 1934 or even 1936. Pieces of the text appear in her 1931–32 and 1934 notebooks, and one part resembles a 1936 sketch (though this fragment may have been part of "The Return Home" before being included in the sketch).

2. The known audience of her notes in the early years included those listed in note 3, as well as Viktor Shklovsky and Nikolai Khardzhiev. During the Blockade, she read to Grigory Makogonenko and Olga Berggolts. In the late Soviet period, among the admirers of her yet-unpublished notes were Alexander Kushner, Andrei Bitov, Elena Shvarts, Eleazar Meletinsky, Irina Paperno, John Malmstad, Kseniia Kumpan, Yakov Gordin, Nina Snetkova, Irena Podol'skaia, Galia Murav'ëva, Nikolai Kononov, Elena Kumpan, Al'bin Konechnyi, Aleksei Mashevsky, Irina Semenko, and Alexander Chudakov. While most of Ginzburg's audience lived in Leningrad, some members were based in Moscow. Audiotapes of Ginzburg reading from her notes and conversing with friends, made in 1983, 1984, 1988, and 1989, were given to me by Kseniia Kumpan, Al'bin Konechnyi, and Irina Paperno.

The fact that her audience included some of Leningrad's most important writers, scholars, and cultural luminaries meanwhile did not prevent Ginzburg from being tortured by the thought that her writings would never reach a broad readership, at least not during her lifetime. On this theme, frequent in the notes, see for example Lidiia Ginzburg, *Zapisnye knizhki. Vospominaniia. Esse.* (St. Petersburg: Iskusstvo-SPb, 2002), 153–55, 188–89, and 269. Henceforth, I refer to this volume as "Ginzburg 2002." In Ginzburg's view, only the prospect of publication could challenge the writer to "achieve socially significant forms of expression." Ibid, 188.

3. Initials are given in Ginzburg's note on this conversation, which is in a small notebook (*obshchaia tetrad'*) with a note "Otzyvy," not catalogued and located in a box with miscellaneous materials. Ginzburg then included a revised version of this dialogue in the draft introductory chapter ("Theoretical Introduction") to her new composition. Descriptions (such as "young poet") of the figures appear in this rendering of the conversation. From these two sources, one can decipher that A.A. is Anna Akhmatova, N.N. is Nikolai Nikolaevich Punin, Gr. is Grigory Gukovsky, M.A. is Matvei Aleksandrovich Gukovsky, B.M. is Boris Mikhailovich Engelgardt, B. is Boris Bukhstab, and O. is Nikolai Oleinikov. There is a Zh. who is probably Evgeny Shvarts, a woman V. who may be Veta Dolukhanova, a woman Ir. who may be Irina Shchegoleva, and a woman L. who may be Lialia or Liza (an as yet-unidentified intimate friend of Ginzburg's). The "Theoretical Introduction" is currently catalogued as op. 2 ed. khr. 63: "Teoreticheskoe vstuplenie." Zametki o literature. V tetradi i otd. listy b.d. ll. I + 51. OR RNB 1377. See pages 29–32.

4. See Ilya Serman, "Writer-Researcher," *Canadian-American Slavic Studies Journal* 19, 2 (1985): 187–92. Also see Andrei Zorin's discussion of this in "Proza L. Ia. Ginzburg i gumanitarnaia mysl' XX veka," *Novoe literaturnoe obozrenie* 76, 6 (2005): 45–46.

5. Small common notebook, uncatalogued; duplicated in "Teoreticheskaia vstuplenie," 30–31. OR RNB 1377.

6. Ginzburg writes, "The main thing for a writer is to reflect the pathos [or emotional content] of a law-governed [regular] human fate" In Russian: "Главное для писателя—отразить пафос закономерной человеческой судьбы." Ginzburg 2002, 61. Original note in ZK III (1928) 58. OR RNB 1377.

7. From the essay "On Old Age and Infantilism," in Ginzburg 2002, 189.

8. David Shepherd discusses the crisis of the novel in Soviet Russia (and how it inspired experimentation with metafiction) in *Beyond Metafiction: Self-Consciousness in Soviet Literature* (Oxford: Clarendon Press, 1992), 17–28.

9. See for example Judith Ryan, "The Vanishing Subject: Empirical Psychology and the Modern Novel," *PMLA* 95, 5 (1980): 857–59.

10. Osip Mandel'shtam, "Konets romana," *Sochineniia v dvukh tomakh*, vol. 2 (Moscow: Khudozhestvennaia literatura, 1990), 201–5. In a similar manner, György Lukács found that elements of "lyricism and psychology" that entered contemporary novels were part of an unproductive, "epigonic imitation" from earlier times. See Georg Lukács, *The Theory of the Novel* (1914–1915), trans. Anna Bostock (Cambridge, MA: MIT Press, 1971), 151.

11. Osip Mandel'shtam, "Konets romana," 201.

12. Shklovsky inserted some of Elsa Triolet's letters (as well as his letter to the Communist Party) into his epistolary novel *Zoo, or Letters Not about Love*. On Pilnyak, see Victor Erlich, "The Novel in Crisis: Boris Pilnyak and Konstantin Fedin," in *The Russian Novel from Pushkin to Pasternak*, ed. John Garrad (New Haven, CT: Yale University Press, 1983), 155–76. See also Viktor Gofman, "Mesto Pil'niaka," in *Boris Pil'niak : Stat'i i Materialy*. Mastera sovremennoi literatury, vol. 3, ed. V. Kazanskii and Iu. Tynianov (Leningrad: Academia, 1928), 5–34.

13. Shklovsky, quoted in Richard Sheldon's introduction to Viktor Shklovsky, *Zoo, or Letters Not about Love*, trans. Richard Sheldon (Chicago, IL: Dalkey Archive Press, 2001

[1971]). Russian in Viktor Shklovskii, "Retsenziia na etu knigu," *Gamburgskii schet* (Leningrad: 1928), 108–9.

14. The phrase "how it's made" comes from the title of Boris Eikhenbaum's article, "Kak sdelana 'Shinel'' Gogolia" (first published in 1919). English translation: Boris Eikhenbaum, "How Gogol's 'Overcoat' Is Made," *Gogol from the Twentieth Century: Eleven Essays*, ed. and trans. Robert Maguire (Princeton, NJ: Princeton University Press, 1974), 267–92.

15. Ginzburg 2002, 35. Original note in ZK 1927 (entry from October of that year). OR RNB 1377.

16. Michel Aucouturier has argued that this was in part because of the "crushing domination of a realist aesthetic" that lingered from the nineteenth century. Michel Aucouturier, "The Theory of the Novel in Russia in the 1930s: Lukács and Bakhtin," in *The Russian Novel from Pushkin to Pasternak*, 227–28. Galin Tihanov has argued that a tradition of Russian theory of the novel had developed in the 1890s–1930s, and that several of the Formalists' ideas about continuity in the history of the novel, about genre more generally and its evolution, and the importance of everyday speech and life for literary systems (the novel, the ode) influenced Bakhtin's theories of the novel. See Galin Tihanov, *The Master and the Slave: Lukács, Bakhtin, and the Ideas of Their Time* (Oxford: Clarendon Press, 2000) 112–61.

17. The quotation is from Shklovsky's essay "Sketch and Anecdote," cited in Tihanov's *The Master and the Slave*, 129.

18. Lukács, whose *Theory of the Novel* had been published in 1916, took part in Moscow debates on the novel in 1935–36. Bakhtin's four important essays on the novel were written between 1935 and 1941. On Soviet theories of the novel, and the debates on genre in the 1930s, see Katerina Clark and Galin Tihanov, "Soviet Literary Theory in the 1930s: Battles over Genre and the Boundaries of Modernity," in *A History of Russian Literary Theory and Criticism: The Soviet Age and Beyond*, ed. Evgeny Dobrenko and Galin Tihanov (Pittsburgh, PA: University of Pittsburgh Press, 2011), 109–43. See also Tihanov's *The Master and the Slave*, which carefully traces and analyzes the debates in 1935–36 around Lukács's entry on the novel for the first Soviet literary encyclopedia, as well as Bakhtin's creative synthesis of certain ideas of Lukács, the Formalists, Veselovskii, Griftsov, and Olga Freidenberg.

Bakhtin's theories of the novel are calibrated to twentieth-century Modernism: they stress linguistic heterogeneity and polyphony, the lack of authoritative discourse, openness of time, and "unfinalizability."

19. Lidiia Ginzburg, "Chelovek za pis'mennym stolom. Po starym zapisnym knizhkam," in *Novyi mir* 6 (June 1982), 235 (from the author's introduction to the publication of notes).

20. Ibid.

21. Iurii Tynianov, "Oda kak oratorskii zhanr" (1922), in *Poetika. Istoriia literatury. Kino*, ed. E. A. Toddes, A. P. Chudakov, and M. Chudakova (Moscow: Nauka, 1977), 228. Its significance is discussed by Tihanov in *The Master and the Slave*, 134–35.

22. Iurii Tynianov, "Literaturnyi fakt," in *Poetika. Istoriia literatury. Kino*, 259 (translation mine). (The article was first published in *Lef* 2 [1924]: 101–16.)

23. For a discussion of how the Formalists studied the Romantic fragment under the influence of the development of montage in the 1920s, see Monika F. Greenleaf, "Tynianov, Pushkin and the Fragment: Through the Lens of Montage," *Cultural Mythologies of Russian Modernism*, ed. Boris Gasparov, Robert P. Hughes, and Irina Paperno

(Berkeley: University of California Press, 1992), 264–92. On the Romantic fragment in relation to Pushkin and Russian Romanticism, see Greenleaf's book, *Pushkin and Romantic Fashion: Fragment, Elegy, Orient, Irony* (Stanford, CA: Stanford University Press, 1994), esp. 1–55. For a discussion of the Romantic concept of the fragment in its philosophical dimentions, see Philippe Lacoue-Labarthe and Jean-Luc Nancy, *The Literary Absolute: The Theory of Literature in German Romanticism*, trans. Philip Barnard and Cheryl Lester (Albany: State University of New York Press, 1988), 39–58.

24. Tynianov, "Literaturnyi fakt," *Poetika. Istoriia literatury. Kino*, 256. Translation from Iurii Tynianov, "The Literary Fact," *Modern Genre Theory*, ed. David Duff, trans. Ann Shukman (New York: Longman, 2000), 31–32.

25. Tynianov defines "the concept of size" as "primarily an energy concept: we tend to call a form on whose construction we have expended more energy a 'large form.'" Tynianov, "The Literary Fact," 31–32. Russian in "Literaturnyi fakt," 256.

26. Tynianov, "Literaturnyi fakt," 261. English in "The Literary Fact," 36. Just as size and energy are taken for granted when speaking about the novel, Tynianov argues that his definition of literature as a "dynamic speech construction" is self-evident. On how the constructive principle is connected to the idea of the whole, see Gary Saul Morson, *The Boundaries of Genre: Dostoevsky's* Diary of a Writer *and the Traditions of Literary Utopia* (Evanston, IL: Northwestern University Press, 1981), 41–42.

27. In Russian: "В своей совокупности бессвязные отрывки 'Записных книжек' почти монументальны—это своего рода большая форма малого жанра." Lidiia Ginzburg, "Viazemskii-literator" (1926), republished in L. Ginzburg, *Raboty dovoennogo vremeni*, ed. Stanislav Savitskii (St. Petersburg: Petropolis, 2007), 101.

28. Yevgeny Zamyatin, "On Literature, Revolution, Entropy, and Other Matters," in *A Soviet Heretic: Essays by Yevgeny Zamyatin*, ed. and trans. Mirra Ginsburg (Chicago: University of Chicago Press, 1970), 112. Russian in Evgenii Zamiatin, "O literature, revoliutsii, entropii i o prochem," in *Sobranie sochinenii v 5 tomakh*, ed. St. Nikonenko and A. Tiurin, vol. 3 (Moscow: Russkaia kniga, 2004), 179.

29. Ginzburg adds, "It's sooner French, though Shklovsky doesn't know French." Ginzburg 2002, 54. There is a fuller note in the original ZK II (1927), 16–17 (surrounded by notes from April 1927). OR RNB 1377.

30. Ginzburg 2002, 19.

31. From Tynianov's letter to Shklovsky in May 1927. In E. A. Toddes, "Neosushchestvlennye zamysly Tynianova," in *Tynianovskii sbornik: Pervye Tynianovskie chteniia* (Riga: Zinatne, 1984), 43–44. Toddes, discussing these unrealized plans, explains that the "rhetorical orientation" (*rechevaia ustanovka*) of Tynianov's small forms would have been the notebook entry. He postulates that what was important to Tynianov was not size, but rather the aspect of the sketch that blurs the distinction between a draft and a finished text. Thanks to Kseniia Kumpan for directing my attention to this publication.

32. In Russian: "Можно переварить скуку трехтомного романа, но в трехстрочной записи скука непереносима." Ginzburg ZK V (1929–31), 173. Sentence underlined by the author (I render her underlining with italics). OR RNB 1377.

33. Ginzburg ZK VIII–2 (1932), 11. OR RNB 1377.

34. Boris Eikhenbaum, "V poiskakh zhanra," *Russkii sovremennik* 3 (1924): 228–31. Meanwhile, for his part Zamyatin declared that "Russian literature in recent years is like Peter Schlemiel who has lost his shadow: there are writers, but there are no critics. The Formalists still don't venture to operate on living people but continue to dissect

corpses." Zamyatin, "The New Russian Prose" (1923), in *A Soviet Heretic*, 92. Russian in Evgenii Zamiatin, "Novaia russkaia proza," in *Sobranie sochinenii v 5 tomakh*, ed. St. Nikonenko and A. Tiurin, vol. 3 (Moscow: Russkaia kniga, 2004), 125.

35. Cf. Tynianov's judgments on how "easily" Ehrenburg puts his novels together in "Promezhutok" (1924): "Sometimes it seems that it was not the writer, but inertia itself that wrote the story," 169, and in "Literaturnoe segodnya" (1924), 153–55. In *Poetika. Istoriia literatury. Kino* (1977).

36. ZK I (1925–26), 100–101. OR RNB 1377. Undated entry, but surrounding entries are from October 1925. A portion of this note was published—see Ginzburg 2002, 23. In this note, Ginzburg writes that the most promising contemporary prose writer is Zamyatin, but that he is "not a major writer" (*on ne bol'shoi pisatel'*): he's good only because he imitates Nikolai Leskov. She also praises the contemporary poetry of Nikolai Tikhonov and Boris Pasternak. The reference to wise snakes goes back to Matthew 10:16 (*bud'te mudry, kak zmii*) and also to Pushkin's "Prorok" (*zhalo mudryia zmei*). The connection from Pushkin to Matthew is made in Michael Wachtel, *A Commentary to Pushkin's Lyric Poetry 1826–1836* (Madison: University of Wisconsin Press, 2011), 26.

37. Translation of Tolstoy's letter in Viktor Shklovsky, *Third Factory*, intro. and trans. Richard Sheldon (Normal, IL: Dalkey Archive Press, 2002), 50; Russian in Viktor Shklovskii, *Tret'ia fabrika* (Letchworth, UK: Prideaux Press, 1978; reprint of 1926 Russian edition by Artel' pisatelei "Krug"), 82–83. Original letter in Lev Tolstoy, *Polnoe sobranie sochinenii v 90 tomakh* (Moscow, 1953–58), vol. LXXVII: 218–20.

38. Quoted in Eikhenbaum, "V poiskakh zhanra," 230. In Russian: "Мне кажется, что современем [sic] вообще перестанут выдумывать художественные произведения. Будет совестно сочинять про какого-нибудь выдуманного Ивана Ивановича или Марью Петровну. Писатели, если они будут, будут не сочинять, а только рассказывать то значительное или интересное, что им случилось наблюдать в жизни." Emphasis in original.

39. In Russian: "Мы говорили долго о непостижимости того, как писать прозу. Уже ничего не может быть постыдней как написать: такой-то подошел к столу и сел. И вообще все существующие способы изображения человека—навеки скомпрометированная фикция." In ZK VIII (1933), 19–20. OR RNB 1377.

40. In Russian: "Выдуманные люди и ситуации < . . . > внушают мне некоторое отвращение." Unpublished fragment temporarily located in a folder with miscellaneous manuscripts from the 1920s and 1930s. OR RNB 1377. Ginzburg follows this with a remark she subsequently crossed out: "There is the form of the *short story*, in the broad sense—that is, an invented story—which is impossible now, because no one knows why or how to invent." In Russian: "Есть форма рассказа, в широком понимании,—то-есть выдуманной истории,—невозможная сейчас, потому что неизвестно зачем и как выдумывать."

41. Tynianov discusses the reader's "über-naturalism" (сверхнатурализм) as a fad that might soon give way to a demand for pure literary fictions. From his piece "Dream" (Сон) from the end of the 1920s, quoted in commentaries to "Literaturnyi fakt," 508.

42. Ginzburg, "On Writers' Notebooks," manuscript, typescript version. Currently miscatalogued in the archive as Op. 3. Ed. khr. 53. Ginzburg L. Ia. *Zapisnaia knizhka* <1940–1950ые> II+46 ll. OR RNB 1377. In *Third Factory*, Shklovsky writes of one possible path for new artistic creation: "The third alternative is to work in newspapers and journals every day, to be unsparing of yourself and caring about the work, to change, to

crossbreed with the material, change some more, crossbreed with the material, process it some more—and then there will be literature." Shklovsky, *Third Factory*, 51–52; Russian in Shklovskii, *Tret'ia fabrika*, 84–85.

43. Iurii Tynianov, "Zhurnal, kritik, chitatel' i pisatel'" (first published in 1924), in *Poetika. Istoriia literatury. Kino* (Moscow: Nauka, 1977), 147–49. Viktor Shklovskii, *Gamburgskii schet* (Leningrad: Izdatel'stvo pisatelei, 1928), 112–17. Both are discussed by Gary Saul Morson in *The Boundaries of Genre*, 57–58.

44. On Eikhenbaum's *My Periodical*, see Carol Any, *Boris Eikhenbaum: Voices of a Russian Formalist* (Stanford, CA: Stanford University Press, 1994), 110–15. As Any argues, Eikhenbaum had by 1929 broken with Brik and the LEF group, and saw documentary literature as "a means to finding new literary forms," whereas Brik saw them "as an end in themselves, a Soviet literature of fact that fulfilled the new society's needs and surpassed European and prerevolutionary Russian literature." Any, 115. See also Alyson Tapp, "'Как быть писателем?': Boris Eikhenbaum's Response to the Crisis of the Novel in the 1920s," *Slavonica* 15, 1 (April 2009): 32–47. Tapp argues that *Moi vremennik* constitutes Eikhenbaum's search for an active writerly existence ("How to Be a Writer") in the context of the novel's crisis through "the blending of scholarly, autobiographical, and fictional modes," 45.

45. In Russian: "Мы воспринимаем сейчас как литературу мемуары, ощущая их эстетически. < . . . > Конечно, сейчас существует и будет существовать сюжетная проза, но она существует на запасе старых навыков," in *Tret'ia fabrika*, 9. I have altered Sheldon's translation (Shklovsky, *Third Factory*, 4). Galin Tihanov has noted that in their literary theories, the Formalists saw plot as playing a subservient role to devices; Bakhtin, too, subordinates the plot—in his case, it serves to bring different discourses into contact with one another. Tihanov, *The Master and the Slave*, 144.

46. See Eikhenbaum and Goffman, ibid. Also see the articles in *Literatura fakta: Pervyi sbornik materialov rabotnikov LEFa* (Moscow: Federatsia, 1929, republished by I. V. Zakharov, 2000), especially N. Chuzhak, "Pisatel'skaia pamiatka," 9–28; S. Tret'iakov, "Novyi Lev Tolstoi," 29–33, and "Biografiia veshchi," 68–72; O. Brik "Blizhe k faktu," 80–85, and "Razlozhenie siuzheta," 226–28, and V. Shklovskii, "K tekhnike vnesiuzhetnoi prozy," 229–334.

47. Osip Brik, "Razlozhenie siuzheta" ("The Disintegration of Plot"), in *Literatura fakta: Pervyi sbornik materialov rabotnikov LEFa*, 226–27.

48. In Russian: "Литература фактов, в которую верует Брик (если верует), вместо эстетики (буржуазной) имеет потребность в этике. Она должна быть честной." Ginzburg 2002, 32.

49. In Russian: "В этой теории подкупает ее очевидная абсурдность. Она настолько антилитературна, что испытываешь потребность дойти до каких-то ее здравых корней." Ibid. The original, in ZK I 193 (OR RNB 1377), is slightly different, calling the theory not just anti-literary but also "primitive," and adding in the desire to seek out "fresh" and healthy roots.

50. In Russian: "Дело не в материале, а в создании новой структуры смыслов и в повышении познавательных возможностей литературного слова." Ginzburg, draft article on Proust, page not numbered. OR RNB 1377.

51. Small selections from Vyazemsky's notebooks were published in journals and in a collected edition during his lifetime. A fuller version came out posthumously in three volumes of collected works.

52. Lidiia Ginzburg, introduction in P. Viazemskii, *Staraia zapisnaia knizhka*, 11.

53. On oral speech as the closest "extra-literary series" to the literary system, see

Tynianov, "Oda kak oratorskii zhanr" (1922) in *Poetika. Istoriia literatury. Kino*, 228. On ideas about center and periphery in literary evolution, see Tynianov's "Literaturnyi fakt" in ibid., 257–58.

54. In Russian: "Тогда же эти занятия навели меня на мысль начать самой нечто вроде записной книжки." Lidiia Ginzburg, "Chelovek za pis'mennym stolom. Po starym zapisnym knizhkam" in *Novyi mir* 6 (June 1982): 235. The notes were published in the section of the journal called "Literary Criticism." Also see Ginzburg 2002, 303.

55. See Pëtr Viazemskii, *Staraia zapisnaia knizhka* (ed. Ginzburg), 59, 94. In both notes, he discusses literature as the reflection or expression of society, and laments the deficiency of good writers and writing in Russia. He calls for the necessity of documenting oral culture, including rumors.

56. Ibid., 222. Meanwhile, Vyazemsky completely failed to recognize the importance of the Russian psychological novel that emerged during his lifetime.

57. Lidiia Ginzburg, introduction in P. Viazemskii, *Staraia zapisnaia knizhka*, ed. and comment. L. Ginzburg (Leningrad: Izdatel'stvo pisatelei, 1929), 36–37. Comparisons between the literary scene in the 1920s and 1830s were common in this period. David Shepherd comments on this in *Beyond Metafiction: Self-Consciousness in Soviet Literature*, 19–20.

58. In Russian: "литература поступила в промежуточный период, период использования, переработки и преодоления высоких достижений предыдущих десятилетий." Ginzburg, introduction to P. Viazemskii, *Staraia zapisnaia knizhka*, 39. Tynianov's article "Promezhutok" (1924) treats poetry, and the lack of definite poetic schools in this period. Surveying a number of contemporary poets, he concludes that "In the period of the interval, what is valuable to us are not at all 'successes' or 'readymade things.' We don't know what to do with these well-made things, just as children don't know what to do with toys that are too good. We need an exit. 'Things' can be 'unsuccessful,' but what is important is that they bring the possibility of 'success' closer." Tynianov, "Promezhutok," in *Poetika. Istoriia literatury. Kino*, 195.

59. In 1929, as Ginzburg edited Vyazemsky, LEF published the collection of essays *Literature of Fact* (*Literatura fakta*), a volume that turned out to be the swan song of the movement. Many of the articles here had been published in 1927–1928. See Maria Zalambani, *Literatura Fakta: Ot Avangarda k sotsrealizmu* (St. Petersburg: Akademicheskii proekt, 2006), 41. This book is a translation of Zalambani, *La More del Romanzo: Dall' Avanguardia Al Realismo Socialista* (Rome: Carocci Editore, 2003).

60. Ginzburg, introduction in P. Viazemskii, *Staraia zapisnaia knizhka*, 41. In her article, Ginzburg uses the phrase "literature of facts" (*literatura faktov*) rather than "literature of fact" as the movement was known. Vyazemsky had once used the same phrase. Stanislav Savitsky has wondered whether this phrase may have been picked up from Vyazemsky by LEF. Stanislav Savitskii, "Zhivaia literatura faktov: spor L. Ginzburg i B. Bukhshtaba o 'Liricheskom otstuplenii' N. Aseeva," *Novoe literaturnoe obozrenie* 89, 1 (2008): 22–23. In his book, Savitsky attempts to put Ginzburg's notes in the context of the montage techniques of Vertov and others. Savitskii, *Chastnyi chelovek: L. Ia. Ginzburg v kontse 1920-kh–nachale 1930-kh godov* (St. Petersburg: Evropeiskii universitet, 2013), 78–79. My review of this book, "Fragmenty s otstupleniiami: Lidiia Ginzburg v nachale puti" appears in *Novoe literaturnoe obozrenie* 128, 4 (2014): 328–36.

61. In Russian: "Создать законченные словесные конструкции, не убивая и не пролитературивая факта—в этом пафос «Записных книжек», и в этом же их основная техническая проблема." Lidiia Ginzburg, introduction to *Staraia zapisnaia knizhka*, 42. Note how, like Tynianov in his definition of literature as "dynamic speech

constructions," Ginzburg uses the Latinate *konstruktsiia* here. She would later come to prefer the word *postroenie*, especially when describing personality constructs.

62. In Russian, "автор полностью брал на себя ответственность за словесный строй своих записей." Ginzburg, introduction to *Staraia zapisnaia knizhka*, 42.

63. Ginzburg's argument runs counter to that of other scholars such as Lauren Leighton, who describes Vyazemsky's anecdotes (in contrast to Pushkin's demonstrations of brevity and stylistic flair) as relatively long, oriented toward capturing the speech of others and toward collecting material. Lauren Leighton, "The Anecdote in Russia: Pushkin, Vjazemskij, and Davydov," *Slavic and East European Journal* 10, 2 (Summer 1966): 155–66.

64. See Ginzburg's edition, *Staraia zapisnaia knizhka*, 296 n. 15.

65. Gary Saul Morson, *The Long and Short of It: From Aphorism to Novel* (Stanford, CA: Stanford University Press), 71–73.

66. This article exists as a handwritten outline/draft, currently miscatalogued in the archive as Op. 3. Ed. khr. 53. Гинзбург Л.Я. Записная книжка. <1940–1950ые> II+46 лл. and as a typescript (in another section of the archives). The typescript is in purple ink. The article dates to sometime between late 1930 and early 1932. So, for instance, Ginzburg makes reference to a 1930 review (by Pertsovich) of Lavrukhin's "In the Hero's Footsteps." And in a note from 3 January 1932, Ginzburg writes: "I have been writing for a long time now: last year *Pinkerton*, before that an ill-fated article about 'Notebooks,' and before that there was 'Children's Literature' and ill-fated articles about Proust and Aseev—all the way back to Venevitinov." In Russian: "Я очень давно пишу: последний год «Пинкертона», до этого злосчастную статью о «Записных Книжках», до этого была «Детская Литература» и злосчастные Пруст и Асеев—вплоть до Веневитинова." ZK VI (1931–32), 38–39. OR RNB 1377. Other parts of this note were published in Ginzburg 2002, 98–100.

67. See for example a book on the realist French novel, *Frantsuzskii realisticheskii roman XIX veka*, ed. Vasilii A. Desnitskii (Moscow/Leningrad: Gosudarstvennoe izdatel'svto khudozhestvennoi literatury, 1932). In his introduction, Desnitskii justified the book as being of use for "proletarian literature," 6, and writes, "The French Realist novel offers real interest for Marxist-Leninist literary scholarship not only for its historical significance in the dialectic of the literary process. The European realist novel forms under the slogan of acquiring a materialist method in the sphere of literary creation," 3.

68. In Russian: "Чему учиться: Самому принципу обостренного наблюдения мира. Свободному противостоянию материалу, извлекаемому из пролитературенных ассоциаций." Ginzburg, draft article "On Writers' Notebooks" ("*O zapisnykh knizhkak pisatelei*"), manuscript version. OR RNB 1377.

69. In Russian: "Всякий знает, что записная книжка—это тетрадка, блокнот или книжечка особого (и непременно малого) формата, которую носят в кармане и куда записывают разные вещи, о которых не следует забывать." Ginzburg, "On Writers' Notebooks" ("*O zapisnykh knizhkak pisatelei*"), typescript version, OR RNB 1377.

70. Ginzburg's move reflects Tynianov's attention to *byt* and anticipates issues raised by Foucault in "What Is an Author?" (first published in French in 1969).

71. Ginzburg, "On Writers' Notebooks," typescript version. OR RNB 1377. In Russian: "давление на подбор материала, на способы его распределения и сочетания, наконец, на характер отдельной записи."

72. Ginzburg, introduction to Viazemskii, *Staraia zapisnaia knizhka*, 47.

73. "On Writers' Notebooks," typescript version. OR RNB 1377.

74. In Russian: "для меня всякий процесс писания—это процесс наилучшего разрешения задачи." Ginzburg ZK VII (1932), 41. OR RNB 1377. This belongs to a note the rest of which was published in Ginzburg 2002, 107–8. In a youthful diary, Ginzburg had established the goal of making every notebook entry "be of practical necessity to me, that is, not go beyond the boundaries of that circle of questions that I am attempting to resolve at a given moment." Small notebook, 15 September 1922 (second page, not numbered). This note is discussed by Stanislav Savitsky, who through probable typographical error omits the particle "not" in the phrase "not go beyond" ("не выходить за пределы"). Savitskii, *Chastnyi chelovek,* 15. The full draft was published by Savitsky in "'Zritel' sobstvennoi mysli': o zametke L. Ginzburg 1922 goda," *Varietas et Concordia: Essays in Honour of Pekka Pesonen,* ed. Ben Hellman, Tomi Huttunen, and Gennady Obatnin (Helsinki: University of Helsinki, 2007), 444–67 (see pp. 460–67). The error appears here as well, on 460.

75. Some of these drafts in pencil and pen on scraps of paper have survived in the archives. From the 1950s to 1980s, Ginzburg would first use ink on paper and then type up notes. As another example of drafting techniques, the end of the 1932–33 notebooks contains in draft form (and pencil) the first several entries that she includes in a more polished way at the beginning of the 1933–35 notebook. This echoes Vyazemsky's methods (he kept separate notebooks for his drafts). See Ginzburg's draft article "On Writers' Notebooks," typescript version. OR RNB 1377.

76. "Person at a Writing Table" was also the title of Ginzburg's very first publication of notes in *Novyi mir.* Lidiia Ginzburg, "Chelovek za pis'mennym stolom. Po starym zapisnym knizhkam," *Novyi mir* 6 (June 1982): 235–45.

77. Ginzburg remarks that Leonid Grossman, publishing Chekhov's notebooks, compared them to a fragmentary novel. *Zapisnye knizhki A.P. Chekhova,* prepared by E. N. Konshin, ed. and intro. L. P. Grossman (Moscow: Gosudarstvennaia akademiia khudozhestvennykh nauk, 1927), 5–10; see especially p. 5.

78. In Russian: "в *наше время трудно оперировать понятием чистого материала, настолько он имеет тенденцию конструктивно осознаваться.*" "On Writers' Notebooks," notebook version. OR RNB 1377. Emphasis in original.

79. In Russian: "Каждый автор, ведущий сейчас те или иные документальные записи ощущает их двойную обращенность (иногда тех же записей)–в сторону конструкции и в сторону заготовки." Ibid.

80. In Russian: "И самое прекрасное, что не знаешь, для чего именно понадобятся эти слепки любви и боли, победы и унижения,—потому что еще не знаешь, что ты можешь и чего не можешь написать." Ginzburg 2002, 264. Essay dated 1973.

81. Ginzburg ZK II (1927–28), 149. OR RNB 1377. The entry is undated, but occurs between entries dated 17 August and 10 September 1927. In Russian: "Я, например, знаю, что напишу роман,—и это одно из тех ожиданий, страшных по существу, которые не страшат только в силу своей естественности. Так люди думают о том, что они неизбежно постареют, переживут своих близких, умрут." When later publishing the note within which this statement originally appeared, Ginzburg edited out this excessively confident remark—one thinks, because the "inevitability" did not come to pass.

82. She signed a contract with the publishing house Young Guards (*Molodaia Gvardiia*) for *The Pinkerton Agency* on August 13, 1930. See ZK V (1929–31), 126 (notebook entry dated 4 September 1930). Her notebooks from late 1930 to late 1932 document the

"plot" of her writing, revisions, and dealings with the publishers. Evgeny Shvarts remarked in February 1933, as a private reader of Ginzburg's notebooks: "it's good that the fate of *Pinkerton* threads through your Notebooks. *Pinkerton!* They suppress it, then they allow it . . . in turns. A plot interest is formed." ZK VIII (1933), 1. OR RNB 1377. Savitsky charts Ginzburg's difficulties with her Pinkerton novel in *Chastnyi chelovek*, 96–109, attributing perhaps excessive importance to her work on this novel as a creative turning point. He also writes (mistakenly) on page 100 that Ginzburg worked together with Veta Dolukhanova on the novel, misreading her notebook entry—in fact, it was with Viktor Gofman. See Ginzburg 2002, 93, and also ZK V (1929–30), 142. OR RNB 1377.

83. See for example Ginzburg's notebook from 1933–35 (ZK VIII/IX): "A person's possibilities are defined by what he cannot do, at least as much as by what he can do. A writer is a person who cannot experience life without writing." In Russian: "Возможности человека определяется тем, чего он не может, по крайней мере настолько же как и тем, что он может. Писатель—это человек, который не может переживать жизнь не пиша." 67 (ca. 1934). The fragment in which this was drafted is similar to material in "Zametki o proze." For example: "The correspondence between the impossible, the possible, and the insistently necessary forms the line of fate." In Russian: "Соотношение невозможного, возможного, настоятельно нужного образует линию судьбы." Ginzburg 2002, 150.

84. Ginzburg 2002, 110. From ZK VIII–2, p. 4 (entry that dates near the end of September 1932).

85. ZK VIII–2 (1932), 9. OR RNB 1377. In Russian: "При каждом движении все просвечивает и напоминает—не вещи, которые можно назвать по имени, но абстрагированные жанровые начала."

86. Ibid., 19. OR RNB 1377. Entry is not dated, but comes after entries of late March 1933.

87. Ginzburg 2002, 399–400. Original note in ZK 1928 (III), 57–58. OR RNB 1377.

88. "In particular I am irritated by my style. It is still only eloquence and wit, and not at all cognition and expression of reality. I will have to change everything completely." In Russian: "В частности меня раздражает мой слог. Это еще только красноречие и остроумие, отнюдь не познание и выражение действительности. Придется совершенно все переменить." Ginzburg ZK VIII (1933), 14. OR RNB 1377. Compare to a similar statement from 1934, published in L. Ginzburg, "Iz zapisnykh knizhek (1925–34)," *Zvezda* 3 (2002): 123.

89. Ginzburg ZK VIII (1933), 25. OR RNB 1377. In Russian: "Записные книжки и проч.—литература импотентов. Следовательно—мне невозможно жить, не пиша роман. Но писать роман, как я сейчас понимаю, тоже почти невозможно. Я не вижу той реальности, даже следов той реальности, какая может быть образована из слов, имеющихся в моем распоряжении."

90. Ginzburg 2002, 141, in "Notes on Prose" ("Zametki o proze"). In Russian: "Пишущий дневник продвигается наугад, не зная еще ни своей судьбы, ни судьбы своих знакомых. Это поступательная динамика, исполненная случайностей и непроверенных событий. Роман обладает ретроспективной динамикой, предполагающей закономерности и оценки." Drafts contain interesting variations on these phrases, including one that shows hesitation over whether the backward glance is indeed distinctive to the novel. She writes: "I was wrong to define the novel's dynamic as retrospective; it is retrospective and gradual at the same time. Because everything—not just what happened, but what could possibly have happened—should ultimately be

packed within the compass of the final understanding." In Russian: "Я не правильно определила динамику романа, как ретроспективную; она и ретроспективная и поступательная в то же время. Потому что в охвате конечного понимания должно уложиться не только все случившееся, но и все могущее имеющее случиться." Draft located in folder of miscellaneous writings from 1920s and 1930s. OR RNB 1377.

91. Notebook entry in ZK VIII (1933), 23, which bears a resemblance to the passage in her "Theoretical Introduction" (subsequently published as "Notes on Prose"). OR RNB 1377. Ginzburg's view of the novel as finalizable, complete, and in possession of a retrospective dynamic contrasts strikingly with Bakhtin's theory, developed around the same time, of the novel as unfinalizable and temporally and structurally open.

92. Ginzburg 2002, 142. ". . . the cold of remote time . . . ." In Russian: " . . . Холод отодвинутого времени . . . ."

93. Ibid.

94. In Russian: "Если бы—не выдумывая и не вспоминая—фиксировать протекание жизни . . . чувство протекания, чувство настоящего, подлинность множественных и нерасторжимых элементов бытия. В переводе на специальную терминологию получается опять не то: *роман по типу дневника или, что мне все-таки больше нравится,—дневник по типу романа.*" Ibid. Italics added.

95. The title in Russian, *Dom i mir*, alludes to Tolstoy's *Voina i mir*, which if one follows the old orthography translates as *War and the World* (world meaning "society") rather than *War and Peace*. There are drafts and stray sheets elsewhere in the archive that seem to relate to *Home and the World*; these include etudes on "characters" in Ginzburg's milieu who would have figured in this/these narrative/s, for example, sketches of "K." (Rina [Ekaterina] Zelyonaya) and "S." (Selli Dolukhanova), as well as notes on Akhmatova and Gukovsky. Also mentioned in the outlines are "Method for Examining a Person" from 1935 (extant, see chapter 4) and fragments such as "Dialogue about Love" (see chapter 3). To judge from the contents, handwriting, and paper, all of the materials in the "Dom i mir" file date from the 1930s. There are content-based overlaps with other manuscripts such as the essay "Stages of Love" ["Stadii liubvi"], dated 1934 and mentioned in one of the *Home and the World* outlines. The character Otter figures first in "The Return Home" (dated 1931 by the author, but containing fragments that appear to have been written before and after), whose earlier title, "Return to the Homeland," is mentioned in the *Home and the World* outlines. The notebook with a long sketch of Rina Zelyonaya ("K.") is dated 1936. One of Ginzburg's contemporaries, L. M. Andrievskaia, noted in a diary entry on 5 March 1939 that Ginzburg was writing a long novel, "one chapter a year, and soon she'll have a third chapter of a novel without beginning or end." See Savitskii, *Chastnyi chelovek*, 58. For more information, see also Emily Van Buskirk, "V poiskakh romana: Lidiia Ginzburg v 1930-e gody," *Novoe literaturnoe obozrenie* 88, 6 (2007): 154–60.

96. In some inventories of characters, she lists three groups: (1) "Les intellectuelles"; (2) "Povrezhdennye," elsewhere as "iskazhennye"; and (3) "zhenshchiny." The intellectuals are described in terms of the "generation," and the separate groups of teachers ("Metry") (Shklovsky), three promising students ("Tri luchshikh": "Otter," Gukovsky, and Bukhstab), and others ("Zh.," probably Zhirmunsky, and "St.," possibly Stepanov). The "povrezhdennye" or "iskazhennye" include a Poetess (abbreviated as V.V., probably upside-down A's, standing for Anna Andreevna Akhmatova), a philosopher Be (probably Boris Engegardt), a "snob" (M., possibly Matvei Gukovsky, Grigory's brother), and "svetskaia zhenshchina" (S., probably Selli Dolukhanova, Ginzburg's

neighbor and at one time wife of Matvei Gukovsky). The third group, women, includes Otter's three loves (the first of whom is clearly Rina Zelyonaya, the second is referred to as Liza, and the third, present one is "Lialia"), and somewhat separately, Tetka, Otter's aunt (modeled on Ginzburg's mother).

97. The text in angle brackets was crossed out in the manuscript. "M." most likely stands for Mandelstam. Manuscripts in the folder "Dom i mir." OR RNB 1377. There is a full draft of the "Theoretical Introduction" in the archive, which greatly resembles what eventually was published as "Notes on Prose." "Return to the Homeland" (*Vozvrashchenie na rodinu*) appears to have later become "The Return Home" (*Vozvrashchenie domoi*). Entry three ("Death") probably refers to "Delusion of the Will" and possibly to "The Thought That Drew a Circle," two narratives that at one point Ginzburg planned to join together (eventually publishing "Delusion . . ." as a variation to "The Thought . . .").

98. "Home and the World I" would treat *byt* and love, and "Home and the World II" would be about profession and creativity, followed by an epilogue about self-consciousness.

99. Aside from the narratives mentioned in note 123, Ginzburg's reader knows some pieces that emerged from these 1930s experiments as "Psychological Sketches (From the Life of A.)" ("Psikhologicheskie chertezhi [iz zhizni A.]") and the recently published writings on love ("The Stages of Love" ["Stadii liubvi"] and "Conversation about Love" ["Razgovor o liubvi"]).

100. Ginzburg would later use the "day in the life" structure for the 1940s version of *Notes of a Blockade Person*, which features an autobiographical hero similar to the one in *Home and the World*.

101. Ginzburg 2002, 317–18. The reader was Makogonenko, and the time was the blockade, as one can ascertain from a note in ZK IX (1943–45). OR RNB 1377. See Ginzburg 2011, 155.

102. In Russian: "Я хожу только на свои доклады,—говорит Виноградов,—и то не всегда." Ginzburg 2002, 58. Original in ZK III (1928), 53. OR RNB 1277.

103. On the tradition of the anecdote to which Ginzburg is indebted, see Lauren Leighton, "The Anecdote in Russia: Pushkin, Vjazemskij, and Davydov." Leighton summarizes: "In general, it may be said that the anecdote is marked by a delight in gossip and in human foibles, that its basis is often a pun or play on words, that usually it is short, and that it is always unconducive to digression. It need not be humorous, but it is often both humorous and risqué. It should be marked by a confidential tone that includes even the uninitiated reader in an intimate circle. In its most usual form it comprises an opening line which imparts the essential facts in a seemingly inadvertent manner, a narrative body which presents and develops the content, and a concluding or 'punch' line. No part is essential, however, for any one may be merged with another or even entirely omitted. An anecdote may comprise a single line or several paragraphs," 156–57.

104. Ginzburg 2002, 310. A partial draft of this essay, published with notes from the 1980s, exists in the archives in the handwriting and paper of the 1930s. The draft is followed by a list of several maxims Ginzburg copied out from La Rochefoucauld (whom she also quotes also in the draft narratives of the 1930s). See the folder catalogued as Razgovor. La Rochefoucauld. Esse 50–60gg. OR RNB 1377.

105. In order, these "formulae" can be found in Ginzburg 2002, 149 (late 1930s), 297 (undated, but published with notes from 1980), and 150 (late 1930s).

106. Barthes made a similar observation about his own aphorisms: "I write maxims

(or I sketch their movement) *in order to reassure myself*: when some disturbance arises, I attenuate it by confiding myself to a fixity which exceeds my powers: *'Actually, it's always like that'*: and the maxim is born. The maxim is a sort of *sentence-name*, and to name is to pacify." *Roland Barthes by Roland Barthes*, trans. Richard Howard (Berkeley: University of California Press, 1994), 179.

107. Passages about emotionality, generalization and the novel can be found in the notebook from 1933 (ZK VIII) (see p. 23) and in drafts of what became "Zametki o proze." OR RNB 1377.

108. In Russian: "все психофизиологически и исторически закономерное. Фатум человека, как точка пересечения всеобщих тенденций." Ginzburg 2002, 60.

109. Referring to work in the physical sciences, Lotman writes of *sluchainost'* and *zakonomernost'* as potential states of one and the same object or event, depending on the degree of equilibrium in the environment (a stable political situation versus a revolution, for example). Iurii Lotman, "Istoricheskie zakonomernosti i struktura teksta," *Semiosfera* (St. Petersburg: Iskusstvo-SPB, 2004), 348–49.

110. Ginzburg 2002, 61. In Russian: "Что касается дневников, записных книжек, то автор их принужден идти по пятам за собственной жизнью, которая не обязалась быть поучительной."

111. Ibid., 74. Original note in ZK V (1929–31) 24–27. OR RNB 1377. The entry is undated, but is between two others from August 1929.

112. Tynianov discusses the contemporary trend of seeing plot (*siuzhet*) in compositions that have a minimal story (*minimal'naia fabula*) in "Literaturnyi fakt," *Poetika. Istoriia literatury. Kino*, 267.

113. In Russian: "Общее краткое определение какого-либо положения, закона, отношения и т.п., приложимое к частным случаям; краткое, точное словесное выражение, определение чего-либо." *Slovar' sovremennogo russkogo literaturnogo iazyka*, Insitut Russkogo iazyka (Moscow: Izdatel'stvo Akademii Nauk SSSR, 1950–65), vol. 16, 1506.

114. Ginzburg 2002, 47. For other examples of formulae used by the masses recorded by Ginzburg, see 2002, 81 and 190.

115. Ginzburg is discussing the summation of Tynianov's "Problems of Poetic Language" into the formula about the "closeness and unity of the poetic series" ("теснота и единство стихового ряда") in "Tynianov-literaturoved," Ginzburg 2002, 447.

116. In Russian: "Усвойте себе общий взгляд, общую формулу, и вы почти никогда не ошибетесь в частном приложении." *Slovar' sovremennogo russkogo literaturnogo iazyka*, vol. 16, 1506. The Herzen example comes from *Poriadok torzhestvuet!* The four-volume Ushakov dictionary has a similar first definition: "A general short and exact expression (of a thought, law), a definition (bookish)." In Russian: "Общее краткое и точное выражение (мысли, закона), определение (книжн.)." *Tolkovyi slovar' russkogo iazyka*, ed. D. N. Ushakov (Moscow: Gosudarstvennyi institut "Sovetskaia entsiklopediia," 1935), vol. 4, 1103.

117. See for example the usage in Ginzburg 2002, 258.

118. He meant it admiringly, as he found that it was precisely the unlikely combination of lyricism and pseudo-science in Ginzburg's prose that made it unique, enjoyable, and interesting. Aleksandr Zholkovskii, "Mezhdu zhanrami (L. Ia. Ginzburg)," in Zholkovskii, *Inventsii* (Moscow: Gendal'f, 1995), 154–57. English version "Between Genres," in *Lydia Ginzburg's Alternative Literary Identities*, ed. Emily Van Buskirk and Andrei Zorin (Oxford: Peter Lang AG, 2012), 33–37.

119. Iurii Lotman, "Istoricheskie zakonomernosti i struktura teksta," 354. Lotman argues further that the scholarly (*nauchnyi*) text looks at the world "retrospectively," as if it were already made (and thus itself does not require interpretation).

120. Barbara Hernnstein Smith, *On the Margins of Discourse: The Relation of Literature to Language* (Chicago: University of Chicago Press, 1978), 12.

121. I have modified Rosengrant's translation from Lydia Ginzburg, *On Psychological Prose,* trans. and ed. Judson Rosengrant (Princeton, NJ: Princeton University Press, 1991), 9–10. Henceforth, "Ginzburg 1991." Russian in Lidiia Ginzburg, *O psikhologicheskoi proze* (Leningrad: Khudozhestvennaia literatura, 1977), 13–14. Henceforth, "Ginzburg 1977."

122. In Russian: "Чужие слова всегда находка—их берут такими, какие они есть; их все равно нельзя улучшить и переделать. Чужие слова, хотя бы отдаленно и неточно выражающие нашу мысль, действуют, как откровение или как давно искомая и обретенная формула." Ginzburg 2002, 18. Original undated note appears together with notes from the spring of 1925 in ZK I (1925–26), 19. OR RNB 1377.

123. In Russian, "... так жить, как я живу, нельзя, нельзя и нельзя,—это одно было правда». Вот она, формула личной нравственной ответственности за социальное зло. Формула действительного гуманизма. Предпосылка жалости. Формула утраченная." Ibid., 180. This appears to be an inexact quotation from Tolstoy's "What Then Should We Do?" ("Tak chto zhe nam delat'?"). See Lev Tolstoy, *Sobranie sochinenii v 22 tomakh,* vol. 16 (Moscow: Khudozhestvennaia literatura, 1983), 175.

124. Ginzburg 2011, 357.

125. For a concise summary of some basic contrasts between the essay and scientific scholarship, see Anthony J. Cascardi, *The Cambridge Introduction to Literature and Philosophy* (Cambridge, UK: Cambridge University Press, 2014), 180.

126. In Russian: "все как-то обнажается, и осознаешь себя минутами тем, чем являешься всегда—затерянным человеком, окруженным тысячью угроз." Diary I (1920–22), 156–57. May–June 1922. The end of the passage has been rewritten by Ginzburg in handwriting of the 1980s, seeming to replace and rewrite a page that was cut out of the notebook.

127. It seems not coincidental that when in 1929 she described the frustration she felt as a writer at her inability to "formulate" a scene, Ginzburg selects a scene from nature as what stumps her (recall my discussion of the passage "When I see a beautiful landscape, not having a formula for it . . .").

128. In Russian: "Я предпочитаю море в широком и тусклом блеске солнца, поднимающегося к зениту, утреннее море морского цвета < . . . > ." Ginzburg 2002, 521.

129. In Russian: "который нельзя с чем-нибудь сравнить или назвать иначе (вообще много сравнивать бесполезно)." Ibid.

130. In Russian: "опасность безответственных сравнений, фальшивых масштабов, кунсткамерности и остроумия." Ibid., 75. She recalls one of her own metaphors, where she wrote of birch logs that "lying in their light gray bark, as in fine factory packaging," and takes herself to task for making "the most confused thing merrily replace a simple and good one" (вещь самая путаная радостно замещается простой и хорошенькой).

131. In Russian: "море морского цвета, в короткой и крепкой волне, помогает найти формулу здоровья и формулу преодоления страха. Здоровье—мужество организма, который живет, хотя знает о бедствиях возможных и неизбежных, в том числе о собственной смерти." Ibid., 522.

132. Drafts of "Zametki o proze" are designated by Ginzburg as the preamble ("Teoreticheskii razdel") to "Vozvrashchenie domoi." A partial draft is in a folder with miscellaneous materials from the 1920s and 30s, OR RNB 1377. A full draft is currently catalogued as op. khr. 63: *"Teoreticheskoe vstuplenie." Zametki o literature.* (The passage in question appears on p. 33, after a comparison of the writer to Proust's intellectual hero.) Ginzburg published parts of this piece as "Notes on Prose" in *Person at a Writing Table,* within a section of "Fragments" from the end of the 1920s to 1930s, thus reintegrating more novelistic prose back into the "notebooks." See Ginzburg 2002, 142.

133. Ibid., 147.

134. Alexander Zholkovsky has examined a different passage of Ginzburg's for its unique combination of "quasi-poetry" and "quasi-science." Alexander Zholkovsky, "Between Genres," in *Canadian-American Slavic Studies* 28, 2–3 (Summer–Fall 1994): 157–60. Republished in *Lydia Ginzburg's Alternative Literary Identities,* ed. Emily Van Buskirk and Andrei Zorin (Oxford: Peter Lang AG, 2012), 33–37. In Russian: Aleksandr Zholkovskii, "Mezhdu zhanrami (L. Ia. Ginzburg)," in Zholkovskii, *Inventsii* (Moscow: Gendal'f, 1995), 154–57. First published in a different version in *Literaturnoe obozrenie* 10 (October 1989): 83.

135. Temporal expansion in Tolstoy's autobiographical "A History of Yesterday" has been productively studied by Irina Paperno in "'Who, What Is I?': Tolstoy in His Diaries," *Tolstoy Studies Journal* 9 (1999): 32–54.

136. Ginzburg 1991 (*On Psychological Prose*), 254. Russian in idem 1977, 311.

137. Ibid., 226. The passage comes from the essay "Does One Need to Travel?" ("Nuzhno li puteshestvovat'?"), which considers (among other topics) whether one gains anything in knowledge or experience by traveling, or whether one can make more penetrating observations when in one's local context. See my discussion in Lidiia Ginzburg, "Zapisi 50–60-kh godov," publication, introduction, and commentaries by E. Van Buskirk, *Seans* 51–52 (2012): 310–21.

138. On this basis, Richard Gustafson dubbed her "one of the great recyclers in modern Russian letters." Gustafson, "Lidiia Ginzburg and Tolstoi," *Canadian-American Slavic Studies* 28, 2–3 (Summer–Fall 1994): 210.

139. See Ginzburg 2002, 103. In Russian: "У меня было много уже придумано про жизнь; много заготовок, в частности описаний. Следовательно, неотступный соблазн—вставить." Original version in ZK VIII-2 (1932), 11. OR RNB 1377.

140. Lidiia Ginzburg, *Agentstvo Pinkertona* (Moscow/Leningrad: OGIZ Molodaia Gvardiia, 1932), 11–12.

141. Ginzburg writes about hunger in her youthful diaries. See for example, Diary I (19 August 1920–4 September 1922), 22, and Diary II (23 September 1922–14 May 1923), 45 and 69. Her discussion of hunger in Diary II, 69, follows a discussion of a story by Knut Hamsun (not his 1890 novel *Hunger,* but the association may have been there). OR RNB 1377. She refers to *Hunger* in *Notes of a Blockade Person.* See Ginzburg 2002, 646. See "Delusion of the Will" for a treatment of her alter-ego's hunger in his student years (ibid., 593) and his support of his "father."

142. Ginzburg 2002, 645. She repeats this observation a few times within the *Zapiski.* For example, see 657.

143. Ginzburg 1991, 7. In Russian: "Для эстетической значимости не обязателен вымысел и обязательна организация—отбор и творческое сочетание элементов, отраженных и преображенных словом." Ginzburg 1977, 10.

144. "Dve vstrechi," in *Petropol: Al'manakh,* issue 1 (Leningrad: Vasil'evskii ostrov, 1990): 71–76. Reprinted in *Pretvorenie opyta* (1991) and in Ginzburg 2002, 338–41.

145. She wrote: "I would like to believe that the reader will find in these fragments from half a century ago facts and thoughts that have not lost their relevance even now, having a direct relationship to the tasks and concerns of our literature today." In Russian: "Хочется верить, что в этих записях уже полувековой давности читатель найдет факты и соображения, не утратившие актуальности и теперь, имеющие непосредственное отношение к делам и заботам сегодняшней нашей литературы." In *Novyi mir* (1982): 236.

146. Ginzburg 1979, 6, 14. Ginzburg mentions that the current period was experiencing an opening up of the boundaries of literary genres and a heightened interest in the theory of documentary prose, naming several publications on the topic.

147. For a survey and analysis of the robust growth of memoirs and diaries in the late Soviet period, and their intellectual traditions (including a discussion of Alexander Herzen and Lydia Ginzburg), see Irina Paperno, "Personal Accounts of the Soviet Experience," *Kritika: Explorations in Russian and Eurasian History* 3, 4 (Fall 2002): 577–610. See also Paperno's book, *Stories of the Soviet Experience: Memoirs, Diaries, Dreams* (Ithaca, NY: Cornell University Press, 2009). Alexander Chudakov, in his commentary to a publication of Ginzbrg's notes, draws a connection between the interest in "literature of fact" in the 1920s, and the wave of popularity of nonfiction in the 1980s. He also describes the twentieth century in terms of the flourishing of in-between literature in Russia (mentioning Gorky, Remizov, Olesha, Kataev, Solzhenitsyn, Siniavksy, Bitov, and Voinovich). Lidiia Ginzburg, "Zapisi 20–30-x godov," intr. Alexander Kushner, comm. Alexander Chudakov, *Novyi mir* 6 (1992): 179–80.

148. Barbara Walker, "On Reading Soviet Memoirs: A History of the 'Contemporaries' Genre as an Institution of Russian Intelligentsia Culture from the 1790s to the 1970s," *Russian Review* 59, 3 (July 2000): 327–52.

149. For example, the six notes about Akhmatova are published in the following order: 1933, 1933, 1935, 1929, 1927, 1929.

150. "Chelovek za pis'mennym stolom: Po starym zapisnym knizhkam," *Novyi mir* (1982): 236. Also see Ginzburg 2002, 34.

151. L. Ginzburg, "Chelovek . . . ," *Novyi mir* (1982): 245. Also see Ginzburg 2002, 71.

152. L. Ginzburg, *Chelovek za pis'mennym stolom* (Leningrad: Sovetskii pisatel', 1989), 4.

153. Kirill Kobrin notes that one can read the notebooks in two ways: (1) as typical notebooks à la Vyazemsky, where reflections, chance observations, and notes on famous people mix together; (2) as a complexly organized tract about the history and fates of Soviet "people of the 20s." He suggests that Ginzburg probably counted on the first type of reader in the 1920s, and in the 1980s, on the second. Kobrin, "M. L. Gasparovu—70 let. O Gasparove. Universal'naia kniga," in *Novoe literaturnoe obozrenie* 73, 3 (2005): 166.

154. The note begins, "Someone said that there are two types of fools: winter and summer." Ginzburg explains that "summer" fools are recognizable from afar, whereas "winter" fools reveal themselves more slowly (they must first disrobe of all those layers). And then "V." adds a new category: "tropical" fools. Ginzburg *Chelovek za pis'mennym stolom* (1989), 9. Henceforth, I will refer to this volume as "Ginzburg 1989." (Also see Ginzburg 2002, 15.) In the original notebook, Ginzburg identifies the source of this witticism as Veta Dolukhanova, an important friend. But in print, she creates two different sources: the anonymous "someone" (*kto-to*), and V., who thus appears even wittier.

155. See Ginzburg 2002, 15, or Ginzburg 1989, 9. Originals in ZK I (1925–26) 151, 107. OR RNB 1377.

156. These divisions also reflect the fact the Ginzburg stopped writing in actual notebooks after the war, which in turn is related to the trend that her essays become less intensely linked to a particular year or historical event.

157. For instance, the final note under the division "1931" was in fact dated "31 January 1932" in the original. Publication under the wrong year is justified by the fact that Ginzburg is reflecting, morosely, on the previous year (a consistent habit of her notes around the New Year). She writes of a cessation of activity, emptiness ("*vide complet*"), the loss of her profession. As another example, a note about Shklovsky from June 1935 appears (without a date) as one of three meager notes that comprise the entire year 1934. Shklovsky thus serves as the subject of all three fragments from this year.

158. Ginzburg 2002, 14.

159. Barbara Hernnstein Smith, 47, 8.

160. The first note is in ZK I (1925–26), 108 (probably written in October 1925, though it is uncertain, since this individual entry is not dated, pages are mixed up, and the ink changes). The second note was written in ZK I, 33, near notes written in April 1925. However, it is in a different pen and may have been added in 1926, when she added (and dated) commentary to another note on Shklovsky (that appears in 2002, 13). Shklovsky's descriptions of *Zoo*, which Ginzburg culled from two different notebooks, ZK I, 67, and ZK II, 14, both appear to be from 1927. The final note comes from ZK I, 193–94. OR RNB 1377.

161. This note was published posthumously, in *Zvezda* 3 (2002): 106. The reason Ginzburg did not publish it during her lifetime was probably the negative sketch of Shklovsky's wife Vasiliia Georgievna, and V. G. Shklovskaia-Kordi's negative epithet for Eikhenbaum, "Aunt Boria."

162. The fragment about *Third Factory* was published on a different page of *Person at a Writing Table* under the heading "From Conversations in Moscow in Fall 1926." Ginzburg 1989, 30, and Ginzburg 2002, 32.

163. Herzen used the informal term *zapiski* ("notes") to describe the writings that went into his generically heterogeneous and multivolume memoir, *My Past and Thoughts*. See Lydia Ginzburg, *On Psychological Prose*, trans. Judson Rosengrant (Princeton, NJ: Princeton University Press, 1991), 199. In Russian: L. Ginzburg, *O psikhologicheskoi proze*, 2nd ed. (Leningrad: Khudozhestvennaia literatura, 1977), 247.

164. Russian editions of Montaigne's *Essays* have been published in Russian as *Opyty*, which can be translated as "experiment," "experience," "trial," or "attempt" (the root, *pyt*, meaning "to try or test"). Ginzburg, a Francophile, uses the word "essay" (*esse* in Russian) instead. Michel Montaigne, *Opyty*, 3 vols. (Moscow: Nauka, 1979, 1981).

165. Reda Bensmaïa, *The Barthes Effect: The Essay as Reflective Text*, trans. Pat Fedkiew, intr. Michèle Richman (Minneapolis: University of Minnesota, 1987), 95. In *The Literary Absolute*, Lacoue-Labarthe and Nancy also discuss the essay as a fragment that "does not pretend to be exhaustive," 42.

166. Georg Lukacs, "On the Nature and Form of the Essay," *Soul and Form*, trans. Anna Bostock (Cambridge, MA: MIT Press, 1974), 7. Theodor W. Adorno, "The Essay as Form," *The Adorno Reader*, ed. Brian O'Connor, trans. Samuel and Shierry Weber (Oxford, UK: Blackwell Publishers, 2000), 94, 105. See also Bensmaïa, 95.

167. Bensmaïa, 96. Like the word *opyt*, the French word *essai* or *essaier* (in modern French, *essayer*) means to "try," or "test," and has since the Renaissance been linked to

experimental science. The French word *essai* comes from the Latin *exagium*, which signifies exact weighing, examination, or an ordeal. In his book, Bensmaïa recounts a thorough definition and concise history of the French essay.

168. Lukacs wrote of the essay that it treats experiences "which cannot be expressed by any gesture and which yet long for expression. From all that has been said you will know what experiences I mean and of what kind they are. I mean intellectuality, conceptuality as sensed experience, as immediate reality, as spontaneous principle of existence; the worldview in its undisguised purity as an event of the soul, as the motive force of life." Such a description of the essay reminds one, for example, of Ginzburg's fragment, "There are plots that do not lend themselves to prose," analyzed by Alexander Zholkovsky in "Between Genres," *Lydia Ginzburg's Alternative Literary Identities*, 33–37. On Ginzburg's generic fluidity, including a reading of the scholarly essays as autobiography, see Sarah Pratt, "Lydia Ginzburg and the Fluidity of Genre," in *Autobiographical Statements in Twentieth-Century Russian Literature*, ed. Jane Gary Harris (Princeton, NJ: Princeton University Press, 1990), 207–16.

169. Bensmaïa argues that it is precisely this loose arrangement that generates their meaning, 8–9. See also ibid., xxxi.

170. According to Bensmaïa, essays do not combine preexisting genres, but are *prior* to genre and contain the seeds of forms that may become actualized as genres. Ibid., 92. His description demonstrates why the essay is an appropriate form for innovation in periods of literary history (like the early or late twentieth century) when established genres are in crisis.

171. Quoted in Bensmaïa, 5–6, from Montaigne's book III, 9, 761.

172. Bensmaïa, 12–13.

173. Ginzburg, *Chelovek za pis'mennym stolom*, 9. This note appears directly after the one-liner discussed earlier, "How strange that we see one another so rarely and part so often (from a letter)." For a treatment of "Poets," see Andrew Kahn, "Lydia Ginzburg's 'Lives of the Poets': Mandelstam in Profile," in *Lydia Ginzburg's Alternative Literary Identities*, 171–73.

174. See Jane Gary Harris, "'The Direct Conversation about Life': Lidiia Ginzburg's Journal as a Contemporary Literary Genre," in *Neo-Formalist Papers: Contributions to the Silver Jubilee Conference to Mark 25 Years of the Neo-Formalist Circle*, ed. Joe Andrew and Robert Reid (Rodopi: 1998), 45, 52. Harris refers to the work of Hélène Cixous, Rebecca Hogan, Sidonie Smith, Robert Fothergill, and others.

175. I have in mind works such as Gasparov's *Zapisi i vypiski* (Moscow: Novoe literaturnoe obozrenie, 2001); Zholkovsky's *Erosiped i drugie vin'etki* (Moscow: Volodei, 2003); and Bezrodny's *Konets tsitaty* (St. Petersburg: Izdatel'stvo Ivana Limbakha, 1996).

176. Kirill Kobrin has written about Lydia Ginzburg as being potentially of great interest and importance in the post-Soviet environment, but believes that readers (current thirty-somethings) are passing up her type of historical understanding. He suggests that Ginzburg's notes are resistant to "eclectic" or "post-modernist" readings in a way that Mikhail Gasparov's *Zapisi i vypisky* are not. See Kirill Kobrin, "Nenuzhnaia Lidiia Ginzburg," *Neprikosnovennyi zapas* 2 (2004), at http://magazines.russ.ru/nz/2004/34/kobr12.html, accessed 27 September 2008); and Kobrin, "Universal'naia kniga," 166–69. Ilya Kukulin has written about Ginzburg as a "domestic classic" and a Russian equivalent to Georges Bataille, Simone Weil, or Roland Barthes. I. Kukulin, "Dnevniki na peske: Lidiia Ginzburg v roli domashnego klassika," *NG: Ex libris* 22 (7 April 2002): 4.

177. Lidiia Ginzburg, *Pretvorenie opyta* (Riga: Avots, 1991). It has four sections: "Notes of a Blockade Person," which contains part II of the work, largely consisting of recorded speech that is analyzed; "Notes from the 1940s," which contains titled essays extracted from Ginzburg's 1943–46 notebook, and published out of order; "Notes of Various Years," containing essays of the 1970s and 1980s; and "On Writers," with essays on literature and reminiscences on literary figures. In an interview, Nikolai Kononov told me that he invented some of the titles of essays, and also that Ginzburg was frail and made corrections to typescripts while lying down, in the final weeks of her life.

178. In Russian, Kononov's description ("Мысль, осуществляющая себя самое") clearly echoes one of her titles, "The Thought That Drew a Circle" ("Мысль, описавшая круг"). It also refers to her Proustian aspirations. Nikolai Kononov, "Korotko o knigakh," *Russkaia mysl' (La Pensée russe)* 2, 3852 (November 1990), "Literaturnoe prilozhenie no. 11": xiv.

179. Ginzburg 2002, 321. The section "Notes from Various Years" in the 2002 book (321–67) replicates this division in *Transformation of Experience (Pretvorenie opyta).*

180. Alexander Kushner, preface to Lidiia Ginzburg, "Zapisi 20–30-x godov," *Novyi mir* 6 (1992): 144–45. See also Aleksander Kushner, "Tsel'nost': o tvorchestve L. Ia. Ginzburg," *Literaturnoe obozrenie* 10 (October 1989): 84–86, reprinted in *Canadian-American Slavic Studies* 28, 2–3 (1994): 234–35.

181. Lidiia Ginzburg, "From The Journals," trans. Jane Gary Harris, in *Russian Women Writers*, vol. 2, ed. Christine D. Tomei (New York: Garland, 1999), 1166–78. This publication includes fifteen fragments in chronological order from the 1920s to the 1970s, with editorial headings such as "On friendship" or "On laws and logic." It also provides a bibliography of Ginzburg's works. The second publication of Ginzburg's essays in English, in the book *Lydia Ginzburg's Alternative Literary Identities* (2012), takes a different course, publishing only longer, titled essays and narratives that can more or less stand alone, with the remark that "the notes are perhaps best experienced in a larger selection." *Lydia Ginzburg's Alternative Literary Identities: A Collection of Articles and New Translations*, ed. Emily Van Buskirk and Andrei Zorin (Oxford: Peter Lang AG, 2012), 20. The book contains translations of a longer narrative ("The Return Home"), essays unpublished by the author during her lifetime ("Conversations about Love," "The Jewish Question," "The State of Literature near the End of the War"), and famous essays of the later period ("Generation at a Turning Point," "At One with the Legal Order").

182. Lidiia Ginzburg, *Zapisnye knizhki: Novoe sobranie* (Moscow: Zakharov, 1999). It contains prose from *Person at a Writing Table*, the 1992 *Novyi Mir* selection, and *Transformation of Experience*. The book exists in two slightly different versions. One, apparently produced for domestic distribution, lists a print-run of 5,000; the second, apparently produced for international distribution, lists a print run of 3,000.

183. Kobrin, "Nenuzhnaia Lidiia Ginzburg."

184. Ibid.

185. The volume was reissued in 2011.

186. The book separates notes published by Ginzburg (including notes from the 1940s from *Transformation of Experience*, which are inserted chronologically within the body of *Person at a Writing Table* in a new section devoted to this decade) from those published posthumously. The latter division contains notes more or less in the order in which they appear in Ginzburg's notebooks (and the typescripts made from the notebooks during her lifetime, which skipped over many notes), though there are some errors (the first note published under 1931 is in fact a note from 1933). Most notes in this

division from the 1920s and 1930s were originally published in *Novyi mir* in the same order. Lidiia Ginzburg, "Zapisi 20–30-x godov," pub. Alexander Kushner, comm. Alexander Chudakov, *Novyi mir* 6 (1992): 144–86. A few others were inserted from the publication "Iz dnevnikov Lidii Ginzburg: 'To li my eshche videli . . . ,'" ed. A. Kushner, *Literaturnaia gazeta* 41, 5469 (13 October 1993): 6, at www.belousenko.com/books/litera/ginzburg_dnevniki.htm, accessed 1 May 2015.

187. Kushner writes, "I remember how Lidiia Iakovlevna sought advice about whether to include this or that fragment from those who helped her type notes up in the 1960s through the 1980s, and I see that we could have convinced her to be more generous and indulgent to herself." Alexander Kushner's preface in Lidiia Ginzburg, "Iz zapisnykh knizhek (1925–34)," *Zvezda* 3 (2002), pub. A. Kushner, comm. D. Ustinov, 104. Alexander Kushner and Denis Ustinov made the selections and chose to protect the identity of some of Ginzburg's "characters." In another publication for *Literaturnaia gazeta* in 1993, Kushner justifies the fragmentary publication of Ginzburg's notes by appealing to the whole: "The notes presented here are only the most insignificant part of her legacy. . . . The sharpness of some utterances would be canceled out [*pogashena*] by the whole enormous context of her essays." Kushner, intro. to "Iz dnevnikov Lidii Ginzburg," at www.belousenko.com/books/litera/ginzburg_dnevniki.htm, accessed 1 May 2015.

188. For comparisons to the novel, see Nikolai Kononov, "Korotko o knigakh"; Andrei Zorin, "Proza L. Ia. Ginzburg i gumanitarnaia mysl' XX veka," *Novoe literaturnoe obozrenie* 76, 6 (2005): 45–46; Alexander Kushner, "Tsel'nost': o tvorchestve L.Ia. Ginzburg," *Canadian-American Slavic Studies* 28, 2/3 (Summer–Fall 1994): 233–35.

189. Ginzburg writes, "A novel is a writer's conversation about life. In essence it does not make sense to write novels on different themes during a lifetime, because there's only one life, and there can only be one theme." Ginzburg ZK VIII (1933), 22. OR RNB 1377. Similar to the note published in Ginzburg 2002, 141. At times, she spoke of her writings as dividing into a "conversation about literature" and a "conversation about life." In Russian: "двойной разговор—о жизни и о литературе" (Ginzburg 2002, 269). At others, she divided her writings into finer categories of hackwork, professional work, and creative work. See Ginzburg 2011, 170.

190. In Russian: "Между жанрами обеих частей я не ощущаю непроходимого разрыва. Все это для меня разновидности прозы." L. Ginzburg, *Literatura v poiskakh real'nosti* (Leningrad: Sovetskii pisatel', 1987), 2.

191. In *Chastnyi chelovek*, Savitsky discusses why the notebooks have elements of the diary on 33 and 81, but then he slips into calling the notebooks diaries, as for example on 145. Strangely, Savitsky then refers to Ginzburg's youthful diaries (which were in fact diaries) as "notebooks" on 86.

192. Svetlana Boym exemplifies this trend in her frequent reference to thoughts and observations from the notebooks, to which she sometimes refers as "diaries." See for example Svetlana Boym, "'Banality of Evil,' Mimicry, and the Soviet Subject," *Slavic Review* 67, 2 (Summer 2008): 345; and Boym, *The Future of Nostalgia* (New York: Basic Books, 2001), 291.

193. Sarah Pratt, "Lidija Ginzburg's *O starom i novom* as Autobiography," *Slavic and East European Journal* 30, 1 (1986): 45–53. Reprinted with modifications as "Lydia Ginzburg and the Fluidity of Genre," in *Autobiographical Statements in Twentieth-Century Russian Literature*, ed. Jane Gary Harris (Princeton, NJ: Princeton University Press, 1990), 207–16.

194. Lidiia Ginzburg, "Stadii liubvi," intro. Denis Ustinov, *Kriticheskaia massa* 1

(2002): 34–38; "Chetvertyi razgovor o liubvi," intro. Emily Van Buskirk, *Novoe literaturnoe obozrenie* 88, 6 (2007): 154–68; "Lidiia Ginzburg on Elena Shvarts," *Slavonica* 16, 2 (November 2010): 139–43; "Prezumptsia sotsializma," intro. and commentary Emily Van Buskirk and Andrei Zorin, *Novoe literaturnoe obozrenie* 116, 4 (2012): 416–26; "Zapisi 50–60-kh godov," publication, introduction, and commentaries by Van Buskirk, *Seans (Séance)* 51–52 (2012): 310–21.

195. *Prokhodiashchie kharaktery. Zapiski blokadnogo cheloveka. Proza voennykh let.*, ed. Emily Van Buskirk and Andrei Zorin (Moscow: Novoe izdatel'stvo, 2011), contains Ginzburg's notes, sketches, "A Story of Pity and Cruelty," and early drafts of *Notes of a Blockade Person* (called "Otter's Day"), pieced together from the archival manuscripts. The volume also presents, in the commentaries, variants from the typescripts made in the 1960s and 1970s, as well as the published versions of the notes and *Notes of a Blockade Person* itself. Recent years have also seen other publications: Lidiia Ginzburg, *Raboty dovoennogo vremeni*, ed. Stanislav Savitskii (St. Petersburg: Petropolis, 2007), containing her scholarly articles from the 1920s and 1930s and her book *Lermontov's Creative Path*; a reissuing of the 2002 book—Lidiia Ginzburg, *Zapisnye knizhki. Vospominaniia. Esse* (St. Petersburg: Iskusstvo-SPb, 2011); Lidiia Ginzburg, *Zapiski blokadnogo cheloveka. Vospominaniia* (Moscow: Eksmo, 2014), a new commercial edition that contains *Notes of a Blockade Person* together with the book *On the Lyric* and several reiminiscences.

196. I. Bulkina, "Fragment o fragmentakh" (a review of Savitsky's *Chastnyi chelovek*), *Novoe literaturnoe obozrenie* 128, 4 (2014): 326–38.

197. The entire 2002 book was available online in a downloadable zip file at www.srcc.msu.su/uni-persona/site/authors/ginzburg/ginzburg.htm, accessed 6 February 2006. Last attempt to access on 1 May 2015 shows that the book is no longer available at this website.

198. Members of the "Lydia Ginzburg Community" upload and comment on individual notes, or single lines extracted from notes, which receive dates according to the time of their posting (2004 to the present), at http://community.livejournal.com/lidia_ginsburg, accessed 1 May 2015. See Paperno, *Stories of the Soviet Experience: Memoirs, Diaries, Dreams*, 51–55.

199. The note on "pre-spring" is published in Ginzburg 2002, 221. The fragment about the blockade winter is in Ginzburg 2002, 735; the fragment of "Otsepenenie" is from "Vokrug *Zapisok blokadnogo cheloveka*."

200. See http://lidia-ginsburg.livejournal.com/92319.html#comments, accessed 6 October 2013.

201. Barthes 1994, 99.

202. In Russian: "В сфере художественного вымысла образ возникает в движении от идеи к выражающему его единичному, в литературе документальной—от данного единичного и конкретного к обобщающей мысли." Ginzburg 1979, 7.

203. ZK VIII (1933), 24–25. OR RNB 1377.

204. Ibid.

205. In Russian: "Этот будущий роман напишу во всяком случае не я. Его напишут люди положительных идей, у которых я недостойна развязать ремень обуви . . . ." Written on a page (not in a notebook) in a folder containing miscellaneous fragments from the 1920s and 1930s. Near the drafts for "Zametki o proze," and a note about a conversation with Oleinikov (O.) about the novel. OR RNB 1377.

206. She wrote, "I have broad tastes for poetry. I am not a poet. But in prose I am

driven mad even by very good things (Giraudoux, for example). This does not mean I am a prose writer. But it does mean that I still have hope of becoming a prose writer. Irritation is a necessary, but not sufficient, condition. Alas." In Russian: "На стихи у меня очень широкий вкус. Я не поэт. Но в прозе меня бесят и очень хорошие вещи (Жироду, например). Это не значит, что я прозаик. Но значит, что я еще имею надежду стать прозаиком. Раздражение—условие необходимое, но, увы, недостаточное." In ZK 1933 (VIII), 13–14. And elsewhere, from her note on the problem with her unpublishable article on Proust: "I am not a writer," in ZK V (1929–31), 154. OR RNB 1377. Published posthumously in Ginzburg 2002, 414.

207. As she wrote, "If only—without invention or recollection—one could fix the flow of life . . . the feeling of flow, the feeling of the present, the authenticity of multiple and indissoluble aspects of being." This passage is discussed earlier in this chapter.

208. Ginzburg wrote about how we "auto-correct" and edit even when we are trying to faithfully, stenographically record oral speech. Lidiia Ginzburg, "Ustnaia rech' i khudozhestvennaia proza," *Semiotika ustnoi rechi. Lingvisticheskaia semantika i semiotika II* (Tartu: Tartuskii gosudarstvennyi universitet, 1979), 54–55. Cf. also the exchange with Andrei Bitov about the "inventedness" of her own notes on others' conversations. Ginzburg 2002, 321.

209. For example, Proust reinvents the psychological novel about adultery without the moralizing; he elaborates on every detail but then brushes aside the most important factual or plot events (mentioning them merely in passing); his main hero is all the time lying in bed. Ginzburg 2002, 43. When Ginzburg reads Blok's letters to his mother, she delights in another negative principle—lack of stylization. Ibid., 52–53. Ginzburg writes that in contrast to his letters to friends, Blok had no need for "round phrases," crafted introductions, or sorting out of different kinds of facts—he relates everything with the confidence that it would simply be interesting to his mother.

210. Barthes writes, "The writerly is the novelistic without the novel, poetry without the poem, the essay without the dissertation, writing without style, production without product, structuration without structure." Roland Barthes, *S/Z*, trans. Richard Miller (London: Jonathan Cape, 1975), 5. Elsewhere, he notes, "Snare of infatuation: to suggest that he is willing to consider what he writes as a work, an '*oeuvre*,'—to move from the contingency of writings to the transcendence of a unitary, sacred product. . . . I delight continuously, endlessly, in writing as in perpetual production, in an unconditional dispersion. . . . But in our mercantile society, one must end up with a work, an '*oeuvre*': one must construct, i.e., *complete*, a piece of merchandise. . . . How to write, given all the snares set by the collective image of the work? Why, *blindly*." Roland Barthes, *Roland Barthes by Roland Barthes*, trans. Richard Howard (Berkeley: University of California Press, 1994), 136.

211. Lacoue-Labarthe and Nancy, *The Literary Absolute*, 42.

212. Ginzburg 2002, 400.

CHAPTER 3. MARGINALITY IN THE MAINSTREAM, LESBIAN LOVE IN THE THIRD PERSON

1. Lidiia Ginzburg, *Zapisnye knizhki. Vospominaniia. Esse* (St. Petersburg: Iskusstvo-SPb, 2002), 372. Henceforth, "Ginzburg 2002." The first commercial edition of Gide's *Corydon*, which Ginzburg read, was published in 1925. For more details on the early

history of the work's circulation, see the "Translator's Note" in *Corydon*, trans. and with preface by Richard Howard (New York: Farrar, Straus & Giroux, 1983), xiv.

2. Gide distinguishes "normal pederasts" from "inverts," seemingly on the bases of their self-image. Corydon says, "The doctors who usually write about the subject treat only uranists who are ashamed of themselves—pathetic inverts, sick men. They're the only ones who consult doctors" (Gide, 18). His terminology is idiosyncratic.

3. Ginzburg 2002, 371–73.

4. Lidiia Ginzburg, "Chetvertyi 'Razgovor o liubvi' Lidiia Ginzburg (text, publication, introductory article by E. Van Buskirk, trans. E. Kanishchevoi)," *Novoe literaturnoe obozrenie* 88, 6 (2007): 161. Henceforth, "Chevertyi 'Razgovor o liubvi.'" Translation by E. Van Buskirk and A. Tapp in *Lydia Ginzburg's Alternative Literary Identities* (Oxford: Peter Lang AG, 2012), 348. While Ginzburg later used the title "Conversation about Love," her 1930s piece was tentatively titled "Dialogue about Love," the name I have chosen to use here.

5. "Chetvertyi 'Razgovor o liubvi,'" 163 (Russian); English in *Lydia Ginzburg's Alternative Literary Identities*, 350–51. It bears emphasizing that Ginzburg is speaking of the psychological needs of the "normal woman" in the 1930s.

6. Gide, 7.

7. "Chetvertyi 'Razgovor o liubvi,'" 164 (Russian); *Lydia Ginzburg's Alternative Literary Identities*, 351.

8. See my short article "V poiskakh romana: Lidiia Ginzburg v 1930-e gody" ("In Search of the Novel: Lydia Ginzburg in the 1930s"), which introduces the publication of Lidiia Ginzburg's "Chetvertyi 'Razgovor o liubvi.'"

9. Igor Kon, *Liki i maski odnopoloi liubvi: lunnyi svet na zare*, 2nd, expanded ed. (Moscow: Astrel', 2006), 362.

10. One can use the reception of Kuzmin's (quite chaste) gay bildungsroman *Wings* as a case study demonstrating the homophobic atmosphere among the more general literary elite. See John Malmstad, "Bathhouses, Hustlers, and a Sex Club: The Reception of Mikhail Kuzmin's *Wings*," *Journal of the History of Sexuality* 9, 1–2 (2000): 85–104.

11. Simon Karlinsky, "Russia's Gay History and Literature from the Eleventh to the Twentieth Centuries," in Winston Leyland, ed., *Gay Roots: Twenty Years of Gay Sunshine* (San Francisco: Gay Sunshine Press, 1991–93), 103.

12. Simon Karlinsky, "Russia's Gay Literature and Culture: The Impact of the October Revolution," in Martin Duberman Martha Vicinus, and George Chauncey, Jr., eds., *Hidden from History: Reclaiming the Gay and Lesbian Past* (New York: NAL Books, 1989), 360.

13. Ibid., 362. Dan Healey, in a revisionist historical work that seeks to complicate our notions of gender and sexuality in the Stalinist era, and to find a "usable past" for vulnerable groups in post-communist society, has found that a "continuous and concealed sociability among homosexuals persisted" in the 1930s. His research concerns male homosexuality. Dan Healey, "Sexual and Gender Dissent: Homosexuality as Resistance in Stalin's Russia," *Contending with Stalinism: Soviet Power and Popular Resistance in the 1930s*, ed. Lynne Viola (Ithaca, NY: Cornell University Press, 2002,) 139–69, see 159, 168.

14. Igor Kon, "Sexual Minorities," in Igor Kon and James Riordan, eds., *Sex and Russian Society* (London: Pluto Press, 1993), 103.

15. Diana Burgin, *"Ottiagotela . . .": Russkie zhenshchiny za predelami obydennoi zhizni* (St. Petersburg: Inapress, 2004), 62.

16. Only in a few unpublished drafts does one find "Vasya" (1920s) and "Alexander Ilych" (1940s).

17. "Otter" appears in unpublished drafts of the 1930s and 40s. In some early drafts, Ginzburg writes "Oter," which helps to make it unmistakably clear that she did not mean to evoke a sea otter, but rather was transliterating a foreign word phonetically. See, for example, the drafts in the folder labeled "Razgovor. 'La Rochefoucauld.' Esse 50–60 gg." (which in fact contains drafts from the 1930s as well). OR RNB 1377.

18. It is telling that on many occasions, when editing her essays for publication, Ginzburg excised and replaced instances of "I" with "he," with initials, or with "*chelovek*."

19. Michael Lucey, *Never Say I: Sexuality and the First Person in Colette, Gide, and Proust* (Durham, NC: Duke University Press, 2006), 17. Lucey describes this book as the first in a two-volume work on "the queer first person in twentieth-century French literature," 4.

20. I follow Lucey in preferring "same-sex" as slightly better than the alternatives. While not neutral, it nevertheless marks "the nonneutrality of the word *homosexual* and its cognates," ibid., 8.

21. Proust's words are quoted in *Never Say I*, 1, and come from André Gide's 1921 journal entry, where he records a conversation with Proust on the subject of *Corydon*.

22. Gérard Genette, *Narrative Discourse: An Essay in Method*, trans. Jane E. Lewin (Ithaca, NY: Cornell University Press, 1980), 249, as quoted in Lucey, *Never Say I*, 199.

23. Dorrit Cohn has argued convincingly for the impossibility of reading Proust's work either as purely fictional or as purely autobiographical in *The Distinction of Fiction* (Baltimore, MD: Johns Hopkins University Press, 1999), 58–78, partially through an analysis of one of the two "naming" scenes in *Recherche*. Several scholars have discussed the abstraction of Proust's "je." Cohn (72) refers to a linguistic study of Proust's work by A. Gréllison, J. L. Lebrave, and C. Viollet, *Proust à la lettre*. Lucey in *Never Say I* describes the "abstracting work" that Proust does in terms of expressing same-sex sexuality (1–26), and shows how Proust draws attention to the referential function of pronouns in discourse (215–49). In *Narrative Discourse*, Genette writes of Proust's "conquest of the 'I'" as a distancing project, as opposed to a move toward subjectivity (249).

24. The most obvious inconsistency is the third-person omniscience in "Swann in Love," but there are other examples. Lucey argues that Proust deliberately plays with levels of omniscience in the narrative whenever the scenes have some homosexual content, such as the sex scene between Charlus and Jupien, and the scene where the doorman recognizes the Duc de Châtellerault from a sexual encounter. Lucey, *Never Say I*, 234–49.

25. Ginzburg, "Chetvertyi 'Razgovor o liubvi,'" 164; in *Lydia Ginzburg's Alternative Literary Identities*, 351–52. A challenge to this view is put forth by Elisabeth Ladenson in *Proust's Lesbianism* (Ithaca, NY: Cornell University Press, 1999). Landenson argues that Proust's represention of female sexuality posits "a sexual economy that is not based on a phallic standard," 134. Landenson also argues against the "transposition theory," 10–27, and discusses Proust's concepts of "inversion," 36–43.

26. *Never Say I*, 199, from Lucey's summary of Genette's argument.

27. Lucey, *Never Say I*, 14.

28. Ginzburg discusses three basic kinds of authorial inclusion in *O lirike*, while ac-

knowledging the existence of in-between forms. In scholarly prose, the author's image or personality remains *za tekstom*, outside or behind the text. In "artistic" (*khudozhestvennaia*) prose and epic, the author typically is "included" in a "hidden" way (*skrytoe vkliuchenie avtora*), airing her views and values in the mediated form of a "second reality," to which a fictional narrator belongs. Finally, in "lyric prose or the prose of meditations, and in the lyrical digressions of poetic epics," the author is "included" in an "open" way (*otkrytoe vkliuchenie avtora*). Ginzburg, *O lirike*, 2nd ed. (Leningrad: Sovetskii pisatel', 1974), 7–8.

29. See Michael Lucey, *Never Say I*, 1–27, and especially 19–21, where he cites the work of Erving Goffman.

30. Ginzburg 2002, 247–48. English in *Lydia Ginzburg's Alternative Literary Identities*, 345–46.

31. Ginzburg 2002, 137.

32. Ibid., 101.

33. Natalia Sokolova, Lydia Ginzburg's niece and Viktor Tipot's daughter, published a portion of her memoirs (which are in RGALI) about Krot, which she dates as existing from 1920–21. It seems (from Ginzburg's diaries) that the troupe survived at least until 1922. N. Sokolova, "Ogliadyvaias' nazad . . . ," *Voprosy literatury* 5 (1994): 285–92. On Krot, see also Rina Zelënaia, *Razroznennye strannitsy* (Moscow: Zebra E, 2010), 43–49.

34. Ibid., 101–2. Ginzburg's play, called "Philosophy Lesson" (*Urok filosofii*), features a dialogue between a student and a skeleton. Excerpts were published by Sokolova in "Ogliadyvaias' nazad . . . ."

35. Ginzburg 2002, 120.

36. See Katerina Clark, *Petersburg, Crucible of Cultural Revolution* (Cambridge, MA: Harvard University Press, 1995), 103–5. Ginzburg mentions Evreinov's works in *On Psychological Prose*, trans. and ed. Judson Rosengrant (Princeton, NJ: Princeton University Press, 1991), 369 n. 29. Henceforth, I refer to this book as "Ginzburg 1991." Russian in *O psikhologicheskoi proze* (Leningrad: Khudozhestvennaia literatura, 1977), 29 n. 1. Henceforth, "Ginzburg 1977."

37. I make parenthetical references to these diaries as "Diary I" (19 August 1920–4 September 1922) and "Diary II" (23 September 1922–14 May 1923) with the page numeration made by Ginzburg. The archive contains smaller diaries preceding these two (the earliest begins on 26 December 1918 and is roughly 50 pages long) and separate drafts made during this period, but these are the two primary diaries, much more substantial than any others. OR RNB 1377. Rina Zelyonaya's birth year was not recorded at birth in Tashkent; she invented the year 1902 when filling out forms. According to relatives she was born in 1901, but by some accounts it was earlier. In one of Ginzburg's sketches, she appears three years older than the author (b. 1902). After acting in Krot in Odessa (1919–21), Zelyonaya acted in cabarets in Moscow (*Nerydai*) and Petersburg/Petrograd (*Balaganchik*) (1922–23), the Moscow Satirical Theater (1924–28), and a series of Moscow theaters and concert halls. Starting in 1939 with *Podkidysh* (*Foundling*), she appeared in a number of Soviet films. She is also remembered for her radio programs, and for her convincing imitations of children's voices. See *Estrada v Rossii. XX Vek. Entsiklopediia*, ed. Elizaveta Uvarova (Moscow: Olma-Press, 2004), 236–37.

38. Ginzburg's note, left with her 1920–23 diaries when sealing them for a decade after her death. OR RNB 1377. In the note, she also mentions letters. So far, I have found only a small number of unsent letters in the archives.

39. Ibid.

40. I have been unable to establish the exact date of their meeting or of the inception of Ginzburg's infatuation, but "E" is mentioned in the first entry of "Diary I" on 19 August 1920 in the context of a relationship or infatuation. The year of Zelyonaya's arrival in Odessa is not given in her memoir, but was in winter, either in late 1919 (the year given in the encyclopedia entry cited in note 37) or early 1920.

41. See Sokolova, "Ogliadyvaias' nazad . . . ," and the manuscript of "Urok filosofii" in Sokolova's archive in RGALI, F. 2897.

42. Rina Zelyonaya's description of her Odessa life accentuates the complete destitution of her existence, with a light-heartedness that agrees with Ginzburg's descriptions of her. One passage where Zelyonaya describes sleeping in a freezing cold room under a pile of clothing (with a theatrical flair) seems unwittingly to travesty a scene in Ginzburg's *Zapiski blokadnogo cheloveka*. See Zelënaia, 22.

43. Zelënaia, 46–47. Sokolova describes Ginzburg as "strong and sporty" (*Ogliadyvaias'* . . . , 88). Zelyonaya and Sokolova may be trying to hint at Ginzburg's sexuality with these descriptions.

44. There is a secondhand account of this relationship in Natalia Sokolova's unpublished memoir. The basic contours are the same ones Ginzburg depicts: humiliation on one side, rejection on the other. "At one point, according to rumor, Liusia was desperately in love with Rina Zelyonaya, pursued her, humiliated herself. But naturally I don't remember this, I was too young. Rina, who was untouchable [*nedotroga*], an unusually chaste and wholesome person, rejected all of Liusia's solicitations [*domogatel'stva*]. In my memory, they were always joined by a good strong friendship and mutual respect." "Lidiia Ginzburg, rodnia, znakomye: Materialy k biografii," RGALI F. 3270. Sokolova N. V. Op. 1 ed. khr. 27. l.l. 29–30.

45. This alternation from E. and K. to R. can be explained by the fact that Ekaterina became known as Rina after moving to Moscow in 1922. For her own story about her name, see Zelënaia, 50–51.

46. Zelyonaya discusses in her memoir how after moving to Moscow she sent to Odessa for her family and Tipot's, and then the five of them (Rina, her younger sister, her mother, Viktor Tipot, and his wife, Nadezhda Bliumenfel'd) lived in a single room of 6 square meters (Zelënaia, 64). It is possible there were other periods of cohabitation as well.

47. Ginzburg, ZK V (1929–31), 113. OR RNB 1377. Compare this to the generalized version published in Ginzburg 2002, 82.

48. Ginzburg's diary entry from 10 December 1920 incorporates a quotation from Blok's 1914 poem, "Nu, chto zhe! Ustalo zalomleny slabye ruki" ("Well, what now! My hands are wearily wrung"). She would quote different lines from the same poem in her blockade essay "Résumé of Failures" ("Itogi neudach"). See Ginzburg 2011, 167.

49. Ginzburg 2002, 225. The quotation is from Blok's play in verse "The Rose and the Cross" ("Roza i krest' ").

50. Ginzburg writes: "In essence I want nothing more than to sit in Pargolovo and keep warm, eat, and write my paper, but I go to the city, in order to *see* Petersburg [*sic*] on the anniversary of October. I go to a Mystery Play, in the crowd I don't see a damned thing and don't experience the least bit of pleasure, but I don't care—after all, an understanding is acquired." Diary I, 54, 10 November 1920 (two days after the mass spectacle). OR RNB 1377. For an account of the spectacle, see Clark, *Petersburg*, 122–39.

51. It is significant that to the extent that she takes part in the apocalyptic spirit of Symbolism, she is motivated by a drive to possess a consciousness that encompasses all

of history: "I imagine that if I were a still disembodied spirit, presented with a choice of epochs in which to become incarnate, then I would choose the latest possible one, completely independently of the conditions and such that my death would be the death of the world, so that afterward—there would be nothing." Ginzburg, Diary I, 55. OR RNB 1377.

52. See Ginzburg 2002, 474.

53. Ibid., 21.

54. This passage, and Ginzburg's confrontation with the question of "Tolstoy vs. Dostoevsky," have been discussed by Caryl Emerson in "Lydia Ginzburg on Tolstoy and Lermontov (with Dostoevsky as the Distant Ground," in E. Van Buskirk and A. Zorin, eds., *Lydia Ginzburg's Alternative Literary Identities* (Oxford: Peter Lang AG, 2012), 39–82: see esp. 52–54 (diary entries that I shared with the author are part of the discussion).

55. "Many of my notes, and all of my letters to N [filled in later Nina] bear the traces of this kind of befuddlement of the self with a romantic lexicon, in which, unfortunately, it is one step from the beautiful to the vulgar, and which you therefore have to handle with the utmost care. Incidentally, my sensitivity to a counterfeit word returns to me rather quickly, but it's useless, all the same I cannot hold back—the false sound of these words almost physically caresses my strained nerves." Diary I, 48–49. OR RNB 1377. This Nina is Nina Lazarevna Gurfinkel', a close childhood friend of Ginzburg's who later emigrated to Paris. For biographical information about Nina Gourfinkel (as her name was spelled in emigration) and a bibliography of her works as a Slavist, see R. Schatzman, "Nina Gourfinkel," *Revue des études slaves*, Paris, LXIII, 3 (1991): 705–23.

56. Ginzburg 2002, 225. Evidence from the diaries of her early reading of Freud includes an entry on December 1920, where she writes: "I learned to consider everything, down to the most trivial, especially after Freud" (Diary I, 76). In February 1923, Ginzburg acknowledges (in passing) Freud's notion of the erotic nature of the attachment to the mother (Diary II, 117). OR RNB 1377.

57. See Evgenii Bershtein's doctoral dissertation, "Western Models of Sexuality in Russian Modernism" (University of California, Berkeley, 1998), and his article, "*Psychopathia Sexualis* v Rossii nachala veka: politika i zhanr," in M. Levitt and A. Toporkov, eds., *Eros and Pornography in Russian Culture* (Moscow: Ladomir, 1999), 414–41. On understandings of female sexuality in pre-Revolutionary Russia, including the influence of Western notions, see Laura Engelstein, *The Keys to Happiness: Sex and the Search for Modernity in Fin-de-Siècle Russia* (Ithaca, NY: Cornell University Press, 1992), esp.128–64.

58. Ibid. (Evgenii Bershtein's dissertation and article.)

59. Ginzburg, "Chetvertyi 'Razgovor o liubvi,'" 162. Translation in *Lydia Ginzburg's Alternative Literary Identities*, 348.

60. Ibid., 161; English on 347.

61. Sigmund Freud, "The Psychogenesis of a Case of Homosexuality in a Woman," in *Freud on Women: A Reader*, ed. Elisabeth Young-Bruehl (New York: W.W. Norton & Co., 1990), 246.

62. Ginzburg 2002, 218, 282–83.

63. Freud, *The Standard Edition of the Complete Psychological Works of Sigmund Freud*, trans. and ed. James Strachey, vol. VII (1901–5) (London: Hogarth Press and the Institute of Psychoanalysis, 1953), 165. See also Young-Bruehl, introduction to *Freud on Women*, 12.

64. Ginzburg 2002, 372.

65. A few of those terms were invert, pederast, uranist, unisexual, homosexual, ambisexual, tribade, lesbian, and sapphist. See Lucey, *Never Say I,* 36, where the focus is on France, and also all of chapters 1 and 2. Burgin finds these words in the Russian discourse: *lesbianka* ("lesbian"), *izvrashchenka* ("female pervert"), *sodomitka* ("female sodomite"), *selenitka* ("lunarian"), *tribadka* ("tribade"), and *gomoseksualistka* ("female homosexualist") (Burgin, 45).

66. Ginzburg wrote this essay in the 1930s, but edited it slightly in the 1960s, when it was typed up. She left the word "invert" unmodified. In her 1925 essay on André Gide's *Corydon,* she uses a broader range of terms: *gomoseksual'nost'* ("homosexuality"), *gomoseksualist* ("homosexualist"), *lesbiiskaia liubov'* ("lesbian love"), *odnopolaia liubov'* ("same-sex love"). Ginzburg 2002, 371–72.

67. Quotation from Freud, *Complete Standard Edition,* vol. VII, 148. Freud writes of "inverts" and "inversion" in "Three Essays on the Theory of Sexuality" (first edition 1905, further ones in 1910, 1915, 1920). He distinguishes "mental" or "character" inversion from sexual inversion as such. Ibid., 142, and see also Young-Bruehl, introduction to *Freud on Women,* 13. Krafft-Ebing writes about "congenital sexual inversion" in *Psychopathia Sexualis* (1886); Weininger writes of "inverted sexual attraction" in "homosexuals" in *Sex and Character*; Havelock Ellis titles the second volume of his *Studies in the Psychology of Sex* "Sexual Inversion" (1897), and F. W. Stella Browne publishes "Studies in Sexual Inversion" in 1923. For a brief survey of the major contributions of Weininger, Havelock Ellis, Stella Browne, and others to this discourse, see *Sexology Uncensored,* ed. Lucy Bland and Laura Doan (Cambridge, UK: Polity Press, 1998), 39–65. For a discussion of the concept of inversion in reference to the "birth of homosexuality" in 1870, see Eve Kosofsky Sedgwick's discussion of Foucault in *Epistemology of the Closet* (Berkeley: University of California Press, 2008), 44–46.

68. In this entry, she discusses and adopts as a motto Weininger's quotation from Friedrich Hebbel: "What do you pay for more dearly, the lie or the truth? The former costs you your self, the latter at the most your happiness." In Otto Weininger, *Sex and Character: An Investigation of Fundamental Principles,* trans. Ladislaus Löb (Bloomington: Indiana University Press, 2005), 140.

69. Ginzburg cites the Russian title (*Pol i kharakter*), but she may have read it in German. The same diary entry includes a discussion of Moll's concepts of "Detumeszenztrieb" and "Kontrektationstrieb," quoting from a German text. Weininger discusses Moll's theories of the "detumescence drive" and "contrectation drive" in *Sex and Character,* 77–79.

70. Weininger, 75–81.

71. Ibid., 57–65.

72. See Judy Greenway, "It's What You Do with It That Counts: Interpretations of Otto Weininger," in *Sexology in Culture: Labelling Bodies and Desires,* ed. Lucy Bland and Laura Doan (Cambridge, UK: Polity Press, 1998), 31, 33. In a footnote to his discussion of morality and fecundity, Weininger (311, 424) mentions Tolstoy's "On the Sexual Question" ("Über die sexuelle Frage," Leipzig, 1901); in a discussion of prostitution, he mentions *Resurrection* (203). In his 1910 essay "O bezumii," Tolstoy accuses Weininger (along with Hamsun, Darwin, Marx, Nietzsche, and others) of leading young readers, searching for the meaning of life, to despair and suicide. Lev Tolstoy, "O bezumii," in *Polnoe sobranie sochinenii,* vol. 38 (Moscow: Khudozhestvennaia literatura, 1936), 395–411.

73. In Pargolovo in September 1920, Ginzburg writes of a wish for an alternative fu-

ture that recalls the career of Nadezhda Durova: "I know that if I were a man (no, better not get carried away, because with such an 'if' I would no longer be myself), well, simply if they accepted women, or if I could disguise myself—I wouldn't hesitate for a moment, and would go to nautical school. Even better, naval school. I *know* that I would not be afraid for one minute. That's why I love the sea, because it is the one thing I do not fear. But whether this would be happiness—I don't know." Diary I, 46–47. OR RNB 1377.

In early 1923, Ginzburg laments not being a man in order to take revenge on her unrequited love, and on R.'s flirtatious romance with Viktor. She wishes for hidden spheres in herself that would be less transparent to another woman: "Oh, if only I were a man [. . .] if I appeared as a man I could announce myself, vent my rage not on her, not on him, not on myself, but on the order of things. A man always has a part of his life that is special, independent, and inaccessible to women, which even the most arrogant woman fears and over which she envies the most unfortunate of men. I remember how once the three of us were walking—she, S. and I. S. [a man] was talking about the abundance of brothels in Odessa and about the authorities' attitude toward them; she listened silently, and then asked bluntly: 'and how do you know such details?'—in such questions there is fear, disgust, curiosity and jealousy, the jealousy not of betrayal, but of a man's freedom. And in contrast my life is for her completely comprehensible and transparent. The fact that I have some intellectual interests and occupations that are inaccessible to her [. . .] well, this only makes a person more ridiculous. Never did a book seem to me so vapid, so imposing, such a surrogate, for a lack of better things, a surrogate of genuine experience." Diary II, 82–83, 2 January 1923. OR RNB 1377.

74. Ginzburg reflects that women have been scorned by nature as well as culture: "being predestined to give happiness (satisfaction, pleasure), she is little adapted to receive pleasure. Nature and people by some kind of unspoken worldwide agreement scorn the individual female worldview. Let's begin with nature: menstruation, the difficulty of childbirth, pregnancy, and nursing, the abundance of female illnesses, frequently the torture of the first sexual act, even the first several—how can this not be offensive?" Diary II, 21. OR RNB 1377.

75. In her famous essay "Visual Pleasure and Narrative Cinema," Mulvey writes of the "patriarchal" order of narrative cinema, in light of a similarly patriarchal psychoanalysis. In the same vein as Ginzburg, but with a greater emphasis on visual effects, she writes: "In a world ordered by sexual imbalance, pleasure in looking has been split between active/male and passive/female. The determining male gaze projects its fantasy onto the female figure, which is stylized accordingly. In their traditional exhibitionist role women are simultaneously looked at and displayed, with their appearance coded for strong visual and erotic impact so that they can be said to connote *to-be-looked-at-ness*," in *Visual and Other Pleasures* (London: Macmillan Press, 1989), 19.

76. Mulvey, "Visual Pleasure and Narrative Cinema," 33. She continues, "However, this Nature does not sit easily and shifts restlessly in its borrowed transvestite clothes." Ginzburg might argue against this second statement.

77. Ginzburg continues: "Now what remains to me is only the regret that I did not submit [my life] to a scheme that was even greater, more artistic, and more symbolic [. . .]." Diary II, 35.

78. Catriona Kelly, *A History of Russian Women's Writing: 1820–1992* (Oxford: Clarendon Press, 1994), 172. Eric Naiman has argued that Weininger's popularity in Russia was due to a likeminded view of women that already existed there in "Historectomies: On

the Metaphysics of Reproduction in a Utopian Age," in *Sexuality and the Body in Russian Culture,* ed. Jane T. Costlow, Stephanie Sandler, and Judith Vowles. (Stanford, CA: Stanford University Press, 1993), 255–76 (see particularly 262–70). Evgenii Bershtein discusses Weininger's influence in Russia extensively in his dissertation, "Western Models of Sexuality in Russian Modernism," 111–58.

79. Olga Matich has investigated the details of this celebrated marriage, which was an object of obsession for a group of Symbolists who hoped that Alexander Blok, Liubov' Dmitrievna Mendeleeva, and Andrei Bely in their triangular love would forgo physical consummation, embodying the ideas of Vladimir Solovyov concerning a higher spiritual union, and thereby bringing about the apocalypse. See Olga Matich, "The Case of Alexander Blok: Marriage, Genealogy, Degeneration," in *Erotic Utopia: The Decadent Imagination in Russia's Fin de Siècle* (Madison: University of Wisconsin Press, 2005), 89–125. Ginzburg may or may not have been privy to the facts of Blok's family life. As of December 1921, she was still something of an outsider in literary circles. She also writes of her first sojourn in Petrograd: "In those days, I had no literary connections in Petrograd. I did not make it once to the Institute for the History of Arts, but somehow I made it to Gumilyov's workshop. I went there a few times, did not meet anyone and did not speak a single word." Ginzburg 2002, 21.

80. J. Douglas Clayton, *Pierrot in Petrograd: The Commedia dell'Arte/*Balagan *in Twentieth-Century Russian Theatre and Drama* (Montreal: McGill-Queen's University Press, 1993), 9.

81. Recall the line from Ginzburg's "Conversations about Love": "The classic first love of an intellectual is grand, unrequited, unrealized (secretly it does not want to be realized)." *Lydia Ginzburg's Alternative Literary Identities,* 345. Russian in Ginzburg 2002, 248.

82. It is possible that Zelyonaya played this role in "Krot," which (according to Sokolova) put on Harlequinades, and where she played a Russian *matryoshka* doll in one of Inber's plays. See Sokolova, "Ogliadyvaias' nazad . . . ," 285–92. She also later (in 1923) worked in the theater with the name "Puppet Booth" (*Balaganchik*) in Petrograd (Zelënaia, 66–79).

83. Blok's poem "Neznakomka" ("The Stranger") from 1906 portrays a poet's encounter in a bar with a beautiful and mysterious woman, whose features include delicate (or narrow) hands, silks, perfume, and an ostrich-feathered hat.

84. See my discussion in chapter 4.

85. Ginzburg, *O lirike,* 284.

86. For a discussion of the destruction of theatrical illusion in "The Puppet Booth," see Stuart Goldberg, *Mandelstam, Blok, and the Boundaries of Mythopoetic Symbolism* (Columbus: Ohio State University Press, 2011), 189. For an interpretation of Blok's death as an instance of a staged tragedy that turns real, see Boris Eikhenbaum, "Sud'ba Bloka" [1921], in *O literature: Raboty raznykh let* (Moscow: Sovetskii pisatel', 1987), 355.

87. See Ginzburg, *Prokhodiashchie kharaktery. Proza voennykh Let. Zapiski blokadnogo cheloveka,* ed. Zorin and Van Buskirk (Moscow: Novizdat, 2011), 153–54. Henceforth, "Ginzburg 2011." A similar discussion of the "artificial" values of Symbolism, as compared to Classicism and Romanticism, can be found in her book *On the Lyric,* where her concept of "stylization" closely resembles the discussion of "*poshlost'*" from her notebooks. See Ginzburg, *O lirike,* 309–10. *Poshlost'* is famously (and differently) explicated by Nabokov in *Nikolai Gogol* (New York: New Directions, 1961 [1944]), 63–74; and in

"Philistines and Philistinism," *Lectures on Russian Literature*, ed. Fredson Bowers (New York: Harcourt, Inc., 1981), 309–14.

88. I am referring to what Ginzburg posits as an increasing structural organization of reality as one moves from everyday life to human documents to the novel. Ginzburg 1991, 8–9. Russian in idem 1977, 12–13.

89. I date the manuscript based on its fictionalized treatment of Zelyonaya's departure from Odessa to Moscow in June 1922. The piece was labeled, in much later handwriting, "Drafts. Excerpts" [*Zagotovki. Vypiski*].

90. Genette, *Narrative Discourse*, 238.

91. Ginzburg, "Iz besporiadochnykh zapisok N.N.," 5–6. OR RNB 1377. The pages in the manuscript were not numbered. I have assigned them numbers, from, 1–40. Henceforth, I give these page numbers in parenthetical references.

92. As she writes, the meaning of a dialogue in Tolstoy "is formulated only through the accompanying authorial explanation, which frequently alters that meaning by removing the dialogue to another, hidden context." Ginzburg 1991, 294. Russian in idem 1977, 357.

93. The rest of the sentence after "consciously" is illegible in the manuscript.

94. The original draft is in Diary II, 104–12. The later draft was tucked into the notebook, and has separate page numbering. OR RNB 1377.

95. By the time she added her later title, she must have known Mikhail Zoshchenko's story from 1925, "Nervnye liudi." There was in the mid-1920s a widespread crisis of "nervousness," treated in part as a sexual disorder. See Frances Lee Bernstein, *The Dictatorship of Sex: Lifestyle Advice for the Soviet Masses* (DeKalb, IL: Northern Illinois University Press, 2007), 73–99.

96. "Razgovor (nochnoi) . . . ." I quote from the 1923 draft (Diary II, 110–11). In the later version, the main difference (aside from the exclusion of pronouns) is the excision of the phrase "You just said it yourself" in the final utterance. OR RNB 1377.

97. Ginzburg 2002, 74. Original in ZK V (1929–31), 24. OR RNB 1377.

98. Ginzburg 2002, 635. From *Notes of a Blockade Person*. The statement is repeated in Ginzburg 1991, 286; Russian in idem 1977, 348.

99. Ginzburg 2002, 46.

100. Ibid.

101. See my biographical sketch in the introduction.

102. Unpublished essay from 1933 in Ginzburg, ZK VIII–IV (1933–35). OR RNB 1377.

103. Ginzburg 2002, 56.

104. "Conversations about Love," in *Lydia Ginzburg's Alternative Literary Identities*, 345–46. Russian in Ginzburg 2002, 247–48.

105. Lidiia Ginzburg, "Stadii liubvi," publication and introduction by Denis Ustinov, *Kriticheskaia massa* 1 (2002): 37–38.

106. Ginzburg, ZK VIII (1933), 24–25. OR RNB 1377.

107. Ibid., 25. See my discussion of Ginzburg's move toward the novel in chapter 2.

108. Ginzburg 2002, 98 (the note is from 1931).

109. Ginzburg writes: "[Our generation] acquired the age-old culture of love and carried it into an altogether different age of catastrophe. How things will fare with future generations is unclear; among other things, they never have free time, which is essential for a culture of love." In the third "Conversation about Love," Ginzburg 2002, 248. English translation in *Lydia Ginzburg's Alternative Literary Identities*, 345.

110. Keith Livers, *Constructing the Stalinist Body: Fictional Representations of Corporeality in the Stalinist 1930s* (New York: Lexington Books, 2004), 91–152. The earnest attempts of Soviet citizens to become ideal subjects are analyzed by Jochen Hellbeck in *Revolution on My Mind: Writing a Diary under Stalin* (Cambridge, MA: Harvard University Press, 2009).

111. Ginzburg, ZK V (1929–31), 114. OR RNB 1377. Ginzburg has in mind ethical and behavioral norms, as she does when she writes: "The norm is good because it mechanically imparts value to the behavior of the average person, value that he is not in a position to obtain on his own. This behavior is raised up to vast ideas of social good, family, and individual conscience, which are elaborated outside of the given person. Deviations from the norm are forgiven for those who replace values in general use with individual ones. Great poets, very beautiful women, brave people, and the rich have obliged others to accept their eccentricity." Ibid., 55. She notes the exceptions to the rule—curiously including "beautiful women" alongside great poets (according to Romantic stereotypes)—as a statement of fact, without judging whether these exceptions are justified.

112. Ginzburg, ZK V (1929–31) 114–15. Emphasis in original. OR RNB 1377. Cf. Ginzburg 2002, 82–83.

113. She writes in ZK IV (1928–29), 55, in Russian: "В руках нашего поколения она [норма] механизируется и грубеет; ее прекрасная схема обрастает нечистым мясом равнодушия; к сожалению, только в уклонениях мы сохраняем нашу человечность." OR RNB 1377.

114. The poem refers back to Alexander Pushkin's "Stansy (V nadezhde slavy i dobra)," written in 1828 and addressed to Nicholas I, containing flattering comparisons of the tsar to Peter the Great and a muted plea for a merciful release of the Decembrists from Siberia. Pasternak, in turning to Pushkin, renewed the perennial Russian dilemma of how a writer should interact with, relate to, or exert influence on an authoritarian ruler.

115. See Ginzburg 2002, 149–50, 349.

116. Ibid., 115. Bukhstab answered that Freud's theory did not suit his ambitions.

117. Ginzburg, 1934 essay in ZK VIII–IX (1933–35). OR RNB 1377.

118. According to Ginzburg, writers belonging to the "active" type are driven by the desire to stir their audiences, to "intervene with reality" through their word (*vmeshatel'stvo slova v deistvitel'nost'*). Shklovsky and Tolstoy serve as examples.

119. Ginzburg, "Chetvertyi razgovor o liubvi," 162. English in *Lydia Ginzburg's Alternative Literary Identities*, 349.

120. In her note criticizing Gide, Ginzburg concedes that homosexuals—along with "bachelors, old maids, and even women who do not want children"—can be rightfully accused of being "useless" in society because they do not advance its central aims (Ginzburg 2002, 372–73). In an unpublished essay on the death of Natalia Rykova, Ginzburg discusses the value of childbirth (Folder of miscellaneous drafts from the 1920s to 1930s, OR RNB 1377).

121. Ginzburg, ZK V (1929–31) 114–15. OR RNB 1377.

122. Ginzburg writes that she and Shklovsky developed a friendship beginning in 1924, and were in close contact through the later 1920s and 1930s, as well as in the 1950s and 1960s. In Russian: "С 1924 года, примерно, у меня с Виктором Борисовичем установились не только литературно-научные, но и личные отношения. Мы много

общались в 20–30-х годах, общались и потом в 50–60-х." Ginzburg, "O Shklovskom." OR RNB 1377.

In Ginzburg's letter to Shklovsky dated 1929 (but written, it seems, in January 1930), she quotes from a part of *Zoo* that appeared in the second (1924), third, and fourth editions but not in the first. Published by Denis Ustinov, *Novoe literaturnoe obozrenie* 50, 4 (2001): 319. Nevertheless, she alludes to *Zoo* in a draft letter to Zelyonaya, which was most likely written in 1923. Ginzburg, small blue notebook titled "Zametki o literature." OR RNB 1377.

123. Ginzburg writes: "In general, there are books we read with varying degrees of satisfaction, and there are books with which we live. And then it is not about satisfaction, but about how a book will take charge of our consciousness [о том, как книга распорядится нашим сознанием]. This happened to me at various times and to varying degrees with Tolstoy, Proust, Heine, Pasternak, with *Zoo* it seems, in part with Rousseau's *Confessions*." Ginzburg 2002, 96–97 (from 1931).

124. Viktor Shklovsky, *Zoo, or Letters Not about Love*, trans. Richard Sheldon (Chicago: Dalkey Archive Press, 2001), 73. In Russian, Shklovskii, *Eshche nichego ne konchilos'*, ed. A. Galushkin (Moscow: Progaganda, 2002), 313.

125. Shklovsky, *Zoo*, 84. Russian in Shklovskii, *Eshche nichego ne konchilos'*, 320.

126. Ginzburg reminds us of Shklovsky's motivation for writing not just for art's sake, but for revenge, when she repeats his refrain "Words avenge" ("Слова мстят") in "Zametki o proze," Ginzburg 2002, 149. Original, with slight variations, in ZK 1932 (VII), 11. OR RNB 1377.

127. See Richard Sheldon's introduction, *Zoo*, xxv–xxvi.

128. Ginzburg 2002, 43. The note is from 1927.

129. She writes, "—You don't think that Shklovsky really used the formalist method to write *Zoo*—the most tender book of our time?" Ibid., 65. Note from 1928. The original version was longer: "I have had occasion to hear how Shklovsky has been called (and perhaps not without grounds) a traitor, a lout, a sexual maniac, an unprincipled professional,—but I do not bear it, I cannot bear it, when he is considered a fool. Do these people really think that he used the Formalist method to write *Zoo*, the tenderest book of our time!" Ginzburg 2002, 405.

130. These notes become the basis for her essay-reminiscence that she published in several forms in the late 1980s. See Judson Rosengrant, "L. Ya. Ginzburg: An International Chronological Bibliography of Primary and Secondary Work," in *Russian Review* 54, 4 (October 1995): 587–600.

131. Ginzburg 2002, 496. "Nikolai Oleinikov."

132. Ibid., 489.

133. The Russian idiom literally reads "beat yourself into a flatbread," which harmonizes with Oleinikov's frequent theme of food and hunger. Ginzburg notes that Oleinikov agreed with her assessment, countering those interpretations of him as a simple purveyor of satire and levity.

134. In Russian: "Он употребляет [галантерейный язык], чтобы в щепки скомпрометировать наследственные символистические смыслы. Потому что ничем на свете нельзя так испохабить идеологию, как галантерейностью." ZK VIII (1933). OR RNB 1377.

135. In her 1933 analysis (ZK VIII, OR RNB 1377), Ginzburg declares that the last three strophes are as utterly lacking in parody as Gavriil Derzhavin's ode "God" (1784). Perhaps this explains how she was able to cite the final line uttered by the

corpse, "And the world will turn its other side" in her Blockade piece "Paralysis." Ginzburg 2011, 434.

136. Ginzburg 2002, 470. The 1936 translation was by Evgeniia Kalashnikova. Ilya Ehrenburg recalls that in 1937, Hemingway was named by the majority of writers surveyed by *International Literature* as the most important contemporary author in the West. Ilya Ehrenburg, "Saturday Review" (29 July 1961), in *Hemingway: the Critical Heritage*, ed. Jeffrey Meyers (London: Routledge & Kegan Paul), 433–36.

137. These paragraphs were published under the title "Remarks about Prose," in *Person at a Writing Table*. See Ginzburg 2002, 143–45. See also Ginzburg, "Teoreticheskoe vstuplenie" (archival manuscript), 20–27. OR RNB 1377.

138. Ginzburg 2002, 143–44.

139. Ibid., 144. Ginzburg writes: "Compositions ripen or disintegrate in the desk drawer for decades—and it is not surprising that they gradually acquire predecessors." Ginzburg 2011, 453. She is speaking of her composition that became *Notes of a Blockade Person* (1942–1962–1983), in relation to Solzhenitsyn's *One Day in the Life of Ivan Denisevich* (1962).

140. Here, she imagines the result of a Proust "assimilated to the traditions of the psychological novel," which would be "problematic self-analysis [*problemnyi samoanaliz*], something alien to Proust's spirit." Ginzburg 2002, 43. The year 1927 was when Frankovsky's translations of the first volume appeared. Ginzburg's draft article from 1929–30 shows that she proceeded to read the entire work in French. It is unclear if she was aware of its unfinished aspects; in any case she writes, "Proust's literary fate is unusual: his novel (in eight [*sic*] volumes and sixteen books), finished almost 8 years ago and then only partially published, gained notoriety only in 1919 (? years before the author's death [a note in the margins reads "? year of author's death"]) and even later gained a reader . . . ." OR RNB 1377.

141. The draft article on Proust is written on several small notebooks and loose sheets tucked into a notebook. The roughly sixty pages of the draft are in relative disarray and there are at least two paginations, corresponding most likely to different sections of the article, but at times there exist multiple revisions of a single passage. The draft is inside a larger folder of various materials currently catalogued as "Realizatsia v slove. Teoriia slova. O L.N. Tolstom i drugie chernovye avtorgrafy." OR RNB 1377. Ginzburg included certain arguments from this article in the section on Proust in *On Psychological Prose*.

142. Ginzburg, draft article on Proust (1929–30). She cautions against imitating Proust too closely, since "his literary manner is wholly unthinkable outside of his personal genius." OR RNB 1377.

143. Ginzburg 1991, 310. Russian in idem 1977, 376.

144. Ginzburg, draft article on Proust (1929–30), various pages (most of them not numbered, though the page on Tolstoy's *Childhood* is numbered 20). OR RNB 1377. It is worth mentioning that Ginzburg's article is sprinkled with German terminology (Ich-Erzählung, Darstellung, Berricht), and that she cites Leo Spitzer (without mentioning the specific work, though it is possible she read his *Stilstudien* and its chapter on Proust). Her friend Viktor Zhirmunsky was importing and translating Spitzer's work, for example, as the editor of *Problemy literaturnoi formy (sbornik statei O. Val'tselia, V. Dibeliusa, K. Fosslera, L. Shpitzera)* (Leningrad: Academia 1928). Ginzburg translated an article for this volume by Dibelius on Dickens.

145. Ginzburg 1991, 309. Russian in idem 1977, 374.

146. Ginzburg, draft article on Proust, page not numbered. OR RNB 1377. See my discussion of this statement in chapter 2.

147. Ginzburg uses the terms "sociological" and "linguistic" when writing of Proust in 1933. ZK VIII (1933), 20. OR RNB 1377.

148. Ginzburg writes: "to search for 'indecency' in *À la recherche* . . . is senseless, just as it is senseless to search for it in an anatomical atlas. You can find it in both cases, but not otherwise than by releasing a thing from its function [не иначе, как отрешив вещь от ее назначения]." ZK II (1927–28), 48. OR RNB 1377. She adds that "for a post-revolutionary *intelligent* skeptic who wants to (and most convincingly, who sometimes can) overcome the original sin of *intelligent* romanticism, there is something captivating about this French 'soullessness' [нечто пленительное в этом французском «бездушии»]." Ibid., 40.

149. As quoted in Michael Lucey, "Simone de Beauvoir and Sexuality in the Third Person," *Representations* 109, 1 (Winter 2010): 100. Sartre writes also that Proust "believes in the existence of universal passions whose mechanism does not vary substantially when there is a change in the sexual characteristics, social condition, nation, or era of the individuals experiencing them. [. . .] Faithful to the postulates of the analytic cast of mind, he does not even imagine that there might be a dialectic of feelings—he imagines only a mechanics." Ibid. Cited from Jean-Paul Sartre, "Introducing *Les Temps modernes*," in *"What Is Literature?" and Other Essays*, trans. Jeffrey Mehlman (Cambridge, MA: Harvard University Press, 1988), 258–59.

150. For a discussion of the structure of this work, see chapter 2.

151. This fragment can be found within the drafts for "Mysl', opisavshaia krug" ("The Thought That Drew a Circle"), envisioned as part of *Home and the World*. OR RNB 1377.

152. Written in pencil on a loose page tucked into a folder with one of the drafts for "Mysl', opisavshaia krug." OR RNB 1377.

153. Ginzburg, "Dom i mir" folder. The pages in this folder were not numbered. OR RNB 1377.

154. It is possible that other sections of this narrative remain to be discovered in the archive, although they may have been destroyed, lost, or never drafted. In October 2012, I found several pages sketching the characters of Gukovsky and Bukhstab, who are mentioned as part of the plan for the sections on profession, as well as dialogues and analyses of Anna Akhmatova, who was to be a character in *Dom i mir*. I found these in a folder that is labeled as "Esse raznykh let. Fragmenty. Chernovoi avtograf. 1950-e–1960e. 94 ll." Several drafts here, including those on Gukovsky, Bukhstab, and Akhmatova, are from the 1930s.

155. Ginzburg 1991, 327; Russian in idem 1977, 396.

156. Ginzburg 2002, 149–50.

157. Ginzburg, "Dom i mir" manuscript, 1930s. OR RNB 1377.

158. Ginzburg's letters and unpublished prose sketches suggest that this critique may have emerged from her disapproval of women who thought that marriage was not a binding choice, that it was not an obstacle to carrying on lesbian relationships. In a folder currently labeled "Esse raznykh let. Fragmenty. Chernovoi avtograf. 1950-e–1 960-e. 94 ll.," there is a sketch under the title "Personalia" of a woman who tried (and failed) to maintain her relationship with X. (who seems to stand in for the author) even after she married Y., and here Ginzburg writes that it is typical of women to think that they can have it all without making a choice.

159. Ginzburg, "Dom i mir" manuscript, 1930s. OR RNB 1377.

160. Ginzburg 2002, 370.

161. Ginzburg 1977, 204. English in idem 1991, 163.

162. Ginzburg 2002, 370.

163. Another narrative of this same later period, "Psychological Sketches (from the life of A.)" ("Психологические чертежи [из жизни А.]"), connects both to "The Stages of Love" and to *Home and the World*. See Ginzburg 2002, 138.

164. Ginzburg, "Stadii liubvi," *Kriticheskaia massa* 1 (2002): 34–35.

165. Ibid., 37.

166. Ginzburg, "Chetvertyi razgovor o liubvi," 163. English in *Lydia Ginzburg's Alternative Literary Identities*, 350.

167. Ginzburg, "Stadii liubvi," 35.

168. In the draft "Theoretical Introduction," Ginzburg writes: "Notebooks, diaries, fragments and so on—are not independent. And not emotional. The emotion with which they are written belongs to the author personally; it is not obligatory for the reader. The most emotional thing of all—a person's fate." In Russian: "Записные книжки, дневники, фрагменты и проч.—не самостоятельны. И не эмоциональны. Волнение, с которым их пишут, принадлежит лично автору; оно не для читателя обязательно. Самое эмоциональное из всего—судьба человека," 3. OR RNB 1377.

169. Ginzburg, "Stadii liubvi," 38.

170. "The Thought That Drew a Circle" ("Mysl', opisavshaia krug") is different. It contains a gendered (feminine) first person singular, as well as historically identified personages. In this sense, it is less of a fiction than these other narratives, and its planned connection to them as part of *Home and the World* brings the whole opus closer to the "diary-novel."

171. The only explicit marker of his apparent masculinity is a derogatory generalization he makes in his diary: "Women exhibit this stupid carelessness in how they treat people." In Russian: "У женщин есть в обращении с людьми дурацкая неосторожность." Ginzburg 2002, 534. This sentence was inadvertently omitted from the translation in *Lydia Ginzburg's Alternative Literary Identities*.

172. Thus, Igrek writes about the three illusions that sustain love—"the illusions of eternity, irreplaceability and inexhaustibility," and then the author elaborates a few pages later on "the inexhaustibility hypothesis," which he/she calls "the most important of all the hypotheses of love." Ginzburg, "The Return Home," in *Lydia Ginzburg's Alternative Literary Identities*, 329 and 334. Russian in Ginzburg 2002, 532 and 536. The "irreplaceability" illusion is also explored in "The Stages of Love." Ginzburg, "Stadii liubvi," 37.

173. Genette, *Narrative Discourse*, 246.

174. It is possible that certain of Ginzburg's friends were hesitant to speak on this topic out of reluctance to feed any public discussion of what for them may have been a private matter. The topic of gay, lesbian, bisexual, and transgender identities remains a taboo topic in Russian society, and public discussions of homosexuality have been outlawed recently in Putin's Russia.

175. The note is not dated, but is located in a folder of typescripts from 1955–65. OR RNB 1377.

176. Nataliia Sokolova, "Lidiia Ginzburg, rodnia, znakomye: Materialy k biografii," 30. RGALI F. 3270. Sokolova N.V. Op. 1 ed. khr. 27. Gippius is an interesting choice because of her inscription of lesbian love into heterosexual representations, and her ambivalence about female creativity and femininity. See Jennifer Presto, *Beyond the Flesh:*

Alexander Blok, Zinaida Gippius, and the Symbolist Sublimation of Sex (Madison: University of Wisconsin Press, 2008), esp. chapter 6.

177. Ginzburg 2002, 734.

178. See Ginzburg 2011, 283–92.

179. See quotation from Genette in Lucey, *Never Say I*, 195: "The *Recherche du temps perdu* . . . cannot but appear . . . as an immense text, at once allusive, metonymic, synecdochic, (metaphoric, of course) and disavowing, of involuntary avowal, in which are revealed, but by concealment and disguise in innumerable transformations, a small number of simple statements concerning its author, his origins, his ambitions, his morals [*moeurs*: also habits], everything he shares secretly with Bloch, with Legrandin, with Charlus, and of which he has carefully exempted his hero, the colorless, yet idealized image of himself."

180. Ginzburg 1991, 21. Russian in idem 1977, 29.

181. She wrote of this kind of indifference in the essay "At One with the Legal Order," ibid., 285. The speaker of her 1930s "Conversation about Love" argues that authors who write about same-sex desire, such as Mikhail Kuzmin, appeal to homosexual readers less than Pushkin, Heine, or Blok. History has proven Ginzburg wrong, as Kuzmin is now a cult figure in the small tradition of gay Russian literature.

182. Ginzburg, "Chetvertyi 'Razgovor o liubvi,'" 164. English in *Lydia Ginzburg's Alternative Literary Identities*, 352.

CHAPTER 4. PASSING CHARACTERS

Some of the material for this chapter originally appeared in the chapter "Varieties of Failure: Lydia Ginzburg's Character Analyses from the 1930s and 1940s," in Emily Van Buskirk and Andrei Zorin (eds), *Lydia Ginzburg's Alternative Literary Identities* (Oxford: Peter Lang AG, 2012), 125–62, and is reproduced here with permission.

1. *O psikhologicheskoi proze* (Leningrad: Khudozhestvennaia literatura, 1977), 16, 20. Henceforth, "Ginzburg 1977." English translation: *On Psychological Prose*, trans. and ed. Judson Rosengrant (Princeton, NJ: Princeton University Press, 1991), 11, 14. Henceforth, "Ginzburg 1991."

2. Ginzburg 1977, 21; English in idem 1991, 15.

3. My translation, in *Lydia Ginzburg's Alternative Literary Identities*, ed. Emily Van Buskirk and Andrei Zorin (Oxford: Peter Lang AG, 2012), 376 (italics added). Russian in Lidiia Ginzburg, *Zapisnye knizhki. Vospominaniia. Esse.* (St. Petersburg: Iskusstvo-SPb, 2002), 281. Henceforth, "Ginzburg 2002." The essay "Generation at a Turning Point" was written in 1979 and first published in 1986.

4. Ginzburg 1977, 20. English in idem 1991, 15.

5. Lydia Ginzburg set apart *On Psychological Prose* from her previous books of literary scholarship by calling it her first "book" in an unpublished note from 1974, written at age seventy-two (before the publication of her essays/prose, and also before *On the Literary Hero*): "All the same *On Psychological Prose* is the only book of mine which I genuinely like. Because it is my only *book*. And *On the Lyric*—that is still literary scholarship. Good scholarship, but nonetheless. That which I do not want. And it [scholarship] won't leave me be; it must be that it won't let go of me—as long as I am able to work." Ginzburg folder labeled "1970s–80s," containing typescripts of essays from 1973–89. OR RNB 1377.

6. Ginzburg, ZK VIII–IX (July 1933–January 1935) 37–38. OR RNB 1377. Ginzburg also writes in this notebook entry that she was content neither to "accept in 'novelistic' characterization a method inappropriate for history," nor to "accept in history a method that in infinite abridgment cannot explain character."

7. Ibid. This portion of the note was published by Denis Ustinov in Ginzburg, "Stadii liubvi," *Kriticheskaia massa*, 1 (2002): 34.

8. Sociology did not develop as a discipline in Russia until the 1960s. Before the Revolution, it was part of the discipline of philosophy. After the Revolution, it was gradually replaced by historical materialism, a distorted variant of Marxist sociology. Sociology was criticized for its bourgeois origins, and for being too abstract and metaphysical. From the mid-1930s to the mid-1950s, sociology was nonexistent as an independent academic discipline, though ethnography and anthropology continued in some form. See Elizabeth Weinberg, *Sociology in the Soviet Union and Beyond: Social Enquiry and Social Change*, rev. ed. (Burlington, VT: Ashgate, 2004), 1–10. See also William Mills Todd III, "Between Marxism and Semiotics: Lidiia Ginzburg and Soviet Literary Sociology," *Canadian-American Slavic Studies* 19, 2 (1985): 159–66. On psychology, see Aleksandr Luriia, *Etapy proidennogo puti: Nauchnaia avtobiografia* (Moscow: Izdatel'stvo Moskovskogo universiteta, 2001); and David Joravsky, *Russian Psychology: A Critical History* (Oxford: Basil Blackwell, 1989).

9. For a concise treatment of Ginzburg's relationship to many of these influences, see Andrei Zorin, "Proza L.Ia. Ginzburg i gumanitarnaia mysl' XX veka," in *Novoe literaturnoe obozrenie* 76, 6 (2005): 45–68. For an expanded survey of the convergences and comparisons between Ginzburg's theories and those of German and American social psychologists, including Eduard Spranger, Alfred Adler, William James, George Herbert Mead, Kurt Lewin, Gordon Allport, Henry Murray, Kurt Goldstein, Abraham Maslow, and Carl Rogers, see Zorin's article "Ginzburg as Psychologist," in *Lydia Ginzburg's Alternative Literary Identities*, 83–123. He argues that Ginzburg was on the cutting edge of the sociopsychological theory being developed by her contemporaries in the 1930s and 1940s, even if she may not have been directly aware of them. On Bergson's influence on Russian Modernism, see Hilary Fink, *Bergson and Russian Modernism, 1900–1930* (Evanston, IL: Northwestern University Press, 1999). On Nietzsche, see *Nietzsche and Soviet Culture: Ally and Adversary*, ed. Bernice Glatzer Rosenthal (Cambridge, UK: Cambridge University Press, 1994).

10. See Ginzburg 1979, 6, where she references Mead's *Mind, Self and Society* (Chicago: University of Chicago Press, 1934). On the Mead-Ginzburg connection, see Andrei Zorin, "Ginzburg as Psychologist," *Lydia Ginzburg's Alternative Literary Identities*, 109–11.

11. On the functioning of hierarchies in Stalinist culture, see for example Sheila Fitzpatrick, *Everyday Stalinism: Ordinary Life in Extraordinary Times: Soviet Russia in the 1930s* (Oxford: Oxford University Press, 1999).

12. These are "passing" characters in a third sense as well: in the blockade, she was writing about "minor" characters in her projected novel, where she planned to focus on Bukhstab, Gukovsky, Ginzburg herself, Anna Akhmatova, and a few others. These "major" characters (other than Ginzburg) were evacuated at various points in the Blockade.

13. Ginzburg 1991, 127. Russian in idem 1977, 161.

14. See Ginzburg 1977, 325–29; English in idem 1991, 266–70. The first three volumes of *Klim Samgin* (1925–36) predated the official adoption of Socialist Realism in 1932, but

served as a model. As Katerina Clark points out, "negative heroes" such as Klim Samgin (a pre-Revolutionary character) became less popular in works of the 1930s and later. See Clark, *The Soviet Novel: History as Ritual,* 3rd ed. (Bloomington: Indiana University Press, 2000), 27, 45.

15. See Ginzburg, "The State of Literature near the End of the War," in *Lydia Ginzburg's Alternative Literary Identities,* 360–61. For the Russian, see Lidiia Ginzburg, *Prokhodiashchie kharaktery. Proza voennykh let. Zapiski blokadnogo cheloveka,* ed. Emily Van Buskirk and Andrei Zorin (Moscow: Novizdat, 2011), 100–101. Henceforth, "Ginzburg 2011." Andrei Zorin discusses this essay in terms of the larger dynamics of Socialist Realism in "Iz predystoria izucheniia sotsialistichekogo realizma (V. Khodasevich i L. Ginzburg o sovetskoi literature)," *Varietas et Concordia: Essays in Honour of Pekka Pesonen* (Helsinki: Slavic Helsingiensia, 2007), 322–27.

16. Ginzburg 2002, 277. I quote Joseph Brodsky's translation here from "In a Room and a Half," *Less than One* (New York: Farrar, Straus & Giroux, 1987), 482. Brodsky introduces Akhmatova's poem when discussing his parents' biographies and fates in the harsh and limited possibilities of the Soviet era. Ginzburg's discussion appears in English in "Generation at a Turning Point" in *Lydia Ginzburg's Alternative Literary Identities,* 370.

17. Ginzburg 2011, 74.

18. All of these waves of terror and mass extermination are in fact mentioned in some of Ginzburg's later essays, for example "At One with the Legal Order" (1980), where she tries to explain their absence from her earlier notes. See Ginzburg 2002, 285–96, esp. 287. Translation in *Lydia Ginzburg's Alternative Literary Identities,* 383–99, esp. 387.

19. See Irina Sandomirskaia's discussion, "The Leviathan, or Language in Besiegement: Lydia Ginzburg's Prolegomena to Critical Discourse Analysis," in *Lydia Ginzburg's Alternative Literary Identities,* 193–234.

20. In *Lydia Ginzburg's Alternative Literary Identities,* 360; Russian in Ginzburg 2011, 101.

21. Alexander Zholkovsky, "The Obverse of Stalinism: Akhmatova's Self-Serving Charisma of Selflessness," in *Self and Story in Russian History,* ed. Laura Engelstein and Stephanie Sandler (Ithaca, NY: Cornell University Press, 2000), 64–65. In this provocative piece on Anna Akhmatova, Zholkovsky argues that the poet adopted the strategies of a "despot" to survive totalitarian times. Ginzburg, in her notes on Akhmatova, interprets the poet's self-image as a remnant from an earlier epoch (see Ginzburg 2002, 44). Later, in the summer of 1945, Ginzburg remarks that Akhmatova advertises her moral superiority by ceaselessly reminding others that her "prosperity" comes from her victory over the state, which has retreated before her spiritual strength (Ginzburg 2011, 139), an observation much in line with Zholkovsky's portrayal. Ginzburg's notes from the late 1930s contain critical analyses of Akhmatova's methods of self-assertion in several dialogues. These may have been related to Ginzburg's work on *Home and the World,* in which Akhmatova would have been a character. As of October 2012, these dialogues are (mis-)catalogued as follows: Ginzburg Lidiia Iakovlevna. <Povedenie geroicheskoe i normal'noe>. Fragmenty esse raznykh let. Avtograf, mashinopis' s avtorskoi pravkoi. 1950-e–1980-e. 68 l.l. Op. 3 ed. khr. 57. OR RNB 1377. For some observations on Ginzburg's Akhmatova, see Andrew Kahn, "Lydia Ginzburg's 'Lives of the Poets': Mandelstam in Profile," in *Lydia Ginzburg's Alternative Literary Identities,* 183–84.

22. Mandelstam herself describes experiencing the opposite reaction: self-

effacement. Nadezhda Mandelstam, *Hope Abandoned,* trans. Max Hayward (New York: Atheneum, 1974), 6. In Russian: "Из этого следует, что выше всего стоит инстинкт самосохранения—спасайся, кто может и какими угодно способами.< . . . > Потеря "я" выразилась в ущербности (мой случай) или в открытом индивидуализме—ведь эгоцентризм и самоутверждение его крайние проявления." N. Mandel'shtam, *Vtoraia kniga: Vospominaniia,* ed. M. K. Polivanova (Moscow: Moskovskii rabochii, 1990), 12.

23. Ginzburg, "At One with the Legal Order," trans. Alyson Tapp, *Lydia Ginzburg's Alternative Literary Identities,* 384; Russian in Ginzburg 2002, 285.

24. Ginzburg's mode of being does not fit in with any of those Zholkovsky summarizes as belonging to such luminaries as Mandelstam, Pasternak, Eisenstein, and Mayakovsky (for example, enthusiasm, defiance, submission, exile, suicide).

25. She writes in "At One with the Legal Order": "In my case the justifying mechanism was less developed than the others; it was hindered by an inherent analytical propensity. The indifference mechanism, on the other hand, worked without a hitch." *Lydia Ginzburg's Alternative Literary Identities,* 394; Russian in Ginzburg 2002, 292.

26. On the importance of the hidden over the visible as a feature of individuation in Soviet society, see Oleg Kharkhordin's treatment of dissimulation in his book, *The Collective and the Individual in Russia: A Study of Practices* (Berkeley: University of California Press, 1999), 270–78.

27. See Sandomirskaia, "The Leviathan," in *Lydia Ginzburg's Alternative Literary Identities,* 193–234. Also see Andrei Zorin's comments in the roundtable "Analitika zhiznetvorchestva: Iu. M. Lotman i L. Ia. Ginzburg. Kul'turnye kody, sotsial'nye strategii i literaturnye tsenarii," *Novoe literaturnoe obozrenie* 82, 6 (2006): 93–121.

28. Ginzburg specified that this "readiness to suffer" emerged not from "personal moral qualities (which goes without saying), but was an indispensable condition, the most important constituent part of this social model." In Russian: "Интеллигенция в классическом понимании—это сознательные носители целенаправленной общественной мысли. Если таков основной интеллектуальный признак русской интеллигенции, то основной ее этический признак—готовность претерпеть. Она возникла не из личных нравственных качеств (это само собой), но была непременным условием, важнейшей составной частью этой социальной модели." Ginzburg 2002, 349–50.

29. After the Revolution, the term "intelligentsia" continued to be used, but in a completely new sense: as Malia writes, the Soviets defined the intelligentsia as "one of the three pillars of the socialist order, together with the proletariat and the toiling peasantry," referring to "all those who 'toil' with their minds instead of with their hands, that is the technological, liberal-professional, managerial, administrative, or merely white-collar personnel of the state." Martin Malia, "What Is the Intelligentsia?" in *The Russian Intelligentsia,* ed. Richard Pipes (New York: Columbia University Press, 1961), 2–3.

30. Ginzburg explains Herzen's term thus: "He was fond of speaking of human 'strata' and even invented the term 'constrators' [*soplastniki*]. 'Constrators' were not merely contemporaries, but fellow members of a particular historical stratum." Ginzburg 1991, 17; idem 1977, 23.

31. "And back there, in the glow of legends / Fool, hero, intelligent . . . / . . . and back there, in the glow of legends / The idealist-*intelligent* / Printed and penned placards / About the joy of his own sunset." In Russian: "А сзади, в зареве легенд / Дурак, герой, интеллигент . . . / . . . А сзади, в зареве легенд / Идеалист-интеллигент / Печатал и

писал плакаты / Про радость своего заката." The poem has two dates, 1923 and 1928. For the full poem and commentary, see Boris Pasternak, *Stikhotvoreniia i poemy v dvukh tomakh,* vol. 1 (Leningrad: Sovetskii pisatel', 1990), 238–46, 481–82. Cited in Ginzburg 2002, 284, in the essay "Generation at a Turning Point" ("Pokolenie na povorote"). Ginzburg also notes elsewhere that Pastnerak's "hero, fool, *intelligent*" was a type she studied "in its minutest details" ("разновидность, до тонкости нами изученная"). See Ginzburg 2002, 353.

32. These lines are from Pasternak's 1931 poem "More than a Century Ago—Not Yesterday" ("Stolet'e s lishnim—ne vchera"). See *Lydia Ginzburg's Alternative Literary Identities,* 389; Russian in Ginzburg 2002, 289.

33. In an unpublished essay from 1933, she writes:

"The history of the relationship of the humanities intelligentsia to the revolution is inconsistent and agonizing. It is the history of answers to two questions:

Can the Russian intelligentsia function outside of the pathways of the October Revolution?

and: Can the Russian intelligentsia function on the pathways of the revolution?

I, a person with a ruined literary fate, perhaps one whose creative life is over, say firmly: by age sixteen the answer to the first question was received—the Russian intelligentsia cannot function outside the pathways of the October Revolution.

Our fate holds an answer to the second question in the balance. And that's why this generation's fate is tragic."

In Russian: "История отношения гуманитарной интеллигенции к революции сбивчива и мучительна. Это история ответов на два вопроса:

Может ли русская интеллигенция функционировать вне путей Октябрьской революции?

и: Может ли русская интеллигенция функционировать на путях революции?

Я, человек с испорченной литературной судьбой, быть может, творчески погибший,—говорю твердо: к 16 годовщине ответ на первый вопрос получен—русская интеллигенция не может функционировать вне путей Октябрьской революции.

Наша судьба задерживает ответ на второй вопрос. Этим судьба поколения трагична."

Loose manuscript tucked into ZK VIII-2 (1933), and a later typescript of the same. OR RNB 1377.

34. Ginzburg 1936 notebook with sketch of "K." OR RNB 1377.

35. Ginzburg 2011, 70–71.

36. The high stakes may explain why Ginzburg, while similar to Erving Goffman in describing life in terms of a game or as drama, does not at all suggest that the acting out of a role could constitute what the latter calls the "bureaucratization" of self, which is uncomfortable for the fluid subject. See *The Goffman Reader,* ed. Charles Lemert and Ann Branaman (Oxford: Blackwell Publishing, 1997) 101–2.

37. Ginzburg 2011, 38. In the Blockade narrative "A Story of Pity and Cruelty," the hero mistakenly discounts his aunt's emotions as false: "The aberration consisted in the fact that his aunt was not a genuine person and that all of her reactions in life were just playful fictions [*igrovye fiktsii*]."

38. Ginzburg 2002, 60.

39. Unpublished essay "Metod rassmotreniia cheloveka," 5 January 1935. She writes, "I. A person is examined in relation to the values that define his desires, and in relation to the possibility for realizing these values. The differentiation of typological structures

of a person (the active type, the sensual type, the emotional type and so on) is based on how someone experiences life's values." In Russian: "I. Человек рассматривается в отношении ценностей, определяющих его желания, и в отношении возможности реализации этих ценностей. Различение типовых структур человека (активный тип, чувственный тип, эмоциональный тип и т.п.) основано на типе переживания жизненной ценности." Ginzburg ZK VIII–IX (1933–35), 82–85. OR RNB 1377.

40. Ginzburg writes, "Let us assume that a person is constructed by way of coordinating his social function with his biological and inherited traits. Let us assume that all of this is set in motion by the primary human need to realize the maximum of one's abilities—as a social being. A person realizes himself socially, finds a 'place,' assimilating and producing that which he experiences as a *value*." In Russian: "Допустим, что человек составляется во взаимодействии его социальной функции с его биологическими и наследственными предпосылками. Допустим, что все это приводится в движение первичной человеческой потребностью реализовать максимум своих возможностей—как существа социального. Человек социально реализуется, находит «место», воспринимая и продуцируя то, что переживается им как ценность." Unpublished essay from ZK VIII–IX (1933–35), dated 16 February 1934. OR RNB 1377.

41. A few years later (as it appears, though the notebook is not dated), when writing a sketch of S., Ginzburg reduced her typology to four types: active, emotional, sensitive, and intellectual. OR RNB 1377.

42. Eduard Spranger's "Ideally Basic Types of Individuality" are Theoretic, Economic, Aesthetic, Social, Political, and Religious (listed as "The Theoretic Attitude," and so on). Eduard Spranger, *Types of Men: The Psychology and Ethics of Personality*, authorized trans. by Paul J. W. Pigors (Halle: Max Niemeyer Verlag, 1928). Ginzburg also refers in her sketch of S. to Hippocrates' four humors as beginning this tradition of typology.

43. Like Ginzburg's, Martin Malia's definition of the intelligentsia hinges on the "primacy of the ideological." See Malia, 2.

44. Ginzburg describes intellectual types as aesthetes, dilettantes, individualists, and in her words, people with "sexual defects." See chapter 3.

45. Ginzburg uses the examples of Belinsky and Tolstoy. Of Belinsky, she writes: "There are few people who remain so unchanged in their lifetimes as Belinsky; but the reinterpretation carried out by *intelligents* of Belinsky's activities into a single liberal stream (with corrections for mistakes made during his period of reconciliation with reality)—is a huge mistake, and has made Belinsky completely incomprehensible." In Russian: "Мало кто быт всю жизнь так человечески неизменен как Белинский; но произведенное интеллигентами превращение деятельности Белинского в единый либеральный поток (с поправками на ошибки периода примирения с действительностью)—великая ошибка, от которой Белинский стал вообще непонятен." On Tolstoy, she argues that the young libertine and skeptic Tolstoy had the same psychological structure as Tolstoy the ascetic preacher in his seventies, but that their activities took place in drastically different historical contexts. Her view thus differs from the dominant interpretation of Tolstoy's spiritual crisis and conversion. Ibid.

46. Ginzburg 2002, 82. The original note is from ZK V (June 1929–January 1931), 112–13. OR RNB 1377.

47. Ginzburg 2002, 83.

48. See Keith Livers, *Constructing the Stalinist Body: Fictional Representations of Corporeality in the Stalinist 1930s* (New York: Lexington Books, 2004), 91–152. In his discus-

sion, Livers refers inter alia to Katerina Clark's discussion of nature versus culture in *The Soviet Novel* and Jochen Hellbeck's treatment of Soviet subjectivity in *Revolution on My Mind: Writing a Diary under Stalin* (Cambridge, MA: Harvard University Press, 2009).

49. Fyodor Dostoevsky, *The Brothers Karamazov*, trans. Constance Garnett, revised by Ralph E. Matlaw (New York: W.W. Norton & Company, 1976).

50. As McDuff also notes, *nadryv* derives from the French *déchirement*, meaning "breaking, tearing, and straining beneath an intolerable weight of mental, emotional and spiritual suffering." McDuff's footnote is quoted in Irina Levontina and Anna Zalizniak, "Human Emotions Viewed through the Russian Language," in *Emotions in Crosslinguistic Perspective*, ed. Jean Harkins and Anna Wierzbicka (Berlin: Mouton de Gruyter, 2001), 304.

51. Belknap writes that whereas "the buffoon makes himself laughable in order to make others so," the *nadryv* "causes a person to hurt himself in order to hurt others, or, perversely, to hurt others in order to hurt himself." Robert Belknap, *The Structure of the Brothers Karamazov* (The Hague: Mouton, 1967), 46.

52. The linguists Irina Levontina and Anna Zalizniak (who use a cognitive approach to language, aiming to describe emotions through language, following Anna Wierzbicka) write that *nadryv* has two opposite meanings: "an uncontrolled emotional outburst or an expression of forced and inauthentic emotions." In the second case, *nadryv* "verges on falseness or grotesque." Levontina and Zalizniak, "Human Emotions Viewed through the Russian Language," 303–4.

53. Ginzburg 2002, 493.

54. Ibid., 388. Ginzburg aligns the aesthetics of the Symbolists (particularly in a passage on Blok and Bely) with *nadryv*, whereas the aesthetics of Acmeism are the opposite—about filtering emotions through and making them dry. Ginzburg stylistically approaches Akhmatova and Mandelstam in certain ways. See also Levontina, "Dostoevskii nadryv," in *Kliuchevye idei russkoii iazykovoi kartiny mira*, ed. A. A. Zalizniak, I. B. Levontina, and A. D. Shmelev (Moscow: Iazyki slavianskoi kul'tury, 2005), 257.

55. On the significance of proper names in in-between prose as making what Dorrit Cohn calls "the distinction of fiction," see Lidiia Ginzburg, *O literaturnom geroe* (Leningrad: Sovetskii pisatel', 1979), 11–12. Henceforth, "Ginzburg 1979."

56. See chapter 3.

57. The Russian word *byt* is not directly synonymous with "everyday life." It signifies everyday routine, the domestic sphere, and stagnation, as opposed to *bytie* ("spiritual being," "transcendence"), and it became a target for both Symbolists and revolutionaries. See Svetlana Boym, *Common Places: Mythologies of Everyday Life in Russia* (Cambridge, MA: Harvard University Press, 1994), 29–40. See also Roman Jakobson, "On a Generation That Squandered Its Poets," in *Language and Literature*, ed. Krystyna Pomorska and Stephen Rudy (Cambridge, MA: Harvard University Press, 1987), 277, where Jakobson calls *byt* the element of "stagnating slime" that stabilizes the present.

58. Ginzburg added to her 1936 draft a much later footnote—probably in the 1980s, judging from the handwriting—correcting her error in seeing K.'s career as doomed: "This turned out not to be true (i.e., it was just a phase. Later she worked and achieved success)." 1936 notebook with sketch of "K." OR RNB 1377.

59. Levontina and Zalizniak write about the relationship between *nadryv* and the verb *nadryvat'sia*, meaning "to do something with a great effort." But this effort occurs not in the context of work, they tell us, but rather in "shouting, crying, and especially

coughing." Levontina and Zalizniak, "Human Emotions Viewed through the Russian Language," 303.

60. 1936 notebook with sketch of "K." OR RNB 1377.

61. Ibid.

62. Ginzburg, Blue notebook from approximately 1943–44 ("Svetoch"—12 listov, 10 kopeks) containing a sketch of "G.B." Currently located in a folder not yet catalogued, and mislabeled "Zapiski blokadnogo cheloveka. Esse. Chernovoi avtograf. 452 l." Also contains other unpublished character sketches from the blockade period. OR RNB 1377.

63. For a feminist treatment of Ginzburg's analysis of G.B. (who is disguised as "P.V." in part 2 of *Zapiski blokadnogo cheloveka*), see Irina Sandomirskaia, "Rage in the City of Hunger: Body, Talk, and the Politics of Womanliness in Lidia Ginzburg's Notes from the Siege of Leningrad," in *Embracing Arms: Cultural Representation of Slavic and Balkan Women in War*, ed. Helena Goscilo with Yana Hashamova (Budapest/New York: Central European University Press, 2012), 131–51.

64. In her book *On Psychological Prose*, Ginzburg uses the hero of *Notes from Underground* as an example of "a reverse form of self-affirmation" [*oprokinutaia forma samoutverzhdeniia*]. It is significant that she associates *nadryv* with Dostoevsky's hero, who creates an elevating aesthetic out of "deliberate foolishness, self-abasement, and hysterical display" [*iurodstvo, samounichizhenie, nadryv*]. See Ginzburg 1991, 286; Russian in idem 1977: 348.

65. In Russian: "Хамство тем и отличается от грубости, наглости и нахальства, что оно непобедимо, что с ним невозможно бороться, что перед ним можно только отступить < . . . > хамство есть не что иное, как грубость, наглость, нахальство, вместе взятые, но при этом—умноженные на безнаказанность < . . . > Именно безнаказанностью своей хамство и убивает вас наповал, вам нечего ему противопоставить, кроме собственного унижения, потому что хамство—это всегда «сверху вниз», это всегда «от сильного—слабому», потому что хамство—это беспомощность одного и безнаказанность другого, потому что хамство—это неравенство." Sergei Dovlatov, "Eto neperevodimoe slovo—'khamstvo,'" in *Sobranie sochinenii v chetyrekh tomakh*, vol. 4 (St. Petersburg: Azbuka, 2002), 324–25. I would like to thank Rebecca Frumkina for pointing me to Dovlatov, for the definition of "offensive boldness," and for helpful e-mail correspondence on the subject in January 2011.

66. Unlike Herzen, Merezhkovsky believed the savior must be the "approaching Christ," who would be at home in a religious community fostered by the "heart and conscience" of the Russian intelligentsia. See Dmitrii Merezhkovskii, "Griadushchii kham," in *Polnoe sobranie sochinenii*, vol. 11 (St. Petersburg: Izdanie T-va M.O Vol'f, 1911) 31, 36.

67. Iurii Lotman, "Besedy o russkoi kul'ture. Televizionnye lektsii. Tsikl 2: Kul'tura i intelligentnost'," in *Vospitanie dushi* (St. Petersburg: Isskustvo-SPb, 2003), 473.

68. Ibid., 472.

69. If one understands a *kham* as a petty tyrant who might also be found among peasants and the lower social classes, one finds examples in the plays of Anton Chekhov from the turn of the twentieth century. In *The Cherry Orchard*, for example, the young servant Yasha is a consistent *kham*, with a sneer and an insult for everyone, especially his inferiors. Though a lackey, he thinks highly of himself, since he has traveled abroad. To the 87-year-old servant Firs's touching speech about his mortality and health, Yasha

replies, "How you weary me, Grandad! [*Yawns.*] I wish you'd go away and die soon." Anton Chekhov, *Plays*, trans. Elisaveta Fen (London: Penguin Books, 1959), 378.

70. See for example the traveler in Zoshchenko's story "Khamstvo," the rude "lady aristocrat" in Zoshchenko's eponymous story ("Aristokratka" in Russian), the customers as well as the bath attendant in "The Bathhouse," and the young man who is rude to his elderly mother in "The Grimace of NEP." Mikhail Zoshchenko, *Sobranie sochinenii v trekh tomakh*, vol. 1 (Moscow: Terra, 1994), 170–73, 278–80, 400–402.

71. The scholars of rhetoric Svetlana and Georgii Khazagerov have written of *khamstvo* (and its depiction in Zoshchenko) as a product of the first stage of a "dehumanitarianization" in the Stalinist subject who lacks Christian morality, national roots, and the cultural forms of the *intelligent*, and therefore displays "short-sighted pragmatism." Svetlana and Georgii Khazagerov, "Kul'tura-1, Kul'tura 2 i gumanitarnaia kul'tura," *Znamia* 3, at http://khazagerov.com/cultural-situation/107-culture1–2.html, accessed 31 December 2013.

72. Ginzburg 1991, 335; Russian in idem 1977, 406.

73. As Ginzburg writes while quoting from Shklovsky's *Zoo*, "Words avenge" (*Slova mstiat*): "and that means—you say that 'it [my love, for example] is meaningless' to you, and I will describe how you say this, I will describe, if I want to, how you open your mouth and what you are thinking when you say it." Ginzburg 2002, 149.

74. Ginzburg 1991, 335; Russian in idem 1977, 406.

75. Vladislav Khodasevich, "Dekol'tirovannaia loshchad'" (1927), in *Sobranie sochinenii v chetyrekh tomakh*, vol. 2 (Moscow: Soglasie, 1996), 162.

76. Zholkovsky also calls Mayakovsky the myth an "extremist—avant-gardist—terrorist." He explicates themes such as violence and misogyny that make Mayakovsky's poetry far from moral or pure. Alexander Zholkovsky, "O genii i zlodeistve, o babe i vserossiiskom masshtabe (Progulki po Maiakovskomu)," in *Izbrannye stat'i o russkoi poezii: Invarianty, struktury, strategii, interteksty* (Moscow: Rossiiskii gosudarstvennyi gumanitarnyi universitet, 2005), 208–9.

77. Ginzburg 2002, 427. She issued this definition within a critique of Zholkovksy's article on the proletarian poet (the article first appeared in 1986). Ginzburg sided with Roman Jakobson's characterization of Mayakovsky in "A Generation That Squandered Its Poets."

78. After Mayakovsky's suicide in 1930, Ginzburg recorded a conversation in which Shklovsky said to her: "Everyone around [Mayakovsky] wrote in their diaries that he was an unsympathetic person. And you wanted to write an article about him as a wonderful poet, but ended up not writing it. I didn't write one either. But maybe that's what Volodya [Mayakovsky] needed?" Ginzburg 2002, 80.

79. Ginzburg 2011, 87. Reshetov's wife was Tatyana Georgievna Paiusova, who headed the cultural section of the Leningrad City Committee VKP(b).

80. Ibid., 88.

81. Based on the paper and handwriting, the sketch appears to have been composed in the late 1930s, perhaps as late as 1940, judging from the fact that S.'s real-life counterpart was born in 1901, and her age is given as "approaching forty" (*pod sorok*).

82. Ginzburg notebook "S," 16 pages, from the late 1930s or 1940. OR RNB 1377.

83. Ginzburg writes a note that seems to contradict this portrait in her 1936 notebook (which I believe to predate this sketch of S.). She writes of drinking vodka with S., who opens up about her difficult relationship with a man who turned out to be impotent. The note ends: "This story surprised me, since I considered that S. was an interest-

ing woman because she lived without love and even without affairs—on the order of some kind of eccentricity. My mistake confirms a methodological premise for me: every person, independent from outward appearance, lives approximately according to the laws of nature." 1936 notebook with sketch of "K." (27 pages). OR RNB 1377.

84. In Russian: "оно [мышление] перекладывает вину на обстоятельства и озлобляется на обстоятельства. Гедонистической жизни не может быть, следовательно жизнь ужасна, все обман, лучше бы собственно умереть." Ginzburg, notebook with sketch of "S." OR RNB 1377.

85. Ibid.

86. The blockade produced a life estrangement: toward one's body, the city, and language. Ginzburg uses the devices of estrangement in her blockade prose, *Notes of a Blockade Person*. See chapters 1 and 5. In the words of Shklovsky, "Habitualization devours works, clothes, furniture, one's wife, and the fear of war." Shklovsky's 1917 essay "Art as Technique" in *Russian Formalist Criticism: Four Essays* (Lincoln: University of Nebraska Press, 1965), 12.

87. Ginzburg 2011, 60. The siege diarist Sofiia Ostrovskaia describes the process of recovering one's identity in a more literal way: "one sees fewer and fewer of those terrifying dystrophics: they've died out—or they're recovering and, instead of naked skulls, they're again beginning to wear a face" In Russian: "Жутких дистрофиков встречается все меньше: вымерли—или поправляются и, вместо обнажающегося черепа, вновь начинают носить лицо." Sofiia Ostrovskaia, *Dnevnik*, ed. P. Iu. Barskova and T. S. Pozdniakova (Moscow: Novoe literaturnoe obozrenie, 2013), 345.

88. The euphemistic term diverted responsibility from the state for the death of the citizenry. For a discussion of dystrophy, see Sandomirskaia, "The Leviathan, or Language in Besiegement," 193–99, who refers to Mikhail Chernorutskii, ed., *Alimentarnaia distrofiia v blokirovannom Leningrade* (Leningrad: Medgiz, 1947). See also *Writing the Siege of Leningrad*, ed. Cynthia Simmons and Nina Perlina (Pittsburgh, PA: University of Pittsburgh Press, 2002), xxx, and 225–26 n. 56–57.

89. Ginzburg 2011, 75.

90. Esfir' Levina, "Dnevnik 12 ianvaria 1942–6 iunia 1943," in *Chelovek v blokade: novye svidetel'stva* (St. Petersburg: Ostrov, 2008), 159. As another exemplary usage of this term, the diarist Liubov' Shaporina writes of how she reacted to stories of cannibalism with the idea "of starting an album dedicated to those of my friends and acquaintances who have lived through these two years here and did not dystrophy morally [*moral'no ne distrofirovali*]." Entry from 17 July 1943 in Liubov' Shaporina, *Dnevnik*, vol. 1, ed. V. F. Petrova and V. N. Sazhin (Moscow: Novoe literaturnoe obozrenie, 2011), 402–3.

91. Ginzburg 2011, 69.

92. The semiautobiographical fragment called "Otsepenenie" ("Torpor") is subtitled "Confessions of a Recovered Dystrophic."

93. Ginzburg 2011, 60–61.

94. One wonders about the influence of Zinaida Gippius on the number of female Don Juans Ginzburg identifies in her milieu. On Gippius as "female dandy," see Jenifer Presto, *Beyond the Flesh: Alexander Blok, Zinaida Gippius, and the Symbolist Sublimation of Sex* (Madison: University of Wisconsin Press, 2008), 160–89. See also Olga Matich, *Erotic Utopia: The Decadent Imagination in Russia's Fin de Siècle* (Madison: University of Wisconsin Press, 2005), 162–212. Matich's discussion of Gippius draws connections to a Dostoevsky character known for *nadryv*, Nastas'ia Filipovna.

95. T.'s story takes unexpected turns over the course of Ginzburg's notes. She suffers

a greater catastrophe: hit by a bomb in December 1943, she survived, but at the cost of losing a leg. Surprisingly, as Ginzburg realizes on a hospital visit after the amputation, this tragedy served as the catalyst for a new romance with a female member of the hospital staff. This new highpoint (even higher because unexpected) returns her self-image specifically through catastrophe. She avoids pity, and is loved instead. At least this is a *peredyshka* before any further hardships, Ginzburg writes. Ginzburg 2011, 121–28.

96. Ibid., 74.

97. Ibid., 75.

98. She writes, after an "interview" with N.P.: "Beyond this biological life-affirmation, *intelligents* occasionally, when it is their lot—construct self-conceptions of troglodytism, fatalism, etc., to make things beautiful and interesting." Ibid., 71.

99. See, for instance, the diary of Anna Likhacheva, who writes that "Life during those months made fatalists of us all," in *Writing the Siege of Leningrad*, 61. See also Liubov' Shaporina, "Everyone's used to it, all have become fatalists and pay no attention to the din and to the impending danger." Entry from 4 June 1941 in Liubov' Shaporina, *Dnevnik*, vol. 1, 327.

100. Ginzburg 2011, 70.

101. Ilya Utekhin uses this term in "O smysle vkliuchennogo nabliudeniia povsednevnosti," *Istoriia povsednevnosti* (St. Petersburg: Evropeiskii universitet v Sankt Peterburge, Aleteiia, 2003), 15–24.

102. The essay was first published in *Pretvorenie opyta* (*Transformation of Experience*), the book that was edited by Nikolai Kononov and came out shortly after Ginzburg's death. As I determined through an interview and through studying handwriting, Kononov himself created the titles for some essays in this publication. It is unclear whether the title for this essay is his, but in the archival typescript, the essay is untitled. The setting for the initial observations and reflections is a meeting at the Writers' Union, but Ginzburg moves to other scenes from there. The typescript is dated, in what appears to be Kushner's handwriting, spring 1975; the published version has the date 1974. Ginzburg scribbled a note about Saint-Simon on the typescript of the essay. Difficult to decipher, it appears to say "in Saint-Simon, the king's brother with tactics and fearlessness" ("у Сен-Симона брат короля с тактиками [?] и бесстрашием"). OR RNB 1377.

103. Ginzburg 1991, 135. Russian in idem 1977, 171. In Russian: ". . . где-то в основе—наиболее общая социально-моральная типология эпохи, затем изученная Сен-Симоном при французском дворе «социальная механика», которую он и считал главным предметом истории, и личный характер, в котором индивидуальные, иногда причудливые черты вплетаются в сеть повторяющихся формул. Устойчивая типологическая схема и ее непрестанные дифференцирующие нарушения—вот метод Сен-Симона."

104. Ginzburg 1991, 141; idem in Ginzburg 1977, 178. As Ginzburg notes, Saint-Simon's memoirs were allowed into print only some one hundred years after they were written, since the government of Louis XV feared their impact (Ginzburg 1991, 107; Ginzburg 1977, 135).

105. Ginzburg 1991, 138; Russian in idem 1977, 174–75. I consistently use Rosengrant's English translation, but here I correct his "attribute" in the singular to the appropriate plural form.

106. Ibid. In Russian: ". . . положение в расстановке сил сенсимоновского мира, в основных конфликтах этого обширного, но замкнутого мира, где непрерывно про-

исходит столкновение начал положительных [высшая аристократия] и отрицательных [буржуазные выскочки, королевские чиновники . . . .”

107. Sarah Pratt, “Lidiia Ginzburg, A Russian Democrat at the Rendezvous,” *Canadian-American Slavic Studies* 28, 2–3 (1996): 186. This article has appeared in Russian: Sara Pratt, “Lidiia Ginzburg, russkii democrat na rendez-vous,” trans. Ia. Tokareva, *Novoe literaturnoe obozrenie* 49, 3 (2001): 387–400. Pratt explains this phenomenon based on a confluence of circumstances, including Ginzburg’s “ethnic background, her sex . . . and her marital status,” all of which separated her from the establishment.

108. Pratt (English), 195.

109. Kirill Kobrin, “ ‘Chelovek 20-x godov’: Sluchai Lidii Ginzburg (K postanovke problemy),” *Novoe literaturnoe obozrenie* 78, 2 (2006): 60–83. The quotation comes from p. 67. In Russian: “Важнейшая часть характеристики «людей 20-х»—беспредельный энтузиазм, бешеная энергия, удивительный пафос, то, что вообще считается чуть ли не главными признаками этого советского десятилетия.”

110. Kobrin, 66.

111. Ginzburg writes of the tradition among “students of OPOYAZ” of combining skepticism and decency in Ginzburg 2002, 26. On irony, see for example the amusing note in ibid., 407.

112. “Sobranie,” Ginzburg 2002, 346.

113. She writes, “Contemporary sociology has shown that a person is a social organization, governed not by the tyranny of personal desires and even less by logic, but by various mechanisms which are instilled in him through group values and norms (this idea goes back to Marx, with his lesson about how interests are transformed into ideals).” In Russian: “Современная социология показала, что человек—это социальное устройство, управляемое не личным произволом, еще менее логикой, но разными механизмами, внушающими ему групповые ценности и нормы (так уже у Маркса, с его учением о превращении интересов в идеалы).” Ibid., 347. She started using the expressions “group consciousness” and “group self-concept” already in the Leningrad Blockade. See for example Ginzburg 2002, 184. She writes also of “group consciousness” and “group values” in her 1979 book *On the Literary Hero*, where she shows an extensive knowledge of Western sociology.

114. Ginzburg 1991, 138; Ginzburg 1977, 175.

115. Ginzburg 2002, 351.

116. Ibid., 359.

117. The full passage reads: “We shall leave aside the different mental gradations. But a schematic gradation is yielded for example by my old theory of dividing people into decent people (who basically have not survived), half-decent people, scoundrels who wanted to do what they did, and half-scoundrels, who unwillingly did what they did, and therefore did it a bit less.” In Russian: “Оставим в покое разные душевные градации. Но схематическую градацию дает хотя бы моя старая теория разделения людей на порядочных (которые в основном не сохранились), полупорядочных, мерзавцев, которые хотели делать то, что они делали, полумерзавцев, которые не хотели делать то, что они делали, и потому делали немного меньше.” Ibid.

118. Ginzburg 2002, 346.

119. Ibid., 351.

120. Ibid.

121. Ibid.

122. In Russian: “Подмененные темы выполняют разные функции. Они создают

видимость деятельности, что собравшимся практически нужно, и видимость высказываний, разумных, даже либеральных и благородных,—что всегда приятно высказывающимся." Ibid.

123. Ibid., 352.

124. For a short biography of Plotkin, see *Pushkinskii Dom: Materialy k istorii. 1905–2005* (St. Petersburg: Bulanina, 2005), 505–6. On Plotkin's role in Leningrad literary life of the 1940s, see P. A. Druzhinin, *Ideologiia i filologiia: Leningrad, 1940-e gody*, 2 vols. (Moscow: Novoe literaturnoe obozrenie, 2012). For Plotkin's role in Eikhenbaum's postwar difficulties, see Carol Any, *Boris Eikhenbaum: Voices of a Russian Formalist* (Stanford, CA: Stanford University Press, 1994), 175, 200.

125. Ginzburg 2002, 354.

126. On Bazanov, Makogonenko, and the other figures Ginzburg analyzes here, as well as for a deep treatment (with substantial archival documentation) of the Leningrad literary establishment in the 1940s, see P. A. Druzhinin, *Ideologiia i filologiia: Leningrad, 1940-e gody*.

127. Viktor Vinogradov, too, makes a brief appearance as V-ov (serving as an example of a "bad dignitary," as opposed to Orlov). Ginzburg 2002, 359. In the typescript, there is a coda on Dmitry Yevgenievich Maksimov (1904–87), cut from the final version. OR RNB 1377.

128. Ginzburg 2002, 363.

129. Ibid. In Russian: "Волеизъявление их опосредствовано продуктами их творчества и труда."

130. Ginzburg imagines that if Eikhenbaum had survived to his "renaissance," he would have become a "patriarch" surrounded by admirers of his person and charm, and Gukovsky would have returned to his original methods of ravishing minds. Ibid., 366.

131. There are many testimonies to Gukovsky's unparalleled talents as a lecturer. See for example Lidiia M. Lotman, *Vospominaniia* (St. Petersburg: Nestor-Istoriia, 2007), 100–117.

132. Ginzburg 2002, 361.

133. Though Ginzburg does not discuss it here, Gukovsky was capable not only of producing great scholarship and mentoring great students but also of standing up against the positions of official Soviet scholarship. For example, together with Eikhenbaum and V. V. Gippius, he was a strong opponent at the defense of Dymshits's dissertation, which was meant to serve as a Soviet-style model. See Lidiia Lotman, 116–17. Dymshits's odious behavior is a subject of many of Ginzburg's wartime notes. See for example Ginzburg 2011, 194, 207.

134. In Russian: "Зато поведение общественное единственное в своем роде. Поведение было возведено в осознанную историческую роль. Ценою лишений и риска платил он за то, чтобы сберечь person'у. Это был истинно бесстрашный человек. Что не противоречит натуре—избалованные женщины бывали порой особенно бесстрашны. Собрание. Ритуальная формула председательствующего. Кто за? Кто против?—Никого против. Единогласно. И вот почти в нулевом промежутке между «никого против» и «единогласно» он поднимает руку—один в задержавшем дыхание зале." Ginzburg 2002, 365.

135. In Russian: "Еще позднее он иногда уступал, но тогда уже все перешло человеческий предел. Притом научные ориентиры были потеряны. Школа ушла из-под ног." Archival typescript for "Sobranie," 1974/5, in the folder of essays from the 1970s and 1980s. OR RNB 1377.

136. This sketch, written ca. June 1945 and titled "Intellectual Egoists Who Have Stopped Thinking" ("Intellektual'nye egoisty, perestavshie dumat'"), was unpublished in Ginzburg's lifetime: it is included in Ginzburg 2011, 139–47. The poignancy of this critical portrait issues from Lydia Ginzburg's earlier admiration for her teacher, and her disappointment in what she saw as his current "incapacity to elaborate large, interconnected concepts." Ibid., 139.

137. To demonstrate this, Ginzburg reproduces a conversation where Eikhenbaum is overeager to advertise his ironic relationship to his bureaucratic position. When she has to deliver to him for review her *tvorcheskii otchet*, a kind of report on her work of the past few years, he jokes, "Why don't they just request these for our whole lifetime in advance, already?" He further quips that this will not be one of her "works" that holds particular interest for him, and so he will not read it, but will sign it blindly. Ibid., 141.

138. In Russian: "Не получив ничего, можно замкнуться в гордом и насмешливом равнодушии, но раз попав в иерархический механизм, этого уже нельзя. Иерархическое ощущение, особенно в беспокойной и неустойчивой обстановке, это непрестанное ощущение двустороннего нажима. Снизу вас вздымает наверх, а сверху опять жмет и отбрасывает вниз." Ibid., 142.

139. This is a quotation from Gogol's satirical play *The Inspector General* (*Revizor*): "Why are you laughing? It is at yourselves that you laugh!"

140. In Russian: "Таким образом, у них два противоречивых начала—одно неудержимый восторг, соответствующий их реальной функции и ситуации чиновников; другое—насмешка (над собой смеетесь . . .), соответствующая их фиктивной (призрачной) функции интеллигентов с ее фиктивными традициями. Причем это начало поддерживается профессиональной необходимостью и привычкой все время умиляться по поводу традиций, как раз запрещающих этот восторг. Не следует также забывать, что второе начало несет в себе столь дорогое для человека переживание собственного морального превосходства." Ginzburg 2011, 142.

141. In the section on Eikhenbaum in the published essay "A Meeting," Ginzburg is more charitable. She writes: "Later he took a liking for appointments and marks of distinction. But he related to them partially as a game or as something exotic, as something that did not become him and was therefore interesting for his audience. They sometimes gave him these toys, sometimes took them away. When they gave them, he was vainglorious, and when they took them away, he was always well-prepared with his magnificent stubbornness." In Russian: "Позднее ему стали нравиться должности и знаки отличия. Но относился он к ним отчасти как к игре или к экзотике, то есть к чему-то ему неподобающему и поэтому для аудитории занимательному. Игрушки эти ему то давали, то опять отбирали. Когда давали, тщеславился; когда отбирали, у него тут же, всегда наготове, было его великолепное упрямство." Ginzburg 2002, 365.

142. Ibid., 350. By this measure, she excludes the Decembrists: they protested, but greeted their punishment with surprise. Ginzburg also writes that the Decembrists were too close to power—the classic intelligentsia position is to be separated from power by an abyss (ibid.). Martin Malia agrees that the Decembrists predated the intelligentsia's rise, and he too points out this proximity to power, but not the readiness to suffer. Malia, 9.

143. Ginzburg 2002, 350.

144. Cf. her essay "Résumé of Failure," from January 1944 in Ginzburg 2011, 164–74.

145. Marietta Chudakova discussed the period from 1943–45 or early 1946 in Soviet

literature as a “short thaw” in *Izbrannye raboty*, vol. 1 (Moscow: Iazyki russkoi kul’tury, 2001), 363, 384. See also Andrei Zorin, “Iz predistoriia izucheniia sotsialistichekogo realizma (V. Khodasevich i L. Ginzburg o sovetskoi literature).”

146. Ginzburg 2002, 360. In Russian: “О таких говорят ласково, с интонацией самоосуждения: «Этого человека я уважаю. Он построил свою жизнь, как хотел». Да, как хотел. Только большая часть этой жизни ушла на темную работу, только порой он не имел рубля на обед. Но вам он не сообщал об этом.” One should recall that at the time of composition, Ginzburg was still an unpublished author.

147. Ibid., 354. I believe this passage to be self-referential. This section contrasts Gukovsky, Bukhstab (as can be guessed with certainty), and Ginzburg. These three were to be characters who were compared on this basis—three friends, top students at the Institute, whose fates diverged considerably based on their different personalities—in *Home and the World*. OR RNB 1377.

148. Ginzburg 2002, 348.

149. In *Lydia Ginzburg's Alternative Literary Identities*, 399. Russian in Ginzburg 2002, 296.

CHAPTER 5. TRANSFORMATIONS OF EXPERIENCE

1. Lidiia Ginzburg, “<Gruppovoe soznanie Leningradtsev>,” from the 1943–46 notebook, published in *Prokhodiashchie kharaktery. Proza voennykh let. Zapiski blokadnogo cheloveka*, ed. Van Buskirk and Zorin (Moscow: Novizdat, 2011), 188. Henceforth, “Ginzburg 2011.” The essay was first published in *Pretvorenie opyta* (Riga, 1991) as “Leningradskaia situatsia” and reprinted in Lidiia Ginzburg, *Zapisnye knizhki. Vospominaniia. Esse* (St. Petersburg, 2002), 184–86. Henceforth, “Ginzburg 2002.” The siege was lifted on 27 January 1944.

2. Ginzburg 2011, 188–89. A draft letter in the archive indicates that Ginzburg herself made attempts to leave Leningrad temporarily in July 1943, seeking help from the Writers’ Union and from her brother. She states clearly that she did not want to part with the city for good; but she seems to dread another winter in Blockade Leningrad. Ginzburg in fact never left the city during the siege. See Ginzburg Lidiia Iakovlevna. Pis’mo bratu Viktoru Ginzburgu. 20.07.b.g. 2 l. l. OR RNB 1377, ed. khr. 84.

3. Ginzburg 2011, 189.

4. Ibid., 106. English in *Lydia Ginzburg's Alternative Literary Identities*, 367.

5. Ginzburg 2011, 107.

6. Ibid., 105.

7. Ibid., 113. Ginzburg did not know Olga Berggolts’s private diaries, first published in the 1991 in the almanac *Aprel’* 4 (1991). New excerpts came out recently in *Ol’ga. Zapretnyi dnevnik*, ed. Nataliia Sokolovskaia (St. Petersburg: Azbuka-klassika, 2010).

8. This composition remains Ginzburg’s most translated work. A Dutch translation by Jan Robert Braat appeared in 1988 as *Omsingeld: notities van een belegerde*. The first English translation (1990) was “The Siege of Leningrad: Notes of a Survivor,” by Gerald Mikelson and Margaret Winchell, in *Soviet Women Writing*. The second was Alan Myers’s *Blockade Diary* (which will be republished, edited by E. Van Buskirk, with “A Story of Pity and Cruelty” [translated by Angela Livingstone] as *Notes from the Leningrad Blockade* by Random House). A German translation by Gerhard Hacker appeared in 1997 as *Aufzeichnungen eines Blockademenschen*. In 2014, Suhrkamp published a new edition of *Aufzeichnungen eines Blockademenschen*, which includes a translation of “A Story

of Pity and Cruelty." A French translation by Christian Bourgois was published in 1998, as *Journal du siège de Léningrad*. A Swedish translation appeared in 1999 as *Anteckningar från belägringen*, by Karin Grelz. A Finnish translation, *Leningradin piirityksen päiväkirja*, was published in 2011. On the earlier publications see Judson Rosengrant, "L. Ia. Ginzburg: An International Chronological Bibliography of Primary and Secondary Works," *Russian Review* 54, 4 (October 1995): 587–600.

9. For a full history of the text and Ginzburg's revisions, see Ginzburg 2011, 545–56. The text originally published in 1984 (*Neva* 1) as "Zapiski blokadnogo cheloveka" was republished, with slight modifications, in *Literatura v poikskakh real'nosti* (Leningrad: Sovetskii pisatel', 1987) and *Chelovek za pis'mennym stolom* (Leningrad: Sovetskii pisatel', 1989). In the latter book, Ginzburg added the section "Vokrug *Zapisok blokadnogo cheloveka*" (Around *Notes of a Blockade Person*). At the time of her death, she was working with the assistance of Nikolai Kononov to publish "Part 2" of *Notes* (and essays from the 1940s), which came out in 1991 in *Pretvorenie opyta*. All three parts appear together in Ginzburg 2002.

10. Ginzburg 2011, 327, 343.

11. Ibid., 311.

12. A phrase used in relation to Rousseau and Herzen in Lidiia Ginzburg, *O psikhologicheskoi proze*, 2nd ed. (Leningrad: Khudozhestvennaia literatura, 1977). Henceforth, "Ginzburg 1977." See for example p. 204. English in *On Psychological Prose*, trans. Judson Rosengrant (Princeton, NJ: Princeton University Press, 1991), 163. Henceforth, "Ginzburg 1991."

13. Ginzburg 1991, 7; Russian in idem 1977, 10.

14. See Leona Toker, "Toward a Poetics of Documentary Prose—from the Perspective of Gulag Testimonies," *Poetics Today* 18, 2 (Summer 1997): 187–222. Susan Suleiman treats issues of generic heterogeneity in memoirs of the Holocaust (which she defines as a collective historical trauma) in *Crises of Memory and the Second World War* (Cambridge, MA: Harvard University Press, 2006). See especially 160–61.

15. I found the text we titled "Rasskaz o zhalosti i o zhestokosti" in spring 2006, in the portion of the Ginzburg archive then held by Alexander Kushner. The manuscript was lying in a folder behind a draft of "Delusion of the Will"; it had been misclassified as a variant of the same. The two texts may have been stored together by Ginzburg herself, or they may have been placed in the single folder by Al'bin Konechnyi (one of the first to organize the archive) or Kushner. None of the friends of Ginzburg I interviewed knew of this text or the story contained in it. The story was published for the first time in Ginzburg 2011, 17–59. For a detailed description of the manuscript, see ibid. 557–58.

16. Though Ginzburg did not write a title on her blockade era drafts, the narrative we have titled "Den' Ottera" was labeled in one place by her in handwriting of the 1960s, indicating the change of hero, in the following way: "Den' Ottera—N" "(Otter's—N's Day)." See Ginzburg 2011, 208–82, and also 568.

17. Ginzburg 2011, 353. In the 1960s draft, there is an elusive continuation of this passage: "But I will yet return to the blockade story of O., a story of pity and of cruelty." Ibid.

18. One exception is the diaries of Yura Riabinkin (included in Ales' Adamovich and Daniil Granin's *Blokadnaia kniga*), in which the child recounts suspicions that his mother was dividing food inequitably, and describes the tenor of their conversations as follows: "No matter what the conversation touched upon—there was swearing, shout-

ing, hysterics, something of the sort." *Blokadnaia kniga*, ed. Ales' Adamovich and Daniil Granin, 5th ed. (Leningrad, 1989), 378. Ginzburg suggests that the *Book of the Blockade* (*Blokadnaia kniga*) encouraged her own pursuit of publication in 1984, and singles out the diary of Riabinkin as a "very strong testimony." Interview with G. Silina, *Literaturnaia gazeta* 3, 5069 (15 January 1986). Fragments from Riabinkin's diaries were published in *Smena* in 1970 (see *Blokadnaia kniga*, 266). *Blokadnaia kniga* made it past the Moscow censors, with many cuts, in 1979, and more fully in 1982; it was printed in Leningrad in 1984. See Arlen Blium, *Kak eto delalos' v Leningrade: Tsenzura v gody ottepeli, zastoia i perestroika 1953–1991* (St. Petersburg: Akademicheskii proekt, 2005), 167.

19. Ginzburg 2011, 35.

20. Ibid., 313–14.

21. Alexander Zholkovsky explicates the relationship of analysis to lyricism using one passage from Ginzburg's prose in "Between Genres," *Canadian-American Slavic Studies* 28, 2–3 (Summer–Fall 1994): 147–60. This essay was republished in *Lydia Ginzburg's Alternative Literary Identities*, ed. Emily Van Buskirk and Andrei Zorin (Oxford: Peter Lang AG, 2012), 33–37.

22. Karin Grelz has written about how Ginzburg builds her observations into sentences that have the quality of formulae or axioms—and how this "closed system" mirrors the Blockade. See Grel'ts, "Osazhdennyi smysl," in *Novoe literaturnoe obozrenie* 49, 3 (2001): 401–2.

23. Ginzburg 2011, 356.

24. See my discussion in chapter 1 about Ginzburg's theories of guilt and remorse as a source of art.

25. Ginzburg 2011, 358. An alternative translation would be: "In the abyss of lost time is time found." In Russian: "В бездне потерянного времени—найденное."

26. Irina Paperno, "Sovetskii opyt, avtobiograficheskoe pis'mo i istoricheskoe soznanie: Ginzburg, Gertsen, Gegel'," *Novoe literaturnoe obozrenie* 68, 4 (2004): 102–27, esp. 109–10. Ilya Kukulin has further argued that both Herzen and Ginzburg were "reformers" or even "revolutionaries" of their genres of notes, in part because of how their self-understanding diverged from that of their respective generations. Il'ia Kukulin, "Traditsiia intellektual'nogo odinochestva: Gertsen. Povorot bez pokoleniia: Aleksandr Gertsen i Lidiia Ginzburg kak revoliutsionery zhanrov," *Novoe literaturnoe obozrenie* 58, 6 (2002): 111–22.

27. Lidiia Ginzburg, "Gertsen—sozdatel' 'Bylogo i dum,'" *Zvezda* 2 (1944): 129–35.

28. Ginzburg defended her candidate's dissertation in 1940 on Mikhail Lermontov, and from 1944–1947 was a doctoral student at the Institute of Literature of the Academy of Sciences, working on Herzen. In the late 1940s and early 1950s, she participated in the thirty-volume edition of Herzen's *Collected Works*. For political and ideological reasons, defending and publishing her work on Herzen created difficulties for her; this situation was finally resolved in 1957 with the publication of her book: Byloe i dumy *Gertsena* (Leningrad: Gosudarstvennoe izdatel'stvo khudozhestvennoi literatury, 1957). About her relationship to this book, see Ginzburg 2002, 294. See also Ginzburg 2011, 501–5.

29. Ibid., 623. A scribbling from the 1960s on the back of one of the pages of "Otter's Day" includes three planned epigraphs: Herzen's saying and lines from Nikolai Nekrasov and from Nikolai Oleinikov. OR RNB 1377. For Herzen's saying in the original, see A. I. Gertsen, *Sobranie sochinenii v tridsati tomakh*, vol. 10 (Moscow: Izdatel'stvo Akademii nauk SSSR, 1956), 26.

30. Edward Acton underscores the relationship between remembering and writing

for Herzen in *Alexander Herzen and the Role of the Intellectual Revolutionary* (Cambridge, UK: Cambridge University Press, 1979), 99.

31. For a thorough account of the long and complicated publication history of "<A Story of a Family Drama>" and its interpretations by Soviet scholars, see Irina Paperno, "Introduction: Intimacy and History. The Gercen Family Drama Reconsidered," in *Russian Literature* LXI–I/II (Special Issue), ed. Irina Paperno, 1 January–15 February 2007: 1–66. The six articles in this special issue devoted to the family drama show in different ways (as Paperno describes it) how, "by way of literature, intimacy was converted into history: the history of the failed 1848 revolution, underwritten by socialist Romanticism, the proto-socialist adultery novel, and Romantic and Post-Romantic philosophy." Ibid., 50.

32. Herzen's minimal references to his own guilt may stem in part from the fact that he was writing a virtual legal self-defense against rumors initiated by Herwegh (and spreading across Europe) to the effect that Herzen was tyrannizing over his wife and preventing her from leaving him for Herwegh.

33. Ginzburg 1991, 216. Rosengrant uses "delayed memory" for *pytka zamedlennym vospominaniem,* whereas "slow remembering" is more accurate. Russian in Ginzburg 1977, 267. See also Byloe i dumy *Gertsena,* 308–13.

34. Some have suggested that Ginzburg was generous to a fault in her reading of Herzen through the lens of lofty artistic explanations. See Acton, 101–3, and also Ulrich Schmid, "The Family Drama as an Interpretive Pattern in Aleksandr Gercen's *Byloe i dumy,*" in *Russian Literature* LXI–I/II: 88.

35. Byloe i dumy *Gertsena,* 294–303; and also Ginzburg 1991, 209–17, and idem 1977, 258–68.

36. Ginzburg 1991, 211. Russian in idem 1977, 261.

37. Ginzburg writes, "those impulses which led Herzen to *My Past and Thoughts* were reworked and disappeared [*pererabotalis' i ischezli*] in the poetic and philosophical unity of a great epic." Byloe i dumy *Gertsena,* 312–13.

38. Ibid., 311.

39. Alexander Herzen, *My Past and Thoughts,* trans. Constance Garnett, rev. Humphrey Higgens, vol. 2 (New York, 1968), 857.

40. Ginzburg 1991, 217. Russian in idem 1977, 267–68. See a similar passage in Byloe i dumy *Gertsena,* 312–13.

41. In addition, it is significant that Herzen kept journals in which he blames himself for "murdering" his wife while trying to save her. Ginzburg 1991, 216; Russian in idem 1977, 267.

42. I have consulted the English translation *Blockade Diary,* trans. Alan Myers (London: Harvill Press, 1995), for the translation of *vnelichnyi* as "what is outside the self," rather than the slightly more literal "extra-personal." However, as a translation of the title of Ginzburg's work, I prefer *Notes of a Blockade Person,* to preserve the reference to the form (not a diary), to the typical blockade dweller, and to Dostoevsky's *Notes from Underground.*

43. The triple dates, added for publication in *Neva,* remained unchanged in subsequent publications.

44. Interview with G. Silina, *Literaturnaia gazeta.*

45. Ginzburg 2011, 20.

46. Post-traumatic psychotherapy was initiated by Pierre Janet near the beginning of the twentieth century. See Bessel van der Kolk and Onno van der Hart, "The Intrusive

Past: The Flexibility of Memory and the Engraving of Trauma" in *Trauma: Explorations in Memory*, ed. Cathy Caruth (Baltimore, MD: Johns Hopkins University Press, 1995), 158–82.

47. Otter's presence in several fragmentary narratives may be evidence that Ginzburg envisioned them as a kind of a novel or a cycle, *Home and the World*. See chapter 2.

48. Ginzburg 2011, 429.

49. In "A Story of Pity and Cruelty," Otter experiences a "direct feeling of his vital obligation [*krovnogo svoego obiazatel'stva*—which could also be translated as "his obligation as a blood relative"] to support Aunt's life," and yet Ginzburg writes that he needed and lacked "adherence to a principle, a firm sense of duty" [*printsipial'nost', tverdoe chuvstvo dolga*]." See Ginzburg 2011, 23, 32.

50. Ginzburg 2002, 198.

51. See my discussion in chapter 1.

52. For an exploration of Ginzburg's concept of *sotsial'nost'*, partially in the context of *Notes of a Blockade Person*, see Sarah Pratt, "Lidiia Ginzburg, a Russian Democrat at the Rendezvous," *Canadian-American Slavic Studies* 28, 2–3 (Summer–Fall 1994): 183–203.

53. The phrase "working egoism" (*rabochii egoizm*) comes within Ginzburg's description of the creative type of person in a 1970s essay. Ginzburg 2002, 364.

54. Ginzburg writes: "Maybe, to love and save this pitiful life, closely related by blood, it was worth paying the price of his cruel creativity. This is something he does not know and never can verify. There was no love, and nowhere to get it from." "Rasskaz o zhalosti i o zhestokosti." Ginzburg 2011, 54.

55. There are two occurrences of the word "mother" in the text, but they are in fact figurative. Aunt exclaims in exasperation, "all this is cursed motherhood" (*vse materinstvo prokliatoe*); and in Otter's view, she pretends to be a victim and a selfless mother ("*ei nuzhno izobrazhat' zhertvu i samootverzhennuiu mat'* ") in order to torture him more effectively. Ibid., 37, 48.

56. Nataliia Sokolova, "Lidiia Ginzburg, rodnia, znakomye: Materialy k biographii." RGALI F. 3270. Sokolova N. V. Op. 1 ed. khr. 27.

57. An entry with the month and year of death of Ginzburg (Gol'denberg) Raisa (Rakhil') Davydovna (1867–1942) can be found in *Blokada, 1941–1944. Leningrad. Kniga pamiati*, vol. 6 (St. Petersburg: Pravitel'stvo Sankt Peterburga, 1999). Available online; the page with Rakhil' Davydovna Ginzburg's data, http://visz.nlr.ru/search/lists/blkd/227_230.html, accessed 3 May 2015. In Ginzburg's archives, there is a slip for a money transfer from 22 December 1942. Natalia (Ata) Viktorovna Sokolova sent 800 rubles to Ginzburg from her place of evacuation in Chistopol' along with the following message: "Liusa, my dearest friend, we found out about the old woman's death, and it is very sad. Her final months were immensely difficult. We hope you are in good health. You should write us about yourself, even just a few words. My mother sends her regards. Ata." OR RNB 1377. The contents of "A Story of Pity and Cruelty" suggest that Aunt was alive in late summer, leaving the date of death unspecified.

58. There are letters in the archive between Lydia Ginzburg and her brother Viktor Tipot concerning money for Raisa Ginzburg. See for example RGALI F. 2897 op. 1. ed. xr. 88. l. 3 (1936) and F. 3270 op. 1 ed. khr. 82 l. 1.

59. N. V. Sokolova, "Lidiia Ginzburg, rodnia, znakomye," 6. As mentioned in the introduction, Sokolova relates a joke about their contrasting characters: "One of Liusia's friends said this about Raisa Davidovna and Liusa: a hen laid an eagle's egg." Ibid. One

of Ginzburg's notes, published posthumously, puns on her mother's light-spirited character: "Khardzhiev told me: 'Your mother has such an easy character that it must be very hard to live with her.'" Ginzburg 2002, 395.

60. Natalia Viktorovna had a son, Aleksei, with her first husband, Konstantin Simonov, in the 1930s. She then married Pavel Illarionovich Sokolov, who died at the front. Natalia Viktorovna's second child, Pavel Pavlovich Sokolov, was born during the war while she was in evacuation in Chistopol'. (This information comes from the introduction to the Sokolova archive in RGALI, F. 3270.)

61. Other biographical correspondences in "A Story . . ." include the description of Raisa's sister. According to Sokolova, Raisa's sister Liuba, who lived through the war, was physically unattractive and never married. In "A Story . . . ," Aunt sees her unmarriageable sister as inferior. Aunt's idea that she sacrificed everything for her "nephews" corresponds to an argument between Lydia Ginzburg and her mother, which Sokolova quotes. Finally, Sokolova's description of Mark Ginzburg as gentle and meek corresponds to the old man (*starik* in "Delusion of the Will") and "A Story . . . ," where he is "a person with a weak life force" (*chelovek slabogo napora*).

62. The biographical information about Ginzburg's uncle/stepfather's death in *Detskoe selo* comes from one of Lydia Ginzburg's "autobiographies," written for official purposes, in the archives. Ginzburg 2011, 503.

63. RGALI F. 3270. Sokolova N. V. Op. 1 ed. khr. 27. l. l. 23–25.

64. Ginzburg wrote in drafts related to "Zametki o proze," ca. 1934: "Invented [*vydumannye*] people and situations [. . .] fill me with a certain disgust." OR RNB 1377.

65. *My Past and Thoughts*, vol. 2, 858 (Garnett translation). A. I. Gertsen, *Sobranie sochinenii v tridsati tomakh*, vol. 10, 238. The literal translation would be "psychic pathology."

66. See Ginzburg 1991, 212–16.

67. Ginzburg, Byloe i dumy *Gertsena*, 305.

68. Ginzburg 2011, 17, and Herzen, *My Past and Thoughts*, vol. 2., 845. Here are some more examples of resemblances between the texts. The page numbers refer to these two editions.

Herzen: "This life was my whole fortune [*dostoianie*] . . . ." (748)

Ginzburg: "They had ruined her life, his successful composition [proizvedenie] *. . . ."* (32)

Herzen (after Natalie's death): "A home I had no longer. With the departure of the children the last trace of family life vanished. Everything had assumed the appearance of bachelorhood." (920)

Ginzburg's Otter (after Aunt's death): "With this death he lost the last trace of youth. He lost the stable foundation of daily life, a small element of family belonging, which oppressed him, irritated him, but nevertheless was solid and enduring; surviving affairs and breakups, it had given form to daily existence." "Yes, he had lost the remnants of youth and of humanity, day-to-day existence and home." (20)

A detail in *My Past and Thoughts* where Herzen tries to minister some orange juice to the dying Natalie (which Ginzburg quotes in 1957, 309) partially resembles a scene in Ginzburg's "Delusion of the Will," Ginzburg 2002, 602.

69. Ginzburg, Byloe i dumy *Gertsena*, 308.

70. Ginzburg 2011, 46.

71. Ibid., 47.

72. Ibid., 35.

73. Gertsen, *Sobranie sochinenii v tridsati tomakh*, 10: 274. Garnett's translation is dif-

ferent: "the happenings that can never be obliterated from the memory." *My Past and Thoughts* 2: 893. Quoted in *On Psychological Prose*, 217.

74. Herzen, *My Past and Thoughts* 2: 911.

75. Ginzburg 1991, 216; Russian in idem 1977, 267.

76. Ginzburg, "Otter's Day," in Ginzburg 2011, 212.

77. When Ginzburg renewed work on her Blockade manuscripts in 1962, she drafted a preamble that included mention of Tolstoy and Solzhenitsyn: "During the quarter century in which these drafts/draft variants /preparations of this day [Ginzburg's variants] lay in my writing table, another immediate predecessor appeared: 'One Day in the Life of Ivan Denisovich.' I cannot accept this composition; I cannot accept this implausible, grimacing, opposed-to-reason imaginary direct speech in which the whole thing is written. But I know that the social significance of this composition is tremendous, it is very important for its details, its patient exposition. Of course there is an analogy between the circle of the labor camp and the circle of the blockade. But my composition is about something else." Ginzburg 2011, 451.

78. Half of the city's inhabitants who had remained in Leningrad perished during this unusually cold winter. See Richard Bidlack, "Foreword: Historical Background to the Siege of Leningrad," in *Writing the Siege of Leningrad*, ed. Cynthia Simmons and Nina Perlina (Pittsburgh, PA: University of Pittsburgh Press, 2002), xv.

79. Ginzburg also describes the circle this way in "Otter's Day": "waking up, domestic chores, breakfast, trip to work, lunch, trip home with Aunt's lunch, return to work, return home, supper, sleep, waking up, domestic chores, breakfast . . . ." Ginzburg 2011, 277.

80. Ibid., 352.

81. Ibid., 440.

82. Interview with G. Silina, 1986.

83. Ginzburg 2011, 322.

84. Ibid., 353. This passage builds on the synopsis of Otter and Aunt's relationship from "Otter's Day," and comes at the same place in the narrative.

85. Ibid., 358. For further textual comparisons between *Notes* and "A Story of Pity and Cruelty," see my chart in "'Samo-otstranenie' kak eticheskii i esteticheskii printsip v proze L. Ia. Ginzburg," *Novoe literaturnoe obozrenie* 81, 5 (2006): 281.

86. Ginzburg 2011, 58.

87. Ibid., 245.

88. Ibid., 348.

89. Ibid., 47.

90. Ibid., 259.

91. Ibid., 359.

92. Ibid.

93. In drafts for "Paralysis," one of the first texts Ginzburg wrote about the blockade, there is another scene with containers, where the hero's will is so traumatized that he can barely bring himself to wash them (Ginzburg 2011, 286). He also has trouble organizing his bag and coupons (this latter part is in the published version too; see ibid., 434). The different experience may be one reason she decided to keep this narrative separate, with a different hero.

94. Andrei Zorin, "Lidiia Ginzburg: opyt 'primireniia s deistvitel'nost'iu,' " in *Novoe literaturnoe obozrenie* 101, 1 (2010): 32–51, esp. 33. While I agree with most of Zorin's positions, I am not entirely convinced of the dateable appearance and disappearance of

Ginzburg's "justification" of the Soviet state and its policies. The note from late 1944 about Grigory Gukovsky, which Zorin uses to argue that Ginzburg's "historiosophical optimism" had come to an end, relates to Ginzburg's reflections on the contamination of an artist's and intellectual's activities by compromises made or work done in other spheres. As such, it seems to represent not a change but a continuation of her views on the subject. I share Zorin's observation that these historically optimistic passages appear in certain blockade writings, and cannot be found in her notes of other periods.

95. In Russian: "Интеллигент теперь должен был сам захотеть того самого, чего от него хотело общее. Старая утопическая задача (как она увлекала Герцена!)—не разрешится ли она синтезом логики государства с логическим абсурдом самоценной личности?" Ginzburg 2011, 431.

96. See ibid., 189.

97. In Russian: "И люди поняли. То есть поняли пока отдельные люди, а большинство внутренне созрело, чтобы понять—что эгоизм как мерило поведения подобен смерти, что гедонистический индивидуализм и гуманистический социализм несостоятельны; и это в силу двух настойчиво открывшихся человеку факторов—иллюзорности индивидуального существования и неизбывности социального зла." Draft "Teoreticheskii razdel" to "Den' Ottera." Ibid., 294.

98. Ibid., 463.

99. In Russian: "Людям казалось, что они изменятся, им страстно хотелось измениться, но это не вышло < . . . > Но они созрели для изменения, и лучшие понимают необходимость перерождения человека." From an outline for the work that became "Den' Ottera" and eventually *Notes of a Blockade Person*. Ibid., 303.

100. Herzen writes in "Diletantizm v nauke": "The life of people in the flourishing epoch of the ancient world was radiantly clear, like the life of nature. Indistinct melancholy, agonizing excavations of the self, painful egoism—none of this existed for them. They suffered from real causes, shed tears from sincere losses. The person of the individual was lost in the citizen, and the citizen was an organ, an atom of the other, sacred, deified person—the person of the city. They trembled not for their own 'I,' but for the 'I' of Athens, Sparta, Rome: such was the broad, free worldview of the Greco-Roman world, humanly sublime *in its confines*. It had to make way for a new worldview, because it was limited. The ancient world equated the external and the internal—as it is in nature, but not in truth—the spirit rules over form." In Russian: "Жизнь людей в цветущую эпоху древнего мира была беспечно ясна, как жизнь природы. Неопределенная тоска, мучительные углубления в себя, болезненный эгоизм—для них не существовали. Они страдали от реальных причин, лили слезы от истинных потерь. Личность индивидуума терялась в гражданине, а гражданин был орган, атом другой, священной, обоготворяемой личности—личности города. Трепетали не за свое "я", а за "я" Афин, Спарты, Рима: таково было широкое, вольное воззрение греко-римского мира, человечески прекрасное в своих границах. Оно должно было уступить иному воззрению, потому что оно было ограниченно. Древний мир поставил внешнее на одну доску с внутренним—так оно и есть в природе, но не так в истине—дух господствует над формой." Aleksandr Gertsen, *Sobranie sochinenii v tridtsati tomakh*, vol. 3 (Moscow: Izdatel'stvo Akademii nauk SSSR, 1954), 30–31.

Another of Ginzburg's favorite writers, Rousseau, writes of the model of Sparta in *The Social Contract* and "Discourse on the Sciences and the Arts."

101. In Russian: "Остается новое гражданское сознание, новое спартанство, которое не отрицает неизбежность зла и несвободы. И прямо требует, чтобы еди-

ничный человек отдал себя в распоряжение общего. Оно ищет правильной диалектики социального зла, заменителей, наиболее благоприятных для данной исторической формации." Ginzburg 2011, 211–12. The idea of looking for the lesser evil, the loopholes in the necessary social evil, is expressed many times in Ginzburg's notes and is related to the individual's relationship to a powerful state. For a treatment of how Ginzburg expresses the relationship between the individual and "Leviathan," see Irina Sandomirskaia, "The Leviathan, or Language in Besiegement: Lydia Ginzburg's Prolegomena to Critical Discourse Analysis," in *Lydia Ginzburg's Alternative Literary Identities*, ed. Van Buskirk and Zorin (Oxford: Peter Lang AG, 2012), 193–234.

102. In Russian: "Гражданственность в качестве положительного содержания слишком абстрактна, рационалистична. По настоящему она овладевала человеческой массой только в религиозном своем варианте (древний мир). В абстрактности—порочность и чистой государственности и социальных утопий. <. . . > Сознанию человека нового времени из форм общей жизни особенно близко, адекватна идея родины, народа. Родина—связь эмоциональная, не боящаяся иррациональных, логически неразложимых остатков." From the essay "Povedenie," in ZK 1943–46. Ginzburg 2011, 177.

103. In Russian: "Они торопливо, жадно хватаются за все знаки различия, за все, что теперь должно их выделить, оградить." 1943–46 notebook in ibid., 484.

104. Ibid., 463.

105. In Russian: "Этот человек думает не о будущих формах самосознания, но думает и с толком—о том, как он будет жить, как ему выйти из того социально-пониженного положения, в котором он очутился." Ibid., 76.

106. "Несмотря на становление общей воли, все продолжает совершаться казенным и бюрократическим порядком. При всех ее недостатках, это выработанная форма, которую не момент сейчас пересматривать, да и неизвестно будет ли она пересматриваться в сколько-нибудь ближайшем будущем." From "Zasedanie na iskhode voiny." Ibid., 85.

107. In Russian: "Истребляемый, испытуемый катастрофами человек не в силах верить в красоту и абсолютную ценность единичной души. Гораздо естественнее ему испытывать отвращение к этой голой душе и горькую и тщетную жажду очищения во всеобщем, в некоей искомой системе связей—в религии? В экзистенциальном самопроектировании? В новой гражданственности?" Ibid., 429.

108. In Russian: "Под артиллерийским обстрелом нормально работали механизмы общественного зла, вместе с мужеством, вместе с терпением. Это истерзанная страна побеждала. И она же, сама того не зная, готовилась войти в новый разгул социального зла." Ibid., 425.

109. One exception to this rule is Boris Gasparov, who terms *Notes* an essay, which combines the "characteristics of a diary, of a literary-philosophical essay and of analytic psychological prose." Gasparov, "On 'Notes from the Leningrad Blockade,'" *Canadian-American Slavic Studies* 28, 2–3 (Summer–Fall 1994): 216.

110. See in particular Cynthia Simmons, "Leningrad Culture under Siege (1941–1944)," in *Preserving Petersburg: History, Memory, Nostalgia*, ed. Helena Goscilo and Stephen M. Norris (Bloomington: Indiana University Press, 2008), 164–81.

111. Cynthia Simmons uses Ginzburg as a central text in "Leningrad Culture under Siege." Simmons and Nina Perlina use Ginzburg's work as a central and definitive example of women's representations of the siege in their book *Writing the Siege of Leningrad: Women's Diaries, Memoirs, and Documentary Prose*, xxxi. Lisa Kirschenbaum, in *The*

Legacy of the Siege of Leningrad, 1941–1995 (Cambridge, UK: Cambridge University Press, 2006), shows how Ginzburg's account aligns with others on several elements of the blockade experience, for example, bodily changes (182), the impulse to document food preparation (27), the vivid memory of Molotov's voice over the loudspeaker (42–43), the importance of *War and Peace* (29), and the wartime press (46).

112. Interview with Liudmila Titova in *Smena* 262, 19/12 (13 November 1988): 2.

113. This note is dated 2 October 1985. Ginzburg 2011, 510.

114. Sarah Pratt interprets Ginzburg's writing about N., instead of about "I" differently: as emblematic of women's autobiography and of the Russian Orthodox tradition, both of which put forth "the notion of finding oneself through something outside the self." Pratt, "Angels in the Stalinist House: Nadezhda Mandelstam, Lidiia Chukovskaia, Lidiia Ginzburg, and Russian Women's Autobiography," *Auto/biography Studies* 11, 2 (1996): 74, 81.

115. A page with two draft versions of this note (one of them is crossed out; I am providing the other, clearly a revision) was lying loose in a miscellaneous folder of manuscripts. Its place in the 1960s drafts of "Blokada" (as the piece was called then) would have been after the "Preamble" (which resembles what was later published as "Zapiski v dni blokady" in *Vokrug* "Zapisok blokadnogo cheloveka"), and immediately preceding the fragment "Paralysis" ("Otsepenenie"), the shorter story that served as an "interlude" before the longer narrative of N.'s day (later to become part 1). See Ginzburg 2011, 551.

116. Ibid., 433.

117. Ibid.

118. For one take on Ginzburg's notion of authorship and literary character, see William Mills Todd II, "Between Marxism and Semiotics: Lidiia Ginzburg and Soviet Literary Sociology," *Canadian-American Slavic Studies* 19, 2 (1985): 178–86.

119. Ginzburg 2002, 400.

120. Ibid.

121. Ginzburg 2011, 294.

CONCLUSION: SUSTAINING A HUMAN IMAGE

1. In Russian: "Когда ты ропщешь на социальное зло, посмотри, не является ли оно заменителем зла, еще более смертельного." Lidiia Ginzburg, *Prokhodiashchie kharaktery. Proza voennykh let. Zapiski blokadnogo cheloveka*, ed. Emily Van Buskirk and Andrei Zorin (Moscow: Novoe izdatel'stvo, 2011), 211. Henceforth, "Ginzburg 2011."

2. In Russian: "Возможности человека определяется тем, чего он не может, по крайней мере настолько же как и тем, что он может. Писатель—это человек, который не может переживать жизнь не пиша."

Ginzburg, ZK VIII/IX (1933–35), 67. OR RNB 1377.

3. Lidiia Ginzburg, *Zapisnye knizhki. Vospominaniia. Esse* (St. Petersburg: Iskusstvo-SPb, 2002), 74. Henceforth, "Ginzburg 2002."

4. Lydia Ginzburg *On Psychological Prose*, trans. and ed. Judson Rosengrant (Princeton, NJ: Princeton University Press, 1991), 323–24; original Russian in *O psikhologicheskoi proze* (Leningrad: Khudozhestvennaia literatura, 1977), 392–93.

5. Alexander Zholkovsky, "Between Genres," reprinted in *Lydia Ginzburg's Alternative Literary Identities*, ed. Emily Van Buskirk and Andrei Zorin (Oxford: Peter Lang AG, 2012), 37.

6. Lidiia Ginzburg, *O literaturnom geroe* (Leningrad: Sovetskii pisatel', 1979), 81. Henceforth, "Ginzburg 1979."

7. Lidiia Ginzburg, "Iz zapisnykh knizhek," pub. Aleksandr Kushner and Denis Ustinov (K 100-letiiu so dnia rozhdeniia L. Ia. Ginzburg), *Zvezda* 3 (2002): 123. In Russian: "Натуралистический-психологический роман важен. Но тут надо одолеть свойственную натурализму грубую фикцию объективности изображаемого. Объективность ощущений, мыслительного процесса, людей, которые садятся и встают со стола. Людей, понимаемых не как построяемая [sic] система, а как вещь." This 1934 note overlaps in theme with the 1933 note recording a conversation with Oleinikov, discussed in chapter 2.

8. Ginzburg 1979, 141. Ginzburg writes of how Samuel Beckett brought the novel to a destructive endpoint in *L'innomable*, creating an isolated character who is nothing more than pure speech, testifying to an almost animal or even vegetable existence; but as she points out, Beckett's creation of this novel proves his own inability to escape the social act of writing, to escape character-shaping values. Ibid., 142–43.

9. Pushkin, "O proze," *Polnoe sobranie sochinenii v 10 tomakh*, vol. 7 (Leningrad: Nauka, 1977–79), 12–13.

10. In Russian: ". . . новое познание действительности возможно только <тогда>, когда каждая словесная формулировка добывается на новом опыте; не как разматывание неудержимого словесного клубка, но как очередное отношение к вещи (этим беспрерывно возобновляемым соизмерением слов и реалий в опыте страшно силен Толстой)." Ginzburg, ZK VIII–IV (1933–35), note from 1934. OR RNB 1377. Published in 2002 in Lidiia Ginzburg, "Iz zapisnykh knizhek," *Zvezda* 3 (2002): 123. Tolstoy had written in a letter to Leonid Andreev that "you should write, in the first place, only when the thought that you want to express is so obsessive that, until you express it as best you can, it will give you no peace." He also wrote that "simplicity is the essential condition of the beautiful." Translation of Tolstoy's letter in Viktor Shklovsky, *Third Factory*, intro. and trans. Richard Sheldon (Normal, IL: Dalkey Archive Press, 2002), 50; Russian in Viktor Shklovskii, *Tret'ia fabrika* (Letchworth, UK: Prideaux Press, 1978; reprint of 1926 Russian edition by Artel' pisatelei "Krug"), 82–83. Original in Lev Tolstoy, *Polnoe sobranie sochinenii v 90 tomakh*, vol. LXXVII (Moscow, 1953–58), 218–20.

11. Lidiia Ginzburg, "Literaturnye sovremenniki i potomki," *Literatura v poiskakh real'nosti* (Leningrad: Sovetskii pisatel', 1987), 115–16.

12. In Russian: "Никто не говорит о том, о чем не говорят." Ginzburg 2002, 287.

13. Ibid., 294. English in *Lydia Ginzburg's Alternative Literary Identities*, 397. I have adjusted Alyson Tapp's translation by one word: from "compatability" to "agreement."

14. Ginzburg 2011, 82. In Russian: "В условиях абсолютной несвободы очень трудно и очень легко быть смелым. Ибо все есть смелость, каждое неотрегулированное дыхание есть смелость."

15. Jerrold Seigel, in his survey of Western European selfhood from the seventeenth century onward, distinguishes three primary dimensions of the self: (1) bodily or material; (2) relational/social/cultural; and (3) reflective. Seigel, *The Idea of the Self* (Cambridge, UK: Cambridge University Press, 2005), 5–6.

16. See for example Sarah Pratt, "Review of *Lydia Ginzburg's Alternative Literary Identities*," *Modern Language Review*, 109, 1 (January 2014): 305–7.

17. Ginzburg writes in 1927: "I'm afraid we [literary scholars] are parasites who, in order not to die from insufficient food (or from boredom), have to nourish ourselves either with sociology (Eikhenbaum's 'literary environment' and so on), linguistics (Vi-

nogradov and others), or contemporary literature. For those who think of themselves not as literary historians or theorists primarily, but more broadly—as *littérateurs*, professionals of the word—an absence of the last kind of connections and impulses is fatal." In Russian: "Боюсь, что мы паразиты, которым для того, чтобы не умереть от недостатка пищи (или от скуки), необходимо питаться либо социологией (эйхенбаумовский «литературный быт» и проч.), либо лингвистикой (Виноградов и проч.), либо текущей литературой. Для тех, кто ощущает себя не историками или теоретиками литературы по преимуществу, но шире того—литераторами, профессионалами слова,—отсутствие последнего рода связей и импульсов—губительно." Ginzburg 2002, 36.

18. Sergei Kozlov, "Lydia Ginzburg's Victory and Defeat," in *Lydia Ginzburg's Alternative Literary Identities*, 26.

19. I am thinking of projects of the type Druzhinin undertook with Leningrad's academic and literary scene in the 1940s. He writes of the misfortune of being unable to access Ginzburg's archive. Petr Druzhinin, *Ideologiia i filologiia: Leningrad, 1940-e gody*, 2 vols (Moscow: Novoe literaturnoe obozrenie, 2012).

20. In Russian: "Под пустой некогда оболочкой как бы образуется постепенно соответствующее ей живое ядро." Ginzburg 2011, 188, 493.

21. Ibid., 187. She writes: "There forms an ideal concept of oneself as a member of a collective. And this concept is binding. Genuine supra-personal, collective motivations develop from this notion, almost in reverse order. This is a value that has been gained forever, the basis of moral development." In Russian: "Идеальное представление о себе самом как представителе коллектива. И это представление обязывает. От него, как бы в обратном порядке, развиваются подлинно сверхличные, коллективистические побуждения. Это навсегда заработанная ценность, основа морального развития."

BIBLIOGRAPHY

Acton, Edward. *Alexander Herzen and the Role of the Intellectual Revolutionary*. Cambridge, UK: Cambridge University Press, 1979.

Adamovich, Adam, and Daniil Granin. *Blokadnaia kniga*, 5th ed. Leningrad: Lenizdat, 1989.

Adler, Alfred. *The Individual Psychology of Alfred Adler: A Systematic Presentation in Selections from His Writings*. Edited and annotated by Heinz L. Ansbacher and Rowena R. Ansbacher. New York: Harper & Row, 1964.

Adorno, Theodor. "The Essay as Form." In *The Adorno Reader*, edited by Brian O'Connor, translated by Samuel and Shierry Weber. Oxford: Blackwell Publishers, 2000, 91–111.

"Analitika zhiznetvorchestva: Iu. M. Lotman i L. Ia. Ginzburg. Kul'turnye kody, sotsial'nye strategii i literaturnye tsenarii." Roundtable. *Novoe literaturnoe obozrenie* 82 (2006): 93–121.

Andrievskaia, Lidiia Mikhailovna. *Stranichki iz dnevnika. 1934–41*. St. Petersburg: Niva, 2006.

Any, Carol. *Boris Eikhenbaum: Voices of a Russian Formalist*. Stanford, CA: Stanford University Press, 1994.

Aucouturier, Michel. "The Theory of the Novel in Russia in the 1930s: Lukács and Bakhtin." In *The Russian Novel from Pushkin to Pasternak*, edited by John Garrad. New Haven, CT: Yale University Press, 1983, 227–40.

Bakhtin, M. M. *Art and Answerability: Early Philosophical Essays by M. M. Bakhtin*. Edited by Michael Holquist and Vadim Liapunov, translated by Vadim Liapunov. Austin: University of Texas Press, 1990.

———. *Sobranie sochinenii v semi tomakh*. Edited by S. G. Bocharov and L. A. Gogotishvili. Moscow: Russkie slovari, 1996–.

Bakhtin, Vladimir. *Leningradskie pisateli-frontoviki 1941–1945*. Leningrad: Sovetskii pisatel', 1985.

Barskova, Polina. "Avgust, kotorogo ne bylo, i mekhanizm kalendarnoi travmy: razmyshleniia o blokadnykh khronologiiakh." *Novoe literaturnoe obozrenie* 116, 4 (2012): 130–45.

———. "Chernyi svet: problema temnoty v blokadnom Leningrade." *Neprikosnovennyi zapas* 2, 70 (2010): 122–38.

———. "Nastoiashchee nastoiashchee: o vospriiatii vremeni v blokadnom Leningrade." *Neprikosnovennyi zapas* 2, 76 (2011): 200–213.

Barthes, Roland. "The Death of the Author." In *Authorship: From Plato to the Postmodern*, edited by Seán Burke. Edinburgh: Edinburgh University Press, 1995, 125–30.

———. *Roland Barthes by Roland Barthes*. Translated by Richard Howard. Berkeley: University of California Press, 1994.

———. *S/Z*. Translated by Richard Miller. London: Jonathan Cape, 1975.

Belknap, Robert. *The Structure of the Brothers Karamazov*. The Hague: Mouton, 1967.

Bensmaïa, Réda. *The Barthes Effect: The Essay as Reflective Text*. Translated by Pat Fedkiew, introduction by Michèle Richman. Theory and History of Literature, vol. 54. Minneapolis: University of Minnesota Press, 1987.

Bergson, Henri. *Essai sur les données immédiates de la conscience.* Paris, 1888.

Bernstein, Frances Lee. *The Dictatorship of Sex: Lifestyle Advice for the Soviet Masses.* DeKalb: Northern Illinois University Press, 2007.

Bershtein, Evgenii. "*Psychopathia Sexualis* v Rossii nachala veka: politika i zhanr." In *Eros and Pornography in Russian Culture*, edited by M. Levitt and A. Toporkov. Moscow: Ladomir, 1999, 414–41.

———. "Western Models of Sexuality in Russian Modernism." Doctoral Dissertation, University of California, Berkeley, 1998.

Bezrodnyi, Mikhail. *Konets tsitaty.* St. Petersburg: Izdatel'stvo Ivana Limbakha, 1996.

Bibler, V. S. "Umerla Lidiia Ginzburg." In *Odissei: Chelovek v istorii. Lichnost' i obshchestvo*. Moscow: Nauka, 1990, 217–18.

Bidlack, Richard. "Foreword: Historical Background to the Siege of Leningrad." In *Writing the Siege of Leningrad*, edited by Cynthia Simmons and Nina Perlina. Pittsburgh, PA: University of Pittsburgh Press, 2002, ix–xxvi.

Bland, Lucy, and Laura Doan, eds. *Sexology Uncensored.* Cambridge, UK: Polity Press, 1998.

Blium, Arlen. *Kak eto delalos' v Leningrade: Tsenzura v gody ottepeli, zastoia i perestroika 1953–1991.* St. Petersburg: Akademicheskii proekt, 2005.

Blokada, 1941–1944. Leningrad. Kniga pamiati. 35 vols. St. Petersburg: Pravitel'stvo Sankt Peterburga, 1998–2006.

Bocharov, Sergei. "Vspominaia Lidiiu Iakovlevnu." *Novoe literaturnoe obozrenie* 49, 3 (2001): 306–13.

Boym, Svetlana. "'Banality of Evil,' Mimicry, and the Soviet Subject." *Slavic Review* 67, 2 (Summer 2008): 342–63.

———. *Common Places: Mythologies of Everyday Life in Russia.* Cambridge, MA: Harvard University Press, 1994.

———. *The Future of Nostalgia.* New York: Basic Books, 2001.

———. "Poetics and Politics of Estrangement: Viktor Shklovsky and Hannah Arendt." *Poetics Today* 26, 4 (Winter 2005): 581–611.

Brandist, Craig. *The Bakhtin Circle: Philosophy, Culture and Politics.* London: Pluto Press, 2002.

Brik, Osip. "Razlozhenie siuzheta." *Literatura fakta: Pervyi sbornik materialov rabotnikov LEFa.* Moscow: Federatsia, 1929, republished by I. V. Zakharov, 2000, 226–28.

Brodsky, Joseph. *Less Than One.* New York: Farrar, Straus & Giroux, 1987.

Brooks, Peter. *Enigmas of Identity.* Princeton, NJ: Princeton University Press, 2011.

Bulkina, Inna. "Fragment o fragmentakh. Review of *Chastnyi chelovek: L. Ia. Ginzburg v kontse 1920-kh—nachale 1930-kh godov* by Stanislav Savitskii." *Novoe literaturnoe obozrenie* 128, 4 (2014): 326–38.

Burgin, Diana. *"Ottiagotela . . .": Russkie zhenshchiny za predelami obydennoi zhizni.* St. Petersburg: Inapress, 2004.

Butler, Judith. *Gender Trouble: Feminism and the Subversion of Identity.* New York: Routledge, 1999.

———. *The Psychic Life of Power: Theories in Subjection.* Stanford, CA: Stanford University Press, 1997.

Canadian-American Slavic Studies Journal. Lydia Ginzburg's Contribution to Literary Criticism. Edited by Sarah Pratt. Vol. 19, 2 (Summer 1985).

———. *Lidiia Iakovlevna Ginzburg: In Memoriam.* Edited by Jane Gary Harris. Vol. 28, 2–3 (Summer–Fall 1994).

Cascardi, Anthony J. *The Cambridge Introduction to Literature and Philosophy*. Cambridge, UK: Cambridge University Press, 2014.

Chekhov, Anton. *Plays*. Translated by Elisaveta Fen. London: Penguin Books, 1959.

———. *Zapisnye knizhki A. P. Chekhova*. Prepared by E. N. Konshin, edited by L. P. Grossman. Moscow: Gosudarstvennaia akademiia khudozhestvennykh nauk, 1927.

Chernorutskii, Mikhail, ed. *Alimentarnaia distrofiia v blokirovannom Leningrade*. Leningrad: Medgiz, 1947.

Chudakov, Alexander. Untitled, in "Tsel'nost': o tvorchestve L.Ia. Ginzburg." *Canadian-American Slavic Studies* 28, 2–3 (Summer–Fall 1994): 246–49.

Chudakova, Marietta. *Izbrannye raboty*, vol. 1. Moscow: Iazyki russkoi kul'tury, 2001.

Chukovskaia, Lydia. *Zapiski ob Anne Akhmatovoi: v trekh tomakh*. Moscow: Soglasie, 1997.

Clark, Katarina. *Petersburg, Crucible of Cultural Revolution*. Cambridge, MA: Harvard University Press, 1995.

———. *The Soviet Novel: History as Ritual*. 3rd ed. Bloomington: Indiana University Press, 2000.

Clark, Katarina, and Galin Tihanov. "Soviet Literary Theory in the 1930s: Battles over Genre and the Boundaries of Modernity." In *A History of Russian Literary Theory and Criticism: The Soviet Age and Beyond*, edited by Evgeny Dobrenko and Galin Tihanov. Pittsburgh, PA: University of Pittsburgh Press, 2011, 109–43.

Clayton, J. Douglas. *Pierrot in Petrograd: The Commedia Dell'arte/Balagan in Twentieth-Century Russian Theatre and Drama*. Montreal: McGill-Queen's University Press, 1993.

Cohn, Dorrit. *The Distinction of Fiction*. Baltimore, MD: Johns Hopkins University Press, 1999.

de Man, Paul. *Allegories of Reading: Figural Language in Rousseau, Nietzsche, Rilke, and Proust*. New Haven, CT: Yale University Press, 1979.

———. "Autobiography as De-Facement." In *The Rhetoric of Romanticism*. New York: Columbia University Press, 1984, 67–81.

Depretto, Catherine. *Le Formalisme en Russie*. Paris: Institut d'Etudes Slaves, 2009.

Desnitskii, Vasilii A. *Frantsuzskii realisticheskii roman XIX veka*. Moscow/Leningrad: Gosudarstvennoe izdatel'svto khudozhestvennoi literatury, 1932.

Dilthey, Wilhelm. *Descriptive Psychology and Historical Understanding*. Translated by Richard Zaner and Kenneth Heiges. The Hague: Martinus Nijhoff, 1977.

———. *Pattern & Meaning in History; Thoughts on History & Society*. Edited by H. P. Rickman. New York: Harper, 1962.

Dobrenko, Evgeny, and Galin Tihanov. *A History of Russian Literary Theory and Criticism: The Soviet Age and Beyond*. Pittsburgh, PA: University of Pittsburgh Press, 2011.

———. *Istoriia russkoi literaturnoi kritiki: sovetskaia i postsovetskaia epokhi*. Moscow: Novoe literaturnoe obozrenie, 2011.

Dostoevsky, Fyodor. *The Brothers Karamazov*. Translated by Constance Garnett, revised by Ralph E. Matlaw. New York: W.W. Norton & Company, 1976.

———. *The Brothers Karamazov*. Translated by David McDuff. New York: Penguin Books, 1993.

———. *The Brothers Karamazov*. Translated by Richard Pevear and Larissa Volokhonsky. New York: Vintage Classics, 1990.

Dovlatov, Sergei. "Eto neperevodimoe slovo—'khamstvo.'" In *Sobranie sochinenii v chetyrekh tomakh*, vol. 4. St. Petersburg: Azbuka, 2002, 323–27.

Druzhinin, P. A. *Ideologiia i filologiia: Leningrad, 1940-e gody*, 2 vols. Moscow: Novoe literaturnoe obozrenie, 2012.

Eakin, Paul John. *How Our Lives Become Stories: Making Selves*. Ithaca, NY: Cornell University Press, 1999.

———. *Living Autobiographically: How We Create Identity in Narrative.* Ithaca, NY: Cornell University Press, 2008.

Ehrenburg, Ilya. "Saturday Review" (29 July 1961). In *Hemingway: The Critical Heritage*, edited by Jeffrey Meyers. London: Routledge & Kegan Paul, 433–36.

Eikhenbaum, Boris. "How Gogol's 'Overcoat' Is Made." In *Gogol from the Twentieth Century: Eleven Essays*, edited and translated by Robert Maguire. Princeton, NJ: Princeton University Press, 1974, 267–92.

———. "Sud'ba Bloka" [1921]. In *O literature: Raboty raznykh let*, edited by O. B. Eikhenbaum and E. A. Toddes, commentaries by E. A. Toddes, M. O. Chudakova, and A. P. Chudakov. Moscow: Sovetskii pisatel', 1987, 353–65.

———. "V poiskakh zhanra." *Russkii sovremennik* 3 (1924): 228–31.

Emerson, Caryl. "Bakhtin, Lotman, Vygotsky, and Lydia Ginzburg." In *Self and Story in Russian History*, edited by Laura Engelstein and Stephanie Sandler. Ithaca, NY: Cornell University Press, 2000, 20–45.

———. "Lydia Ginzburg on Tolstoy and Lermontov (with Dostoevsky as the Distant Ground)." In *Lydia Ginzburg's Alternative Literary Identities*, edited by Emily Van Buskirk and Andrei Zorin. Oxford: Peter Lang AG, 2012, 39–82.

———. "Shklovsky's *ostranenie*, Bakhtin's *vnenakhodimost'* (How Distance Serves an Aesthetics of Arousal Differently from an Aesthetics Based on Pain)." *Poetics Today* 26, 4 (Winter 2005): 637–64.

Engelstein, Laura. *The Keys to Happiness: Sex and the Search for Modernity in Fin-de-Siècle Russia.* Ithaca, NY: Cornell University Press, 1992.

Erlich, Victor. "The Novel in Crisis: Boris Pilnyak and Konstantin Fedin." In *The Russian Novel from Pushkin to Pasternak*, edited by John Garrad. New Haven, CT: Yale University Press, 1983, 155–76.

———. *Russian Formalism: History, Doctrine*. New Haven, CT: Yale University Press, 1981.

Fink, Hilary. *Bergson and Russian Modernism, 1900–1930*. Evanston, IL: Northwestern University Press, 1999.

Fitzpatrick, Sheila. *Everyday Stalinism: Ordinary Life in Extraordinary Times: Soviet Russia in the 1930s*. New York: Oxford University Press, 1999.

Folkenflik, Robert. "The Self as Other." In *The Culture of Autobiography: Constructions of Self-Representation*, edited by Robert Folkenflik. Stanford, CA: Stanford University Press, 1993, 215–36.

Foucault, Michel. *The History of Sexuality*. London: Penguin, 1990.

———. "Self Writing." In *Ethics: Subjectivity and Truth*, edited by Paul Rabinow, translated by Robert Hurley and others. *Essential Works of Michel Foucault 1954–84*, vol. 1. New York: New York Press, 1997, 207–23.

———. "What Is an Author?" In *Authorship: From Plato to the Postmodern*, edited by Seán Burke. Edinburgh: Edinburgh University Press, 1995, 233–46.

Frank, Joseph. "Subversive Activities." *New York Review of Books* (1 December 1994): 44–48.

Freud, Sigmund. "The Psychogenesis of a Case of Homosexuality in a Woman." In

Freud on Women: A Reader, edited by Elisabeth Young-Bruehl. New York: W.W. Norton & Co., 1990, 241–66.

———. *The Standard Edition of the Complete Psychological Works of Sigmund Freud*, translated and edited by James Strachey, vol. VII (1901–1905). London: Hogarth Press and the Institute of Psychoanalysis, 1953.

Gasparov, Boris. "On 'Notes from the Leningrad Blockade.'" *Canadian-American Slavic Studies* 28, 2–3 (Summer–Fall 1994): 216–20.

———. Untitled, in "Tsel'nost': O tvorchestve L. Ia. Ginzburg." *Canadian-American Slavic Studies* 28, 2–3 (Summer–Fall 1994): 250–51.

Gasparov, Boris, Robert P. Hughes, and Irina Paperno, eds. *Cultural Mythologies of Russian Modernism: From the Golden Age to the Silver Age*. California Slavic Studies, vol. 15. Berkeley: University of California Press, 1992.

Gasparov, Mikhail. *Zapisi i vypiski*. Moscow: Novoe literaturnoe obozrenie, 2001.

Genette, Gerard. *Palimpsests: Literature in the Second Degree*. Translated by Channa Newman and Claude Doubinsky. Lincoln: University of Nebraska Press, 1997.

Genette, Gerard. *Narrative Discourse: An Essay in Method*. Translated by Jane E. Lewin. Ithaca, NY: Cornell University Press, 1980.

———. *Palimpsests: Literature in the Second Degree*. Translated by Channa Newman and Claude Doubinsky. Lincoln: University of Nebraska Press, 1997.

Gide, André. *Corydon*. Translated and with preface by Richard Howard. New York: Farrar, Straus & Giroux, 1983.

Ginzburg, Lidiia [also Ginzburg, Lydia]. *Agenstvo Pinkertona*. Moscow, Leningrad: OGIZ Molodaia Gvardiia, 1932.

———. Byloe i dumy *Gertsena*. Leningrad: Gosudarstvennoe izdatel'stvo khudozhestvennoi literatury, 1957.

———. *Chelovek za pis'mennym stolom: esse, iz vospominanii, chetyre povestvovaniia*. Leningrad: Sovetskii pisatel', 1989.

———. "Chelovek za pis'mennym stolom. Po starym zapisnym knizhkam." *Novyi mir* 6 (June 1982): 235–45.

———. "Dolgii den'. Otryvok." *Avrora* 4 (1989): 103–6.

———. "Dve vstrechi." In *Petropol: Al'manakh*, issue 1. Leningrad: Vasil'evskii ostrov, 1990, 71–76.

———. Introduction in Petr Viazemskii, *Staraia zapisnaia knizhka*, edited and with commentaries by L. Ginzburg. Leningrad: Izdatel'stvo pisatelei, 1929.

———. "Iz dnevnikov Lidii Ginzburg: 'To li my eshche videli. . . .'" Edited by A. Kushner. *Literaturnaia gazeta*, 13 October (41 [5469]).

———. "Iz zapisnykh knizhek." Published by Aleksandr Kushner and Denis Ustinov (K 100-letiiu so dnia rozhdeniia L. Ia. Ginzburg). *Zvezda* 3 (2002): 104–32.

———. *Literatura v poiskakh real'nosti: stat'i, esse, zametki*. Moscow: Sovetskii pisatel', 1987.

———. "'Nikto ne plachet nad tem, chto ego ne kasaetsia': Chetvertyi 'Razgovor o liubvi' Lidii Ginzburg (podgotovka teksta, publikatsia i vstupitel'naia stat'ia Emily Van Buskirk. Perevod E. Kanishchevoi) ("'No one cries over what doesn't concern him': Lydia Ginzburg's Fourth 'Conversation about Love'": text, publication, and introductory article by Emily Van Buskirk), *Novoe literaturnoe obozrenie* 88, 6 (2007): 154–68.

———. *O lirike*. 2nd ed. Leningrad: Sovetskii pisatel', 1974.

———. *O literaturnom geroe*. Leningrad: Sovetskii pisatel', 1979.

———. *O psikhologicheskoi proze.* 2nd ed. Leningrad: Khudozhestvennaia literatura, 1977.

———. "Opyt filosofskoi liriki." In *Raboty dovoennogo vremeni: Stat'i. Retsenzii. Monografiia,* edited by Stanislav Savitskii. St. Petersburg: ID "Petropolis" 2007, 126–59.

———. "Opyt filosofskoi liriki (Venevitinov)." In *Poetika,* edited by V. Zhirmunskii. Leningrad: Academia, 1929, 72–104.

———. *O starom i novom: stat'i i ocherki.* Leningrad: Sovetskii pisatel', 1982.

———. "Pis'ma L. Ia. Ginzburg B. Ia. Bukhshtabu." Commentary and introduction by Denis Ustinov. *Novoe literaturnoe obozrenie* 49, 3 (2002): 325–86.

———. *Pretvorenie opyta.* Riga: Avots, 1991.

———. "Prezumptsia sotsializma" ("The Presumption of Socialism"). Publication, commentary, and introductory article "Ginzburg i perestroika" ("Ginzburg and Perestroika") by Emily Van Buskirk and Andrei Zorin. *Novoe literaturnoe obozrenie* 116, 4 (2012), 416–26.

———. *Prokhodiashchie kharaktery. Proza voennykh let. Zapiski blokadnogo cheloveka.* Edited by Emily Van Buskirk and Andrei Zorin. Moscow: Novoe izdatel'stvo, 2011.

———. *Raboty dovoennogo vremeni: Stat'i. Retsenzii. Monografiia.* Edited by Stanislav Savitskii. St. Petersburg: Petropolis, 2007.

———. "Stadii liubvi." Introduction by Denis Ustinov. *Kriticheskaia massa* 1 (2002): 34–38.

———. *Tvorcheskii put' Lermontova.* Leningrad: Khudozhestvennaia literatura, 1940.

———. "Ustnaia rech' i khudozhestvennaia proza." In *Semiotika ustnoi rechi. Lingvisticheskaia semantika i semiotika II.* Tartu: Tartuskii gosudarstvennyi universitet, 1979, 54–88.

———. "Zapisi 20–30-x godov." Introduction by Alexander Kushner, commentary by Alexander Chudakov. *Novyi mir* 6 (1992): 144–86.

———. "Zapisi 50–60-kh godov." Publication, introduction, and commentaries by E. Van Buskirk. *Seans* 51–52 (2012): 310–21.

———. *Zapisnye knizhki. Vospominaniia. Esse.* St. Petersburg: Iskusstvo-SPb, 2002.

———. *Zapisnye knizhki: Novoe Sobranie.* Moscow: Zakharov, 1999.

[TRANSLATIONS]

Ginzburg, Lidiia [also Ginzburg, Lydia]. "At One with the Legal Order." Translated by Alyson Tapp. In *Lydia Ginzburg's Alternative Literary Identities,* edited by Emily Van Buskirk and Andrei Zorin. Oxford: Peter Lang AG, 2012.

———. *Blockade Diary.* Translated by Alan Myers. London: Harvill Press, 1995.

———. "Conscience Deluded." In *Present Imperfect: Stories by Russian Women,* edited by Ayesha Kagal and Nataliia Perova, introduction by Helena Goscilo. Boulder, CO: Westview Press, 1996, 41–68.

———. "Conversations about Love." Translated by Alyson Tapp and Emily Van Buskirk. In *Lydia Ginzburg's Alternative Literary Identities,* edited by Emily Van Buskirk and Andrei Zorin. Oxford: Peter Lang AG, 2012, 343–52.

———. "From The Journals." Translated by Jane Gary Harris. In *Russian Women Writers,* vol. 2, edited by Christine D. Tomei. New York and London: Garland Pubishing, 1999, 1166–78.

———. "Generation at a Turning Point." Translated by Emily Van Buskirk. In *Lydia Ginzburg's Alternative Literary Identities,* edited by Emily Van Buskirk and Andrei Zorin. Oxford: Peter Lang AG, 2012, 369–82.

———. *On Psychological Prose*. Translated by Judson Rosengrant. Princeton, NJ: Princeton University Press, 1991.

———. "The Return Home." Translated by Alyson Tapp. In *Lydia Ginzburg's Alternative Literary Identities*, edited by Emily Van Buskirk and Andrei Zorin. Oxford: Peter Lang AG, 2012, 313–42.

[INTERVIEWS]

Ginzburg, Lidiia [also Ginzburg, Lydia]. Interview with G. Silina. *Literaturnaia gazeta* 3, 5069 (15 January 1986): 7.

———. Interview with Liudmila Titova. *Smena* 262, 19112 (13 November 1988): 2.

———. "Nravstvennost' svobodnogo cheloveka." Interview with Il'ia Foniakov. *Literaturnaia panorama* 2, 5224 (14 January 1989): 7.

———. "Pisatel'skaia mysl' i sovremennost': Chto est' chto?" Interview. *Literaturnaia Rossiia* 51, 1351 (23 December 1988): 8.

Goffman, Erving. *The Goffman Reader*. Edited by Charles Lemert and Ann Branaman. Oxford: Blackwell Publishing, 1997.

Gofman, Viktor, "Mesto Pil'niaka." In *Bor. Pil'niak : Stat'i i Materialy*, Mastera sovremennoi literatury, vol. 3, edited by V. Kazanskii and Iuri Tynianov. Leningrad: Academia, 1928, 5–34.

Goldberg, Stuart. *Mandelstam, Blok, and the Boundaries of Mythopoetic Symbolism*. Columbus: Ohio State University Press, 2011.

Gol'dshtein, Aleksandr. "Chelovek za pis'mennym stolom." *Okna: Ezhenedel'noe prilozhenie k gazete "Vesti"* (Tel Aviv, 11 March 1993): 16–19.

Golubeva, I. V. "Fragment Rechevogo Portreta L. Ia. Ginzburg." In *Aktual'nye problemy filologii i metodiki prepodavaniia*, edited by V. Iu. Melikian. Rostov on Don: Rostovskii gosudarstvennyi pedagogicheskii universitet, 2001, 33–39.

Greenleaf, Monika. *Pushkin and Romantic Fashion: Fragment, Elegy, Orient, Irony*. Stanford, CA: Stanford University Press, 1994.

———. "Tynianov, Pushkin, and the Fragment: Through the Lens of Montage." In *Cultural Mythologies of Russian Modernism from the Golden Age to the Silver Age*, edited by Boris Gasparov, Robert P. Hughes, and Irina Paperno. Berkeley: University of California, 1992, 264–92.

Greenway, Judy. "It's What You Do with It That Counts: Interpretations of Otto Weininger." In *Sexology in Culture: Labelling Bodies and Desires*, edited by Lucy Bland and Laura Doan. Cambridge, UK: Polity Press, 1998, 27–43.

Grekova, I. "Proza uchenogo." *Oktiabr'* 2 (February 1985): 203–5.

———. "Samoosuzhdenie i samoopravdanie." *Oktiabr'* 4 (April 1989): 200–202.

Grel'ts, Karin. "Osazhdennyi smysl." *Novoe literaturnoe obozrenie* 49, 3 (2001): 401–5.

Grossman, Joan Delaney, and Ruth Rischin. *William James in Russian Culture*. Lanham, MD: Lexington Books, 2003.

Grossman, Joan Delaney, and Irina Paperno, eds. *Creating Life: The Aesthetic Utopia of Russian Modernism*. Stanford, CA: Stanford University Press, 1994.

Grossman, Vasily [Vasilii]. *Life and Fate*. Translated by Robert Chandler. New York: New York Review of Books, 2006 [1995].

———. *Zhizn' i sud'ba*. Moscow: Knizhnaia palata, 1989.

Gubailovskii, V. "Poema bez fabuly (Zagadka Lidii Ginzburg)." *Ario: Zhurnal poezii* 3 (2003): 72–79.

Gustafson, Richard F. "Ginzburg's Theory of the Lyric." *Canadian-American Slavic Studies* 19, 2 (Summer 1985): 135–39.

———. "Lidiia Ginzburg and Tolstoi." *Canadian-American Slavic Studies* 28, 2–3 (Summer–Fall 1994): 204–15.

Guyau, Jean-Marie. *A Sketch of Morality Independent of Obligation or Sanction*. Translated from French (2nd ed.) by Gertrude Kapteyn. London: Watts & Co., 1898.

Harris, Jane Garry. "A Biographical Introduction." In *In Memoriam: Lidiia Ginzburg*, edited by Jane G. Harris. *Canadian-American Slavic Studies*, Special Issue 28 (Summer 1994): 126–45.

———. "'The Direct Conversation about Life': Lidiia Ginzburg's Journal as a Contemporary Literary Genre." In *Neo-Formalist Papers: Contributions to the Silver Jubilee Conference to Mark 25 Years of the Neo-Formalist Circle*, edited by Joe Andrew and Robert Reid. Amsterdam: Rodopi, 1998: 45–64.

———. "Lidiia Ginzburg: Images of the Intelligentsia." In *The Russian Memoir: History and Literature*, edited by Beth Holmgren. Evanston, IL: Northwestern University Press, 2003, 5–34.

Harris, Jane Garry, ed. *Autobiographical Statements in Twentieth-Century Russian Literature*. Princeton, NJ: Princeton University Press, 1990, 3–35.

Healey, Dan. "Sexual and Gender Dissent: Homosexuality as Resistance in Stalin's Russia." In *Contending with Stalinism: Soviet Power and Popular Resistance in the 1930s*, edited by Lynne Viola. Ithaca, NY: Cornell University Press, 2002, 139–69.

Hegel, Georg Wilhelm Friedrich. "Vorlesungen über die Ästhetik." In *Werke II*, vol. 13. Berlin: Hegel-Institut, 1999, 2002, 104. Electronic Resource: Charlottesville, VA: InteLex Corporation, 1999–.

Hellbeck, Jochen. *Revolution on My Mind: Writing a Diary under Stalin*. Cambridge, MA: Harvard University Press, 2009.

Herzen, Alexander [also Gertsen, Aleksandr]. *My Past and Thoughts*. Translated by Constance Garnett. Berkeley: University of California Press, 1982.

———. *Polnoe sobranie sochinenii i pisem*. Petrograd: Literaturno-izdatel'skii otdel Narkomprosa, 1919.

———. *Sobranie sochinenii v tridtsati tomakh*. Moscow: Izdatel'stvo Akademii nauk SSSR, 1954–65.

Holmgren, Beth. *The Russian Memoir: History and Literature*. Evanston, IL: Northwestern University Press, 2003.

———. *Women's Works in Stalin's Time: On Lidiia Chukovskaia and Nadezhda Mandelstam*. Bloomington/Indianapolis: Indiana University Press, 1993.

Iarov, Sergei. *Blokadnaia etika: Predstavleniia o morali v Leningrade v 1941–1942 g.g.* Moscow: Tsentrpoligraf, 2012.

Jakobson, Roman. *Language in Literature*. Edited by Krystyna Pomorska and Stephen Rudy. Cambridge, MA: Belknap Press of Harvard University Press, 1987.

James, William. *The Writings of William James*. Edited by John J. McDermott. Chicago: University of Chicago Press, 1967.

———. *Psychology: Briefer Course*. Cambridge, MA: Harvard University Press, 1984.

Janet, Pierre. *L'Automatisme Psychologique: Essai de Psychologie Expérimentale sur les Formes Inférieures de l'Activité Humaine*. Paris: Alcan, 1889.

———. *Principles of Psychotherapy*. Translated by H. M. Guthrie and E. R. Guthrie. New York: Macmillan, 1924.

Joravsky, David. *Russian Psychology: A Critical History*. Oxford: Basil Blackwell, 1989.

Kahn, Andrew. "Lydia Ginzburg's 'Lives of the Poets': Mandelstam in Profile." In *Lydia Ginzburg's Alternative Literary Identities*, edited by Emily Van Buskirk and Andrei Zorin. Oxford: Peter Lang AG, 2012, 163–92.

Kant, Immanuel. *Critique of Pure Reason*. Translated, edited, and introduced by Marcus Weigelt. Based on translation by Max Muller. New York: Penguin Books, 2007.

Karlinsky, Simon. "Russia's Gay History and Literature from the Eleventh to the Twentieth Centuries." In *Gay Roots: Twenty Years of Gay Sunshine*, edited by Winston Leyland. San Francisco: Gay Sunshine Press, 1991–93, 81–104.

———. "Russia's Gay Literature and Culture: The Impact of the October Revolution." In *Hidden from History: Reclaiming the Gay and Lesbian Past*, edited by Martin Duberman, Martha Vicinus, and George Chauncey, Jr. New York: NAL Books, 1989, 347–64.

Kelly, Catriona. *A History of Russian Women's Writing: 1820–1992*. Oxford: Clarendon Press, 1994.

Kharkhordin, Oleg. *The Collective and the Individual in Russia: A Study of Practices*. Berkeley: University of California Press, 1999.

———. *Oblichat' i litsemerit': genealogiia rossiisskoi lichnosti*. St. Petersburg: Evropeiskii universitet v Sankt-Peterburge, 2002.

Khazagerov, Svetlana, and Georgii. "Kul'tura-1, Kul'tura 2 i gumanitarnaia kul'tura." *Znamia* 3, at http://khazagerov.com/cultural-situation/107-culture1-2.html, accessed 31 December 2013.

Khodasevich, Vladislav. "Dekol'tirovannaia loshchad'" [1927]. In *Sobranie sochinenii v chetyrekh tomakh*, vol. 2. Edited by A. P. Andreeva, S. I. Bogatyreva, S. G. Bocharov, and I. P. Khabarov. Moscow: Soglasie, 1996, 159–67.

———. "Konets renaty." *Tiazhëlaia lira*. Edited by S. G. Bocharov and I. Z. Surat. Moscow: Panorama, 2000, 241–52.

Kirschenbaum, Lisa. *The Legacy of the Siege of Leningrad, 1941–1995*. Cambridge, UK: Cambridge University Press, 2006.

Kobrin, Kirill. "'Chelovek 20-x godov': Sluchai Lidii Ginzburg (K postanovke problemy)." *Novoe literaturnoe obozrenie* 78, 2 (2006): 60–83.

———. "M. L. Gasparovu—70 let. O Gasparove. Universal'naia kniga." *Novoe literaturnoe obozrenie* 73, 3 (2005): 166–69.

———. "Nenuzhnaia Lidiia Ginzburg," *Neprikosnovennyi zapas* 2 (2004), at http://magazines.russ.ru/nz/2004/34/kobr12.html, accessed 27 September 2008.

———. "To Create a Circle and to Break It ('Blockade Person's' World of Rituals)." In *Lydia Ginzburg's Alternative Literary Identities*, edited by Emily Van Buskirk and Andrei Zorin. Oxford: Peter Lang AG, 2012, 235–62.

Kolk, Bessel van der, and Onno van der Hart. "The Intrusive Past: The Flexibility of Memory and the Engraving of Trauma." In *Trauma: Explorations in Memory*, edited by Cathy Caruth. Baltimore, MD: Johns Hopkins University Press, 1995, 158–82.

Kon, Igor. *Liki i maski odnopoloi liubvi: lunnyi svet na zare*. 2nd, expanded ed. Moscow: Astrel', 2006.

———. "Sexual Minorities." In *Sex and Russian Society*, edited by Igor Kon and James Riordan. London: Pluto Press, 1993, 89–115.

Kononov, Nikolai. "Korotko o knigakh." *Russkaia mysl' (La Pensée russe)* 2, 3852 (November 1990), "Literaturnoe prilozhenie no. 11": xiv.

Kozlov, Sergei. "Lydia Ginzburg's Victory and Defeat." Translated by Emily Van Buskirk. In *Lydia Ginzburg's Alternative Literary Identities*, edited by Emily Van Buskirk and Andrei Zorin. Oxford: Peter Lang AG, 2012, 23–26.

Kukulin, Il'ia."Dnevniki na peske: Lidiia Ginzburg v roli domashnego klassika." *NG: Ex libris* 22 (7 April 2002): 4.

———. "Traditsiia intellektual'nogo odinochestva: Gertsen. Povorot bez pokoleniia: Aleksandr Gertsen i Lidiia Ginzburg kak revoliutsionery zhanrov." *Novoe literaturnoe obozrenie* 58, 6 (2002): 111–22.

"Kul'turnye kody, sotsial'nye strategii i literaturnye stsenarii," Roundtable. *Novoe literaturnoe obozrenie* 82, 6 (2006): 93–121.

Kumpan, Elena. *Blizhnii podstup k legende.* St. Petersburg: Izdatel'stvo zhurnala "Zvezda," 2005.

———. "Vspominaia Lidiiu Iakovlevnu." *Zvezda* 3 (2002): 135–56.

Kumpan, Kseniia. "Institut istorii iskusstv na rubezhe 1920-x–1930-x godov." In *Instituty kul'tury Leningrada na perelome ot 1920-x k 1930-m godam* (2011), at www.pushkinskij dom.ru/LinkClick.aspx?fileticket=lSfRoURS2-k%3d&tabid=10460, accessed 4 May 2015.

Kushner, Alexander. Untitled, in "Tsel'nost': o tvorchestve L.Ia. Ginzburg." *Canadian-American Slavic Studies* 28, 2–3 (Summer–Fall 1994): 233–45.

La Bruyère, Jean de. *Characters.* Translated by Henri Van Laun. New York: Howard Fertig, 1992.

Lacoue-Labarthe, Philippe, and Jean-Luc Nancy. *The Literary Absolute: The Theory of Literature in German Romanticism.* Translation, introduction, and notes by Philip Barnard and Cheryl Lester. Albany: State University of New York Press, 1988.

Ladenson, Elisabeth. *Proust's Lesbianism.* Ithaca, NY: Cornell University Press, 1999.

Lang, Candace. "Autobiography in the Aftermath of Romanticism." *Diacritics* 12, 4 (Winter 1982): 2–16.

Leighton, Lauren. "The Anecdote in Russia: Pushkin, Vjazemskij, and Davydov." *Slavic and East European Journal* 10, 2 (Summer 1966): 155–66.

———. "The Great Soviet Debate over Romanticism: 1957–1964." *Studies in Romanticism* 22, 1 (Spring 1983): 41–64.

Lejeune, Philippe. *On Autobiography.* Edited by Paul John Eakin, translated by Katherine Leary. Theory and History of Literature, vol. 52. Minneapolis: University of Minnesota Press, 1989.

Lemon, Lee T., and Marion J. Reis. *Russian Formalist Criticism: Four Essays.* Lincoln: University of Nebraska Press, 1965.

Levina, Esfir'. "Dnevnik 12 ianvaria 1942–6 iunia 1943." In *Chelovek v blokade: novye svidetel'stva,* edited by V. M. Koval'chuk, A. I. Rupasov, and A. N. Chistikov. St. Petersburg: Ostrov, 2008, 145–214.

Levkin, Andrei. "Shkola dlia umnykh." *Novoe literaturnoe obozrene* 49, 3 (2001): 421–26.

Levontina, Irina. "Dostoevskii nadryv." In *Kliuchevye idei russkoi iazykovoi kartiny mira,* edited by A. A. Zalizniak, I. B. Levontina, and A. D. Shmelev. Moscow: Iazyki slavianskoi kul'tury, 2005, 247–58.

Levontina, Irina, and Anna Zalizniak. "Human Emotions Viewed through the Russian Language." In *Emotions in Crosslinguistic Perspective,* edited by Jean Harkins and Anna Wierzbicka. Berlin: Mouton de Gruyter, 2001, 291–336.

Literatura Fakta: pervyi sbornik materialov rabotnikov LEF-a. Edited by N. F. Chuzhak. Moscow: Zakharov, 2000.

Livers, Keith. *Constructing the Stalinist Body: Fictional Representations of Corporeality in the Stalinist 1930s*. New York: Lexington Books, 2004.

Lotman, Iurii. "Besedy o russkoi kul'ture. Televizionnye lektsii. Tsikl 2: Kul'tura i intelligentnost'." In *Vospitanie dushi*. St. Petersburg: Isskustvo-SPb, 2003.

———. *Semiosfera*. St. Petersburg: Iskusstvo-SPb, 2004.

———. *Universe of the Mind: A Semiotic Theory of Culture*. Translated by Ann Shukman. Bloomington: Indiana University Press, 1990.

Lotman, Iurii M., Lidiia Ia. Ginzburg, and Boris A. Uspenskii. *The Semiotics of Russian Cultural History: Essays*. Edited by Alexander D. Nakhimovsky and Alice S. Nakhimovsky. Ithaca, NY: Cornell University Press, 1985.

Lotman, Lidiia. *Vospominaniia*. St. Petersburg: Nestor-Istoriia, 2007.

Lucey, Michael. *Never Say I: Sexuality and the First Person in Colette, Gide, and Proust*. Durham, NC: Duke University Press, 2006.

———. "Simone de Beauvoir and Sexuality in the Third Person." *Representations* 109, 1 (Winter 2010): 95–121.

Lukács, György. *Soul and Form*. Translated by Anna Bostock. Cambridge, MA: MIT Press, 1978.

———. *The Theory of the Novel*. Translated by Anna Bostock. Cambridge, MA: MIT Press, 1971.

Lukes, Steven. "The Meanings of 'Individualism.'" *Journal of the History of Ideas* 32, 1 (January–March 1971): 45–66.

Luriia, Aleksandr. *Etapy proidennogo puti: Nauchnaia avtobiografia*. Moscow: Izdatel'stvo Moskovskogo universiteta, 2001.

Malia, Martin. "What Is the Intelligentsia?" In *The Russian Intelligentsia*, edited by Richard Pipes. New York: Columbia University Press, 1961, 1–18.

Malmstad, John E. "Bathhouses, Hustlers, and a Sex Club: The Reception of Mikhail Kuzmin's *Wings*." *Journal of the History of Sexuality* 9, 1–2 (2000): 85–104.

Mandel'shtam, Nadezhda. *Vospominaniia*. New York: Izdatel'stvo im. Chekhova, 1979.

Mandel'shtam, Osip [also Mandelstam, Osip]. "The End of the Novel." In *Mandelstam: The Complete Critical Prose and Letters*, edited by Jane Gary Harris, translated by J. G. Harris and Constance Link. Ann Arbor, MI: Ardis, 1979, 198–201.

———. "Konets romana." In *Sochineniia v dvukh tomakh*, vol. 2, edited by P. M. Nerler. Moscow: Khudozhestvennaia literatura, 1990, 201–5.

———. *The Noise of Time: Selected Prose*. Translated by Clarence Brown. Evanston, IL: Northwestern University Press, 2002.

———. *Slovo i kul'tura*. Moscow: Sovetskii pisatel', 1987.

———. *Stikhotvoreniia*. Leningrad: Sovetskii pisatel', 1974.

Martens, Lorna. *The Diary Novel*. Cambridge, UK: Cambridge University Press, 1985.

Marx, Karl. "Preface" to *A Contribution to the Critique of Political Economy*. In *The Marx-Engels Reader*, 2nd ed., edited by Robert C. Tucker. New York: Norton, 1978, 3–6.

Mashevskii, Aleksei. "Prervannyi dialog." *Canadian-American Slavic Studies* 28, 2–3 (Summer–Fall 1994): 253–62.

Matich, Olga. *Erotic Utopia: The Decadent Imagination in Russia's Fin-De-Siècle*. Madison: University of Wisconsin Press, 2005.

Mead, George Herbert. *Mind, Self, and Society*. Edited by Charles W. Morris. Chicago: University of Chicago Press, 1934.

Merezhkovskii, Dmitrii. "Griadushchii kham." In *Polnoe sobranie sochinenii*, vol. 11. St. Petersburg: Izdanie T-va M.O Vol'f, 1911–13, 1–36.

Mink, Louis O. "History and Fiction as Modes of Comprehension." *New Literary History* 3 (Spring 1970): 541–58.

Montaigne, Michel. *The Complete Works of Montaigne: Essays, Travel Journals, Letters*. Translated by Donald M. Frame. Stanford, CA: Stanford University Press, 1958.

———. *Opyty*. 3 vols. Moscow: Nauka, 1979, 1981.

Morson, Gary Saul. *The Boundaries of Genre*. Evanston, IL: Northwestern University Press, 1981.

———. *The Long and Short of It: From Aphorism to Novel*. Stanford, CA: Stanford University Press, 2012.

Morson, Gary Saul, and Caryl Emerson. *Mikhail Bakhtin: Creation of a Prosaics*. Stanford, CA: Stanford University Press, 1990.

Mulvey, Laura. *Visual and Other Pleasures*. Bloomington: Indiana University Press, 1989.

Nabokov, Vladimir. *Nikolai Gogol*. New York: New Directions, 1961 [1944].

———. "Philistines and Philistinism." In *Lectures on Russian Literature*, edited by Fredson Bowers. New York: Harcourt, 1981, 309–14.

Naiman, Eric. "Historectomies: On the Metaphysics of Reproduction in a Utopian Age." In *Sexuality and the Body in Russian Culture*, edited by Jane T. Costlow, Stephanie Sandler, and Judith Vowles. Stanford, CA: Stanford University Press, 1993, 255–76.

Neisser, Ulric. "Five Kinds of Self-Knowledge." *Philosophical Psychology* 1, 1 (1988): 35–59.

Nevzgliadova, Elena. "Razgovory s L.Ia. Ginzburg." *Zvezda* 3 (2002): 157–67.

Nussbaum, Martha C. *Love's Knowledge: Essays on Philosophy and Literature*. New York: Oxford University Press, 1990.

Offord, Derek. "Lichnost': Notions of Individual Identity." In *Constructing Russian Culture in the Age of Revolution: 1881–1940*, edited by Catriona Kelly and David Shepherd. Oxford: Oxford University Press, 1998, 13–25.

Olney, James, ed. *Autobiography, Essays Theoretical and Critical*. Princeton, NJ: Princeton University Press, 1980.

Oosterhuis, Harry. *Stepchildren of Nature: Krafft-Ebing, Psychiatry, and the Making of Sexual Identity*. Chicago: University of Chicago Press, 2000.

Ostrovskaia, Sofiia. *Dnevnik*. Edited by Polina Iu. Barskova and T. S. Pozdniakova. Moscow: Novoe literaturnoe obozrenie, 2013.

Paperno, Irina. "Beyond Literary Criticism." *Canadian-American Slavic Studies* 19, 2 (1985), 176–86.

———. *Chernyshevsky and the Age of Realism*. Stanford, CA: Stanford University Press, 1988.

———. "Introduction: Intimacy and History. The Gercen Family Drama Reconsidered." *Russian Literature* LXI, I/II (1 January–15 February 2007): 1–66.

———. "Personal Accounts of the Soviet Experience." *Kritika: Explorations in Russian and Eurasian History* 3, 4 (Fall 2002): 577–610.

———. "Sovetskii opyt, avtobiograficheskoe pis'mo, istoricheskoe soznanie: Ginzburg-Gertsen-Gegel'." *Novoe literaturnoe obozrenie* 68, 4 (2004): 102–27.

———. *Stories of the Soviet Experience: Memoirs, Diaries, Dreams*. Ithaca, NY: Cornell University Press, 2009.

———. "'Who, What Is I?': Tolstoy in His Diaries." *Tolstoy Studies Journal* 9 (1999): 32–54.

Pasternak, Boris Leonidovich. *Pozhiznennaia priviazannost': Perepiska s O. M. Freidenberg,* edited by E. V. and E. B. Pasternak. Moscow: ART-FLEKS, 2000.

———. *Stikhotvoreniia i poemy v dvukh tomakh,* vol. 1. Leningrad: Sovetskii pisatel', 1990.

Pipes, Richard. *The Russian Intelligentsia.* New York: Columbia University Press, 1961.

Plotnikov, Nikolai. "Ot 'individual'nosti' k 'identichnosti' (istoriia poniatii personal'nosti v russkoi kul'ture)." *Novoe literaturnoe obrzenie* 91, 3 (2008): 64–83.

Poole, Brian. "From Phenomenology to Dialogue: Max Scheler's Phenomenological Tradition and Mikhail Bakhtin's Development from 'Toward a Philosophy of the Act' to His Study of Dostoevsky." In *Bakhtin and Cultural Theory,* edited by Ken Hirschkop and David Shepherd. Manchester, UK: Manchester University Press, 2001, 109–35.

Pratt, Sarah. "Angels in the Stalinist House: Nadezhda Mandelstam, Lidiia Chukovskaia, Lidiia Ginzburg, and Russian Women's Autobiography." *Auto/biography Studies* 11, 2 (1996): 68–87.

———. "Lidiia Ginzburg, a Russian Democrat at the Rendezvous." *Canadian-American Slavic Studies* 28, 2–3 (Summer–Fall 1994): 183–203.

———. "Lidija Ginzburg's *O starom i novom* as Autobiography." *Slavic and East European Journal* 30, 1 (1986): 45–53. Reprinted with modifications as "Lydia Ginzburg and the Fluidity of Genre," in *Autobiographical Statements in Twentieth-Century Russian Literature,* edited by Jane Gary Harris. Princeton, NJ: Princeton University Press, 1990, 207–16.

———. "Review of *Lydia Ginzburg's Alternative Literary Identities.*" *Modern Language Review* 109, 1 (January 2014): 305–7.

Presto, Jenifer. *Beyond the Flesh: Alexander Blok, Zinaida Gippius, and the Symbolist Sublimation of Sex.* Madison: University of Wisconsin Press, 2008.

Proust, Marcel. *In Search of Lost Time.* Translated by C. K. Scott Moncrieff and Terence Kilmartin. New York: Modern Library, 1992.

———. *À la recherche du temps perdu.* Paris: Omnibus, 2011.

Pushkin, Alexander. "O proze." In *Polnoe sobranie sochinenii v 10 tomakh,* 4th ed., vol. 7, edited by USSR Academy of Sciences. Leningrad: Nauka, 1977–79, 12–13.

Pushkinskii Dom: Materialy k istorii. 1905–2005. St. Petersburg: Bulanina, 2005.

Ricoeur, Paul. "Narrative Identity." In *On Paul Ricoeur: Narrative and Interpretation,* edited by David Wood. London: Routledge, 1991, 188–99.

———. *Oneself as Another.* Chicago: University of Chicago Press, 1992.

Rochefoucauld, Duke de la. *Moral Maxims.* Translation from 1749 English edition, published by A. Millar in London. Newark, DE: University of Delaware Press, 2003.

Rosengrant, Judson. "L. Ia. Ginzburg. An International Chronological Bibliography of Primary and Secondary Works." *Russian Review* 54, 4 (October 1995): 587–600.

Rosenthal, Bernice Glatzer, ed. *Nietzsche and Soviet Culture: Ally and Adversary.* Cambridge, UK: Cambridge University Press, 1994.

Rothberg, Michael. "After Adorno: Culture in the Wake of Catastrophe." *New German Critique* 72 (Fall 1997): 45–81.

Rozanov, V. V. *Liudi lunnogo sveta: Metafizika khristianstva.* Moscow: Druzhba narodov, 1990.

———. *Uedinennoe.* Edited by A. N. Nikoliukina. Moscow: Politizdat, 1990.

Ryan, Judith. "The Vanishing Subject: Empirical Psychology and the Modern Novel." *PMLA* 95, 5 (October 1980): 857–69.

Sacks, Oliver. *The Man Who Mistook His Wife for a Hat*. New York: Simon & Schuster, 1998.

———. *A Leg to Stand On*. New York: Harper Perennial, 1994.

Saint-Simon, Duc de. *Memoirs: A Shortened Version*, 3 vols. Edited and translated by Lucy Norton. London: Prion Books Ltd., 2000.

Sandomirskaia, Irina. *Blokada v slove: Ocherki kriticheskoi teorii i biopolitiki iazyka*. Moscow: Novoe literaturnoe obozrenie, 2013.

———. "The Leviathan, or Language in Besiegement: Lydia Ginzburg's Prolegomena to Critical Discourse Analysis." In *Lydia Ginzburg's Alternative Literary Identities*, edited by Emily Van Buskirk and Andrei Zorin. Oxford: Peter Lang AG, 2012, 193–234.

———. "Rage in the City of Hunger: Body, Talk, and the Politics of Womanliness in Lidia Ginzburg's *Notes from the Siege of Leningrad*." In *Embracing Arms: Cultural Representation of Slavic and Balkan Women in War*, edited by Helena Goscilo with Yana Hashamova. Budapest/New York: Central European University Press, 2012, 131–51.

Sandler, Stephanie. "Speaking Volumes: Pushkin, Coleridge, and Table Talk." *Comparative Literature* 43, 3 (1991): 230–45.

Sandler, Stephanie, and Laura Engelstein, eds. *Self and Story in Russian History*. Ithaca, NY: Cornell University Press, 2000.

Sartre, Jean Paul. *What Is Literature?* Translated by Bernard Frechtman, introduction by David Caute. London/New York: Routledge, 2001.

———. "Introducing *Les Temps modernes*." In *"What Is Literature?" and Other Essays*, translated by Jeffrey Mehlman. Cambridge, MA: Harvard University Press, 1988, 247–68.

Savitskii, Stanislav. *Chastnyi chelovek: L. Ia. Ginzburg v kontse 1920-kh–nachale 1930-kh godov*. St. Petersburg: Evropeiskii universitet, 2013.

———. "Spor s uchitelem: nachalo literaturnogo/issledovatel'skogo proekta L.Ginzburg." *Novoe literaturnoe obozrenie* 82, 6 (2006): 129–54.

———. "Zhivaia literatura faktov: spor L. Ginzburg i B. Bukhshtaba o 'Liricheskom otstuplenii' N. Aseeva." *Novoe literaturnoe obozrenie* 89, 1 (2008): 8–37.

———. " 'Zritel' sobstvennoi mysli': o zametke L. Ginzburg 1922 goda." In *Varietas et Concordia: Essays in Honour of Pekka Pesonen*, edited by Ben Hellman, Tomi Huttunen, and Gennady Obatnin. Helsinki: University of Helsinki, 2007, 444–67.

Schatzman, R. "Nina Gourfinkel." *Revue des études slaves*, Paris, LXIII, 3 (1991): 705–23.

Scheler, Max. "Repentance and Rebirth." In *On the Eternal in Man*, translated by Bernard Noble. London: SCM Press Ltd, 1960, 35–65.

Schmid, Ulrich. "The Family Drama as an Interpretive Pattern in Aleksandr Gercen's *Byloe i dumy*." *Russian Literature* LXI, I/II (1 January–15 February 2007): 67–102.

Sedgwick, Eve Kosofsky. *Epistemology of the Closet*. Berkeley: University of California Press, 1990.

Seigel, Jerrold. *The Idea of the Self: Thought and Experience in Western Europe since the Seventeenth Century*. Cambridge, UK: Cambridge University Press, 2005.

Sepman, I. V., ed. *Rossiiskii institut istorii iskusstv v memuarakh*. St. Petersburg: RIII, 2003.

Serman, Ilya. "Writer-Researcher." *Canadian-American Slavic Studies Journal* 19, 2 (Summer 1985): 187–92.

Shalamov, Varlam. *Kolyma Tales*. Translated by John Glad. New York: Penguin Classics, 1995.

———. "O proze" (1965). In *Sobranie sochinenii v shesti tomakh*, vol. 5, edited by I. Sirotinskaia. Moscow: Terra—Knizhnyi klub, 2005, 144–57.

Shaporina, Liubov'. *Dnevnik*. Edited by V. F. Petrova and V. N. Sazhin. Moscow: Novoe literaturnoe obozrenie, 2011.

Shepherd, David. *Beyond Metafiction: Self-consciousness in Soviet Literature*. Oxford: Clarendon Press, 1992.

Shklovskii [also Shklovsky], Viktor. *"Eshche nichego ne konchilos'."* Commentary by A. Galushkin and V. Nekhotin. Moscow: Propaganda, 2002.

———. *Gamburgskii Schet*. Leningrad: Izdatel'stvo pisatelei v Leningrade, 1928.

———. *Gamburgskii schet: Stat'i–vospominaniia–esse (1914–1933)*. Moscow: Sovetskii pisatel', 1990.

———. *Izbrannoe v dvukh tomakh*, vol. 2. Moscow: Khudozhestvennaia literatura, 1983.

———. *Theory of Prose*. Translated by Benjamin Sher. Normal, IL: Dalkey Archive Press, 1990.

———. *Third Factory*. Introduced and translated by Richard Sheldon. Chicago: Dalkey Archive Press, 2002.

———. *Tret'ia fabrika*. Russian Titles for the Specialist No. 141. Letchworth, UK: Prideaux Press, 1978. Reprint of 1926 Russian edition by Artel' pisatelei "Krug."

———. *Zoo, or Letters Not about Love*. Translated by Richard Sheldon. Chicago: Dalkey Archive Press, 2001.

Simmel, Georg. "Individual and Society in Eighteenth- and Nineteenth-Century Views of Life: an Example of Philosophical Sociology." In *The Sociology of Georg Simmel*, translated and edited by Kurt H. Wolff. Glencoe, IL: Free Press, 1950, 78–83.

———. *On Individuality and Social Forms; Selected Writings*. Edited by Donald Levine. Chicago: University of Chicago Press, 1971.

Simmons, Cynthia. "Leningrad Culture under Siege (1941–1944)." In *Preserving Petersburg: History, Memory, Nostalgia*, edited by Helena Goscilo and Stephen M. Norris. Bloomington: Indiana University Press, 2008, 164–81.

Simmons, Cynthia, and Nina Perlina, eds. *Writing the Siege of Leningrad: Women's Diaries, Memoirs, and Documentary Prose*. Pittsburgh, PA: University of Pittsburgh Press, 2002.

Slovar' sovremennogo russkogo literaturnogo iazyka, Institut Russkogo iazyka. Moscow: Izdatel'stvo Akademii Nauk SSSR, 1950–65.

Smith, Barbara Herrnstein. *On the Margins of Discourse: The Relation of Literature to Language*. Chicago: University of Chicago Press, 1978.

Smith, Sidonie, and Julia Watson. *Reading Autobiography: A Guide for Interpreting Life Narratives*. Minneapolis: University of Minnesota Press, 2001.

Sokolova, Nataliia Viktorovna. "Lidiia Ginzburg, rodnia, znakomye. Materialy k biografii." 1990s, 93 pages. RGALI. F. 3270 Op. 1, delo 27.

———. "Ogliadyvaias' nazad. . . ." *Voprosy literatury* 5 (1994): 285–92.

Sokolovskaia, Natal'ia, ed. *Ol'ga. Zapretnyi dnevnik. Dnevniki, pis'ma, proza, izbrannye stikhotvoreniia i poemy Ol'gi Berggol'ts*. St. Petersburg: Azbuka-klassika, 2010.

Solovyov, Vladimir. *The Justification of the Good: An Essay on Moral Philosophy*. Translated by Nathalie Duddington, edited by Boris Jakim. Grand Rapids, MI: William B. Eerdmans, 2005.

———. "The Meaning of Love." In *Russian Philosophy*, vol. III, edited by James Edie, James Scanlan, and Mary-Barbara Zeldin. Chicago: Quadrangle Books, 1965, 85–98.

———. *The Meaning of Love*. Edited and translated by Thomas R. Beyer. West Stockbridge, MA: Lindisfarne Press Publisher, 1985.

———. "Smysl liubvi." In *Russkii Eros ili filosofiia liubvi v Rossii*, edited by V. P. Shestakov and A. N. Bogoslovskii. Moscow: Progress, 1991, 19–76.

Spranger, Eduard. *Types of Men: the Psychology and Ethics of Personality*, authorized translation by Paul J. W. Pigors. Halle: Max Niemeyer Verlag, 1928.

Starobinski, Jean. "The Style of Autobiography." Translated by Seymour Chatman. In *Autobiography: Essays Theoretical and Critical*, edited by James Olney. Princeton, NJ: Princeton University Press, 1980, 73–83.

Steiner, Peter. *Russian Formalism: A Metapoetics*. Ithaca, NY: Cornell University Press, 1984.

Striedter, Jurij. *Literary Structure, Evolution, and Value: Russian Formalism and Czech Structuralism Reconsidered*. Cambridge, MA: Harvard University Press, 1989.

Suleiman, Susan. *Crises of Memory and the Second World War*. Cambridge, MA: Harvard University Press, 2006.

Tapp, Alyson. "'Как быть писателем?': Boris Eikhenbaum's Response to the Crisis of the Novel in the 1920s." *Slavonica* 15, 1 (April 2009): 32–47.

Taylor, Charles. *Sources of the Self: The Making of the Modern Identity*. Cambridge, MA: Harvard University Press, 1989.

Tihanov, Galin. *The Master and the Slave: Lukács, Bakhtin and the Ideas of Their Time*. New York: Oxford University Press; Oxford: Clarendon Press.

———. "The Politics of Estrangement: The Case of the Early Shklovsky." *Poetics Today* 26, 4 (Winter 2005): 665–96.

Todd, William Mills III. "Between Marxism and Semiotics: Lidiia Ginzburg and Soviet Literary Sociology." *Canadian-American Slavic Studies* 19, 2 (1985): 178–86.

———. "Discoveries and Advances in Literary Theory, 1960s–1980s." In *A History of Russian Literary Criticism and Theory*, edited by Evgeny Dobrenko and Galin Tihanov. Pittsburgh, PA: University of Pittsburgh Press, 2011, 230–49.

———. "Soviet Sociology of Literature: Conceptions of a Changing World." *Soviet Studies in Literature* 25, 3 (Summer 1989): 5–20.

Toddes, E. A. "Neosushchestvlennye zamysly Tynianova." In *Tynianovskii sbornik: Pervye Tynianovskie chteniia*. Riga: Zinatne, 1984, 25–45.

Toker, Leona. "Toward a Poetics of Documentary Prose—from the Perspective of Gulag Testimonies." *Poetics Today* 18, 2 (Summer 1997): 187–222.

Tolstoy, Lev. "O bezumii." In *Polnoe sobranie sochinenii*, edited by V. T. Chertkov, vol. 38. Moscow: Khudozhestvennaia literatura, 1936, 395–411.

———. *Polnoe sobranie sochinenii v 90 tomakh*, vol. LXXVII. Moscow, 1953–58.

———. *Sobranie sochinenii v 22 tomakh*, vol. 16. Moscow: Khudozhestvennaia literatura, 1983.

Tynianov, Iuri. "The Literary Fact." Translated by Ann Shukman. In *Modern Genre Theory*, edited by David Duff. New York: Longman, 2000, 29–49.

———. *Poetika. Istoriia literatury. Kino*. Edited by E. A. Toddes, A. P. Chudakov, and M. O. Chudakova. Moscow: Nauka, 1977.

Ushakov, D. N., ed. *Tolkovyi slovar' russkogo iazyka*. Moscow: Gosudarstvennyi institut "Sovetskaia entsiklopediia," 1935.

Ustinov, Denis. "1920-e gody kak intellektual'nyi resurs: v pole Formalizma. Formalizm i mladoformalisty." *Novoe literaturnoe obozrenie* 50, 4 (2001): 296–321.

———. "1920-e gody kak intellektual'nyi resurs: v pole Formalizma. Materialy disputa 'Marksizm i Formal'nyi metod.'" *Novoe literaturnoe obozrenie* 50, 4 (2001): 247–78.

Utekhin, Il'ia. "O smysle vkliuchennogo nabliudeniia povsednevnosti." In *Istoriia povsednevnosti*. St. Petersburg: Evropeiskii universitet v Sankt Peterburge, Aleteiia, 2003, 15–24.

Uvarova, Elizaveta D. *Estrada v Rossii. XX Vek. Entsiklopedia*. Moscow: Olma-Press, 2004, 236–37.

Uznadze, D. N. *Psikhologicheskie issledovaniia*. Moscow: Nauka, 1966.

Van Buskirk, Emily. "Fragmenty s otstupleniiami: Lidiia Ginzburg v nachale puti." Review of Stanislav Savitskii, *Chastnyi chelovek: Lidiia Ginzburg v kontse 1920-x–nachale 1930-x godov. Novoe literaturnoe obozrenie* 128, 4 (2014): 328–36.

———. "Lichnyi i istoricheskii opyt v blokadnoi prozy Lidii Ginzburg." *Prokhodiashchie kharaktery. Proza voennykh let. Zapiski blokadnogo cheloveka*, edited by Emily Van Buskirk and Andrei Zorin. Moscow: Novoe izdatel'stvo, 2011.

———. "Lidiia Ginzburg on Elena Shvarts." *Slavonica* 16, 2 (November 2010): 139–43.

———. "Reality in Search of Literature: Lydia Ginzburg's In-Between Prose." PhD Dissertation, Harvard University, 2008.

———. "Recovering the Past for the Future: Guilt, Memory, and Lidiia Ginzburg's *Notes of a Blockade Person*." *Slavic Review* 69, 2 (Summer 2010): 281–305.

———. " 'Samo-otstranenie' kak eticheskii i esteticheskii printsip v proze L. Ia. Ginzburg." *Novoe literaturnoe obozrenie* 81, 5 (2006): 261–81.

———. "Varieties of Failure: Lydia Ginzburg's Character Analyses from the 1930s and 1940s." In *Lydia Ginzburg's Alternative Literary Identities*, edited by Emily Van Buskirk and Andrei Zorin. Oxford: Peter Lang AG, 2012, 125–62.

———. "V poiskakh romana: Lidiia Ginzburg v 1930-e gody." *Novoe literaturnoe obozrenie* 88, 6 (2007): 154–68.

———. "Zapisi 50–60-kh godov." Publication, introduction, and commentaries. *Seans* (*Séance*) 51–52 (2012): 310–21.

Van Buskirk, Emily, and Andrei Zorin, eds. *Lydia Ginzburg's Alternative Literary Identities*. Russian Transformations: Literature, Thought, Culture, vol. 3. Oxford: Peter Lang AG, 2012.

Verheul, Kees. "Chelovek v severnom svete (Po povodu smerti L. Ia. Ginzburg)." *Russkaia mysl' (La Pensée russe)* (2 November 1990), "Literaturnoe prilozhenie no. 11": xiv–xv.

Vestnik vinokureniia 6 (30 May 1910): 62–67, and 20 (31 December 1909). Obituaries of Iakov M. Ginzburg.

Viazemskii, Petr Andreevich. *Staraia zapisnaia knizhka*. Edited, introduction, and commentary by Lidiia Ginzburg. Leningrad: Izdatel'stvo pisatelei, 1929.

———. *Polnoe sobranie sochinenii*. St. Petersburg: Izdatel'stvo grafa Sheremeteva, 1878–96.

Vinokur, G. O. *Biografiia i kul'tura; Russkoe stsenicheskoe proiznoshenie*. Moscow: Russkie slovari, 1997, 5–96.

Voloshinov, V. N. *Freudianism: A Marxist Critique*. Translated by I. R. Titunik. New York: Academic Press, 1976.

———. *Marxism and the Philosophy of Language*. Translated by Ladislav Matejka and I. R. Titunik. Cambridge, MA: Harvard University Press, 1986.

———. *Marksizm i filosofiia iazyka*. Moscow: Labirint, 1993.

Wachtel, Michael. *A Commentary to Pushkin's Lyric Poetry 1826–1836*. Madison: University of Wisconsin Press, 2011.

Walicki, Andrzej. "Variants of Positivism." In *A History of Russian Thought from the Enlightenment to Marxism*. Stanford, CA: Stanford University Press, 349–70.

Walker, Barbara. "On Reading Soviet Memoirs: A History of the 'Contemporaries' Genre as an Institution of Russian Intelligentsia Culture from the 1790s to the 1970s." *Russian Review* 59, 3 (July 2000): 327–52.

Weinberg, Elizabeth. *Sociology in the Soviet Union and Beyond: Social Enquiry and Social Change*, rev. ed. Burlington, VT: Ashgate, 2004.

Weininger, Otto. *Sex and Character: An Investigation of Fundamental Principles* [1906]. Translated by Ladislaus Löb. Bloomington: Indiana University Press, 2005.

Weintraub, Karl. "Autobiography and Historical Consciousness." *Critical Inquiry* 1, 4 (June 1975): 821–48.

———. *Value of the Individual: Self and Circumstance in Autobiography*. Chicago: University of Chicago Press, 1978.

Zalambani, Maria. *Literatura Fakta: Ot Avangarda k sotsrealizmu*. St. Petersburg: Akademicheskii proekt, 2006.

Zamyatin, Yevgeny [also Zamiatin, Evgenii]. "The Cave." In *The Portable Twentieth-Century Russian Reader*, edited by Clarence Brown. New York: Penguin Books, 2003, 90–102.

———. *Sobranie sochinenii v 5 tomakh*. Moscow: Russkaia kniga, 2003.

———. *A Soviet Heretic: Essays by Yevgeny Zamyatin*, edited and translated by Mirra Ginsburg. Chicago: University of Chicago Press, 1970.

Zelënaia, Rina. *Razroznennye stranitsy* [1987]. Moscow: Zebra E, 2010.

Zhirmunskii, Viktor, ed. *Problemy literaturnoi formy (sbornik statei O. Val'tselia, V. Dibeliusa, K. Fosslera, L. Shpitzera)*. Leningrad: Academia 1928.

Zhivov, Viktor. "Post scriptum k poetike bytovogo povedeniia i k posviashchennomu ei proekta L. Ia. Ginzburg." *Novoe literaturnoe obozrenie* 82, 6 (2006): 122–28.

Zholkovsky [also Zholkovskii], Alexander. "Between Genres." *Canadian-American Slavic Studies* 28, 2–3 (Summer–Fall 1994): 147–60. Reprinted in *Lydia Ginzburg's Alternative Literary Identities*, edited by Emily Van Buskirk and Andrei Zorin. Oxford: Peter Lang AG, 2012, 33–37.

———. *Erosiped i drugie vin'etki*. Moscow: Volodei, 2003.

———. "Mezhdu zhanrami (L. Ia. Ginzburg)." In *Inventsii*. Moscow: Gendal'f, 1995, 154–57.

———. "The Obverse of Stalinism: Akhmatova's Self-Serving Charisma of Selflessness." In *Self and Story in Russian History*, edited by Laura Engelstein and Stephanie Sandler. Ithaca, NY: Cornell University Press, 2000, 46–68.

———. "O genii i zlodeistve, o babe i vserossiiskom masshtabe (Progulki po Maiakovskomu)." In *Izbrannye stat'i o russkoi poezii: Invarianty, struktury, strategii, interteksty*. Moscow: Rossiiskii gosudarstvennyi gumanitarnyi universitet, 2005, 255–78.

Zorin, Andrei. "Ginzburg as Psychologist." In *Lydia Ginzburg's Alternative Literary Identities*, edited by Emily Van Buskirk and Andrei Zorin. Oxford: Peter Lang AG, 2012, 83–123.

———. "Iz predystoria izucheniia sotsialistichekogo realizma (V. Khodasevich i L. Ginzburg o sovetskoi literature)." In *Varietas et Concordia: Essays in Honour of Pekka Pesonen*. Helsinki: Slavic Helsingiensia, 2007, 322–37.

———. "Lidiia Ginzburg: opyt 'primireniia s deistvitel'nost'iu." *Novoe literaturnoe obozrenie* 101, 1 (2010): 32–51.

———. "Proza L. Ia. Ginzburg i gumanitarnaia mysl' XX veka." *Novoe literaturnoe obozrenie* 76, 6 (2005): 45–68.

Zoshchenko, Mikhail. *Sobranie sochinenii v trekh tomakh*, vol. 1. Moscow: Terra, 1994.

INDEX